COUNSELING
Children &
Adolescents

FOURTH EDITION

Ann Vernon
University of Northern Iowa

LOVE PUBLISHING COMPANY®
Denver • London • Singapore

This book is dedicated with love to my young granddaughter, Elia Kavic Vernon, whose vibrant personality has already impacted my life. Elia, I look forward to watching you develop as you forge your journey through life.

Published by Love Publishing Company
P.O. Box 22353
Denver, Colorado 80222
www.lovepublishing.com

Library of Congress Catalog Card Number 2008927447

Copyright © 2009 by Love Publishing Company
Printed in the United States of America
ISBN 978-0-89108-340-5

Contents

4 Play Therapy   123

Terry Kottman

5 Brief Counseling in Action With Children and Adolescents   147

John M. Littrell and Kirk Zinck

6 Applications of Rational–Emotive Behavior Therapy With Children and Adolescents   173

Ann Vernon

7 Counseling With Exceptional Children   203

Shari Tarver-Behring and Michael E. Spagna

8   Counseling Children From Diverse Backgrounds   255

Darcie Davis-Gage

9   Counseling Children and Adolescents With Special Needs   287

William McFarland and Toni Tollerud

10   Counseling At-Risk Children and Adolescents   335

Ellen Hawley McWhirter and Jason J. Burrow-Sanchez

11   Small-Group Counseling   359

James J. Bergin and James F. Klein

Preface

Times have changed. Children not so many years ago entertained themselves by capturing fireflies in a jar, soaring high on a tire swing, or playing hide-and-go-seek and tag. These simple pleasures were inexpensive, creative, and healthy—in sharp contrast to what many of today's youth do for fun. Without DVDs, game cubes, or video games, they seem lost—and even more so if families can't afford these entertainment devices.

In so many ways the world is more complex than it was even 15 years ago when the first edition of this book was published. At that time I wrote that children and adolescents faced many challenges. In addition to normal growing-up problems, young people had to deal with the complexities of our contemporary society. The same holds true today—but to a much greater extent. Now children seem to have lost their innocence and have to deal with issues far beyond their level of comprehension. They grow up too fast and too soon, and though they may be young chronologically, they are exposed to adult issues through the media and the Internet, as well as day-to-day experiences that they are not developmentally equipped to deal with.

In addition, they are more fearful and feel more vulnerable after the events of 9/11 and the increasing violence in schools. School and mental health counselors must play an increasing role in helping young people deal with the challenges of growing up today. Clearly, we must find effective ways to teach children how to be resilient and equip them with tools to handle the typical developmental problems as well as the more serious problems that so many will encounter. By listening to their stories, employing effective interventions, advocating for them, and informing parents and other professionals about child and adolescent development and other important issues, we can make their journey through life easier.

The contributing authors have revised all chapters, and this fourth edition builds on the earlier editions in several ways. More case studies illustrate application of the principles discussed. Chapter 8, in particular, has been updated in keeping with the growing numbers of children with various cultural backgrounds. And readers working in school settings should find the Chapter 12 discussion of the developmental counseling curriculum to be particularly helpful in program implementation. As a foundation for work with children, readers are directed to Chapter 5 (brief counseling), Chapter 6 (rational emotive behavior therapy), and Chapter 4 (play therapy), as well as significant revisions to Chapter 2 (individual counseling). Chapters 13 and

14 (working with parents and families) emphasize the necessity of working with the entire system.

The authors of this book are all well respected authorities in their fields and have provided pertinent, up-to-date information that will increase the reader's knowledge about effective counseling strategies for children and adolescents. Each chapter contains practical as well as theoretical information, along with case studies or sample group/classroom activities to illustrate the application of concepts. This fourth edition, we hope, will be a valuable resource that will help students and practitioners make a positive difference for today's children and families.

Ann Vernon

Meet the Editor

Ann Vernon, PhD, NCC, LMHC, is Professor Emeritus, University of Northern Iowa where she served as professor and coordinator of the School and Mental Health Counseling Programs for 25 years. During her tenure there, she taught courses related to counseling children and adolescents, counseling skills and theory, and practicum and internship in school counseling. Dr. Vernon has published numerous books, chapters, and articles about counseling children and adolescents, including *What Works When With Children and Adolescents: A Handbook of Individual Counseling Techniques,* and the *Thinking, Feeling, Behaving* emotional education curriculums. Dr. Vernon is the recipient of several awards for outstanding service to the counseling profession and has held leadership positions in state, regional, and national associations. Dr. Vernon is Vice President of the Albert Ellis Board of Trustees and is considered one of the few leading experts on applications of REBT with children and adolescents. She currently conducts REBT training programs in Europe, Mexico and South America, Singapore, and Australia. Until last year when she moved to Arizona, she maintained a very successful private practice in Iowa where she specialized in working with children, adolescents, and parents.

Meet the Contributors

James J. Bergin, EdD, is a professor of Counselor Education at Georgia Southern University in Statesborso. Dr. Bergin is a past president of the Georgia School Counselors Association (GSCA). In addition to authoring several articles and book chapters, Dr. Bergin has served as the editor of the *GSCA Journal* and has held several other leadership positions in state and national counseling associations, including supervisor/postsecondary president of ASCA.

Loretta J. Bradley, PhD, is Paul Whitfield Horn Professor and Coordinator of Counselor Education at Texas Tech University. She has authored or coauthored seven books and more than 200 articles and conference presentations. She is a past president of the American Counseling Association (ACA) and the Association for Counselor Education and Supervision (ACES). She is a corecipient of the ACA Research Award and the BACP (British Association for Counselling and Psychotherapy) Research Award. Dr. Bradley was selected as a counseling leader who has made significant contributions to the counseling profession and was featured in the book,

Leaders and Legacies. Dr. Bradley is a National Certified Counselor (NCC), Texas LPC, Texas Licensed Marriage and Family Counselor, TX-LMFC-Supervisor. She also has certification as a school counselor and teacher.

Jason J. Burrow-Sanchez, PhD, is an assistant professor of Counseling Psychology in the Educational Psychology Department at the University of Utah. He is a licensed psychologist, and his research interest is the prevention and treatment of substance abuse problems with adolescent populations in school and community settings. He is coauthor of the book *Helping Students Overcome Substance Abuse: Effective Practices for Prevention and Intervention.*

Charles R. Crews, PhD, is an assistant professor at Texas Tech University and the director of the Professional School Counseling Program. He has been a counselor in K–12 schools, a university counseling center, and community counseling centers. Dr. Crews teaches school counseling, career development, and assessment for counselors. His research interests include special topics in school counseling such as ethics, dealing with difficult students, school guidance curriculum, and technology compulsion.

Darcie Davis-Gage, PhD, LPC, is an assistant professor in Counseling at the University of Northern Iowa. Her research interests are in the area of group counseling, clinical supervision, and diversity issues related to counselor education and practice. Dr. Davis-Gage has nine years of professional counseling experience working with children, adolescents, and young adults. She is also an active member of ACA and ACES. She has authored or coauthored several articles and book chapters.

C. Bret Hendricks, EdD, LPC, is an assistant professor and the clinical director of Counselor Education at Texas Tech University. Dr. Hendricks currently serves as the president of the International Association of Marriage and Family Counselors (IAMFC), and he serves on the board of directors for the Texas Counseling Association and the West Texas Counseling Association. He has been named Family Counselor of the Year by the IAMFC. His major areas of research include adolescent studies, at-risk adolescents, substance abuse treatment, and the use of music therapy techniques in counseling.

James F. Klein, EdD, NCC, is an assistant professor in the Human Development Counseling Program at the University of Illinois, Springfield. His research interests are related to school counseling, spirituality and counseling, and the common factors of counseling.

Terry Kottman, PhD, NCC, RPT-S, LMHC, founded The Encouragement Zone, a center where she provides play therapy training, counseling, coaching, and "playshops" for adults. Dr. Kottman developed Adlerian play therapy, an approach to counseling children that combines the ideas and techniques of Individual Psychology and play therapy. She is the author of *Partners in Play: An Adlerian Approach to Play Therapy, Play Therapy: Basics and Beyond,* and coauthor of *Adventures in Guidance* with Drs. Jeff Ashby and Don DeGraaf. Dr. Kottman has two new books coming out in 2008: *Counseling Theories: Practical Applications with Children and*

Adolescents in Schools (edited with Dr. Ann Vernon) and *Active Intervention for Kids and Teens* (written with Drs. Jeff Ashby and Don DeGraaf).

John M. Littrell, EdD, Professor and Program Coordinator, Counseling and Career Development, Colorado State University, has been a counselor educator for 33 years. Dr. Littrell is the author of two books (*Brief Counseling in Action*, and *Portrait and Model of a School Counselor* with Jean Peterson). He has authored more than 30 refereed articles in major journals (e.g., *Professional School Counseling, Journal of Counseling and Development, Counselor Education and Supervision, Journal of Multicultural Counseling and Development*). In addition, he has authored 10 book chapters and produced six counseling videotapes for professional audiences. He has served on the editorial boards of *Professional School Counseling* and *Counselor Education and Supervision.* His specialty is the topic of brief, solution-focused counseling. In his spare time he is writing short story murder mysteries about famous counselors/therapists who, using their own theoretical frameworks, solve murders that occur in their practices.

William P. McFarland, EdD, LCPC, NCC, has been a school counselor and counselor educator for 27 years. He teaches graduate courses in school counseling, counseling children and adolescents, career development, and assessment techniques. He has been published in state and national journals on topics related to school counseling.

Ellen Hawley McWhirter, PhD, is an associate professor and the Director of Training for the Counseling Psychology Program at the University of Oregon. She authored *Counseling for Empowerment*, coauthored *At-Risk Youth: A Comprehensive Response,* 4th ed., and has over 50 refereed journal publications and book chapters. She was a 2004 Fulbright Scholar to Chile, conducting research on Chilean youth, providing consultation and training in the community, and serving as a visiting professor to the *Universidad de Chile* in Santiago. Her scholarship focuses on adolescent vocational development, youth at risk, and applications of the construct of empowerment to counseling, training, and consultation.

Robert J. Nejedlo, PhD, is Professor Emeritus at Northern Illinois University. He was a school counselor in Skokie, Illinois, and later was professor of Counseling and Director of the Student Development Center at Northern Illinois University. After retiring in 1997, he was a visiting professor at Governor's State University. Dr. Nejedlo was president of the Illinois Counseling Association, the Association for Counselor Education and Supervision, and the American Counseling Association.

Jean Sunde Peterson, PhD, NCC, LMHC, is an associate professor and coordinator of the School Counseling program at Purdue University. Her 70 publications include models for clinical practice and research related to the social and emotional development of at-risk, high-ability youth. Among her seven books are *Portrait and Model of a School Counselor* (with Dr. John Littrell) and *Models of Counseling Gifted Children, Adolescents, and Young Adults.* She has received national research awards from NAGC and American Mensa.

Carol Klose Smith, PhD, LPC, NCC, completed her doctoral studies at the University of Iowa and is currently an assistant professor in the Counselor Education Program at Winona State University. Her research interests include interpersonal violence, group counseling, social class concerns in counselor education, and academic transitions.

Michael Spagna, Professor, received his PhD in special education with concentrations in reading disabilities, public policy, and psychological/educational measurement and assessment from the University of California, Berkley–San Francisco State joint doctoral program. Dr. Spagna is the author of several articles and texts, including *Curriculum, Assessment, and Instruction for Students With Disabilities,* and several chapters on learning disorders in the two-volume *Comprehensive Textbook of Psychiatry.* Dr. Spagna is the first Eisner Endowed Chair in Teaching and Learning, a premier center with a mission of keeping Cal State University Northridge at the forefront of cutting edge innovations in preparing teachers, administrators, as well as school counselors and school psychologists.

Shari Tarver-Behring, PhD, is a professor and school counseling coordinator at California State University, Northridge. Dr. Tarver-Behring is a credentialed psychologist and school counselor. In addition to her extensive clinical and teaching experience in the area of child and adolescent psychology, Dr. Tarver-Behring has published and presented in the areas of school consultation with diverse youth, the school counselor's role in full inclusion, and school interventions for at-risk youth. She has recently begun working in the area of transdisciplinary team assessment and interventions with children, adolescents, and their families.

Toni R. Tollerud, PhD, LCPC, NCC, NCSC, ACS, has been a professor of Counselor Education for 17 years, with a specialty in school counseling and supervision. She is a noted consultant and speaker across the state of Illinois and has been a strong advocate for legislation that has benefited school counselors, and has promoted the inclusion of the developmental model for all schools in the state. In 2007 she took the position as Director of Training for the Center for Child Welfare and Education, where she supervises education advisors who work with kids in foster care and adoption to ensure that their educational needs and rights are being met. On a personal note, she loves music, Italian food, and traveling.

Kirk Zinck, PhD, LMFT is an assistant professor at the University of Texas at Tyler and director for graduate programs in Marriage and Family Therapy and School Counseling. He also serves as a family consultant to Smith County Juvenile Services in Tyler, where he works with a team on developing a family-centered approach to treating sexually abused youth. Dr. Zinck's background includes school counseling, clinical counseling, and counselor supervision. He has coauthored seven brief counseling publications and a nationally distributed videotape with Dr. John Littrell. Prior to starting his university teaching, he served as an itinerant mental health clinician to three Alaskan villages.

Working With Children, Adolescents, and Their Parents: Practical Application of Developmental Theory

Ann Vernon

The counselor met with a single-parent father and his 15-year-old son. The dad told the counselor that he and his son, Dustin had recently begun to have some major arguments about the boy's curfew and chores. They both wanted to address these problems before they escalated. The counselor, who had seen Dustin previously in regard to school performance and sibling relationship issues, thought him to be a "good kid" who was concerned about his grades but had to work hard to keep them up. The counselor recalled that, although Dustin said he had trouble controlling his temper when his younger brother did things that annoyed him, Dustin said he had learned new ways to handle his anger and frustration.

As the counselor listened to the father and son describing their recent conflict, she became aware that the father perceived his son's refusal to do assigned chores as defiant and assumed that this defiant behavior would begin to surface in other areas as well. When the counselor asked Dustin to talk from his perspective, she began to sense that, although this adolescent did not necessarily like doing chores, the real issue was the arbitrary way in which his dad was instructing him. Dustin also told the counselor that he resented his curfew being earlier than most of his friends' curfews, but he admitted that he had not talked to his dad about this because Dustin assumed it wouldn't do any good. Instead, he sometimes stayed out later than his curfew and then argued with Dad at being grounded for coming in late.

Based on what father and son had related, the counselor concluded that many of the problems they were experiencing were a result of the difficulties inherent in the transition from childhood to adolescence. She explained to them that significant changes occur in parent–child relationships during this time, one of which is that adolescents are naturally struggling to achieve independence and need an opportunity to make some of their own decisions. Therefore, when parents tell their children what, when, and how to do things, adolescents hear their parents' words as commands and feel like they are being treated as children who are not responsible enough to make their own decisions.

The counselor suggested to the dad that his son probably would be less defiant if the dad were to phrase his requests in a way that would allow Dustin to take more control of the tasks. She also explained that, at Dustin's age, many adolescents assume things without checking them out and do not have the cognitive ability to analyze situations and anticipate consequences carefully. Therefore, it was normal for Dustin to assume that his dad would not negotiate on curfew and instead take matters into his own hands by ignoring his curfew.

Assimilating this information about adolescent development, Dustin's father was able to reframe the issue of defiance and recognize that his son was attempting to assert his independence—normal for that age. At this point, Dustin and his dad were able to work out a contract for chores and curfew that had reasonable timelines and consequences if Dustin were to fail to do what they had agreed upon.

As this vignette illustrates, knowledge about developmental characteristics is essential in assessment and intervention with children, adolescents, and their parents. Without this perspective, problems can be easily misconstrued. Parents in particular may assume that the symptom or behavior they see is indicative of something more pervasive if they fail to take into account that their children should be expected to change over time and what the parents have been accustomed to as "normal" will differ at later stages of development.

A Model of Developmental Levels

Children's level of development influences how they respond to their attaining basic needs, as well as to normal developmental issues and more significant situational problems. According to Maslow (1968), among the needs of all human beings are safety, belongingness, love, and respect. When these basic needs are not met, children respond to the deficits depending on their developmental level in one or more of the areas listed in the next level: self, emotional, cognitive, physical, and social. The model in Figure 1.1 illustrates this concept more specifically.

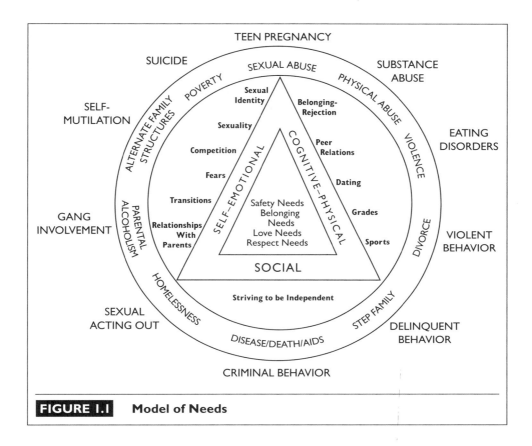

FIGURE 1.1 Model of Needs

Thus, young children in the preoperational stage of development will respond very differently to a basic need for safety than will adolescents who have begun to develop abstract thinking skills. Young children do not have the ability to clearly identify or express their feelings, do not understand all of the ramifications of the situation, and have difficulty generating effective coping skills. The implication, therefore, is that the experience itself is mediated by the level of development and impacts children differently depending on that level.

The level of development also influences how children respond to the normal developmental problems that most children and adolescents experience to some extent and are listed in the first circle of the model: puberty, friendship, grades, mastery and competition, and so forth. Once again, how children respond to these typical problems depends upon their level of development. For instance, self-conscious pre-teens whose abstract thinking skills are limited can easily overgeneralize about the horror of giving a speech in front of peers. Instead of realizing that their classmates probably feel very much the same way and that not everyone will be staring at them or noticing their acne, they assume that their only option is to skip class to avoid the situation. Had they been at a more advanced level of cognitive develop-ment, they would have been able to identify alternative ways to deal with this typi-cal problem associated with puberty and physical development.

The same observation applies to how children respond to the situational prob-lems listed in the next circle: living with divorced or alcoholic parents, being home-less, or being a victim of abuse. Fortunately, not all children have these problems, but how they respond also depends on their developmental level. For example, an 8-year-old whose mother abandoned the family will have difficulty understanding how her mother could do this if she loves her daughter. The 8-year-old's thinking is con-crete and dichotomous: Her mother either loves her and stays with the family or she doesn't love her daughter and leaves. A 17-year-old whose cognitive skills are more advanced would be able to recognize other relevant factors and issues that influenced her mother's decision and would not automatically assume that just because her mother left did not mean that she did not love her daughter.

Finally, how children interpret and respond to basic needs, as well as typical and situational problems, can result in various self-defeating behaviors, as listed around the outside edges of the circles in Figure 1.1 and illustrated in the following example.

After 9-year-old Rosa's parents lost their jobs, the family was homeless for several months. On many nights Rosa could not sleep because she was cold, hungry, or frightened. Even though her parents usually made sure that Rosa went to school, she was embarrassed because she was dirty and disheveled and felt bad about being teased and taunted by her peers. Rosa kept her feelings to herself, but as the humiliation increased, her self-worth plummeted. She believed she was as ugly and worthless as her classmates claimed.

Eventually Rosa's parents both secured new jobs, and the family moved into an apartment. Still, Rosa's situation at school did not improve. She lacked both the confidence and the social skills to be accepted by her peers.

In junior high Rosa began to develop physically, and suddenly she became the center of attention because boys were attracted to her. For the first time she felt like she belonged. Before long she became sexually active, which was her way to feel loved and respected. Unfortunately, her physical maturity was not accompanied by maturity in other areas of development. She didn't think about the consequences of her sexual activity, lacked the social skills to assertively deal with the pressure to have sex, and illogically attributed her popularity with boys as the way to feel worthwhile. By age 15 she was preg-nant and dropped out of school.

As this vignette illustrates, the way youngsters process the experiences depicted in Figure 1.1 is influenced by their developmental maturity. Helping professionals have to recognize this reality and take an active role in helping their counselees develop the social, emotional, cognitive, and self-development skills needed to handle the normal and situational challenges of growing up at the different developmental levels. To some extent, the importance of incorporating a developmental perspective into the counseling process with clients of all ages has been acknowledged, but developmental theory has been applied primarily through comprehensive counseling programs that focus on prevention through classroom and small-group work rather than assessment and intervention in individual counseling (Vernon & Clemente, 2005).

Although the preventive focus is extremely important, counselors must also consider developmental factors in conceptualizing problems, in designing or selecting age-appropriate assessment instruments, and in developing interventions that take into account the child's developmental capabilities. In addition, because adult models of assessment and treatment cannot be extrapolated to young clients, knowledge of development is essential in selecting appropriate interventions that will engage children in the counseling process (Vernon, 2002; Vernon & Clemente, 2005).

As illustrated in the vignette at the beginning of this chapter, counselors must convey information about developmental norms and competencies in their consultations with parents. If parents have a better understanding about what to expect with their children at various stages of development, they are more able to assess symptoms they see as problematic.

This chapter covers characteristics and applications in counseling and consulting for early childhood, middle childhood, early adolescence, and mid-adolescence. Typical characteristics and developmental problems are described for these children, ages 4–18, in five areas of development: physical, cognitive, self, social, and emotional.

Developmental Characteristics of Early Childhood

Physical Development

Young children seem to be in perpetual motion as they explore their world and direct their energy to a variety of things. Although physical growth is slower during the preschool years than in earlier years, gross motor skills such as running, jumping, hopping, throwing, and climbing improve dramatically during this period (Berger, 2003; Trawick-Smith, 2000). Fine-motor skills develop more slowly but also improve dramatically during early childhood.

Drawing, writing, and using scissors are more difficult to master because they involve small body movements (Berger, 2003). Nevertheless, 4-year-olds can copy designs, and 5-year-olds can reproduce letters and copy short words (Owens, 2002).

Although their muscles have increased in size and strength, children at this level still have immature functioning compared to children in middle childhood. Gradually, 4- and 5-year-olds lose their baby fat, and by age 6 their body proportions are similar to those of adults (Owens, 2002). Because their growth has slowed, preschoolers tend to have diminished appetites.

Cognitive Development

To 4- and 5-year-old preschoolers, the world is a fascinating place. With their imaginations and vivid fantasies, anything is possible. Ordinary playrooms become transformed into museums, and imaginary friends are frequent dinner-table guests. Typical preschoolers are curious, energetic, and eager.

The cognitive development of preschoolers is characterized by preoperational thinking (Berk, 2003; McDevitt & Ormrod, 2002). Although they are beginning to reason more logically if they are asked to think about familiar things in a familiar context, they still rely heavily on solving problems based on what they hear or see rather than by logical reasoning. McDevitt and Ormrod noted, however, that preschoolers can think more logically than Piaget suggested and that they can draw logically valid conclusions such as making appropriate inferences when they listen to a story. They do have difficulty with abstract concepts such as divorce and death (Berk, 2001).

Also characteristic of their cognitive style is unidimensional thought (Trawick–Smith, 2000), the tendency to center on their perceptions, or on one aspect of the situation, rather than taking a broader view. This style of thinking interferes with their ability to understand cause and effect, and to see that the same object or situation can have two identities. For example, many preschoolers cannot grasp the concept that their teacher could also be a parent.

Two additional characteristics of preschoolers' thinking are *animism* and *artificialism* (Rathus, 2004). Animism refers to the attribution of lifelike qualities to inanimate objects, such as comforting a doll when it falls. Artificialism is the belief that people cause natural phenomena, such as thinking that rain occurs because fire fighters are spraying water from the sky. Both of these characteristics contribute to preschoolers' ability to engage in make-believe play.

An important facet of cognitive development during this period is language. By age 5, children can understand almost anything explained to them in context if the examples are specific (Bjorklund, 2000). They are able to introduce new topics into a conversation but have difficulty maintaining a sustained dialogue about one idea (Owens, 1996). They also struggle with abstract nouns and concepts such as time and space, as characterized by the frequent question, "Are we there yet?"

Self-Development

Preschoolers are egocentric. They assume that everyone thinks and feels the same way they do and have difficulty seeing things from another's perspective. This egocentrism is reflected in their excessive use of "my" and "mine." Their self-esteem is quite high (McDevitt & Ormrod, 2002), and they tend to overestimate their own abilities, thinking that they are competent in everything (Berger, 2003). This belief is advantageous at this stage, when the children have so many new tasks to master. With each mastery, their sense of initiative and competence increases.

Another self-development issue relates to preschoolers' self-control, which improves during this period. Preschoolers are better at modifying and controlling their own impulses and are not as frustrated and intolerant if their needs are not met immediately (Berger, 2003; Berk, 2001). Preschoolers also show more initiative during this period. As children enter preschool, they face more challenges and assume more responsibilities. In turn, their self-initiated behaviors increase.

Social Development

At this age play serves an extremely important function. Most of the play of 4-year-olds is associative; they interact and share, and although they are engaging in a common activity, they do not assign roles and do not have clear goals (Owens, 2002).

By age 5, they begin to engage in more cooperative play—taking turns, creating games, sharing, dealing with conflict, and forming groups to do something (Rathus, 2004). They also engage in more structured games that are based on reality (Newman & Newman, 2006).

Children at this age do not understand give-and-take. They are likely to be egocentric and unable to see another child's point of view (Kaplan, 2000). Because they also have difficulty understanding intentionality, they may misinterpret others' behavior and respond inappropriately.

Gender differences are quite apparent. At this age, in the United States as well as in other parts of the world, children prefer same-gender playmates (Newman & Newman, 2006). Boys engage more readily in rough, noisy, competitive, aggressive play, whereas girls are more nurturing and cooperative (Feldman, 2003; Rathus, 2004). By age 5 toughness is associated with males and gentleness with females (Owens, 2002).

Emotional Development

Although their vocabularies are expanding and they are beginning to understand which emotions are appropriate to specific situations (Izard & Ackerman, 2000), preschoolers still have a rather limited vocabulary for expressing how they feel. As a result, they often express their feelings behaviorally. Children at this age have difficulty understanding that they can experience different emotions about a situation simultaneously, although they can understand the concept of experiencing different emotions at different times (Berk, 1999). They are still quite literal and cannot clearly differentiate what someone is expressing overtly and what they may be feeling (Cobb, 2001).

Toward the end of the preschool period, children have a better understanding of why others are upset, and they begin to respond verbally or physically to others' emotions. Their understanding of other people's emotions is limited, however, by their perception, and they tend to perceive only the most obvious aspects of an emotional situation, such as being angry, happy, or sad (Vernon & Clemente, 2005).

Counseling Applications for Early Childhood

Helping professionals who work with 4- and 5-year-olds must remain cognizant of the physical, intellectual, social, emotional, and self-development characteristics of young children during both assessment and intervention. Because preschoolers have a limited attention span, counselors should use a variety of techniques to engage these children. Also, at this age children require concrete approaches. Their ability to remember concepts is enhanced if they can manipulate objects, have a visual representation of the concept, or engage in some form of play to help them resolve issues. Traditional forms of counseling that rely primarily on talking and listening do not work well with young children (DiGiuseppe, 1999; Vernon, 2002). Consequently, counselors will find themselves using multiple forms of play media, including puppetry, games, art and music activities, as well as role playing and movement activities. Teaching them to identify and describe emotions using flash cards or feeling games is also helpful given their limited feeling vocabulary. Chapters 3 and 4 of this book describe in detail appropriate interventions to use with young children.

Typical Problems During Early Childhood

The social and emotional development of preschoolers may be manifested by difficulty engaging in cooperative play. These children sometimes have trouble getting along because of their limited ability to understand give-and-take or to see situations from perspectives other than their own egocentric view. In addition, the tendency of young children to take things literally can result in fear. For example, parents who tell their preschooler that Grandma "went to sleep" when in reality she died should not be surprised when their child is afraid to go to sleep at night.

Elkind (1991) related the example of a young child who refused to go home from preschool because he was going to meet his new "half brother." In discussing his fear, it became apparent that the boy actually thought he would be seeing half of a brother! This type of thinking, characteristic of preschoolers, is similar to many other fears and uncertainties of 4- and 5-year-olds because of their preoperational thinking— fear of dark rooms, fear of noises at night, fear of monsters, fear of "bad people" (Bee, 2000). In addition, they may hesitate to leave the house to play in the yard, visit a friend, or be left at preschool because they are afraid of being separated from a parent.

In addition to these typical problems, many situational problems, such as divorce, abuse, and parental alcoholism, affect the lives of children. Counselors must keep in mind that the way children process typical developmental problems as well as more serious situational issues is directly related to the developmental capabilities of these young children.

Case Studies of Young Children

██████Manuel

Manuel, age 5, had started refusing to go outdoors to play in the yard. This behavior was confusing to his parents because until the past month, he had showed no hesitation about playing in the neighborhood with his friends. The parents were not aware of any traumatic incident when Manuel was playing outside, and they did not see any other problematic symptoms. They contacted a counselor for help.

The counselor first reassured the parents that this problem is common in children of this age because they have a vivid imagination, take things literally, and have a limited ability to process concepts. She explained that she first would attempt to determine specifically what Manuel was afraid of and then develop some interventions to help him deal with the problem.

In working with Manuel, the counselor had him draw a picture of himself playing in the yard. He readily drew himself with several friends playing in the sand pile. The counselor told him that she knew he did not want to play outside much any more and asked if he were afraid of something in the yard. At first Manuel denied being afraid of anything and said he didn't want to go outside because it was too cold or because his friends weren't allowed to go outdoors at that time. The counselor then read Manuel a book, *Something Might Happen* (Lester, 2003), to help him cope with his anxieties.

After hearing the story, Manuel did admit that he was a little scared to go outside but couldn't verbalize why, so the counselor asked him to draw a picture to show what he thought might happen. The picture showed "bogeymen" hiding in the trees.

To empower Manuel to handle the fear of bogeymen, as well as other fears he might have, the counselor used a combination of empowerment strategies, self-talk, and puppet play, specifically addressing the imaginative fear that seemed very real to this 5-year-old. First, she asked Manuel if he could think of anything that he could put in the yard or on the fence that might scare away the bogeymen. After some brainstorming, he and the counselor decided that Manuel could make scary masks to hang around the yard. The counselor also knew that Manuel had a dog, so the counselor suggested that Manuel put up a sign reading, "This is a bogeyman guard dog."

Next, the counselor helped Manuel generate some statements he could say to himself when he was going outside: "My dog will scare them away," "The masks will scare them away," and "Even if they aren't scared away, my friends are there with me and we can protect each other." The counselor also suggested that Manuel buy a whistle to alert his parents if he felt threatened. Finally, the counselor asked Manuel to use puppets to act out different ways he could react if he thought he saw a bogeyman in the yard.

In conferring with Manuel's parents, the counselor again emphasized that his behavior seemed normal for a child of his age and that they might see some of this fear transferred to monsters in his room at night. She emphasized that these fears do seem very real and probable to a young child and cautioned them to take the fear seriously and not let his siblings tease him about it. The counselor asked the parents to help Manuel rehearse his self-talk and make the masks. She concluded by saying that if these interventions were unsuccessful, other approaches could be tried.

As this case illustrates, the counselor conceptualized the problem by taking into account how children at this age experience the world and process experiences. The interventions she suggested and implemented were concrete and addressed the problem in a variety of ways.

Amaya

When kindergarten started in the fall, 5-year-old Amaya was excited and looked forward to going each day. After the third week of school, however, she began to have difficulty falling asleep and told her parents that she didn't want to go to school again. The father called the school counselor to express his concern and ask for help. In talking with him, the counselor determined that there had been no changes in routine at home and no new developments, so together they assumed that something at school was causing the anxiety.

Prior to seeing this young client individually, the counselor selected Amaya and two of her classmates to visit with in the playroom. During this session the counselor put out a Fisher Price schoolhouse and some blocks and invited the children to play with the toys. Amaya chose to play with blocks while the other two children were engaged with the schoolhouse. The purpose of this session was to get somewhat acquainted with Amaya so she would feel more comfortable when the counselor would meet with her alone. The counselor also took other small groups of children and a few individuals over the next several days, to normalize the experience of going to the counselor's playroom.

When the counselor met with Amaya individually, she brought out several paper plates and markers. On different plates she drew a sad face, a worried/scared face, an angry face, and a happy face, discussing the feelings as she drew. Then she asked Tanya to pick out the paper-plate faces that described how she felt about going to a birthday party, going swimming, going shopping with her parents, going to the doctor, and going to school.

Amaya readily selected the worried/scared face for going to school, and the counselor gently asked if she could describe what scared her about this. Amaya just shrugged her shoulders, so the counselor said that they would play a little guessing game. She said that she has had kindergarteners in the past who have been afraid of going to school, so she was going to think hard about what they were scared about and see if Amaya had the same fears. To engage Amaya, together they selected 8 colored buttons from a large jar and put them in a smaller container. Then the counselor explained that she would have Amaya close her eyes while she put one of the buttons in her hand and closed her fist over it. Amaya's job was to guess the color of the button (without looking in the container) and if was correct, the counselor would make a guess about what worried Amaya about going to school. Amaya liked the game, and it seemed to help her relax. It took several tries before she identified the correct color, and several guesses before the counselor hit on Amaya's fear: strangers snatching her as she walked from the school to the bus.

Knowing that the local police had recently talked to the class about "stranger danger," the counselor asked Amaya if she would tell more about what she was afraid would happen. Amanda replied that "these policemen told us to be scared of strangers, and I don't know the lady who walks us to the bus, so she must be a stranger." Amandas response is a typical example of preoperational thinking—taking things literally.

Prior to the next session the counselor asked the teacher to take a picture of all the "helpers" who worked with this class. Then the counselor mixed in pictures of people who would be strangers to Amaya and contacted the parents to get photos of close friends and relatives. When they met for the next session, the counselor laid out the following pictures and asked Amaya to sort them into three categories and paste them on a sorting board: people I know very well, people I don't know at all, and people who I know a little bit because they are helpers at school. After correctly identifying the helpers and sorting the pictures, they talked about the difference between strangers—people you don't know at all—and people who you know a little bit because they have contact with you in some way and are there to help you. She asked Amaya to take the poster home to show her parents, and maybe they could add to it if she were interested in doing that.

Another intervention the counselor used was to have Amaya be a "detective." Every day, instead of worrying that the stranger lady would snatch her, Amaya was asked to pay close attention to what the stranger lady did. Did she take any kids? Was she mean? When the counselor saw Amaya two days later, Amaya said she had been a really good detective and she didn't see the stranger lady do anything bad. The counselor encouraged Amayato keep up the good work and checked with the parents to see if their daughter was sleeping better and not complaining about going to school. They confirmed that things seemed to be better and had posted Amaya's sorting board in her room so they could continue to review the concepts and discuss them as needed.

Developmental Characteristics of Middle Childhood

Physical Development

During middle childhood, ages 6–11, physical growth is relatively stable (Bee, 2000; McDevitt & Ormrod, 2002). Children do grow taller, their body proportions change, and their muscles become stronger (Schickendanz, Schickendanz, Forsyth, & Forsyth, 1998), but because of the slower rate of growth, they have more self-control over their bodies. Movement becomes more controlled and complex (Owens, 2002). Children at this level are able to master most motor skills and become much more agile and adept at running, skipping, jumping, and riding a bike. By the end of this period, they show a major improvement in their fine-motor skills as well.

Because children's bodies mature at different rates, some 10- and 11-year-olds are entering puberty (Rathaus, 2004). Height and weight growth spurts, which begin at different times for different children, contribute to self-consciousness and embarrassment (Vernon & Al-Mabuk, 1995).

Cognitive Development

According to Piaget (1967), children undergo a transitional period between preoperational and concrete operational thought between the ages of 5 and 7. By age 8, they have become concrete operational thinkers, which Berk (2003) considered a "major turning point" (p. 241) because their thinking is becoming more like that of adults. As a result, they are able to understand reversibility, reciprocity, identity, and classification. They also develop the skill of conservation, the ability to understand that the quantity remains the same even if the appearance changes (Owens, 2002). They begin to apply these principles in a variety of contexts such as friendships, rules in games, and team play, as well as in academic contexts (Vernon, 1993).

During this period of development, children's thinking becomes more logical, and their problem-solving abilities are enhanced. However, their problem-solving abilities are somewhat limited because they do not consider other possible solutions (Siegler, DeLoache, & Eisenberg, 2003). Because they are concrete thinkers, however, they still cannot reason abstractly, and they make assumptions and jump to conclusions, which influences the way they approach situations. For example, if their best friend does not sit by them, they assume that they did something that made the friend angry, rather than consider a variety of other possibilities.

In middle childhood, children learn best by questioning, exploring, and engaging in guided participation through social interaction (Gauvain, 2001). Their language development continues; they begin to understand more abstract concepts; and they use vocabulary in more sophisticated ways (Berk, 1999). By the end of middle childhood, children's vocabularies will expand to more than 40,000 words (Owens, 2002). Even in middle childhood, children rely on intonation more than context to help them understand another person's intent (Shwe, 1999).

Self-Development

Children's self-understanding expands during this period, and instead of describing themselves superficially, they have a multidimensional view of themselves (Owens, 2002). Consequently, they are able to describe themselves in terms of several competencies at once: "I'm short, a good reader, and a fast runner." Further, they can provide justification for their attributes: "I'm smart because I got an A on a test." During middle childhood they begin to see themselves as having more complex personalities (Harter, Waters, & Whitesell, 1998; Siegler et al., 2003) and start to develop more of an internal locus of control (Vernon & Al-Mabuk, 1995).

As they enter school and begin to compare themselves to others, they become self-critical, feel inferior, and may develop lower self-esteem (Cole & Cole, 1996). They may be more inhibited about trying new things, and they are sensitive to feedback from peers. As they become aware of their specific areas of competence and more aware of their personal strengths and weaknesses, they may experience either self-confidence or self-doubt (Bee, 2000).

At around age 8 children develop a concept of their overall worth (Harter, 1996). Their self-esteem begins to solidify, and they behave according to their preconceived ideas of themselves (Harter, Waters, & Whitesell, 1998).

Social Development

During the primary school years, socialization with peers is a major issue. Being accepted in a group and having a "best friend" contribute to children's sense of competence. As they learn to deal with peer pressure, rejection, approval, and conformity, they begin to formulate values, behaviors, and beliefs that facilitate their social development (Pruitt, 1998). Associating with peers who are different from them with regard to abilities, religion, ethnicity, and personality enhances their perspective-taking skills (Berk, 2003)

Friendships serve other important functions, too. Through associations with peers, children develop a broader view of the world, experiment with ideas and roles, and learn important interaction skills. As they participate in activities, they learn to cooperate and compromise, to make and break rules, to assume roles as leaders and followers, and to understand others' points of view (Berger, 2003).

By age 7, children begin to outgrow their egocentrism and adopt more prosocial behaviors. According to Selman (1980) and Selman and Schultz (1990), children in this stage of development realize that other people have thoughts and feelings that may differ from their own, although these children still have overly simplistic perceptions of others' perspectives. In the upper elementary grades, they begin to realize that others may have mixed or contradictory feelings about a situation, and they understand that how people act may not reflect accurately what they feel (McDevitt & Ormrod, 2002).

As children continue to mature and develop an ability to see things from another's perspective, they become more adept at interpreting social cues and evaluating input (Cole & Cole, 1996; Pruitt, 1998). Therefore, they become better able to resolve conflicts and solve social problems.

Emotional Development

During this period children begin to have more complex emotions, such as guilt, shame, and pride. They also are increasingly aware that people are capable of having more than one emotion at the same time, that feelings can change, and that they are not the cause of another's emotional discomfort (Kaplan, 2000). Children at this age are more adept at hiding their emotions when they don't want to hurt someone's feelings (Berk, 1999).

Generally, children at this age are more sensitive, empathic, and better able to recognize and communicate their feelings to others. Children who are more sociable and assertive have more empathy toward others (Berk, 2003). During middle childhood, fears and anxieties are related to real-life as opposed to imaginary issues. For example, because they are experiencing many new situations that require mastery, anxiety about school performance or peer inclusion is common (Vernon & Clemente, 2005).

Counseling Applications for Middle Childhood

Middle childhood spans a number of years and has many "firsts," particularly those associated with school and friends. School and mental health professionals should keep in mind that children in the concrete stage of development have limited ability to think logically and see possibilities.

This point was brought to light when a 10-year-old and her father visited with the mental health counselor about a situation that had arisen. The father was upset because, instead of coming home from school immediately to deliver newspapers to her customers, she stayed for an additional basketball practice. The frustrated father asked, "Why didn't you can home and ask someone else to do it rather than just not show up?" His daughter replied, "I honestly didn't think about that. The coach said we wouldn't get to play if we didn't stay, so that's what I did."

This case is a good example that, despite the gradual improvement in their problem-solving abilities, these children continue to need adult guidance to apply their skills consistently to common problems.

Professionals working with this age group should continue to employ concrete interventions to help the children resolve problems. For example, playing a board game and identifying positive and negative study skills at each "stop" along the Road to Achievement (Vernon, 2002, pp. 202–203) is a creative way to help children learn good study skills. Singing "procrastination pointers" to the tune of *Mary Had a Little Lamb* is an engaging way for them to learn more about how to deal with procrastination (Vernon, 2002, p. 185). Creating an anger alarm using various art media is an effective way to teach children how to recognize what "sets off" their anger (Vernon, 2002, p. 162), and engaging them in "I Can, I Can't" experiments helps them learn that everyone has strengths and weaknesses (Vernon, 2002, p. 71). In addition, as described in Chapter 3, bibliotherapy, art activities, puppets, role play, and games are appropriate interventions for this age group.

Typical Problems During Middle Childhood

The most common stressors for children during middle childhood are school-related—failing a test, getting a bad report card, or not receiving the teacher's approval (Owens, 2002). Owens noted other stressors that were related to the family—arguing, sibling issues, and parental separation. Appearance and health issues, too, were cited as stressors. Porter (1999) identified additional typical concerns of children at this age. In particular, this author noted issues surrounding peer relationships—being different from other children, losing friends, being accepted by peers, being picked on, or being lonely. These children also worry about needing to be perfect, struggle with self-confidence, and are frustrated in becoming more independent (Porter, 1999).

Far too many young children also must deal with more serious situational problems, such as growing up in abusive or alcoholic homes, living in poverty, or dealing with difficult adjustments to parental divorce and remarriage. Regardless of the type of problem, whether it is a normal challenge of growing up or a more serious situational problem, counselors should design interventions that are concrete in nature to engage the child in problem solving regardless of the type of problem. During middle childhood, simply talking about the problem is usually not effective (Vernon, 2002).

Case Studies from Middle Childhood

▓▓▓Jessica

Jessica, age 9, was referred to a counselor because she was afraid to perform in front of others. This was problematic for her because she was a talented dancer and ice skater, but she became so anxious prior to and during a performance that she sometimes missed school on the day of the performance. She felt sick to her stomach as the performance date approached. Jessica was self-critical and hard on herself if she didn't perform perfectly.

To get a more accurate assessment of the problem, the counselor asked Jessica to describe the following:

What she is thinking prior to performing
What she is feeling physically prior to performing

What she imagines will happen as she performs
How she feels emotionally before and during the performance

The counselor also asked Jessica what she had tried to do to solve the problem. Based on what Jessica said, the counselor confirmed her hypothesis that Jessica was perfectionistic and looked at the performance situation as an "all or nothing, pass/fail" event. In addition, Jessica imagined the worst, even though she seldom received less than a perfect score. This sort of absolutist thinking is common in children of Jessica's age, and counselors should help them see that there is a range of possibilities. To help Jessica with this, the counselor placed a strip of masking tape on the floor and positioned note cards stating the following along the line in the order shown here:

1. Fail by getting everything wrong
2. Get a bad score and make lots of wrong moves
3. Get an average score and make quite a few wrong moves
4. Get a very high score but still make some wrong moves
5. Get a perfect score and do everything absolutely right

Next, the counselor asked Jessica to stand at the position on the line that represented where her scores were most of the time. Then the counselor asked her to stand on the spot that represented where she was if she didn't get a perfect score. As the counselor suspected, Jessica stood first at the far end of the line (top score, everything right), then at the next level down.

The counselor then gave Jessica two pairs of old eyeglasses. She described one pair as the "doom and gloom" glasses and said that when Jessica put them on, she would imagine only terrible things happening when she performed. She asked Jessica to put on the glasses and verbalize those thoughts while the counselor recorded them. Then she asked Jessica to put on the other pair, which the counselor described as "rose-colored" glasses. When Jessica had these glasses on, things would look very good. The counselor asked Jessica to verbalize her thoughts when she wore the rose-colored glasses.

The counselor explained to Jessica that because she had never totally failed a performance in the past, nor had she ever received an average or below-average score, Jessica probably didn't need to wear the "doom-and-gloom" glasses. The counselor pointed out that if Jessica pretended to put on the rose-colored glasses before each performance, she could say positive things to herself, such as, "I usually do very well, so why should I even think I won't do well this time?" "Even if I mess up a little, does this mean I'm a terrible dancer or skater?" "If I get too nervous, I'll worry too much and make myself sick, but if I just work hard and focus, I'll probably do okay." After the counselor modeled these rational self-statements to Jessica, the two of them generated a few more together and put them on note cards that Jessica could look at prior to a performance.

As a final intervention, the counselor taught Jessica how to do progressive muscle relaxation and other deep-breathing techniques (Copeland, 2001). The counselor also had Jessica interview her older sister and her aunt, both of whom had been dancers, about whether they had ever scored less than perfect and how they handled that, as well as what they saw as their individual strengths and weaknesses. This activity helped Jessica see that other people had strong and weak areas, that they made mistakes, and that they had scored less than perfect in dance recitals and it hadn't been a catastrophe.

The counselor explained to Jessica's parents that it was normal for her to feel more pressure at age 9 than she had previously because she was more aware of her performance in relation to others. The counselor emphasized the importance of the parents' sharing some of their "less than perfect" experiences with Jessica, reinforcing the importance of effort versus the final score, and helping her avoid thinking the worst by looking at her "track record" of performance. The counselor also recommended that they read together the story "The Less Than Perfect Prince" from *Color Us Rational* (Waters, 1979), a story about a prince who learns that he and the world can't be perfect. Finally, the counselor explained the relaxation exercises she had taught Jessica so the parents could help their daughter use them at home.

Ian

Ian, a second-grader, visited the school counselor because he said that everyone was picking on him. To get a more accurate picture of the problem, the counselor asked Ian to act out, with 15 small action figures, what happened when others picked on him. When Ian acted out the situation, the counselor noted that of the 15 action figures involved in the game, only a few seemed to be actively involved in picking on Ian—calling him names and trying to prevent him from participating in the game. When questioned about this, Ian agreed that not everyone picked on him but said that he didn't want to go out for recess because the kids were so mean to him.

The counselor then asked Ian to tell him more specifically how these kids picked on him. Ian related in detail some of the things they did to him. He said that what bothered him the most was when they called him a pig and said he was fat and ugly and couldn't run fast. The counselor listened carefully to Ian, then took out a mirror and handed it to him. "Ian," he said, "look into this mirror and tell me what you see."

Ian looked in the mirror and said that he saw himself.

"Do you see a fat, ugly kid?"

"No," Ian responded.

The counselor then asked, "Do you see something with pink ears and a snout in the mirror?"

"No!" Ian laughed.

"Then, Ian, if you aren't what they say you are, what is there to be upset about?"

Ian responded that the kids shouldn't call him names, and the counselor agreed that it wasn't nice to call others names but stressed that usually we can't control what others do. He explained to Ian that together they might be able to come up with some ideas that Ian could use so he didn't upset himself so much when others behaved badly toward him.

Together, Ian and the counselor brainstormed some things that might help him, including making up a silly song or a limerick that he could say to himself to make him laugh instead of feeling upset when others called him names that he knew weren't true. Ian liked the idea of the limerick and, with a little help from the counselor, he wrote the following:

You shouldn't call me a pig,
But if you do, it's nothing big.
I'm not what you say,
So have it your way,
But I'm not a pig in a hole that I dig.

After developing the limerick, the counselor asked Ian to repeat it aloud several times until he had memorized it. They agreed that Ian would say this to himself the next time his classmates teased him so he could laugh instead of getting so upset. Before sending him back to the classroom, the counselor asked Ian what he had learned during their session. Ian immediately stated that he knew he didn't have to be upset if others teased him about things that weren't true and that he felt better because he had a plan to try.

Developmental Characteristics of Early Adolescence

Physical Development

During early adolescence (ages 10 to 14) physical changes take place more rapidly than at any other time in the lifespan with the exception of infancy (Meece, 2002). These changes are dramatic (Susman & Rogel, 2004). The increased production of sex hormones and the changes associated with puberty begin at about age 10 for females and 12 for males, although this varies considerably. Given that the rate of puberty is earlier for girls, boys and girls of the same chronological age are at different places relative to physical development, which has implications for how they relate to each other (Wigfield, Lutz, & Wagner (2005).

Following the onset of puberty, the reproductive system matures (the ovaries in females and the testes in males), and secondary sex characteristics (growth of pubic hair, development of facial hair and voice change in males, breast development and widening of the hips in females) appear. Also, this age is characterized by a growth spurt that lasts approximately 3 years, beginning about 2 years earlier in girls than in boys (Cobb, 2001).

Although young adolescents' rates of maturity vary tremendously, self-consciousness and anxiety are common. Males and females alike may become clumsy and uncoordinated for a time because the size of their hands and feet may be disproportionate to other body parts. In addition, their rates of physical change affect how they see themselves (McDevitt & Ormrod, 2002). Early adolescents want to be like everyone else and are painfully aware of appearing awkward or different (Owens, 2002). Because they don't want others to see their bodies, "locker room phobia" is common during this period of development (Jaffe, 1998).

According to Ge and colleagues (2003), the variation in maturation rates has multiple ramifications. For example, early-maturing boys reported more depressive symptoms than those maturing on time or late, up until seventh grade. Early-maturing girls also are more prone to depression and other adjustment issues because they feel different from their peers.

The physical and hormonal changes characteristic of early adolescence can cause early adolescents to become confused. Sexual thoughts and feelings abound, often accompanied by feelings of shame and guilt. Young adolescents are curious about sex and wonder if others feel the same way they do. Straightforward information about sex is extremely important prior to and during early adolescence.

Cognitive Development

The shift from concrete to formal operational thinking begins during early adolescence. Although this change actually begins at about age 11, children do not attain formal operational thinking until age 15 to 20 (Kaplan, 2000). As they move into more formal operational thinking, adolescents begin to think more abstractly, develop the ability to hypothesize, and consider alternatives (Dusek, 1996; Kaplan, 2000; Wigfield et al., 2003). They also can reason more logically and can predict consequences of events and behaviors, but they do not always apply these skills to themselves. Thus, they may apply their skill in logic to their work in mathematics but not logically assume that if they stay out past their curfew, there might be a consequence (Vernon & Clemente, 2005).

Young adolescents are unable to link events, feelings, and situations. Schave and Schave (1989) labeled this as the "time warp." As a result, young adolescents may fail to connect flunking a test with not studying for it, or not associate being grounded with coming in late. If they were to associate these events, they might be overwhelmed by guilt, shame, or anger, so the time warp allows them to avoid responsibility.

According to Schave and Schave (1989), the shift from concrete to formal operational thinking is "the most drastic and dramatic change in cognition that occurs in anyone's life" (p. 7). With these new abilities, young adolescents are able to detect inconsistencies, think about future changes, see possibilities, think of logical rebuttals, and hypothesize about the logical sequence of events (Bee, 2000; Cobb, 2001). Counselors should keep in mind that the extent to which formal operational thinking is attained and applied consistently varies considerably during early adolescence (Cobb, 2001). Because it is easy to assume that these adolescents are capable of more mature cognitive thought than they actually are, working with them can be confusing.

Self-Development

The task of self-definition and integration begins during early adolescence (Dusek, 1996; Jaffe, 1998; Martin, 2003). This is the time when they "begin to think about their own identity and where they fit in the world," according to Holcomb-McCoy (2005), who noted that ethnicity can play a critical role in the identity development of minority youth. Ponterotto and Pederson (cited in Homcomb-McCoy, 2005) stressed that "ethnic identity development is as fundamental to the establishment of and adults' healthy self-concept and positive intercultural attitudes as are more researched areas such as occupational identity and political identity (p. 120).

As early adolescents engage in their self-development search, they push for autonomy (Cobb, 2001). At the same time, they are still immature and lack life experience (Weisfeld, 1999). These contrasts, coupled with their cognitive, physical, and pubertal changes, leave them vulnerable. As a result, they show increased dependency, which can be confusing to them and to the adults in their lives.

In some ways young adolescents contradict themselves. They want to be unique, yet they want to look like everyone else. They are both self-conscious (McDevitt & Ormrod, 2002; Meece, 2002) and egocentric, assuming that everyone is looking at them or thinking about them (Dusek, 1996). Elkind (1988) termed this belief that others are as concerned with us as we are the "imaginary audience." As a result of this type of thinking, early adolescents fantasize about how others will react to them and become overly sensitive about their performance and appearance. Because they feel awkward and ugly, self-esteem usually diminishes during this period of development and is more pronounced in young females than males (Vernon & Clemente, 2005). Eccles (2004) stressed that self-esteem is especially low at the beginning of middle school, when there are multiple transitions including puberty, as well as a change in schools and peer relationships.

At the same time, early adolescents can be highly egocentric, seeing themselves as more important than they really are or assuming that no one else experiences things the way they do (Bjorklund, 2000; Owens, 2002). They also assume that because they are unique, they are also invulnerable. Elkind (1984) labeled this the "personal fable": Because adolescents believe they are special, they think bad things can happen to others but not to them. The personal fable accounts for self-deprecating as well as self-aggrandizing behavior, in which the adolescent assumes that he or she will be heroic and world-famous.

Social Development

Peers play an increasingly significant role in young adolescents' lives and are an important part of their socialization. This is the period when cliques and distinct groups emerge, with specific "rules" about how to dress and behave. Because young adolescents look to peers as a source of support (McDevitt & Ormrod, 2002; Rubin, Coplan, Chen, Buskirk, & Wojslawowicz, 2005), so they are sensitive and vulnerable to humiliation by peers (Vernon & Al-Mabuk, 1995). Thus, while peer relationships can be a source of pleasure, they also can be negative, and dealing with rejection is a major stressor at this age. Further, bullying and fighting increase in middle school, which have many negative outcomes (Juyonen, Le, Kaganoff, Augustine, & Constant, 2004). Because they have a strong need to belong and to be accepted (Cobb, 2001; Meece, 2002), young adolescents have to learn to contend with peer pressure and decisions about which group to associate with. Wigfield and colleagues (2005) noted that the assumption that peer groups exert negative pressure during adolescence has been challenged by Brown (2004), whose studies indicated that ineffective parenting is the reason that young teens associate with bad peer groups rather than the peer group's influencing their poor decision making.

As adolescents mature, their relationships become more complex (Weisfeld, 1999). Some adolescents still have difficulty stepping outside themselves and looking at their own behavior objectively, so they may behave in obnoxious ways. This, in turn, influences how others respond to them. They also continue to have trouble taking others' viewpoints into account because they still are preoccupied with their own needs (Jaffe, 1998; Vernon & Clemente, 2005).

Young adolescents also struggle with popularity. Being good in sports contributes to popularity for boys, and being a social leader is important for girls (Cobb, 2001). Fitting into a group seems to be based on figuring out what the group is doing; the better able the adolescent is to do this, the more popular he or she will be.

Emotional Development

Early adolescents often ride an emotional roller coaster. They are more emotionally volatile (McDevitt & Ormrod, 2002) and moody, accompanied by emotional outbursts (Cobb, 2001; Siegler et al., 2003). Troublesome emotions, such as anxiety, shame, depression, guilt, and anger, also occur more frequently (Vernon & Clemente, 2005). These negative emotions can be overwhelming and cause adolescents to feel vulnerable, so they often mask their feelings of fear and vulnerability with anger. This response tends to distance people and often results in increased conflict with adults, who all too often react to the anger and fail to recognize the underlying feelings.

The increased intensity of emotions permeates all facets of young adolescents' lives. They feel anxious about their emotions, but because they are unable to think abstractly for the most part, they tend to view situations from an "either–or" perspective. They do not make good choices about how to deal with the anxiety because they are unable to generate alternatives. This, in turn, may result in more anxiety or guilt and shame.

Adults who interact with young adolescents must recognize their emotional vulnerability and not exacerbate the problem by reacting insensitively. Educating young adolescents about what they are experiencing is also essential because it is far too easy for them to feel overwhelmed by their negative emotions and deal with them in unconstructive ways.

Counseling Applications for Early Adolescence

Working with young adolescents is challenging because they mask their anger, apathy, or acting out. Helping professionals have to remember that the attainment of formal operational thinking occurs gradually, and that many of the problem behaviors they see are a result of incompetencies in thinking and reasoning. The rapid achievement of physical maturity often leads adults to assume that adolescents are more mature than they actually are.

Despite all the worries and concerns accompanying the many significant changes during early adolescence, many researchers contend that this is part of a normal, healthy, developmental process (Jaffe, 1998; Kaplan, 2000). Further, most adolescents do not resort to drug dependence, delinquent acting-out, school failure, sexual promiscuity, or other self-destructive behaviors (Owens, 2002). Nevertheless, adult guidance is useful for helping adolescents deal with their worries and problems, whether typical or more severe.

Given that young adolescents have to contend with many significant issues unique to this age level, school counselors must strive to be responsive to their needs. Akos (2005) contended that middle school counselors actively promote early adolescent development by teaching decision-making skills, educating parents about identify formation, and conducting growing-up groups to help young adolescents learn more about puberty. In addition, counselors should consult with school personnel about implementing advisory groups, teaming, and experiential learning, which are developmentally responsive practices.

In addition to a comprehensive program that includes a guidance curriculum based on adolescents' developmental needs, counselors should help students with anger management, conflict resolution, and peer relationships. Counseling interventions, whether applied in classrooms and groups or individually, should be engaging and experiential. For example, rewriting happier lyrics to sad songs is helpful in dealing with depression (Vernon, 2002, p. 135), as is making a depression "toolbox" (Vernon, 2006a) or using a sorting board activity to help identify rational and irrational beliefs that affect relationships (Vernon, 2006b, pp. 151–153).

Typical Problems During Early Adolescence

Young adolescents are easily overwhelmed by their feelings, and many of their problems result from their inability to deal effectively with these feelings. Anger, depression, and mood swings are common (Vernon, 2002; 2006a). Being overly sensitive, early adolescents may overreact to relationship issues involving friends and parents. They worry excessively about how they look, how they act, and whether they belong. They also have concerns about dealing with their own sexuality.

Relationships can be difficult during this period. As adolescents struggle for independence, they may be loving and affectionate with parents one minute and hostile and rejecting the next (Vernon & Al-Mabuk, 1995). They sometimes change friends in attempt to piece together their identity and see where they fit in socially. They typically resist authority, signifying their need to assert their independence.

Adults often overreact to adolescents' behavior, assuming that their illogical actions are intentional. Such overreaction creates additional problems for adolescents, and they may respond with defiance or withdrawal. Mental health professionals working with adolescents must keep in mind that adolescents are confused and that concrete strategies may be necessary to help them look at cause and effect, alternative behaviors, and long-range implications.

Case Studies of Young Adolescents

▰▰▰Casey

Casey's mother referred her eighth-grade son to a counselor at a local mental health center because the school had called to inform her that he had skipped school for the last 5 days. For several years the mother has had to leave for work before it was time for Casey to go to school, but his school attendance had not been a problem. She said that he "seems happy at home and has several close friends." He had struggled some with grades in seventh grade but generally got average grades. There had been no major changes in his life other than the transition to junior high last year.

When the counselor saw Casey for the first time, it was immediately apparent that although he was very tall, his feet and hands were large for his body, which made him appear clumsy and awkward. He had noticeable acne and seemed somewhat immature compared to other eighth-graders the counselor had worked with. Casey didn't deny skipping school, but he wasn't willing to talk about why he did it. To try to elicit more information from him, the counselor asked Casey to complete the following sentences:

1. When I go to school, I feel _____.
2. The part of the school day I like best is _____.
3. The part of the school day I like least is _____.

4. The subject I like best is _____.
5. The subject that is easiest for me is _____.
6. The subject I like least is _____.
7. The subject that is hardest for me is_____.
8. If I could change something about school, I would change _____.
9. Other kids in this school _____.
10. Teachers in this school _____.

Casey's responses to these questions indicated two problem areas: speech class and physical education. The counselor hypothesized that Casey was overly sensitive about his body and didn't want to change clothes in the locker room before and after physical education. Likewise, the counselor surmised that Casey wanted to skip speech class because he was self-conscious about getting up in front of the other 25 students to give a speech.

After some discussion, Casey admitted that he felt self-conscious in these classes. The counselor explained the concept of the "imaginary audience" to him and assured Casey that his classmates probably had the same concerns. He asked Casey to assess how helpful skipping school had been in dealing with these problems and obtained a commitment from Casey to work on more productive ways to handle the situation.

The counselor then had Casey work on an adaptation of an activity called "Magnify" (Pincus, 1990). The counselor listed several events and instructed Casey to magnify their importance by turning them into catastrophes. For example:

1. You walk to the front of the room to give a speech.
   Catastrophic thoughts: _____
2. You go into the locker room to change for physical education.
   Catastrophic thoughts: _____

After Casey identified the worst-case scenarios, the counselor taught him to look at the probable situation by having him work on an adaptation of an activity called "Getting Straight Our Magnifications" (Pincus, 1990). In this activity, best-case, worst-case, and probable scenarios were identified. For example:

You walk to the front of the room to give a speech.

Best-case scenario: _____
Worst-case scenario: _____
Probable scenario: _____

As he identified the best, worst, and probable outcomes and identified his catastrophic thoughts for several different situations, Casey began to question some of his anxieties about speech and physical education. Next, the counselor helped Casey develop self-statements to deal with the anxiety. Among these were the following:

Even though it seems like everyone is looking at me when I give a speech,
    probably only a few people are, and that's not the end of the world.
If I mess up when I'm giving a speech, I'm not a total jerk.
If I'm embarrassed to undress in physical education, probably other kids
    are too, so it's not worth skipping school over.

Following these activities, Casey and the counselor looked at the consequences of skipping school and brainstormed better ways for Casey to handle his anxiety. The counselor recommended that he read *Life Happens* (McCoy & Wibbelsman, 1996) to help him see that these thoughts and feelings are normal. Together they drew up a contract for school attendance.

Consulting with Casey's mother, the counselor explained the concept of the imaginary audience and assured her that her son's solution to the problem no doubt seemed logical to him because of the cognitive incompetencies characteristic of youth at this stage of development. The counselor suggested that she visit with the speech teacher to discuss the possibility of utilizing small groups for some of the speech activities because students in the small group wouldn't feel as anxious about their performances. Finally, the counselor praised the mother for being firm about Casey's school attendance while being understanding about why Casey had chosen to behave as he had.

Maria

Maria, a sixth-grader, referred herself to the school counselor because she was having problems with friends. First, her best friend had been ignoring her and wasn't spending much time with her. Although this bothered Maria a lot, she was more upset that some girls had started an "I Hate Maria" club, and that to get into the club, her classmates had to say bad things about her.

Although Maria was highly verbal, she rambled a lot. To help her focus on some of her thoughts and feelings about these issues, the counselor asked her to fill in the blanks in the following series of open-ended sentences:

1. If my best friend doesn't do things with me, it means that

_____

2. If some kids in my class join the "I Hate Maria" club, I feel
    _____ and I think that _____

3. If other kids say mean things about me, I feel
    _____ and I think_____

4. What I wish would happen is _____

5. What I think I can control about this situation is _____

Based on her responses, Maria seemed to feel helpless, sad, angry, and inadequate. These are normal responses for early adolescents, who place great importance on peer relationships.

Because Marta felt inadequate, the counselor chose to concentrate on her self-concept and what she thought being rejected by some friends said about her. He took a dry sponge and asked her to hold it, specifically focusing on how heavy it felt. Then he asked her to soak that sponge in a pan of water and compare how heavy it was now to when it was dry. Then he explained to Marta that when she soaked the sponge in water and it got heavy, an analogy could be made to what she did when her peers teased her and said bad things about her: She soaked it all up. He then asked her what happened when she wrung out the sponge, and she said that it wasn't as heavy. The counselor told her that she should look at herself and ask herself whether she was what her peers said she was—in effect, she needed to "wring out" her sponge instead of soaking in all the bad things people were saying.

The counselor asked Marta for some examples of what she thought others were saying about her, and then asked her to prove to him that she was stupid, that she was a stuck-up snob, and that she couldn't rollerblade well. Marta admitted that none of these things said about her was true. and the counselor challenged her: "If none of those things are true, why do you soak them up and upset yourself?" Marta gave a few more examples but admitted that they weren't true about her either, so the counselor suggested that she remember that "who I am isn't what they say I am"—so even if others thought they were, it didn't have to change who she was.

Then the counselor talked to Marta about what she could and could not control in this situation, and he helped her see that she could control her own thoughts by reminding herself that she wasn't what some of her classmates said she was, but that she couldn't control her classmates. He encouraged her to make up or recall a short saying or a song, such as, "Sticks and stones can break my bones, but words will never hurt me unless I let them." Marta, who really liked music, wrote the following words to the tune of the ABC song: "I am not a stupid geek. I don't smell, and I don't squeak. If you have to say terrible words, say them to some imaginary nerds."

Next, the counselor helped Marta put the problem in perspective by having her make a list of all the boys and girls in her class. He then asked her to cross out the names of the kids in the club, put an asterisk beside the names of the kids who were still nice to her, and put a star next to the names of the kids she could still consider good friends. By doing this, Marta realized that only a small percentage of her classmates were in the club, that most of them were still nice to her, and that she still had several good friends. This activity helped her to see that she had been overgeneralizing about the club. She'd been thinking that everyone was against her.

As a final intervention, the counselor helped Maria deal with her anger by asking her to make a list of all the things that angered her about this situation. Next he asked how she dealt with her anger and how it helped her.

Developmental Characteristics of Mid-Adolescence

Physical Development

Typically at about age 15 for females and 17 for males, the growth spurt ends (McDevitt & Ormrod, 2002). Depending on when he or she entered puberty, however, the 15- to 18-year-old's physical development might continue rather rapidly or slow down gradually. Because males typically lag behind females in the rate of physical development in early adolescence, females tend to tower over males until this trend is reversed in mid-adolescence (Jaffe, 1998). By mid-adolescence, females usually have achieved full breast growth, have started to menstruate, and have pubic hair (Dusek, 1996). By age 15 the male voice lowers (McDevitt & Ormrod, 2002), and facial hair appears approximately a year later (Kaplan, 2000).

During mid-adolescence, sexual urges are strong, and this can evoke anxiety in adolescents and their parents. Becoming sexually active is often unplanned, and, although most adolescents are aware of the risks of sexually transmitted diseases and pregnancy (Owens, 2002), unprotected sex is common because they see themselves as immune from the consequences (Vernon & Al-Mabuk, 1995). Although most teenagers aren't obsessed by sex or having intercourse on a regular basis, good sex education is imperative (Kaplan, 2000).

Cognitive Development

Formal operational thinking continues to develop during mid-adolescence, and their new cognitive capabilities allow 15- to 18-year-olds to think and behave in ways that are significantly different than before. For example, as they develop the ability to think more abstractly, they can hypothesize, can think about the future, and are less likely to conceptualize everything in either–or terms because their thought processes are more flexible (Newman & Newman, 2006). Formal operational thinking moves adolescents into the realm of possibility; their thinking is more multidimensional and relativistic (Owens, 2002). During mid-adolescence, they are capable of pondering and philosophizing about moral, social, and political issues and are better able to distinguish the real and concrete from the abstract and possible (Frankel, 1998; Jaffe, 1998).

Although their cognitive abilities have improved considerably since early adolescence, adolescents at ages 15 to 18 are still likely to be inconsistent in their thinking and behaving (Cobb, 2001). They might be able to see alternatives but lack the experience or self-understanding to make appropriate choices.

Self-Development

Adolescents at this stage are preoccupied with achieving independence and finding their identity—discovering who they are and are not (Cobb, 2001). Finding themselves involves establishing a vocational, political, social, sexual, moral, and religious identity (Erikson, 1968). They do this by trying on various roles and responsibilities; engaging in discussions; observing adults and peers; speculating about possibilities; dreaming about the future; and doing a lot of self-questioning, experimenting, and exploring. During this period of development, they may spend more time alone, contemplating ideas and trying to clarify their values, beliefs, and direction in life.

Children at mid-adolescence generally are more self-confident than they were previously and do not feel the need to look like carbon copies of their peers. Actually, they may strive to do the opposite—dying their hair green or wearing quirky clothes from secondhand stores to "make a statement." This self-assertion extends to other areas as well. Mid-adolescents are more capable of resisting peer pressure because of their greater self-confidence and their ability to look beyond the immediate present and speculate about long-term consequences (Vernon & Clemente, 2005).

Whether the genders differ in the process of identity formation has been the topic of considerable discussion. Cobb (2001) summarized the research, suggesting that the process is comparable for both sexes but the specific content that adolescents address in achieving their identify can differ for either gender. Cultural values also contribute to identity development, as our sense of self reflects an awareness of how others see us (Cobb, 2001). Meece (2002) noted that identity development may be more difficult for ethnic minority adolescents who often struggle to juxtapose the values of their culture and society at large. Meece also pointed out that developing a sexual identity may be difficult and anxiety-provoking.

Social Development

Peer relationships continue to be important during this stage of development. Mid-adolescents spend more time with peers, and this serves the important functions of trying out various roles (Broderick & Blewitt, 2006), learning to tolerate individual differences, and preparing themselves for adult interactions as they form more intimate relationships (Dusek, 1996).

If they have attained formal operational thinking, adolescents at this stage approach relationships with more wisdom and maturity. With their higher level of self-confidence, they do not depend as much on friends for emotional support, and by the end of this period, they begin to select friendships based on compatibility, common interests, shared experiences, and what they can contribute to the relationship (Dusek, 1996; Jaffe, 1998).

During this time, intimate friendships increase, which helps mid-adolescents become more socially sensitive. Females seek intimate friendships sooner than males do; these relationships are more intense; and their development of intimacy is more advanced than it is for males (Dusek, 1996). As they become less egocentric, mid-adolescents are better able to recognize and deal with shortcomings in relationships. As a result, friendship patterns become more stable and less exclusive (Broderick & Blewitt, 2006). Dating and sexual experimentation generally increase during this period (Cobb, 2001).

Emotional Development

As they attain formal operational thinking, mid-adolescents have fewer rapid mood fluctuations and, therefore, are not as overwhelmed by their emotions. They tend to be less defensive and are more capable of expressing their feelings rather than acting them out behaviorally. The increased emotional complexity during this period enables adolescents to identify, understand, and express their emotions more effectively, as well as to be more empathic (Kang & Shaver, 2004). A compounding factor in adolescents' emotional development is depression According to Newman and Newman (2006), 35% of adolescents experience depression to some extent.

Toward the end of this developmental stage, many adolescents are lonely and ambivalent. As their needs and interests change, they may be gradually growing away from their friends. As high school graduation approaches, they might be apprehensive about the future. Some experience self-doubt and insecurity if they compare themselves to peers or when they explore the skills and abilities they need to qualify for a certain job or for postsecondary education.

Once they have developed formal operational thinking skills, adolescents are better able to deal with emotionally charged issues. They are not as impulsive or as likely to behave irrationally or erratically in response to emotional upsets. How adolescents at this stage of development manage their emotions varies widely depending on their level of cognitive maturation.

Counseling Applications for Mid-Adolescence

Counseling the mid-adolescent is easier than working with the 11- to 14-year-old, but a lot depends on the extent to which the adolescent has attained formal operational thinking. In general, the older adolescent does not feel as vulnerable, is better able to express feelings rather than masking them through acting out, and is more willing to be in counseling. That is not to say that all older adolescents are this way. A lot depends on the nature of the problem and the adolescent's personality. For the most part, though, adolescents are better able to express themselves verbally, and it is easy to assume that concepts don't have to be reinforced in concrete ways.

Because the level of maturity of adolescents varies, and because some are visual learners rather than auditory learners, it is still appropriate to use activities to illustrate points.

They benefit from individual or group activities that address developmental issues, such as a sorting board that helps them clarify future goals (Vernon, 2002, pp. 281–283), a visual activity that helps them look more realistically at relationships (Vernon, 2002, pp. 235–237), role plays that facilitate their understanding of parent–adolescent relationships, (Vernon, 2002, pp. 238–239), or imagery exercises that help them learn to identify and express feelings associated with the transition from high school. Reading short poems or stories about how other teens have dealt with depression or anxiety is also helpful, as is writing about their own experiences through structured or unstructured journaling.

Typical Problems During Mid-Adolescence

Although the emotional turbulence lessens significantly during mid-adolescence, a new set of circumstances can create problems for 15- to 18-year-olds. Specifically, adolescents in this age-group are dealing with more complex relationships that may involve sexual intimacy (Owens, 2002) and with decisions about their future. Teenagers are concerned with getting enough out of high school to prepare them for life (Kaplan, 2000). They also express confusion about career choice, and they worry about money. The transition from high school to postsecondary plans results in mixed feelings of elation, ambivalence, and loss (Vernon & Al-Mabuk, 1995). Relationships with their families may be strained as they push for more autonomy, yet are anxious about being too independent.

Mid-adolescence serves as a stepping stone to the young adult world with its even greater challenges and new opportunities. Although this can be an exciting time, it also can give rise to anxiety. Mental health professionals working with adolescents have to be aware of the ambivalence that mid-adolescents likely feel. Counselors must be sensitive to both the anxiety and the excitement that many adolescents feel about making a significant transition that will involve a change in roles, relationships, routine, and assessment of self.

Case Studies of Mid-Adolescents

Annie

Annie, age 17, initiated contact with the school counselor to discuss her relationship with her boyfriend, James. She said the relationship had been very good for the first few months, but lately they had been arguing so much that she was afraid he would break up with her. Whenever they went out, she constantly wanted reassurance that he cared about her, which irritated him. When she persisted, he ignored her. If he didn't call when he said he would, Annie became anxious, and she got upset if he didn't return her phone calls right away. She was certain that he was seeing other girls and she assumed that something was wrong with her. Her response to this situation was to sit at home and wait for his phone calls, to call his friends to try to find out where he was, and to stay awake at night thinking about the situation. She felt depressed and anxious.

In talking further with Annie, it became apparent that most of their arguments seemed to arise because Annie wanted to spend all her time with James, and he was insisting on some space. When Annie expressed concern about what he would do if he wasn't with her as much, the counselor asked her to make a list of all the possible things that could happen. Then the counselor asked Annie to put a checkmark next to the things she could prove had happened. After Annie completed this task, the counselor explained the difference between probability and possibility and explained that one way of distinguishing between them would be to look at past evidence.

For example, although James possibly could be taking out another girl, to Annie's knowledge had he ever done this? And he possibly could get killed in a car accident, but had he ever driven recklessly or while drunk when she had been with him? The counselor instructed Annie to use this type of self-questioning to help her deal with her anxiety about things that could happen when James wasn't with her. Many of them, she would find, were unlikely based on her past history and her information about James.

Next, the counselor discussed issues of control in the relationship. She tied some strings to her arms and legs and asked Annie to pull on them. The harder Annie pulled, the more the counselor resisted. They discussed the idea that Annie's attempts to control James would probably drive him away—which Annie acknowledged had happened once already.

To help Annie deal with this, the counselor helped her make a list of things she could say to herself when she felt like she wanted to control her boyfriend, such as: "Will it do more harm than good to control?" "What's the worst thing that could happen if I don't control him?" "Can I really control another person?"

As Annie talked about her relationship with James, she brought up times when she wasn't being controlling but James still was not treating her with respect. The counselor gave Annie some handouts on personal rights and assertion and explained the concepts. They then role-played assertive and nonassertive responses to some issues that Annie generated.

When Annie left the session, she admitted feeling less anxious. She indicated that she would work on several things to help her deal with these relationship issues.

▉▉Marcus

Marcus's father referred him to a mental health counselor because Marcus was a senior in high school and had no idea what he wanted to do after graduation. The father also suspected that Marcus was depressed because he spent a lot of time alone in his room and had withdrawn considerably from his peers. In addition, his grades had dropped and he had no interest in going out for track, which had been his favorite sport and one in which he excelled. Marcus refused to talk to his dad about what was going on, but he noted that Marcus seemed to be increasingly anxious whenever anyone asked about his future plans.

Marcus was reluctant to talk and resented being in counseling, so the first thing the counselor did was to share with Marcus that his dad sensed some anxiety about his after-high school plans and the counselor reassured Marcus that he often worked with high school seniors who had ambivalent or confused feelings about the future. She invited Marcus to read several short journal entries written by another student, who had given consent to share his writings without his identity being revealed. The counselor believed that this would help normalize Marcus's feelings and perhaps set him more at ease.

After Marcus finished reading, the counselor gave him paper and pencil and invited him to jot down any reactions, specifying that he didn't have to share these if that was his desire. Although Marcus did not share, he did write quite a bit, so the counselor perceived some progress. After Marcus had finished writing, the counselor suggested a sorting activity that might help Marcus with his future plans and asked if he would be willing to take a look at it. Once again, the counselor assured him that he wouldn't have to share unless he chose to do so. Marcus agreed, and the counselor handed him a *What's Next?* sorting board divided into three columns: very likely, somewhat likely, not very likely, and a packet of cards that contained various after-high-school options such as full-time job in the community, trade or technical school, two-year college, four-year college, and so forth (Vernon, 2002, pp. 281–283). She instructed Marcus to read the cards and place them in the categories according to his priorities. This intervention, which required no verbalization on Marcus's part, seemed to interest him and he appeared to take it quite seriously.

By the end of the first session, although Marcus hadn't related much at all, the counselor sensed that he was more relaxed and probably had gained some insights from these interventions. She asked Marcus if he would be willing to come back again to work more on his future plans, and he said yes. The counselor casually mentioned that it might be helpful during the week for Marcus to jot down any reactions to the activities he had completed during this session or any thoughts related to graduation and the future. At this point the counselor said nothing about Marcus's depression because she thought that he would gain more ground by dealing with the other issue first.

During the second session, the counselor first asked Marcus if he had thought at all about his impending graduation, and Marcus replied that he hadn't. The counselor then explained that in any transition, roles, relationships, routine, and responsibilities change. She handed Marcus a sheet of paper divided into four squares, with one of these words listed in each. She invited Marcus to write whatever came to mind relative to the changes in each of these four areas. She also asked him to list several "feeling words" that described how he felt about graduating.

Based on Marcus's responses, he seemed to have a lot of ambivalence about graduating, coupled with feelings of loss. The counselor explained that, because high school graduation is such a major transition, having mixed feelings is normal, and Marcus, like other high school graduates, would be experiencing losses: the loss of a familiar routine, loss of friendships as people branch off in new directions, and loss of status, as Marcus probably would no longer be participating competitively in the sports in which he excelled.

This activity helped Marcus identify his feelings, some of which he was willing to discuss with the counselor. As a follow-up activity, the counselor asked Marcus if he would be willing to complete a "loss graph" to help him deal more effectively with his feelings. Marcus agreed to do this during the next session.

At the third session the counselor reviewed some of the things they had discussed during the initial session and then asked Marcus to draw a line across a sheet of paper. At one end of the line he was to put a date signifying the beginning of middle school, as Marcus had said in the previous session that he had been with his current friends since that time. The counselor then asked Marcus to put his graduation date at the other end of the line. After he had done this, he was to divide the line into specific grade levels and make separate markers for significant events, both positive and negative.

The counselor asked Marcus to write on the graph several words about each event, placing the positive words above the line and the negative ones below it. She explained to Marcus that the purpose of this activity was to help him get more in touch with his memories about middle school and high school. Once Marcus had done so, they could begin looking ahead to the future. The counselor encouraged him to look back through scrapbooks as a way to help him remember these years.

Marcus spent considerable time on this activity and was willing to talk about some of his memories with the counselor. Together they discussed how things wouldn't be the same again and identified some ways by which Marcus could reach closure with friends who were leaving the state—for example, by emailing them, telling them what their relationship had meant to him, and planning a special outing with them.

During the next session, Marcus was more open about discussing things they had talked about up to this point. Because she sensed that Marcus was becoming somewhat overwhelmed with everything involved in the transition to life after high school, the counselor suggested that Marcus get three envelopes and label them as follows: this week, this month, and in the future. She explained that when Marcus felt overwhelmed or worried about any aspect of graduation and future planning, he write down the worry and then put it in the appropriate envelope. In this way, Marcus could stop himself from thinking about everything at once and would be able to manage things more effectively. As a homework assignment, she suggested that Marcus visit with the school counselor to review the interest inventories he had completed during his junior year and to get some scholarship applications.

Since she sensed that Marcus was more comfortable in counseling, during the next session the counselor asked Marcus about feeling depressed, indicating that his father had expressed some concern about this in his initial phone call. Marcus just shrugged, saying he didn't know, but he was willing to complete a short checklist based on DSM characteristics. His responses revealed some minor depression, but because he seemed hesitant to talk about it, the counselor simply shared that it did not seem to be a major issue, encouraged him to keep track of the level of depression using a form (Vernon, 2002, p. 133), and read the *Will I Ever Get Better?* story written by former client (Vernon, 2002, p. 134).

Prior to the next visit, the counselor contacted Marcus's father to ask if he was seeing any changes in his son. He indicated that Marcus was going out more and appeared a little happier. This was confirmed during the next session when Marcus shared his chart indicating level of depressed feelings. At this point, the counselor believed the depression wasn't a major issue and that he had some tools to use relative to the transition from high school, so she suggested that Marcus come back for a check-up visit in a month. At that time they would evaluate to see what progress he was making in dealing with the practical and the emotional challenges associated with this major transition.

Summary

Children at various developmental levels have some physical, cognitive, self, social, and emotional characteristics in common. These levels are delineated here as early childhood, mid-childhood, early adolescence, and mid-adolescence. Armed with developmental information, counselors can make more accurate assessments and design more helpful interventions. In assessment, age-specific developmental characteristics can serve as a barometer to indicate how a child is progressing relative to normal developmental guidelines. Without such a barometer, parents and professionals can easily misconstrue or misdiagnose problems. With this knowledge, they have a general sense of what's "normal."

Developmental knowledge is also crucial in designing effective interventions. Children and adolescents don't respond well to many of the counseling approaches that work with adults. Because the attention span of children is more limited than the adult attention span—at least until adolescence—helping professionals who work with children must be more creative and use visual and kinesthetic methods as well as auditory methods. Games, art activities, play, simulation activities, music, and drama—all are examples of interventions that take into consideration the developmental capabilities of children and adolescents. These interventions are described in greater detail in subsequent chapters.

Too often, parents and teachers think children (adolescents in particular) are being obnoxious when they actually are acting the way they are because that is the best way they know to process information in the given situation. Growing up is challenging, and most children experience the normal developmental issues identified in this chapter. Beyond these normal passages, many children today have significant situational concerns such as growing up in abusive or alcoholic families, adjusting to parental divorce or remarriage, being homeless, or living in poverty. How children respond to these problems in addition to their basic needs has a bearing on whether they will or will not engage in self-defeating behaviors. Helping professionals who are well grounded in developmental theory will be better equipped to understand how young people process information and how to work most effectively with them to resolve problems.

References

Akos, P. (2005). The unique nature of middle school counseling. *Professional School Counseling, 9*, 95–105.

Bee, H. (2000). *The developing child* (9th ed.). Needham Heights, MA: Allyn & Bacon.

Berger, K. S. (2003). The developing person through childhood (3rd ed.). New York: Worth.

Berk, L. E. (1999). *Infants and children*. Boston: Allyn & Bacon.

Berk, L. E. (2001). *Awakening children's minds*. New York: Oxford University Press.

Berk, L. E. (2003). *Child development* (6th ed.). Boston, MA: Allyn & Bacon.

Bjorklund, D. F. (2000). *Children's thinking: Developmental function and individual differences* (3rd ed.). Belmont, CA: Wadsworth.

Broderick, P. C., & Blewitt, P. (2006). *The life span: Human development for helping professionals* (2nd ed.). Upper Saddle River, NJ. Pearson Education.

Brown, B. B. (2004) Adolescents' relationships with peers. In R. M. Lerner & L. D. Steinberg (Eds.), *Handbook of adolescent psychology* (2nd ed., pp. 363–394). New York: Wiley.

Cobb, N. J. (2001). *Adolescence: Continuity, change, and diversity* (4th ed.). Mountain View, CA: Mayfield.

Cole, M., & Cole, S. R. (1996). *The development of children* (3rd ed.). New York: W. H. Freeman.

Copeland, M.E. (2001). *The depression workbook* (2nd ed.). Oakland, CA: New Harbinger.

DiGiuseppe, R. (1999). Rational emotive behavior therapy. In H. T. Prout & D. T. Brown, *Counseling and psychotherapy with children and adolescents: Theory and practice for school settings* (pp. 252–293). New York: John Wiley & Sons.

Dusek, J. B. (1996). *Adolescent development and behavior* (3rd ed.). Upper Saddle River, NJ: Prentice–Hall.

Eccles, J. S. (2004). Schools, academic motivation, and stage–environment fit. In R. M. Lerner & L. D. Steinberg (Eds.), *Handbook of adolescent psychology* (2nd ed.), pp. 125–153). New York: Wiley

Elkind, D. (1984). *All grown up and no place to go: Teenagers in crisis.* Reading, MA: Addison–Wesley.

Elkind, D. (1988). *The hurried child: Growing up too fast too soon.* Reading, MA: Addison–Wesley.

Elkind, D. (1991). Development in early childhood. *Elementary School Guidance and Counseling, 26*, 12–21.

Erikson, E. (1968). *Identity: Youth and crisis.* New York: W. W. Norton.

Feldman, R.S. (2003). *Development across the life span* (3rd ed.). Upper Saddle River, NJ: Pearson Education.

Frankel, R. (1998). *The adolescent psyche.* New York: Routledge.

Gauvain, M. (2001). *The social context of cognitive development.* New York: Guilford Press.

Ge, X., Kim, I. J., Brody, G., Conger, R. D., Simons, R. L., Gibbons, F. X., et al. (2003). It's about timing and change. Pubertal transition effects on symptoms of major depression among African American youths. *Developmental Psychology, 38*, 430–439.

Harter, S. (1996). *The construction of the self: A developmental perspective.* New York: Guilford.

Harter, S., Waters, P., & Whitesell, N. R. (1998). Relationship self-worth: Differences in perceived worth as a person across interpersonal contexts among adolescents. *Child Development, 69*, 756–766.

Holcomb-McCoy, C. (2005). Ethnic identity development in early adolescence: Implications and recommendations for middle school counselors. *Professional School Counseling, 9*, 120–127.

Izard, C. E., & Ackerman, B. P. (2000). Motivation, organization, and regulatory functions of discrete emotions. In M. Lewis & J. M. Haviland–Jones (Eds.), *Handbook of emotions* (pp. 253–264). New York: Guilford Press.

Jaffe, M. L. (1998). *Adolescence.* Danvers, MA: John Wiley & Sons.

Juvonen, J., Le, V. N., Kaganoff, T., Augustine, C., & Constant, L. (2004). *Focus on the wonder years: Challenges facing the American middle school.* Santa Monica, CA: Rand.

Kang, S. M., & Shaver, P. R., (2004). Individual differences in emotional complexity: Their psychological implications. *Journal of Personality, 72*, 687–726

Kaplan, P. S. (2000). *A child's odyssey* (3rd ed.). Belmont, CA: Wadsworth.

Lester, H., (2003). *Something might happen.* New York: Houghton Mifflin.

Martin, D. G. (2003). *Clinical practice with adolescents.* Pacific Grove, CA: Brooks/Cole.

Maslow, A. H. (1968). *Toward a psychology of being* (2nd ed.). Princeton, NJ: D. Van Nostrand.

McCoy, K., & Wibbelsman, C. (1996). *Life happens.* New York: Perigee Press

McDevitt, T. M., & Ormrod, J. E. (2002). *Child development and education.* Upper Saddle River, NJ: Pearson Education.

Meece, J. L. (2002). *Child and adolescent development for educators* (2nd ed.). New York: McGraw Hill.

Newman, B. M., & Newman, P. R., 2006. *Development through life: A psychosocial approach* (9th ed.). Belmont, CA: Thompson Wadsworth.

Owens, K. B. (2002). *Child and adolescent development: An integrated approach.* Belmont, CA: Wadsworth.

Owens, R. E., Jr. (1996). *Language development* (4th ed.). Boston: Allyn & Bacon.

Piaget, J. (1967). *Six psychological studies.* New York: Random House.

Pincus, D. (1990). *Feeling good about yourself.* Carthage, IL: Good Apple.

Porter, L. (1999). *Young children's behavior: Practical approaches for caregivers and teachers.* Sydney, Australia.

Pruitt, D. B. (Ed.) (1998). *Your child: What every parent needs to know about childhood development from birth to preadolescence.* New York: HarperCollins.

Rathus, S.A., (2004). *Voyages in childhood.* Belmont, CA: Wadsworth.

Rubin, K. H., Coplan, R., Chen, X., Buskirk, A. A., & Wojslawowicz, J. D. (2005). Peer relationships in childhood. In M. Bornsten & M. Lamb (Eds.), *Developmental science: An advanced textbook* (5th ed., pp. 469–512). Mahwah, NJ: Earlbaum.

Schave, D., & Schave, B. F. (1989). *Early adolescence and the search for self: A developmental perspective.* New York: Praeger.

Schickendanz, J. A., Schickendanz, D. J., Forsyth, P. D., & Forsyth, G. A. (1998). *Understanding children and adolescents* (3rd ed.). Needham Heights, MA: Allyn & Bacon.

Selman, R. (1980). *The growth of interpersonal understanding: Developmental and clinical analyses.* New York: Academic Press.

Selman, R. L., & Schultz, L. J. (1990). *Making a friend in youth: Developmental theory and pair therapy.* Chicago: University of Chicago Press.

Shwe, H. I. (1999). Gricean pragmatics in preschoolers: Young children's understanding of sarcasm and irony. *Dissertation Abstracts International, 59,* Sciences and Engineering.

Siegler, R., DeLoache, J., & Eisenberg, N. (2003). *How children develop.* New York: McGraw Hill.

Susman, E. J., & Rogel, A. (2004). Puberty and psychological development. In R. M. Lerner & L. D. Steinberg (Eds.). *Handbook of adolescent psychology* (2nd ed., pp. 15–44). New York: Wiley.

Trawick-Smith, J. (2000). *Early childhood development* (2nd ed.). Upper Saddle River, NJ: Prentice–Hall.

Vernon, A. (2002). *What works when with children and adolescents: A handbook of individual counseling techniques.* Champaign, IL: Research Press.

Vernon, A. (2006a). Depression in children and adolescents: REBT approaches to assessment and treatment. In A. Ellis & M. E. Bernard (Eds.), *Rational emotive behavioral approaches to childhood disorders: Theory, practice, and research* (pp. 212–231). New York: Springer.

Vernon, A. (2006b). *Thinking, feeling, behaving: An emotional education curriculum for adolescents.* Champaign, IL: Research Press.

Vernon, A., & Al-Mabuk, R. H. (1995). *What growing up is all about: A parent's guide to child and adolescent development.* Champaign, IL: Research Press.

Vernon, A., & Clemente, R. (2005). *Assessment and intervention with children and adolescents: Developmental and multicultural approaches.* Alexandria, VA: American Counseling Association.

Waters, V. (1979). *Color us rational.* New York: Institute for Rational Living.

Weisfeld, G. (1999). *Evolutionary principles of human adolescence.* New York: Basic Books.

Wigfield, A., Lutz, S. L., & Wagner, A. L. (2005). Early adolescents' development across the middle school years: Implications for school counselors. *Professional School Counseling, 9,* 112–119.

The Individual Counseling Process

Jean Peterson

A 5-year-old girl's teacher brings her to the school counselor after the girl's mother was killed in a tornado.

A gifted 6-year-old is referred to a counselor because he has "meltdowns" whenever he makes an error on a spelling test.

A 7-year-old asks the school counselor if kids with dark skin can go to college.

An 8-year-old sees an agency counselor because of aggressive behavior.

A 9-year-old asks to see a school counselor because of family tension during his parents' divorce proceedings.

A 10-year-old girl is referred by the courts for counseling because of her drug use and shoplifting.

An 11-year-old boy finally sees a school counselor after being bullied relentlessly by a group of classmates outside of school for the past 5 years.

A 12-year-old girl with physical and cognitive disabilities is referred to an agency counselor after being raped by a special-services bus driver.

A 12-year-old is sent to a counselor by her parents because of her perfectionism, anxiety, and insomnia.

A 13-year-old, after wondering since age 11, is now convinced he is gay and sees his school counselor because he is thinking of suicide.

A 14-year-old reveals in an essay that she has been date-raped. Her teacher, who also suspects the girl has an eating disorder, refers the girl to the school counselor.

School and agency counselors see children with issues like these daily. Some professionals have had training in interventions geared specifically to children and adolescents and have developed a repertoire of effective strategies. They have an affinity for working with the problems typical of this age group. Other counselors working with youngsters are uncomfortable with this age-group and their issues. They have had little or no training or supervision in counseling children and adolescents, which reflects and contributes to an "enormous service delivery shortfall" (Prout, 2007, p. 4). They chafe against their clients' lack of autonomy and may not understand child and adolescent development. During counseling sessions they feel inept. In return, the children or adolescents they counsel are uncomfortable, untrusting, and unresponsive.

Like typical counselors of a few decades ago (Vernon, 2002), these counselors may apply strategies that are appropriate only for adults, with the result that the counselor and the young child alike feel frustrated. What works for adults probably will not be effective with children and adolescents, signifying the need for significant adaptations. Effective work with young clients requires specific skills and knowledge (Hutchinson, 2007).

Children and adolescents may present with any of a multitude of issues, as reflected in the table of contents of a current school counseling textbook (Parsons, 2007)—disruptive behavior, dishonesty, lack of motivation, social issues, aggression and bullying, noncompliance, poor social behavior, high-risk sexual behavior, and loss—in addition to symptoms of psychiatric disorders. One in five children and adolescents is affected by mental health problems, and two-thirds may not be getting the help they need (National Institute of Mental Health, 2005). This chapter addresses some of what counselors need to know to counsel children and adolescents effectively. The emphasis is on building a relationship with younger clientele and adapting counseling skills for these clients.

Basic Guidelines for Working With Young Clients

Some guidelines offered by various scholars for counseling children and adolescents are the following.

1. Children often lack information about counseling and may feel fearful or anxious about it. After perhaps asking what a child knows about counseling, counselors might include information about what counselors do (e.g., listen carefully) and what children can expect to happen in counseling (working together to figure out what to do with worries or troubles or things that are confusing) (Thompson & Henderson, 2007).
2. Children are socially embedded. Therefore, a systemic perspective is useful, including consulting with some significant adults in their life (Clark, 2002), especially when working with cultural groups characterized by collective interdependence or using network therapy (Ivey, Ivey, Myers, & Sweeney, 2005).

3. Counselors have to be aware of their clients' developmental stage and use interventions appropriate for their developmental level (O'Brien & Burnett, 2000).

4. Counselors should differentiate counseling approaches according to ability level, covering students along the entire ability spectrum (Heckenberg, 2007; Milsom, 2006; Peterson, 2006).

5. Active listening is more important than expert questioning (Thompson & Henderson, 2007).

6. Reluctance and resistance from children are common and are normal responses. Respecting these protective behaviors helps to build trust (cf. Clark, 2002; O'Malley, 2002; Teyber, 2005).

7. When working with children, especially difficult children, patience is essential (Clark, 2002; Thompson & Henderson, 2007).

8. Because elementary teachers see children for the entire school day, they are able to observe extensively and can make crucial referrals to counselors (Schmidt, 2008).

9. A strong counselor–client relationship is a "necessary but not sufficient condition" for change (Semrud-Clikeman, 1995, p. 91).

10. Specific, research-based intervention strategies can be effective (Parsons, 2007), but forcing a strategy on a young client can be counterproductive (Murphy, 2006).

11. Emphasis on the here-and-now is more powerful and exciting for the client but also is more threatening than there-and-then statements, which diffuses the intensity of the present (Myrick, 1997).

12. Paying attention to strengths (Peterson, 2007a) and eventually helping children to apply their strengths in making changes is an effective counseling strategy (Murphy, 2006).

13. Counselors who work in schools should be sensitive to teachers' time constraints and their need for information about the counseling process (Muro & Kottman, 1995).

14. The length of sessions should be adapted to the setting and the client's needs (Hutchinson, 2007).

15. Counselors should listen to young clients' metaphors and join their language, even with young children (Winslade & Monk, 2007).

16. Counselors should be even more "real" and spontaneous with children and adolescents than with older clients (Hutchinson, 2007).

17. Counselors can play a mentor role with young clients, as well as find other mentors for them (Hutchinson, 2007).

Counselors who work with children and adolescents should be aware of how easily counselors can become enmeshed or overinvolved in their lives. Counselors may want to "rescue" children and adolescents, second-guess their parents, and lose objectivity, particularly when the counselor connects at an emotional level with the issues at hand, including a young person's vulnerability and lack of autonomy. But excessive reassurances, consoling, and even humor and teasing actually might communicate a lack of understanding or the counselor's own discomfort (Erdman & Lampe, 1996). Repeated reassurances can inadvertently suggest that there is indeed something to fear. With children in particular, counselors should maintain objectivity and clear boundaries, not just to be of maximum assistance but for the counselor's own long-term health as well.

Also, counselors also may be tempted to give "treats" to children. Turley (1993) stated that a counselor's gift to a child is, instead, "time, a caring person, a place where there [are] unusual freedoms, togetherness" (p. 199). To establish a habit of giving material gifts or food, even if only small and seemingly inconsequential, may obscure boundaries, create expectations, foster manipulation of either client or counselor, or distort the idea of counseling.

Resistance

Trust is essential to productive therapy (O'Malley, 2002). Because children and adolescents are often referred involuntarily for counseling, they may feel uncertain or reluctant during the sessions. Counselors should expect some distrust, and therefore resistance, and consider these reactions to be reasonable (Clark, 2002; Fall, 2002). Orton (1997) defined resistance as

> the child's attempts at self-protection through the use of defensive behavior. . . . When children are threatened, they protect themselves by withdrawing, acting out, regressing, or evidencing other problem behaviors. Rather than challenging a child's resistance to treatment, the therapist should explore the reasons for the resistance. Children may refuse to participate because they fear reprisals from parents for revealing "family secrets," they have not been adequately prepared about what to expect, their previous experiences with adults have been hurtful and disappointing, or they have a strong belief that they are (as one youngster put it) "a hopeless case." (p. 178)

Resistance is also a common response to a counselor's moving too quickly or interpreting prematurely. Children and adolescents may show resistance through fantasy, crises, silence, chattering, belligerence, storytelling, or other avoidant maneuverings, including missing sessions. They may resist because they do not desire to change (Herlihy, 2002) or because they feel a need for control in response to perceptions that adults are trying to "fix" them. Some young clients also resist counselor interpretations (Clark, 2002), such as statements linking the past to the present, because of the level of abstraction of these statements or as a reaction to uncomfortable or overwhelming feelings. In general, even though they are miserable, and even though constructive change probably would be positive, the child may not perceive change as desirable, especially at the outset (Egan, 2007).

For Peterson (2007a), resistance reflects a lack of readiness or capability for what the counselor is incorporating. The counselor is responsible for ascertaining the child's readiness and making appropriate adjustments. Concentrating on building a relationship lessens the need to resist (Thompson & Henderson, 2007), as does collaborative goal-setting rather than imposing the goals of a third party (Young, 2005). In addition, resistance does not necessarily reflect negative feelings about the counselor (Egan, 2007). Instead, it can be reframed as self-affirmation. Ivey, Ivey, Myers, and Sweeney (2005), however, made a case for the value of "perturbing" in counseling in the interest of provoking change. This includes careful listening, accurate mirroring, and challenging thought patterns—after support and connection are in place.

Defenses are functional, protecting the ego from pressure and anxiety (Thompson & Henderson, 2007), and are not necessarily maladaptive. According to Semrud-Clikeman (1995), defenses may help children or adolescents cope with daily life. Stripping their defenses away is not always healthy. Counselors must sort out which mechanisms are adaptive and which inhibit growth and development and must challenge the latter appropriately and constructively.

Several authors have offered suggestions for working with resistance and making it therapeutically useful. Orton (1997) encouraged counselors to respect young clients' refusal to allow access to their private thoughts and feelings, suggesting that this respect helps to build trust and reduce anxiety. Thompson and Henderson (2007) noted that a trusting relationship "undermines the client's need to resist the counselor's attempts to be helpful" (p. 95).

Strategies that might be used to address resistance in young clients include play therapy, role-playing, the counselor's self-disclosure about resistance, the counselor's comment about a probable cause for the resistance, and confrontation. Structured exercises also may move the counseling relationship forward to counteract resistance (Peterson, 2007b), especially with chronologically or developmentally young children (Thompson & Henderson). Ritchie (1994) suggested gaining the young client's commitment to change through indirect confrontation using puppets, media, or stories; through paradox and reframing; and through modeling and role-plays. Oaklander (1997) argued that strengthening children's inner support structure is essential to their being able to work through deep-seated emotions.

With a resistant adolescent, another effective and empowering strategy is to acknowledge and "go with" the reluctance, leaving room for choice. This strategy is illustrated by the following statement by a veteran counselor of adolescents:

> I know you don't feel like talking today. We can just sit here together. I'm not going to go away. You can choose to talk, or you can say nothing. If you choose not to talk, I might sit here with you, or I might just leave you alone and work quietly at my desk over there, if it seems that you'd prefer that. I'll decide later. You can decide about the talking. It's your time here, and you can use it as you like.

Thompson and Henderson (2007) commented that sometimes a child simply does not feel like talking or does not have anything to discuss. They encouraged counselors to come to sessions with a tentative plan that they can turn to during unexpected silent periods. In general, counselors should evaluate what is happening when sessions become blocked and whether a lack of skill or lack of planning may be contributing.

Parents, too, may demonstrate resistance. Thompson and Henderson's (2007) six-step model for a counseling interview included the possibility of involving parents initially to "build bridges between the child's world and the counseling office" (p. 44). Parents may resist necessary treatment for a child or attempt to sit in on their child's session (Semrud-Clikeman, 1995). They may also object to their own involvement in the counseling process, deny connections between their own issues and their child's presenting problem (Kottman, 2002), and even sabotage therapy out of envy, jealousy, competition, or narcissism (Hailparn & Hailparn, 2000). If the services are rejected, alternatives can be explored.

Parent Expectations

Parents' pretreatment expectancies for their child also play a role in their child's treatment participation, attendance, and premature termination. Those expectations may be less in situations reflecting socioeconomic disadvantage, ethnic minority status, severity of child dysfunction, the child's age, and parental stress and depression (Nock & Kazdin, 2001). Children's lack of participation might reflect concern about seeming to be disloyal to parents who oppose counseling (Thompson & Henderson, 2007). With these realities in mind, counselors should consider establishing contact with parents during the initial stages of counseling to lessen the latter's anxieties (Semrud-Clikeman, 1995). In general, working with significant adults in the larger system can enhance the counseling process (cf. Clark, 2002). Hutchinson (2007) noted that working with children "is inextricably tied to working with their parents and guardians" (p. 298) and that, typically, the counselor's posture should be as a parental ally. When children's problems seem to reflect family problems, parents can be involved in the counseling process directly. Indirect strategies may also be helpful. In addition to generating cooperation, involving parents of at-risk children as helpers at school can effect change (Littrell & Peterson, 2005). Counselors using narrative counseling strategies—linking past, present, and future—can involve teachers and parents in creating an alternative, positive personal story for a troubled child or family to replace a problem-filled, cultural-deficit, or other-deficit story (Winslade & Monk, 2007).

The Counseling Process

Typically, the counseling process moves through the following stages:

1. Intake
2. Meeting for the first session
3. Establishing a relationship and developing focus
4. Working together toward change
5. Closure

Intake

The intake process may involve a telephone interview with one parent, a face-to-face interview with the child and one or more members of the family, a meeting with just the child, or a combination of these and other possible scenarios. What and how much is discussed in regard to informed consent and confidentiality depends on who is present. Orton (1997) pointed out that the intake process may involve one or several sessions, depending on the counselor's orientation and whether other members of the child's family are to be interviewed. She emphasized the importance of non-judgmental respect for the verbal and nonverbal expressions of everyone who is interviewed. According to Orton, the intake interview is

> an essential part of the counseling process because it helps the counselor establish a relationship with the child and the family that will form the basis for all future counseling and therapy. A successful intake interview offers a glimpse into the interpersonal world of the child and provides valuable insight into the family dynamics. Most practitioners, regardless of their theoretical orientation, use the interview process to gather information that will help them conceptualize the case and design an appropriate treatment plan. (p. 148)

Intake information typically includes the age and grade of the child or adolescent, the reason for referral, the child's date of birth and birth order, names and ages of siblings and parents, parents' employment, the child's birth and medical history, any medications, developmental history, strengths and weaknesses, family and school relationships, activities, and other information pertinent to the reason for referral. If the child is of school age, the counselor might ask the parents to request applicable information from school records or ask them to sign a release of information giving the counselor permission to make that request. (If the child is being seen in a school setting, the type of intake interview described here may not be feasible.)

After gathering pertinent data, the counselor might ask the parents what they expect from the counseling experience for their child and whether they have had counseling experiences themselves (Semrud-Clikeman, 1995). The counselor should explain that children might not experience counseling in the same way that adults do. If the child is not present, the counselor might suggest how the parents can explain to their child what to expect in counseling. At ages 3 to 5 it is appropriate to refer to "playing games," but with older children it is best to say that they will, for example, "see an adult who works with children who may have some problems in school" (p. 34). Telling children and adolescents about their counseling session only the night before or the morning of the first interview will give them less time to worry.

Informing Clients and Others About "Counseling"

Thompson and Henderson (2007) recommended telling the child the length of the sessions, ascertaining the child's expectations for counseling, and communicating what the counselor can offer. Counselors should talk about what counseling *is* with children and adolescents and also with their parents if the parents have anxieties about the process. Children may be confused about what they will experience, and adults, too, may not know what to expect from counseling or may have misconceptions, such as that counselors "give advice." As part of informed consent, some discussion of the counseling process is warranted, even with very young children.

With children, as with adults, the counselor's "definition" of counseling, his or her behaviors, and the goals set forth should be in accord with the client's culture and worldview (Herring, 1997; Ivey, Ivey, & Simek-Morgan, 1997; Sue, Ivey, & Pedersen, 1996) and level of cognitive development (Thompson & Henderson, 2007). Given the commonly held premise that counseling is collaborative (Teyber, 2005), an explanation of the process may help to demystify it for the client and consequently empower the client. A group of my graduate students, based on what they had learned in their courses, developed the following list of ways to explain the counseling process to children, some more understandable to children than others. The words used in such explanations—as is true in all aspects of counseling—should be developmentally appropriate and, therefore, some may have to be adapted.

> Counseling is for normal people who have "something to work on" in their lives.
> Counseling can help people to feel better and be more effective in life.
> Counseling can help people "not to feel stuck anymore" about something.
> Counseling can help people make changes.
> Counselors can help people discover their strengths, what they can rely on.
> Counseling can help to prevent problems.
> Counselors listen carefully to people to learn what they feel, what they think about, what they enjoy and dislike, and what they are confused about.
> Counselors can help people make sense of confusing, complicated things.
> Counselors support and look for good things in people, instead of judging, criticizing, or looking for what is wrong with them.
> Counselors believe that, with a little help, people can figure out how to move ahead.
> Rather than giving advice, counselors usually try to help people solve their own problems.

Developmental Considerations

Children and adolescents go through many developmental changes during the preschool and school years. Even small age increments may translate into significant developmental differences in behavior. Therefore, as noted by Prout (2007), counselors need to be knowledgeable about child and adolescent development, and able to distinguish between pathology and normal developmental deviation and minor crises. The counselor must think carefully about the presumed physical, cognitive, social, and emotional development of the child before the first meeting, and then continue to consider developmental aspects throughout the counseling process. Play media, structured and unstructured activities, vocabulary, and cognitive strategies— all should be developmentally appropriate if they are to be optimally effective.

In addition, counselors should be alert to asynchronous development (Olenchak & Reis, 2002)—in which intellectual, social, physical, and emotional development are at varying levels—and to other anomalies as well. Models of counseling differentiated for gifted children and adolescents are available now, addressing asynchrony and other pertinent phenomena (Mendaglio & Peterson, 2007), as well as literature related to working with children with disabilities (Milsom, 2006; Taub, 2006). In schools, counselors may work more with the latter children's parents than with the children themselves. In addition, the potential diversity of developmental trajectories among nonheterosexual children and adolescents should be recognized, along with their differences from heterosexual youth (Peterson & Rischar, 2000; Savin-Williams & Diamond, 1999).

In general, counselors can normalize development with young clients, helping them to make sense of themselves and those around them (Peterson, 2007a). Counselors can also relate information about development to teachers and parents (Murphy, 2006).

Ethical and Legal Concerns

Taking into consideration clients' age and maturity, counselors should work toward regarding children as equal partners in the counseling relationship with the right to participate in setting goals and planning treatment, the right to expect privacy and feedback, and the right to refuse or end treatment. Nevertheless, a number of difficulties regarding equal partnership are inherent in the relationship.

> First, children generally do not have sufficient understanding and ability to make informed decisions on their own about whether to accept or refuse different therapeutic interventions; second, young children are not considered legally competent because they have not reached the statutory age; and third, children rarely come to therapy voluntarily. (Orton, 1997, p. 357)

In addition to having a professional obligation to the child, the counselor has an obligation to the parents. During the intake interview and later sessions, parents may resist the counselor's treatment approach, a least-restrictive alternative to placement, or even counseling in general; the last situation is supported by law if there are no extenuating circumstances (Thompson & Henderson, 2007). Legally, a parent usually must give consent for counseling, and counselors should also involve children in the agreement to participate, as well as later in care decisions (Welfel, 2006). Parents' wishes can be overridden if the state decides that they are not providing adequately for a child's physical or psychosocial needs (Swenson, 1993). When substance abuse, sexual abuse, pregnancy, sexually transmitted diseases, and contraception are issues, or when gaining parental consent is likely to preclude treatment, minors may be allowed to consent to treatment without parental knowledge or approval.

Treatment for emancipated minors, emergency treatment, and court-ordered treatment also are recognized as general exceptions to the requirement for parental consent (Thompson & Henderson, 2007), as well as when the state is the child's guardian. Such access typically involves medical treatment of some kind (Prout & Brown, 2007). The age at which a child is considered competent to give informed consent varies from state to state, and counselors are responsible for knowing the laws and statutes of the states in which they practice (Orton, 1997).

In regard to informed consent, counselors must make sure that the child and parents alike understand the types of services available, fees (if applicable), and potential risks and benefits, and that written permission will be sought if there is need to release information to other professionals (Orton, 1997). All of these areas should be covered in a written professional-services agreement to be signed prior to the start of therapy. Even though a child's signature may not be legally binding, having the child sign a consent form reinforces the counselor's responsibility to inform all who are involved about the counseling process and reinforces the rights of both child and parents.

Because adults often become involved when a child or adolescent is being counseled, confidentiality issues must be clarified with them prior to the start of counseling. Adults' involvement may take many forms. For example, the counselor may contact the parents to gain information about the family system and how the parents perceive their child. Or the parents may contact the counselor for information about their child. School counselors, in particular, should expect teachers, principals, and other school personnel to request information about students. Huss (2001) highly recommended that counselors take advantage of opportunities to educate school personnel and parents about confidentiality guidelines. All too often, teachers and counselors assume that the rules of confidentiality do not apply to very young children.

Counselors should be aware that all pertinent ethical codes emphasize the right to privacy for all clients and client choice about who shall receive information (e.g., American Association for Marriage and Family Therapy, 2001; American Counseling Association, 2005; American Psychological Association, 2002; American School Counselor Association, 2004), with the following significant exceptions: when there is a duty to warn or protect; when the client consents to disclosure; when reimbursement or other legal rules require it; when there is an emergency; or when the client has waived confidentiality by bringing a lawsuit, for example (Stone, 2005).

Young children may not understand the need for confidentiality, but adolescents may be quite concerned about privacy (Remley & Herlihy, 2005). As mentioned previously, though, whatever the age of the child or adolescent, at the outset of the counseling relationship, confidentiality guidelines should be clarified with any involved parents or guardians. Even though parents have a legal right to information about their child's life, the counselor should make some or all of the following points to them, reflecting the admonitions of several scholars (Schmidt, 2008; Semrud-Clike-man, 1995; Thompson & Henderson, 2007):

- Any inquiry for information by a parent will be discussed first with the client and must be agreed to by the client.
- A counselor's sharing information is not in the client's best interest except when the counselor believes it is necessary to protect the welfare of the child or others.
- A trusting relationship is basic to effective counseling, and insisting that information be shared may undermine the counseling relationship and the counseling process alike.
- School-age children often want their parents to know what they are saying in sessions, and no assumption will be made to the contrary; however, the child should have the choice regarding what is shared, except when necessary to protect the client or others from clear and imminent danger.
- The counseling process promotes empowerment through choice, and the child or adolescent will explore issues and decisions emphasizing choice and with a goal of empowerment.
- The counselor will try to help children tell their parents what they need to know, even practicing the telling, if appropriate, but the parents should recognize that telling or not telling is the client's choice.
- A joint session, involving counselor, client, and parent(s), is an option, when appropriate, for discussing an issue.
- If parents object to any of these points, they may decide, if counseling is not mandated, not to initiate or to discontinue counseling.

Most parents are sensitive to their child's right to privacy and accept that specifics from sessions will not be related to them, as long as they are kept generally informed about their child's progress (McWhirter, 2002).

About another issue related to confidentiality, Stone (2005) underscored that a noncustodial parent has the same rights as a custodial parent unless a court order states otherwise, but the counselor should consider context and history when communicating with both parents. Also, counselors are reminded that documentation is potentially public information. According to Thompson and Henderson (2007), in states that have no licensure law providing for privileged communication, counselors have no recourse except to reveal information if subpoenaed, although there may be exceptions:

> Some courts are more tolerant than others, allowing the counselor to share the privileged information with the judge in private to determine whether the information is necessary to the proceeding or whether public disclosure would be too hurtful to those involved, such as children who are a part of the case. (p. 620)

Regarding confidentiality, children and adolescents may be told that, even though the counselor will not divulge to parents, teachers, or administrators *what* they say in sessions, the counselor may think it is appropriate to share the child's *feelings* about certain situations (Huey & Remley, 1988), especially situations in which the child seems to have been misunderstood or in which significant adults do not seem to be aware of the impact of an event.

In general, counselors should recognize that their explanation of confidentiality will be processed differently at each level of a child's cognitive development and, therefore, requires appropriate vocabulary. Adolescents may have an automatic distrust of confidentiality. Young children actually may be frightened by something that is presented to them by adults with a serious demeanor. Wording such as the following probably will not induce fear and usually is effective:

> What we talk about here I don't tell anybody else. Everything you say is confidential. That means I don't talk about it with other people. If anyone asks me about what I talk about with kids, I check it out with the kids—whether they want me to say anything. And I go by what they say. At times I have to tell somebody, though, if I think you're a danger to yourself or if you're going to hurt someone else. If I believe you're being abused or hurt or someone is putting you in danger, I'd also have to tell that to someone who could do something about it. The law says I have to do that. Otherwise, what we talk about is kept confidential. So what do you think of these rules that I have to go by?

Semrud-Clikeman (1995) emphasized the ethical principle of counselor competence and recommended that counselors seek supervision from an experienced colleague or establish a network for consultation whenever they feel unsure about their ability to be effective with children or adolescents. She also called attention to the issue of establishing who will participate in counseling—the child/adolescent, the parent, the teacher, or perhaps some combination of these. In a school, the referring teacher, for example, might be the sole participant if the child is resistant, especially if the aim is to improve the teacher–student relationship. Because the cooperation and assistance of adults in a child's life usually are necessary requisites for changes in behavior, contact with at least one significant adult during the counseling process is important.

A parent might establish "unspoken boundaries" to maintain parent–child enmeshment and to prevent a close relationship from developing between the child and the counselor (Semrud-Clikeman, 1995). Involving parents early in the process can alleviate this problem.

Conceptualizing the Client as Part of a System

Everyone is part of various systems, such as family, work environment, school, social groups, and ethnic group. Although systemic considerations are important when counseling any client, they are especially important when counseling children and adolescents because many of their problems are found within the context of a system. The child's family, for example, might play an integral role in the child's developing and maintaining anxiety, a symptom that has a potentially deleterious impact on the child's success in school and peer relationships (Bolton, 2000).

Before meeting with children, the counselor should attempt to obtain information about the systems in which they are involved. Adults are the best source for this important information, because children, especially very young children, often lack the ability to articulate it. School counselors can ask teachers for this information or can look at school records. Counselors can interview parents by phone or in person or make inquiries during the initial phone contact if a parent initiated the call. Semrud-Clikeman (1995) emphasized the need for counselors to determine whether calling a parent at work is permissible, asking if they are calling at a convenient time, and leaving messages that contain no more than their name and number for returning the call. Orton (1997) advocated building a partnership with parents during this contact, validating and valuing them and simultaneously gaining insight about their parenting style and interaction with the child. In addition, the counselor may form hypotheses about the potential impact of family structure and marital and other family conflict on the child (Buchanan & Waizenhofer, 2001).

Ben

Ben, age 7, has been referred for counseling because he is having difficulty concentrating in school. Prior to the start of counseling, the counselor should know that Ben is his divorced parents' only child and that he lives 3 days each week with Mom and 4 days with Dad. Each parent remarried recently, and Ben now has four stepsiblings, two in each household. The stepgrandmother babysits for Ben and his stepsiblings before and after school. Ben's stepfather is considering a job transfer to a city 2 hours distant.

Ben rarely interacts in the classroom and recently became agitated and cried uncontrollably when a classmate wanted to look at a small toy Ben had brought to school. Ben's recent written assignments have been incomplete, and he has difficulty staying on task.

Before meeting with a child, the counselor should consider some hypotheses. Might a reported problem have a function (e.g., to escape, to call attention to a situation, to provoke adults to communicate, to avoid feeling)? Given the circumstances, what might a problem protect or deflect (e.g., others' concerns, uncomfortable feelings) or express (e.g., grief, agitation)? What additional factors might be contributing to a problem?

Ben, for instance, might be grieving losses associated with his new living arrangements, which may translate to his having little time alone with either parent and sharing space with stepsiblings. Perhaps he is concerned that if his mother and stepfather move, he will have less time with his father. He could be angry about all of the changes in his life, and he might not be sleeping well at night because of everything taking place in his family system. Both households may have marital tensions, and Ben may fear further unsettling both households if he expresses strong feelings.

Even though forming tentative hypotheses can be helpful, more comprehensive assessment is necessary before considering the direction the school should take. To isolate specific family factors in accounting for children's issues is difficult, given the circularity of influences, the complex structures of families, and the simultaneous developmental transitions within individuals and families (Minuchin, 2001). Counselors should resist the temptation to label a child or adolescent based only on the situation described by the referral source. In Ben's case, for instance, systemic factors at school also could be involved in his lack of concentration. Changing the conditions, interactions, and relationships in a child's environment, instead of the child, can potentially move children and their families forward (Dunn & Levy, 2002). In general, counselors should consider the power of language in applying labels (Saunders, 2007; Winslade & Monk, 2007) and also recognizing, when a diagnosis is required for insurance purposes, that the nonstigmatizing term adjustment disorder acknowledges a short-term response to a difficult situation (McWhirter, 2002).

Among many pertinent systemic factors, counselors should consider cultural context when conceptualizing a family. This would include, for example, acculturation status, ethnic composition of the neighborhood, language preference and facility, education, religion, and cultural explanation of the presenting problem (Ponterotto, Gretchen, & Chauhan, 2001). Sociocultural environment also affects cultural groups' perceptions of ideal family functioning (Garcia & Peralbo, 2000).

Papilia, Olds, and Feldman (1998) noted that preferred gender roles in families may reflect cultural values, gender behaviors in a person's household, and media stereotypes. They also observed that, in general, disciplinary methods vary according to geographical location, socioeconomic circumstances, and religious affiliation. Narrative counseling locates problems in a cultural landscape (Winslade & Monk, 2007). Counselors have to consider their own and the child's "cultural positioning" when conceptualizing the situations presented. Granato (2002) pointed out the importance of a systemic perspective, including culture, religion, and the immigrant experience, in addition to the counselor's role in facilitating family communication and improved school performance.

Meeting for the First Session

The Physical Setting

Regardless of the age of a child or adolescent, the counselor should create a physically and psychologically comfortable environment for counseling (Erdman & Lampe, 1996). The meeting room should be cheerful and should contain furnishings, sturdy toys, and activities that offer choice and that are appropriate for children and adolescents of various age levels, as well as for their parents (Orton, 1997). The toys in the room should meet a variety of interests and promote exploration and creative expression (Presbury, McKee, & Echterling, 2007). Counselors should sit at their clients' eye level, inquire about their comfort, and have office furniture that does not contribute to the "disempowering and intimidating" feeling of having feet dangling or "sinking down into large chairs or couches" (Erdman & Lampe, 1996, p. 375).

Building Rapport and Defining the Problem

When working with young people, counselors often direct the first few sessions toward becoming acquainted. Children are more sensitive than are adults to others' feelings and attitudes and "intuitively trust and open up to those who like and understand them" (Thompson & Henderson, 2007, p. 169). Developing a working relationship, however, tends to take longer with children than with adults, as children typically need more time to accept the counselor as someone who can help them (Orton, 1997). Regardless of the situation, cooperation, or progress, the counselor should stay focused on the relationship (Clark, 2002).

Counselors should follow the client's lead and offer facilitative comments and responses (Myrick, 1997). For example, if the child or adolescent has self-referred, the counselor might ask, "What did you want to see me about?" If the client has been referred by someone else, the counselor should clarify the reasons for the referral, check the child's perceptions of the referral, not attempt to speak for teachers or others, and instead concentrate on the child's input. Semrud-Clikeman (1995) suggested a mini-interview format for gaining an understanding of the child's or adolescent's personal experiences, worldview, and family environment. The information gained may be useful in later sessions when exploring the child's feelings and situations in the present.

Relationship. Paying attention to the counselor–client relationship is important when working with children and adolescents, particularly young children who are guarded and defensive (Erdman & Lampe, 1996) or who have little knowledge about the counseling process and why they are to be involved (Myrick, 1997). The child initially may see the counselor as just one more rule-making, disciplinary authority figure, especially if an adult has sent him or her to the counselor (Kottman, 1990).

When a child is troubled and highly resistant, the "joining" process may take time. Several sessions may have no immediate goal other than to forge a trusting, unconditional relationship with a child in whose world adults are perhaps highly reactive, conditional, unpredictable, critical, and even abusive. Even though a client can make significant progress quickly, especially when using brief techniques, counselors have to beware of pushing young clients toward immediate results, simply to satisfy the adults, not to help the child (Hobson, 2002).

For the child to learn that a trusting relationship is possible, helpful, and satisfying may itself be a worthy goal—a corrective emotional experience (Merydith, 2007). Helping a child learn to trust and feel valued, described by Semrud-Clikeman (1995) as "align[ing] early experiences into a different mold" (p. 11), may help the child function more effectively in the classroom and elsewhere. Vernon (1993) offered a number of suggestions for building rapport in these and other situations—for example, chatting about hobbies, activities, and pastimes; being personal but not a "buddy"; showing genuine interest and concern; and taking the client's lead in comfortable seating. Vernon (2002b) also recommended playing games.

Active listening is basic to both building rapport and defining the problem (Peterson, 2007a). From the outset counselors should listen for a problem that has not been solved, associated feelings, and expectations about what the counselor should do about the problem (Thompson & Henderson, 2007). Giving a young client feedback in the form of clarification and paraphrasing helps to confirm the counselor's understanding of the problem.

Counselors should be aware, too, that sometimes a child or adolescent needs time to sort out what has been said. In these situations silence can be useful and productive. Clients may use the time to consider their responses (Orton, 1997; Thompson & Henderson) or, motivated by anxiety, move "to deeper levels of thinking, feeling, and self-disclosure" (Gumaer, 1984). Silence allows the counselor to consider what has been said and can convey that the client is indeed free to speak (Skovolt & Rivers, 2004). In general, counselors should monitor whether they are talking too much. With young children, however, the counselor's talking slightly more than usual may help them to verbalize (Ivey & Ivey, 1999).

Cultural differences.   When working with children and adolescents, as with adults, the counselor should be aware of cultural differences in eye contact, proximity preferences, response to stress, socioeconomic and sociocultural circumstances (Semrud-Clikeman, 1995), and even how circumstances are interpreted (Garbarino & Stott, 1989). Culturally responsive counselors keep acculturation and ethnic identity in mind, both of these on a continuum (Prout & Prout, 2007). Recent-immigrant children and families, for instance, will probably be high in ethnic identity and low in acculturation. In addition to language and other differences, counselors should recognize the likelihood of loss issues related to relocation.

Peterson (1999) delineated the values of various cultures, which remain relevant today. As examples: Latinos value arts as expression, not as performance; African American value selfless contributions to the neighborhood and handiwork; low-income Anglo Americans place priorities on helping, listening, advising, and childrearing.

Mosley-Howard and Burgan Evans (2000) pointed out that African-Americans emphasize indigenous cultural strengths—connection with extended family, pride in heritage, negotiation between two cultures, and spirituality and involvement with the church. Non-Hispanic counselors' relationships with Hispanic children are likely to be enhanced if counselors respect their clients' preferences for interpersonal distance, develop a smooth and pleasant relationship, and do not exploit the child's deference in that relationship. The cultural value of familialism—namely, strong identification with, attachment to, and natural support system in nuclear and extended families (Triandis, Marin, Betancourt, Lisandky, & Chang, 1982)—also can be important if family-related reasons can be connected to desired behavioral changes (Herring, 1997).

Issues related to school achievement, including oral classroom participation, should also be seen in the context of the values of humility for Latinos, and not "standing out" for American Indians (Peterson, 1999). Counselors might seek out individuals who are similar in background to that of a client from an unfamiliar culture and question them about the culture's various behaviors and values (Semrud-Clikeman, 1995). Ethnically matching the helping professional and the client, too, may result in improved functioning (Chapman, 2000).

Sidney

Ten-year-old Sidney had been referred to Sarah, a school counselor in a large elementary school, because he had been absent from school for several days, had fallen far behind his class in assignments, and seemed listless and uncommunicative. His already low level of interaction with his mostly Anglo classmates, and even with the one other Native American boy in class, had also declined. His teacher had communicated to the counselor about a death in the family recently but could not understand why Sidney wasn't "snapping out of it," as it was "just his grandmother."

The counselor recognized that Sidney's lack of eye contact denoted deference and respect, and she noted his flat affect as he sat before her. To avoid being uncomfortably direct in her approach, she offered a few gentle "small-talk" comments, then apologized for not being aware until an hour earlier that his grandmother had died. After she invited Sidney to tell her about his grandmother, he began to explain that she had essentially raised him and his siblings after his mother developed a disabling condition shortly after Sidney was born.

Sarah recognized Sidney's deep grief and listened attentively as he responded quietly to her open-ended questions. He explained various extended-family relationships and told her about the recent days of community mourning. Near the end of the session, Sarah asked Sidney if he thought she should talk with his aunt, who now seemed to be the family leader. With his permission, Sarah contacted the aunt and made an important connection between school and family, learning at the same time that the family had been concerned about Sidney's emotional withdrawal. Sidney also gave Sarah permission to tell his teacher about his closeness to his grandmother and his grief.

Assessment

Some form of early and ongoing assessment is needed to allow accurate client conceptualization and effective strategic planning. Assessment is potentially therapeutic in itself (Newsome & Gladding, 2003). Vernon (1993) advocated creative and practical developmental assessment, describing it as qualitative, based on developmental theory, interactive with the counseling process, and involving child, practitioner, and significant other adults. Developmental assessment can assess the concerns that bring a child or adolescent to counseling and also motor, cognitive, emotional, and social development relative to expectations at different ages; school and family relationships; attitudes about and performance at school; and support systems (Orton, 1997).

CACREP (Council for the Accreditation of Counseling and Related Educational Programs, 2008) has included ability and extreme ability in the 2009 standards, among many aspects in which counselors have to be knowledgeable and skilled. Counselors should know about laws, diagnoses, needs, and transitions related to children with special needs, including children whose cognitive, social, or emotional development is not commensurate with their physical development (Milsom, 2006), and who have additional awareness of cultural issues and implications related to services (Barona & Barona, 2006).

Counselors, too, should be aware of the potential of gifted children for asynchronous development, reflected in this population as cognitive development far ahead of social, emotional, and physical development. These children may not be emotionally mature enough to deal with precocious existential concerns, may have intense responses to troublesome situations, or may demonstrate a highly developed talent at a young age (Grobman, 2006). When assessing needs, counselors must be aware that the sensitivity, intensity, and various overexcitabilities (Piechowski, 1997) associated with rapid information-processing (Mendaglio, 2007) may actually be misdiagnosed as pathology (Webb et al., 2005). Awareness of the possibility of *twice-exceptionality*, that giftedness can coincide with learning disability, is also important, since, for example, giftedness can coincide with learning disability (Assouline, Nicpon, & Huber, 2006).

Informal and formal assessment procedures can both be used. Myrick (1997) considered informal assessment valuable in the areas of physical development (including manner, grooming, posture, and energy level), social development (including speech flow, attitudes, and friendships), cognitive development (including logic, sense of reality, consequences, and values), cultural development (including religious and environmental influences and sense of stigmatization), history (including relevant events), future perspective (including goals, sense of responsibility, and sense of control), and the presenting problem, noting that some school counselors develop their own norms in these areas.

Other tools useful in informal assessment include art, puppets, storytelling, board games, free play, unfinished-sentence activities, role-play activities, play-therapy strategies (Gitlin-Weiner, Sandgrund, & Schaefer, 2000), writing activities, and artwork (Schmidt, 2008). Narrative descriptions of family systems in response to story stems can provide valuable information related to marital conflict, parental acceptance, and behavioral control in relation to the presenting issues (Shamir, DuRocher Schudlich, & Cummings, 2001). Drawing the ideal self encourages youngsters to be actively involved in the therapeutic process and can enhance self-understanding (Moran, 2001). A multiple-intelligences framework can tap into varied talents during and following assessment with young children (O'Brien & Burnett, 2000). Autobiographical outlines and family-roles activities (Peterson, 2007b) can elicit valuable information about pertinent family-systemic factors.

Orton (1997) discussed the usefulness of observation by teachers and counselors, ideally in several home and school settings, focusing on learning style, attention span, mood and affect, expression of emotions, and interactions with parents, teachers, and peers. Semrud-Clikeman (1995) recommended observing not only the child but also his or her peers to make behavioral comparisons. Observing parent–child interaction also can be helpful in forming treatment goals and strategies and also in assessing how various behaviors may be affecting the parent–child relationship.

Formal, structured assessment might involve tests, surveys, and scales related to the child's interests, values, study habits, social acceptance, behavior, and personality type. Observations can be helpful in assessing frequency, duration, and severity of behaviors. Psychological and educational tests, including intelligence, aptitude, and achievement instruments, are common assessments (Thompson & Henderson, 2007); scores on the last two usually are available to school counselors. Schmidt (1999) suggested that school records (e.g., grade and attendance reports and health cards) can be incorporated into comprehensive assessment of development and needs, and students' classroom products might also be assessed. He argued for caution with self-report instruments related to personality, given the potential for inaccurate or distorted portrayals, the lack of insight in individuals who have poor social functioning, and the possibility of respondents' multiple interpretations of items. Instruments should be used as one component in a comprehensive appraisal.

Clinicians involved with third-party reimbursement should refer to the *Diagnostic and Statistical Manual of Mental Disorders* (DSM–IV-TM) (American Psychiatric Association, 2000). For organizing and communicating clinical information, this volume presents a standardized format based on a multiaxial system of assessment. Indeed, all counselors, including school counselors, should be familiar with diagnostic terminology and with common diagnoses in children and adolescents, such as attention deficit/hyperactivity disorder, post-traumatic stress disorder, conduct disorder, depressive disorders, and anorexia nervosa, as well as less common disorders. When young clients show symptoms of depression, for example, counselors with knowledge of pertinent diagnoses can administer an appropriate assessment or make informal inquiries with specific symptoms in mind. Based on their assessments, counselors should be prepared to provide referrals to other service providers when appropriate (Erford, 2003).

Gathering More Information

Regardless of the client's age, culture, or level of cognitive and emotional development, a trusting relationship between counselor and client is the hallmark of effective counseling. With this in mind, a counselor might sense that focusing on "the problem" should be delayed. However, directly addressing the reason for a referral, for instance, may be appropriate. The counselor can acknowledge whatever information the referral source has provided and indicate readiness to discuss the situation (Thompson & Henderson, 2007). A less direct approach, allowing the child or adolescent to explain the referral, may reveal a problem that differs from the one noted in the referral. Giving children choices can restore some of the control they "might have thought they lost by coming to counseling; for example, allowing them to choose where to sit or what to discuss" (p. 42).

When interviewing children, listening is more important than questioning (Erford, 2003). One of the purposes in the initial session is to show the child that he or she is in a safe environment and will be listened to, so a bond can develop. Some children form bonds easily and talk readily about their feelings and concerns. Others require time before they feel safe enough to share confidences (Semrud-Clikeman, 1995). Beginning counselors in particular might feel defensive and frustrated when a child does not want to talk. Even reluctant or disinclined adolescents, however, may respond to approaches incorporating interests and media, as Herlihy's (2002) client did through music, which seemed to be the client's "world."

Children are "extremely sensitive to adult moods and can recognize insincerity or lack of concern quickly" (Thompson & Henderson, 2007, p. 40). In addition, forcing attention on "therapeutic issues" may be counterproductive: "When children are forced to do things, they become angry, resistant, and oppositional in an attempt to regain control … reacting normally to a strange situation" (p. 41).

Interviewing style may be an additional issue. When a child answers a question, many counselors follow the response with another question. More effective is to paraphrase or summarize, as those strategies encourage expanding on the previous response. Erdman and Lampe (1996) warned against becoming impatient at delayed rapport. Abused children, in particular, may be alert to the possibility of deception (Bugental, Shennum, Frank, & Ekman, 2001) and therefore slow to trust a counselor.

In general, the counselor has to be open to children's needs and concerns, paying attention to what the child is expressing and exploring how to help with that expression without having a rigid agenda for a session and without making judgments (e.g., "This isn't at all what she should be dealing with"). When a counselor reflects feelings accurately (e.g., "You seem happy about that"; "You sound sad today"; "I sense that you're worried about your dad"), young clients feel heard. When a child assumes incorrectly that "the problem" should be obvious to a counselor, such as in situations of self-referral to a school counselor, the counselor might say, "I'm guessing that there's something you'd like to talk to me about. Could you help me, because I'm not sure what it is?"

Matthew

Matthew, age 10, was being bullied at school. He came to see the school counselor because his teacher noticed that he was not doing his schoolwork and was unresponsive in class. Neither she nor Matthew's parents were aware of any cause. In meeting with the counselor, Matthew seemed shy and nervous, perhaps even frightened. While he and the counselor put together a puzzle, they talked about the people he lived with, his teacher, his dog, and what he did when he could do anything he wanted. He then worked with some clay. As he did this, the counselor asked him if he wondered what counselors do.

In response to Matthew's affirmative head nod, the counselor said, "Kids can talk to counselors about anything they wonder about, or think about, or are upset about. Counselors are good listeners. But what kids say is up to them."

Matthew then chose some markers and began to draw designs on a paper. As he drew, the counselor made nonevaluative statements about the colors and shapes.

When the counselor prepared to send Matthew back to class, she told him that she enjoyed being with him and would like to do that again sometime. Matthew, however, seemed reluctant to leave and took another sheet of paper to draw on. Suddenly, with tears welling in his eyes, he told her about the bullying.

"That sounds scary," the counselor said.

Matthew told her he was afraid his dad and older brother would call him a sissy and said he knew his parents would argue over what he should do. He said his older brother punched him regularly to "teach me not to be a wimp."

"You don't feel very good about that," the counselor replied, responding with empathy to his sad, serious expression.

Matthew admitted that he felt angry and hurt.

In the next session the two interacted further, with the counselor following Matthew's lead, validating his feelings, and asking open-ended questions to become informed about sequences and situations related to the bullying.

Maya

Maya's teacher referred the 10-year-old to the school counselor because the teacher noticed dark circles under Maya's eyes and observed that she had a flat affect. Maya and the counselor began by exploring the toys in the counseling office and conversing about Maya's siblings, her friends, and her interests. During a subsequent get-acquainted activity involving completing sentence stems ("When I was little…; now…."), Maya said, "When I was little, I was afraid of monsters; now I'm afraid of the dark." She added, "I'm *really* afraid of the dark!"

Further conversation revealed Maya's sleep problems, fears about accidents, fears about death, and her parents' nonvalidation of her fears. The counselor normalized Maya's fears by saying, "A lot of kids are scared of the dark—or of something. That's okay. There's nothing wrong with you. I wonder what we can do to help you with your fear of the dark."

They decided that Maya would ask her parents for a flashlight and ask if they would read her a calm story before bedtime. The counselor expressed confidence that, with practice, Maya would get better and better at being able to deal with her fears. They agreed that Maya would return in a week to tell the counselor how her "practicing" was coming along.

With Maya's permission, the counselor met a few days later with Maya's mother. During their meeting he normalized the fears, engaged the mother in an exploration of coping strategies for Maya, and discussed other possible sources of her anxiety. The mother reported that she had been on the phone a great deal lately, talking with relatives in India, where a cousin recently had an accident and was hospitalized. The counselor noticed the mother's use of "awfulizing language" and gently explored with her the possibility that catastrophizing in "scary" family talk might be having an impact on Maya. Maya's mother said she had been overprotective of Maya since the accident and might be anxious herself at bedtime.

At the conclusion of the conversation, the counselor sent the mother a message of confidence, saying, "I'm sure you'll figure out how to help Maya relax at bedtime and how to let her know that you'll be there to take care of her. We get smarter and smarter about these things." As a result of this discussion, the counselor was more informed, although he planned not to discuss the cousin's accident in subsequent sessions until or unless Maya brought it up.

Teachers and administrators frequently expect school counselors to "fix" a classroom behavior problem quickly, perhaps in just 15 minutes. When a quick solution seems possible, and best, the counselor may apply a brief-counseling model (see chapter 5). The counselor may decide, however, that the best course initially is to work on establishing a relationship. Unpressured interaction, even for a few minutes a few times a week, can be a key to other "progress." An apparently no-agenda approach, including reframing the presenting problem, might get the attention of a reluctant child. This approach was used in the following scenario of a child who had just been removed from a physical education class because of problematic behavior:

> You look like an interesting kid, and I like interesting kids. They're usually nice to get to know. Sometimes they're full of surprises, and that makes my work interesting. That's good. Sounds like you've got some spunk. Do you think so? Maybe we can just hang out here for a while and get a start on knowing each other.

When counselors allow pressure from parents or teachers to dictate pace and process of initial sessions, and when interventions are premature, a trusting relationship with young clients may not develop sufficiently for effective work. A counselor self-disclosure about experiencing a negative situation similar to the child client's, meant to move the relationship forward, may seem too intimate before a relationship has been sufficiently established. Even when there seems to be urgency, it is important to "trust the counseling process and remain solidly focused on the relationship" (Clark, 2002, p. 58).

Asking Questions

Garbarino and Stott (1989) recommended that, with preschoolers, counselors use the child's name and the child's terms in their questions; rephrase, not repeat, questions that the child does not understand; avoid time-sequence questions; not ask a question following every answer the child gives; and use questions that are only slightly longer than the sentences the children use. This is timeless advice.

Thompson and Henderson (2007) pointed out that adults' questions often reflect curiosity rather than a desire to help; that questions can be used to judge, blame, or criticize; that "why" questions often are associated with blame and contribute to defensiveness; and that children easily fall into a pattern of answering and then waiting for the next question. Lamb, Sternberg, Orbach, Esplin, and Mitchell (2002) acknowledged that direct questions can be appropriate for gaining factual information or clarification but noted that open-ended questions generate more information and promote spontaneous expression.

Counselors can respond to cryptic comments with open-ended requests for more information. As examples of open inquiry, Evans, Hearn, Uhlemann, and Ivey (1998, pp. 39–50) offered the following question stems, beginning with *could, what, can, and how*:

"Could you help me understand . . .";
"What do you feel like doing when . . .";
"Can you tell me more about . . .";
"How do you feel about . . .";
"What do you . . .";
"What sorts of things . . . ."

Entire sessions may be facilitated by reflective statements with no, or almost no, questions used at all (Peterson, 2007b).

Park (2001) found that during interviews with child witnesses, developmentally appropriate questions elicited accurate responses whereas questions beyond the cognitive capabilities of the children led to difficulties with accuracy. Open-ended questions also generate more accurate responses in children within and across interviews (Fivush, Peterson, & Schwarzmueller, 2002) and fewer contradictions across multiple interviews than do closed questions (requiring a yes/no response), particularly questions that provide options or are suggestive (Lamb & Fauchier, 2001). According to one study (Waterman, Blades, & Spencer, 2001), children may answer closed questions even when questions are unanswerable, while readily acknowledging that they do not know the answer to questions requiring specific details. Accuracy may also be compromised over time by parental pressures or misleading questioning (Henderson, 2001).

Establishing the Relationship and Developing a Focus

Using Media

Many children, and even some adolescents, benefit by having "something to fiddle with" in the counselor's office. Therefore, counselors in schools should have available an array of developmentally appropriate toys, materials for creative expression, drawing paper and markers, and puzzles for those who feel the need to be distracted from the intensity of the situation at hand, need something to diminish their self-consciousness, or need media to help with expression. (See chapter 4 for a discussion of play therapy.)

Aaron

When Aaron, age 13, arrived for his first counseling session, he appeared nervous. He made no eye contact with the counselor and responded with only monosyllables when she tried to engage him in light conversation. The counselor knew that Aaron's middle-class family had recently been traumatized by his father, whose behavior had deteriorated after being laid off by his employer. To help Aaron feel at ease, the counselor moved a shallow tub of Legos® between them and began to construct something, inviting Aaron to do the same. Soon just Aaron was involved with the Legos.

After some small talk, the counselor said, "I understand that your life has been difficult lately. But I don't know much about it. What should I understand to get an idea of what it's been like?"

Aaron continued to keep his hands busy with the Legos while he gradually became engaged in dialogue, talking about his fears as an oldest child trying to protect his siblings. His comments were incisive. Although he still made no eye contact, he seemed less self-conscious and more able to concentrate on his feelings and thoughts when his hands were busy.

Sonja

Play media were essential during the first session with Sonja, age 9, who had been diagnosed with attention-deficit/hyperactivity disorder (ADHD) and was reported to be increasingly disruptive in the classroom. The counselor asked Sonja if she would like to sit with her on the floor and play with dolls and miniature dishes. As Sonja played, the two talked quietly about her interests and what she liked to do with her parents, who had been divorced for 2 years.

The counselor commented, "It sounds like you and your parents have worked it out so you can be with both of them every week. How's that going for you?"

Sonja was articulate and calm when talking about the divorce but was agitated and tearful when talking about her mother's new baby. Playing seemed to help her concentrate and express her feelings instead of being overwhelmed by them. She lapsed momentarily into baby talk but stayed with the issue of the baby and her relationship with her mother. The counselor did not remark on the 9-year-old's play during the session.

Regardless of the purpose of play media, the counselor should not make evaluative judgments about the quality of constructions, drawings, or play. Adolescents, especially, are often so concerned about evaluations of what they are doing that the process ceases to be either expression or distraction. Further, children's artwork should be viewed only in conjunction with their other behaviors. Although drawings can be revealing, they also can simply be creative expression for the sake of creative expression. In addition, having a creative outlet and having something to be busy with can help to build the counseling relationship with a child or adolescent (Orton, 1997). Sometimes, of course, the content of the drawings may provide basic information about family members, portray school relationships, or convey requests. For example, one 6-year-old, unsolicited, drew his preferred custody arrangement during a counseling session with me and invited me to guess what he had drawn.

Giving Feedback

Children need to receive information and feedback about themselves so they can make sense of their feelings and their own and others' behavior. Ivey and Ivey (2003) described a "strength inventory," whereby clients focus on cultural, gender, family, and personal strengths and, for example, form images of people who have demonstrated courage and support. Timely, credible comments help to build the client–counselor relationship. Genuine, sincere compliments about behaviors and strengths demonstrated in sessions can help children gain confidence (Peterson, 2007b). Qualities to watch for include the ability to express complicated thoughts and feelings, courage, compassion, kindness, wisdom, common sense, responsibility, and problem-solving abilities (p. 17).

▰▰▰Talia

Talia, age 15, had been sexually abused by an older boy several years before coming to see me. Her parents were ashamed and blamed her. The message she received was, "It's your fault. There's something wrong with you."

That key information was incorrect. I told her that she was not bad or wrong. Her family just didn't know what to do about what had happened. They were afraid, so they reacted in a wrong way, I said. It made sense that Talia was upset. It also made sense that they had misunderstood.

Then I described a hypothetical scenario in which Talia's mother had responded appropriately. In this scene, Talia told her mom what had happened, and her mom rocked, comforted, and soothed her, listened to her story, told her it was not her fault, and that she would protect her and get her help. In this scenario Talia's mom called the police, and the police talked to both Mom and Talia to get all the pertinent information. The police then arrested the boy, and Talia's mom took her to their family doctor, who helped them. Every day Talia's mom comforted her and told her it wasn't her fault and that she wasn't a bad person.

I encouraged Talia to imagine that scene every day and to rock herself, as she was too old to be rocked by her mother now. But she could get hugs from her mom—real hugs. The next week she reported that she and her mom had their first sustained conversation ever about the incident. Both had cried, and they hugged. Talia said she eventually might be able to understand and forgive her mother.

By providing Talia with accurate feedback and affirming her, the counselor helped her to make sense of a troubling situation. This empowered her to move forward.

Unconditional Affirmation

Counselors must enter the world of the young person, poised and nonjudgmental (Peterson, 2007a). Unconditional positive regard, congruence, and empathy—the basic tenets of person-centered therapy (Rogers, 1965)—are essential in counseling relationships. Counselors applying unconditional positive regard refrain from moralizing, making judgments, diagnosing, or searching for solutions. Talia, in the case study, seemed to benefit from the counselor's affirmation and unconditional acceptance.

In discussing how Rogers's person-centered approach can be applied to working with children, Thompson and Henderson (2007) countered critics of a nonconfrontational approach by emphasizing that Rogers advised creating a safe counseling environment in which clients could begin to direct their own lives. They viewed children as "effective problem-solvers and decision-makers when they have the opportunity to be in a nonthreatening counseling atmosphere with a counselor who listens and provides guidance" (p. 5). They noted that, although some situations require counselors to take an active role, "even young children can distinguish between positive and negative behaviors and are able to choose the positive behaviors once the counselor has established an open dialogue in which feelings and emotions can be aired and conflicts resolved" (p. 169). This approach is most effective when the counselor practices active listening and uses summary and reflection statements. In this way, the counselor communicates that the client is worth hearing and understanding.

Children and adolescents may need mainly to have someone "stand beside them" during a difficult period (Peterson & Servaty-Seib, 2008). A teen who was sexually abused as a child might not be ready to talk at length about it but may need someone to offer uncritical acceptance (Peterson, 2007a). A child experiencing his parents' divorce may need reassurance that his feelings are normal and that he is a worthy human being. A depressed adolescent may be unable to name the problem, but a counselor can provide credible affirmation and a secure, crucial base.

Although school counselors usually have shorter-term involvement than agency counselors over time, they do have opportunities to connect frequently and informally with children at school. Despite their constraints, agency counselors, too, can offer significant support, perhaps even with feedback in the form of a letter between sessions, affirming strengths (Winslade & Monk, 2007). I have observed numerous instances in and out of school settings in which children and adolescents survived extended periods of suicidal ideation while leaning periodically on a counselor and later, spontaneous resolution as young adults.

Telling the Truth

Counselors face a dilemma when children tell extraordinary stories. Are the stories meant to gain attention or sympathy or even simply to help the child to be interesting (Thompson & Henderson, 2007)? Directly challenging a statement or story may interfere with a trusting relationship, and all or part of a story might actually be true. One strategy is to use immediacy—offering personal reactions to a client's comments or behaviors in the present—saying, for example, "That story bothers me. It seems like a strange thing to happen. I'll have to think about that one." A response like this gives the child a chance to alter the story while avoiding a direct challenge. Other effective responses could be: "Which parts of that story do you think I should think about the most?" "I would like you to tell me more about that"; "I'll bet some people think that was strange for someone your age." All of these offer an opportunity for the child to expand or retract.

Counselor Self-Disclosure

Counselor self-disclosure remains a controversial topic in the profession. Counselors should be judicious in their use of self-disclosure with children and adolescents, striking a therapeutically effective balance between rigid self-distancing and careless, unthinking, and unnecessary self-disclosures (Renik, 1999). Counseling should stay focused on the client and not be displaced onto the counselor. Every self-disclosure takes attention away from the client momentarily and also may not be as helpful as the counselor thinks (Peterson, 2007b).

In general, the use of immediacy is usually an appropriate form of self-disclosure and has been supported by research. Ivey and Ivey (1999) acknowledge that, when used carefully, self-disclosure can contribute to trust, openness, and a sense of equality. In contrast, self-disclosure of personal experiences in the past may be viewed as self-focused (Cashwell, Shcherbakova, & Cashwell, 2003), inappropriate confessions (Thompson & Henderson, 2007), or simply not listening.

Few adolescents believe that anyone else, particularly someone older than they are, could have had an experience similar to theirs (Elkind, 1981). Young clients need an objective, nonjudgmental listener who validates their experience as unique and important. At-risk children and adolescents in particular appreciate a stable listener who is not self-absorbed. Counselors, however, should be aware that cultural attitudes about self-disclosure vary. Asian, Native Americans, and Hispanics, for example, may equate self-disclosure to a stranger with lack of maturity and wisdom (Zhang, 1999). Children and adolescents within cultures also may differ considerably regarding counselor self-disclosure—and client self-disclosure as well (Egan, 2007).

A "One-Down" Position

By taking a one-down, "not-knowing" position (Murphy, 2006; Peterson, 2007b), the counselor can elicit information from children while empowering them. Counselors do not know the child's or adolescent's world, and they will not learn about it from an authoritative one-up position. More effective is: "Teach me about [your life; your sadness; being 13; your sleep problems]." Counselors are trained to explore the phenomenological world of clients, including children and adolescents. In these explorations, being "clueless" can be extremely helpful. Comments such as the following can elicit information about their clients' world:

"I can't imagine what it's like to be nine years old and have your mom tell you that she and your dad are going to get a divorce."
"Help me understand what going to the hospital to visit your dad is like."
"I'm not in your world, so I don't know what kinds of drugs are out there. What should adults understand about drugs these days?"
"Maybe you could take me down to the auto-mechanics room and show me around. I'm not very smart about cars."
"I would like to understand more about what it's like for you and your family to have come from Mexico to this town in the Midwest. Could you help me?"

When telling about their world, children and adolescents might benefit from suggestions for words to describe their feelings. Relevant comments could include the following:

"If I were in your shoes, I'd probably be feeling a little scared."
"That sounds really confusing."
"I think if someone were teasing me like that, I might get very angry."
"Some kids I've known have felt sad when that happened to them."

Using "Process" Questions

Process-oriented comments and questions, which look at internal and external processes, are beneficial in dealing with awkward moments, revelations, expressions of intense feelings, moments of insight, counselor "error," and silences. Processing provides an opportunity for the child or adolescent to learn to articulate emotions (Peterson, 2008a, p. 10). The following are examples of process questions:

"Tell me how that felt."
"What were you thinking just now?"
"What feelings do you have now—after all that hard work?"
"What was it like to challenge me like that?"
"Tell me about what just happened in here. Did I invade your space?"
"I didn't say that very well. What did that sound like to you?"

Processing punctuates moments in the counseling relationship and significant moments of personal growth. It also can be used to stop long narratives and reestablish the focus on feelings or a presenting issue, as in this instance: "I'd like to put a period at the end of what you've told me so far. I can see that it was disturbing to talk about what happened. What were you feeling when you told me that?"

Using Structured Exercises

Although using structured exercises (e.g., Peterson, 2007b) can be effective with all children and adolescents, it is especially helpful with those who are reluctant. Counselors can overuse and abuse structure, of course, but well-crafted pencil-and-paper or oral activities such as the following have great potential for building trust, eliciting information, helping shy and unassertive children and adolescents find words to say, and providing information about ability and development:

1. Sentence stems (e.g., "Something I have that is special to me is….."; "I'm probably most myself when I…. "; "I would like to give myself permission to…." (Peterson, 2007b).
2. Open-ended questions (e.g., "What would happen if you suddenly became an achiever?") (Peterson, 2008b).
3. Checklists (for child or parent, including statements such as, "My child seems rested each morning when he/she begins the day"; "I often feel uncomfortable at school.")
4. Continuum exercises (e.g., "On a scale of 1 to 10, how much do you agree with the following statements? Move physically to where you'd rate yourself for each statement, with 1 being there and 10 being over there.") (Peterson, 2007b).
5. Stress-sorters (e.g., drawing 6 boxes in a column, each connected by a line to a box on the right; writing one current stressor in each box on the left; making a "lightning line" on each existing line, with width showing degree of stress; marking each right-column box to indicate either a long- or short-term stressor, either potentially controllable or not; and telling about each stressor, assisted by the drawing) (Peterson, 2007b).
6. Role-plays (e.g., "You be yourself, and I'll pretend I'm a bully in gym class. Let's practice with some of the strategies we've been talking about.").
7. Written scenarios presenting problematic situations such as date rape, aggressive behavior, or not being appropriately assertive (Peterson, 2007b) or decision-making dilemmas (Vernon, 1993).
8. Self-description sheets (e.g., "My mom thinks I am…."; "My dad thinks I am…."; "My teachers think I am…."; "My friends think I am…."; "I think I am….") (Peterson, 2008b).
9. Self-monitoring exercises (e.g., related to self-talk, feelings) (Vernon, 1993, p. 30).
10. Family role-exploration checklist (e.g., "peacemaker," "worrier," "rule-maker," "leader," "joker," "easy to raise," "difficult to raise," "social") (Peterson, 2007b)
11. Diaries, logs, and journals; self-composed songs, poems, and stories (Vernon, 1993, pp. 27–28).
12. "Word-movies" (weekly storytelling by client and counselor, customized to fit client circumstances, with attention to encoded developmental information helpful for reaching therapeutic goals) (Spees, 2002)

Developmentally appropriate activities provide a good beginning for self-exploration and also can be used throughout the counseling relationship to raise children's awareness of self and others and assist in problem-solving.

Special Considerations When Working With Adolescents

Adolescents require approaches different from those used with younger children. Trust is often harder to achieve with adolescents than with children, and rapport may be more tenuous. Though some adolescents are suspicious of unbusiness-like conversation, it actually might be productive and may result in unexpected personal connections. For example, a counselor and an adolescent client stumbled into a discussion of motorcycles, about which both had considerable interest and experience. The boy became animated. Several minutes later the counselor successfully used a "biker" metaphor to access an important issue, and the adolescent's behavior improved noticeably thereafter.

Counselors should show interest in adolescents personally but not be patronizing. When coming to counseling, many adolescents feel like they have been "written off" by family, teachers, administrators, and perhaps even their peers. Therefore, they should feel like they are taken seriously, respected, and not judged. They want to be accepted unconditionally, no matter how odd or unusual their self-presentation may be. In addition, they accept direction, when it comes, much more readily when they think it is their own idea, not the counselor's.

During sessions, effective counselors react to comments and behaviors by being respectful, nonreactive, collaborative, and not argumentative. In addition, counselors respect adolescents' need for personal space and individual expression. These counselor behaviors might be new to many adolescents who are accustomed to "walking on eggshells" with adults. The following examples of counselor responses illustrate low reactivity and respect:

"I stole a Toyota once." (Counselor: "So what was going on in your life when you stole the Toyota?")

"Like when you came to our class and talked about violence with a guy you're going out with? That's happened to me." (Counselor: "I'm so sorry that you had to go through that. It may have been hard to tell me, but I'm glad you did. Do you feel like talking about it?")

"Sometimes I feel so bad that I get scared at how bad I feel." (Counselor: "That sounds frightening—to feel that bad. Tell me more about it. What do you think about? What's scary?")

Verbal "bombshells," such as those in the previous examples, may be meant to test counselors personally or to find out whether something actually can be talked about. For the counselor, good listening requires hard work and low emotional reactivity (Peterson, 2007b). The counselor's attentive responses can help adolescents know that it is okay to bring up and talk about difficult issues. Perhaps, quite unlike the high reactivity the adolescent faces at home, the counselor's poise, attention, affirmation, and validation will lead to trust.

A counselor might validate the adolescent by saying, "Wow! That sounds like a really difficult situation!" This sort of statement can provide needed validation to the adolescent. The counselor also should be on the lookout for any statements that indicate possible suicidal ideation, and respond at an appropriate time, "How much should I worry about you?"

Adolescents may be used to having adults judge them and leave them, so counselors must demonstrate that they are there "for the long haul." Authority figures in adolescents' lives may have been capricious and inconsistent, modeling displaced anger, scapegoating, mood instability, and unhealthy coping. Counselors should be careful not to mimic the ineffective and problem-creating behaviors of adult figures in the adolescents' lives, including emotional enmeshment, high reactivity, and rejection. In psychodynamic terms, when counselors do not behave in ways the adolescents are used to from adults in authority, this can be a corrective emotional experience (Merydith, 2007).

Adolescents are moving through uncertain territory, including differentiating from parents. Counselors can acknowledge and normalize the discomfort and uncertainty of adolescents at this developmental stage. Another kind of correction can happen when the counselor provides important information in the safety of a counseling session, as in the following example, involving a 17-year-old girl:

Client: "I did what you said. I told my dad I wanted to talk about seeing my boyfriend [outside of school]. He grounded me for a month."

Counselor: "Your dad may be scared for you, and he might not know how to protect you except by being very strict and keeping you at home. But that was a good thing you did—asking to talk to him. I'm glad you believe that talking can be helpful—like here. I hope you'll be able to talk with him about things like this sometime. I'm sorry you were grounded."

Working Together Toward Change

Developing Interventions

Developing interventions should not be done in a haphazard manner. Careful planning, design, implementation, and evaluation are essential. After exploring the presenting problem with the client, the counselor begins to plan the interventions, based on current goals, awareness of unsuccessful previous interventions, counselor skills, client ability and developmental level, client learning style, and time constraints.

Implementation might entail homework assignments "to bridge counseling sessions and daily living" (Mendaglio, 2007, p. 56). At the time of implementation, however, the counselor may have to make adjustments in the intervention as a result of timing and lack of client readiness. Later, evaluation should involve a systematic, deliberate appraisal of the intervention. Myrick (1997) suggested asking questions such as, "What did you like best about what you did?" "If you were to change things, what would you do differently?" (p. 154).

School counselors, in particular, are often called upon to solve students' problems. Myrick (1997) presented a systematic problem-solving model consisting of four questions to ask in an interview:

1. What is the problem?

2. What have you tried?
3. What else could you do?
4. What is your next step?

He acknowledged that the presenting problem may not be the "real problem," but is nevertheless a place to begin. When a child presents with multiple problems, Myrick cautioned against "flooding," instead suggesting that the child select only a few of the problems to work on and take a few steps with them.

A school-counseling exemplar (Littrell & Peterson, 2005) used "clear, focused questions, which requested highly specific responses" (p. 75). She asked third- and fourth-graders two questions: "Did your solution make the problem bigger or smaller?" and "What can you do to make the problem smaller?" Elementary-level students responded eagerly and ingenuously to these questions, especially after she had thoroughly normalized "having problems" in the school. In this context, she could informally check in before or after school or in the halls, asking, "How are you doing with the problem?"

Eventually, no matter what problem-solving model is followed, counselors put to use what they have learned while working with the client, applying patterns and themes heard and observed, helping young clients gain insight (Orton, 1997), and, depending on the theoretical approach, focusing on goals and the "next step." For instance, a basic tenet of a solution-focused approach is that even a small change can generate a larger change: "Big problems do not necessarily require big solutions" (Murphy, 2006, p. 41). Subsequent positive behaviors are more likely if the client has made a commitment to try a problem-solving idea (Thompson & Henderson, 2007).

Some authors have advocated brief-counseling approaches for use in the schools. This is the topic of chapter 5. Chapter 6 addresses the use of rational–emotive behavior therapy with children and adolescents. Both of those approaches work well with childrens because, among other reasons, they fit children's developmental conceptualization of time. For them, a problem today may not be a problem tomorrow.

Many schools also have embraced choice theory reality therapy (Glasser, 2005). This approach emphasizes basic needs, logical consequences, the importance of focusing on one's own instead of others' behavior, and the idea that irresponsible behavior contributes to mental illness rather than vice versa.

Interventions applied during this stage in counseling may encompass a wide variety of developmentally appropriate approaches—play therapy, bibliotherapy, shared viewing of film clips, therapeutic writing, music, art, and structured experiences—some of which were referred to earlier in this chapter. Chapter 3 provides a more detailed discussion of appropriate interventions for working with children and adolescents.

Giving Advice

A common public perception of counselors is that they are advice-givers. Especially with young children, it is indeed often tempting to offer advice. These children often expect it, and they are young and a captive audience. Thompson and Henderson (2007) urged counselors to resist this temptation:

> Counselors who believe in the uniqueness, worth, dignity, and responsi-bility of the individual and who believe that, given the right conditions, individuals can make correct choices for themselves are reluctant to give advice on solving life's problems. Instead, they use their counseling knowledge and skills to help clients make responsible choices of their own and, in effect, learn how to become their own counselor. (pp. 52–53)

These authors emphasized the danger of creating dependency and overconformity in young clients as a result of encouraging them to rely on adults to make decisions for them. In mild contrast, Winslade and Monk (2007) argued, in connection with nar-rative counseling, that a tentative, curious posture when giving suggestions can give the client permission to agree or disagree.

When clients, even young children, feel in charge of their own growth, they are more likely to continue to grow, sustain their exploration independently, and find their own strengths and strategies in the future. Counselors can empower young clients by affirming their strengths and by stepping back periodically and explaining to them "what just happened" in the session, while minimizing the counselor's role.

In the case of 9-year-old Sonja, whose case was summarized earlier in this chap-ter, the counselor might say:

> I'm really impressed with what you just did. You said something that was very, very important, and you said it in grown-up language. You told me how you felt—that you didn't feel very good about the new baby. That was beautiful. I'm surprised, because I didn't know you could do that. You didn't whine, and you didn't get upset. You just said it! I asked a question that you could have answered any way you chose. And you knew how to do it. That's so important to be able to tell people exactly what you feel. When you need to do that again, you'll be ready. How did it feel to tell me that?

Here-and-Now Focus

Myrick (1997) distinguished between here-and-now and then-and-there comments during counseling. The former relate to what is happening in the present between the counselor and the client, and the latter to feelings and events in the past. The coun-selor's here-and-now statements help the client explore matters in depth and are likely to be intense, intimate, and personal. These statements are potentially threat-ening but also are powerful and exciting. The counselor can use then-and-there state-ments to diffuse the intensity of the present moment, and they also may be appropriate at the outset of counseling, as they are less threatening.

Here-and-now statements can be effective with reluctant clients: "Tell me what you're feeling right now. I'm sensing a reaction to what I said." In contrast to pres-ent-focused approaches, narrative counseling is an approach that does not privilege here-and-now, instead purposefully linking past, present, and future (Winslade & Monk, 2007).

Affirming Resilience

Counselors can empower young clients by affirming their resilience (e.g., Benard, 2004; Werner & Smith, 2001; Masten, 2001), Thompson and Henderson (2007, p. 19) defined resilience as "a self-righting tendency toward health not limited to any ethnicity, social class, or geographic boundary." Resilience can mediate the effects of difficult circumstances. Even though no one may have noticed a child's strengths in this regard, these strengths might be crucial to day-to-day survival.

Among many factors of resilience noted by scholars are social strengths, problem-solving ability, autonomy, and a sense of purpose (Benard, 2004), as well as caring and support, high expectations, and opportunities for participation (Lewis, 2006). A counselor who notices these strengths and speaks confidently of their place in "a better future" offers optimism at a critical time during development while not losing sight of potential mental-health issues.

A counselor may have a long-term impact on children or adolescents simply by being a stable, caring figure who acknowledges their difficult circumstances, affirms their personal strengths and resilience, and shows confidence in them. In general, counselors have credibility if their comments are based on information and observations from sessions, as in this situation involving a 12-year-old African American boy:

> In what you've told me today, I've noticed many things that give me confidence that things will work out for you. You have a grandma you can count on. You've found ways to get other adults to pay attention to you and help you—in the neighborhood and here at school. You think well. You're a survivor. You make sense of complicated situations. And your mom took good care of you before she died when you were very young. All of those are good things in your life, and they help to make you strong. That's why I'm so hopeful for you.

At the same time, counselors may have to point out that, although certain "survival skills" may have been essential in the past, they now are likely to interfere with relationships. For example, lying might have been necessary to avoid beatings, manipulation might have been critical to engaging helpful adults, bottling emotions might have ensured short-term calm in the family, self-medicating through substances might have dulled pain, and aggressive behavior might have offered some self-protection. But these behaviors now might be contributing to problems at home, at school, with friends, in relationships, or on the job.

Reframing the problematic behaviors into the more affirmative perspective of "using your intelligence" offers a functional view, probably quite different from other adults' feedback. Then, collaboratively helping young clients recognize that their behaviors are no longer effective might generate openness to strategies for making positive changes.

Closure

Referral

After careful attention to the scope of the problem, to responses to current interventions, and to what would be best for the child or adolescent (Semrud-Clikeman, 1995), a counselor may determine that his or her counseling competence or institutional resources are not adequate to meet the child's or adolescent's needs. In such cases, referral to other services, such as substance abuse or mental health facilities, residential treatment centers, or social services, is in order. The counselor is responsible for organizing information to ensure a smooth transition and to provide parents or guardians with accurate information about the referral site and services offered.

Termination

Counseling ends for many reasons. Insurance and personal finances may be factors. The school year might be over, or school children might move to a new school, district, or city. Parents or the child may call a halt to counseling for a variety of reasons. A counselor may make a referral to another professional. Some children and adolescents simply do not return after intake, or they discontinue treatment with no explanation. Christy (2001) found that low family income and history of truancy or runaway behaviors were associated with self-termination. We are referring in this discussion to situations in which counselors can facilitate termination of young clients that is satisfactory to counselor and client alike.

Often, the counseling relationship is a powerful presence in the lives of children and adolescents, and they become anxious as the counseling process draws to a close. For children for whom change has meant upheaval or for whom endings have meant abandonment, termination of counseling may be especially difficult. Therefore, the counselor should prepare the young client for the end of counseling in advance of the final session whenever possible, including, as discussed by Somody (2007), a process of weaning when preparing to transfer a child to a new counselor. The counselor should help the child process his or her feelings associated with the ending, perhaps arranging some sort of concluding ritual, and should reassure the child that he or she will remain in the counselor's thoughts. In doing so, the counselor communicates an important message: The counseling process has been a significant experience, and the child is worthy of it. Even though agitation, anger, and anxiety are normal reactions to termination (Semrud-Clikeman, 1995), these reactions should be explored to determine if termination is premature or calls for more processing, particularly when the counselor is the one who initiates the termination.

As termination nears, various issues can be addressed. When both child and counselor will remain in proximity and the counselor will be available, the child can be made aware that future counseling can be arranged if needed. Based on the client's progress in counseling, the counselor can predict his or her continued success and potential developmental challenges—the latter to prepare the client for "normal stumbling." Progress made during the sessions can be noted and celebrated, with the counselor emphasizing what the child did for himself or herself. The relationship between counselor and client can be affirmed and validated. The counselor can model genuine feelings about terminating a relationship and also model saying good-bye. Some counselors ask children or adolescents how their leave-taking should be concluded. Semrud-Clikeman (1995) has used the "graduation" metaphor with children, explaining that endings reflect "success, not just loss" (p. 144). At the end of the final meeting with a preadolescent, the counselor might say something like this:

> I've really enjoyed working with you. You've done a lot of hard work over the past few weeks, and I respect that very much. I'll remember you as having lots of interesting parts that go together to make someone really beautiful—like pieces in a quilt. Some pieces are velvety-soft, some rough and nubby, some in between. I've seen lots of different pieces in you. Thank you for sharing those with me.

> What do you think you'll remember from our conversations together? What has been helpful? . . . .

> I imagine there will be times when you'll worry that things will go back to the way they were when things were bad—like if you have to move again. It will be normal to worry. But you've worked hard here, and I know you'll remember some of the things you've learned about yourself. And you'll remember all the things you did to survive your last move and what you can do again. [The counselor then would list them.] If you ever feel you need to talk to a counselor, don't hesitate to be in touch with me, if you're here, or with another counselor.

> What would be the best way to say good-bye right now? You can choose. I'm open to a handshake, a hug, a smile, a good-bye—whatever you'd like.

When concluding counseling with clients of any age, the counselor may have unsettling thoughts and feelings, including thoughts about endings and loss. This may be especially true when the clients are children and adolescents. The feelings arise because the counseling relationship has been satisfying and productive and also because the counselor knows that the young client may continue to be vulnerable in a complex and troublesome environment. The caring counselor consequently may have anxiety about the loss of counseling support for the child. Helping professionals must monitor themselves during these transitions, validating their own feelings and needs and paying attention to boundary and dependency issues. When working with children and adolescents, counselors should also consider that termination is not a final step, as young clients have considered their issues only at their developmental stage (Oaklander, 1997).

In some cases, counseling is better phased out gradually, perhaps by increasing the length of time between sessions rather than ending counseling more abruptly. The counselor also may schedule occasional "check-up" visits to monitor progress, especially in school settings.

Summary

When working with children and adolescents, as with adults, counselors must pay attention to ethical and legal concerns. In addition, they have to assess physical, emotional, social, and cognitive development, as well as the family system, school context, and social milieu. As counseling continues, they have to build rapport; develop focus; plan, implement, and assess intervention strategies; and prepare the client for termination. Building a relationship with children and adolescents differs from developing a relationship with adults. Toys, manipulatives, and other media may be used as the "language" or to mitigate emotional intensity. Structured exercises may be effective in building a relationship and also in eliciting information and exploring issues.

The process of building a relationship may itself result in therapeutic gain. By actively listening, giving feedback, providing accurate and developmentally appropriate information, and generating corrective emotional experiences, counselors can model important relationship skills and affirm clients' strengths and resilience. Counselors should assume that significant adults in the lives of children and adolescents will be involved in the counseling process at some point.

References

American Association for Marriage and Family Therapy. (2001). *AAMFT code of ethics*. Washington, DC: Author.

American Counseling Association. (2005). *ACA Code of ethics*. Alexandria, VA: Author.

American Psychiatric Association. (2000). *Diagnostic and statistical manual of mental disorders (4th ed.): Text revision* Washington, DC: Author

American Psychological Association. (2002). *Ethical principles of psychologists and code of conduct*. Washington, DC: Author.

American School Counselor Association. (2004). *ASCA code of ethics: Ethical standards for school counselors*. Alexandria, VA: Author.

Assouline, S. G., Nicpon, M. F., & Huber, D. H. (2006). The impact of vulnerabilities and strengths on the academic experiences of twice-exceptional students: A message to school counselors. *Professional School Counseling, 10*, 14–24.

Barona, M., & Barona, A. (2006). School counselors and school psychologists: Collaborating to ensure minority students receive appropriate consideration for special education programs. *Professional School Counseling, 10*, 3–13.

Benard, B. (2004). *Resiliency: What we have learned*. San Francisco: WestEd.

Bolton, J. E. (2000). Attachment theory and family systems theory: An integrative approach to treating childhood anxiety. *Dissertation Abstracts International, 61*(4–B), 2191.

Buchanan, C. M., & Waizenhofer, R. (2001). The impact of interparental conflict on adolescent children: Considerations of family systems and family structure. In A. Booth & A. C. Crouter (Eds.), *Couples in conflict* (pp. 149–160). Mahwah, NJ: Erlbaum.

Bugental, D. B., Shennum, W., Frank, M., & Ekman, P. (2001). True lies: Children's abuse history and power attributions as influences on deception detection. In V. Manusov & J. H. Harvey (Eds.), *Attribution, communication behavior, and close relationships. Advances in personal relations* (pp. 248–265). New York: Cambridge University Press.

Cashwell, C. S., Shcherbakova, J., & Cashwell, T. H. (2003). Effect of client and counselor ethnicity on preference for counselor disclosure. *Journal of Counseling & Development, 81*, 196–201.

Chapman, C. R. (2000). Ethnic match and depression. *Dissertation Abstracts International, 61*(5–B), 2815.

Christy, V. F. (2001). Factors associated with premature termination of psychotherapy in children and adolescents. *Dissertation Abstracts International, 61*(12–B), 6698.

Clark, A. J. (2002). The defense never rests. In L. Golden (Ed.), *Case studies in child and adolescent counseling* (pp. 48–59). Upper Saddle River, NJ: Merrill/Prentice Hall.

Council for Accreditation of Counseling and Related Educational Programs (2008). *2009 CACREP standards.* Retrieved September 1, 2008, from www.cacrep.org/2009standards.doc

Dunn, B. P., & Levy, R. L. (2002).The girl with painful steps. In L. Golden (Ed.), *Case studies in child and adolescent counseling* (pp. 90–99). Upper Saddle River, NJ: Merrill/Prentice Hall.

Egan, G. (2007). *The skilled helper: A problem-management and opportunity-development approach to helping.* Belmont, CA: Brooks/Cole.

Elkind, D. (1981). *Children and adolescents. Interpretive essays on Jean Piaget* (3rd ed.). New York: Oxford University Press.

Erdman, P., & Lampe, R. (1996). Adapting basic skills to counsel children. *Journal of Counseling & Development, 74*, 374–377.

Erford, B. T. (2003). *Transforming the school counseling profession.* Upper Saddle River, NJ: Merrill/Prentice Hall.

Evans, D. R., Hearn, M. T., Uhlemann, M. R., & Ivey, A. E. (1998). *Essential interviewing: A programmed approach to effective communication.* Pacific Grove, CA: Brooks/Cole.

Fall, M. (2002). Where do I fit? In L. Golden (Ed.), *Case studies in child and adolescent counseling* (pp. 127–134). Upper Saddle River, NJ: Merrill/Prentice Hall.

Fivush, R., Peterson, C., & Schwarzmueller, A. (2002). Questions and answers: The credibility of child witnesses in the context of specific questioning techniques. In M. L. Eisen & J. A. Quas (Eds.), *Memory and suggestibility in the forensic interview* (pp. 331–354). Mahwah, NJ: Erlbaum.

Garbarino, J., & Stott, E. (1989). *What children can tell us.* San Francisco: Jossey–Bass.

Garcia, M., & Peralbo, M. (2000). Culture, acculturation, and perception of family relationships (Cultura, aculturacion y percepcion de las relaciones familiares). *Infancia y Aprendizaje, 89*, 81–101.

Gitlin-Weiner, K., Sandgrund, K., & Schaefer, C. (Eds.) (2000). *Play diagnosis and assessment* (2nd ed.). New York: John Wiley & Sons.

Glasser, W. (2005). *Treating mental health as a public health problem: A new leadership role for the helping professions.* Chatsworth, CA: William Glasser.

Grenato, L. A. (2002). Family secrets. In L. Golden (Ed.), *Case studies in child and adolescent counseling.* Upper Saddle River, NJ: Merrill/Prentice Hall.

Grobman, J. (2006). Underachievement in exceptionally gifted adolescents and young adults: A psychiatrist's view. *Journal of Secondary Gifted Education. 17*, 199–210.

Gumaer, J. (1984). *Counseling and therapy for children.* New York: Free Press.

Hailparn, D. F., & Hailparn, M. (2000). Parent as saboteur in the therapeutic treatment of children. *Journal of Contemporary Psychotherapy, 30*, 341–351.

Heckenberg, L. (2007). We two can be teachers. In L. B. Golden & P. Henderson (Eds.), *Case studies in school counseling.* Upper Saddle River, NJ: Merrill/Prentice Hall.

Henderson, A. L. (2001). The role of parental pressures and interviewing techniques on children's eyewitness reports. *Dissertation Abstracts International, 61*(9–B), 4985.

Herlihy, B. (2002). Mandy: Out in the world. In L. B. Golden (Ed.), *Case studies in child & adolescent counseling* (pp. 60–69). Upper Saddle River, NJ: Prentice-Hall.

Herring, R. D. (1997). *Counseling diverse ethnic youth.* Ft. Worth, TX: Harcourt Brace.

Higgins, G. O. (1994). *Resilient adults.* San Francisco: Jossey-Bass.

Hobson, S. M. (2002). The flight of the Lego plane. In L. Golden (Ed.), *Case studies in child and adolescent counseling* (3rd ed., pp. 1–7). Upper Saddle River, NJ: Merrill/Prentice Hall.

Huey, W. C., & Remley, I. P. (1988). *Ethical & legal issues in school counseling.* Alexandria, VA: American School Counselor Association.

Huss, S. N. (2001). Navigating the quagmire of inherent ethical dilemmas present in elementary school counseling programs. In D. S. Sandhu (Ed.), *Elementary school counseling in the new millennium* (pp. 15–25). Alexandria, VA: American Counseling Association.

Hutchinson, D. (2007). *The essential counselor: Process, skills, & Techniques.* Boston: Houghton Mifflin/Lahaska Press.

Ivey, A. E., & Ivey, M. B. (2003). *Intentional interviewing & counseling: Facilitating client development in a multicultural society* (5th ed.). Pacific Grove, CA: Brooks/Cole-Thomson Learning.

Ivey, A., Ivey, M., Myers, J., & Sweeney, T. (2005). *Developmental counseling & therapy: Promoting wellness over the lifespan.* Boston: Houghton Mifflin/Lahaska Press.

Ivey, A. E., Ivey, M. B., & Simek–Morgan, L. (1997). *Counseling and psychotherapy: A multicultural perspective* (4th ed.). Boston: Allyn & Bacon.

Kottman, T. (1990). Counseling middle school students: Techniques that work. *Elementary School Guidance and Counseling, 25,* 138–145.

Kottman, T. (2002). Billy, the teddy bear boy. In L. B. Golden (Ed.), *Case studies in child and adolescent counseling* (pp. 8–20). Upper Saddle River, NJ: Prentice-Hall.

Lamb, M. E., & Fauchier, A. (2001). The effects of question type on self-contradictions by children in the course of forensic interviews. *Applied Cognitive Psychology, 15,* 483–491.

Lamb, M. E., Sternberg, K. J., Orbach, Y., Esplin, P. W., & Mitchell, S. (2002). Is ongoing feedback necessary to maintain the quality of investigative interviews with allegedly abused children? *Applied Developmental Science, 6,* 35–41.

Lewis, R. E. (2006). Resilience: Individual, family, school, and community perspectives. In D. Capuzzi & D. R. Gross (Eds.), *Youth at risk: A prevention resource for counselors, teachers, and parents* (4th ed.) (pp. 35–68). Upper Saddle River, NJ: Pearson.

Littrell, J. M., & Peterson, J. S. (2005). *Portrait and model of a school counselor.* Boston: Houghton Mifflin/Lahaska Press.

Masten, A. (2001). Ordinary magic: Resilience processes in development. *American Psychologist, 56,* 227–238.

McWhirter, J. J. (2002). Will he choose life? In L. Golden (Ed.), *Case studies in child and adolescent counseling* (pp. 81–89). Upper Saddle River, NJ: Merrill/Prentice Hall.

Mendaglio, S. (2007). Affective-cognitive therapy for counseling gifted individuals. In S. Mendaglio & J. S. Peterson (Eds.), *Models of counseling gifted children, adolescents, and young adults* (pp. 35–68). Waco, TX: Prufrock.

Mendaglio, S., & Peterson, J. S. (2007). *Models of counseling gifted children, adolescents, and young adults.* Austin, TX: Prufrock.

Merydith, S. P. (2007). Psychodynamic approaches. In H. T. Prout & D. T. Brown (Eds.), *Counseling & psychotherapy with children & adolescents: Theory & practice for school and clinical settings* (pp. 94–130). Hoboken, NJ: Wiley.

Milsom, A. (2006). Creating positive school experiences for students with disabilities. *Professional School Counseling, 10,* 66–72.

Minuchin, P. (2001). Looking toward the horizon: Present and future in the study of family systems. In J. P. McHale & W. S. Grolnick (Eds.), *Retrospect and prospect in the psychological study of families* (pp. 259–278). Mahwah, NJ: Erlbaum.

Moran, H. (2001). Who do you think you are? Drawing the ideal self: A technique to explore a child's sense of self. *Clinical Child Psychology & Psychiatry, 6,* 599–604.

Mosley–Howard, G. S., & Burgan Evans, C. (2000). Relationships and contemporary experiences of the African American family: An ethnographic case study. *Journal of Black Studies, 30,* 428–452.

Muro, J. J., & Kottman, I. (1995). *Guidance and counseling in the elementary and middle schools: A practical approach.* Madison, WI: Brown & Benchmark.

Murphy, J. J. (2006). *Solution-focused counseling in middle and high schools.* Upper Saddle river, NJ: Merrill/Prentice Hall.

Myrick, R. D. (1997). *Developmental guidance and counseling: A practical approach* (3rd ed.). Minneapolis: Educational Media.

National Institute of Mental Health. (2005). *Children's mental health statistics.* Retrieved from www1.nmha.org/children/prevent/stats.cfm on August 22, 2007.

Newsome, D. W., & Gladding, S. T. (2003). Counseling individuals and groups in schools. In B. Erford (Ed.), *Transforming the school counseling profession* (pp. 209-230). Upper Saddle River, NJ: Merrill/Prentice Hall.

Nock, M. K., & Kazdin, A. E. (2001). Parent expectancies for child therapy: Assessment and relation to participation in treatment. *Journal of Child & Family Studies, 10,* 155–180.

Oaklander, V. (1997). The therapeutic process with children and adolescents. *Gestalt Review, 1,* 292–317.

O'Brien, P., & Burnett, P. C. (2000). Counseling children using a multiple intelligences framework. *British Journal of Guidance and Counseling, 28,* 353–371.

Olenchak, F. R., & Reis, S. M. (2002). Gifted students with learning disabilities. In M. Mann, R. L. (2006). Effective teaching strategies for gifted/learning-disabled students with spatial strengths. *Journal of Secondary Gifted Education, 17*(2), 112–121.

O'Malley, P. (2002). Raising Martin. In L. Golden (Ed.), *Case studies in child and adolescent counseling* (pp. 142-152). Upper Saddle River, NJ: Merrill/Prentice Hall.

Orton, G. L. (1997). *Strategies for counseling with children and their parents.* Pacific Grove, CA: Brooks/Cole.

Papilia, D. E., Olds, S. W., & Feldman, R. D. (1998). *Human development* (7th ed.). Boston: McGraw Hill.

Park, L. (2001). The child witness of sexual abuse: Recognizing developmental differences and creating a forum for eliciting accurate testimony. *Dissertation Abstracts International, 62*(2–B), 1117.

Parsons, R. D. (2007). *Counseling strategies that work!: Evidence-based interventions for school counselors.* Boston: Pearson/Allyn & Bacon.

Peterson, J. S. (1999). Gifted—through whose cultural lens? An application of the postpositivistic mode of inquiry. *Journal for the Education of the Gifted, 22,* 354–383.

Peterson, J. S. (2006). Addressing counseling needs of gifted students. *Professional School Counseling, 10,* 43–51.

Peterson, J. S. (2007a). A developmental perspective. In S. Mendaglio & J. S. Peterson (Eds.), *Models of counseling gifted children, adolescents, and young adults* (pp. 97–126). Waco, TX: Prufrock.

Peterson, J. S. (2007b). *The essential guide to talking with teens: Ready-to-use discussions for school and youth groups.* Minneapolis: Free Spirit.

Peterson, J. S. (2008a). *Gifted and traumatized: A study of development.* Manuscript submitted for publication.

Peterson, J. S. (2008b). The essential guide to talking with gifted teens: *Ready-to-use group discussions about identity, stress, relationships, and more.* Minneapolis: Free Spirit.

Peterson, J. S., & Rischar, H. (2000). Gifted and gay: A study of the adolescent experience. *Gifted Child Quarterly, 44,* 149–164.

Peterson, J. S.. & Servaty-Seib, H. (In press). Focused, but flexible: A developmental approach to small group work in schools. In H. L. K. Coleman & C. J. Yeh (Eds.), *Handbook of school counseling* (pp. 409–428). Mahwah, NJ: Lawrence Erlbaum Associates, Inc.

Piechowski, M. M. (1997). Emotional giftedness: The measure of intrapersonal intelligence. In N. Colangelo & G. A. Davis (Eds.), *Handbook of gifted education* (2nd ed., pp. 366–381). Boston: Allyn and Bacon.

Ponterotto, J. G., Gretchen, D., & Chauhan, R. V. (2001). Cultural identity and multicultural assessment: Quantitative and qualitative tools for the clinician. In L. A. Suzuki, J. G. Ponterotto, & P. J. Meller (Eds.), *Handbook of multicultural assessment* (2nd ed., pp. 67–69). San Francisco: Jossey-Bass.

Presbury, J. H., McKee, J. E., & Echterling, L. G. (2007). Person-centered approaches. In H. T. Prout & D. T. Brown (Eds.), *Counseling and psychotherapy with children and adolescents: Theory and practice for school and clinical settings* (pp. 180–240). Hoboken, NJ: Wiley.

Prout, H. T. (2007). Counseling and psychotherapy with children and adolescents: Historical developmental, integrative, and effectiveness perspectives. In H. T. Prout & D. T. Brown (Eds.), *Counseling and psychotherapy with children and adolescents: Theory & practice for school and clinical settings* (pp. 1–31). Hoboken, NJ: Wiley.

Prout, S. M., & Prout, H. T. (2007). Ethical and legal issues in psychological interventions with children and adolescents. In H. T. Prout & D. T. Brown (Eds.), *Counseling & psychotherapy with children and adolescents: Theory & practice for school and clinical settings* (pp. 32–63). Hoboken, NJ: Wiley.

Remley, T. P., Jr., & Herlihy, B. (2005). *Ethical, legal, and professional issues in counseling* (2nd ed.). Upper Saddle River, NJ: Merrill/Prentice Hall.

Renik, W. (1999). Das ideal des anonymen analytikers und das problem der selbstenthuellung. *Psyche: Zeitschrift Fuer Psychoanalyse und Ihre Anwendungen, 53,* 929–957.

Ritchie, M. H. (1994). Counselling difficult children. *Canadian Journal of Counselling, 28,* 58–68.

Rogers, C. R. (1965). *Client-centered therapy: Its current practice, implications, and theory.* Boston: Houghton Mifflin.

Saunders, C. (2007). Counseling underachieving students and their parents. In S. Mendaglio & J. S. Peterson (Eds.), *Models of counseling gifted children, adolescents, & young adults* (pp. 127–152). Waco, TX: Prufrock.

Savin-Williams, R. C., & Diamond, L. M. (1999). Sexual orientation. In W. K. Silverman & T. H. Ollendick (Eds.), *Developmental issues in the clinical treatment of children* (pp. 241–258). Needham Heights, MA: Allyn & Bacon.

Schmidt, J. J. (1999). *Counseling in schools: Essential services and comprehensive programs* (3rd ed.). Boston: Allyn & Bacon.

Schmidt, J. J. (2008). *Counseling in schools: Comprehensive programs of responsive services for all students*. Boston: Pearson.

Semrud-Clikeman, M. (1995). *Child and adolescent therapy*. Boston: Allyn & Bacon.

Shamir, H., DuRocher Schudlich, T., & Cummings, E. M. (2001). Marital conflict, parenting styles, and children's representations of family relationships. Parenting*: Science & Practice, 1*, 123–151.

Skovolt, T. M., & Rivers, D. A. (2004). *Skills and strategies for the helping professions*. Denver: Love Publishing.

Somody, C. (2007). The boy who wanted to call me "Mom." In L. B. Golden & P. Henderson (Eds.), *Case studies in school counseling* (pp. 69-81). Upper Saddle River, NJ: Merrill/Prentice Hall.

Spees, E. K. (2002). Word movies: Strategy and resources for therapeutic storytelling with children and adolescents. *Annals of the American Psychotherapy Association, 5*(1), 14–21.

Stone, C. (2005). *School counseling principles: Ethics and law.* Alexandria, VA: American School Counseling Association.

Sue, D. W., Ivey, A. E., & Pedersen, R. B. (1996). *A theory of multicultural counseling and therapy*. Pacific Grove, CA: Brooks/Cole.

Swenson, L. C. (1993). *Psychology and law for the helping professions*. Pacific Grove, CA: Brooks/Cole.

Taub, D. J. (2006). Understanding the concerns of parents of students with disabilities: Challenges and roles for school counselors. *Professional School Counseling, 10*, 52–57.

Teyber, E. (2005). *Interpersonal process in therapy: An integrative model*. Belmont, CA: Thomson.

Thompson, C. L., & Henderson, D. A.. (2007). *Counseling children* (7th ed.). Pacific Grove, CA: Brooks/Cole.

Triandis, H. C., Marin, G., Betancourt, H., Lisansky, J., & Chang, B. (1982). *Dimensions of familialism among Hispanic and mainstream Navy recruits*. Chicago: University of Illinois, Department of Psychology.

Turley, D. L. (1993). Frederika: Wrapped in burgundy wool. In L. B. Golden & M. L. Norwood (Eds.), *Case studies in child counseling* (pp. 187–209). Upper Saddle River, NJ: Prentice-Hall.

Vernon, A. (1993). *Developmental assessment & intervention with children & adolescents*. Alexandria, VA: American Counseling Association.

Vernon, A. (2002a). Foreword. In L. B. Golden (Ed.), *Case studies in child & adolescent counseling* (3rd ed.). Upper Saddle River, NJ: Merrill/Prentice Hall.

Vernon, A. (2002b). *What works when with children and adolescents: A handbook of individual counseling techniques*. Champaign, IL: Research Press.

Wagner, C. (1981). Confidentiality and the school counselor. *Personnel and Guidance Journal, 51*, 305–310.

Waterman, A. H., Blades, M., & Spencer, C. (2001). Interviewing children and adults: The effect of question format on the tendency to speculate. *Applied Cognitive Psychology, 15*, 521–531.

Webb, J. R., Amend, E. R., Webb, N. E., Goerss, J., Beljan, P., & Olenchak, F. R. (2005). *Misdiagnosis and dual diagnosis of gifted children and adults: ADHD, Bipolar, OCD, Asperger's, depression, and other disorders*. Scottsdale, AZ: Great Potential Press.

Welfel, E. R. (2006). *Ethics in counseling & psychotherapy: Standards, research, & emerging issues* (3rd ed.). Belmont, CA: Thomson.

Werner, E. E., & Smith, R. S. (2001). *Journeys from childhood to the midlife: Risk, resilience, and recovery.* New York: Cornell University Press.

Winslade, J. M., & Monk, G. D. (2007). *Narrative counseling in schools* (2nd ed.). Thousand Oaks, CA: Corwin Press.

Young, M. E. (2005). *Learning the art of helping: Building blocks and techniques.* Upper Saddle River, NJ: Merrill/Prentice Hall.

Zhang, HN. (1999). Is so much self-disclosure appropriate? In A. E. Ivey & M. B. Ivey, *Intentional interviewing & counseling: Facilitating client development in a multicultural society* (4th ed.) (pp. 290–291). Pacific Grove, CA: Brooks/Cole.

Expressive Techniques: Counseling Interventions for Children and Adolescents

Loretta J. Bradley, C. Bret Hendricks, and Charles R. Crews

Tracy sits in the counselor's office and refuses to speak. Despite many verbal attempts by the counselor, this young child remains unresponsive. José, who was referred to the school counselor, is quick to inform her that he doesn't want to be there. Amanda definitely lets the counselor know that she doesn't need to be there because she doesn't have a problem; she thinks her family is the problem. John challenges the counselor: "Fix me if you can . . . but I've been in counseling before, and it didn't work."

What is the common denominator with these four children? Clearly, none of them wants to be in counseling—because all of them are uncomfortable with the process, or they don't think they have a problem, or they question whether counseling can be effective. Despite the best verbal techniques the counselor might use, they may not be effective in engaging clients because verbal approaches have limitations (Dunn & Griggs, 1995, as cited in Vernon, 2005). Gladding (2005) concurred, noting that verbal techniques are especially ineffective with reluctant and nonverbal clients. Further, because their verbal abilities may be limited in accordance with their developmental level (Vernon & Clemente, 2005), children and adolescents may need different types of interventions (Okun, 2007).

Gladding (2005) stressed the importance of using expressive, creative arts because these techniques help engage clients in the counseling process and are effective with a variety of clients. He added that these approaches combine theory and practice in flexible ways that facilitate change and problem solving.

For centuries, the helping professions have utilized innovative, expressive techniques such as music, drawing, and literature (Frostig & Essex, 1998; Okun, 2007;

Thompson, 2003). The Romans used poetry as a means of calming troubled people, and the ancient Egyptians played and listened to music to treat people with mental illness (Gladding, 2005). In recent times, too, counselors have become increasingly interested in more creative, expressive techniques because these methods facilitate insight and communication, and they encourage originality and allow freedom of expression, which in turn facilitate identification of feelings and encourage self-awareness (Cheek, Bradley, Parr, & Lan, 2003; Franklin, 2000; Hendricks, Bradley, Robinson, & Davis, 1997; Jensen, 2001; Vernon, 2005). Music, drawing, story-telling, and drama enable clients to express feelings and thoughts that otherwise might be unidentified.

Regardless of the counseling approach or theory, counselors often encounter challenges when working with youth, in part because the developmental levels of children and adolescents limit their ability to express themselves verbally. Often, children have not reached the level of cognitive development that allows for sponta-neous introspection or the ability to express themselves. Further, they often have a limited attention span, so they easily become bored or distracted. For these reasons, using developmentally appropriate interventions is vital (Vernon & Clemente, 2005).

This chapter describes the following expressive counseling interventions appli-cable to children and adolescents: art, bibliotherapy, games, activity books and worksheets, music, drama and role-playing, storytelling, metaphors, and therapeutic writing. In addition, interventions are suggested incorporating multicultural tech-niques and career exploration, as well as issues common to children and adolescents, such as anger and aggression, grief and loss, low self-awareness and self-esteem, stress and anxiety, and incorporating the new technology.

Art

Children have difficulty verbally communicating their needs because they have not yet developed the skills and coping mechanisms of adults. Art therapy techniques facilitate communication, allow clients to express anger and hostility with less guilt, and enable clients to perceive themselves and those around them more clearly (Bur-rick & McKelvey, 2004; Kwiatkowska, 2001; Weiser, 2001; Withrow, 2004). Art therapy techniques also enable the counselor to examine the client's inner language, giving the counselor and the client increased insight (Lev-Wiesel & Daphna-Tekoha, 2000).

Gladding (1995, 2005) described art techniques that have been utilized with diverse populations and concluded that these techniques can transcend cultural boundaries. These techniques have been found to be especially useful in treating a variety of child and adolescent problems including trauma, grief, depression, stress, and low self-esteem (Chapman et al., 2001; Jordan, 2001; Withrow, 2004). Art is both relaxing and soothing, facilitates the manipulation of various media, and can lubricate verbal communication of thoughts and feelings. "Art, like talk, is simply a way to get to know each other, another mode of communication" (Rubin, 1988, p.

181). In using art, counselors should permit clients to select the medium they want to use; and the counselors' suggestions should be limited.

Art media should not be limited to drawings. Other effective media include sculpture using clay, soap, and other media. Collages using construction paper or pictures from magazines and paintings also are effective. At the end of any session involving art techniques, counselors should allow time for the client to discuss his or her work (Sontag, 2001). Because some children are concerned that their art products will not be good enough, counselors must emphasize the importance of progress, not the product or artistic skill (Dalley, 1990).

Counselors must be aware of ethical considerations unique to art therapy. Artwork should be viewed as "symbolic speech" and be given the same consideration as any form of speech (Hammond & Gantt, 1998). Consequently, the artwork the client produces should be accorded the same protection and consideration as all other forms of communications. As in any counseling relationship, the client's right to privacy and confidentiality has to be observed and protected. Descriptions of several specific art interventions follow. Depending on the client's age and developmental level, some adaptation may be necessary.

Color Your Life (O'Connor, 1983)

Purpose: To identify feelings associated with life.
Materials: A large sheet of plain white paper and any type of coloring instruments (paint, crayons, chalk, pencils); available colors must include yellow, green, blue, black, red, purple, brown, and gray.
Procedure: Ask the child to pair an emotion or feeling with a color.

If the child seems to be having trouble, the counselor may offer a prompt: "What feeling might go with the color red?" Have the child continue to pair emotions with color. The most common associations are red/anger, purple/rage, blue/sad, black/very sad, green/jealous, brown/bored, gray/lonesome, yellow/happy. Combinations are limited only by the child's knowledge of feelings and colors, imagination, and ingenuity. Usually, however, the counselor should limit the associations to eight or nine pairs.

Once the pairs are established, give the child a sheet of white paper and ask him or her to fill the paper with colors to portray the feelings he or she has had during the past week. The counselor might ask, "As you remember last week, how much of your life was happy? Color that much of your paper yellow." The child is to color the paper in whatever designs he or she wishes until it is completely covered with colors. Encourage the child to verbalize his or her thoughts and feelings during the activity.

Windows (Gladding, 1995)

Purpose: To help the child examine what he or she is focusing on in life at this time.

Materials: Plain white paper and pencil.

Procedure: Instruct the child to draw a window on a sheet of white paper. Explain that this is a window into his or her life. Ask the child to "look" through the window and draw what he or she sees. After the drawing has been completed, explore what the child is focusing on in the present and what he or she wants to see for the future.

Bibliotherapy

Literature has been integrated into counseling for many years and in a variety of ways. It has been used to establish relationships with clients, explore clients' lifestyles, promote clients' insight, and educate and reorient clients (Jackson, 2000). Bibliotherapy is designed to help individuals solve problems and better understand themselves through reading (Shechtman, 2006). Bibliotherapy techniques can help children and adolescents in many ways (Gladding, 2005, Pardeck, 1995; Pereira & Smith, 2006; Prater et al., 2006). For example, although children might be unable to verbalize their thoughts and feelings, they often gain insight as they identify with characters or themes in literature. Bibliotherapy techniques also may be used to explore relationships, deal with unfinished business, alleviate depression, reduce compulsive behaviors, and enhance school achievement (Black, 2007; Frieswijk et al., 2006; Jones, 2006; Nugent, 2000; Quackenbush, 1991).

Bibliotherapy techniques are best used to promote interaction and exploration of important issues and concerns while providing ample opportunity for feedback. Children may accept themselves as they accept fictional characters. Or the reverse could be the case: The fiction may produce anxiety in which the children condemn and reject the characters. Therefore, the counselor should be cautious when implementing these techniques by using appropriate interventions that will facilitate positive communication and therapeutic interventions. The counselor should ask questions such as: What is your impression of the book? With which characters did you most or least identify with? What meaning does the story have for you?

School counselors may wish to consult with the school librarian to select books for the library and to keep abreast of new books dealing with students' concerns and problems. National bookstore chains also have extensive bibliotherapy selections, as does the Self-Esteem Shop (www.selfesteemshop.com) and Paperbacks for Educators (www.paperbacksforeducators.com).

Super Action Heroes

Super Action Heroes is adapted from work presented by Jackson (2000).

Procedure: Ask the child to name his or her favorite action figure (e.g., Superman, Spiderman, Batman, Wonder Woman, Power Rangers). Then have the child list at least three characteristics that describe the "superhero."

After the client has identified these characteristics, ask: Name one person who has made a positive difference in your life. Why? Name some people you admire, and tell me why you admire them. What makes someone a superhero? Who would you consider a "real live" superhero? How hard is it to name positive characteristics about someone? What is a role model? What impact do role models have on our lives? How should you choose role models? Could you be someone's hero? Why or why not?

The following case study illustrates how using action figures facilitate the counseling process.

▌Brian

Brian, a 9-year-old, went to see Ms. Perry, the school counselor, because he was failing two subjects. Usually a good student, Brian had said he stopped doing his assignments. When he arrived at Ms. Perry's office, he sat in a chair across the room and appeared withdrawn. Ms. Perry asked him what he wanted to talk about with her, but he didn't respond. After several minutes, she pointed to an assortment of action figures (Superman, Spiderman, etc.). Brian said he liked Spiderman best.

Ms. Perry pointed out that Spiderman helps people and does good deeds. She asked Brian what he would do to help people. He said that he would like to help his grandmother, who has been sick lately. He told the counselor that he has been so worried about his grandma that he has not been doing his schoolwork. Ms. Perry suggested that they brainstorm things he might be able to do, and Brian identified several things—making a card for her, calling her in her hospital room, and visiting her at the hospital after school. Brian decided to make the card first, and Ms. Perry told him that he could work on it during his next counseling session. When Brian left the session, he said he was feeling better already just knowing that he can do something to cheer up his grandma while she is sick.

As Ms. Perry reflected on the session, she realized that the action figure activity was a catalyst for Brian to start talking about his grandmother. In turn, Ms. Perry was able to understand why Brian was not completing his assignments. She concluded that if she had not introduced the action figures, Brian may not have opened up about his worries in this session.

Games

Games serve a variety of functions in counseling. Friedberg (1986) noted that games are "appropriate interventions for various children's problems" (p. 12) and posited that they are helpful in working with externalizing disorders (aggression, impulsivity, attention disorders) and internalizing problems (depression, anxiety). According to Friedberg, games are particularly helpful with resistant children, verbally deficient children, resistant children who are in denial, and anxious and inhibited children. Games can be used to teach new behaviors, facilitate verbalization, and address specific concerns. For example, a child who is having a hard time with problem solving would benefit by playing "Who Knew That Problem Solving Could Be This Much Fun?" (Childswork, Childsplay, 1998), and a young adolescent struggling with relationship and sexuality issues could benefit by playing "Crossroads: A Game on Teenage Sexuality and Relationships" (Childswork, Childsplay, 1998). Although Frieberg's work is more than two decades old, Chung (2006) and Mazza (2007) agreed that games have much therapeutic merit.

Counselors are encouraged to be creative and design their own board games. A simple game (Vernon, 2002) to help young clients express their feelings can be created by stapling four paper plates to the middle of a large sheet of tagboard. On one plate draw a happy face, and place a yellow dot beside it. On another plate draw an angry face, and put a red dot beside it. On the third plate draw a sad face and place a blue dot beside it. On the last plate draw a worried face, and label it with a green dot. Then place a path of 20–25 colored dots (red, blue, green, and yellow, in random order) around the edge of the tagboard. The client and counselor take turns rolling a dice and moving a marker the designated number of dots. When a player lands on a dot, the player talks about a time he or she has had the feeling that corresponds to the color of the dot (e.g., red/angry).

Friedberg (1986) suggested that games are more effective when they are incorporated into counseling sessions rather than being presented at the beginning or end of a session. Friedberg also noted that games are most effective when they are tailored to individual problems.

Nickerson and O'Laughlin (1983) offered the following guidelines for selecting games to be used in counseling.

- The game should be familiar or easy to learn.
- The game should be appropriate for the client's age and developmental level.
- The game should have clear, inherent properties related to the therapeutic goals of counseling.

Frey (1986) also proposed three categories of games:

1. interpersonal communication games;
2. games for specialized populations; and
3. games with specific theoretical orientations.

The following advantages of games in the counseling process have been identified (Frey, 1986; Friedberg, 1986; Nickerson & O'Laughlin, 1983).

- Because gaming formats are familiar and nonthreatening, they are effective in establishing rapport with children and adolescents.
- Games have diagnostic value because the counselor may observe a variety of behaviors, thoughts, and feelings as the game is being played.

- Games can enhance clients' egos by allowing them to receive positive feedback, gain a sense of mastery, and indulge in a pleasurable experience.
- Games permit clients to test reality by playing different roles and selecting solutions in a safe environment.
- Games allow clients to come to terms with situations and learn to work within a system of rules and limits.

Friedberg (1986) identified some possible disadvantages of using games in counseling.

- If the games are used in an artificial and stilted manner, they do not enhance the counseling process.
- Inflexible game play disconnected from the client's problems is ineffective and may reflect avoidance of difficult and painful topics.
- Complicated games with a myriad of rules are likely to be counterproductive because they can be confusing.
- Older children and adolescents may find games condescending. Therefore, counselors must consider the developmental appropriateness of any game they are considering using in counseling.

Counselors can create their own games from posterboard, and checkers or small toys may be used as markers. Commercially developed games may be found in catalogs such as the Self Esteem Shop (www.selfesteemshop.com) and Childswork/Childsplay (www.sunburstvm.com). In addition, games often are available at professional conferences. The following games, "Me Too" and "Soup Cans," can be played with items that are obtained easily and inexpensively.

Me Too

"Me Too" can be used with an individual client or as a group technique. With individual clients, the counselor writes statements on separate index cards that relate to identified problems. For example, if a child is having problems with his or her parents, topics for the cards might include statements such as: "Sometimes I feel sad when I see my dad"; "Sometimes I feel mad when I see my mom." If the child agrees with each statement as each card is read, he or she is to say, "Me too." Then the counselor encourages the child to discuss and process these statements.

As a variation of this game in a group setting, the counselor explains the game by saying, "When you hear someone say something that you identify with, say, 'Me too!'" For example, a member of the group might say, "My name is Amanda, and math is my favorite class." Anyone in the group who agrees with the class preference stands up and says, "Me too!" This game is a good icebreaker, especially for new members of the group.

Soup Cans

Materials required for "Soup Cans" are several clean soup cans with the labels removed. In place of the labels, the counselor attaches to the front of each can a picture representing a family member. The picture may be drawn, or it may be from a magazine. For example, if the child comes from a family with a mother, father, and brother, three soup cans are needed to represent each member of the family.

The counselor explains to the child that they are going to play a game involving the soup cans, some tokens, and a few questions. The counselor develops approximately 10–12 questions individualized to address the child's presenting problem. For example, if the child feels neglected, the counselor might initiate questions around belonging or inclusion, such as: Who would you like to spend more time with? If you could go to your favorite movie, which family member would you choose to go with you? If the child replies, "I want to spend more time with Mom," the client is instructed to drop a token inside the can with the mother's picture on it. This game continues until all questions have been asked and all tokens have been dispersed into the soup cans.

The counselor should have the questions written prior to the counseling session, and each of the tokens should be labeled with numbers corresponding to the questions. In this way, after the questions have been asked, the counselor can match the token number with the respective question. This game can be revealing by the child's showing the family member(s) with whom he or she wants to spend time and also family member(s) the child wants to avoid.

A variation of this game might be to include peers. If, for example, the child feels isolated from his or her friends at school, the pictures on the soup can could represent classmates. The questions could be posed to ascertain why the child feels isolated or omitted from activities with peers.

Activity Books and Worksheets

Activity books are a valuable resource for counselors because they provide a format that is adaptable, flexible, and nonthreatening. Activity books are widely available and easy to obtain. In addition, techniques from activity books may be adapted for use with children representing a variety of developmental levels and ages. The purpose of activity books is to provide counselors with therapeutic worksheets that children may complete during a counseling session or outside a counseling session as "homework." These worksheets enable the child or adolescent to gain stronger awareness and understanding of issues pertinent to topics encountered in counseling.

Some activity books, such as the *Student's Workbook for Exploring the Spiritual Journey* (Atkinson, 2001), deal with specific areas. Other activity books provide topics on broader areas. For example, the Passport series (Vernon, 1998a, b, c) consists of worksheets on many topics including anger management, feelings, self-esteem, social skills, and cognitive development.

Other activity books that counselors find useful are *Getting Along With Others* (Jackson, Jackson, & Monroe, 2002) and *Thinking, Feeling, and Behaving* (Vernon, 2006). An example of a worksheet activity from the Passport series (Vernon, 1998a, pp. 217–219) is provided below.

Solutions for Sad Feelings

"Solutions for Sad Feelings" is a group activity appropriate for use with first-grade through fifth-grade children. It is designed to enable them to identify effective ways of dealing with sad feelings.

Have the participants divide into pairs. Hand out a worksheet to each pair of students and explain that the worksheets are dealing with sad situations and their job is to help the child in the situation feel less sad. After reading the first situation, allow a short time for the pairs to discuss what they could do to deal with the sad feelings. They may write this on the worksheet or simply talk about the ideas. Then ask the paired participants to discuss their ideas with the whole group. Some examples of the situations described on the worksheets are:

> Carlos's dog just got run over by a car. What would you suggest to help Carlos feel less sad?

> Annie's grandma fell and broke her leg and is in the hospital. What would you suggest to help Annie feel less sad?

> Theresa's best friend is moving to another town. What could you suggest that might help Theresa feel less sad?

The activity book also includes content questions to be used for discussion and personalization questions that facilitate participants' self-awareness and encourage personal application of the activity. Examples of content questions (related to a feelings worksheet) are:

- Do you think that everyone feels sad about the same things?
- Were you surprised at the number of different ideas you came up with to deal with sad feelings?
- Do you think it is possible to feel less sad about sad situations if you find some good ways to help you deal with them?

Examples of personalization questions are:

- Have you tried any of the ideas that were suggested today? If so, which ones have worked best for you?
- Of the ideas presented today, which ones would you like to try the next time you feel sad?

Music

Adolescents spend an average of 3 hours a day listening to music (Gladding, 2005; Jensen, 2001). Music alleviates feelings of depression, anxiety, loneliness, and grief, and clarifies developmental issues and identity. Music plays an important role in healing and nurturing and is considered to be an effective adjunct to counseling with children and adolescents (Newcomb, 1994). For example, music is used in counseling to increase awareness of affect, intensify understanding, reduce anxiety, and increase verbal disclosure (Jensen, 2001). Gladding (1992) described music as "therapeutic to the verbal approaches to counseling" (p. 14), and Newcomb (1994) suggested that music is an ideal approach with clients who have difficulty expressing themselves verbally.

Counselors may use music-listening exercises in counseling to reduce depression and increase self-concept (Hendricks, 2000). Music often is used in conjunction with other techniques to elicit memories, fantasies, and visual imagery. Songs help to teach children about their feelings, cope with their fears, and gain self-understanding. Although many music techniques are designed for group work, they can be adapted for individual counseling (Hendricks, 2000; Hendricks, Bradley, Robinson, & Davis, 1997). In addition, counselors have found that background music in the counseling environment enhances positive mood, increases self-disclosure, and decreases negative self-talk (Jensen, 2001). Overall, music has been found to be therapeutic. The following activities are counseling interventions using music.

Music and Color

In the "Music and Color" activity, the child is asked to listen to a piece of recorded music that has personal meaning. Then the child is asked to visualize colors that he or she associates with the music. After the colors are identified, the child is asked to discuss the colors and explain what the colors might represent.

Music Listening

In "Music Listening" the counselor asks the child to select a song that has strong personal meaning for him or her. Together, the counselor and the child listen to the music. Afterward, the counselor asks the child questions about the feelings and thoughts the song evoked and way(s) by which the feelings and thoughts contribute to the child's present life functioning. For example, a song describing friendship might elicit feelings of comfort and pleasure for the child, who then would identify ways by which these feelings could be helpful in combating stress and anxiety about friendships or any other applicable situation. This technique gives the child and counselor alike insight into the child's life situation, history, and functioning.

Reframing

In "Reframing," the therapist and child generate new, positive, cognitive understandings or frames of reference for a given situation or experience. For example, an adolescent who is having trouble understanding a curfew time might reframe his or her misunderstanding to focus on the parents' concern for their child's safety. After identifying the reframe, the teen is asked to find a piece of written or recorded music that describes some of the feelings identified in the reframing process. The adolescent and the counselor then listen to the music. Afterward, the adolescent talks about why he or she chose the music and what feelings the music evoked.

Songs as Lessons

In using "Songs as Lessons," the counselor selects a song with a positive, useful message. The song may be one that is popular currently or one written expressly for children, such as Bowman's (1985) "I Have Lots of Feelings and They're OK." After teaching the children the song, the counselor invites them to stand and sing the song. Movement and gestures may be incorporated to go along with the lyrics. For example, in Bowman's song, the children might be asked to jump when singing "jump" or to bring a finger and thumb together when singing "They're okay." After the children sing the song, the counselor leads a discussion about the feelings identified in the song.

The following case study illustrates how music can be used to establish rapport and clarify goals for change.

▋▋Melinda

Melinda is a 15-year-old ninth-grade student. Until recently she has been a high-achieving student but currently is failing two subject. Mr. Johnson, her school counselor, is concerned and asks to see Melinda. She reluctantly agrees. During the session Melinda is withdrawn and sullen. To build rapport, he asks her if she likes to listen to music. Melinda says she enjoys music and describes her favorite song. The counselor asks her to bring the CD with that song to the next session. At that session Melinda brings "A Change Would Do You Good" (Sheryl Crow). Melinda and Mr. Johnson listen to the music together and after the song is played, he asks her to describe what the song means to her.

Soon Melinda is describing the lyrics with animation. The lyrics refer to the positive aspects of change and the ways in which routine can be stifling. Melinda begins to talk about her own routine and how she is bored much of the time. She suggests that a change would do her good. When Mr. Johnson asks her about school, Melinda replies that school is "boring," and teachers should change the way(s) they do things. Specifically, she complains that her biology class is not "fun" and the teacher should do more interesting things.

The counselor inquires about what would make biology class more interesting for Melinda, and she says she would like to study butterflies and moths. Mr. Johnson asks her if she thinks there is a possibility that the class will study this, and she says she will have to ask her teacher. The counselor then engages her in a role-play about how to do this effectively.

At this point Melinda begins to talk excitedly about the ways she could collect information for the project and present the project to the class. She proudly says she could be the "insects expert" in her class. Mr. Johnson sees for the first time that Melinda is excited about her schoolwork and enthusiastic about completing a project.

In the next session Melinda reports that she has talked to Ms. Teeter. She agreed that a butterfly project was "just what the class needs" and that Melinda can be the leader of this project that will involve the entire class.

As Mr. Johnson and Melinda begin to set new goals, Melinda's enthusiasm about school builds. For reinforcement, Mr. Johnson asks Melinda to play the piece of music she brought to counseling. As she plays the song a second time, Melinda announces that it has become her "theme song" and that she is convinced more than ever that "change can do you good."

Drama and Role-Play

The use of drama in counseling involves spontaneous, highly personalized improvisation. The children may choose a role that represents themselves, others in their life, or symbolic character types. The counselor gains information from the way the client plays the role. Drama encourages safe expression of strong feelings, both positive and negative, and allows clients to learn from externalizing experiences. In addition, role-play encourages social interaction, learning, awareness, creativity, and spontaneity (Goh & Wahl, 2007). At the same time, these techniques function as a medium for dialogue and narrative (Chesner & Hahn, 2002). With groups, drama is useful in facilitating interaction among group members and has many uses in establishing and maintaining rapport. Counselors may use costumes to facilitate role-play and aid children in switching roles (e.g., passive to aggressive, strong to weak, appropriate to inappropriate).

Role-play provides clients with a way to rehearse new skills and practice stressful situations without undue stress (Lane & Rollnick, 2007; Thompson, 2003). Role-play may be initiated in several ways. The counselor could present the client with a dilemma and ask the client to act it out. The situation may be one that the client has or has not experienced or one that he or she is anxious about. For example, the counselor might suggest a situation in which an adolescent has a conflict with a parent. In this situation, the adolescent might role-play ways to initiate a conversation with the parent about the conflict. To achieve insight, the adolescent could play the roles of both self and parent. This type of role-play gives clients opportunities to practice strategies and increase their coping abilities (Akande, Akande, & Odewale, 1994; Shurts et al., 2006).

In a form of role-play, *role reversal*, the child or adolescent is asked to play the role of someone significant in his or her life (parent, sibling, teacher) with whom the child is having difficulty. Similarly, Hackney and Cormier (2004) suggested a role-play in which the youngster plays two part—the public self and the private self. This type of role-play encourages children to confront aspects of their own personality and behavior.

Empty Chair Dialoguing (Okun, 2007)

"Empty Chair Dialoguing," influenced by Gestalt therapy constructs, is an example of the way in which drama and role-play may be integrated into a counseling relationship. This type of role-play is especially valuable in helping children and adolescents deal with conflict situations.

Materials: Two chairs.
Procedure: Ask the client to speak to an empty chair as if it is someone in his or her life (parent, sibling, friend, teacher). If a child has difficulty speaking to an empty chair, the counselor may have the child speak to a stuffed animal.

The following case study illustrates this technique.

Tony

Tony is a shy eighth-grader new to his school. Several of his teachers have noticed that he is not making friends and avoids getting involved in school activities. The school counselor, Mr. DiBrito, is concerned that Tony is feeling alienated from the other students and asks him to stop by his office. After talking with Tony about his previous school, Mr. DiBrito determines that Tony was shy in that environment as well. He asks Tony, "If things here at school could be different, what would you change?"

Tony thinks a minute, then answers, "I'd be one of the guys—involved in sports and school stuff."

"What do you think keeps you from being that way?" Mr. DiBrito asks.

Tony looks at the floor and says, "I just don't know what to say or do. I get tongue-tied and make an idiot of myself. So it's easier not to say anything."

Mr. DiBrito assures him that many adolescents feel self-conscious and adds that it seems like Tony's self-consciousness is really getting in his way. The counselor takes a piece of paper and divides it into three columns. At the top of the first column, he writes "Activity." On the second he writes, "Positive Results." On the third column he writes, "Negative Results." He hands the paper to Tony and says, "I want you to list in the 'Activity' column at least five things you 'd like to do. Then, in the appropriate columns, list at least three possible good results from each activity and three possible bad results. Bring this paper back to our next session."

At the next session Tony shows the counselor his list, which includes joining the computer club and talking with another student. Mr. DiBrito asks, "Tony, if you were to talk to another student, who would you choose, and what would you like to say?"

Tony thinks for a minute, then says he would like to talk to Tom, who is in his history class and on the football team.

"Tony, can you pretend that Tom is sitting in this empty chair and imagine saying something to him?" Mr. DiBrito asks. He goes on to explain that sometimes when people are having problems talking to someone, they find it easier to do it in real life if they practice it first.

Tony seems a little dubious but agrees to try. He looks at the empty chair and says, "Hi, Tom. My name is Tony, and I just moved here. I went to the game yesterday and thought you played really well."

When Tony finishes speaking, Mr. DiBrito tells him it is a good beginning and encourages him to continue talking. Tony looks at the empty chair again and talks more about the game. Over the next several sessions they repeat this empty chair dialoguing, branching out to other students Tony says he wants to meet, and they set goals for him to practice in real life.

Several weeks later Mr. DiBrito notices Tony hanging out in the lunchroom with a small group of students. Later in the month, Tony stops by Mr. DiBrito's office and tells him he is getting along well with his schoolmates and has even joined the computer club.

Storytelling

Storytelling, used as a means of communication for centuries, provides a way for individuals to express their identities (Carlson, 2001; Padulo & Rees, 2006; Salvatore, Dimaggio, & Semerari, 2004; Wiitala & Dansereau, 2004). Storytelling is a powerful means for exploring painful experiences and can help children and young adolescents gain personal understanding and self-acceptance. Stories can be about a myriad of subjects: the client, the client's family, events in the client's life, fictional characters from books, cartoons, television, or movies, or characters the child has invented. The only limit to the topic of a story is the imagination of the client or the counselor.

Mutual Storytelling Technique

The mutual storytelling technique, described early by Gardner (1979), has been used effectively with depressed and suicidal children and is most appropriate for children between the ages of 9 and 14 years (Kottman & Skyles, 1990).

Materials: Recorder (tape/digital).
Procedure: Ask the child if he or she would like to work with you to record a make-believe TV or radio show in which the child is the guest of honor. Turn on the recorder and make a few brief statements of introduction. To help put the child at ease, ask the child to state his or her name, age, school, and grade. Then ask the child to tell a story.

Most children will begin immediately, but some need time to think or want help getting started. If the child needs help, ask him or her about interests, hobbies, family, and so forth. While the child tells his or her story, take notes on the story's content and possible meaning. After the child has finished the story, ask if it might have a "lesson." Ask for more details or information about specific items.

Comment about the story, such as how good (exciting, interesting, unusual, etc.) it was.

Turn off the recorder and discuss the child's story with him or her to get the information you need to prepare your own version of the story. Have the child determine which figures in the story represent him or her and which represent significant others in his or her life, what symbols the child uses, and the overall "feel" of the setting and atmosphere of the story.

Take into account the emotional reactions the child showed while telling the story. Use the moral lesson the child stated in selecting the story's theme. Consider healthier resolutions or adaptations to problems than those in the story.

Turn on recorder again, and tell the revised story, which should involve the same characters, settings, and initial situation as the original story but have a better resolution of conflict. In the story identify alternatives to problems and indicate that behavior can change. The story should emphasize healthier adaptations. Play the story for the child and discuss it.

A variation of the storytelling procedure is to use sentence starters within the context of a very short story to encourage client self-expression as described next.

Completing the Story

Telling a story has long been identified as an effective technique for encouraging clients to tell personal stories as an aid to discussing and working through issues (Carey & Dimmitt, 2004; Carlson, 2001; Cohen, 2002; Lane & Rollnick, 2007; Marszalek & Myers, 2006; Nadeau, 2006; Padulo & Rees, 2006; Payne, 2004; Salvatore, Dimaggio, & Semerari, 2004). The following are examples.

My Favorite Day

Purpose: To identify feelings and thoughts associated with life events.
Materials: Pencil and paper with story starters.
Procedure: Ask the child to complete the story you start. After the child has completed the story, ask him or her to talk about memories and feelings associated with the story.

Story starters:

As I think back on the days in my life, my favorite day was….
This day was my favorite because….
The people that spent this favorite day with me were….
If I could have another favorite day, it would be a day of….
This favorite day would be filled with….
The people who would be there on my favorite day are….
The nicest thing about this day will be….

My Very Own Magic Wand

Purpose: To identify feelings/thoughts associated with life events.
Materials: Pencil and paper with story starters.
Procedure: Ask the child to complete the story. After he or she has completed the
            story, ask the child to talk about memories and feelings associated with
            the story.

Story starters:

If I had my very own magic wand, I would name the wand….
My feelings about having a magic wand are….
If I could have the magic wand grant me three wishes, the wishes would be….
If I could ask the magic wand to change three things in my life, they would be….
If I could keep three things in my life just the way they are now, they would be….
If I could ask the magic wand to grant me 3 more wishes, they would be….

Metaphors

Counselors frequently use metaphors in counseling children and adolescents, as they
add richness to description and provide memorable symbols for the child. Metaphors
often are used to describe individual or group characteristics, processes, and products
in terms familiar to the child. In addition, metaphors help the child understand experiences that are not easily described in literal terms. Metaphors are abundant in children's literature, fairy tales, cartoons, movies, and television shows that contain
important social and emotional lessons. Metaphors are useful in expressing empathic
understanding of a problem (such as shyness), presenting feedback (using an object
to both compliment the positive aspects of behavior and confront the negative aspects
of behavior), and giving affirmations (emphasizing personal strengths rather than specific behaviors) (Bowman, 1995; Hansen, 2006; Nadeau, 2006; Sandoz, 2006).

   The counselor should determine the child's preferences (favorite games, hobbies, animals, etc.) and, from previous counseling sessions, determine the child's
problem areas, challenges, and personal strengths. The counselor also should assess
the client's primary sensory learning style (visual, auditory, kinesthetic). Then the
counselor constructs a story that interweaves this information and style. The story

should be brief and to the point. The counselor should not interpret or explain the story to the child. Rather, the child should be encouraged to explore new possibilities (different endings, etc.) by bringing the story back to reality.

Therapeutic Writing

Writing has been used for decades to help individuals develop perspective (Vernon, 2005). In counseling, writing enhances awareness by helping clients organize their thoughts and feelings, providing cathartic emotional release, and contributing to personal integration and self-validation. Writing is particularly beneficial for adults and older children. Counselors often find that writing can be used effectively with young children, too, if the writing is simplistic. In using this technique with younger children, the counselor may serve as the recorder (Wiitala & Dansereau, 2004; Vernon, 1997, 2002, 2005).

Examples of therapeutic writing include

- correspondence, which may be used when the client is unable or unwilling to sustain a verbal dialogue with another person;
- journal writing, which may be a stream of consciousness or structured in some manner;
- creative writing, prose, or poetry, which may be used to clarify projections, explore problems and solutions, or fantasize; and
- structured writing, including making lists, writing instructions, responding to open-ended sentences, or filling out questionnaires or inventories.

Autobiography

Autobiographies can describe a specific aspect of a person's life, or they can cover the entire lifespan. Autobiographies help clients express feelings, clarify concerns, and work toward resolving problems. In developing an autobiography, the counselor might suggest that the young child try to organize his or her life into 2-year intervals and write about that time. For older children, the intervals might be 3–4 years. Although the counselor doesn't want to stifle or interrupt creativity with younger children, some structure may be helpful. The counselor might begin by suggesting that children tell where and when they were born.

Lifeline

In the lifeline exercise the counselor asks the client to draw a long line across a large sheet of paper and place a symbol of a baby at one end of the line to indicate birth. Then the client is to place symbols above (good events) or below (challenging events) the line to indicate the best and the most troublesome things. Then the client is asked to write/describe these events next to each symbol. Finally the counselor discusses with the client these events in his or her life.

Outer/Inner Exercise

For the outer/inner exercise the counselor asks the client to draw a line down the middle of a sheet of paper, making two columns, then to label the columns "outer" and "inner." The outer column represents memorable events that occurred at a certain point in time. The inner column represents the client's feelings in relation to these events. The client is to fill in the columns as a stimulus for discussion. For example, if a child states that he or she moved at a certain time, that would go in the outer column. The feelings the child associates with the move would be in the inner column. The counselor should help the child continue to process the feelings associated with words in the columns.

Uninterrupted, Sustained, Silent Writing

For this writing technique, the counselor asks the client to write down everything related to feelings that comes to mind until the counselor tells him or her to stop. (A typical time is 3–5 minutes). At the end of the exercise, the counselor and the client discuss this writing. For example, if the child writes words related to negative feelings (sad, mad, scared), the counselor could explore why he or she has these feelings and try to set goals enabling the child to change these feelings. If the child writes about positive feelings, the counselor could talk with him or her about where these feelings came from and devise strategies to sustain them.

Multicultural Techniques

Children and adolescents who are aware of multicultural issues are more tolerant and less critical of others (Moses, 2002). They are less likely to create negative stereotypes and more likely to be tolerant of differences between persons. The following activities may be used to create and enhance multicultural awareness in children and adolescents.

Diversity Bingo

Purpose: To become more aware of cultural diversity.
Activity: Group.
Materials :   Pencil, paper, and bingo card with 25 squares.
Procedure: As in bingo, the first person to complete all the squares wins. In playing Diversity Bingo the counselor asks the group members to find someone in the group who meets one of the following criteria and write that person's name in the box.

As with any game of Bingo, the first player to complete all squares wins the game. The first square is a "free" square, so the players focus on the remaining 24 bingo squares, which ask questions such as:

Who in this group…

has parents or grandparents who lived outside the USA?
has met someone who is a Native American?
has met someone who is African American?
has met someone who is Hispanic American?
has met someone who is Asian American?
knows someone who was born outside the USA?
has visited a country outside the USA?

The questions should be tailored to meet the group's characteristics and needs.

Dream Catcher

Dreams are an integral part of the world of children and adolescents. The Dream Catcher activity is borrowed from Native American culture, which emphasizes that dreams can be good or bad. Some Native Americans have a tradition of keeping a dream catcher in their home, usually in the bedroom, so that during the night the dream catcher can catch both good and bad dreams. According to tradition, the good dreams know how to slip out of the dream catcher's web and escape by way of the feather attached to the dream catcher. In contrast, the bad dreams do not know how to get out of the web, so they remain caught in the web until the next morning, when they perish at the first light of dawn.

This activity offers an opportunity for clients to discuss their dreams. Counselors may use this technique to elicit both good and bad feelings and, in addition, allay fears associated with dreams. Further, this technique offers an opportunity to involve parents in the counseling process.

Purpose: To identify feelings associated with dreams.
Materials: Enough pipe cleaners to make a circle with a 2–4 inch diameter; string or thread long enough to make a web inside the pipe cleaners; a feather 1–3 inches long. Colorful threads, pipe cleaners, and feathers seem to appeal to children.
Procedure: Construct the dream catcher together. Then ask the child to describe a dream that he or she has had. Ask him or her to pair an emotion or feeling with the dream. Talk with the child about the role of the dream catcher in catching the bad dreams and freeing the good dreams. Have the child talk more about the dream, focusing on the reality of the dream. Discuss how having a dream catcher in his or her room might be helpful. In future counseling sessions follow up on the role of the dream catcher

Multicultural Circle

Multicultural Circles may be used in either individual or group counseling. As the counselor names the topics or issues, the child moves to the center of the circle if he or she identifies with the topic or issue. For example, the counselor might say: "Please move to the center of the circle if you… are a Native American,…have a family member who is Hispanic,… have lived in a country other than the USA, and so on. After calling all the items, the counselor helps the participants process the thoughts and feelings evoked in this activity.

Although this exercise is conducted most often in a group setting, it can be used with individual clients and topics. For example, if the counselor is working with a client on anger management, the questions would focus on anger, in which the counselor might start with: "If you want to hit someone when you get angry, please move to the center of the circle…; If you count to 10 when you're angry, please move to the center of the circle." Regardless of the topic, this technique is powerful in helping children see with what and with whom they identify and associate.

You Are Dealt a Hand in Life

This activity, which may be used with individuals or groups, is especially effective with adolescents.

Purpose: To increase awareness of diversity and challenge stereotypes
Materials: Two decks of cards of different colors shuffled together
Procedure: The card dealt first refers to gender. For example, if the first card dealt to is red, the client is a female, and if the card is blue, the client is a male. The second card refers to height. If the second card dealt is a club, the client is taller than 6' 6". If the second card is a heart, the client is 6' tall. A diamond indicates that the client is 5' 2" tall, and a spade indicates that the client is under 5' 2" tall. The third card indicates age. This is determined by totaling the amount on the face cards. For example, an ace = 1 point, a king = 10, a queen = 10, a jack = 10. If the card is a 2, 3, 4, 5, 6, 7, 8, 9, or 10, the value is the face value on the card (e.g., 2 = 2 points, 9 = 9 points). If the total points are an odd number, the client is 10 years of age or younger. If the total is an even number, the client is over 10 years old. The fourth category in the profile is that of physical challenge. If the rank of the fourth card dealt to the client is an ace, king, or queen, the person has a debilitating long-term disease that causes physical impairment, such as multiple sclerosis or cerebral palsy. If the rank of the card is a jack or 10, the client has a weight issue. If the rank of the card is 9, 8, or 7, the client has a physical appearance issue. If the rank of the card is 6, 5, or 4, the client has an eating disorder, and if the rank of the card is 3 or 2, the client has a fashion issue.

The counselor discusses the profiles. For example, after the profile is obtained from the cards that have been dealt, the counselor may ask the following questions:

What do you think about the profile you obtained?

Based on the profile, what do you think is the most positive aspect of your life?

What is the least positive aspect of your life?

What is your great hope for the world?

If you could change one of the cards you were dealt, which card would it be? Explain.

What's in a Name?

This activity can be used in either individual or group counseling. It is an easy exercise in which clients tell how they received their first name. For example, a boy might say, "I'm David, and I was named David because my father's favorite Biblical character was David." A girl might say that she was named Maria because the family has a tradition of naming the oldest daughter after her grandmother. This exercise can be helpful in identifying important family dynamics such as religion, values, traditions, family histories, and cultural awareness.

Interventions for Specific Issues

Career Exploration

Career exploration is important in working with children and adolescents. Counselors should encourage free expression to identify their interests for further exploration. Experiential learning provides clients with insights and awareness that they might not achieve through more conventional means (Lane & Rollnick, 2007; Macera & Cohen, 2006; Reed, Bruch, & Haase, 2004; Riemer-Reiss, 2000 Soper & Von-Bergen, 2001; Turner et al., 2006). Creative techniques provide validation and act as catalysts for change (Hartung, 2005). Several counseling interventions that facilitate clients' self-expression regarding career and lifestyle choices are described here. These exercises clarify career choices through prioritization of interest areas, identification of previously unidentified careers, and definition of lifestyle preferences.

Budgeting: How Much Does It Cost?

Purpose: To illustrate the importance of budgeting and career goal-setting.

Activity: Individual, most suitable for older adolescents.

Materials: Paper, pen or pencil, and calculator.

Procedure: Ask the student to make a list of all the clothing that he or she is wearing at the time, including items such as shoes, belt, and purse, if applicable; the list should not include jewelry, cell phones, or other electronic devices. The student should estimate the original cost of each item and use the calculator to arrive at a grand total.

Discuss the cost by asking the following questions:

Are you surprised how much your items add up to?

If you are working and receiving minimum wage, how many hours would you have
  to work to pay for the items on your list?
How does this information impact your career goals?
What jobs would enable you to buy the things you want?
Where would you find this information?

Classified Ads

Purpose: Career goal setting, best suited for adolescents.
Activity: Individual.
Materials: Employment section of the newspaper, paper, pen or pencil.
Procedure: Have the student identify at least two jobs he or she is interested in pur-
              suing, using the employment section of the newspaper. Once the client
              has selected two job notices, discuss these choices by asking the fol-
              lowing questions:

> What does a person with this job do, and where could you find more
>   information about it?
> What interests you about this job?
> Which factors are important to you—money, hours, challenge, pres-
>   tige, and so forth?
> Do you know someone who does this job? If so, how has this influ-
>   enced your choice of this job?
> Have the student draw a simple bridge, leaving enough room to write
>   around it. Have the student write "points of knowledge" (informa-
>   tion attained in this session) on the left side of the bridge. Then ask
>   the student to write his or her career hopes and dreams on the right
>   side of the bridge. Serve as facilitator while the client completes the
>   drawing.

After the student has done this, ask if he or she has any further comments related
to the exercise and/or any unfinished business to process verbally. Typically, students
disclose many things while drawing, although some remain silent while drawing. If
the student does not say anything while drawing, the counselor should encourage
(not coerce) some discussion regarding the drawing. Using the student's cues, the
counselor should invite the student to talk by saying, for example, "Your design is
very detailed. How does this design represent your hopes or dreams about your
career?"

Many times, students need to take some time before articulating their answers.
The counselor must respect students' need for silence at times before answering
questions or elaborating about the drawing. If the counselor "rushes" the student to
talk too soon, he or she may show active resistance and refuse to talk at all or passive resistance, merely telling the counselor what he or she thinks the counselor
wants to hear. In short, counselors should follow students' pace during the session
and encourage them to take the time they need.

Cribs

Purpose: Career goal setting and life planning

Activity: Individual

Materials: Real estate listing booklets with illustrations of houses for sale in the immediate area; paper; pen or pencil.

Procedure: Ask the student to identify at least two houses he or she would like to live in using illustrated real estate flyers. As the student searches the listings, the counselor might ask

How much does the house cost?

What job(s) and/or career(s) might provide the salary necessary to afford this house?

Where is the house located?

What factors would be important for you in considering the location? For example, is it important for you to live near shopping? Is it important to live near your work? Is it important to live near your family?

Anger and Aggression

Children and adolescents often have trouble finding acceptable ways to express negative emotions and behaviors. Inappropriate expression of anger often results in discipline problems and difficulties with interpersonal relationships. The following techniques are helpful in working with children and adolescents who have problems with anger and aggression.

Basic Relaxation

Procedure:

1. Instruct the student to close his or her eyes. Say: "Begin to relax by breathing evenly and slowly. Think of your feet. Feel your feet as they begin to relax. Ignore any worries, anxieties, or thoughts that come to you, and concentrate on keeping your breathing even and slow. Now think of your legs. Feel your legs relax."
2. Continue through the trunk of the body, back, arms, neck, and head.
3. After about 10 minutes, lead the client back to the counseling room, saying, "Now that you have relaxed, sit quietly for a moment. Now open your eyes."

This technique may be used to induce meditation by having the client repeat a meaningless word again and again (Thompson, 2003).

The following case study illustrates the use of relaxation.

■■■Michael

Michael, age 11, walks slowly into Serena's office. A professional counselor in private practice, Serena has seen Michael four times for counseling related to his anxiety. She observes that he is lethargic and has a blunt affect. This is in sharp contrast to Michael's usual presentation, which has been active and animated. Concerned, Serena asks Michael how he is feeling. In response, he merely shrugs, bows his head, looks at the floor, and sits heavily in a chair.

She says, "Michael, here's a pencil. Hold it by the eraser with your left hand. Close your eyes and put your right hand over your heart." After asking Michael if he can feel his heartbeat, she asks him to describe it. "Is your heart beating fast or slow?"

Michael tells her that his heart is beating fast.

Serena then asks him to open his eyes and lightly tap the rhythm of his heartbeat on the tabletop next to him, using the end of the pencil he is holding. She directs Michael to look at the "feelings poster" and tell her which feeling he is feeling.

"I'm feeling mad. Matt pushed me down the hall at school, and the teacher thought I started it, and she got mad at me and made me go to the office. The principal got real mad, and he wouldn't listen to me." He pauses, then adds, "It's not fair."

With this information, Serena and Michael talk about ways to deal with his anger. At the conclusion of the session, Serena asks Michael to tap the rhythm of his heartbeat again.

Michael exclaims, "Wow! It's way different! It's a lot slower now!" He points to the feelings chart and says, "I feel one of those feelings that means 'cool.'"

The following activities utilize simple, inexpensive items—nerf balls, animal sounds, pillows and old telephone books—to help clients rechannel their anger.

Nerf Balls

The counselor gives the child several Nerf balls to throw across the room. Small objects that will do no damage (rubber balls, plastic figures, beanbags) may be substituted. This exercise allows children to externalize anger in a safe way and at the same time attach a physical action to the feeling. For example, the child might think of several things that she gets angry about and then throws the ball across the room (yard) as a way to release angry energy.

Parallels with Animals

This activity is for young children who are unable to express their anger. For example, the counselor may ask, "How does a dog act when it's mad?" Then the counselor growls and barks like a dog and asks the child to join in. Other animals that might be used in this activity are bears, tigers, lions, and cats. This activity also may be used with other emotions such as happiness, sadness, and loneliness.

Punch It Out

Children can rechannel anger and aggression by hitting, punching, or kicking a pillow or a punching bag. "Punch It Out" provides an acceptable way of releasing the pent-up anger. The counselor might point out that when they are angry, they often have "hot thoughts" (thoughts that trigger the anger).

After they have calmed down, the counselor helps them identify "cool thoughts" (thoughts that aren't as upsetting). The counselor helps them make a plan to think cool thoughts when they begin to get angry.

Tear It Up

The counselor gives children something they can tear up, such as old telephone books, magazines, or newspapers. The counselor instructs the children to verbalize their angry thoughts and feelings as they "tear it up." For example, the client might verbalize anger about having a conflict with a peer while he is tearing up the phone book.

Loss and Grief

When someone significant in the child's life dies or when the child experiences a loss such as in the parents' divorcing, or the child's moving to a different area and school, children and adolescents may feel abandoned, angry, sad, or guilty. For most children and adolescents these feelings are confusing and disturbing.

Interventions that work well with grieving children and adolescents include bibliotherapy, music, art, writing poetry, making a collage, and identifying and resolving unfinished business through journaling.

Creating a Playlist

The counselor invites the child to compile a list of songs that were especially meaningful to the person who left or died, or songs the child thinks this person would have enjoyed. For example, if a child's grandfather dies, the list may include songs that were a part of a generation in which the grandfather lived. The counselor may enlist the parents in recording these songs for the child to play back when needed.

Letter Writing

The counselor invites the child to write a letter to the person who has died (moved, left), describing what he or she misses the most about that person and how life is different without him or her. The counselor informs the client that he or she has the choice of whether to share the letter with the counselor or anyone else (Thompson, 2003).

Making a Collage

The counselor encourages the child to collect pictures or small memorabilia representing the person who left or died, and use these materials to make a collage of memories (Vernon, 1997). For instance, if a child has fond memories of her uncle taking her to the circus, the child might make a collage of pictures that depict the circus. The counselor then discusses with the child how the visit to the circus made her happy and how these memories provide a source of comfort to her.

Saying Good-Bye

The counselor asks the child if he or she would like to say anything to the person who is gone. If the child is unable to think of anything , the counselor might consider a short story about death (divorce, moving, etc.). If the child is unable to verbalize his or her feelings, the counselor might consider using the empty chair technique described earlier in this chapter (Thompson, 2003).

Birthdays, Anniversaries, Holidays

Many times people who have lost a loved one find themselves reexperiencing the death of a loved one during their birthdays and holidays. A way to redirect some of the emotional mourning may be to encourage a remembrance activity.

Purpose: To decrease feelings of despair and reexperience the grief process.
Materials: Calendar, pencil/pen.
Procedure: Have the child identify the dates during the year that are of significance to the loss. After the dates have been identified, instruct the child that, on those days, to do something special for themselves to remember the loved one. As an example, on the loved one's birthday, instruct the child to purchase a small birthday present for himself or herself as a lasting remembrance.

Self-Awareness and Self-Esteem

Low self-esteem is prevalent in children and adolescents. In the child's environment, low self-esteem can be debilitating because it can contribute to violence, poor academic performance, substance abuse, and teenage pregnancy, In contrast, higher self-esteem correlates with higher achievement and better adaptive social behaviors (Duys & Hobson, 2004). Parents and other adults sometimes inadvertently foster low self-esteem by placing too much emphasis on school performance or peer relationships. Many techniques, such as the following, can assist in building self-esteem and helping develop self-awareness.

How To Be, How Not To Be

The counselor asks the child to title one piece of paper "How To Be" and another "How Not To Be." The child will have about 10 minutes to list on the papers everything he or she can remember that significant adults (parents, teachers) have told him or her about how to behave. After the child has completed the lists, the counselor discusses what he or she has been taught, to determine if the child is dwelling on negatives and mistakes. The counselor discusses the positives and successes from the lists, emphasizing the need to put more energy into success than failure (Frey & Carlock, 1999).

Lifeboat

The Lifeboat game can be used in individual or group counseling. The counselor tells the client that he or she is in a lifeboat and the lifeboat cannot handle that many people at a time. Therefore, to avoid sinking, someone must leave the boat. The counselor asks the client to discuss the unique talents that he or she has to justify remaining in the boat. This exercise is valuable in helping the child recognize his or her unique contributions and in bolstering self-esteem, especially with older children and adolescents.

Magic Box (Canfield & Wells, 1994)

In the "Magic Box" activity the counselor asks the child to place a mirror in any type of box so it will reflect the face of whomever looks inside. The counselor says to the child, "I have a magic box that will show anyone who looks inside the most important person in the world." Then the counselor asks the child who he or she thinks is the most important person in the world and invites the child to look inside the box. After the child looks into the box, the counselor comments on his or her reaction and asks what he or she thought when seeing himself or herself. The counselor explains that the box is valuable because it allows the child to see himself or herself as a special person

Positive Mantra

The counselor asks the child to close his or her eyes and repeat the following sentence: "No matter what you say or do to me, I'm still a worthwhile person." Although the "Positive Mantra" exercise seems simple, it can have a profound impact when done repeatedly. Each time the child begins the sentence, the counselor asks him or her to imagine the face of someone who has put him or her down in the past. The counselor instructs the child to stick out his or her chin and repeat the sentence in a strong, convincing voice.

After the child has become familiar and comfortable with the sentence, the counselor interjects statements such as, "You're stupid… ugly… lazy" (whatever the client says was directed to him or her), while the client responds, "No matter what you say or do to me, I'm still a worthwhile person" (Canfield & Wells, 1994).

Pride Line

In the Pride Line activity the counselor makes a positive statement about a specific area of the child's behavior. For example, the counselor might say, "I'd like you to tell me something about your free time that you're proud of." Then the counselor instructs the child to say, "I'm proud that I…." Specific behavior areas that might be highlighted include homework, schoolwork, sports, music, something the child owns, a habit, an accomplishment, or something the child has done for someone else. For example, if an adolescent says she is proud of going to basketball practice every day without missing any practices, the counselor talks to her about what an accomplishment this is, and that she should be proud of the accomplishment.

Unconditional Self-Acceptance

In this technique the counselor labels a paper bag "USA" and places inside it five strips of paper, each with one of the following terms written on it: school performance, peer relationships, sports, music and drama, jobs or chores, girl or boy. When the child discusses his or her failures, the counselor hands the child the paper bag. The counselor introduces the concept of unconditional self-acceptance, which means accepting yourself as a worthwhile person and not rating yourself as either "all good" or "all bad." The child is invited to open the bag, take out the strips of paper, and rate himself or herself 1 (low) to 5 (high) in each area.

The counselor encourages the child to think about his or her performance in these areas over time, rather than one or two isolated incidents. The child is encouraged to talk about the ratings. The counselor emphasizes that all of these dimensions contribute to who the child is and that what he or she may judge as poor in one area does not make him or her a bad person, that we all perform better in some areas than others, and it is important to accept ourselves unconditionally with our strong and weak points (Vernon, 2002).

What If...

The counselor asks the child "What If" questions such as: "What if your bike could talk? What do you think it would say about you?" The "talking item" could be a toothbrush, a bed, a dog, a TV, a school desk, a coat, a computer, or anything the child might recognize. Through the use of projection, this activity allows the child to become aware of his or her feelings about the self.

An alternative technique is to substitute people in the client's life for the objects. Whether this alternative can be used effectively depends on how trusting and open the child is and on the strength of the therapeutic relationship between the counselor and the child.

Stress and Anxiety

Stop, Drop, and Roll (Cheek, Bradley, Reynolds, & Coy, 2002)

Purpose: To help elementary students reduce test anxiety.
Procedure: Instruct the students that they will learn how to deal with situational test anxiety. They are to use this coping skill when they feel anxious while taking a test. They are to follow the fire safety safeguard of

Stop—Stop the test and put down your pencil.

Drop—Drop your head and close your eyes.

Roll—Roll your head slightly while inhaling and exhaling three deep breaths.

Once they have done this, they are instructed to take one more deep breath, open their eyes, smile big, and begin working again.

This intervention was conducted as part of a school guidance project in which 16 elementary students who failed a portion of a check-point test were identified as participants. Following the intervention and statewide testing, 14 of the original students passed a section of the test that they had failed previously. The students reported less stress, and parents and teachers verified less stress reactions by the students.

The Price of Perfection (Vernon, 2002)

Purpose: To reduce the emotional trauma caused by an irrational belief in perfectionism. It also is used to help clients view realistic expectations of self.

Materials: Paper and pencil.

Procedure: Have the child write on the paper the "cost" or "price" he or she pays while striving to be perfect. Also ask the child to list the emotional, physical, and behavioral consequences of striving for perfection. Following completion of the lists, ask the child typical process questions such as: What if you aren't perfect? Is the cost of becoming perfect worth it? What is an alternative to feeling anxiety about perfection?

This intervention may work well with children of varying ages, but some children may need more explanation of the term "cost." A good follow-up to this intervention is to have a meeting with the parents in which the counselor outlines some of the pressures that parents put on children that may hurt the child.

Paradoxical Intervention (adapted from Thompson, 2003)

The counselor might consider "Paradoxical Intervention" (also called "Exaggeration") with children who worry excessively. The counselor asks the child to exaggerate a thought or behavior that is disruptive and instructs him or her to set aside a specific time each day to worry about everything. For example, the counselor might get the child to agree to write down daily worries that arise and revisit them before school every day. For children who fear speaking out in class, ask them to sit in the back of the room and say nothing at all. By exaggerating the behavior, clients are confronted with how they react in certain situations and the consequences of that behavior.

Special Place Relaxation

The counselor asks the child to imagine a special place that belongs only to him or her. Then the counselor says, "Imagine being in that place that is yours. Tell me what you see around you."

After the child describes the special place, the counselor asks him or her to describe the feelings about the place. Then the counselor discusses how the special place helps the child relax and points out that the child may "go there" when the stress level gets uncomfortable. If the child has trouble imagining a special place, the counselor might suggest a quiet lake, the mountains, or floating on clouds (St. Denis, Orlick, & McCaffrey, 1996).

Preparing for the Future (adapted from Vernon, 2002)

Purpose: To help secondary students understand how cognitions influence behaviors, which influence emotions. Specifically, this intervention helps students who may be going through a transition prepare for the emotions associated with the process of change.

Materials: Goggles, paper, writing utensil.

Procedure: Instruct the student to put on the goggles. Have him or her discuss and list future events and the associated emotions. Ask the student to be as specific as possible, such as moving away to college, going to a new high school, or having a new resource teacher. Ask him or her about each of the items listed and how he or she truly feels about the events. For example: "When you see yourself leaving for college, what goes on in your mind?"

Confront the student about the irrational beliefs behind the feelings. For example, if the student reports stress as an emotion behind moving to a new school because he or she does not know anyone there, ask: "How long will it will take before you meet anyone?" Help the student identify negative feelings, and encourage positive responses to the negative concerns.

In school counseling this activity can be used during any of the transitions a student may go through. The goggles keep the student tied to the concrete feeling of having lenses on. Once the goggles are removed, the student can see in a different way the problem that was once negative.

Burst or Bounce Back (adapted from Vernon, 2002)

This concrete, creative intervention utilizes tangible objects to represent a child's resiliency. Sometimes children and adolescents struggle with growing up. It's not easy being a kid!

Materials: A large balloon; a safety pin or other sharp object; a ball that will bounce.

Procedure: Explain to the child the significance of the objects.

balloon: represents the client's life; it expands and contracts depending on the pressures the client receives from the world.

safety pin or other sharp object: represents the final event that comes along that a person cannot handle.

a ball that will bounce: things in our lives that will bounce back even though we drop them.

Ask the child to hold the deflated balloon. Then ask him or her to recall events that cause stress and anxiety. After each event is recalled, have the child blow air into the balloon. Once the balloon is fully inflated, have him or her tie it up. Ask the child to pretend that he or she is the balloon, and each time he or she experiences a stressful or anxiety-provoking situation, it causes his or her life to inflate a little bit. Sometimes an event comes along and bursts the balloon (have the child pop the balloon). It is helpful to identify those situations before they arise so we can learn to cope with them.

Have the child pick up the bouncy ball. Ask him or her to recall the same situations that filled up the balloon. Once all the situations are recalled, ask the child to try to pop the bouncy ball. Discuss the results—that the bouncy ball will not pop, and it will bounce back if dropped.

Discuss the differences between the balloon and the bouncy ball. Which would the child want to be, and what will it take to be like that object (hopefully, they chose the bouncy ball!)? Explore with the child the coping skills related to anxiety and stress discussed in this chapter.

The concreteness of this intervention may be reinforced by having the child take the ball from the session as a reminder that bouncing back is possible even though the world bursts.

Mild Social Anxiety

Sometimes middle school-aged children do not like talking to others because of the internal voice in their heads talking to them about social appropriateness. Counselors can intervene by teaching appropriate responses to common situations.

Materials: Index cards, writing utensil.
Procedure: Discuss with the child the situations that produce anxiety. Examples: talking to other people, talking in class, eating lunch with others, making new friends, reaching out to others, sitting with someone on the school bus. Have the child write down each situation on the blank side of the index card. Typically, a theme will be produced in which the counselor can identify. Once the theme is identified, take each note card and collaborate on a solution for each problem. Write a step-by-step solution to each situation. Have the child review the cards at home or in your office as needed.

Technology

Technology provides a new modality for interacting with clients. Incorporating technology into counseling through various methods has been advocated by Carlson, Portman, and Bartlett (2006), Chester and Glass (2006), Elleven and Allen (2004), Kim (2007), Layne & Hohenshil, (2005), Wagner, Knaevelsrud, and Maercker (2006). The Internet has changed the way people seek mental health services, as well as how they spend their time (Sheese, Brown, & Graziano, 2004). Children and adolescents spend a lot of time on the Internet doing schoolwork, playing games, shopping, and downloading music (Whitlock, Powers, & Eckenrode, 2006). This tells us that the Internet may be an effective vehicle for counselors to use.

The following interventions use the tools of technology native to young clients. Because a solid counseling relationship is fundamental to using technology, the counselor must be well versed in the ethical guidelines concerning technology and counseling set forth by licensing bodies. Computer technology may affect counseling interventions because of how feelings are translated from the client's writing ability to the therapist's interpretation of the test. Below are some ways to incorporate technology into counseling (Hill, Zack, Rochlen, McCready, & Dematasis, 2003; Kolt, Schofield, Kerse, Garrett, Oliver, & Melody, 2007; Trepal, Haberstroh, Duffey, & Evans, 2007; Van Horn & Myrick, 2001).

Online Biographical or Social Networking Page

Purpose: To increase awareness of the image the child portrays (or wants to portray) publicly on the Internet.

Materials: Computer with Internet access.

Procedure: Ask the student if he or she has a biographical or social networking page on the Internet, such as myspace.com, facebook.com, friendster.com, or a personal website, to name a few. If the student does have such a site, ask if he or she will view it with you.

Ask questions about music, colors, and picture sections. For example: "What does this web page say about you?" can open up a deep dialogue if the student is inclined to disclose this information to you. Discussion questions may include

What do your parents think of your page?
What is the best/worst thing someone has written on your page?
Tell me about how this site makes you look to the world?

Once the student has described the web page, ask him or her if there is a difference in what is on the site and how he or she currently behaves or feels in real life.

Parents may not know about the information on these types of websites, so therapists should be alert to anything they think parents should know about their child's online activities. Examples are pictures of drugs or alcohol, erotic pictures, and derogatory statements (flaming). If students post such a site to the Internet, they may be impacted by responses from various visitors to the site. Valkenburg, Peter, and Schouten (2006), who conducted research in this area, found that, "adolescents' self-esteem was affected solely by the tone of the feedback that adolescents received on their profiles: Positive feedback enhanced adolescents' self-esteem, and negative feedback decreased their self-esteem" (p. 589).

Slide Show

Purpose: To promote creativity; self exploration and self-expression.
Materials: Computer with a slide show program such as PowerPoint.
Procedure: Ask the student to collect pictures, music, and writing on a topic of choice. Using the software package, have the student create a slide show consisting of pictures, music and text. The child may choose to create the slide show at home and spend some time working on it. Once the show is complete, invite the student to show it to you. Ask questions about the choice of music, content of the pictures, and meaning of the literature selections.

Messaging Technology Encouragement

Purpose: To increase effectiveness of assigned clinical homework, and to help the client be accountable for work conducted outside of a therapeutic session.
Materials: One of the following: a computer with text messaging software, a cell phone that can text message, email addresses, instant mail/messaging account, Internet Relay Chat (IRC) program
Procedure: Invite the student to message you after completing certain portions of behavioral clinical homework.

This intervention has been used, for example, to remind a student about homework.

Video-Conferencing

Purpose: To observe the parent–child interaction of a struggling adolescent
Materials: Computer, broadband Internet connection, web camera
Procedure: Secure a computer with a broadband Internet connection and a web camera. Begin the interaction by introducing yourself and why you are participating. Allow the family to interact through the medium until reaching the time limit. Debrief with the student following the interaction, focusing on emotion and feeling.

The use of a web camera, microphone, and software to communicate across the Internet can be easier by enlisting a consultant to set up the connections (Fraenkel,

2006). Fraenkel stated that through the use of technologies such as distance communication, assessments can be conducted prior to any client entering the office of a trained professional, which saves time and money. In addition, Trull (2007) recommended that various psychological assessments be conducted through distance communications.

This type of therapeutic intervention was used with the son of an active-duty U.S. soldier stationed overseas. The son was exhibiting intense anger and frustration but was unable to express his exact feelings about this situation. He did tell the counselor that he could not play football well because his dad was not there to cheer him on. The child's mother reported that she could not meet during the scheduled meeting time and would not be able to make it to the base to use the military equipment.

The counselor contacted the commanding officer of the boy's father, and the officer allowed us to hold the video-conference at school. A coworker's husband served as an advanced army technology officer who set up the interaction.

Video Game Character Identification

Purpose: To integrate online gaming personality into the real world persona
Materials: Role-playing games (for example, World of Warcraft, by Blizzard Entertainment; EverQuest, by Sony Entertainment; Final Fantasy, by Square Enix).
Procedure: Ask the child about a character in a game he or she plays. Asking questions about the character's name, class, level or rank, combat style, and character design may open up the discussion. Once you have gathered enough information, invite the child to show you his or her character. This can be done by having the client bring in a printed image or by bringing in an image to open on your computer in the office.

Your task as the counselor will be to assess the extent to which your client identifies with the online character. If he or she identifies strongly with the online character, a discussion of the client's character should commence. The discussion may begin with,

"Tell me what your character does that you can't do in your real life."

Webpage Memorial

Purpose: To encourage self-healing and expression after the loss of a loved one; to gain insight into the feelings the child has about the loss
Materials: Photos, scanner, Internet, computer, web page creation software
Procedure: Ask the child to select three pictures that best portray the loved one they want to remember. Instruct the child to type the memories the pictures elicit, using a word-processing program. Ask the child to select colors for a web page. This can be done using the Internet searching

for Hex color codes (6 numbers). Ask the child to select a font to use for the text of the web page. Invite the child to bring a song that reminds him or her of the loved one.

Summary

Counselors can readily utilize a wide spectrum of therapeutic techniques and interventions in the areas of art, bibliotherapy, games, activity books and worksheets, music, role-play/drama, storytelling, metaphors, therapeutic writing, and using new technology in counseling. In addition, interventions can be used with specific problem areas or issues, including career exploration, self-esteem, anger and aggression, stress and anxiety, and grief and loss. Although the techniques and interventions discussed here are directed mainly to children and adolescents in individual counseling, most may be adapted for use in group settings.

Familiarity with a variety of interventions and techniques allows the counselor to select those that most closely match the developmental level of the child or adolescent. Counselors working with elementary school children should avoid interventions or techniques that are too difficult, too complex, or too advanced for that age group. The opposite is also true: Using techniques with adolescents that are appropriate for younger children may offend or bore adolescents. At one end of the continuum, paradoxical interventions or techniques that depend on writing and verbal skills might be too complex for young children and will confuse them. At the other end of the continuum, board games might not be appropriate for some adolescents.

Counselors must recognize that some children and adolescents are responsive to counseling and others are reluctant and hostile to counseling. Using the expressive, creative interventions described in this chapter will more effectively facilitate their ability to engage in counseling and resolve their problems.

References

Abney, P., & Maddux, C. (2004). Counseling and technology: Some thoughts about the controversy. *Journal of Technology in Human Services, 22*, 1–24.

Akande, A., Akande, B., & Odewale, F. (1994). Putting the self back in the child: An African perspective. *Early Child Development and Care, 105*, 103–115.

Atkinson, D. (2001). The student's workbook for exploring the spiritual journey. *American Journal of Health Education, 32*(2), 112–115.

Black, D. W. (2007). A review of compulsive buying disorder. *World Psychiatry, 6*, 14–18.

Bowman, R. (1995). Using metaphors as tools for counseling children. *Elementary School Guidance and Counseling, 29*, 206–216.

Burrick, C. R., & McKelvey, J. B. (2004). Watercolors, pastels and paintbrushes are therapeutic tools. *Behavioral Health Management, 24*, 50–52.

Canfield, J., & Wells, H. C. (1994). *100 ways to enhance self-concept in the classroom: A handbook for teachers, counselors, and group leaders* (2nd ed.). Boston: Allyn & Bacon.

Carey, J., & Dimmitt, C. (2004). The Web and school counseling. *Computers in the Schools, 21*, 69–79.

Carlson, R. (2001). Therapeutic use of story in therapy with children. *Guidance & Counseling, 16*, 92.

Carlson, L., Portman, T., & Bartlett, J. (2006). Professional school counselors' approaches to technology. *Professional School Counseling, 9*, 252–256.

Cattanach, A. (1997). *Children's stories in play therapy*. London: Jessica Kingsley Publishers.

Chapman, L. M., Morabito, D., Ladakakos, C., Schreier, H., & Knudson, M. (2001). The effectiveness of art. Interventions in reducing post-traumatic stress disorder symptoms in pediatric trauma patients. *Art Therapy: Journal of the American Art Therapy Association, 18*, 100–104.

Cheek, J., Bradley, L., Parr, G., & Lan, W. (2003). Using therapy techniques to treat teacher burnout. *Journal of Mental Health Counseling, 25*, 204–217.

Cheek, J., Bradley, L., Reynolds, J., & Coy, D. (2002). An intervention for helping elementary students reduce test anxiety. *Professional School Counseling, 6*, 162–165.

Chesner, A., & Hahn, H. (Eds.). (2002). *Creative advances in group work*. Philadelphia: Kingsley.

Chester, A., & Glass, C. (2006). Online counselling: A descriptive analysis of therapy services on the Internet. *British Journal of Guidance & Counselling, 34*, 145–160.

Childswork, Childsplay. (1998). King of Prussia, PA: Center for Applied Psychology (resource catalog). www.sunburstvm.com

Chung, M. (2006). *Therapeutic games and guided imagery: Tools for mental health and school professionals working with children, adolescents, and families*. Chicago: Lyceum Books.

Cohen, P. F. (2002). The New York inferno: Taking solace from the stories. *Journal of Religion and Health, 41*, 113–120.

Dalley, T. (1990). Images and integration: Art therapy in a multi-cultural school. In C. Case & T. Dalley (Eds.), *Working with children in art therapy* (pp. 161–198). London: Tavistock/ Routledge.

Duys, D. K., & Hobson, S. M. (2004). Reconceptualizing self-esteem: Implications of Kegan's constructive-developmental model for school counseling. *Journal of Humanistic Counseling, Education, and Development, 43*, 152–162.

Edwards, C., & Springate, K. (1995). Encouraging creativity in childhood classrooms. *Dimension of Early Childhood, 22*, 9–12.

Elleven, R., & Allen, J. (2004). Applying technology to online counseling: Suggestions for the beginning e-therapist. *Journal of Instructional Psychology, 31*, 223–226.

Fraenkel, P. (2006). Of shiny boxes and complex processes: Challenges, collaboration, and creativity at the interface of technology and family systems health care. *Families, Systems, & Health, 24*, 299–301.

Franklin, M. (2000). Art practice/psychotherapy practice/contemplative practice: Sitting on the dove's tail. *Guidance and Counseling, 15*, 18–23.

Frey, D. E. (1986). Communication boardgames with children. In C. E. Schaefer & S. E. Reid (Eds.), *Game play: Therapeutic use of childhood games* (pp. 21–39). New York: Wiley.

Frey, D., & Carlock, C. J. (Eds.). (1999). *Enhancing self-esteem* (3rd ed.). Muncie, IN: Accelerated Development.

Friedberg, R. D. (1986). Cognitive-behavioral games and workbooks: Tips for school counselors. *Elementary School Guidance and Counseling, 31*, 11–19.

Frieswijk, N., Steverink, N., Buunk, B. P., & Slaets, J. (2006). The effectiveness of a biblio-therapy in increasing the self-management ability of slightly to moderately frail older people. Patient Education and Counseling, *61*, 219–227.

Frostig, K., & Essex, M. (1998). *Expressive arts therapies in schools: A supervision and program development guide.* Springfield, IL: Charles C Thomas.

Gardner, R. A. (1979). Mutual storytelling technique. In C. E. Schaefer (Ed.), *The therapeutic use of child's play* (pp. 313–321). New York: Jason Aronson.

Gladding, S. (1992). *Counseling as an art: The creative arts in counseling.* Alexandria, VA: American Counseling Association.

Gladding, S. (1995). Creativity in counseling. *Counseling and Human Development, 28*, 1–12.

Gladding, S. (2005). *Counseling as art: The creative arts in counseling* (3rd ed.). Alexandria, VA: American Counseling Association.

Goh, M., & Wahl, K. H. (2007). Working with immigrant students in schools: The role of school counselors in building cross-cultural bridges. *Journal of Multicultural Counseling, 35*, 66–79.

Hackney, H. L., & Cormier, L. S. (2004). *The professional counselor: A process guide to helping* (5th ed.). Boston: Pearson/Allyn & Bacon.

Hammond, L. C., & Gantt, L. (1998). Using art in counseling. *American Journal of Art Therapy, 38*, 20–26.

Hansen, J. T. (2006). Discovery and creation within the counseling process: Reflections on the timeless nature of the helping encounter. *Journal of Mental Health Counseling, 28*, 289–308.

Hartung, P. J. (2005). Toward integrated career assessment: Using story to appraise career dispositions and adaptability. *Journal of Career Assessment, 13*, 439–451.

Hendricks, B. (2000). A study of the use of music therapy techniques in a group for the treatment of adolescent depression. *Dissertation Abstracts International, 62*, 107.

Hendricks, B., Bradley, L. J., Robinson, B., & Davis, K. (1997). Using music techniques to treat adolescent depression. *Journal of Humanistic Education and Counseling, 38*, 39–46.

Hill, C. E., Zack, J. S., Rochlen, A. B., McCready, T., & Dematasis, A. (2003). Using the Hill Cognitive-Experiential Model. A comparison of computer-assisted therapist empathy and therapist empathy and input conditions. *Journal of Counseling Psychology, 50*, 211–221.

Jackson, N. F., Jackson, D. A., & Monroe, C. (2002). *Getting along with others: Teaching social effectiveness to children.* Champaign, IL: Research Press.

Jackson, T. (2000). *Still more activities that teach.* Salt Lake City: Red Rock Publishing.

Jensen, K. L. (2001). The effects of selected classical music on self-disclosure. *Journal of Music Therapy, 38*, 2–27.

Jones, J. L. (2006). A closer look at bibliotherapy. *Young Adult Library Services, 5,* 24–27.

Jordan, K. (2001). The joint family holiday drawing. *Family Journal, 9*, 52–54.

Kim, J. (2007). A reality therapy group counseling program as an internet addiction recovery method for college students in Korea. *International Journal of Reality Therapy, 26*, 3–9.

Kolt, G. S., Schofield, G. M., Kerse, N., Garrett, N., Oliver, M., & Melody. (2007). Effects of technology counseling on physical activity for low-active older people in primary care: A randomized controlled trial. *Journal of the American Geriatrics Society, 55*, 986–992.

Kottman, T., & Skyles, K. (1990). The mutual storytelling technique: An Adlerian application in child therapy. *Journal of Individual Psychology, 46*, 148–156.

Kwiatkowska, H. (2001). Family art therapy: Experiments with new techniques. *American Journal of Art Therapy, 40*, 27–39.

Lane, C., & Rollnick, S. (2007). The use of simulated patients and role-play in communication skills training: A review of the literature to August 2005. *Patient Education & Counseling, 67*, 13–20.

Layne, C. M., & Hohenshil, T. H. (2005). High tech counseling: Revisited. *Journal of Counseling and Development, 83*, 222–226.

Lev-Wiesel, R., & Daphna-Tekoha, S. (2000). The self-revelation through color technique: Understanding client's relationships with significant others through the use of color. *American Journal of Art Therapy, 39*, 35–41.

Macera, M. H., & Cohen, S. H. (2006). Psychology as a profession: An effective career exploration and orientation course for undergraduate psychology majors. *Career Development Quarterly, 54*, 367–371.

Marszalek, J., & Myers, J. E. (2006). Dream interpretation: A developmental counseling and therapy approach. *Journal of Mental Health Counseling, 28*, 18–37.

Mazza, E. (2007). Review of therapeutic games and guided imagery: Tools for mental health and school professionals working with children, adolescents, and their families. *Social Work Education, 26*, 321–322.

Miles, R. (1993). I've got a song to sing. *Elementary School Counseling and Guidance, 28*, 71–75.

Moses, M. S. (2002). *Embracing race: Why we need race-conscious education policy*. Williston, VT: Teachers College Press.

Nadeau, J. W. (2006). Metaphorically speaking: The use of metaphors in grief therapy. *Illness, Crisis, & Loss, 14*, 201–221.

Newcomb, N. S. (1994). Music: A powerful resource for the elementary school counselor. *Elementary School Guidance and Counseling, 29*, 150–155.

Nickerson, E. T., & O'Laughlin, K. S. (1983). The therapeutic use of games. In C. E. Schaefer & K. J. O'Connor (Eds.), *Handbook of play therapy* (pp. 234–250). New York: Wiley.

Nugent, S. A. (2000). Perfectionism: Its manifestations and classroom based interventions. *Journal of Secondary Gifted Education, 11*, 215–221.

O'Connor, K. J. (1983). The color-your-life technique. In C. E. Schaefer & K. J. O'Connor (Eds.), *Handbook of play therapy* (pp. 251–258). New York: Wiley.

Okun, B. F. (2007). *Effective helping, interviewing and counseling techniques* (7th ed.). Pacific Grove, CA: Brooks/Cole.

Padulo, M. K., & Rees, A. M. (2006). Motivating women with disordered eating towards empowerment and change using narratives of archetypal metaphor. *Women & Therapy, 29*, 63–81.

Pardeck, J. (1995). Bibliotherapy: Using books to help children deal with problems. *Early Child Development and Care, 106*, 75–90.

Payne, H. (2004). Student narratives of a dance movement therapy group. *British Journal of Counselling, 32*, 511–532.

Pereira, M. G., & Smith, T. E. (2006). Evolution of the biopsychosocial model in the practice of family therapy. *International Journal of Clinical and Health Psychology, 6*, 455–467.

Prater, M. A., Johnstun, M. L., Dyches, T. T., & Johnstun, M. R. (2006). Using children's books as bibliotherapy for at-risk students: A guide for teachers. *Preventing School Failure, 50*, 5–13.

Quackenbush, R. L. (1991). The prescription of self help books by psychologists: A bibliography of selected bibliotherapy resources. *Psychotherapy, 28*, 671–677.

Reed, M. B., Bruch, M. A., & Haase, R. F. (2004). Five-factor model of personality and career exploration. *Journal of Career Assessment, 12*, 223–238.

Riemer-Reiss, M. (2000). Vocational rehabilitation counseling at a distance: Challenges, strategies, and ethics to consider. Journal of Rehabilitation, *66*, 11–17.

Rubin, J. A. (1988). Art counseling: An alternative. *Elementary School Guidance and Counseling, 22*, 180–185.

Salvatore, G., Dimaggio, G., & Semerari, A. (2004). A model of narrative development: Implications for understanding psychopathology and guiding therapy. *Psychology & Psychotherapy: Theory, Research, & Practice, 77*, 231–254.

Sandoz, J. (2006). Mental imagery and metaphors for recovery. *American Journal of Pastoral Counseling, 8*, 43–53.

Schumacher, R. B., Wantz, R. A., & Taricone, P. E. (1995). Constructing and using interactive workbooks to promote therapeutic goals. *Elementary School Guidance and Counseling, 29*, 303–309.

Shechtman, Z. (2006) The contribution of bibliotherapy to the counseling of aggressive boys. *Psychotherapy Research, 16*, 631–636.

Sheese, B., Brown, E., & Graziano, W. (2004). Emotional expression in cyberspace: Searching for moderators of the Pennebaker disclosure effect via e-mail. *Health Psychology, 23*, 457–464.

Shovlin, K. J. (1999). Discovering a narrative voice through play and art therapy: A case study. *Guidance and Counseling, 14*, 7–9.

Shurts, W. M., Cashwell, C. S., Craig, S., Spurgeon, S. L., Degges-White, S., Barrio, C. A., & Kardatzke, K. N. (2006). Preparing counselors-in-training to work with couples: Using role-plays and reflecting teams. *Family Journal, 14*, 151–157.

Sontag, M. (2001). Art as an evaluative tool: A pilot study. *Art Therapy: Journal of the American Association of Art Therapy, 18*, 37–43.

Soper, B., & VonBergen, C. W. (2001). Employment counseling and life stressors: Coping through expressive writing. *Journal of Employment Counseling, 38*, 150–160.

St. Denis, T. M., Orlick, I., & McCaffrey, W. (1996). Positive perspectives: Interventions with fourth grade children. *Elementary School Guidance and Counseling, 31*, 52–63.

Thompson, R. A. (2003). *Counseling techniques: Improving relationships with others, ourselves, our families, and our environment* (2nd ed.). Philadelphia: Taylor and Frances.

Trepal, H., Haberstroh, S., Duffey, T., & Evans, M. (2007). Considerations and strategies for teaching online counseling skills: Establishing relationships in cyberspace. *Counselor Education and Supervision, 46*, 266–279.

Trull, T. (2007). Expanding the aperture of psychological assessment: Introduction to the special section on innovative clinical assessment technologies and methods. *Psychological Assessment, 19*, 1–3.

Turner, S. L., Trotter, M. J., Lapan, R. T., Czajka, K. A., Pahoua, Y., & Brissett, A. (2006). Vocational skills and outcomes among Native American adolescents: A test of the integrative contextual model of career development. *Career Development Quarterly, 54*, 216–226.

Van Horn, S., & Myrick, R. (2001). Computer technology and the 21st century school counselor. *Professional School Counseling, 5*, 124.

Valkenburg, P., Peter, J., & Schouten, A. (2006). Friend networking sites and their relationship to adolescents' well-being and social self-esteem. *CyberPsychology & Behavior, 9*(5), 584–590.

Vernon, A. (1997). Special approaches to counseling. In D. Capuzzi & D. Gross (Eds.), *Introduction to the counseling profession* (2nd ed., pp. 235–254). Needham Heights, MA: Allyn & Bacon.

Vernon, A. (1998a). *The Passport Program: A journey through emotional, social, cognitive, and self development, grades 1–5.* Champaign, IL: Research Press.

Vernon, A. (1998b). *The Passport Program. A journey through emotional, social, cognitive, and self-development, grades 6–8.* Champaign, IL: Research Press.

Vernon, A. (1998c). The *Passport Program: A journey through emotional, social, cognitive, and self-development, grades 9–12.* Champaign, IL: Research Press.

Vernon, A. (2002). *What works with children and adolescents: A handbook of individual counseling techniques.* Champaign, IL: Research Press.

Vernon, A. (2005). Creative approaches to counseling. In D. Capuzzi & D. Gross (Eds.), *Introduction to the counseling profession* (4th ed., pp 258–286). New York: Pearson.

Vernon, A. (2006). *Thinking, feeling, behaving: An emotional education curricular for children grades 1–6* (rev.) Champaign, IL: Research Press.

Vernon, A., & Clemente, R. (2005). *Assessment and intervention with children and adolescents: Developmental and multicultural considerations.* Alexandria, VA: American Counseling Association.

Wagner, B., Knaevelsrud, C., & Maercker, A. (2006). Internet-based cognitive-behavioral therapy for complicated grief: A randomized controlled trial. *Death Studies, 30,* 429–453.

Weiser, J. (2001) Psychotherapy techniques: Using clients' persona snapshots and family photos as counseling and therapy tools. *Afterimage, 29,* 10–16.

Whitlock, J., Powers, J., & Eckenrode, J. (2006). The virtual cutting edge: The internet and adolescent self-injury. *Developmental Psychology, 42,* 407–417.

Wiitala, W. L., & Dansereau, D. F. (2004). Using popular quotations to enhance therapeutic writing. *Journal of College Counseling, 7,* 187–191.

Withrow, R. L. (2004). The use of color in art therapy. *Journal of Humanistic Counseling, Education, and Development, 43,* 33–40.

Play Therapy

Terry Kottman

In the play therapy approach, the counselor uses toys and play as the primary vehicle for communication with young children. The rationale stems from the belief that young children (under the age of 12)

> have relatively limited ability to verbalize their feelings and thoughts and to use abstract verbal reasoning. Most of them lack the ability to come into a counseling session, sit down, and use words to tell the therapist about their problems…. Children can come into sessions and use toys, art, stories, and other playful tools to communicate with the therapist. (Kottman, 2001, p. 4)

Because play is the natural language of young children, it can be used as a modality for working out problems and communicating with others. This makes play therapy an essential method for counseling children younger than 12 years of age (Thompson & Henderson, 2006). This chapter presents parameters for determining whether play therapy approaches are appropriate in various situations, goals for play therapy, and suggestions on how to set up an ideal play therapy space and choose toys and play materials that can be therapeutic to children. Finally, we will explore the various styles this counseling approach can take.

Appropriate Clients for Play Therapy

Although some play therapists work with adults (Demanchick, Cochran, & Cochran, 2003; Schaefer, 2002), most play therapy is done with children between the ages of

3 and 12. When working with older elementary-age children, preadolescents, and young teens, the counselor might wish to ask whether they would be more comfortable sitting and discussing their situation or playing with toys. The counselor can extend the usual age range of play therapy by adding toys aimed at older children, such as craft supplies, carpentry tools, office supplies and equipment, and more complex games or games designed for specific therapeutic interventions (Gallo-Lopez & Schaefer, 2005; Kottman, 2001; Luke, 2003: Packman & Bratton, 2003).

Several syntheses of play therapy research (Bratton & Ray, 2000; LeBlanc & Richie, 2001; Ray, Bratton, Rhine, & Jones, 2001) have provided support for the effectiveness of play therapy as a therapeutic intervention with many different presenting problems. The professional literature supports the efficacy of play therapy as an intervention with children and adolescents who have the following behavioral or emotional difficulties:

- Aggressive, acting-out behavior (Fischetti, 2001; Herschell & McNeil, 2005; Johnson & Clark, 2001; Lawrence, Condon, Jacobi, & Nicholson, 2006; Packman & Bratton, 2003)
- Attachment disorder (Ryan, 2004)
- Attention deficit-hyperactivity disorder (Kaduson, 2006b; Reddy, Spencer, Hall, & Rubel, 2001)
- Conduct disorders and severe behavior disorders (Cabe, 1997; O'Connor, 1993; Reid, 1993)
- Depression (Baggerly, 2004; Shen, 2002)
- Enuresis and/or encopresis (Briesmeister, 1997; Cuddy-Casey, 1997)
- Specific fears and phobias, such as fear of hospitalization or separation anxiety (Kottman, 2002; Knell, 2000)
- Selective mutism (Spasaro & Schaefer, 2004)

Further, play therapy can be helpful with children who are struggling with life circumstances of: abuse and/or neglect (Gil, 2006; Ginsberg, 2002; Hill, 2006; Kelly & Odenwalt, 2006;); adoption (Bruning, 2007; Kottman, 1997); divorce of parents (Pedro-Carroll & Jones, 2005; Siegel, 2007); family violence (Kot & Tyndall-Lind, 2005; Weinreb & Groves, 2007); grief issues (Thornberg, 2002); hospitalization (Goodman, 1999); chronic or terminal illness (Jones & Landreth, 2002; VanFleet, 2000, 2003); parental deployment (Herzog & Everson, 2007); and severe trauma and post-traumatic stress disorder, such as caused by war, earthquakes, car wrecks, and kidnapping (Gil 2006; Kaduson, 2006a; Shen, 2002).

When deciding whether play therapy interventions are appropriate for specific children, Anderson and Richards (1995) proposed that the play therapist consider the following factors related to the child and his or her issues:

1. Can this child tolerate, form, and utilize a relationship with an adult?
2. Can this child tolerate and accept a protective environment?
3. Does this child have the capacity to learn new methods of dealing with the presenting problem?

4. Does this child have the capacity for insight into his or her behavior and motivation?
5. Does this child have the capacity for insight into the behavior and motivation of others?
6. Does this child have the capacity for sufficient attention and/or cognitive organization to engage in therapeutic activities?
7. Is play therapy the most effective and efficient way to address this child's problems?

In addition, Anderson and Richards (1995) recommended that the play therapist consider the following questions related to his or her own situation and skills:

1. Do I have the necessary skills to work with this child? Is consultation or supervision available if I need it?
2. Is my practice setting devoid of barriers (e.g., not enough space, funding issues, inadequate length of treatment allowed) that might interfere with effective treatment of this child?
3. If effective therapy for this child will involve working with other professionals, can I work within the necessary framework?
4. Is my energy or stress level such that I can fully commit to working with this child?

If the answers to these questions are *yes* and the counselor has no unresolved personal issues that will impact negatively on his or her ability to work with children and their families, he or she should first explain to the child's parent(s) and/or teachers what play therapy is and how it can be helpful and work with the parent(s) and teachers on the specific goals for the play therapy process.

Counselors have to be able to work with children from diverse cultures (Drewes, 2005; Gil & Drewes, 2005; Glover, 2001; Kao & Landreth, 2001; Kottman, 2001). When working with multicultural populations, counselors should (Coleman et al., 1993)

- include materials and toys that convey respect for and understanding of the cultures and ethnic groups represented by the families involved;
- understand the roles of play, art, and storytelling in various cultures and ethnic groups;
- be aware of the values, customs, beliefs, and traditions of the child's culture;
- seek to become more knowledgeable about other cultures and ethnic groups in general; and
- work to find a "match" between each child's cultural background and the techniques used with that child in the play therapy process.

Goals of Play Therapy

Many children who come to play therapy have a negative self-concept and little confidence in their own abilities. They may believe they are worthless. They may think they are unable to contribute anything positive to relationships and unable to take care of their own needs. One goal of play therapy is to build up children's sense of self-efficacy and competence by encouraging them to do things for themselves and make decisions for themselves in the playroom. By showing genuine concern, empathic understanding, and consistent positive regard, the play therapist can further counteract the negative images about self and others that children have incorporated into their worldviews.

Most children who come to play therapy have relatively weak problem-solving and decision-making skills. Another goal of play therapy is to promote their abilities in these areas and to help the children learn to accept responsibility for their own behaviors and decisions.

In sum, typical goals of play therapy are the following.

1. Enhance the child's self-acceptance, self-confidence, and self-reliance.
2. Help the child learn more about himself or herself and others.
3. Help the child explore and express feelings.
4. Increase the child's ability to make self-enhancing decisions.
5. Provide situations in which the child can practice self-control and self-responsibility.
6. Help the child explore alternative perceptions of problem situations and difficult relationships.
7. Help the child learn and practice problem-solving skills and relationship-building skills.
8. Increase the child's "feeling vocabulary" and formation of emotional concepts.

In addition to these broad therapeutic goals, counselors may set specific goals for specific children, depending on the counselor's theoretical orientation and the child's presenting problem (Kottman, 2001).

Setting Up a Play Therapy Space

A counselor who wants to use play therapy as an intervention approach with children can accomplish this no matter what kind of space is available. Although Landreth (2002) described an "ideal" space for play therapy, even a small corner of a school cafeteria can work as long as others are not using it at the same time (to ensure client confidentiality). The counselor must feel comfortable with the space (Kottman, 2001, 2003). If he or she feels safe, happy, and welcome there, the children will sense this and react accordingly.

An "ideal" play therapy space has the following characteristics (Landreth, 2002):

1. Measures approximately 12 feet by 15 feet, with an area of between 150 and 200 square feet, which allows a child room to move freely but is still small

enough so the child will not feel overwhelmed or be able to stray too far from the play therapist.

2. Offers privacy so the children can feel comfortable revealing information and feelings without worrying about others overhearing them.

3. Has washable wall coverings and vinyl floor coverings so children can make a mess without worrying or feeling guilty.

4. Includes many shelves for storing toys and play materials within easy reach of children.

5. Shelves secured to the walls so no one can accidentally or purposefully topple them.

6. Contains a small sink with cold running water.

7. Has some countertop space or a child-size desk with a storage area for artwork.

8. Has a cabinet for storing materials such as paint, clay, and extra paper.

9. Has a marker board or chalkboard (either attached to a wall or propped on an easel).

10. Has a small bathroom attached to the main room.

11. Preferably, is fitted with acoustical ceiling tiles to reduce noise.

12. Has wood or molded plastic furniture designed to accommodate children, as well as some furniture appropriate for the counselor, parents, and teachers.

13. Has a one-way mirror and equipment for observing and videotaping sessions.

14. Is located in a place where noise during the session will not present a major problem to others in the building.

Toy Selection and Arrangement

Landreth (2002) suggested that the toys and play materials selected for play therapy should

- allow for a broad range of emotional and creative expression by children,
- capture the interest of children in some way,
- facilitate children's verbal and nonverbal investigation and expression, and
- encourage mastery experiences for children.

Landreth stressed that the toys be sturdy and safe. The toys and play materials chosen should help children

- establish positive relationships with the counselor (and with other children in groups),
- express a wide range of feelings,
- explore and/or reenact actual experiences and relationships,
- test their limits,
- increase their self-control,
- enhance their understanding of self and others, and
- improve their self-image.

The selection of toys is based on various theoretical orientations. Kottman (2001, 2003) provides the following list that a counselor could use as a framework to stock an "ideal" playroom:

1. Family/nurturing toys
2. Scary toys
3. Aggressive toys
4. Expressive toys
5. Pretend/fantasy toys

Children can use *family/nurturing* toys to build a relationship with the counselor and to explore family relationships. These toys can also represent real-life experiences. Family/nurturing toys include, among others, a dollhouse and dolls of different ethnicities (preferably with removable clothing and bendable bodies), baby clothes, a cradle, animal families, a soft blanket, people puppets, stuffed toys, sand in a sandbox, pots and pans, dishes and dinnerware, empty food containers, and play kitchen appliances (such as a sink and a stove).

Scary toys are suggested to allow children to express their fears and learn to cope with them. These toys could be, for example, plastic or rubber snakes, rats, monsters, dinosaurs, sharks, insects, dragons, alligators, and "fierce" animal puppets (such as wolf, bear, and alligator puppets).

Aggressive toys encourage children to express anger and aggression symbolically, to give them means to protect themselves from objects of fear, and to explore their need for control in various situations. Examples are a bop bag, toy weapons (such as play guns, swords, and knives), toy soldiers and military vehicles, small pillows for pillow fights, foam bats, plastic shields, and handcuffs.

While playing with *expressive* toys, children give voice to their feelings, enhance their sense of mastery, practice problem-solving skills, and express their creativity. These could include an easel and paints, watercolors, crayons, markers, glue, newsprint, Play-Doh® or clay, fingerpaints, scissors, tape, egg cartons, feathers, materials for making masks, and pipe cleaners.

Pretend/fantasy toys allow children to express their feelings, explore a wide range of roles, experiment with varied behaviors and attitudes, and act out real-life situations and relationships. These toys can include masks, costumes, magic wands, hats, jewelry, purses, a doctor kit, telephones, blocks and other building materials, people figures, zoo and farm animals, puppets and a puppet theater, a sandbox, trucks and construction equipment, kitchen appliances, pots, pans, dishes, dinnerware, and empty food containers.

The playroom does not have to include all of these different toys. With one or two toys from each category, the counselor can provide an effective vehicle for communication. Children are highly creative, and they will make the toys they need if they don't see them in the room—by pretending one of the available toys is something else (e.g., a crayon can easily become a magic wand, a gun, or dinnerware) or by constructing them from play materials (e.g., making a doll or a dish from construction paper or pipe cleaners).

Some authors have suggested that toys and play materials should be returned to approximately the same place after every session (e.g., Kottman, 2001, 2003; Landreth, 2002). This structured placement establishes he play therapy setting as a place where the child can count on predictability and consistency. By arranging the toys and play materials by category (e.g., placing all family toys together), the counselor enables easier clean-up and helps children remember where to locate specific toys. Counselors who do not have stationary playrooms can accomplish the same consistent and predictable arrangement by placing the toys in a specific order on the floor or a table in the space that is the current "playroom" (Kottman, 2001). Some play therapists pick up the toys after the child has left the playroom (Landreth, 2002). Others work with the child to clean up the room before the end of the session, using the cleaning-up process as a time for continuing to build a collaborative partnership with the child (Kottman, 2003).

Basic Play Therapy Skills

Most play therapists, regardless of their theoretical orientation, call upon several generic, basic strategies. These include tracking, restating content, reflecting feelings, returning responsibility to the child, using the child's metaphor, and limiting (Kottman, 2001).

Tracking

In tracking, the counselor describes the child's behavior to the child to convey that what the child is doing is important. The ultimate purpose is to build a relationship with the child by communicating caring and a feeling of connection (Kottman, 2001).

When using tracking, the counselor should avoid labeling objects. An object that looks like a snake to the counselor might be a whip, a tightrope, a slingshot, or any of a number of other things to a child. The counselor should keep the description of the behavior relatively vague. A behavior that looks like jumping off a chair to the counselor can, in the child's imagination, be leaping out of a burning building, parachuting out of an airplane, jumping over a river filled with poisonous snakes, or something else. By using pronouns such as "this," "that," "them," "it," and "those" instead of specific nouns, and by using vague descriptions such as "moving over there" and "going up and down" instead of specific verbs such as "jumping" or "flying," the counselor allows the child to project his or her own meaning onto the toys and onto the actions in the playroom.

Some children impose their own vision of the world on things in the playroom despite the counselor's descriptions. Others simply agree with whatever the counselor says rather than asserting their own version of how things are, or they disagree with whatever the counselor says rather than appearing to comply with the counselor's version of how things are. In any case, counselors should reinforce children's need for freedom of self-expression. Avoiding labeling is one means to that end.

The following interactions illustrate the tracking strategy:

Leonard:	(Picks up a mouse and has it hop up and down on the head of a cat.)
Mr. Hawkins:	That one is moving up and down on the other one.
Leonard:	(Buries a snake underneath the sand.)
Mr. Hawkins:	You put that under there.
Leonard:	(Rocks a doll.)
Mr. Hawkins:	You're moving that back and forth.
Leonard:	(Picks up handcuffs and examines them.)
Mr. Hawkins:	You're checking those out.
Leonard:	(Carefully arranges animal figures on the floor.)
Mr. Hawkins:	You know just where you want to put those.

Restating Content

Restating content involves paraphrasing the child's verbalizations. Just as with tracking, the purpose is to build a relationship with the child (Kottman, 2001). By conveying to the child that what he or she has to say is important, the counselor shows concern and understanding.

To avoid parroting the child, the counselor must use his or her own words and intonations but also use vocabulary that the child understands. Otherwise, the child will not feel understood.

The following interaction illustrates restating content:

Steve:	(Starting to hit the bop bag.) I'm going to hit him and beat him up.
Mrs. Barry:	You really want to get him.
Steve:	You seem like a nice person. Can I come in here every day?
Mrs. Barry:	You think I might be a person you can like, and you wish you could come here once a day.
Steve:	I got an A on my math test, but I got an F on my spelling test.
Mrs. Barry:	You did really well on your math test but not so well on your spelling test.
Steve:	We went to my grandma's house this weekend to visit her because she's sick.
Mrs. Barry:	Your grandmother isn't feeling well, so you went to see her.

Reflecting Feelings

By reflecting the child's feelings and the child's feelings projected onto toys or objects in the playroom, the counselor can deepen the counselor–client relationship and at the same time help the child express and understand his or her emotions, learn more about interactions with others, and expand his or her affective vocabulary (Kottman, 2001). With words such as, "You seem kind of sad today," the counselor can reflect the child's feelings directly. By saying, "It seems like you're disappointed, Miss Kitty," or "The kitty seems really disappointed right now," the counselor reflects the feelings of the toys and other objects in the playroom. To help children learn to take responsibility for their own feelings, the counselor should avoid using the phrase "makes you feel." Instead, the counselor should simply state the feeling by saying, "You feel…."

The counselor must watch for both the surface, obvious feelings and the underlying, deeper feelings (Kottman, 2001). In play therapy, deeper feelings sometimes are expressed through the toys and other objects in the playroom. For example, watching a child play with a cat and mouse, a counselor may observe that at first the cat seemed happy that he could catch the mouse, but then he almost seemed disappointed that the mouse didn't run faster.

The counselor also should look for patterns and interactions between children's behavior in the playroom and his or her information about situations outside the playroom. For example, when Sam comes into the playroom and kicks the toys, he might appear to be simply angry. The counselor, however, knows that Sam's dog died over the weekend and suspects that Sam may be feeling sad and lonely. When reflecting deeper, less obvious emotions, the counselor should offer a tentative formulation. By not imposing his or her own viewpoint onto the child, the counselor reduces the possibility of evoking a defensive reaction from the child.

When reflecting feelings, as at all other times, the counselor must adjust his or her vocabulary to the child's developmental level (Muro & Kottman, 1995). Most preschoolers, kindergarteners, and first-graders seem to recognize four main feeling states: sad, mad, glad, and scared. With these children, the counselor, at least initially, should use only these words and simple synonyms when reflecting feelings.

Children in second and third grades typically have a wider range of feeling vocabulary but still might not comprehend or express more subtle feelings. Sometimes children in these grades have a more extensive receptive vocabulary than their expressive vocabulary. Thus, they may understand words such as "frustrated," "disappointed," and "jealous" even though they might not use these words themselves. The counselor can work to expand the affective vocabulary of these children by using a variety of feeling words to describe more subtle affective states.

Some fourth-, fifth-, and sixth-graders have relatively sophisticated feeling vocabularies. With these children the counselor might decide to switch to "talk therapy" or use more structured activities and games rather than play therapy.

The following interaction illustrates the strategy of reflecting feelings:

Julian:	(In an angry voice.) I got into trouble again, and I can't go to the play with the rest of my class.
Ms. Pataki:	Sounds like you're mad because you got into trouble. I'll bet you're feeling disappointed about not getting to go to the movie with the other kids.
Julian:	(Moving an airplane up and down, dive-bombing a cluster of soldiers.) Hahahaha!! I got you. You can't ever hurt me again.
Ms. Pataki:	He's excited that he got all of them. Sounds like he feels like he'll be safe from now on.

Julian:	(Using the dolls in the dollhouse, he has the parents yell at each other and at the children. He moves the smallest doll under the bed.)
Ms. Pataki:	Seems like it's kind of scary when those bigger ones yell and fight.
Julian:	This was really fun. Can I come again tomorrow? I like it in here a lot better than in my classroom.
Ms. Pataki:	You sound really happy. It feels safe and fun in the playroom, and you wish you could come again tomorrow instead of going to class.

Returning Responsibility to the Child

The strategy of returning responsibility to the child is designed to increase children's self-reliance, self-confidence, and self-responsibility (Kottman, 2001; Landreth, 2002). It also can help them practice decision making, give them a sense of accomplishment, and heighten their feelings of mastery and control. The counselor can return responsibility for executing behaviors (e.g., "I think you know how to open the lid to the sandbox yourself,") or for making decisions (e.g., "You can decide what to paint").

In the playroom, children are capable of making most decisions that come up, so counselors usually should return this responsibility to the children. When returning responsibility to a child, however, the counselor has to consider whether the child is capable of accomplishing the task (Kottman, 2001, 2003). Children can be discouraged if an adult tells them they can do something that they truly cannot do. If the counselor is not sure whether children can execute the behavior, he or she can suggest that they work as a team to accomplish the goal or can ask the child to tell the counselor "how to do it." Either way, the counselor lets the child control the execution and does not remove responsibility for the behavior from the child.

Several different techniques can be used to return responsibility to a child (Kottman, 2001). In the direct approach the counselor simply tells the child that he or she is capable of doing the behavior or making the choice. The counselor also employs a less direct approach, returning responsibility to the child by using (a) tracking, restatement of content, or reflection of feelings; (b) the child's metaphor; (c) minimal encouragers or ignoring the child's desire for assistance, or (d) the "Whisper Technique" (Landreth, 1984, personal communication). The following interactions illustrate these techniques.

Martina:	Will you put this furniture in the dollhouse? (asking for help with the execution of a behavior and with a decision)
Mr. Chuppi:	I think you can do that yourself. (direct response)
	You want me to put the furniture in the dollhouse for you. (indirect response; restating content)
	You sound worried that you might not put the doll furniture where it's supposed to go. (indirect response; reflecting feelings)

	Hmm. . . . (indirect response; minimal encourager, ignores child's request)
	(In a whisper.) Where do you think this piece should go? (indirect response; "Whisper Technique")
Martina:	What's this? (asking for help with a decision)
Mr. Chuppi:	In here, it can be anything you want it to be. (direct response)
	I bet you can figure out what you want it to be. (direct response)
	Mmmmmmmm.... What could it be? (indirect response; minimal encourager)
	You're curious about what that could be. (indirect response; reflecting feelings)
	You want me to tell you what that is. (indirect response; restating content)
Martina:	(Using the mouse puppet, brings a pair of scissors and some yarn to the counselor and says in a squeaky voice.) Make me some nice red hair. (asking for help in executing a behavior)
Mr. Chuppi:	Martina, I'll bet you can make the mouse some hair without any help from me. (direct response)
	Ms. Mouse, I think you can figure out how to make some nice red hair for yourself. (indirect response; using child's metaphor)
	Let's work together to make some hair for Ms. Mouse. (Whispers.) What shall we do first to make her some hair? (indirect response; "Whisper Technique")
	(Not taking the scissors and the yarn.) You want to hand those things to me because you want me to make some hair for the mouse. (indirect response; tracking)

Using the Child's Metaphor

Much of the communication in play therapy takes the form of metaphor, in which the child expresses feelings, thoughts, and attitudes and indirectly tells the story of his or her situation and relationships through the words and actions of various toys (Kottman, 2001). Sometimes the counselor will be able to discern the hidden meaning in the play, and at other times the meaning will be a mystery. The counselor's willingness to use the metaphor is much more important than his or her ability to interpret it. "Using a metaphor" means that the counselor tracks, restates content, reflects feelings, and returns responsibility through the child's story without imposing his or her own interpretation of the story's meaning. The counselor must exercise self-restraint and avoid "breaking" the metaphor by going outside the story to the "real" world.

During the following interaction, the counselor uses the child's metaphor to track, restate content, reflect feelings, and return responsibility to the child:

| Jake: | (Brings a stuffed puppy to the counselor and puts it in her lap.) Woof, woof! I'm a puppy, and my name is Little Puppy. |

Ms. Rohlf:	Sounds like you want to tell me who you are, Little Puppy.
Jake:	(Brings a big plastic dinosaur and puts it next to the puppy. Moving the dinosaur, Jake makes growling noises. He then takes Ms. Rohlf's hand and places it over the puppy.)
Ms. Rohlf:	The dinosaur seems kind of fierce, Little Puppy. You look like you're feeling scared and wanting to find a safe place.
Jake:	(Moves the puppy's head and front paws out from under the counselor's hand toward the dinosaur. The puppy barks at the dinosaur, and the dinosaur yelps and runs away. Jake laughs.)
Ms. Rohlf:	Woo! Even though you were kind of scared, Little Puppy, you came out and barked at that dinosaur to let him know you wanted him to go away. It worked. You took care of yourself.

Limiting

Limiting, or setting limits in the playroom, protects the child and the counselor from harm, increases the child's sense of self-control and self-responsibility, and enhances his or her sense of social responsibility (Ginott, 1959; Kottman, 2001, 2003; Landreth, 2002). Appropriate limits in play therapy are those intended to keep the child from (a) physically harming himself or herself, other children, and/or the counselor; (b) deliberately damaging the play therapy facility or play materials; (c) removing toys or play materials from the play therapy setting; (d) leaving the session before the scheduled time; and (e) staying in the session after the time limit has expired. Imposing other limits (e.g., not aiming the toy gun at the therapist, not pouring water into the sandbox, not jumping from the furniture onto the floor) depends on the individual counselor and his or her setting and clientele.

Counselors seldom come into the first session with a long list of rules outlining "appropriate" playroom behavior. Most counselors wait to set a limit until a child is about to break one of the playroom rules. In this way the counselor can avoid inhibiting the timid, withdrawn child or challenging the acting-out child who likes to get into power struggles. Many different strategies can be used for setting limits in play therapy (Kottman, 2001). One widely used method, developed by Ginott (1959), involves the following four steps:

33.1.1.1. Reflecting the child's wishes, desires, and feelings (e.g., "You're really mad and would like to shoot me with the dart gun.")

33.1.1.2. Stating the limit in a nonjudgmental manner, using a passive voice formulation (e.g., "I'm not for shooting at people.")

33.1.1.3. Redirecting the child to more appropriate behavior (e.g., "You can shoot the dart at the target or the big doll.")

33.1.1.4. Helping the child express any feelings of anger or resentment at being limited (e.g., "I can tell you're really mad that I told you I'm not for shooting at people.")

In another method of setting limits, described in Kottman (2003), the child is engaged in redirecting his or her own inappropriate behavior. This strategy also has four steps:

33.1.1.5. Stating the limit in a nonjudgmental way that reflects the social reality of the play therapy setting. (e.g., "It's against the playroom rules to shoot darts at people.")

33.1.1.6. Reflecting the child's feelings and guessing about the purpose of his or her behavior. (e.g., "You're feeling kind of mad at me, and you want to show me that I can't tell you what to do.")

33.1.1.7. Engaging the child in redirecting his or her behavior by asking for suggestions for more socially appropriate behavior choices. (e.g., "I'll bet you can think of something you can shoot that won't be against the playroom rules.") In many cases the child will come to an agreement with the counselor about appropriate behaviors, will abide by that agreement, and the counselor will not have to take further action. If the child chooses to break the agreement, however, the counselor would move to the fourth step.

33.1.1.8. Setting up logical consequences that the child can enforce. (e.g., "We need to think of a consequence just in case you decide to shoot the dart at me again. What do you think would be a fair consequence?") Examples of consequences are: lose the privilege to play with the toy, sit quietly for several minutes, or lose the privilege to play with certain other playroom materials.

Theoretical Approaches to Play Therapy

The many different theoretical approaches to play therapy range on a continuum from nondirective to directive (Kottman, 2001). The following are brief descriptions of several selected approaches: child-centered play therapy, which represents the nondirective end of the continuum; Adlerian and cognitive–behavioral play therapy, both of which combine nondirective and directive elements and represent the middle of the continuum; and Theraplay, which represents the directive end of the continuum.

Child-Centered Play Therapy

In developing nondirective, child-centered play therapy, Virginia Axline (1947, 1969, 1971) applied the basic concepts of client-centered therapy developed by Rogers (1959). Axline (1969) delineated the following principles for practitioners of client-centered play therapy.

1. The therapist must build a warm, friendly, genuine relationship with the child, facilitating strong therapeutic rapport.
2. The therapist must be utterly accepting of the child and have no desire for the child to change.

3. The therapist must develop and maintain a permissive environment that encourages the child to feel free in exploring and expressing emotions.
4. The therapist must constantly attend to the child's feelings and reflect them in a way that encourages the child to gain insight and increase his or her self-understanding.
5. The therapist must respect the child's ability to solve problems if the child has the opportunity and the necessary resources. In doing so, the therapist must remember that the child must be completely responsible for decisions about whether and when to make changes.
6. The therapist must follow the child's lead in play therapy. The responsibility and privilege of leading the way belong solely to the child.
7. The therapist must be patient with the therapy process and not attempt to speed it up.
8. The therapist must set only those limits essential for connecting the play therapy to reality.

In the words of Landreth and Sweeney (1997), child-centered play therapy is

> a philosophy resulting in attitudes and behaviors for living one's life in relationships with children. It is both a basic philosophy of the innate human capacity of the child to strive toward growth and maturity and an attitude of deep and abiding belief in the child's ability to be constructively self-directing. (p. 17)

Practitioners have found that children's behavior in child-centered play therapy goes through five distinct phases (Landreth & Sweeney, 1997).

1. Children use play to express diffuse negative feelings.
2. Children use play to express ambivalent feelings, usually anxiety or hostility.
3. Children again express mostly negative feelings, but the focus has shifted to specific targets—parents, siblings, or the therapist.
4. Ambivalent feelings (positive and negative) resurface but now are targeted toward parents, siblings, the therapist, and others.
5. Positive feelings predominate, but the child expresses realistic negative attitudes in appropriate situations.

In child-centered play therapy the counselor "maintains an active role in the process of play therapy, not in the sense of directing or managing the experience but by being directly involved and genuinely interested in all of the child's feelings, actions, and decisions" (Landreth, 1991, p. 99). The counselor's main function is to provide the child with the core conditions of unconditional positive regard, empathic understanding, and genuineness. Client-centered play therapists believe that by communicating acceptance and belief in the child, they can activate the child's innate capacity for solving problems and moving toward optimal living.

Child-centered play therapists depend on the skills of tracking, restating content, reflecting feelings, returning responsibility to the child, and setting limits. They avoid skills that lead the child in any way, such as interpretation, design of therapeutic metaphors, bibliotherapy, and other more directive techniques.

Adlerian Play Therapy

In using Adlerian play therapy (Kottman, 1993, 1994, 1997, 2003), counselors combine the principles and strategies of individual psychology with the basic concepts and skills of play therapy. They conceptualize children through Adlerian constructs and communicate with them through toys and play materials.

Adlerian play therapy has four phases (Kottman, 2003):

33.1.1.9. The counselor builds an egalitarian relationship with the child, using tracking, restating content, reflecting feelings, returning responsibility to the child, encouraging, limiting, answering questions, and cleaning the room together.

33.1.1.10. The counselor, using the play interaction, the child's metaphors, and art techniques, gains an understanding of the child's lifestyle and how the child sees himself or herself, others, and the world.

33.1.1.11. The counselor, based on hypotheses he or she has formulated from the information gathered in the second phase, helps the child gain insight into his or her lifestyle, using metaphors, stories, metacommunication, artwork, role-playing, and so forth.

33.1.1.12. The counselor provides reorientation and reeducation for the child, which may involve helping the child learn and practice new skills and attitudes.

In Adlerian play therapy, consultation with parents and teachers is essential. The process is parallel to that of play therapy. In the first phase the counselor builds a relationship with the important adults in the child's life. During the second phase, the counselor explores the adults' lifestyles and their perception of the child's typical ways of interacting with others. Based on an understanding of the child and the adults in his or her life, during the third and fourth phases the counselor helps parents and teachers gain insight into the child's patterns and their own lifestyles and teaches parenting skills.

Cognitive–Behavioral Play Therapy

Cognitive–behavioral play therapy (CBPT), developed by Susan Knell (1993a, 1993b, 1994, 1997), combines cognitive and behavioral strategies within a play therapy delivery system. Using interventions derived from cognitive therapy and behavior therapy, cognitive-behavioral play therapists integrate play activities with verbal and nonverbal communication.

Knell (1994) delineated six specific principles essential to CBPT:

33.1.1.13. The counselor involves the child in the therapy through play. The child is an active partner in the therapeutic process.

33.1.1.14. The counselor examines the child's thoughts, feelings, fantasies, and environment. Rather than being client-focused, CBPT is problem-focused.

33.1.1.15. The counselor helps the child develop more adaptive thoughts and behaviors and more effective strategies for solving problems.

33.1.1.16. CBPT is structured, directive, and goal-oriented.

33.1.1.17. The counselor uses specific behavioral and cognitive interventions that have empirical support for efficacy with specific problems.

33.1.1.18. The counselor designs interventions using baseline and follow-up measurements of behavior to provide empirical support for the effectiveness of treatment.

Cognitive–behavioral play therapy has four stages, delineated by Knell (1993a, 1994):

1. Assessment
2. Introduction/orientation to play therapy
3. Middle stage
4. Termination.

During the assessment stage the counselor employs formal and informal instruments to gather baseline data about the child's current level of functioning, the child's development, the presenting problem, the attitude of parent(s) and child toward the presenting problem, and their understanding of it (Knell, 1994). As part of this process, the counselor may use parent report inventories, clinical interviews, play observation, cognitive/developmental scales, and projective assessment methods (Knell, 1993a, 1994).

In the next phase, introduction/orientation to play therapy, the counselor gives the parent(s) an initial evaluation of the child based on the data gathered during the assessment stage. Then and there they collaborate in devising a treatment plan that includes outcome goals and treatment strategies (Knell, 1993a, 1994).

During the middle stage of CBPT, the counselor combines play activities and interactions with specific cognitive and behavioral intervention techniques (including modeling, role-playing, and behavioral contingency) to teach children more adaptive behaviors for dealing with specific situations, problems, issues, or stressors (Knell, 1993a, 1994). In addition, the counselor uses strategies that will help the child generalize his or her new skills to situations and settings in the "real" world. One of the main functions of the counselor during this phase is to compare the child's current functioning with his or her baseline functioning and assess the child's progress toward therapeutic goals.

During the termination stage the counselor helps the child develop plans for coping with various situations after counseling ends. The counselor uses behavioral techniques to reinforce changes in the child's thinking, feeling, and behaving and encourages the child to practice strategies for generalizing the progress he or she has made in the playroom to other relationships.

Theraplay

As defined by Koller and Booth (1997), Theraplay is an engaging, playful treatment method

> modeled on the healthy interaction between parents and their children. It is an intensive, short-term approach that actively involves parents—first as observers and later as co-therapists. The goal is to enhance attachment, self-esteem, trust, and joyful engagement and to empower parents to continue, on their own, the health-promoting interactions of the treatment sessions. (p. 204)

Healthy parent-child interactions serve as the model for the directive Theraplay dimensions of structure, challenge, intrusion/engagement, and nurture. Play therapists following this approach use activities and materials that facilitate these dimensions to remedy problems in the attachment process that create intrapersonal and interpersonal struggles for children (Jernberg & Jernberg, 1993).

Counselors demonstrate the dimension of *structure* by setting limits and clear rules for safety and by employing experiences that have a beginning, a middle, and an end (e.g., singing games) and activities designed to define body boundaries (Jernberg & Booth, 1999). The dimension of *challenge* is facilitated by, for example, helping the child take an age-appropriate risk to strengthen the child's sense of mastery and self-confidence (Jernberg & Booth, 1999). The counselor exhibits the dimension of *intrusion/engagement* when, for example, he or she engages the child in playful, spontaneous interactions to show the child that the world is fun and stimulating and that other people can be simultaneously exciting and trustworthy. To facilitate the *nurture* dimension, the counselor initiates interactions designed to soothe, calm, quiet, and reassure the child by meeting his or her early, unsatisfied emotional needs. Such interactions include feeding, making lotion handprints, swinging the child in a blanket, and so forth.

Theraplay is directive, intensive, and brief. Usually the counselor meets first with the parents for an initial interview and assessment of the parent/child relationship, using the Marschak Interaction Method (MIM) (Marschak, 1960). They then meet again so the counselor can explain the Theraplay philosophy, begin to build rapport with the parents, provide feedback from the initial assessment, and develop a treatment plan in collaboration with the parent(s). This session is followed by eight to 12 Theraplay sessions, half an hour each, involving the child and parents (Koller, 1994; Koller & Booth, 1997).

In the standard arrangement for Theraplay work, each session has two counselors. The *Theraplay counselor* works directly with the child, and the *interpreting counselor* works directly with the parents. During the entire 30 minutes of the first four Theraplay sessions and the first 15 minutes of each of the remaining sessions, the parents and the interpreting counselor observe the interactions of the child and the Theraplay counselor from behind a one-way mirror or from a corner of the playroom. The interpreting counselor describes to the parents what is happening between the Theraplay counselor and the child and suggests ways in which the parents can use the Theraplay dimensions demonstrated in the sessions in their everyday interactions with the child. Starting with the fifth Theraplay session, the parents and the interpreting counselor join the child and the Theraplay counselor in the play during the last 15 minutes of each session so the parents can practice the Theraplay dimensions under the counselor's supervision.

In the first session with the child, the Theraplay counselor communicates by demonstration and/or explanation of the rules of Theraplay (Koller, 1994):

1. The therapist is in charge of the session.
2. Sessions are fun.
3. Sessions are active.
4. Sessions are predictable and structured.
5. Sessions never involve physical hurting.

Theraplay counselors are constantly active and directive. They do not talk much. Instead, action is the focus of Theraplay sessions. The Theraplay counselor plans activities and materials that facilitate the various dimensions of each session, and are tailored specifically to the needs of the individual child. The counselor decides how much time during the session to spend on each dimension, based on the problems and interactional patterns of the child and his or her family. During the session, the counselor may change or adapt some of the activities in response to the child's attitude and/or reactions to the therapeutic process (Jernberg & Booth, 1999; Koller & Booth, 1997).

The interpreting counselor's role is both verbal and directive. During each Theraplay session he or she explains to the parents the interaction between the child and the Theraplay counselor, makes suggestions to the parents of activities that could help the child at home, comments on how specific Theraplay dimensions could enhance the parent–child relationship, coaches the parents when they participate in activities, and provides support and encouragement when the parents begin to incorporate the Theraplay dimensions in their parenting.

Pedro

Pedro, a 7-year-old Latino male, was brought to play therapy by his parents, Mr. and Mrs. Rodriguez, who had concerns about his behavior. Pedro's parents reported that he invariably expected to have his own way and threw hour-long tantrums if his whims were not indulged. Mr. and Mrs. Rodriguez reported that they probably had spoiled Pedro, especially before the birth of his 1-year-old sister. They tended to give in to their son's demands, especially when he had tantrums in public.

In the first several play therapy sessions Pedro exhibited behavior typical of a child newly introduced to a playroom. He played briefly with many of the toys, exploring the room and the play and art materials. As he did this, his play therapist, Carol, tracked Pedro's behavior (told him what he was doing), restated content, and reflected his feelings. She had to limit him several times when he wanted to pour sand on the floor and when he started to fling paint at the easel. He argued with Carol about why he should get to do whatever he wanted, but she was firm, reflecting his feelings, and he finally acquiesced with the limits.

By the third session Carol had noticed themes in Pedro's interaction with her and in his metaphors of needing to be powerful and in control in his play. He frequently chose to use a lion puppet to represent himself. The lion, which he named Leo, was bossy and domineering with the other puppets, played by Carol. When Carol used the Whisper Technique to let Pedro control the play, he directed her to have the other puppets do whatever Leo wanted. When Carol chose not to use a whisper to find out what she was supposed to do next and had a kitten puppet ignore Leo's demands, Pedro first used the puppet to berate the kitten and then told Carol, "You're always supposed to check with me." When she reflected his feelings of being angry and wanting to be in charge in the playroom, he replied, "Sure, I was mad. I should always run everything, and it makes me mad when people don't remember that."

Several times in subsequent sessions, Pedro had tantrums in the playroom when Carol limited his behavior. Because his behavior during these tantrums did not constitute a threat to anyone's safety or to the contents of the playroom, Carol chose to simply reflect his feelings, hoping that he would feel heard and understood. Because she did not want to reinforce this behavior, she remained firm in the limit, without conveying disapproval for his behavior.

In Sessions 4 through 20 Carol continued to work with Pedro on his feelings of entitlement through his metaphors and in his relationship with her. She consistently limited his inappropriate behavior, tracked, restated content, returned responsibility to him, and made interpretations about his perceived need for control. Sometimes she chose to use the Whisper Technique, and sometimes she chose to make her own decisions about how to play. Her goal was for Pedro to become more comfortable with sharing power with others, to find that he could be safe even when he was not in control, to learn skills for communicating about his feelings and desires using words rather than tantrums.

Carol designed several therapeutic stories about the difficulties Leo the lion got into with his controlling behavior and used the metaphor of his troubles to suggest different ways of interacting with others. Pedro liked these stories so much that he and Carol collaborated on an illustrated book chronicling the life and times of Leo. Pedro gradually started suggesting ways by which Leo could get his way without losing friends or hurting the other animals' feelings. Carol also consulted with Pedro's parents, and suggested that they use more consistent limits and resist the temptation to let their son have his way when he had a tantrum.

By Session 20 Carol recognized, based on feedback from Mr. and Mrs. Rodriguez and Pedro's teacher and her own observations of Pedro's behavior in play therapy sessions, that Pedro was ready for termination. His behavior had improved significantly. His temper tantrums were reduced from one or two per week to one every other week or so. She and Pedro started a countdown—making a chart so they could mark off the next 2 weeks as their final sessions. As is typical with most children, Pedro "replayed" many of the themes from his entire course of play therapy. He concluded the last session by looking at Carol, smiling, and saying, "What would you like to do for our last 10 minutes? You can be the boss in here for right now."

Training and Experience

Counselors cannot learn how to conduct play therapy effectively by reading books or attending a workshop or two. This approach to counseling children requires an entirely different mindset than talk therapy. To make the paradigm shift from thinking about words and verbal interactions as the primary modality for communication to thinking about play and toys as the primary modality for communication takes concentrated training and practice. The Association for Play Therapy provides guidelines for registration or certification as a professional play therapist that include educational requirements and clinical experience.

Summary

Play therapy is an approach to counseling young children that uses toys and play materials as the primary vehicle of communication. The choice of play as a treatment modality is based on children's natural affinity toward toys and play materials and their developmental inability or limitations to an abstract discussion of issues and relationships. The professional literature provides both empirical and anecdotal support for using play therapy as a therapeutic intervention with a wide range of emotional and behavioral problems and life situations. In deciding whether play therapy is appropriate to use with a specific child, the counselor must consider a number of factors related to the child and his or her situation and family, as well as a number of factors related to himself or herself and his or her skills, issues, and work setting.

The ideal playroom contains many different toys and play materials. The most important factor in creating and effectively using a play therapy space, however, is the counselor's own sense of comfort and appropriateness. Personal preference and beliefs about people and how they develop and move toward mental health will dictate the counselor's choice of play therapy strategies and his or her theoretical approach. Basic play therapy skills include tracking, restating content, reflecting feelings, returning responsibility to the child, using the child's metaphor, and limiting. Theoretical approaches to play therapy include child-centered play therapy, Adlerian play therapy, cognitive–behavioral play therapy, and Theraplay.

References

Anderson, J., & Richards, N. (1995, October). *Play therapy in the real world: Coping with managed care, challenging children, skeptical colleagues, time and space constraints.* Paper presented at first annual conference of Iowa Association of Play Therapy, Iowa City, IA.

Axline, V. (1947). *Play therapy: The inner dynamics of childhood.* Boston: Houghton Mifflin.

Axline, V. (1969). *Play therapy* (rev. ed.). New York: Ballantine.

Axline, V. (1971). *Dibs: In search of self.* New York: Ballantine.

Baggerly, J. (2004). The effects of child-centered group play therapy on self-concept, depression, and anxiety of children who are homeless. *International Journal of Play Therapy, 13*(2). 31–51.

Bratton, S., & Ray, D. (2000). What the research shows about play therapy. *International Journal of Play Therapy, 9*(1), 47–88.

Briesmeister, J. (1997). Play therapy with depressed children. In H. Kaduson, D. Cangelosi, & C. Schaefer (Eds.), *The playing cure: Individual play therapy for specific childhood problems* (pp. 3–28). Northvale. NJ: Jason Aronson.

Cabe, N. (1997). Conduct disorder: Grounded play therapy. In H. Kaduson, D. Cangelosi, & C. Schaefer (Eds.), *The playing cure: Individual play therapy for specific childhood problems* (pp. 229–254). Northvale, NJ: Jason Aronson.

Coleman, V., Parmer, T., & Barker, S. (1993). Play therapy for multicultural populations: Guidelines for mental health professionals. *International Journal of Play Therapy, 2*(1), 63–74.

Cuddy-Casey, M. (1997). A case study using child-centered play therapy approach to treat enuresis and encopresis. *Elementary School Guidance and Counseling, 31*, 220–225.

Demanchick, S.P., Cochran, N., & Cochran, J. (2003). Person-centered play therapy with adults with developmental disabilities. *International Journal of Play Therapy, 12*(1), 47–65.

Drewes, A. (2005). Play in selected cultures: Diversity and universality. In E. Gil & A. Drewes (Eds.), *Cultural issues in play therapy* (pp. 26–71). New York: Guilford.

Fischetti, B. (2001). Use of play therapy for anger management in the school setting. In A. Drewes, L. Carey, & C. Schaefer (Eds.), *School-based play therapy* (pp. 238–256). New York: John Wiley and Sons.

Gallo-Lopez, L., & Schaefer, C. (Eds.) (2005). *Play therapy with adolescents.* Lanham, MI: Rowman & Littlefield.

Gil, E. (2006). *Helping abused and traumatized children: Integrating directive and nondirective approaches.* New York: Guilford.

Gil, E., & Drewes, A. (Eds.) (2005). *Cultural issues in play therapy.* New York: Guilford.

Ginott, H. G. (1959). Therapeutic intervention in child treatment. *Journal of Consulting Psychology, 23,*160–166.

Ginsberg, B. (2002). The power of filial relationship enhancement therapy as an intervention in child abuse and neglect. *International Journal of Play Therapy, 11*(1), 65–78.

Glover, G. (2001). Cultural considerations in play therapy. In G. Landreth (Ed.), *Innovations in play therapy: Issues, process, and special populations* (pp. 31–41). Philadelphia: Brunner–Routledge.

Goodman, R. (1999). Childhood cancer and the family: Case of Tim, age 6, and follow-up at age 15. In N. B. Webb (Ed.), *Play therapy with children in crisis* (2nd ed., pp. 380–406). New York: Guilford.

Herschell, A., & McNeil, C. (2005). Parent-child interaction therapy for children experiencing externalizing behavior problems. In L.A. Reddy, T.M. Files-Hall, & C.E. Schaefer (Eds.), *Empirically based play interventions for children* (pp. 169–190). Washington, DC: American Psychological Association.

Hill, A. (2006). Play therapy with sexually abused children: Including parents in therapeutic play. *Child and Family Social Work, 11*, 316–324.

Jernberg, A., & Booth, P. (1999). *Theraplay* (2nd ed.). San Francisco: Jossey–Bass.

Jernberg, A., & Jernberg, E. (1993). Family Theraplay for the family tyrant. In T. Kottman & C. Schaefer (Eds.), *Play therapy in action: A casebook for practitioners* (pp. 45–96). Northvale, NJ: Jason Aronson.

Johnson, S., & Clark, P. (2001). Play therapy with aggressive acting-out children. In G. Landreth (Ed.), *Innovations in play therapy: Issues, process, and special populations* (pp. 323–333). Philadelphia: Taylor & Francis.

Jones, E. M., & Landreth, G. (2002). The efficacy of intensive individual play therapy for chronically ill children. *International Journal of Play Therapy, 10*(2), 117–140.

Kaduson, H. (2006a). Release play therapy for children with Posttraumatic Stress Disorder. In H. Kaduson & C. Schaefer (Eds.), *Short-term play therapy for children* (2nd ed., pp. 3–21). New York: Guiford.

Kaduson, H. (2006b). Short-term play therapy for children with Attention-Deficit/Hyperactivity Disorder. In H. Kaduson & C. Schaefer (Eds.), *Short-term play therapy for children* (2nd ed., pp. 22-45). New York: Guiford.

Kao, S., & Landreth, G. (2001). Play therapy with Chinese children. In G. Landreth (Ed.), *Innovations in play therapy: Issues, process, and special populations* (pp. 43–49). Philadelphia: Brunner–Routledge.

Kelly, M., & Odenwalt, H. (2006). Treatment of sexually abused children. In C. Schaefer & H. Kaduson (Eds.), *Contemporary play therapy: Theory, research, and practice* (pp. 186–211). New York: Guilford.

Knell, S. (1993a). *Cognitive–behavioral play therapy.* Northvale, NJ: Jason Aronson.

Knell, S. (1993b). To show and not tell: Cognitive–behavioral play therapy. In T. Kottman & C. Schaefer (Eds.), *Play therapy in action: A casebook for practitioners* (pp. 169–208). Northvale, NJ: Jason Aronson.

Knell, S. (1994). Cognitive–behavioral play therapy. In K. O'Connor & C. Schaefer (Eds.), *Handbook of play therapy: Vol 2. Advances and innovations* (pp. 111–142). New York: Wiley.

Knell, S. (1997). Cognitive–behavioral play therapy. In K. O'Connor & L. M. Braverman (Eds.), *Play therapy theory and practice: A comparative presentation* (pp. 79–99). New York: Wiley.

Knell, S. (2000). Cognitive-behavioral play therapy for childhood fears and phobias. In H. Kaduson & C. Schaefer (Eds.), *Short-term play therapy for children* (pp. 3–27). New York: Guilford.

Koller, T. (1994). Adolescent Theraplay. In K. O'Connor & C. Schaefer (Eds.), *Handbook of play therapy: Vol 2. Advances and innovations* (pp. 159–188). New York: Wiley

Koller, T., & Booth, P. (1997). Fostering attachment through family Theraplay. In K. O'Connor & L. M. Braverman (Eds.), *Play therapy theory and practice: A comparative presentation* (pp. 204–233). New York: Wiley.

Kot, S., & Tyndall-Lind, A. (2005). Intensive play therapy with child witnesses of domestic violence. In L. Reddy, T. Files-Hall, & C. Schaefer (Eds.), *Empirically based play interventions for children* (pp. 31–49). Washington, DC: American Psychological Association.

Kottman, T. (1993). The king of rock and roll. In T. Kottman & C. Schaefer (Eds.), *Play therapy in action: A casebook for practitioners* (pp. 133–167). Northvale, NJ: Jason Aronson.

Kottman, T. (1994). Adlerian play therapy. In K. O'Connor & C. Schaefer (Eds.), *Handbook of play therapy: Vol. 2. Advances and innovations* (pp. 3–26). New York: Wiley.

Kottman, T. (1997). Building a family: Play therapy with adopted children and their parents. In H. Kaduson, D. Cangelosi, & C. Schaefer (Eds.), *The playing cure: Individual play therapy for specific childhood problems* (pp. 337–370). Northvale, NJ: Jason Aronson.

Kottman, T. (2001). *Play therapy: Basics and beyond.* New York: Guilford.

Kottman, T. (2002). Billy, the teddy bear boy. In L. Golden (Ed.), *Case studies in child and adolescent counseling* (3rd ed., pp. 8–20). Columbus, OH: Merrill Prentice Hall.

Kottman, T. (2003). *Partners in play: An Adlerian approach to play therapy* (2nd ed). Alexandria, VA: American Counseling Association.

Landreth, G. (1991). *Play therapy: The art of the relationship.* Muncie, IN: Accelerated Development.

Landreth, G. (2002). *Play therapy: The art of the relationship* (2nd ed.). New York: Brunner-Routledge.

Landreth, G., & Sweeney, D. (1997). Child-centered play therapy. In K. O'Connor & L.M. Braverman (Eds.), *Play therapy theory and practice. A comparative presentation* (pp. 17–45). New York: Wiley.

Lawrence, M., Condon, K., Jacobi, K., & Nicholson, E. (2006). Play therapy for girls displaying social aggression. In C.E. Schaefer & H.G. Kaduson (Eds.), *Contemporary play therapy* (pp. 212–237). New York: Guilford.

LeBlanc, M., & Richie, M. (2001). A meta-analysis of play therapy outcomes. *Counseling Psychology Quarterly, 14*(2), 149–163.

Luke, M. (2003). A catalyst: Play therapy with adolescents. *International Journal of Play Therapy, 12*(2). 11–12.

Marschak, M. (1960). A method for evaluating child–parent interaction under controlled conditions. *Journal of Genetic Psychology, 97,* 3–22.

Muro, J., & Kottman, T. (1995). *Guidance and counseling in the elementary and middle schools: A practical approach.* Dubuque, IA: Brown & Benchmark.

O'Connor, K. (1993). Child, protector, confidant: Structured group ecosystemic play therapy, In T. Kottman & C. Schaefer (Eds.), *Play therapy in action: A casebook for practitioners* (pp. 245–282). Northvale, NJ: Jason Aronson.

Packman, J., & Bratton, S. (2003). A school-based group play/activity therapy intervention with learning disabled preadolescents exhibiting behavior problems. *International Journal of Play Therapy, 12*(2), 7–29.

Pedro-Carroll, J., & Jones, S. (2005). A preventive play intervention to foster children's resilience in the aftermath of divorce. In L. Reddy, T. Files-Hall, & C. Schaefer (Eds.), *Empirically based play interventions for children* (pp. 51–75). Washington, DC: American Psychological Association.

Ray, D., Bratton, S., Rhine, T., & Jones, L. (2001). The effectiveness of play therapy: Responding to the critics. *International Journal of Play Therapy, 10*(1), 85–108.

Reddy, L., Spencer, P., Hall, T., & Rubel, E. (2001). Use of developmentally appropriate games in a child group training program for young children with attention-deficit/hyperactivity disorder. In A. Drewes, L. Carey, & C. Schaefer (Eds.), *School-based play therapy* (pp. 256–276). New York: John Wiley and Sons.

Reid, S. (1993). It's all in the game: Game play therapy. In T. Kottman & C. Schaefer (Eds.), *Play therapy in action: A casebook for practitioners* (pp. 527–560). Northvale, NJ: Jason Aronson.

Rogers, C. (1959). A theory of therapy, personality, and interpersonal relationships as developed in the client-centered framework. In S. Koch (Ed.), *Psychology: A study of a science. Study L Conceptual and systematic: Vol. 3. Formulation of the person and social context* (pp. 184–256). New York: McGraw Hill.

Ryan, V. (2004). Adapting non-directive play therapy for children with attachment disorder. *Clinical Child Psychology and Psychiatry, 9*(1), 75–87.

Schaefer, C. (Ed.). (2002). *Play therapy with adults*. New York: Wiley.

Shen, Y.–J. (2002). Short-term group play therapy with Chinese earthquake victims: Effects on anxiety, depression, and adjustment. *International Journal of Play Therapy, 10*(2), 43–64.

Spasaro, S., & Schaefer, C. (Eds.). (2004). *Refusal to speak: Treatment of selective mutism in children*. Lanham, MI: Rowman & Littlefield.

Thompson, C., & Henderson, D. (2006). *Counseling children* (7th ed.). Pacific Grove, CA: Wadsworth.

VanFleet, R. (2000). Short-term play therapy for families with chronic illness. In H. Kaduson & C. Schaefer (Eds.), *Short-term play therapy for children* (pp. 175–193). New York: Guilford.

VanFleet, R. (2003). Short-term filial therapy for families with chronic illness. In R. VanFleet & L. Guerney (Eds.), *Casebook of filial therapy* (pp. 65–84). Boiling Springs, PA: Play Therapy Press.

Brief Counseling in Action With Children and Adolescents

John M. Littrell and Kirk Zinck

In an entertaining evening performance by the humorist Tom Bodett, he told about his personal adventures that began after he left college. As it turned out, Tom offered us, beyond entertainment, useful insights for conceptualizing counseling with children and adolescents.

Tom opened his act by reaching into a small wooden box on the table and pulling out a stack of 12 pink cards, each labeled with a key word or phrase. As he explained how a bolt of electricity passed through his body when he climbed to the top of a telephone pole, he threw the cards into the air. Large, pink snowflakes descended to the stage. Tom asked members of the audience to come on stage and randomly point to specific cards. As each person pointed to a card, Tom picked it up, reflected for a moment, and told the story associated with the words written on that card. By the end of the evening, no more pink cards remained on the floor. Tom had told 12 stories, one for each card.

He explained how a bolt of some sort often strikes us. The bolt produces both entrance and exit wounds. Between its entrance and exit, the bolt jumbles and tumbles things out of order. For Tom, tossing the cards into the air represented a bolt that created chaos. Reassembling the cards in a new way was a creative act made possible by the cooperation of Tom and his audience. The parts of Tom's larger story had been reassembled, in this case by random chance. Each of us in the audience heard the disjointed short stories, and we successfully wove them into a coherent larger story. Tom and the audience had experienced together the breaking of a pattern and then worked cooperatively to create new patterns.

Just like the cards scattered over the floor, the order and meaning of life often are strewn about when a bolt hits. The children and adolescents with whom counselors work have entrance and exit wounds—divorcing parents, physical abuse, suicide of friends, blended families, eating disorders, and so forth. They commonly struggle with typical developmental problems such as peer relationships, identity issues, and achievement, to name but a few. When we ask children and adolescents to tell us their stories, they do so in blown-apart fragments, similar to the way Tom Bodett told his story. Unlike the pieces of a shattered vase, which can be put back together like the pieces of a jigsaw puzzle, Bodett's fragments and those of our clients are fragments of meaning that must be put together in a new way.

The children and adolescents we see are struggling with familiar patterns that have been blown apart. Crisis bolts create chaos. Our job as counselors is to assist children and adolescents in creating new and more workable patterns from the shattered fragments of meaning. Bodett's performance provided a model for how, regardless of the entrance and exit wounds, the fragments of meaningful patterns can be collected, reassembled, reorganized, fashioned, constructed, molded, shaped, and understood in many different ways.

Two insights emerged from Tom Bodett's performance that counselors might find useful in helping children and adolescents.

1. Counselors can view the material that clients bring us as fragments of formerly meaningful patterns—often small patterns that worked at one time but no longer do. Meaningful patterns have exploded in clients' lives. The usefulness of the patterns has been shattered. Young people are asking for assistance in creating new patterns that will work in their lives. They want help in putting back what the bolt has jumbled beyond their abilities to repair, to mend, to make whole once again. Initially, clients are unaware that the bolt has rendered impossible a return to the former way of life, and part of our challenge is to help children and youth begin to create new patterns.

2. Life's patterns can be put together in many ways. Bodett began by using a random disruption approach. He assumed that as his audience listened to his stories, we would be able to refashion a larger and more coherent story. His act of throwing the cards and then presenting the small stories in a random fashion guaranteed that the larger story would be reconstructed anew. Although brief counseling avoids the randomness of thrown cards, it echoes his approach in that it breaks away from traditional ways of approaching clients' stories, which often are linear and chronological.

In this chapter we continue to explore how to help children and adolescents by focusing on eight defining characteristics of brief counseling. We illustrate these characteristics as they manifest themselves in three counseling cases.

Characteristics of Brief Counseling

Brief counseling is (a) time-limited, (b) solution-focused, (c) action-based, (d) socially interactive, (e) detail-oriented, (f) humor-eliciting, (g) developmentally attentive, and (h) relationship-based. These eight characteristics define brief counseling as a unique approach (Littrell, 1998). When counselors holistically integrate these eight characteristics into their practice, they can help clients more swiftly alleviate their discomfort and reach their desired states (Littrell, Malia, & Vanderwood, 1995).

Time Limited

School counselors necessarily have been constrained by a limited time within which to do counseling, yet the counseling models presented in graduate school programs often do not reflect the reality of the schools in which counselors will work. Today, managed care has affected the mental health counseling field in a similar way. The brevity to which we refer ranges from a single 10-minute session to five sessions. The brief counseling approach is designed to produce effects in a limited time.

Solution Focused

All solutions are temporary because life continues to present new challenges. Yet, brief counselors find that focusing on solutions is a more productive way to approach issues than dwelling on problems. Seeking solutions generates and mobilizes people's resources and inspires hope. Therefore, brief counselors emphasize what works rather than what does not work in clients' lives.

In brief counseling, counselors assist clients by focusing on three areas: (a) exceptions to the problem (Selekman, 1993), (b) untapped resources, and (c) goals (Littrell & Angera, 1998; Zinck & Littrell, 2002). By emphasizing what clients do that works, instances when clients are not stuck, brief counselors help clients discover how every so often they engage in patterns that are exceptions to their problem states (De Jong & Berg, 1998). Effective interventions accent successful exceptions to encourage clients to do more of what works.

Because exceptions to problems are a potent source of information, brief counselors repeatedly ask questions such as: "When is this not a problem for you?" "How did you do that?" Often clients are amazed when they think about the times their problems were nonexistent or diminished. Usually they have dwelled exclusively on the problem parts of their lives and have failed to notice when these problems are not present.

Brief counselors also guide clients toward their future. Counselors and clients set concrete goals as a way of clarifying clients' desired states. The concreting process shows clients that the future is fluid and that many futures are possible. As new choices become evident, clients begin to experience freedom from being stuck. For some, setting goals is liberating, and they know what they need to do to reach the goals. For others, goal setting is scary because they cannot see how to achieve the goals they have helped to set. These clients would benefit from tapping into their unused resources.

Clients often are unaware of the multitude of internal and external resources they can use to move from their present state to future states. Identifying resources assists clients in believing they can achieve their goals.

Action Based

Brief counselors believe that "client talk" does not equal "client action," and that action is needed before the client will change. Therefore, brief counselors often provide clients with new experiences as quickly as possible. These new experiences let clients know that new patterns of behavior are possible, and hope emerges. Two highly effective methods to provide clients with new experiences are giving directives and assigning tasks.

Socially Interactive

Clients and those around them powerfully influence one another in reciprocal ways. Brief counselors utilize these reciprocal interactions by tapping into need-satisfying qualities of socially supportive relationships. Changes come about more readily when other people support them. Brief counselors help clients utilize others in the change process.

Detail Oriented

Rather than asking for details of what is not working in a client's life, brief counselors ask for details about what *is* working, what the client wants, and what will propel the client to his or her goal. Brief counselors are intrigued by details of their clients' resources, strengths, abilities, and talents and how these will be brought to bear on creating and maintaining new patterns. In short, brief counselors explore in detail what already works, clients' desired states, and methods to reach those desired states.

Humor Eliciting

The indexes of counseling books seldom contain the words "fun," "humor," and "laughter." The notion that counseling always must be serious is a serious mistake. Because pain is a common response to problems, counselors and clients often have assumed that pain must continue while moving toward solutions. In brief counseling, counselors focus less on the pain and more on life-enhancing elements. Attention to the latter tends to bring forth the healing forces of laughter and humor, which are strong indicators of clients' strengths.

Developmentally Attentive

Many of the bolts that hit clients involve developmental growth. Transitions have a way of jumbling and tumbling clients' lives. Brief counselors step back from clients' struggles and listen for developmental themes and challenges. This larger perspective assists counselors in helping clients to construct new solutions that are sound for the developmental stage.

Brief counselors help clients meet the psychological human needs of love/belonging, power, freedom, and fun (Glasser, 1986). They help clients meet their needs for love/belonging by emphasizing the socially interactive nature of counseling (Littrell, Zinck, Nesselhuf, & Yorke, 1997). They help clients meet their needs for power by highlighting the clients' internal and external resources. They stress freedom by having clients continually make their own choices rather than continue to live by the dictates of their internalized "shoulds" or continue to respond unassertively to others' unreasonable demands. Finally, brief counselors help clients meet their need for fun by eliciting humor to solve problems and find solutions. Brief counselors recognize that clients' solutions work best when developmental perspectives and needs are acknowledged and embraced.

Relationship Based

A facilitative counseling relationship contributes considerably more to the success of counseling than do the techniques that counselors use (Sexton, Whiston, Bleuer, & Walz, 1997). Brief counselors, of course, possess and use skills specific to brief counseling but, even more important, they make sure they do not neglect their relationship with their clients. Caring for clients, counselor genuineness, and empathic understanding are not simply frills added to brief counseling techniques. They form a foundation of effective brief counseling.

The MRI Model

Many times, counselors do not have the opportunity to meet with a client for more than a few sessions. Brief counseling is a precise tool that has proven helpful in working within severely limited timeframes. The case of Sneaky Poo, which follows, lasted only one session with three follow-up phone calls, and a total time of about 1 hour. The third phone conversation indicated that the goals of this brief counseling intervention had been met. This case illustrates all eight characteristics of brief counseling (Littrell, 1998).

The brief counseling framework used in the case was developed by the Mental Research Institute (MRI) (Fisch, Weakland, & Segal, 1982; Watzlawick, Weakland, & Fisch, 1974). The MRI model has four steps (Watzlawick et al., 1974):

1. Clearly define the problem in concrete terms.
2. Investigate solutions the client has attempted so far.

3. Clearly define the concrete change to be achieved.
4. Form and implement a plan to produce this change.

To step 2 John Littrell added an exploration of exceptions to the pattern (de Shazer, 1988) and identification of the client's strengths (Littrell, 1998).

Sneaky Poo

Definition of the Problem

Melody phoned and asked if she could consult with me about her 4-year-old son, Randy. We set up a time to meet. During the opening moments of our counseling session, I explained to Melody the basic four-step MRI counseling framework. Then I asked her a question to elicit information about how she saw the problem. I worded the question "What are the most important aspects of this situation that I should be aware of?" deliberately to caution her not to tell me every detail. The question prompted Melody to sift through her understanding and provide the most essential information rather than to offer excruciating details. I acknowledged her thoughts and feelings about the situation but avoided spending too much time talking about them.

Melody told me that Randy still "messed" (wet and soiled) his pants regularly, a problem his 9-year-old sister did not have. This "messing" pattern was not of much concern to Randy, but it was a source of embarrassment and worry to his mother. In Melody's mind, Randy, not she, was the one with the problem.

In the MRI framework, one of the questions asked is: "Who is the customer?" Another wording could be, "Who is willing to work on the concern?" Although Melody perceived the person with the problem to be her son, she was the one who expressed the worry and concern. Therefore, I treated Melody, the parent, as the person who would be most willing to work on the problem. She was my client.

Attempted Solutions, Exceptions, and Strengths

As we entered the second stage of the MRI framework, "What are the client's attempted solutions?" I added a solution-focused question that pinpointed exceptions: When is this *not* a problem? I learned that Melody had been an expert in designing attempted solutions but, unfortunately, none of them had worked. Her most ingenious method had been to invent a game called "Potty Jeopardy." When Randy looked as if he were about to mess his pants, Melody immediately took him to the bathroom and had him sit on the toilet. If he proceeded to go, she offered profuse praise. Although it was a clever idea, Potty Jeopardy did not in practice change Randy's behavior. If Melody did not notice that Randy looked as if he should be heading to the bathroom, he made no attempt to go to the bathroom prior to messing his pants.

I asked Melody about exceptions to Randy's pattern. We discovered that occasionally Randy realized that something didn't feel quite right and he headed to the bathroom. Melody had picked up on this exception and subsequently talked to Randy about how he should go to the bathroom whenever he felt uncomfortable in that way. Melody's attempt to build on the exception met with additional failure.

Brief counselors continually look for clients' strengths. Two of Melody's strengths stood out prominently. First, she was doggedly persistent. Regardless of the frustrating problem situation, she persevered. She continued to look for solutions, illustrated by her seeking my help. Second, Melody had a delightful sense of humor, as evidenced by her inventing Potty Jeopardy. When I pointed out both of these strengths to Melody, she beamed.

Goal Setting

Within 10 minutes of starting our session, Melody and I began to make concrete her desired outcome. We acknowledged that Randy did not seem interested in changing his behavior. Therefore, we conceptualized my role as that of a consultant who would assist Melody in designing more options to bring about a change in Randy's behavior. Melody had to be more effective in "talking" a language that would make more sense to him and that would begin to convince him to change. From what Melody said, humor seemed to be an effective tool for communicating with Randy, but apparently Potty Jeopardy was not quite the right way.

Intervention

When thinking about ways of creating new patterns that will help clients reach their goals, brief counselors do not limit themselves. As Melody talked, I remembered a fascinating description I had read in Michael White and David Epston's (1990) *Narrative Means to Therapeutic Ends,* of how a therapist had helped a child overcome encopresis. The therapist had assisted 6-year-old Nick in defeating Sneaky Poo, who had a tendency to leave an "accident" or have an "incident."

Although I did not clearly remember all of the details in the case of Sneaky Poo, I did remember that the child had been taught to recognize that Sneaky Poo would come when he was least expecting it and make a mess in the boy's pants. The therapist had taught the boy to recognize when Sneaky Poo was coming and to defeat him by going to the bathroom.

Based on my recollection of the Sneaky Poo case, I talked with Melody about an action-based intervention to achieve her goal. I suggested that perhaps her son had to be a better detective (an age-appropriate task) to discover clues of when Sneaky Poo was coming. With those clues he could solve the mystery and catch Sneaky Poo.

In addition, I suggested that a detective would have to know what Sneaky Poo looked like before he left "brown balls and yellow water" in Randy's pants. I added, "Perhaps you and your son can draw a picture of what Sneaky Poo looks like." Because of her sense of humor and that of her son, Melody thought he might really go for this idea. Working together, Melody and I planned the details and discussed how she could carry out this assignment with Randy. The next day I spoke briefly on the phone with Melody, who related the following:

> I talked with Randy last night, and he was really excited about being a detective. I asked him what clues he would spot if Sneaky Poo were around. That's when Randy really surprised me. I had been saying to Randy that if he felt "pressure," that was a message to head to the bathroom. Randy told me that one of the clues would be that it felt "itchy." Then it hit me. I had been using my way of talking, but it hadn't made any sense to him. So now I started using his language of "itchy" to make more sense to him.

Melody and her son seemed to be on the right track, so I went to a bookstore and purchased an age-appropriate children's book about a small bear who acted as a detective looking for clues. I sent the book to Melody with a written homework assignment: "I suggest that you read this book to your son to prepare him to be the best detective in the world as he looks for clues." Melody wrote back, saying that the book and the idea sounded great.

A week later Melody and I talked on the phone for about 15 minutes. During the conversation, she said:

> After I received the book you sent, I decided to work with Randy by drawing a picture of Sneaky Poo. My daughter Sarah, Randy, and I had a picnic in the park, and I brought along crayons and paper. Sarah wanted to make a drawing, too, and that was all right with Randy. All three of us drew Sneaky Poo, and then we voted on which drawing looked the most like Sneaky Poo. We all agreed that Sarah's drawing won the prize. It was a brown figure with scary hands, and it was standing in a pool of yellow water. We were all laughing and having a good time.
>
> Then, last night I read Randy the children's book you gave me. He really liked it. We were just about done reading when Randy looked at me and said, "I think Sneaky Poo is coming." He went to the bathroom

by himself. I was so pleased with him. When he came back into the room, I said, "You're really getting to be a great detective." He smiled the biggest smile.

A follow-up phone call a month later confirmed that Randy had continued to be a "great detective." Melody said she was much more relaxed now that Randy had learned a needed skill. They kept the picture of Sneaky Poo for a back-up reminder if needed, but for now it was simply stored out of sight in Randy's dresser drawer.

Discussion

All eight characteristics of brief counseling found expression in Sneaky Poo Revisited. The characteristics appeared not as separate elements but, instead, as part of a coherent and systematic framework.

1. *Time limited*: We met for only one session, with three follow-up phone calls. The total time was less than 1 hour.
2. *Solution focused*: Melody and I focused on (a) the key exceptions to the problem that Randy had exhibited, (b) Melody's resources of humor and persistence, and (c) Melody's goals.
3. *Action based*: My directives to make a drawing, read a book, and search for clues all served to have Melody and Randy doing something about the situation.
4. *Socially interactive*: Melody involved not only Randy but also Randy's sister in the solution.
5. *Detail oriented*: The drawing of Sneaky Poo, the instructions to find clues, and avoiding "brown balls and yellow water" in Randy's pants are all details focusing on solutions, not the problem.
6. *Humor eliciting*: Melody's description of Potty Jeopardy and the family activity of drawing Sneaky Poo added warm humor to a frustrating problem.
7. *Developmentally attentive*: Recognizing Randy's need to master a developmental task and using the age-appropriate detective book and accompanying task to look for clues indicated attention to developmental stages.
8. *Relationship based*: Even though I didn't ever see Randy or his sister, I did establish and maintain a solid working relationship with their mother. She used her relationship skills within the family to help Randy create a new, age-appropriate pattern.

In the next case, Tim Sumerlin assisted an adolescent to regain his academic motivation and overcome his self-defeating behavior at home and in the classroom environment. As in Sneaky Poo case, this case includes all eight characteristics of brief counseling and explores exceptions to the problem.

Focusing on Matt's Strengths

Definition of the "Problem"

Matt had been on my "radar screen" for 2 years. He was a quiet, talented, and unmotivated 12th grader at a local suburban high school in Colorado. He was performing far below his natural talent and abilities, and not graduating was a serious possibility. Matt lived in the shadow of his older brother, Lance, an academically high-performing, vibrant student, who became a National Merit Finalist and attended a top-flight university.

During the past 2 years I had received phone calls and emails from Matt's parents and teachers, who were concerned about his grades, attitude, and lack of effort at home and in the classroom. They described him as moody and sullen. Despite his parents' and teachers' best efforts, tensions remained high in the home over his almost failing grades. Matt's older brother had been a model student at the same high school several years before, and Matt's parents believed he had "failed to measure up" to Lance's record. Matt was acutely aware of how adults compared him to his older brother. I received a plethora of negative pleas from Matt's parents for me to "fix" their son. An email from Matt's father stated:

> I am very concerned that Matt has simply given up and is deluding himself that it does not matter. I don't know what the problem is, as he won't open up to anyone. He simply has convinced himself that nothing matters. I think that only a very tough approach will work. He has to face reality. He won't listen to us, but he will listen to you because he respects you. Anything you can come up with would be most appreciated.

I felt the need to step up my involvement and help Matt. I hoped for positive change.

Attempted Solutions, Exceptions, and Strengths

After a discussion with Matt's mother, during which she was both negative and emotional, I decided that Matt needed an ally to work with him. Someone had to be there for Matt to emphasize his strengths and successes instead of his weaknesses and problems. The danger was that I believed Matt would see me as his parents' agent and just another authority figure by my sharing their messages with him. If I were to succeed in creating an atmosphere of hope and optimistic expectations, I had to do something different.

With a caseload of more than 400 students, my high school setting allows for only time-limited counseling sessions. Of necessity, the sessions have to be solution focused and goal oriented. I resolved to help Matt change his future by (a) becoming independent of expectations that arose from comparisons with his brother, and (b) breaking the pattern associated with Matt's self-defeating response to his parents' negativity.

Because I perceived that Matt viewed me as another parent in his life—someone to tell him what to do—my first task with Matt was to knock down some walls and build an alliance with him. We spent our first session talking about his goals after graduating from high school. I asked him, "If your parents were a non-factor in your life, what would you be doing after high school?"

Matt's eyes lit up, and he began to discuss his love of photography and the arts. Despite the promising start, though, our discussion turned negative when at one point Matt stated, "I can't measure up to Lance, so why even try?"

I knew that Matt was an entirely different student than Lance, but I wanted Matt to begin making that distinction. While Lance seemed to excel effortlessly, Matt worked hard for every grade he received. When courses proved difficult and the pressure at home increased, Matt grew sullen and hid the reality of his schoolwork. By the end of the first session, we had talked about how different Matt and Lance were, how those differences were to be honored as special and unique, how Matt really did care about his future and was concerned where it was headed.

The respectful position of brief, solution-focused counseling allows for open and honest discussions that are able to move in the direction of taking responsibility for one's actions and eliciting solutions. These discussions do not examine a problem in excruciating detail. I turned to Matt's interests in the arts, his ideal of creating a future for himself independent of his parents, and the goal of graduating from high school and attending college in the fall.

My own goals with Matt were threefold: (a) to build rapport and trust, (b) to help him understand his parents' concern for him apart from the negative environment in the home, and (c) to enhance his sense of power, belonging, freedom, and fun within the context of counseling.

During our first session we had an agreeable and evocative, if somewhat cautious, conversation. I did succeed in building some rapport, however. Matt began to separate me from being his parents' agent.

In a second meeting with Matt, I began asking questions regarding his specific goals and aspirations, such as the following:

- Where do you want to be five years from now?
- What would that look like?
- What are some steps you can see yourself doing today to get there?
- What is it about you that really wants to do these things?

I worked to move Matt into a position where he would focus on his personal goals independent of his family's expectations. I felt as if he were yearning for a chance to stand on his own two feet and yet was being hounded constantly by his parents to perform at a level comparable to his brother. We discussed the times in his life when he did very well in school. I asked him, "What did that look like?" Even though Matt was taking challenging classes, it became apparent to him that motivation to succeed was the problem for him, not the rigor of the coursework.

By the end of our second session, Matt was talking about the "good old days" when life was "simple" and when he actually enjoyed school. Matt became engaged in this conversation, and I quickly saw another side of him—an intelligent, talented, caring person. These characteristics remained hidden when his parents confronted him to do better academically. We concluded our session by setting two specific goals: (1) to complete urgent assignments in classes, and (2) to have a conversation with his brother, who was home for the holidays.

The third time I met with Matt, we discussed his specific goals from our last conversation regarding his academics and how to navigate his parents' wishes and desires for him. Because Matt now was spending the needed time working on his assignments, we proceeded to the topic of his family. Matt discussed a conversation he had with his brother in the past week and how it had helped him to be "more of my own person."

Next our conversation turned to his parents. Matt's mode of dealing with their pressure was to shut down, hide from his parents, and lie about his grades. Naturally, calls from caring teachers and report cards in the mail doomed this strategy. We made a distinction between how what his parents wanted for him was born of a concern and care for his success and how they expressed that in a problematic way. How could an independent, motivated Matt help his parents to "back off" and allow him to make his own decisions?

I emphasized Matt's strengths by offering statements such as, "I'm amazed at your ability to do well in school when you want to" and, "I'm impressed about how resourceful you've been over the years, considering some of the challenges at home." Matt seemed to genuinely appreciate and thrive on my sincere comments. He agreed that he was usually a competent student and enjoyed the times he had been successful in school. He agreed to begin having more honest conversations with his parents.

Goal Setting

Clinical experience and research support the idea that, regardless of the complexity of a problem, a small behavioral change often is sufficient to bring about rapid, profound, and lasting change for an individual or a family (de Shazer, 1988; Maurer 2004; Littrell, 1998). With this in mind,

I expected that small changes in Matt's thinking and behavior might re-ignite the passion and talent he had previously displayed in his academic work.

Matt came up with a plan to have an honest, calm discussion with his brother, parents, and teachers to talk about his change of attitude and his plans for the future after high school. Further discussions with Matt allowed him to explore his own goals and motivations, especially in the area of photography. Matt started demonstrating a determination to "fight his own battles" and regain his work ethic.

Interventions

With Matt's permission I continued to communicate with his parents and teachers via email regarding his academic progress but protected other aspects of our conversations. I believed it was important to allow Matt to stand on his own two feet in these areas. But I did ask his teachers and parents to let me know when they saw Matt's attitude toward his academic work improving. Emails became an important part of this process for two reasons. First, I wanted Matt to know of my desire to help him to navigate these relationships. Second, I wanted to communicate to his teachers and parents a different way to look at Matt. I wanted them to focus on his strengths and abilities instead of his weaknesses. Because he already had academic ability, his grades improved dramatically and Matt quickly found himself receiving mostly A's—even in an Advanced Placement class.

As is often the case in a high school setting, when we see appreciable change in a student, we move on quickly to other "crisis" situations. Matt's progress report showed vast improvement and, honestly, for a few weeks I did not see or think much about him.

I was impressed with Matt's improvements that his mother reported when we visited during the Spring Parent and Teacher Night. She told me about Matt's meaningful changes at home and in the classroom and how happy they were to see him motivated and looking forward to majoring in photography when he started college. Unbeknownst to me, Matt had taken it upon himself to visit the college and arrange for admittance. His mom thanked me for "whatever you said" that helped him change. I assured her that it was Matt's attitude and motivation that had led to the changes.

Two more months passed, and I was in my office gathering items to take home for the summer break. Graduation ceremonies had just ended, and I looked up to see a beaming Matt in my doorway, wearing his purple graduation gown. Matt had dropped by to thank me for all our "good talks" and for "helping me to get though this last year."

All eight characteristics of brief counseling were evident in this case.

1. *Time limited*: Matt and I met for three sessions and had a few follow-up email conversations.
2. *Solution focused*: We focused on (a) previous times of academic success, (b) his resources of relationship negotiation, humor, academic capability, and persistence in carrying out tasks, and (c) his goals for the future.
3. *Action based*: The intervention involved Matt's recovering his academic motivation and having honest conversations with his parents.
4. *Socially interactive*: Though the immediate focus was on Matt's grades, we discussed family relationships and dynamics.
5. *Detail oriented*: We explored Matt's strengths in detail, and exceptions to the problem. The interventions consisted of specific academic changes and how to conduct positive conversations with his parents.
6. *Humor eliciting*: Both Matt and I used humor to reduce some of the tensions he felt from home and to normalize his adolescent development. We laughed about my being an "agent" of his parents.
7. *Developmentally attentive*: The intervention attended to both family and individual development as Matt was making a major developmental transition and the balance in the parent–child relationship was shifting (Becvar & Becvar, 2005).
8. *Relationship based*: Sensing Matt's need for an ally, we formed a friendship style of conversation, which allowed Matt to relate to an adult without feeling the pressure to conform. Discussing Matt's strengths and successes allowed him to be open to the change he desired.

Cultural Considerations

In our final case, Kirk Zinck works with an adolescent who is struggling with how to grieve in a culturally sanctioned manner. As with the other two cases, this one illustrates all eight characteristics of brief counseling and employs the MRI model. The major challenge here is to design interventions that are culturally responsive.

Culture is a complex concept, yet a basic definition offered by Morris and Robinson (1996) will suffice for this discussion. They defined culture as "a frame of reference from which we encounter ourselves, the world, and life" (p. 51).

Cultural Bias

Predominant counseling practices are rooted firmly in the values of European–American middle-class culture (Lee, 2001). Norms by which behavior and attitudes are interpreted adhere to European–American values, with little tolerance for cultural practices that differ from that dominant paradigm. Limitations imposed by this viewpoint may introduce cultural bias into the counseling relationship.

Cultural bias also results from common practices such as ignoring the influence of culture on clients, assigning people to a cultural group based on their appearance, or generalizing certain behaviors and beliefs to all members of a cultural group, with little allowance for variation among individuals and subgroups (Garrett, 1999; Ivey & Ivey, 2006; Lee, 2001; Thomason, 1991). In short, a culturally biased worldview confines normative behavior and attitudes within the parameters of a specific culture. It ignores variations in context, history, level of acculturation, and life experiences within a group of people (Garrett, 1999). In contrast, a culturally responsive worldview allows for variation among the members of any group.

The European–American paradigm is founded on several assumptions about what is normal and socially desirable. Accepting these assumptions may inhibit one's sensitivity to cultural norms, traditions, and beliefs of other cultural groups (Lokken & Twohey, 2004). Morris and Robinson (1996) included, among these assumptions, individualism; small, independent family structures; highly verbal communication; material goods as symbolic of power and status; deemphasis on heritage; a culture-specific view of determinants of "normal" behavior; and highly structured use of time. To these we would add emotional expression (Constantine & Gainor, 2001), open self-disclosure, and the rapid development of trust (Garrett, 1999; Thomason, 1991).

Lee (2001) suggested that people seeking to remedy cultural bias begin with a self-examination of their "cultural blind spots" (p. 262). Many cultural belief systems contradict the European–American worldview. Typical differences include valuing interdependence and connection among all members of the group, viewing independence as detrimental to communal welfare, the prominent use of observation and nonverbal means of communication (Garrett, 1999; Lokken & Twohey, 2004; Turner, Conkel, Reich, Trotter, & Siewart, 2006), and a concept of family as extending beyond biological and nuclear boundaries. Time, viewed as a commodity in European–American culture, is considered plentiful and "impossible to waste" in many cultures (Garrett, 1999; Morris & Robinson, 1996; Thomason, 1991). Further, problem solving may be based on immediate circumstances instead of past or future behavior (Garrett, 1999; Morris & Robinson, 1996; Thomason, 1991).

Expression of emotions also varies. While much of European–American society values cathartic expression in counseling and promotes open self-disclosure, less dominant cultures may lack the words to describe strong emotions, and emotional restraint may be the expected norm (Constantine & Gainor, 2001). Trust is earned over an extended time, despite one's title or position (A. Seville, personal communication, June 10, 2001; Garrett, 1999; Morris & Robinson, 1996).

Cultural Responsiveness

Culturally responsive counseling incorporates interventions that are matched to the client's cultural orientation. Yet, research has demonstrated that three aspects of

the counseling process have been accorded more importance than providing culturally matched interventions (Constantine, 2001a; 2001b; Garrett, 1999; Duncan &
Miller, 2000): (a) the counselor–client relationship, (b) developmentally appropriate
interventions, and (c) counselor flexibility in setting a context, defining problems,
and developing solutions.

Matching interventions to culture requires learning about a client's expectations of counseling and his or her beliefs about what conditions are necessary for
change (Becvar, 2007). Matching may involve appropriately pacing the session,
learning and observing cultural norms or taboos, consulting with traditional healers, and incorporating pertinent rituals within the counseling process. A counselor
must take time to learn which practices and beliefs regarding problems, healing,
and change are important to the client. Clients from minority cultures face a need
to resolve problems in ways that fit both their own culture and the dominant culture
(Garrett, 1999). To resolve problems, cross-cultural clients must develop "bicultural
competencies."

The counselor–client relationship is the foundation upon which change is co-
constructed. According to Duncan and Miller (2000), this relationship accounts for
30% of the contribution to change. Anderson's (1997) collaborative language systems (CLS) is effective across many cultures. In CLS the relationship is primary, as
counselor and client co-create new meanings through a therapeutic conversation that
promotes change. Constantine (2001a) found that theoretical orientation aside, a
counselor whom clients perceive as empathic "is likely to develop effective working
relationships with these individuals, resulting in potentially beneficial counseling
outcomes" (p. 343). Empathy is the communication of caring and understanding
regarding another person's experiences (Constantine, 2001b).

Developmentally appropriate interventions consider a person's stage of development, intellectual functioning, and attention span (Vernon, 2002). These interventions are collaborative in nature and may involve supportive others such as parents,
teachers, family members, or friends. This fits the interdependent character of many
nondominant cultures in which problem resolution is accomplished in a communal
context (Constantine, 2001a; Turner et al., 2006).

Garrett (1999) emphasized the importance of developmental intervention. His
work with Native American youths established that their passage through adolescence is marked by commonalities with other distinct cultures and that the developmental match of counseling interventions is much more important than a cultural
match.

Counselor flexibility refers to the ability to incorporate a variety of conceptual-
izations and treatment strategies with diverse client populations. Flexibility makes
an important contribution to cross-cultural effectiveness (Constantine, 2001b). A
final aspect of cultural responsiveness is multicultural competence, which is
enhanced by extensive multicultural training (Constantine, 2001a, 2001b) and the
counselor's ability to acknowledge and understand the normalcy and significance of
interdependence and ecological connectedness among cultural groups that fall outside of the European–American paradigm.

Making Brief Counseling Culturally Responsive

Much of the aptitude to respond effectively in cross-cultural contexts rests with a counselor's ability to look beyond dominant cultural assumptions (Lee, 2001), to develop a strong relationship with clients (Becvar, 2007; Duncan & Miller, 2000; Garrett, 1999; Thomason, 1991), and to be flexible (Constantine, 2001a, 2001b; Constantine & Gainor, 2001; Thomason, 1991). Empathic skill (Constantine 2001a, 2001b; Duncan & Miller, 2000) and cross-cultural training (Constantine 2001a; 2001b) are also important. These attributes form the foundation upon which counselors can modify and adapt their approach to make it culturally responsive.

In seeking solutions that fit the individual, brief counseling is readily adaptable to the needs of clients from varied cultures (Sklare, 2005). Four of the eight characteristics of brief counseling (Littrell, 1998) are especially pertinent to creating a culturally responsive approach: being socially interactive, developmentally attentive, detail-oriented, and relationship-based. In its attention to these factors, brief counseling is culturally responsive.

The socially interactive aspect of brief counseling enables the counselor to match interventions to the interdependence of many cultural groups. It emphasizes defining and incorporating support and affirmation from the people who inhabit the client's world. The brief counselor often asks, "Who will be the first to notice a change and comment on it?" or "What potential solutions have other people suggested to you?" These kinds of questions lend themselves to developing and involving a community of concerned persons (Freedman & Combs, 1996) in resolving a problem.

As a developmentally attentive intervention, brief counseling addresses problems at the client's level of understanding and capability. Brief counseling is flexible in the attention to details regarding what has worked or is working for the client, what might work, and what will advance the client to his or her goal. In bringing a client's unique resources to bear upon a problem, each intervention is "custom-tailored." One size does not fit all. Finally, because the counselor–client relationship is the foundation for all effective counseling, the brief counselor takes special care to nurture a strong and positive relationship with the client.

Myron

■■■■Definition of the Problem

Myron was stunned. He had just learned of his grandfather's death. This 14-year-old Alaskan Native student was in foster care in a city. Removed from immediate contact with his village and the traditional guidance of village elders, Myron sought me out. As he began coping with his grandfather's death, Myron wanted support and assistance to determine how to mourn his grandfather's passing appropriately and acknowledge the importance of this event with his family and his village community. In most native communities, elders guide their people through the unique blend of cultural traditions and spiritual practices associated with mourning. Removed from his village, Myron was isolated from this guidance, as well as the communal practices that mark the passing of a villager.

As his school counselor, I had enrolled Myron upon his arrival in the city. Intimidated and shy, he entered a school with a student population three times larger than he had left in his village. His foster parent asked me to look after him at school, and I did so willingly.

Unfortunately, court-ordered foster placement in the city left him isolated from the world and the people he knew. His home was a small village where 95% of the inhabitants are native, and most related by blood or marriage. Far from major settlements or roads, the village is seasonally accessible by boat, small plane, or snow machine. In his present circumstances, someone he could connect with—even a relative stranger of a different culture—was desirable. Myron and I had connected at school, and over 3 months our relationship developed into a caring camaraderie.

Now, over the course of four counseling sessions, Myron and I addressed his distress and grief. We looked for ways of expression that were culturally appropriate for him. In his world, when a villager dies, people pull together in support of the immediate family and honor the deceased through established rituals and traditions. As a cultural group, Myron's people share many commonalities, yet villages or small groups of villages in close proximity are cultures in themselves. Language, traditions, and religious practices vary considerably. My cultural responsiveness as a counselor did not equate to knowledge of practices specific to a village. Thus, part of the task ahead was for the two of us to call on his memories of village traditions and to identify any knowledgeable people in his present context to guide him.

Myron and I defined the problems posed by the death of his grandfather: attending the funeral, avoiding trouble, and honoring his deceased grandfather. Many native communities function as an extended family. The death of a village elder brings obligations and traditions that all villagers must observe. Removed from the guidance of village elders, Myron was confused regarding how to honor and mourn the deceased grandfather appropriately.

Attempted Solutions

When he first arrived at my office that morning, Myron did not explain what he wanted. He was distressed about his grandfather's passing and bewildered about how to respond. He expressed a desire to return to his village for the funeral but did not ask me for assistance. He indicated that he did not hold much hope that he would be allowed to travel back to his village. Seeking out the counselor was an attempt to come to terms with his dilemma and stoically verbalize his distress and grief in a supportive, private context. Direct attempts at a solution had been minimal, and Myron had not discussed this situation with his foster parents. Had he been among his own people, a direct request for assistance would have been unnecessary. The villagers simply would have understood and responded to Myron's needs.

Myron's initial response in not making any specific requests was culturally congruent (Turner et. al., 2006), yet unworkable in the predominantly European–American cultural context of his foster care placement. This had an impact on the resolution of his problem. Presenting problems often have a rich history of contemplated, suggested, and attempted solutions to consider when counselor and client join to construct a workable solution, but Myron and I had to develop a solution quickly through brainstorming and networking with other people. We had 2 days to make things happen if Myron were to attend the funeral.

Goal Setting, and Exceptions to the Problem

Having participated in a joint definition of the problems that Myron faced, I facilitated exploration of possible goals. Drawing upon Myron's experience and memories of similar situations in his past, we brainstormed goals in the three problem areas. First, Myron and I identified who must be contacted for permission to attend the funeral and determined how to approach them and request permission and funding to travel.

If permitted to attend the funeral, a related problem presented itself. He had been placed in therapeutic foster care through the juvenile justice system because he was in trouble in his village, stemming from his use of alcohol. Returning to his home would place Myron in a context where he would encounter all the old temptations to drink and engage in other illegal activity. Focusing on the probability that he had also resisted temptation (exceptions to the problem), I inquired about times when Myron had avoided getting into trouble in the village. He responded by describing times when certain people had influenced him positively. He went on to identify individuals who had helped him avoid trouble and households he could visit, where abstinence was the norm.

Finally, we brainstormed ways by which Myron could receive guidance and support on how to appropriately express his loss, his love for his grandfather, and an ongoing (spiritual) connection. He would have received this guidance automatically in the village, but in the context of his foster placement, culturally responsive guidance was not available. Because Myron would be in the village only a few days, we attempted to identify people who could provide ongoing and culturally responsive support after the funeral and upon his return to the foster placement.

▆▆Interventions

Our next step was to develop an action plan, in which Myron would request permission to travel home and attend the funeral. We listed the appropriate people to contact: foster parents, parole officer, and case worker. We reviewed what Myron would say to each of them. I suggested to Myron that he request his foster mother's assistance with making these contacts. As part of the intervention, Myron and I collaboratively planned how he would avoid trouble in the village. He briefly practiced explaining this plan as we anticipated that his probation officer and case worker would inquire about this. Finally, Myron and I discussed making arrangements with his teachers for his absence. Having secured Myron's agreement to make up missed schoolwork, I agreed to talk with his teachers about Myron's possible absence.

Time was short, and we had to move quickly to put the plan into action. Myron phoned his foster mother from my office and explained his desire to attend the funeral. He requested her immediate assistance in contacting the parole officer and the case worker. His foster mother agreed to help. We ended our session and agreed to meet the next morning.

By the next day, Myron and his foster mother had made the necessary contacts and secured permission and funding for him to make a 3-day trip. During a 30-minute session Myron and I reviewed how he would avoid trouble. We also reviewed his agreement to make up missed schoolwork after I informed him that his teachers would provide make-up work and assistance upon his return. We developed a plan for exiting a situation if uncontrolled drinking or some other form of potential trouble were to develop while he was in the village.

Myron, his foster mother (by phone), and I developed a behavioral contract. To solidify and make "public" his intent to avoid trouble (Anderson, 1997), Myron agreed to describe the contract to a trusted uncle and two other supportive people upon his arrival in the village. Making an agreement public tends to elicit communal support and increase a client's commitment to act accordingly (Freedman & Combs, 1996). Myron departed for his village early in the afternoon.

Following his return from the funeral, Myron and I met for a 20-minute session. He reported feeling relieved and grateful that he had been allowed to return to his village. During his visit Myron avoided trouble by requesting support from key people in the village and reviewing our behavioral contract. It had not been necessary to extract himself from a situation where trouble was developing because he conscientiously chose his associations and activities. We celebrated Myron's success with a handshake and some affirming statements.

Although Myron's return to the village satisfied his need to participate in a communal expression of grief, he wanted to honor his grandfather's memory with a personal expression. Recalling our earlier conversation about who could provide culturally appropriate guidance, Myron decided to seek advice from his art teacher. Although the teacher was from an Alaskan Native culture that differed from Myron's, the teacher was knowledgeable and sensitive to the broad cultural issues of native students in general. The teacher and Myron determined that it would be appropriate for Myron to carve a traditional wooden mask to be placed at the gravesite when Myron eventually would return to his village. The teacher offered to provide artistic and spiritual guidance, as traditional masks are personal and powerful expressions of spiritual connections.

In a final 20-minute check-in 2 weeks later, Myron reported feeling satisfied and peaceful with the process of carving a mask. Because I often visited the art room to talk with students and admire their art, I observed Myron's mask in progress. He also reported that his teachers had helped him catch up on what he had missed during his absence.

Over the remaining academic year I saw Myron informally in the hallways during lunch and between classes, in art class, or when he dropped by my office to chat or share a joke. Upon completing his court-ordered rehabilitation, Myron returned to his village, mask in hand.

Discussion

Culture is a way of knowing the world. It is a perspective that is temporally, contextually, and interactionally determined (H. Anderson, personal communication, April 12, 2001; Gergen, 2000). Brief counseling is adapted to individual needs because clients' perceptions guide problem definition, intervention, and action (Sklare, 2005). One aspect of cultural responsiveness is to adopt a "not knowing" stance such that the counselor is always in the process of becoming informed (Anderson, 1997). This allows clients to educate the counselor regarding their unique needs and ideas and theories about what makes change happen and what it looks like. This respectful stance and the emphasis on facilitating client-generated solutions make brief counseling effective across cultural settings.

Cultural responsiveness also included attention to Myron's speech patterns—a deliberate pace typical of rural native people—that cued me to be less verbal and slow down. As a friend of mine explained, "We native people take time to gather our thoughts before we speak" (M. Malchoff, personal communication, May 22, 2002). In comparison to non-native cultures, responses come slowly, so the counselor must be comfortable in allowing significant periods of silence. Responses usually are succinct. Among many native people, "Words are spiritually potent, generative, and…engaged in the continuum of the cosmos, not neutral and disengaged from it" (Suzuki & Knudtson, 1992, p. 78). Words are considered carefully before being spoken.

Another responsive aspect of the intervention was recognizing that mourning may be culturally specific. Myron sought to grieve in ways that fit his culture and satisfied what he knew and felt to be appropriate. Linking Myron with a native elder (the art teacher) provided some culturally informed guidance.

Further adaptation was necessary in planning for the influence of the village community on Myron. While traditional counseling centers on individuals or family units, most Alaskan Native societies are communal in nature, with powerful involvement of the community in childrearing that obliges all adults to model, protect, and correct. Although not all of them act responsibly, a core of adults generally assume broad parental responsibility. In jointly planning Myron's stay in his village, we addressed this communal influence in two ways: First, potentially problematic interactions were identified and a plan was developed to avoid or move away from them; and second, Myron agreed to seek out and interact with people who would affirm and support his efforts to avoid trouble and guide him in the healthy expression of grief.

This case is a specific example of using brief counseling in a cross-cultural context. It demonstrates that brief counseling can be adapted successfully to fit clients from non-Western cultures. Cultural responsiveness requires little modification of the model itself. Of major importance is that cultural responsiveness be linked to the quality of the relationship between counselor and client (Duncan & Miller, 2000; Ivey & Ivey, 2006; Littrell, 1998).

All eight characteristics of brief counseling found expression in the case of Myron. Once again, the characteristics appeared not as separate elements but, rather, as part of a coherent and systematic framework.

1. *Time limited*: We met for four sessions; total time was less than 2.5 hours.
2. *Solution focused*: Rather than looking to the past, the sessions revolved around what Myron wanted and how he could act in the here-and-now to attain his goals. We focused on (a) his knowledge of cultural practices and expectations, (b) identifying people who could assist him in realizing his goals of being present at the funeral and expressing grief in a culturally appropriate way, and (c) developing and acting on a goal.
3. *Action based*: The intervention involved rapid definition of the problem and goal and the immediate creation of a plan. To achieve his goals, Myron was active. He persuaded others to let him travel, negotiated how to avoid trouble, attended the funeral, carved a mask, and eventually delivered the mask to his grandfather's grave.
4. *Socially interactive*: Throughout the intervention the emphasis was on interdependence. Myron had to involve other people in several

contexts (e.g., key people in his village) to realize his multifaceted goal. Rather than left to chance, this support was utilized deliberately.

5. *Detail oriented*: As we worked together, Myron and I developed a detailed plan of action that met the unique requirements of his culture. Attention to detail is a trademark of brief counseling, as each intervention is tied to the individual, and in this case to communal needs and expectations. Individual tailoring resulted in a culturally responsive intervention.

6. *Humor eliciting*: Humor was not used in this intervention itself, but our previous relationship bond and prior interactions included shared humor.

7. *Developmentally attentive*: The intervention attended to the needs of a young man in transition between early and mid-adolescence. It was culturally attentive because it allowed Myron to participate in an important community ritual—taking his place as a young man in the village setting and meeting the appropriate expectations that he would be present and participating. The process also balanced direction and empowerment. By supporting Myron's taking an active role in resolving the problem, it became an interaction within which he developed new skills and competencies.

8. *Relationship based*: Key to any successful counseling is a working relationship between client and counselor. Myron and I had developed a bond prior to this intervention. I talked with him informally, assisted him in negotiating an unfamiliar context, and inquired about his welfare. This early relationship-building led Myron to seek my assistance and support at a time of sorrow and confusion.

Summary

Clinical judgment must enter into the choice of counseling approaches, and brief counseling is but one of many tools in counselors' repertoire. At times it may be a most appropriate tool; at other times it may be most inappropriate.

In using brief counseling, counselors enhance the dignity of children and adolescents by persistently accentuating their strengths rather than their weaknesses. Brief counselors build on what works rather than wallow in what does not work. They point clients toward the future, not the irretrievable past. They find humor in life even as they and their clients struggle to effect change.

Brief counseling offers overwhelmed counselors a possible solution to the recurring question: Where do I find the time to help so many people and not burn out? Counselors using a brief counseling are energized by focusing on what works. In turn, clients respond by living up to the expectations of change because they have been challenged to use their resources. By the very nature of life, children and adolescents are hurt in many different ways. Brief counseling is an effective tool for creating new patterns when old patterns have been damaged. As a bonus, brief counseling helps in less time than other approaches.

References

Anderson, H. (1997). *Conversation, language, and possibilities: A postmodern approach to therapy.* New York: Basic Books.

Becvar, D. S. (2007). *Families that flourish: Facilitating resilience in clinical practice.* New York: W. W. Norton.

Becvar, D. S., & Becvar, R. J. (2005). *Family therapy: A systemic integration* (6th ed.). Boston: Allyn & Bacon.

Constantine, M. G. (2001a). Multicultural training, self-construals, and multicultural competence of school counselors. *Professional School Counseling, 4*(3), 202–208.

Constantine, M. G. (2001b). Theoretical orientation, empathy, and multicultural counseling competence in school counselor trainees. *Professional School Counseling, 4*(5), 342–349.

Constantine, M. G., & Gainor, K. A. (2001). Emotional intelligence and empathy: Their relation to multi-cultural counseling knowledge and awareness. *Professional School Counseling, 5*(2), 131–138.

De Jong, P., & Berg, I. K. (1998). Interviewing for solutions. Pacific Grove, CA: Brooks/Cole.

de Shazer, S. (1988). *Clues: Investigating solutions in brief therapy.* New York: Norton.

Duncan, B. L., & Miller, S. D. (2000). *The heroic client: Doing client-directed, outcome-informed therapy.* San Francisco: Jossey–Bass.

Fisch, R., Weakland, J. H., & Segal, L. (1982). *The tactics of change: Doing therapy briefly.* San Francisco: Jossey–Bass.

Freedman, J., & Combs, G. (1996). *Narrative therapy: The social construction of preferred realities.* New York: W. W. Norton.

Garrett, M. T. (1999). Soaring on wings of the eagle: Wellness of Native American high school students. *Professional School Counseling, 3*(1), 57–65.

Gergen, K. J. (2000). *An invitation to social construction.* Thousand Oaks, CA: Sage.

Glasser, W. (1986). *Control theory in the classroom.* New York: Harper & Row.

Ivey, A. E., & Ivey, M. B. (2006). *Intentional interviewing and counseling: Facilitating client development in a multicultural society* (6th ed.). Belmont, CA: Wadsworth.

Lee, C. C. (2001). Culturally responsive school counselors and programs: Addressing the needs of all students. *Professional School Counseling*, 4(4), 257–262.

Littrell, J. M. (1998). *Brief counseling in action.* New York: W. W. Norton.

Littrell, J. M., & Angera, J. J. (1998). A solution-focused approach in couple and family therapy. In J. D. West, D. L. Bubenzer, & J. R. Bitter (Eds.), *Social construction in couple and family counseling* (pp. 21–53). Alexandria, VA: American Counseling Association.

Littrell, J. M., Malia, J. A., & Vanderwood, M. (1995). Single-session brief counseling in a high school. *Journal of Counseling and Development, 73*(4), 451–458.

Littrell, J. M., Zinck, K., Nesselhuf, D., & Yorke, C. (1997). Integrating brief counselling and adolescents' needs. *Canadian Journal of Counselling*, 32(2), 99–110.

Lokken, J. M. & Twohey, D. (2004). American Indian perspectives of Euro-American counseling behavior. *Journal of Multicultural Counseling and Development, 32*, 320–331.

Maurer, R. (2004). *One small step can change your life: The Kaizen way.* New York: Workman.

Morris, J. R. & Robinson, D. T. (1996). A review of multicultural counseling. *Journal of Humanistic Education and Development, 35*(1), 50–61.

Selekman, M. D. (1993). *Pathways to change: Brief therapy solutions with difficult adolescents.* New York: Guilford Press.

Sexton, T. L., Whiston, S. C., Bleuer, J. C., & Walz, G. R. (1997). *Integrating outcome research into counseling practice and training.* Alexandria, VA: American Counseling Association.

Sklare, G. B. (2005). *Brief counseling that works: A solution-focused approach for school counselors and administrators* (2nd ed.). Thousand Oaks, CA: Corwin.

Suzuki, D., & Knudtson, P. (1992). *Wisdom of the elders: Sacred native stories of nature.* New York: Bantam Books.

Thomason, T. C. (1991). Counseling Native Americans: An introduction for non-Native American counselors. *Journal of Counseling and Development, 69*, 321–327.

Turner, S. L., Conkel, J. L., Reich, A. N., Trotter, M. J., & Siewart, J. J. (2006). Social skills efficacy and proactivity among Native American adolescents. *Professional School Counseling, 10*(2), 189–194.

Vernon, A. (2002). *What works with children and adolescents: A handbook of individual counseling techniques.* Champaign, IL: Research Press.

Watzlawick, R., Weakland, J. H., & Fisch, R. (1974). *Change: Principles of problem formulation and problem resolution.* New York: W. W. Norton.

White, M., & Epston, D. (1990). *Narrative means to therapeutic ends.* New York: W. W. Norton.

Zinck, K., & Littrell, J. M. (2002). A peaceful solution. In L. Golden (Ed.), *Case studies in child and adolescent counseling* (3rd ed., pp. 108–117). Upper Saddle River, NJ: Merrill/Prentice–Hall.

Applications of Rational–Emotive Behavior Therapy With Children and Adolescents

Ann Vernon

On a daily basis helping professionals work with children and adolescents whose problems range from normal developmental concerns to more serious issues that can result in varying degrees of behavioral or emotional maladjustment. Although most young people overcome these problems and master their developmental tasks with minimal adult guidance, others need more professional attention so their problems are not exacerbated, resulting in more serious disturbance. Consequently, professionals should employ the most appropriate approaches and interventions to help children and adolescents deal effectively with their issues.

Rational-emotive behavior therapy (REBT) has been applied effectively and extensively with children and adolescents, in terms of both prevention and intervention, for more than six decades. REBT and its educational derivative, rational–emotive education (REE), have been adopted widely by school and mental health practitioners. Ellis and Bernard (2006) noted that "those who incorporate and integrate REBT in their individual work with young people have seen that REBT's essentials enhance their practice" (p. ix). Because of its educative nature, it is a viable approach in both individual and small-group counseling as well as emotional education in the classroom (Terjesen & Esposito, 2006; Vernon, 2007; Vernon & Bernard, 2006).

This chapter describes individual and group applications of REBT to children and adolescents and identifies numerous reasons why this theory should be considered as one of the most developmentally appropriate approaches to use with school-aged youth.

Rational–Emotive Behavior Therapy: An Overview

Rational–emotive behavior therapy, developed by Albert Ellis in 1955, combines cognitive, emotive, and behavioral techniques in an active–directive therapeutic process (Ellis, 2001a, b; Ellis & Dryden, 1997). Although much of the research, theory, and practice in REBT has addressed the adult population, the professional literature also includes considerable discussion of applications with children and adolescents (Bernard & Joyce, 1984; DiGiuseppe, 1999; Ellis & Bernard, 1983, 2006; Ellis & Wilde, 2002; Vernon, 2002a, 2002b, 2004a, 2004b, 2004c; Waters, 1982; Wilde, 1992, 1995, 1996, 2001). The increasing emphasis on REBT with children has resulted in the development of a number of rational-emotive educational materials that can be used preventively (Bernard, 2001; Knaus, 1974; Pincus, 1990; Vernon, 1998a, b, c; 2006a, b), as well as techniques that can be used in individual counseling (Vernon, 2002a), in consultation with parents and teachers (Barrish & Barrish, 1985, 1989; Joyce, 2006; McInerney & McInerney, 2006), and in school settings (Vernon & Bernard, 2006; Vernon, 2009).

According to REBT theory, emotional distress results from dysfunctional cognitions, and there is a strong interconnectedness between thinking, feeling, and behaving (Dryden, DiGiuseppe, & Neenan, 2003). The primary goal of REBT is to help people develop a rational philosophy of life that enables them to think and feel better and begin to act in self-enhancing ways that will aid them in attaining their personal goals (Dryden & Ellis, 2001; Ellis, 2001a). For counselors to help clients accomplish these goals, they must understand the major components of REBT theory, as follows.

1. An integral part of REBT theory is the A-B-C model, which Ellis created and expanded on to conceptualize the nature of emotional disturbance (Ellis, 1995, 1996, 2001b). In essence, as people attempt to fulfill their goals, they encounter an *activating event* (A) that supports or thwarts their goals. People have beliefs about the activating event, and these beliefs directly influence how they feel and act. It is not the activating event that creates the emotional and behavioral *consequence* (C) but, rather, the *beliefs* (B) about that event.

   To illustrate, imagine that two students take a psychology exam and both fail. The first student catastrophizes, thinking it is the end of the world and proves her incompetence and inadequacy, whereas the second student is not happy about failing but realizes that it has no bearing on his self-worth and that one failing grade isn't the end of the world. As this example shows, beliefs may be rational and contribute to the attainment of goals and to moderate, healthy emotions, or beliefs may be irrational and lead to disturbed emotions and inhibit the attainment of goals and satisfaction in life (Dryden & Ellis, 2001).

   If the emotional and behavioral consequences are strongly negative, the irrational beliefs contributing to these emotions and behaviors must be *disputed* (D) to help clients develop *effective* new beliefs (E) and effective new *feelings* (F).

2. Irrational beliefs derive from three main categories of demandingness: (a) self-demandingness, which implies that people always must perform perfectly to win others' approval, and if they don't, they irrationally believe that they are inadequate and unworthy; (b) other-demandingness, the notion that others should always treat them fairly and nicely, and if they don't, they are bad and unworthy; and (c) world-demandingness, which means that life should be hassle-free and enjoyable, and if it is not, it is awful and unbearable (Dryden et al., 2003).

   To eliminate these dysfunctional thinking patterns, the counselor initiates a process known as *disputing*, which involves challenging the client's irrational beliefs through rigorous questioning and rational self-analysis, utilizing a wide variety of cognitive, emotive, and behavioral techniques (Dryden & Ellis, 2001). The goal of disputation is to help people adopt more adaptive rational beliefs, characterized by a more flexible, nonabsolutistic viewpoint. If this procedure is effective, irrational beliefs are replaced with rational ones and disturbing emotions and self-defeating behaviors are minimized or eliminated (Ellis & MacLaren, 1998).

3. REBT is designed as a self-help, educational therapy that emphasizes the acquisition of skills, which distinguishes it from other forms of therapy (Ellis, 2002). A primary goal is to teach people how to get better rather than simply feel better (Ellis, 2001a, b; Vernon, 2002a), which Ellis claimed can be achieved by using a variety of emotional, behavioral, cognitive, and philosophical methods.

4. REBT is a comprehensive form of therapy, not simply a patchwork approach to problem solving, because it deals with the irrational beliefs that perpetuate the problem so lasting change can be achieved. Counselors help clients maintain change through homework assignments, bibliotherapy, and various self-help materials (Ellis & MacClaren, 1998; Vernon, 2002a).

Applications of REBT with Children and Adolescents

Early in the practice of REBT, Ellis and his colleagues began applying the theory to children to teach positive mental health concepts and the skills to use these concepts (DiGiuseppe, 1999; Vernon, 2007). Because REBT was found to be successful in clinical and experimental investigations, the Living School, a small private grade school, was established in 1970 at the Institute for Rational-Emotive Therapy in New York (Bernard, Ellis, & Terjesen, 2006). During the 5 years of its existence, parents and children benefited from learning rational principles that impacted their emotional adjustment and behavior positively.

   The REBT approach is used extensively throughout the world in schools (Vernon & Bernard, 2006), in child guidance clinics, community mental health facilities, and private practice, on an individual and a small-group basis (Ellis & Dryden, 1997). It has been used successfully with children and adolescents to address a variety of problems, including frustration tolerance (Knaus, 2006), depression (Vernon, 2006c), fear and anxiety (Grieger & Boyd, 2006), aggression (DiGiuseppe & Kelter,

2006), ADHD (Doyle & Terjesen, 2006), underachievement (Bernard, 2006), anger, disruptive behavior, school phobia, low self-concept, test anxiety, interpersonal relationship problems, impulsivity, cheating, withdrawal, and lack of motivation (Vernon, 2002a). Bernard and colleagues (2006) stated that "today, it is abundantly clear that within the fields of school psychology and school counseling and guidance, REBT is a preferred methodology incorporated within the tool boxes of counselors and psychologists who work with children and adolescents" (p. 6).

REBT can be used in two ways with children and adolescents:

1. For school-age children who are not in counseling, REBT can be used preventively through rational–emotive education in the classroom to enhance socioemotional growth and teach rational thinking skills (Bernard, 2001; Vernon, 2004c; Vernon, 2009; Vernon & Bernard, 2006).
2. For children who have been referred to a counselor, social worker, or school psychologist for a specific problem, REBT can be used individually or in small groups to address the problem (DiGiuseppe, 1999; Terjesen & Esposito, 2006; Vernon, 2002a, Vernon, 2007).

Because of the limited ability of young children to process concepts cognitively, some people wonder how applicable REBT is to them. Experience has shown, however, that rational thinking skills can be modeled for children of almost any age. The only limiting factor is the counselor's creativity in adapting REBT to the child's level. According to DiGiuseppe (1999), REBT can be used with children as young as 5 years of age, but the developmental stage must be considered (Bernard et al., 2006; DiGiuseppe, 1999; Vernon, 2002a). Children who have reached the concrete operational stage of thinking are better able to deal with the logic associated with disputing, in contrast to younger children, who respond better to problem-solving strategies and rational coping statements (DiGiuseppe, 1999). Interestingly, more than 4 decades ago, Wagner (1966) argued that REBT is superior to other therapeutic approaches when working with children. REBT practitioners continue to support the following advantages that Wagner enumerated:

1. REBT makes immediate direct intervention possible when it is needed to deal with school problems.
2. The basic principles can be easily understood, applied, and adapted to children of most ages, cultures, and intelligence levels.
3. REBT typically takes less time than other therapies, permitting more effective use of the counselor's time.
4. REBT helps children learn to live in their own environment; it teaches them to deal realistically with what they can and cannot change in their lives. Given that children and adolescents do not have control over many of the events that happen to them, this approach is empowering.

Vernon (2002a) expanded on these advantages, identifying the following additional reasons why REBT is an excellent approach with this population:

5. REBT helps kids "get better," not just feel better, by addressing the core irrational thinking patterns that cause emotional upset.

6. REBT is a developmentally appropriate approach because it employs numerous techniques that help move children beyond their concrete thinking tendencies, enabling them to be more effective problem solvers.

7. REBT teaches behavioral and emotional self-control by teaching the connections between thoughts, feelings, and behaviors.

8. REBT advocates a wide variety of cognitive, emotive, and behavioral techniques to teach the basic principles and help young people dispute irrational beliefs.

9. REBT is effective because it addresses the problem immediately. This is important because children's sense of time is so immediate and their problems often are so pressing that they require swift intervention.

10. REBT can be incorporated in schools in a variety of ways, including individual and small-group counseling, emotional education programs, and workshops for parents and school personnel.

The Counseling Relationship

Although Ellis himself preferred an active-directive therapeutic style with most clients (Ellis, 2002; Dryden, 2003), he did not dogmatically insist on one type of relationship between counselor and client, stressing that the extent to which a counselor is active-directive is a choice (Dryden & Ellis, 2001). Recognizing that all REBT therapists do not share Ellis's preference for an active-directive style, Dryden (2002a, b) encouraged REBT counselors to be flexible, maintaining that counselors can vary the style and adhere to the theoretical principles at the same time.

Particularly in working with children, building the therapeutic alliance is vital (DiGiuseppe & Bernard, 2006; Vernon, 2002a; Young, 2006). According to Bernard and colleagues (2006), "It has always been recognized by child-oriented and adolescent-oriented REBT practitioners that a warm, supportive, empathic relationship with young people is a necessary condition for the full benefits of REBT interventions to be realized." (p. 27). These authors emphasized the importance of listening and offering unconditional positive regard as they get to know the young person. During the initial session, when a combination of relationship building and data gathering take place, counselors should let the client know that they are on his or her side in order to build trust.

Bernard and colleagues (2006) enumerated several ways to build a positive therapeutic alliance:

- Being patient and honest
- Showing genuine interest in their life
- Encouraging mutual self-disclosure
- Using humor
- Working on winning respect
- Respecting resistance

In addition, the counselor might engage the child in activities such as playing a game, drawing a picture, or completing some unfinished sentences as a way of establishing rapport. Vernon (2002a) identified numerous get-acquainted activities that can be used to develop a good working relationship. For example, she described a technique called "Who Are You?" (p. 21), in which the child and counselor take turns asking each other, "Who are you?" As the child asks this question, the counselor might respond, "I'm someone who really likes to read. Who are you?" The child may respond by saying that she really likes pets. As the activity proceeds, the counselor learns important things about the child, which leads to trust through mutual self-disclosure.

Another simple technique, which works with adolescents, too, is to put categories of words, such as the following, on separate index cards: people, places, things, books, movies, food. After placing the cards face down on a table, the counselor and client take turns turning them over and responding with a "favorite" relative to the category.

In working with young children, the counselor should use concrete examples extensively (Vernon, 2002a, b), use the language of the child, and limit the number of "bombarding" questions. Because children typically do not refer themselves for counseling, they may feel uncomfortable. Therefore, the counselor should be friendly, honest, and relaxed to let children see how he or she can help them change some things that might be bothering them (Vernon, 2004a). Young people, particularly adolescents, tend to resist counseling, in part because they often are referred by others and don't think they have a problem (DiGiuseppe, 1999; Vernon, 2002b). Because they may come to counseling feeling defensive, the best strategy is to be straightforward about the problem as he or she understands it: "I understand that you are here because you have some problems getting along with your parents." Simplifying the problem is also helpful, as many adolescents are afraid they are "crazy."

Sometimes adolescents become more willing to open up if the counselor discusses the problem as a hypothetical problem that another teenager had. For example, the counselor might say, "I've worked with some teenagers who really resent being told what to do. Is that how you feel?" In all counseling relationships, it is important to establish mutual goals toward which the counselor and the client will work together to solve the youth's problems (DiGiuseppe, 1999).

Assessing the Problem

Bernard and colleagues (2006) distinguished between *problem identification* and *problem analysis.* During the identification stage, the counselor determines if a problem exists and, if so, who owns it. This is particularly important in working with children and adolescents because they are typically referred by a parent or teacher and, though the child may have an emotional or behavioral problem, the parent or teacher at least may own the problem or share it with the child (Bernard et al., 2006). Because of children's range of behavioral and emotional problems, professionals must examine the frequency, intensity, and duration of the symptoms to determine the extent of the problem and how extensive the intervention has to be. They also have to consider whether the child's problem is representative of his or her age-group and whether the child's emotions and behaviors are normal expressions or atypical responses.

Assuming that there is a problem and after identifying whose problem it is, the next stage is problem analysis. At this time the counselor works with the child and often the parent and/or teacher to determine which emotions and behaviors are problematic, as well as the irrational beliefs that perpetuate the problem.

Distinguishing between practical and emotional problems is another important consideration in assessment (Vernon, 2002a). All too often, counselors look at practical problems—realistic difficulties that involve lack of skills for dealing with the problem—and forget to deal with the emotions behind the problems, which are generated by irrational beliefs. For example, a counselor working with an adolescent who doesn't complete her homework may search for ways to help her get the homework done. A common strategy is to generate a list of good solutions. Many times, however, adolescents fail to follow through because the counselor didn't deal with the frustration stemming from irrational beliefs. In the homework case, the irrational belief might be: "I shouldn't have to work this hard at something that's so boring and irrelevant; I can't stand to do this stupid work."

Or take the example of a young child who repeatedly failed to take his medication at school. His parents and teachers couldn't understand why he didn't remember to take the medicine, and they devised various strategies to assist him. Nothing they suggested had a long-lasting effect until this youngster dealt with his feelings of shame and embarrassment about having to take medication, which he thought made him "different and less than" others. Until he understood that taking medication didn't make him a bad person, the problem continued. By assessing and addressing both the emotional and the practical problems, counselors are better able to get to the heart of the issue.

Assessing Irrational Beliefs

Waters (1982, p. 572) expanded on the three core irrational beliefs—demands on self, others, and the world—and identified the following irrational beliefs common in children:

1. It's awful if others don't like me.
2. I'm bad if I make a mistake.
3. Everything should always go my way; I should get what I want.
4. Things should come easy to me.
5. The world should be fair, and bad people must be punished.
6. I shouldn't show my feelings.
7. Adults should be perfect.
8. There's only one right answer.
9. I must win.
10. I shouldn't have to wait for anything.

Waters (1981, p. 6) enumerated the following irrational beliefs for adolescents:

1. It would be awful if my peers didn't like me. It would be awful to be a social loser.
2. I shouldn't make mistakes, especially social mistakes.
3. It's my parents' fault I'm so miserable.
4. I can't help it. That's just the way I am, and I guess I'll always be this way.
5. The world should be fair.
6. It's awful when things don't go my way.
7. It's better to avoid challenges than to risk failure.
8. I must conform to my peers.
9. I can't stand to be criticized.
10. Others should always be responsible.

Just because a problem exists does not automatically mean that irrational beliefs are causing the negative feelings and behaviors. The way to discern this is to note the emotional intensity and behavioral reaction. For example, it is entirely reasonable for a child to be sad if his or her best friend moves out of the neighborhood. For a short time the child may be listless or cry occasionally, and this is normal. But if he stays in the bedroom, refuses to eat, and cries for days on end, he probably is thinking that this is the worst thing that could ever happen, that new friends cannot replace this one, and that the situation is unbearable. In this case, irrational beliefs are contributing to the more extreme emotional upset.

Therefore, when working with children, the counselor must distinguish between feeling sad, disappointed, regretful, or irritated, and feeling very depressed, guilty, or angry. If the child exhibits the latter feelings or other strong negative emotions or unproductive or self-defeating behaviors, these emanate from irrational beliefs.

To detect irrational beliefs, the REBT counselor must listen discriminately to everything the client says. For instance, when a teenage girl says, "I'll never get a date … I'm a social misfit," she is overgeneralizing, which is indicative of self-downing. Or if an adolescent boy says, "If I'm not picked as class president, it will be terrible," he is making an absolutistic demand. Statements such as, "I can't stand to take tests," "it's too hard to study," and "it's boring" indicate low frustration tolerance—the irrational belief that "things should come easily for me and I shouldn't have to work too hard at anything."

The counselor also must attempt to get to the core irrational beliefs (demands on self, others, and the world) because this is the evaluative component that contributes most to dysfunctional feelings and behaviors. To get a grasp on the evaluative component, the counselor often has to help a child extend his or her thoughts, as this example illustrates:

> A sixth grader was extremely upset because he hadn't been invited to spend the night at a friend's house. When the counselor asked him what he was thinking that made him so upset, the boy replied that it must mean that this friend didn't like him.

> Rather than dispute this overgeneralization—that the friend might like him but might have other reasons for not including him—the counselor asked, "And what does that say about you?" To which the child replied, "That there must be something wrong with me; I must not be good enough for him."

The core belief has to do with the child's self-downing, and disputing the overgeneralization most likely would not address the core belief. Questions such as, "And…?" "And so…?" "And what does that mean?" and "Because…?" will help the counselor dig deeper to get to these core beliefs.

The Individual Counseling Process

After building the relationship and assessing the irrational beliefs and emotional and behavioral consequences, the REBT counselor begins to help children resolve their problems. The goal of REBT is to teach young clients that they have the power to change how they think, which in turn affects how they feel and behave.

Ellis developed the A-B-C model, which conceptualizes the major constructs of the theory and is used to bring about change (Dryden & Ellis, 2001). Specifically, the A is the activating event, which is anything the client experiences or perceives. Although the activating event is assumed to be the cause of the resulting feelings and behaviors, this is not the case, according to REBT. To illustrate, suppose a teacher tells her fourth graders that they cannot go outside for recess because it is raining. Some students may be upset and sulk because they were looking forward to playing soccer, and others are elated and welcome the chance to stay inside and read. The same event resulted in different emotional and behavioral reactions (C) because of what the children were thinking (B).

In accordance with the REBT model, the counselor asks the child or adolescent to describe the activating event but does not encourage him or her to discuss the situation in great detail. Elaboration is unnecessary. More important, the counselor must get a brief sense of the problem, which is not always easy with children for several reasons:

1. They might be ashamed or reluctant to admit that they have a problem.
2. They might not be able to describe the problem because of their limited verbal or cognitive abilities.
3. They might not know what the problem is because they were referred by adults.

In the latter case, the counselor might simply say, "Alejandro, your teacher asked me to visit with you because she thinks others may be picking on you at recess." Or the counselor could invite the client to role-play the problem, write about it, draw a picture, or pretend that this is a rerun of a movie and the child is describing to the counselor what happened.

After getting a brief overview of the activating event, the counselor asks the child how he or she felt and behaved relative to this event. This is more challenging with young children because their feeling vocabularies are limited. Therefore, the counselor could use puppets, feeling word flashcards, bibliotherapy, role play, or other age-appropriate methods to help them identify the emotions (Vernon, 2002a).

The "emotional thermometer" is another good technique to use in assessing the intensity of the emotion: "On a scale of 1 to 10, how strong is your anger?" (DiGiuseppe & Bernard, 2006). If the child has difficulty identifying the emotion, asking how he or she behaved can be effective in ascertaining the feeling, as shown in this example with a second grader:

Counselor:	Ellie, your teacher told me that you have to stay in for recess because you haven't been turning in your assignments. How do you feel about missing recess?
Ellie:	I don't know.
Counselor:	When the teacher told you that you had to stay inside and work on your schoolwork, what did you do?
Ellie:	I got mad and ran out of the room and hid in the bathroom so she couldn't make me do that stupid work."

After determining the emotional and behavioral reaction, the next step in the A-B-C paradigm is to ask the client what he or she thinks about the activating event. This, too, is often difficult for young children, so the counselor may give examples, such as: "Some kids feel angry when they have to stay in for recess because they didn't complete their assignments. They think it isn't fair. They think they should get to do what they want to. Does that sound like something you would think?" The counselor isn't just playing a hunch, as the emotional and behavioral consequences often provide cues to the irrational beliefs. Anger relates to demands or "shoulds": They shouldn't treat me this way; they have to be fair. Guilt and depression are often tied to self-downing beliefs: I should be smarter; my life will never be better because I'm such a loser. Anxiety typically relates to awfulizing or overgeneralizing: I'll never pass this test because it will be so hard.

DiGiuseppe and Bernard (2006) noted that because children may not be aware of their irrational beliefs, counselors will have to be more direct in their questioning, using techniques such as the following:

- Incomplete sentences (when your brother hid your backpack, what were you thinking?)
- Thought bubbles (empty bubbles above the child's head that can be filled in as the counselor asks the child to identify his or her thoughts)
- Instant replay (pretend that we were doing an instant replay of when your classmate told the teacher you cheated. What were you thinking?)

The "D" in the model, disputing irrational beliefs, is the heart and soul of REBT. Again, this can be challenging for children, so the counselor has to employ a variety of developmentally appropriate, creative disputations. Bernard and colleagues (2006) described two basic disputation methods to use with young clients:

1. *Didactic approach*: involves more of an explanation about the REBT theory of emotional disturbance and the difference between rational and irrational beliefs.
2. *Socratic method*: uses questions to help the young client challenge irrational beliefs, illustrated in the following example.

Julia, age 16, was extremely angry and wanted revenge because her boyfriend broke his date with her and took one of her best friends to the movie instead. Her irrational beliefs were: He shouldn't do this. It's not fair. My friend never should have agreed to go out with him. I trusted them, so they should have been loyal to me.

The counselor helped Julia dispute her irrational beliefs in the following way:

Counselor:	Julia, do you know anyone else this has happened to?
Julia:	Yes—it happens a lot.
Counselor:	Is everyone as upset as you are?
Julia:	I don't know; I suppose some are and some aren't.
Counselor:	You're probably right. Some would be as angry and some wouldn't. If they aren't as angry as you are, why do you suppose they aren't?
Julia:	I don't know. Maybe they didn't care about their boyfriend as much as I did.
Counselor:	Right. You really care about him, so of course you'd be more disturbed by this. But if you told yourself that he didn't matter that much to you, you wouldn't be as angry. So do you see that what you think affects how you feel?
Julia:	Yeah, but that doesn't make it better.
Counselor:	It might not make it better, but maybe at least we can reduce your anger, because it's preventing you from doing your schoolwork and having fun with other friends because you're so preoccupied with this.
Julia:	Yeah, I see your point. But I don't see how I can ever get over this.
Counselor:	I know it's hard when something like this happens. It would be nice if there were a law that boyfriends shouldn't do these things, but do you know about any such law?
Julia:	(laughs) No, but I wish there was one!
Counselor:	Right! I bet a lot of your girlfriends would like that, too, but there isn't a law, so how does it help you to insist that he shouldn't have done this or that it isn't fair or that your girlfriend shouldn't have gone out with him?
Julia:	I guess it doesn't help, but it really isn't fair.
Counselor:	You could be right, but have you ever seen the referee make a bad call during your volleyball games—a call that you or others thought was unfair?
Julia:	Sure….

Counselor:	So, whether we like it or not, unfair things do happen, right?
Julia:	Yeah.
Counselor:	And, even though what your boyfriend and good friend did wasn't very nice, how much control do you have over what others do?
Julia:	Not much. But I can't understand why they did it. I never would have done that to them.
Counselor:	It's hard to understand why they did what they did, but you weren't able to control them. What you can do now is to control how you think so you aren't so upset. Of course, you aren't going to like it, or send them a thank-you note for doing what they did, but what could you think that would help you deal with this so you can go on with your life without being so consumed by your anger?
Julia:	I don't know. I suppose I just have to remember that I don't have any control over others and it doesn't do me any good to be so mad when it won't change anything.
Counselor:	Exactly. So do you think it would be helpful to write that down and put it on your mirror or in your backpack to remind you what to think when you feel that anger creeping up on you?
Julia:	I can try that.

As illustrated in the above dialogue, several different disputes were used:

- Functional (how is it helping you to stay so angry that you act out in revenge?)
- Logical (how logical is it for you to assume that everyone should always treat you fairly?)
- Empirical (where is the evidence that this should never have happened?).

Although young clients typically respond well to these types of disputes, they may have to be used repeatedly, or in combination with other age-appropriate techniques for the disputing to be most effective. Suppose that Julia couldn't let go of her irrational demand that unfair things like this shouldn't happen. It might be helpful to give her a homework assignment to interview classmates to see if they have ever gone through anything unfair, or use the reverse role-play technique, in which the counselor keeps insisting that things always should be fair and the client helps dispute this.

The goal of the disputing process is to lessen the intensity of the negative emotions and behaviors and to replace irrational beliefs with more rational ones to promote problem solving and emotional well-being. This is the E (effective new philosophy) and F (effective new feelings) in Ellis's A-B-C-D-E paradigm.

Individual Counseling Techniques

One of the distinct advantages of REBT is that counselors are encouraged to use a variety of culturally and developmentally appropriate techniques as they assess the emotional and behavioral consequences and irrational beliefs and engage clients in the disputation process. Games, bibliotherapy, worksheets, music and art activities, role play, imagery, puppetry, and other nontraditional interventions can be employed effectively to build rapport and reduce resistance, as well as help the client work through the A-B-C model (Vernon, 2002a, 2002b).

In addition, these methods can be used as homework assignments. Homework is integral in the REBT process; DiGiuseppe and Bernard (2006) described it as the "final phase of REBT treatment, practice, and application" (p. 110). Homework assignments reinforce the concepts that clients work on during the counseling session, and as DiGiuseppe and Bernard noted, "these homework activities are crucial in helping them move from cognitive insight to active practice and application of new ways of thinking, feeling, and behaving" (p. 110).

The following case studies feature several individual counseling interventions. Readers are encouraged to refer to *What Works When with Children and Adolescents: A Handbook of Individual Counseling Techniques* (Vernon, 2002a) for additional cases.

Leslie

Leslie is in kindergarten, soon to be in first grade. A perfectionist, she feels bad whenever she makes a mistake. She is worried about going into first grade—afraid that her teacher won't like her and will yell at her for making mistakes, afraid that the work will be too hard and she won't know how to do it, and afraid that other kids will think she's stupid. Even though Leslie is a bright little girl, she is not able to stop worrying. As a result, she has stomachaches and can't sleep at night. Her parents have referred her to the school counselor.

First grade is approaching rapidly, so the counselor suggests that she help Leslie write down all of her worries on separate slips of paper. Then she has Leslie pick out a puppet and asks her to pretend that the puppet is the Worrywart. The counselor explains to Leslie that this Worrywart, which the counselor will hold, is going to help Leslie with her worries. The Worrywart believes that, sometimes, the more we worry about something, the worse it seems. She instructs Leslie to hold out one of the papers to the Worrywart and tell the Worrywart the worry written on it. The counselor explains that the Worrywart will listen and try to help Leslie get rid of the worry so she (the Worrywart) can "gobble it up" and Leslie won't have to worry about it any longer. The exchange goes like this:

Leslie:	(to Worrywart) I know my teacher won't like me.
Worrywart:	How do you know? Just because you think your teacher this year doesn't like you, don't you think next year's teacher can be different?
Leslie:	Well, I'm just worried that she won't like me.

Worrywart:	Do you suppose she might like you? Don't you think maybe this teacher could like you?
Leslie:	Maybe. I just worry about it.
Worrywart:	What good does it do to worry about it? Will it make the teacher be nicer?
Leslie:	No, I guess not. Maybe I don't have to worry so much about that. I suppose she could be nicer than my kindergarten teacher. But I'm scared I'll make mistakes and the teacher and the other kids will think I'm dumb.
Worrywart:	Have you ever made a mistake before? (Leslie nods her head). When you did, did anyone tell you that you're dumb because you made that mistake? (Leslie shakes her head no). And even if they did, does that mean you're dumb? If your new puppy forgets to grab his chew bone when he comes inside, does that mean he's dumb, or does that mean he just forgot?
Leslie:	It means he just forgot.

The dialogue continues in this way, with the counselor demonstrating some simple disputing to help Leslie deal with her worries. At the conclusion of the session, Leslie lets the Worrywart "gobble up" her worries because she isn't as worried about these things any more.

As this case study illustrates, the use of puppets and a concrete approach were effective in helping the young child think more rationally. With very young children, two additional useful techniques are (a) to teach rational coping self-statements, and (b) to challenge beliefs and behaviors with empirical questions (adapted from Vernon, 1983, p. 473). For example, a child who is fearful of the water can be taught to repeat a rational coping statement such as: "Even though I'm afraid of the water, there really isn't anything to be afraid of. The water isn't that deep, and there are people here to watch me." Children can also be helped to understand that some fears are natural but that they will miss out on a lot by not trying new things. This can be achieved through challenging questions, as illustrated in the following exchange.

Child:	But I'm afraid to swim. The water's cold.
Counselor:	How do you know it's cold if you haven't gone in yet?
Child:	Well, I just think it is.
Counselor:	So maybe it isn't as cold as you think. Does it look as if the other children think it's too cold to have fun?
Child:	I guess not.
Counselor:	It must not be too bad or the other children would be shivering, wouldn't they? What else is bothering you about going swimming?
Child:	What if I get in too deep and think I'll drown and no one is there to save me?

Counselor:	Well, let's look around. How many teachers and helpers are walking around supervising?
Child:	There are four teachers or helpers.
Counselor:	That's right. And do you see the rope where some of the other children are standing? That rope shows children how deep they can go before it gets dangerous. Do you see anyone going past the rope?
Child:	Not now. But what if some kids did go outside the rope?
Counselor:	I bet if they went outside the rope, the teacher would blow a whistle and make them come back. What do you think?
Child:	I don't know. I suppose the teacher would make them get back. I'm still sort of scared, though.
Counselor:	It's okay to be scared, but what's the worst thing you think would happen if you got in the water for just a few minutes?
Child:	I would drown.
Counselor:	Well, since you've been watching the other kids swim, has anyone drowned?
Child:	No.
Counselor:	And you said that there are lots of adults around to help if that would happen. So, since the kids look like they're having fun, and you know how far you can go and still be safe because the rope is there, what do you think about getting in for a few minutes and seeing for yourself what it's like?
Child:	I guess I'll try it.

After children first try something new, they should discuss whether it was as bad as they had thought it would be and how they "talked to themselves" to get through it. This type of discussion increases the likelihood that they will apply the coping strategies in future situations.

The next case study describes a type of paradoxical technique used with fourth grade boys.

Antonio and Dave

Antonio and Dave, two fourth graders, were referred to counseling because Dave teased Antonio and Antonio responded with fists flying. All attempts to dispute Antonio's demands about how Dave should act did little good. Dave continued to tease Antonio, and the more Antonio reacted to the teasing, the more victorious Dave felt.

The counselor attempted to work with the two boys together, but Dave wasn't motivated to change. Therefore, the counselor suggested to Antonio that maybe Dave really was doing Antonio a favor because, even though Antonio didn't like the teasing, the experience showed him that he could survive it and he probably wouldn't run into such a terrible tease again. The counselor told Antonio that he had learned some important lessons that maybe he should tell other children with similar problems.

Then Antonio began working on a book that they called *How To Get Along With Friends*. He and the counselor identified ways to tolerate teasing, ways to get along with a difficult person, and what to do to make yourself reasonably happy even though you can't change the other person. In making the book, Antonio was able to reframe the situation somewhat and concentrate on ways he could tolerate what he had considered to be an intolerable situation.

Another effective way to engage younger clients is through games or activities. The interventions in the next case study were used with an anxious third grader.

Sanje

Sanje was perfectionistic and became extremely anxious prior to taking exams, participating in sports or music activities, and completing schoolwork. He insisted that his older brothers always got perfect grades and never made mistakes, and he held himself to these high standards as well.

After several sessions in which they had discussed the possibility of always being perfect and never making mistakes, the counselor invited Sanje to juggle tennis balls. First she gave him two balls, and he juggled them quite well. Then she introduced a third ball and, as might be expected, this was difficult and Sanje wasn't able to juggle them.

To prove her point, the counselor herself tried to do it. She failed. Then the counselor asked Sanje to have his teacher and the school nurse try it. To Sanje's surprise, they couldn't juggle three balls either. He and the counselor discussed whether it was possible to always be perfect, and if there was any such thing as a "perfect" person. The counselor then read a story to him called *Being Perfectly Perfect* (Vernon, 1998a, pp. 129–132) about a child his age who thought she had to be perfect. Knowing that it would take some time to help him give up his need for perfection, the counselor gave Sanje the homework assignment of interviewing family members about whether they considered themselves to be perfect and examples of mistakes they had made.

In the next session the counselor suggested that they work on the anxious feeling and engaged Sanje in a game played like hopscotch. As Sanje discussed being anxious about taking tests, singing in concerts, and doing his schoolwork, the counselor asked him to verbalize all his anxious thoughts, and she wrote them down. Then she invited Sanje to stand on the first square of the hopscotch board (a flannel-backed tablecloth drawn into squares like a hopscotch board), and she read one of his anxious thoughts. She asked him to think of something he could do or think so he wouldn't be so anxious, and state it aloud. If he could do this, he was to jump to the next set of squares. The game proceeded in this way until he reached the end and could shout "Adios, anxiety!" (Vernon, 2002a).

At the end of the game, they discussed the concept of *rational self-statements* as a way of coping with anxiety, stressing that when we are anxious, we usually assume the worst and when we use rational self-talk, we look at things more realistically. For example, a rational self-statement to counter the fear that "I might make a mistake on this assignment" could be, "Everyone makes mistakes. I'll try my best, but I don't have to do it all perfectly."

The following case study provides an explanation of several different interventions to help a depressed adolescent.

Alicia

Alicia, age 14, asked to see the school counselor because she was depressed, which was confirmed by her responses to a brief depression scale, as well as by her noticeably depressed affect. After assessing more thoroughly for suicidal ideation and noting that Alicia did not appear to be suicidal at this point, the counselor asked Alicia to tell her more about feeling depressed and how long she had felt this way. She specifically asked Alicia to rate on a 1 (low) to 10 (high) scale how depressed she had been this past week, which was helpful in determining the intensity of the depression. Alicia then proceeded to tell the school counselor everything that was wrong with her life: She had no friends. Her parents were too strict and hated her. She never got good enough grades. She would never amount to anything.

Given that the counselor knew Alicia, she was aware that until the depression hit, this student's grades actually were quite good, and that although she had typical friendship dilemmas like most of her peers, she did have friends. Rather than confront Alicia's overgeneralizations, the counselor asked her to draw an emotional pie (Merrell, 2001) and divide it into as many different emotions as she had the previous day, in proportion to the intensity of the feeling. Alicia divided the pie into four slices: Depression was the largest, followed by anxiety and anger, and, finally, happiness (a small slice). The counselor then asked Alicia to draw a second pie to illustrate how she wanted her life to be. Alicia drew this pie with small depressed, angry, and anxious slices, and a much larger happiness slice.

The counselor told Alicia that to achieve emotional balance on the second pie, she would have to do some work. She asked Alicia to draw around her hand, and on each finger write something that depressed her. Next, the counselor introduced the concept of disputing, explaining to

Alicia that often when people are depressed, or when they are teenagers, they overgeneralize—make assumptions about things that aren't well founded. She asked Alicia if it really was true that she had *no* friends, or if it just seemed like that because she and her peers got into hassles and were "on again, off again." Alicia agreed that it was like this—that she did have friends, but that they argued a lot.

Then the counselor asked Alicia what she could write beside the "no friends" finger to help her remember that this wasn't really true, but when she didn't stop to think this through and overgeneralized, it depressed her. The counselor asked Alicia to go through each of the fingers and write disputes—more realistic ways of looking at the issue.

In a subsequent session, when Alicia said that when she was depressed, she didn't seem to be able to think of anything good about her life, the counselor suggested that she make a depression toolbox (Vernon, 2006c), in which Alicia first would make a list of the good things in her life and then find concrete objects to represent each of those things. The counselor instructed Alicia to put these items in a box and whenever she got depressed and couldn't recall good things, she could refer to her toolbox. Alicia liked this idea and found it effective.

This next case study incorporates an experiential activity to help a high school student deal with procrastination (Vernon, 2002a, p. 183).

Leo

Leo kept putting things off, both at home and at school. Although he didn't seem to worry much about his procrastination, it had become such a problem that his parents referred him to the counselor because they were concerned that the longer this went on, the more problems it would cause next year, his senior year of high school, and beyond, when the consequences could be much more serious.

After having Leo list the advantages and disadvantages of procrastination and discussing them, it was apparent that he wasn't looking at the long-term or seeing the many probable negative consequences. The counselor therefore asked Leo to imagine that because he really didn't want to change, he wouldn't, and encouraged him to project into next year and the following year by taking photos depicting what his life might be like if he didn't change.

For example, the counselor said Leo could take pictures of the high school because he probably wouldn't graduate if he continued to procrastinate about schoolwork; he could take pictures of his house because he likely would be grounded a lot; and so forth. Although Leo thought this was a stupid homework assignment, the counselor predicted that he would do it because he liked photography and it also was a good excuse for not doing his schoolwork.

Leo did take the photos and, as instructed, made a poster with them. He and the counselor agreed that this intervention seemed to help him be a bit more realistic about the consequences of procrastination. But Leo still was clinging to his irrational beliefs that doing schoolwork was boring, that he had better things to do, that putting things off was no big deal, and so on.

After some disputing, the counselor asked Leo if he would be willing to participate in a short experiment. Leo agreed, and the counselor asked him to make a list of all the things he was currently procrastinating about. Leo did this. Then the counselor asked him to lie on the floor, face up, and explained that Leo was to read the list, one item at a time. As Leo read each item, the counselor piled a newspaper on him. When Leo had read everything on the list, the counselor asked him how he felt with everything piled up on top of him—which is similar to what happens with procrastination. They talked about what Leo would have to do to get out from under the pile. The counselor suggested that Leo come up with a dispute, or something he could tell himself about each item, and as he did, the counselor would remove a newspaper. For example, when Leo thinks school work is too boring, he could say to himself that everything can't be entertaining and that if he wants to graduate from high school, he'd better do the work, boring or not. Leo was able to come up with disputes for the items on his list, and the counselor removed the papers accordingly.

Another effective strategy for helping children, especially those dealing with fear and anxiety, is *rational-emotive imagery*. In adapting adult REBT techniques for use with children, Huber (1981) introduced the concept of the "hero," in which children are asked to identify their fear and the circumstances under which this fear arises. Then they are asked to think of a hero, such as the Incredible Hulk, Wonder Woman, or Spider Man, and to imagine that this hero is experiencing the same fearful sequence of events as the child. Next, the children are asked to imagine that they are the hero who can approach a situation without fear. This type of imagery can be useful for children when they encounter similar fearful circumstances in the future.

Still another useful strategy is to have the client create rational limericks or songs to demonstrate the disputing process or other REBT concepts (Vernon, 2002a). This is fun, and the limericks serve as a concrete way to remember what has been discussed during the counseling session. The following limerick was developed to help a child deal with her anger:

> When I am mad
> I say and do things that are bad
> And later I regret it
> But people can't forget it
> So then I am lonely and sad.

So when I am mad
I need to think that things aren't so bad
Then I can run or scream but not hit
And not act like a firecracker that was lit
And then I won't be so lonely and sad.

When working with young children, the activities that are used must convey REBT concepts in a concrete manner. With older children and adolescents, direct disputation of irrational beliefs is possible but often should be followed by introducing an image or experiment that reinforces the concept and its retention. For instance, an adolescent with numerous irrational beliefs learned to dispute them in counseling. To reinforce the disputing process, the counselor suggested that when he caught himself beginning to think irrationally, he should imagine a bug zapper with his irrational beliefs being "zapped" away. The young man reported that this worked very well, and in a short time he routinely was thinking more rationally.

To reiterate, one of the reasons REBT is so applicable to children and adolescents is that it embraces a wide variety of cognitive, behavioral, and emotive strategies in the intervention (Vernon, 1997; 2002a, 2002b). These techniques can be used to help children identify and dispute irrational beliefs, deal with troublesome emotions and behaviors, and develop effective new coping strategies.

Rational-emotive therapy can be applied to individual clients in school and agency settings. Further, the concepts can be used readily in classroom and small-group counseling settings with rational–emotive education (REE).

Rational-Emotive Education (REE)

Because of the educational nature of rational–emotive behavior therapy, its principles can be incorporated easily and systematically into a classroom or small-group setting to facilitate attitudinal and behavioral changes. Used in this manner, the primary emphasis is on prevention, although groups may have a problem-solving remedial focus. The major goal of rational–emotive education (REE) is to help children and adolescents understand, at an early age, the general principles of emotional health and how to apply these principles to help them deal more effectively with the challenges of growing up.

REE is a social–emotional learning program that helps young people help themselves (Vernon & Bernard, 2006). REE is based on the assumption that children can be taught to cope with life more effectively, providing them with tools they can apply to day-to-day developmental issues as well as more serious situational problems.

Classroom Applications

In the classroom setting, rational–emotive education is typically implemented through a series of structured emotional education lessons that are experientially based, allowing for student involvement and group interaction. Understandings are deduced from the use of games, role-playing, art activities, simulations, bibliotherapy, experiential activities, guided discussions, music and writing activities, and worksheets. In addition, considerable time is spent debriefing the lesson so children can master the content through carefully guided discussions.

Several REE programs have been developed, and their lessons have been used extensively throughout the United States and abroad (Bernard, 2001; Knaus, 1974; Vernon, 1998a, b, c; 2006a, b). These programs emphasize the following:

1. *Feelings*: A critical component of the lessons is learning to understand the connections among thoughts, feelings, and behaviors. Also important is to develop a feeling vocabulary, to learn to deal with emotional overreactions, to assess the intensity of feelings, and to develop appropriate ways to express feelings. REE points out the importance of recognizing that feelings change, that the same event can result in different feelings depending on who experiences the event and how it is perceived, and that having feelings is natural.

2. *Self-acceptance*: REE emphasizes developing an awareness of personal weaknesses as well as strengths, learning that "who I am" is not to be equated with "what I do," and understanding that people are fallible beings who will make mistakes and need to accept their own imperfections.

3. *Beliefs and behaviors*: REE distinguishes between rational and irrational beliefs, and the connection between beliefs and behaviors. It holds that rational beliefs result in moderate emotions and facilitate problem solving, whereas irrational beliefs in the form of demands are self-defeating and result in unproductive behaviors. Children, too, must understand the difference between facts and assumptions. As concrete thinkers, children and many adolescents readily misconstrue events by failing to differentiate fact (she didn't sit by me) and assumption (she's mad at me and doesn't want to be my friend). Because of their impulsive nature, young people all too often act on their assumptions and create more problems when others react to their overreaction.

4. *Disputing beliefs*: A cornerstone of REBT is to teach children to dispute irrational beliefs and thereby achieve a more sensible way of thinking and, in turn, behaving. Through a variety of creative methods, children can be taught various developmentally appropriate disputations that enable them to think more logically and functionally.

5. *Problem solving*: Teaching children to think objectively, tolerate frustration, examine the impact of beliefs on behaviors, and learn alternative ways of problem solving are crucial problem-solving components. This is achieved in REE by teaching children to challenge REE and use new behavioral strategies.

The lessons begin with a brief stimulus activity, such as an imagery activity, a problem-solving task, an art activity, bibliotherapy, a simulation game, writing a rational story, or completing a worksheet. The stimulus activity, designed to introduce the concept specified in the lesson objective, lasts 15–25 minutes depending on the children's age and the time allotted. Following the activity, students engage in a directed discussion about the concept introduced in the stimulus activity.

This discussion is the most important part of the lesson and is organized around two types of questions:

1. *Content questions*: Emphasize the cognitive learnings from the activity.
2. *Personalization questions*: Help the students apply the learnings to their own experiences.

The discussion usually lasts 15–25 minutes, again depending on the children's age and the time period.

The goal of these lessons is to teach the principles of rational thinking and to apply the concepts to common concerns and issues that children encounter in the course of normal development.

An REE Lesson

The goal of this lesson, designed for first and second graders, is to help them learn to differentiate facts from assumptions. The concepts learned in this lesson can be reinforced in the classroom in numerous ways to facilitate rational thinking. This lesson is entitled "Be a Fact Finder" (Vernon, 2006a, p. 53).

Materials

A large ball, a winter coat, a book, and a coloring book, as well as two sheets of poster paper, one labeled "Facts" and one labeled "Assumptions"

Procedure

1. Introduce the lesson by taping the two sheets of poster paper on the board and offering a simple explanation of each term, such as: "A fact is something that we know is true"; and "an assumption is something that we think is true but we don't have proof." Elicit examples from the children.
2. Hold up one of the objects and engage the children in a discussion about the facts. For example: "The ball is round, large, and red." As children state the facts, list them on the poster paper labeled "Facts."
3. After the children have identified several facts, ask what assumptions they have about this object when they look at it: For example: "The ball can bounce high"; "The ball is slippery to hold"; "The ball isn't heavy." Write these on the poster paper labeled "Assumptions." Continue this procedure with several other objects.
4. Explain that they can check out assumptions and that by doing so, they learn more facts. For example, the fact is that the book is thick and has a lot of pages. An assumption is that the book is good, but until they actually read the book, they won't know if it is good or not. Ask for other examples of how to check out facts.

Discussion

Content Questions

1. What is the difference between a fact and an assumption?
2. If you want to know whether an assumption is true, what can you do?
3. Do you think it is difficult or easy to identify facts? How do you do it?
4. Do you think identifying assumptions is hard or easy? How do you do it?
5. Do you think telling the difference between a fact and an assumption is easy or hard? How can you tell the difference?

Personalization Questions

1. Do you think you're good at knowing the difference between a fact and an assumption? If so, how do you do it?
2. What is something you can do next time you want to check out an assumption to see whether or not it is a fact? (Invite sharing of specific examples of things they want to check out.)

Follow-up Activity

The information learned from this REE lesson can be extended by encouraging the children to be "fact detectives" both at home and at school, finding examples of facts and assumptions and sharing them with the class the next day. The teacher can enforce this distinction as situations arise, as illustrated in this example:

Several days after the second graders had participated in the "Be a Fact Finder" lesson, a group of students returned from recess, arguing vehemently about a situation that had erupted on the playground. The teacher pulled them aside to discuss the problem and asked them to describe what they were upset about.

After listening, the teacher asked if they remembered the lesson on facts and assumptions, using several of the examples that had been discussed in the lesson. Then she took out a sheet of paper and asked each student to relate two facts about what had happened on the playground. Then she asked for assumptions. After some discussion, it became apparent to the students that they all agreed on the facts but that they had different assumptions. The teacher helped them challenge these assumptions by looking for more facts, and soon the disagreement was settled.

As this example shows, REE certainly will not eliminate all problems. But this preventive approach will equip children with information that may minimize a problem or help them reach new understandings and resolutions through the use of foundation tools. By using the "teachable moment," this teacher was able to help students apply the rational concepts they had learned in the lesson.

REE emotional education lessons should be implemented regularly with children at both the primary and secondary levels. The topics should be presented sequentially with core ideas introduced and reinforced as developmentally appropriate. For sequentially based lessons, the reader is referred to *Thinking, Feeling,*

Behaving: An Emotional Education Curriculum for Children (Vernon, 2006a), *Thinking, Feeling, Behaving: An Emotional Education Curriculum for Adolescents* (Vernon, 2006b), *The Passport Programs* (Vernon, 1998a, b, c), and *Program Achieve* (Bernard, 2001).

Small-Group Applications

Ellis (2002), a long-time proponent of group applications, claimed that this approach is usually more effective than individual REBT because the children can learn rational principles from multiple people. Terjesen and Esposito (2006) concurred, noting that the group is often mildly competitive, which can motivate members to achieve personal goals and complete homework. In addition, they receive feedback from multiple individuals, thereby learning how to challenge irrational thinking more effectively.

Readers may wish to consult Terjesen and Esposito (2006) on REBT group therapy and Vernon (2007) on REBT groups. Below, two types of rational–emotive groups will be described briefly: (a) problem-centered, and (b) preventive.

The Problem-Centered Group

In the problem-centered group, members raise their current concerns and are taught to apply REBT principles for problem resolution. Group members learn from the problems they present and also by observing how other members' problems are addressed (DiGiuseppe, 1999). The group leader may also use didactic methods to teach the ABCs of REBT, disputational skills, and problem-solving strategies as appropriate. Major objectives include modeling rational attitudes and helping group members apply the basic ideas of REBT. As members learn the concepts, they are involved in group interaction, and they help the individual presenting the problem apply REBT principles. In a problem-centered group, members are typically volunteer participants, although teachers or parents may recommend that they attend. Counselors may also invite members to join a group to follow up on individual counseling.

A variation of the problem-centered group is to select a specific topic that all participants are grappling with, such as anger, procrastination, perfectionism, low tolerance for frustration, or conflict resolution. In addition, topics such as dealing with parental divorce or other types of loss, abuse, or transitions such as moving may be the focus. Group members may volunteer because they identify with the topic, or they may be referred and requested to join.

With this approach the discussion is limited to the specific topic, and the leader helps members apply REBT concepts to deal with current issues relative to the topic. Similar to the homogeneous group identified by DiGiuseppe (1999), group participants are encouraged to help each other, but the leader also assumes a more active role, at least initially, and in keeping with the age and level of participation of the group members. The group setting provides an opportunity for members to learn more about their issues, explore and express their feelings, and learn how their thoughts affect their feelings and behaviors.

The Preventive Group

The REBT group that emphasizes prevention is similar to rational–emotive education except that it is used in small groups of 6 to 10 members, which allows for more interaction and personalization of concepts. In the preventive group the assumption is that participants do not have a serious problem but, instead, are learning skills. This type of group is geared to normal developmental difficulties, and the children and adolescents learn to apply REBT concepts to help them deal with the typical challenges involved in growing up.

Topics may be relationships with parents, peers, or teachers; communication and assertion; school success; problem-solving and decision making; or self-acceptance. The group sessions are structured around an activity with a specific objective, and the children are encouraged to interact and exchange ways in which they can apply concepts from the lesson to their lives.

Another way to conduct this type of group is to organize a series of six to eight sessions in which each session addresses a different topic related to REBT concepts. For example, the sessions might deal with teaching a feeling vocabulary, understanding the thought–feeling connection, identifying irrational beliefs, becoming more rational by learning to challenge beliefs, understanding that no one is "all good or bad," and learning that everyone makes mistakes. All of these concepts can be presented through activities designed to capture group members' interest and at the same time help them to learn rational concepts. Much of the material that has been developed for classroom applications is applicable to small-group sessions.

The specific content of the session must be developmentally and culturally appropriate. This approach is generally more didactic, and various techniques are used to introduce concepts—role-playing, games, simulations, art and music activities, videos, or bibliotherapy, for example. The intent is to teach concepts and engage group members in discussions and activities that facilitate their understanding of rational principles that they can apply to present and future developmental concerns. Some of the topics may be similar to those presented in the general problem-solving groups, but not with the assumption that students who volunteer or are asked to join have a significant problem. This approach is appropriate for anyone and is more preventive than remedial.

In both types of REBT groups, the group leader must develop rapport, create a climate of acceptance, and give positive reinforcement for rational behavior and for learning rational–emotive skills. Grouping children by age is best, because children who differ in age by more than 3 years are at different developmental stages and have different issues (DiGiuseppe, 1999).

Summary

Rational–emotive behavior therapy (REBT) can be used effectively with children and adolescents both therapeutically and preventively. Given the typical developmental milestones that children must master and the increasing stressors of contemporary society, helping professionals must concentrate on children's socioemotional development and provide therapeutic approaches that deal with children's immediate concerns and also help them develop coping skills so they can solve problems independently.

Even though Knaus (1974) summarized the goal of RET more than 3 decades ago, his words still provide an excellent summary of the primary purpose of this approach.

> Permitting a youngster to down himself or herself, and to become afflicted with needless anxiety, depression, guilt, hostility, and lack of discipline, and then taking that individual later in life and attempting to intensively "therapize" him or her in one-to-one encounters or small groups, is indeed a wasteful, tragically inefficient procedure. Far better, if it can be truly done, is to help this youngster to understand, at an early age, some of the general principles of emotional health and to teach him or her to consistently apply these principles to and with self and others. This is now one of the main goals of RET. (p. xii)

Rational–emotive behavior therapy is increasingly being used with children and adolescents to help them "get better," not just "feel better." Professionals concerned with helping today's youth will find this counseling approach extremely viable with young clients.

References

Barrish, H. H., & Barrish, I. J. (1985). *Managing parental anger.* Shawnee Mission, KS: Overland Press.

Barrish, I. J., & Barrish, H. H. (1989). *Surviving and enjoying your adolescent.* Kansas City, MO: Westport.

Bernard, M. E. (2001). *Program achieve: A curriculum of lessons for teaching students how to achieve and develop social–emotional–behavioral well-being* (Vols. 1–6.). Laguna Beach, CA: You Can Do It! Education.

Bernard, M. E., Ellis, A., & Terjesen, M. (2006). Rational-emotive approaches to childhood disorders. In A. Ellis & M. E. Bernard (Eds.), *Rational emotive behavioral approaches to childhood disorders: Theory, practice, and research* (pp. 3-84). New York: Springer.

Bernard, M. E., & Joyce, M. R. (1984). *Rational-emotive therapy with children and adolescents.* New York: Wiley.

DiGiuseppe, R. (1999). Rational emotive behavior therapy. In H. T. Prout & D. T. Brown, *Counseling and psychotherapy with children and adolescents: Theory and practice for school settings* (pp. 252–293). New York: John Wiley & Sons.

DiGiuseppe, R., & Bernard, M. E. (2006). REBT assessment and treatment with children. In A. Ellis and M. E. Bernard (Eds.), *Rational emotive behavioral approaches to childhood disorders: Theory, practice, and research* (pp. 85–114). New York: Springer.

DiGiuseppe, R., & Kelter, J. (2006). Treating aggressive children: A rational-emotive behavior systems approach. In A. Ellis and M. E. Bernard (Eds.), *Rational emotive behavioral approaches to childhood disorders: Theory, practice, and research* (pp. 257–280). New York: Springer.

Doyle, K. A. and Terjesen, M. D. (2006). Rational-emotive behavior therapy and attention deficit hyperactivity disorder. In A. Ellis and M. E. Bernard (Eds.), *Rational emotive behavioral approaches to childhood disorders: Theory, practice, and research* (pp. 281–309). New York: Springer.

Dryden, W. (2002a). Idiosyncratic REBT. In W. Dryden (Ed.), *Idiosyncratic rational emotive behavior therapy* (pp. 2–14). Ross-on-Wye, UK: PCCS Books.

Dyrden, W. (2002b). *Fundamentals of rational emotive behavior therapy: A training handbook.* London: Whurr.

Dryden, W. (Ed.). (2003). *Rational emotive behavior therapy: Theoretical developments.* New York: Brunner-Routledge.

Dryden, W., & Ellis, A. (2001). Rational emotive behavior therapy. In K. S. Dobson (Ed.), *Handbook of cognitive behavioral therapies* (pp. 295–347). New York: Guilford Press.

Dryden, W., DiGiuseppe, R., & Neenan, M. (2003). *A primer on rational emotive therapy* (2nd ed.). Champaign, IL: Research Press.

Dryden, W., & Neenan, M. (2004). *The rational emotive behavioural approach to therapeutic change.* London, Sage.

Ellis, A. (1995). Fundamentals of rational emotive behavior therapy for the 1990's. In W. Dryden (Ed.), *Rational emotive behaviour therapy* (pp. 1–30). London: Sage.

Ellis, A. (1996). *Better, deeper, and more enduring brief therapy: The rational emotive behavior therapy manual.* New York: Brunner/Mazel.

Ellis, A. (2001a). *Overcoming destructive beliefs, feelings, and behaviors.* Amherst, NY: Prometheus Books.

Ellis, A. (2001b). *Overcoming destructive beliefs, feelings, and behaviors.* Amherst, NY: Prometheus Books.

Ellis, A. (2002). *Overcoming resistance: A rational emotive behavior therapy integrated approach.* New York: Springer.

Ellis, A., & Bernard, M. E. (1983). Rational–emotive approaches to the problems of childhood. In A. Ellis & M. E. Bernard (Eds.), *Rational–emotive approaches to the problems of childhood* (pp. 3–36). New York: Plenum.

Ellis, A. & Bernard, M. E. (Eds.). (2006). *Rational emotive behavioral approaches to childhood disorders: Theory, practice, and research.* New York: Springer.

Ellis. A., & Dryden, W. (1997). *The practice of rational–emotive therapy.* New York: Springer.

Ellis, A., & MacLaren, C. (1998). *Rational emotive behavior therapy: A therapist's guide.* Atascadero, CA: Impact.

Ellis, A., & Wilde, J. (2002). *Case studies in rational emotive behavior therapy with children and adolescents.* Columbus, OH: Merrill Prentice Hall.

Grieger, R. M. & Boyd, J. D. (2006). Childhood anxieties, fears, and phobias: A cognitive-beahvioral, psychosituational approach. In A. Ellis & M. E. Bernard (Eds.), *Rational emotive behavioral approaches to childhood disorders: Theory, practice and research* (pp. 232–256). New York: Springer.

Huber, C. H. (1981). Cognitive coping for elementary age children. *RET Work, 1,* 5–10.

Joyce, M. R. (2006). A developmental, rational-emotive behavioral approach for working with parents. In A. Ellis & M. E. Bernard (Eds.), *Rational emotive behavioral approaches to childhood disorders: Theory, practice, and research* (pp. 177–211). New York: Springer.

Knaus, W. J. (1974). *Rational–emotive education: A manual for elementary school teachers.* New York: Institute for Rational Living.

Knaus, W. J. (2006). Frustration tolerance training for children. In A. Ellis & M. E. Bernard (Eds.), *Rational emotive behavioral approaches to childhood disorders: Theory, practice and research* (pp. 133–155). New York: Springer.

McInerney, J. F., & McInerney, B. C. M. (2006). Working with the parents and teachers of exceptional children. In A. Ellis & M. E. Bernard (Eds.), *Rational emotive behavioral approaches to childhood disorders: Theory, practice, and research* (pp. 369–384). New York: Springer.

Merrell, K. W. (2001). *Helping students overcome depression and anxiety: A practical guide.* New York: Guilford Press.

Pincus, D. (1990). *Feeling good about yourself: Strategies to guide young people toward more positive, personal feelings.* Carthage, IL: Good Apple.

Terjesen, M. D., & Esposito, M. A. (2006). Rational-emotive behavior group therapy with children and adolescents. In A. Ellis & M. E. Bernard (Eds.), *Rational emotive behavioral approaches to childhood disorders: Theory, practice, and research* (pp. 385–414). New York: Springer.

Vernon, A. (1983). Rational–emotive education. In A. Ellis & M. E. Bernard (Eds.), *Rational–emotive approaches to the problems of childhood* (pp. 467–483). New York: Plenum.

Vernon, A. (1997). Applications of REBT with children and adolescents. In J. Yankura & W. Dryden (Eds.), *Special populations of REBT—A therapist's casebook* (pp. 11–37). New York: Springer.

Vernon, A. (1998a). *The Passport Program: A journey through social, emotional, cognitive, and self-development (grades 1–5).* Champaign, IL: Research Press.

Vernon, A. (1998b). *The Passport Program: A journey through social, emotional, cognitive, and self-development (grades 6–8).* Champaign, IL: Research Press.

Vernon, A. (1998c). *The Passport Program: A journey through social, emotional, cognitive, and self-development (grades 9–12).* Champaign, IL: Research Press.

Vernon, A. (2002a). *What works when with children and adolescents: A handbook of individual counseling techniques.* Champaign, IL: Research Press.

Vernon, A. (2002b). Idiosyncratic REBT. In W. Dryden (Ed.), *Idiosyncratic rational emotive behaviour therapy* (pp. 143–158). Ros-on-Wye: PCCS Books.

Vernon, A. (2004a). Applications of rational-emotive behavior therapy with children and adolescents. In A. Vernon (Ed.), *Counseling children and adolescents* (3rd ed.) (pp. 140–157). Denver: Love.

Vernon, A. (2004b). Using cognitive behavioral techniques. In B. Erford (Ed.), *Professional school counseling: A handbook of theories, programs, & practice* (pp. 91–99). Austin, TX: Pro-Ed.

Vernon, A. (2004c). Rational emotive education. *Romanian Journal of Cognitive and Behavioral Psychotherapies, 4,* 23–27.

Vernon, A. (2006a). *Thinking, feeling, behaving: An emotional education curriculum for children.* Champaign, IL: Research Press.

Vernon, A. (2006b). *Thinking, feeling, behaving: An emotional education curriculum for adolescents.* Champaign, IL: Research Press.

Vernon, A. (2006c). Depression in children and adolescents: REBT approaches to assessment and treatment. In A. Ellis & M.E. Bernard (Eds.), *Rational emotive behavioral approaches to childhood disorders: Theory, practice, and research* (pp. 212–231). New York: Springer.

Vernon, A. (2007). Application of rational emotive behavior therapy to groups within classrooms and educational settings. In R.W. Christner, J.L. Steward, & A. Freeman (Eds.), *Handbook of cognitive-behavior group therapy with children and adolescents: Specific settings and presenting problems* (pp. 107–128). New York: Routledge.

Vernon, A. (2009). Rational emotive behavior therapy. In A. Vernon and T. Kottman (Eds.), *Counseling theories: Practical applications with children and adolescents in school settings* (pp. 153–184). Denver, CO: Love.

Vernon, A., & Bernard, M. E. (2006). Applications of REBT in schools. In A. Ellis & M. E. Bernard (Eds.), *Rational emotive behavioral approaches to childhood disorders: Theory, practice, and research* (pp. 415-460). New York: Springer.

Wagner, E. E. (1966). Counseling children. *Rational Living, 1*, 26–28.

Waters, V (1981). The living school. *RET Work, 1*, 1–6.

Waters, V (1982). Therapies for children: Rational–emotive therapy. In C. R. Reynolds & T. B. Gutkin (Eds.), *Handbook of school psychology*. New York: Wiley.

Wilde, J. (1992). *Rational counseling with school-aged populations: A practical guide.* Muncie, IN: Accelerated Development.

Wilde, J. (1995). *Anger management in schools: Alternatives to student violence.* Lancaster, PA: Technomic.

Wilde, J. (1996). *Treating anger, anxiety, and depression in children and adolescents: A cognitive–behavioral perspective.* New York: Taylor and Francis.

Wilde, J. (2001). Interventions for children with anger problems. *Journal of Rational–Emotive and Cognitive–Behavior Therapy, 19*(3), 191–197.

Young, H. (2006). REBT assessment and treatment with adolescents. In A. Ellis & M. E. Bernard (Eds.), *Rational emotive behavioral approaches to childhood disorders: Theory, practice, and research* (pp. 115–132). New York: Springer.

Counseling With Exceptional Children

Shari Tarver-Behring and Michael E. Spagna

Children and adolescents who are exceptional have received increasing attention as a group in need of comprehensive, developmental intervention approaches (Milsom & Petterson, 2006). Federal legislation mandates that all counselors who work with children and adolescents, including those who are not working within public school settings, be knowledgeable about the identification of, and services for, students who are considered exceptional because of disabilities, giftedness, or both. In addition, all counselors have a professional and ethical responsibility to be leaders and advocates in promoting the full potential of all individuals, including exceptional groups (Bemak & Chung, 2005; Stone & Clark, 2001: Tarver-Behring & Spagna, 1997). Counselors are among those who can serve children and their families as intended by both legal and professional guidelines (American Psychological Association, 2000; American School Counseling Association, 2005).

In their professional practice, counselors likely will encounter children and adolescents who are exceptional. According to the National Center for Education Statistics (2005), approximately 14% of the school-age population is classified as having a federally recognized disability and, therefore, receiving special education and/or related services. This figure does not include gifted children, who also are significantly different from the norm and in need of identification, curricular modifications, and counseling interventions (Colangelo, 2003). Nor does this figure include students with disabilities who do not qualify for special education but may be eligible for other educational and counseling services. In addition, it is not clear how many twice-exceptional students, who have an identified disability as well as being gifted, are in the schools, because this is a newly recognized group in need (Assouline, Nicpon, & Huber, 2006).

Despite the number of children and adolescents with exceptional needs, many counseling professionals lack the confidence and training to serve these groups. Some are uncomfortable with people with disabilities. Others have incorrect information or prejudices about those with exceptional needs, in particular students from diverse cultures (de Barona & Barona, 2006; Peterson, 2006). In addition, because services to children and adolescents with disabilities are delivered most often by special educational personnel within public schools, counselors may believe that their skills are not needed for these groups (Tarver-Behring, Spagna, & Sullivan, 1998). Most counselors, however, are willing to serve these students and are equipped with the array of the skills needed to work with these children and their families—communication strategies, a background in human development, and experience with a variety of therapeutic techniques (Milsom, 2006).

Counselors can prepare themselves to serve exceptional groups in several ways. First, they must clarify their feelings and attitudes about working with these children and adolescents. Accurate information and direct experience can facilitate their awareness and acceptance of exceptional groups, especially those with diverse backgrounds (de Barona & Barona, 2006; Milsom, 2006). In addition, counselors must obtain knowledge and training for working with specific groups with exceptional needs (Milsom & Peterson, 2006; Tarver-Behring et al., 1998). They can obtain this knowledge through training about federal and state guidelines, consultation and collaboration with professionals and family members, supervision, workshops and literature on best practices, and community resources. Finally, counselors must be prepared to move beyond the traditional counselor model, which is less effective with these populations, to a comprehensive service model coordinated with a collaborative team of community and school professionals, family members, and, when possible, the students themselves.

This chapter first presents a brief legislative history of special education, including recent changes in the laws and definitions; then describes identifying characteristics of children with sensory, physical and neurological, developmental disabilities, hyperactivity, and giftedness; and discusses comprehensive and culturally sensitive counseling approaches that have proven beneficial for specific groups of exceptional children and adolescents.

Overview and History of Special Education

Taking the lead from the civil rights movement of the 1950s, which initiated the process of dismantling racial discrimination, parents of children with disabilities decided in the 1960s and early 1970s that they could achieve better services for their children by taking an activist stance and forcing public schools that previously had segregated students with disabilities to allow their children access to services. Until then, schools had denied admission to public education for students with a range of disabling conditions.

Subsequently, two federal laws were passed that drastically changed this situation: Section 504 of the Rehabilitation Act of 1973 and Public Law 93-380 (Education of the Handicapped Amendments of 1974). These laws, for the first time in modern history, prohibited discrimination by federally funded organizations based on the existence of a disability (Section 504) and required services to be put in place for students with disabilities (PL 93-380). They also laid the foundation for the landmark piece of legislation in 1975, Public Law 94-142, the Education for All Handicapped Children Act. PL 94-142 provided access to public education for all students from ages 3 through 21 with disabilities. Since its enactment, the law has been reauthorized three times, as

Public Law 101-476 (the Individuals with Disabilities Education Act) in 1990;
Public Law 105-17 (also known as the Individuals with Disabilities Education Act) in 1997; and
Public Law 108-446 in 2004.

The original law had six provisions, each designed to allow for a free and appropriate public education for students with disabilities:

1. *Child Find*: Schools were required to seek out all students with disabilities within the boundaries of a given local plan area (usually a district);.
2. *Nondiscriminatory assessment*: Students suspected of having disabilities were to receive a comprehensive and nondiscriminatory assessment to determine their eligibility for special education and/or related services.
3. *Individualized education program (IEP)*: Based on a comprehensive assessment, students found eligible for special education and/or related services were to have an individually designed educational program, addressing their specific educational needs.
4. *Least restrictive environment*: Students were to receive, to the maximum extent possible, education with peers not having disabilities and were to be removed from general education classes only when a multidisciplinary team deemed these classes to be more restrictive to a given student's specific educational program.
5. *Due-process safeguards*: These guidelines ensured that parents and schools were to be equal partners in the education of students with disabilities. (Prior to passage of PL 94-142, schools often made unilateral decisions concerning educational placement and instructional delivery.)
6. *Parental involvement*: Parents were to have equal input into all educational decisions affecting their children and the right to refuse educational placements and services if desired.

All of these provisions have been kept intact through the reauthorizations of PL 94-142. In addition, eligibility was expanded to children ages birth through 3 years of age. The most recent reauthorization, PL 108-446, reflects the following changes (National Center for Learning Disabilities, 2007):

■ a closer alignment with the Elementary and Secondary Education Act of 1965 (No Child Left Behind Act, 2005), including new requirements ranging from the qualifications of special education teachers to assessments of students with disabilities;

- a requirement that complaints be limited to violations that occur not more than 2 years before the date the parent or school district knew or should have known about the alleged action;
- a requirement that if a parent refuses to consent to the provision of services, school districts may not use procedures such as mediation and due process to provide services;
- a change in handling discipline that allows school personnel to make decisions regarding a change in placement on a case-by-case basis;
- a change that now allows the use of mediation without first requiring the filing for a hearing;
- a provision that IEPs must contain measurable annual goals and a description of how the child's progress toward meeting those goals will be measured and reported;
- a requirement that special education and related services be based primarily on peer-reviewed research;
- a new requirement that states have in place policies and procedures designed to prevent the inappropriate overidentification or disproportionate representation by race and ethnicity of children as students with disabilities;
- a new provision that requires schools to provide a summary of a child's academic achievement and functional performance upon termination of services; and
- a new requirement that initial evaluations must be completed within 60 days after receiving parental consent.

Categories of Exceptional Children

Federal law ensures a free and appropriate public education for students with disabilities. According to the Individuals with Disabilities Education Act of 2004, children who fall within the following 10 categories of exceptionality are eligible to receive special education and related services: mental retardation, hearing impairments (including deafness), speech or language impairments, visual impairments (including blindness), serious emotional disturbance, orthopedic impairments, autism, traumatic brain injury, other health impairments, or specific learning disabilities.

Historically, the Commission on Excellence in Special Education (U.S. Department of Education, 2002) has recommended that these 10 eligibility categories be grouped into three major types of disorders—sensory disabilities, physical and neurological disabilities, and developmental disabilities—to facilitate the assessment and identification procedures often associated with students with disabilities.

Section 504 of the Rehabilitation Act

Some children who do not qualify for specific special educational categories under the Individuals with Disabilities Education Act are eligible for educational modifications and services under Section 504 of the Rehabilitation Act of 1973. The Rehabilitation Act of 1973 is in essence a civil rights act that protects the rights of persons with disabilities in settings where federal funds are received, such as public schools (Yell & Shriner, 1997).

Section 504 specifically protects students in educational settings whose disabilities do not affect their educational performance adversely leading to inclusion in a special educational category but who still require reasonable accommodations in the instructional setting to receive an appropriate education. Under Section 504 a qualified person with disabilities is someone who has a physical or mental impairment that substantially limits one or more major life activities (walking, seeing, hearing, speaking, learning, etc.), who has experienced the impairment for some time, and who is perceived as exhibiting the impairment currently.

Examples of students who are eligible for reasonable educational modifications under Section 504 include those with attention deficit/hyperactivity disorder, communicable diseases, behavioral disorders, physical disabilities, chronic asthma, and diabetes. Educational modifications include providing reduced or modified classwork assignments, different approaches in testing, a teacher's aide, seating the student in the front row, a behavior modification plan, building and program accessibility, and computer and technical aids. In addition, students who have met the definitions of qualified disabilities are eligible to be evaluated and to receive a written plan that describes placement and services.

Culturally Diverse Students in Special Education

For many years federal legislation has required that special education services be provided to students in a fair and culturally equitable manner. The most recent reauthorization of IDEA states that inappropriate overidentification or disproportionate representation by race and ethnicity of children as students with disabilities must be prevented through public school policies and procedures.

Despite this mandate, the referral and enrollment of students from culturally and/or linguistically diverse backgrounds within the present-day special education system remains disproportionate (de Barona & Barona, 2006). African American, American Indian, and Latino students are referred and placed in special education programs at a much higher rate than Asian and European American students (American Youth Policy Forum and Center on Educational Policy, 2002). In particular, African American students are identified as having mental retardation three times more often than other students (Losen & Orfield, 2002; Skiba, Poloni-Staudinger, Simmons, Feggins-Azziz, & Chung, 2005).

Cultural inequity in special education referral and placement continues because of

- inadequate teacher training in culturally sensitive methodology (Short & Echevarria, 2005),
- cultural mismatch of the learner with classroom materials and context (Vogt & Shearer, 2003), and

- stereotypical expectations of lower performance toward certain groups by school professionals (Oswald, Coutinho, & Best, 2000; Weinstein, Tomlinson-Clarke, & Curran, 2004),
- inequitable referral practices because of subjective criteria and narrow paradigms (Frasier, Garcia, & Passow, 1995),
- poor educational pedagogy and lack of prereferral interventions in low-income schools (Committee on Minority Representation in Special Education, Donovan, & Cross, et al., 2002), and
- and unfair assessment procedures (Padilla & Medina, 1996).

In addition, school failure and special education referral may be attributable to other cultural variables, such as language differences, the adverse effects of poverty on school performance and study habits (Smith, 2001), and cultural differences in students' and teachers' values and behavioral expectations (Banks, 2004).

In the last decade, the educational field has identified a number of promising practices to correct these inequities, including

1. preservice training for teachers and specialists in effective culturally and linguistically appropriate educational practices, such as peer tutoring, cooperative learning, and cross-cultural meaningful communication in class (Gray & Fleishman, 2005);
2. prereferral culturally sensitive screening and consultation about alternative solutions in the general education classroom, such as sharing culturally relevant information with teachers about specific students, or encouraging the opportunity for group work rather than individual classroom work for diverse students from collectivistic backgrounds (Tarver-Behring, Cabello, Kushida, & Murguia, 2000; Tarver-Behring & Ingraham, 1998);
3. identification procedures for eligibility for special education categories that have been shown to reduce the inequity of minorities in special education using the *responsiveness to intervention* methodology, which measures students' responses to research-based interventions and employs these data to inform instruction (National Joint Committee on Learning Disabilities, 2005);
4. assessment methods that are culturally fair, reflect representative norms, are sensitive to linguistic demands and cultural loading of various tests, and involve the examination of both formal and informal data by a culturally competent interdisciplinary team (de Barona & Barona, 2006);
5. interventions with educational supports when academic risk factors are first evident in students (Echevarria, 2002);
6. culturally sensitive and inclusive school-based programs to support the academic and social success for all students (American Youth Policy Forum and Center on Educational Policy, 2002); and
7. involvement of family members in the education process to better understand the student's home values, learning, language, and interaction style and to foster a supportive, collaborative home-school relationship (de Barona & Barona, 2006).

Counselors can promote culturally equitable special education services by advocating for, and participating in, practices such as those just described.

History of Gifted Education

In 1972 the U.S. Department of Health, Education, and Welfare submitted a report to Congress identifying giftedness as an area of exceptionality and recommending that gifted students receive special services, including counseling. Since then, several federal laws have since been passed outlining services for the gifted population. Public Law 103-382 (1994) continued to support research and programming for gifted and talented students and encouraged the use of these resources for all students as well. More recently, in 2002, the No Child Left Behind Act (NCLB) was passed as the reauthorization of the Elementary and Secondary Education Act. The Javits program, included in NCLB, offers competitive statewide grants for the delivery of gifted and talented education.

The definition of giftedness has changed from a description of a unitary trait into a description of a complex group of talents influenced by culture, age, experience, and sociometric status, and sometimes hidden by variables such as learning disabilities (Shaklee, 1997; Silverman, 1993). The current definition of giftedness contained in the text of NCLB (2002) is as follows:

> Students, children, or youth who give evidence of high achievement capability in areas such as intellectual, creative, artistic, or leadership capacity, or in specific academic fields, and who need services and activities not ordinarily provided by the school in order to fully develop those capabilities. (p. 29)

Gifted education programs historically were designed to match the child's educational needs to a continuum of services similar to the design of special education, such as pullout programs and gifted classrooms. Funding for gifted education, however, has become increasingly limited in most states, resulting in a severe decrease in the educational services available for gifted children and youth. In addition, gifted children are being fully included in the general education classroom more frequently, similar to special education students, often with teachers who lack the time, skills, and resources to serve the gifted adequately (Shaklee, 1997).

Culturally Diverse Students in Gifted Programs

Disproportionately less diversity is found in programs for the academically gifted and talented (de Barona & Barona, 2006). Ford and Granthum (2003) reported findings of between 50% and 70% fewer students from culturally and linguistically different backgrounds in gifted school programs, with significant underrepresentation among African Americans, Latinos, and Native American groups (Committee on Minority Representation in Special Education et al., 2002). This inequity seems to stem in large part from the subjectivity of the selection process, which begins with teacher recommendations. Factors such as low expectations and teachers' lack of multicultural sensitivity, as well as lack of training to understand students' different learning styles among students, may explain why fewer diverse students are referred to gifted programs (de Barona & Barona, 2006).

The assessment of giftedness also can be biased because the often employed global, mainstream understanding of giftedness may miss culturally specific indicators of talent. In addition, professionals who identify giftedness often fail to follow a culturally inclusive selection process that uses multiple, authentic assessment measures (Borland, 2004). The services offered to gifted students, too, must be culturally responsive. Research shows higher dropout rates among minority versus non-minority gifted students (Renzulli & Park, 2002), possibly because the services fail to recognize and foster the unique areas of potential in underrepresented gifted students.

Counselors can advocate for fair and accurate identification and service for diverse gifted students in the following ways.

1. Counselors can facilitate training of school personnel in both gifted and general education in multicultural sensitivity and skills, and in multiple learning styles that have a cultural context, to avoid subjective and inaccurate assumptions about diverse students' educational performance.
2. Counselors should advocate for the identification of gifted abilities to include multiple measures that examine a range of talent and that are sensitive to the student's cultural and linguistic background.
3. Counselors can inform families about gifted services and ensure that they are included in the identification process and subsequent programs.
4. Counselors can advocate for culturally inclusive gifted services that recognize unique abilities to ensure the success of all students.

Twice-Exceptional Students as an Underrepresented Group

Twice-exceptional students are an underrepresented subgroup that is less likely to be referred for either gifted or special education services (Winebrenner, 2003). These students have learning difficulties that qualify them for special education services, as well as academic strengths for gifted and talented placement (Assouline et al., 2006). Only in the most recent revision of IDEA (2004) was this group recognized for the first time by federal legislation. The myth that exceptional academic ability and learning difficulties are mutually exclusive leads to failure to identify twice-exceptional students accurately Too, the conceptualization of gifted as a global area has led to the exclusion of many from gifted programs, even though most students, with or without disabilities, usually are not talented in all areas.

Finally, the assumption that gifted students are motivated and maintain excellent grades eliminates many students with learning disabilities who struggle with organization and academic work but are gifted in specific areas. These common misunderstandings increase the chances that twice-gifted students are overlooked for gifted services and receive services that target only special education needs (Assouline et al., 2006). Twice-exceptional students from diverse backgrounds are even more at risk for underrepresentation in identification and services in gifted programs because of the cultural issues already discussed.

Counselors can support twice-exceptional students by doing the following:

1. Counselors can advocate for the accurate identification of these students by gathering information about strengths and weaknesses from achievement and ability tests, discussing classroom performance with teachers, and consulting with parents, who are the most aware of the unique learning style of these students and the best advocates for appropriate services (Fertig, 2002). Parents and teachers may need support in understanding legal protections and resources in special education and gifted programs for students and how these areas interface.

2. Counselors can facilitate communication among students, parents, and teachers from general, gifted, and special education programs about the student's unique set of strengths and weaknesses, and collaborate to develop academic programming that accommodates these areas (especially programs that include the student in general education settings that are intellectually stimulating but provide supports). Students, in particular, must be encouraged to be aware of their learning style so they are able to self-advocate in educational settings (Assouline et al., 2006).

3. Counselors can assist twice-exceptional students can experience frustration, anxiety, or other psychological challenges as a result of their complex learning style (Olenchak & Reis, 2001). Counselors can offer social/emotional support for these challenges through individual and group counseling at school, consultation with teachers and parents, and referral to community services.

4. Counselors can assist twice-gifted students in vocational and educational planning following high school that takes into consideration the areas of talent and the areas requiring support (Assouline et al., 2006).

Students With Developmental Disabilities

Students with developmental disabilities, according to the Commission on Excellence in Special Education (U.S. Department of Education, 2002), include students having specific learning disabilities, speech and language impairments, emotional disturbance, mild mental retardation, and developmental delay. The categories of specific learning disabilities, emotional disturbance, and mild mental retardation are described in more detail here, which address the cognitive, academic, adaptive, social, perceptual-motor, and language functioning of students with these types of developmental disabilities.

Specific Learning Disabilities

Children and adolescents who have been identified as having specific learning disabilities usually are eligible for special education and related services only if they exhibit average intellectual functioning. This eligibility criterion has created a great deal of controversy, as children and adolescents with above-average intellectual functioning also may benefit from services in some areas. In direct comparison to students with mild mental retardation, who have global deficits in the areas of memory and attention, individuals with specific learning disabilities have difficulties in an encapsulated area or areas of cognitive functioning (e.g., phonemic awareness), referred to as *psychological processing deficits*. These deficits cause academic difficulties and result in achievement significantly below expectations given average intellectual capacity. The incidence of children and adolescents with specific learning disabilities was reported at 5.9% for the 50 states and DC for ages 3–21 during the 2003–04 school year (National Center for Education Statistics, 2005).

Adaptive functioning in students with specific learning disabilities, similar to cognitive ability, is relatively intact. Even though these children and adolescents might exhibit dependency on teachers and parents, they have learned in many instances how to compensate for the impact of their disabilities on life outside of school. Students with specific learning disabilities, similar to those with mild mental retardation, have low self-esteem and generally have a poorly defined self-concept (Elksnin & Elksnin, 2004). Even more than individuals with mild mental retardation, these students desire the acceptance of peers without disabilities, so much so that they place themselves at risk for gang involvement, law-breaking, and substance abuse.

Students with specific learning disabilities may have absolutely no deficits in perceptual-motor functioning, but if their specific learning disability does affect this area of functioning, as in individuals who have dysgraphia, their gross-motor and fine-motor skills may be so involved that even beginning handwriting skills might be affected.

In the area of language functioning, children and adolescents with specific learning disabilities may face any of a multitude of difficulties in both receptive and expressive language. These deficits might be evidenced by an inability to follow oral directions, to ask appropriate questions, to interact with peers socially, and so forth. *Dysnomia*, a type of specific learning disability that involves the inability to retrieve and express vocabulary, results in tip-of-the-tongue difficulties.

Cultural sensitivity should be considered in screening and referring students because a number of racial/ethnic subgroups have been misidentified for specific learning disabilities as a result of language differences, cultural mismatches in educational methodology, learning difficulties related to poverty, and teachers' versus students' cultural differences in behavioral expectations (American Youth Policy Forum and Center on Educational Policy, 2002).

Emotional Disturbance

The second category of children and adolescents identified as having developmental disabilities consists of students with emotional disturbance. Cognitively, these students usually are characterized as having at least low-average to average intellectual functioning and do not exhibit psychological processing deficits. According to the federal definition:

> (i) The term [emotional disturbance] means a condition exhibiting one or more of the following characteristics over a long period of time and to a marked degree that adversely affects a child's educational performance:
>
> (A) An inability to learn that cannot be explained by intellectual, sensory, or health factors.
> (B) An inability to build or maintain satisfactory interpersonal relationships with peers and teachers.
> (C) Inappropriate types of behavior or feelings under normal circumstances.
> (D) A general pervasive mood of unhappiness or depression.
> (E) A tendency to develop physical symptoms or fears associated with personal or school problems.
>
> (ii) The term includes schizophrenia. The term does not apply to children who are socially maladjusted, unless it is determined that they have an emotional disturbance. (IDEA, 1997, sec. 300.7[4])

Students with emotional disturbance fail academically as a direct result of emotional problems or internalized and/or externalized behaviors that impact their performance. For example, students with severe depression or suicidal ideation will encounter academic difficulties, and students who engage in repeated behavioral outbursts (e.g., kicking other students) also will suffer educational consequences—especially if they are suspended or expelled. Indeed, students with emotional disturbance often have discipline problems. The incidence of children and adolescents with emotional disturbance was reported at 1% for the 50 states and DC for ages 3–21 during the 2003–04 school year (National Center for Education Statistics, 2005).

As a result of their behavioral outbursts or generalized withdrawal, students with emotional disturbance generally have poor relationships with their peers without disabilities. Like students with specific learning disabilities, they usually have a poor self-concept and low self-esteem. Often, their behaviors elicit negative reactions in peers, teachers, and parents, resulting in nonacceptance. Thus, these students are particularly susceptible to outside influences and are at risk for substance involvement, gang-related activity, and so forth. Perceptual-motor skills and language functioning in this group generally are intact, but profane language and other behavioral outbursts resulting from emotional problems or socialized aggression can severely limit the interaction of these students with others.

As with the category of specific learning disabilities, African American students have been identified as having emotional difficulties at a higher rate than other cultural groups. Students from all cultural backgrounds must be understood and evaluated for emotional disorders in a culturally fair and appropriate manner (American Youth Policy Forum and Center on Educational Policy, 2002).

Mild Mental Retardation

The incidence of mild mental retardation was approximately 1.2% in the 50 states and Washington, DC for ages 3–21 during the 2003–04 school year (National Center for Education Statistics, 2005). Causes of mental retardation range from organic factors such as Down syndrome, to environmental factors such as fetal alcohol syndrome, malnutrition, and several known maternal infections (e.g., rubella).

Children and adolescents who have been identified as having mild mental retardation are determined to be eligible for special education and related services in accordance with federal law:

> [M]ental retardation means significantly subaverage general intellectual functioning, existing concurrently with deficits in adaptive behavior and manifested during the developmental period, that adversely affects a child's educational performance. (IDEA, 1997, section 300.7[6])

These children and adolescents, as a direct result of their subaverage cognitive functioning, generally learn at a slower pace than their peers without disabilities (Henley et al., 1993). They also do not like to attempt new tasks and use inefficient learning strategies when they are faced with new tasks. To be found eligible for special education and related services, these children and adolescents must be determined to have below-average adaptive behaviors. Some poor adaptive behaviors in students with mild mental retardation include poor self-help skills, low tolerance, low frustration and fatigue levels, and moral judgment commensurate with cognitive functioning.

Generally speaking, students with mild mental retardation are delayed in terms of social and emotional functioning. They usually have lower self-esteem and a more unfavorable self-concept than their peers without mental retardation. Because of their negative view of themselves, adolescents with mild mental retardation are susceptible to negative peer influences. Consequently, they might agree to experiment with foreign substances such as narcotics or to participate in gang-related activities in an attempt to gain peer acceptance (Polloway, Epstein, & Cullinan, 1985).

Perceptual-motor and language functioning also are delayed significantly in children and adolescents with mild mental retardation. This below-average functioning affects their ability to participate fully in physical education activities and negatively curtails their ability to socially communicate and interact with students without mild or moderate mental retardation.

African American students have been found to be identified disproportionately in this category at a much higher rate than other racial/ethnic groups. All students should be screened, referred, and assessed for services with particular attention to approaching the needs of students in a culturally sensitive and fair manner (American Youth Policy Forum and Center on Educational Policy, 2002).

Counseling Students With Developmental Disabilities

The field of counseling is recognizing the importance of serving children and adolescents with developmental disabilities and their families (Milsom, 2006; Scarborough & Gilbride, 2006; Thurneck, Warner, & Cobb, 2007). Although counselors historically have served students with developmental disabilities less often than others, counselor attitudes have become more positive toward interventions with students who have developmental disabilities, as well as toward the inclusion of these students in general education settings (Isaacs, Greene, & Valesky, 1998). This is especially the case when training and resources are available for counselors to work with these groups (Beasley, 2004; Milsom, 2002). Of utmost importance, counselors must understand the characteristics and needs of these students and their families and seek out training and supervision in diagnosis and treatment from colleagues from a range of disciplines (Carpenter, King-Sears, & Keys, 1998).

Also crucial is familiarity with the criteria for qualifying for special educational categories and services, as outlined earlier, and familiarity with the rights of parents and children pertaining to these services. Counselors should advocate for culturally sensitive consultation about alternative solutions in the general education classroom prior to referral and placement in special education (de Barona & Barona, 2006; Tarver-Behring & Ingraham, 1998). Counselors also should support and participate directly in educational supports when academic difficulties are first evident (Echevarria, 2002). Counselors, too, must have general knowledge of culturally fair methods and instruments for assessing children and youth in various categories.

Once an exceptional need has been identified, counselors may provide parents with referrals for various services, such as educational evaluations and services within the public school setting; health screenings; neurological evaluations; psychiatric assessments for medication; speech and language services, physical therapy, and career and vocational resources, both at school and in the community; specialized family counseling services; and support groups. Then counselors can consult with teachers, special educational personnel, parents, and community sources to plan educational and social interventions in a coordinated manner.

The student (especially if he or she is an adolescent) should be included in decision making about educational and therapeutic plans, if feasible. By including the children, they become educated about their strengths and weaknesses and feel mastery in helping to decide how to meet their special needs (Taub, 2006). Whenever possible, children and adolescents with mild and moderate disorders should be fully included in the general education classroom with appropriate modifications to allow for optimal educational and social opportunities (Sciarra, 2004; Ysseldyke, Algozzine, & Thurlow, 2000).

Counselors also can help to promote social and emotional adjustment for children and adolescents with developmental disabilities (Tarver-Behring, Spagna, &

Sullivan, 1998; Taub, 2006). A number of sourcebooks are available offering intervention strategies, describing social skills programs, and listing therapeutic books for counselors to use with these children and adolescents, as well as with their parents and teachers (Albrecht, 1995; Bloomquist, 1996; Klein & Kemp, 2004; Klein & Shive, 2001; Pierangelo & Jacoby, 1996; Rosenberg & Edmond–Rosenberg, 1994; Sinason, 1997; Smith, 1991).

In the school setting, counselors can assist the child or adolescent with developmental disabilities by consulting with teachers about social skills strategies and programs for the entire class. For example, with the guidance of counselors, teachers can act as role models by showing respect for all students, help the class generate ground rules for classroom communication, and give positive feedback to students without disabilities who are engaging in social interaction or academic activities with classmates with disabilities.

In the school setting, collaborative and systemic interventions that are comprehensive and developmental in nature are strongly recommended to address academic, social, and career areas for all students, including those with developmental disabilities (American School Counselor Association, 2004). Schoolwide social inclusion programs are recommended as the most effective method for developing inclusive attitudes, such as those that teach empathy for differences and respect for others through campuswide cooperative interactions among students with and without developmental disabilities (Heinrichs, 2003; Leiberman, James, & Ludwa, 2004). For example, *The Yes I Can* Program for middle school and high school students promotes understanding and acceptance of students with developmental disabilities by their nondisabled peers through structured positive social contact for the entire academic year (Abery et al., 1997). In addition, schoolwide academic programs and a philosophy that promotes success for all students instead of competition, and different learning styles instead of deficiencies, lead to greater acceptance and cooperation (Vaughn, 2002).

Both within and outside the school setting, counselors can work directly with children and adolescents with developmental disabilities through individual and group counseling on key social and emotional areas of difficulty, such as low self-esteem. Counselors can help these children and adolescents build positive self-esteem by modeling appropriate ways to express feelings, teaching them how to think of alternative solutions to a problem, empowering these youngsters to be involved in decision making about themselves, creating opportunities for them to learn positive behavior through rewards and recurring successful experiences, providing them with accurate information about the disability, involving positive role models in counseling, and identifying others with the disability who have succeeded (Pierangelo & Jacoby, 1996; Razza & Tomasulo, 2005; Willner, 2005).

Further, counselors can work with the entire family on physical and emotional well-being, parenting, disability-related support, and positive interactions and acceptance in the home to promote conditions for these families and their children and adolescents to attain optimal quality of life (Turnbull, 2004). Counselors promote emotional adjustment of all family members by encouraging positive feelings for one another within the family, discussing how to balance attention for each child in the family, identifying positive strategies to manage behaviors at home, and specifying methods for support and stress reduction for the parents (Taub, 2006).

Specifically, parents may benefit from assistance with being overprotective and worried about their child being socially accepted by nondisabled peers (Heward, 2003). This can be an issue especially during adolescence, when adolescents with developmental disabilities want to be treated in an age-appropriate manner. Counselors should convey that developing independence and self-advocacy skills are in the adolescent's long-term best interests (Klein & Kemp, 2004; Taub, 2006).

Counseling Students With Specific Learning Disabilities

Because one of the primary difficulties of children and adolescents with specific learning disabilities is in the academic area, counselors who work with these individuals are most effective when collaborating and consulting with a team of teachers, as well as parents and community service providers. Referred to as the *ecological approach*, indirect services such as consultation are used in combination with direct interventions (Dwyer, Osher, & Hoffman, 2000; Meyers, Parsons, & Martin, 1990). The ecological approach emphasizes the interactions among individual, cultural, and environmental factors when assisting students, rather than addressing only individual deficits (Mishna & Muskat, 2004).

The model can be effective when assisting approximately 40% of students with learning disabilities who also struggle with psychosocial issues (Kavale & Forness, 1996). Many of the developmental areas for children and adolescents with specific learning disabilities, however, are entirely normal and may even be areas of strength. These areas can be encouraged within a supportive environmental context to promote their overall adjustment. This is particularly important in counseling with diverse students with disabilities, for whom mainstream services may have to be adjusted to be culturally appropriate and effective (Sue & Sue, 2003).

Federal law mandates that children and adolescents with specific learning disabilities be included in the general education classroom to the fullest extent possible. Students with learning disabilities have been found to perform better both socially and academically when they are included in the general education classroom. Therefore, counselors should support inclusion by collaborating with general education teachers and resource specialists who provide specialized services to students with learning disabilities (Tarver-Behring & Spagna, 1997; Tarver-Behring, Spagna, & Sullivan, 1998). Still applicable are Westman's (1994) suggestions that counselors consult and collaborate with teachers about

- identifying specific academic techniques (e.g., teaching the sequential-step approach to math problems, using repetition, teaching outlining techniques, and instructing students in the use of memory aids);
- implementing classroom accommodations (e.g., administering oral tests, using computers, audiotaping lectures, reducing assignments, and allowing extended time to complete work); and

■ developing motivational approaches (e.g., employing internal and external reinforcers, token economies, and contracts for adolescents) that create a supportive
environment to meet each student's special needs

Counselors who are less skilled in some of these interventions might team with
the resource specialist to offer these services to the general education teacher. The
partnership between special education and general education teachers is necessary
for successful full inclusion, but it often does not happen because of time constraints,
scheduling differences, and the differing roles of school personnel (Eichinger &
Woltman, 1993). Consequently, counselors must assume an active role in advocating
for these students.

Social adjustment can be an area of particular need for students with specific
learning disabilities, either because of weaknesses in social perception or of being
viewed as different because of academic or social difficulties (Taub, 2006). Social
rejection leads to further social problems because these children and adolescents
miss out on important lessons in areas such as communication, responsibility, and
independence when they are excluded from peer-group activities (Sciarra, 2004;
Witt, 2004). Counselors can help teachers promote social inclusion in the classroom
by providing a structured social skills curriculum for positive interactions between
students with and without disabilities, pairing students with learning disabilities with
a peer mentor, creating cooperative work groups, and teaching collaborative problem
solving (Tarver-Behring et al., 1998). When providing services to adolescents who
are fully included in general education, classroom teachers should be alert to the sensitivity to peer acceptance at this age.

Although postsecondary transition planning is critical for adolescents with
learning disabilities, it is often lacking for this population. Unfortunately, when
transition planning does take place, these students infrequently receive career counseling about postsecondary degrees and often are guided toward vocational rather
than university paths (Janiga & Costenbader, 2002). Counselors can act as collabo-
rators, advocates, and direct service providers in transition planning for the postsecondary level (Milsom & Hartley, 2005). Counselors can collaborate with college
admission officers about testing accommodations and courses required for admission into college.

Whenever possible, counselors should attempt to involve both students and parents in postsecondary planning (Sitlington, Clark, & Kolstoe, 2000). In individual
and group counseling, counselors can help students to become aware of their unique
learning styles, acquire knowledge of postsecondary services and educational supports, learn about their rights, and develop self-advocacy skills. Self-advocacy—the
awareness and ability to communicate about one's needs—is especially important
for success in the future (Krebs, 2002). Counselors can coach students in self-advocacy skills by modeling these skills, role-playing the skills, and then having the student practice the skills with teachers (Milsom & Hartley, 2005). Self-advocacy skills
can be particularly beneficial for diverse students with learning disabilities who are
moving to the postsecondary level (Durodoye, Combes, and Bryant, 2004).

Students with learning disabilities sometimes have low self-esteem, anxiety, and depression in relation to academic and social challenges (Orenstein, 2000; Wren & Einhorn, 2000). Counselors can offer individual and group counseling for those who need more support. Career and social emotional counseling approaches may have to be modified to best support individuals with learning disabilities, given each of their unique needs (Milsom & Hartley, 2005). Adjustments might include having shorter sessions and reviewing information when the student has a short attention span, or providing aids such as notes to facilitate comprehension.

Parents of children and adolescents with learning disabilities often experience anxiety and stress because of their child's academic, social, and behavioral challenges (Smith, 2001). Process-oriented counseling groups have been found to be effective in reducing their stress (Shechtman & Gilat, 2005). In addition, counselors can offer parent education programs and community referrals to parents in relation to specific difficulties and demands in the home, such as parenting skills in developing schedules with parents who are frustrated because of their children's lack of organization, and tutorial services to reduce parents' stress surrounding schoolwork demands (Westman, 1994). If the child has attention difficulties in combination with specific learning disabilities, counselors can assist parents with behavioral interventions, as well as environmental accommodations such as short tasks, structured activities, visual aids, minimal distractions, and simple, clear directions. The parents of children who have not responded to other techniques can be referred to a psychiatrist to consider the possibility of prescribing stimulant medication (Barkley, 2006).

Counseling Students With Emotional Disturbance

Children and adolescents with severe emotional disturbance often go undetected and untreated (Reddy & Richardson, 2006). Only about 1% of these children and adolescents receive adequate services in school and community settings and, instead, fail in school and drop out, disrupt the home setting, engage in drug abuse, make poor social adjustment, are involved in the criminal justice system, and commit suicide (U.S. Department of Health and Human Services, 2000; Vander Stoep et al., 2000). Most are in need of stable, supportive environments that offer emotional nurturance, clear behavioral rules, and limits.

Schools, where 75% of services are currently offered, are an ideal setting for addressing the emotional needs of youth (Pollio et al., 2005) because this setting provides access to the majority of youth with emotional disturbances in one location where services can be offered in familiar surroundings for optimal generalization (Masia-Wagner, Nangle, & Hansen, 2006). To maximize the effectiveness of treatment, counselors should be familiar with the various emotional and behavioral disorders of childhood and adolescence and evidenced-based interventions from both an educational and a psychological perspective (American Psychological Association, 2000; Individuals with Disabilities Education Act, 2004).

At school, students with emotional disturbance have been found to perform better in both educational and emotional/social areas if they are included in general education programs and activities that have been properly planned. Because counselors have expertise in assisting with social, emotional, and behavioral adjustment, they can advocate for inclusion of these youth and can participate in the development of schoolwide prevention and intervention supports that promote positive relationships and behaviors for all students, such as social skills training, conflict-resolution programs, and family centers (Martella, Nelson, & Marchand-Martella, 2003). Some programs for elementary students that have shown positive outcomes are First Step to Success (Walker et al., 1998), Parent Teacher Action Teams (Kay & Fitzgerald, 1997), and Integrated Mental Health Program (Roberts et al., 2003). Counselors also can implement evidence-based schoolwide interventions for trauma following disasters such as Hurricane Katrina and the World Trade Center disaster (Masia-Warner et al., 2006).

Another school-based intervention that counselors can offer is consultation with teachers about the challenges presented by children and adolescents with emotional disturbances in the school setting. Conjoint-behavioral consultation is a particularly effective intervention model, in which counselors can include both parents and teachers in planning and intervention (Sheridan, Eagle, & Doll, 2006). Counselors can consult with teachers about how to be appropriate role models, how to pair children with high social-status peer mentors in classroom activities, and how to identify ground rules for communication and behavior for the whole class (Wagner & Davis, 2006).

Counselors can provide teachers with social skills strategies and programs for the classroom, focusing on problem solving, conflict resolution, anger management, and friendship making (Reddy & Richardson, 2006; Tarver-Behring, Spagna, & Sullivan, 1998). An elementary age child with emotional disturbance, for example, could benefit from

- clear classroom rules, rewards and consistent consequences;
- journaling about feelings;
- bibliotherapy;
- discrete prompts from the teacher, such as a gentle touch, to help the child be aware of inappropriate behavior before it escalates;
- brainstorming various solutions and consequences about friendship problems;
- working on goal-oriented projects; and
- participating in activities with other children in areas in which he or she can be successful.

An adolescent would benefit from a reality therapy approach in which the student is given choices and goals to work toward with natural consequences (Passaro, Moon, Weist, & Wong, 2004). Because mental health issues impact school performance for students with emotional disturbance, counselors can consult with teachers about academic supports, such as tutoring, and small-group and individualized instruction for these students.

Early postsecondary planning is also essential for students with emotional disturbance, especially because these students often are disengaged from school. This would include career exploration and skill development for successful transition (Wagner & Davis, 2006). Planning educational and career goals with adolescents, parents, and teachers can provide positive alternatives to help the adolescent with a mild or moderate emotional or behavioral disorder toward long-term adjustment (Kauffman, 1997). Counselors can advocate for authentic learning experiences at school, such as work-linked courses that are aligned with the student's interests and plans to increase student engagement (Phelps, 2003).

In addition, students and their families must be involved in and approve transition plans to enhance the potential for the plans to succeed (Davis, Geller, & Hunt, 2006). IDEA (2004) specifies that by age 16, students with disabilities should have identified vocational goals that reflect their strengths and interests, a course of study, and plans for postsecondary education and service needs to support success. Counselors can coordinate these planning efforts, as well as community resources that support living situations and community adjustment for students with emotional disturbance (Bullis, Tehan, & Clark, 2000). Counselors also can focus on the development of self–advocacy and life skills that are critical for successful adult functioning (Wagner & Davis, 2006).

Counselors, too, may be called upon to provide any of a number of direct counseling services that are vital for the adjustment of children and adolescents with emotional disturbance. Counselors working with these children and their families should have training in crisis counseling and the mandated reporting laws for child abuse, suicidal behavior, and intent to harm others so they can assist students, parents, and teachers competently in these areas if needed. Individual and group counseling can be beneficial with children and adolescents who have mild and moderate emotional problems. Counselors should employ evidence-based interventions, such as cognitive behavioral treatments for depression, which have been found to have positive outcomes in school and community settings alike (Masia-Warner et al., 2006).

Through individual counseling the counselor can build a therapeutic, supportive relationship and work to change the child's or adolescent's negative self-image, depressed or anxious feelings, or relationship difficulties with peers. Group counseling is particularly useful in school settings to help children and adolescents develop a positive self-concept, improve their social skills and academic performance, deal with loss, and increase their motivation.

Further, counselors can offer a number of services to families of children and adolescents with emotional disturbances. Families often experience stress from dealing with the emotional and behavioral challenges of these youth. *Psychoeducation* is a promising intervention in which families are treated as capable partners with valuable resources and experience and are active participants on a support team that includes school and community professionals (Pollio et al., 2005). Counselors on the team can collaborate with other team members to address parents' concerns about behavior management, treatment and medication, and community resources, by offering education, support, and problem-solving skills. Especially helpful for parents of adolescents with emotional disturbance is training in creating and using contracts that clearly specify limits, rules, expected behaviors, privileges, and consequences for inappropriate behaviors. In addition, family therapy is strongly recommended for children and adolescents with emotional disturbances to resolve anger and negative interaction patterns in the family.

Counseling Students With Mild Mental Retardation

Students with mild mental retardation must meet criteria generally aligned with the widely accepted definition of mental retardation proposed by the American Association on Mental Retardation (AAMR, 1992):

> Mental retardation refers to substantial limitations in present functioning. It is characterized by significantly sub-average intellectual functioning, existing concurrently with related limitations in two or more of the following applicable adaptive skill areas: communication, self-care, home living, social skills, community use, self-direction, health and safety, functional academics, leisure and work. Mental retardation manifests before age 18. (p. 1)

Because they have developmental delays in most areas of functioning, children and adolescents with mild mental retardation require multiple services. Counselors can help to coordinate school, home, and community services for all areas of need. In the school setting children and adolescents with mild and moderate mental retardation will benefit in educational and social areas by being fully included in the general educational program. Counselors, therefore, often work with parents, special educators, and teachers to advocate for appropriate educational modifications and resources in the general education classroom.

Counselors can help teachers to promote social adjustment for students with disabilities by providing guidance in how to incorporate peer modeling, self-reliance, age-appropriate social behavior, and friendship-making skills into classroom activities (Tarver-Behring, Spagna, & Sullivan, 1998). They can promote acceptance of differences in peers without disabilities through social skills programs, integrated counseling groups, and classroom modeling and discussion (Frith, Clark, & Miller, 1983; Salend, 1983, Tarver-Behring et al., 1998). Further, they can teach behavioral modification, token economy, and contingency contracting strategies to teachers and parents, to help students develop appropriate academic, social, and self-help behaviors (Heward, 2003).

Behavioral interventions have much support for counseling with children and adolescents with mild mental retardation (Sturmey, 2005). This approach is most effective when assisting lower-functioning individuals, especially children, for a variety of problems including aggression, self-injury, and self-stimulation. Whether other types of counseling, such as cognitive or psychotherapeutic approaches, can be effective with individuals who have developmental disabilities is being debated (Beail, 2003). These approaches address mental health issues not addressed by behavioral approaches.

Although the value of counseling with this group is controversial because of the students' cognitive limitations, counselors surely can offer individual and group counseling directed at self-esteem, self-expression, self-advocacy, and self-determination, all of which are typical areas of need (Hurley, 2005; Turnbull, 2004). In addition, it has been argued that youth with developmental disabilities have the right to have access to all treatment approaches (Taylor, 2005). Psychotherapy and cognitive-behavioral interventions, such as self-management, relaxation techniques, and problem solving, involve mental types of treatment (Hurley, 2005). These approaches have limited support for low-frequency problems with higher-functioning populations (Willner, 2005). Ultimately, the age and specific strengths and weaknesses of individuals with mild mental retardation, as well as the type of problem being addressed, should determine which types of intervention counselors choose to serve this population effectively.

Counselors can help parents in a number of ways. When counseling parents of children and adolescents with mild mental retardation, counselors must remember that families require disability-related, individualized support, an examination of quality-of-life outcomes from this support, and parenting and family dynamics that lead to physical and emotional well-being for all family members (Turnbull, 2004). Counselors can help parents understand and encourage their child's or adolescent's abilities and help the parents cope with the stresses of parenting a child with disabilities through family therapy, group therapy, and parent education. For adolescents, special attention should be directed to their developing independent living skills as well as educational and vocational planning.

Devon

Three of Devon's teachers contacted his school counselor concerning his academic difficulties. They reported that Devon, an African American, struggled with decoding words when reading orally, did not know basic math facts, had difficulty with reasoning and problem-solving skills, and exhibited poor social skills when interacting with his eighth-grade classmates. Although his teachers described Devon as a "good kid," they reported that he was falling behind in classroom and homework assignments, had become increasingly defiant in classes, was openly berating other students, and was not responding to the teacher's redirection prompts.

Initially, the counselor had difficulty contacting Devon's family because the parents both worked long hours. Over time and after several phone contacts, the counselor was able to build a trusting, supportive partnership with one of his primary caregivers, his grandmother. She related that in the past 3 years Devon gradually had become more apathetic about school, no longer expressed interest in academic subjects, and resisted finishing homework assignments of any sort. The grandmother said she had noticed that over the past several months Devon had become more withdrawn and easily agitated when she asked him what was bothering him. She was concerned that Devon had few friends and seemed to be vulnerable to falling in with the wrong crowd.

The grandmother gave the counselor permission to consult with several teachers, in collaboration with the grandmother, about some informal classroom assessment and intervention strategies to determine if these would be effective—thereby removing any need for a formal referral for special education assessment. The teachers had acquired some training in intervention approaches for academics, such as evidenced-based strategies and accommodations. In addition, a popular peer mentor was identified to mentor Devon in social areas. The grandmother and Devon agreed to these plans, and the counselor coordinated home–school communication about Devon's progress.

After several weeks Devon still was having difficulty in achievement and social areas that significantly impacted his academic performance, as documented in the prereferral intervention data. The counselor, in collaboration with the teachers and grandmother, referred Devon for testing and consideration for special education and related services by an interdisciplinary team to include the teachers, the resource specialist, the grandmother, Devon, and the school counselor. The team collaborated in a plan to conduct culturally fair evaluations, as well as authentic informal assessment at home and at school. The finding that Devon had specific learning disabilities in the areas of reading and math qualified him for assistance by the resource specialist. Devon demonstrated strengths in several nonverbal performance areas, which were to be fostered in future academic activities.

The team then designed a program for fully including Devon in the general education classroom with resource support. The resource specialist would collaborate with Devon's teachers in the classroom to identify specific instructional modifications, and work in small groups and with an in-class peer tutor. This specialist also would work with Devon in the resource room one class period each day on academic areas of need.

Further, with the school counselor's help, the resource teacher and the classroom teachers formed an interdisciplinary team with the grandmother and Devon to plan a home–school academic program. This system would allow the resource specialist to offer academic (reduced length of assignments), organizational (notebook organizers), and communication strategies for home and school. The team designed a plan in which Devon would record homework and schoolwork assignments daily in a notebook, and upon completion, his teachers would check it off. Devon's grandmother also would check off the homework assignments and reward Devon upon completion of his homework. The counselor arranged for a staff tutor to work on homework with Devon twice a week during a free period at school. This relieved the tension between the grandmother and Devon stemming from the homework issue.

The team included counseling as a designated instructional service on the individualized education program, and Devon started to attend a conflict-resolution group offered by the school counselor for other adolescents his age. Group members learned how to identify a problem, how to brainstorm a solution, and how to evaluate the outcome. The group members then role-played the problem and identified solutions and discussed other problems that could arise and how they might solve them. In addition, the school counselor offered to assist Devon's teachers with social skills strategies in the classroom through a social skills program promoting positive social behaviors and inclusion of all students, including Devon, which could be instituted in all ninth-grade classrooms as an organizational intervention.

Devon's grandmother decided to attend short-term, culturally sensitive counseling with Devon at a family center on the school campus to better understand and support Devon's needs and to allow him to work individually with the counselor on self-esteem, self-advocacy, and identity development. She also took Devon to a faith-based youth group at the family's church for additional support. Finally, Devon joined the school basketball team, which gave him the opportunity to experience success and provided a healthy social outlet.

Following these interventions, the grandmother and the teachers reported to the school counselor that Devon was completing his academic work more accurately, was less frustrated, and was better adjusted socially. They noted that he recently had developed several positive relationships with friends on his basketball team. The team made plans to review Devon's progress annually, or more often if requested by his family, and to complete a full assessment every 3 years to determine if special education services were still needed or required changes.

As a final intervention, the counselor asked the high school career counselor at the end of the school year to meet with Devon and his grandmother to develop long-range academic and career goals that would help Devon reach his full potential in postsecondary education. This information then was discussed with Devon, his grandmother, and the special education teacher at the transition meeting coordinated by the counselor at the end of eighth grade, to help Devon plan his high school academic program toward successful entry into college.

Students With Physical and Neurological Disabilities

According to the Commission on Excellence in Special Education (U.S. Department of Education, 2002), students with physical and neurological disabilities include those with orthopedic impairments, other health impairments, traumatic brain injury, multiple disabilities, and autism. The categories of orthopedic impairments and multiple disabilities are described here, addressing the cognitive, academic, adaptive, social, perceptual-motor, and language functioning of students with these types of physical and neurological disabilities.

Students With Orthopedic Impairments

The incidence of orthopedic impairments was approximately 0.2% of the 50 states and Washington, DC for ages 3–21 during the 2003–04 school year (National Center for Education Statistics, 2005). Children and adolescents with orthopedic impairments are defined by federal law in the following manner:

> Orthopedic impairment means a severe orthopedic impairment that adversely affects a child's educational performance. The term includes impairments caused by congenital anomaly (e.g., clubfoot, absence of some member, etc.), impairments caused by disease (e.g., poliomyelitis, bone tuberculosis, etc.), and impairments from other causes (e.g., cerebral palsy, amputations, and fractures or burns that cause contractures). (IDEA, 1997, section 300.7[8])

According to Heward (2003), musculoskeletal impairments usually result in severe restriction of movement, typically affecting both gross-motor and fine-motor movements, as a result of stiffening of joints, inflammation of bones, degeneration of muscle fiber and bone structure, and muscle atrophy from lack of use. In addition to influencing range of motion, severe musculoskeletal impairments can cause children and adolescents to become embarrassed and frustrated by their being dependent on others for assistance. Impairments include arthrogryposis multiplex congenita (also known as Pinocchio syndrome because of the wooded appearance of the individuals affected), osteogenesis imperfecta (also known as brittle bone disease), juvenile rheumatoid arthritis, and muscular dystrophy.

Spinal cord impairments, as the name implies, are disabling conditions in which the spinal cord is severed or injured resulting in anything from incoordination to partial to full paralysis below the point of nerve damage. Children and adolescents with severe spinal cord injuries also may have a variety of skin, urinary, and respiratory infections, insensitivity to heat and cold, and inability to control bowel and bladder functions. Severe spinal cord impairments include spina bifida and spinal muscular dystrophy (Heward, 2003).

Cerebral palsy and several seizure disorders are additional orthopedic impairments that can result in severe physical difficulties. Unlike spinal cord impairments, cerebral palsy is a dysfunction of the brain and nervous system (not including the spinal cord) that results in difficulty with gross-motor and fine-motor skills, attention, eye–hand coordination, and so forth (Heward, 2003).

Students With Multiple Disabilities

According to the National Center for Education Statistics (2005), 0.3% of the school-age population in the United States is considered to have multiple disabilities and, therefore, receives special education and related services. Although multiple disabilities may be thought of as an accumulation of several of the categories covered so far, students with multiple disabilities have difficulties that are magnified beyond a simple analysis of the sum of the parts.

The combinations of disabilities are endless. Mild mental retardation, for example, can co-occur with cerebral palsy, with a variety of orthopedic impairments such as those already presented, with a range of severe behavior disorders, as well as with visual and/or hearing impairments. Emotional disturbance also can coexist with a full range of physical, visual, and/or hearing impairments.

Counseling Students With Physical and Neurological Disabilities

Counselors must have an understanding of up-to-date special education, disability, and rehabilitation legislation to be able to best inform children and adolescents who have physical and neurological disabilities and their families about the rights and services available to them (Scarborough & Gilbride, 2006). Counselors can work with school multidisciplinary teams to help identify students with these challenges who qualify for special education services when the child's disability first becomes apparent. This may involve families with very young children with a recently diagnosed condition, or children with recent injuries or illness resulting in a physical or neurological disability.

The best approach for counselors involved with these children and adolescents with physical and neurological disabilities is to work closely with the physicians, community specialists, personnel from governmental services, and the school multidisciplinary team that provides the primary services to these students. These experts can determine the student's strengths and needs and how best to offer support. In conjunction with these experts, counselors should consult with parents and teachers to best understand and advocate for the most appropriate inclusive educational settings and programs that will help children and adolescents to reach their full potential. Students with communication impairments should be in contact with same-aged peers, too (Downing, Eckinger, & Williams, 1997). And counselor consultation can assist with developing and implementing plans at home and at school for accommodations, modifications, and technological aids, such as augmented communication devices for those with cerebral palsy, as well as with vision or hearing impairments.

Finally, counselors should become informed about and collaborate with vocational rehabilitation counselors who offer vocational and psychosocial counseling, post-high school transition planning, and accommodations for individuals whose disability interferes with their future employability (Szymanski & King, 1989). By the time the child with physical and neurological disabilities reaches age 16, a transition plan, which delineates the process by which a student moves from special education into adult services, should be in place as a part of the child's IEP, offering support in work, home, recreation, and community activities and promoting optimal long-term adjustment (Downing, 1996).

Children and adolescents with physical and neurological disabilities benefit from direct individual and group counseling that addresses their social, emotional, behavioral, career, and communication challenges (Amos, 2004). Training in self-advocacy skills also is beneficial to post-high school success (Eisenman, 2003). Positive behavioral support interventions may be effective with some children and adolescents who have a neurological impairment, such as autism, given the nature of the disorder (Wetherby & Prizant, 1999). This approach first involves understanding the purpose of challenging behavior, then assisting in the development of new skills that reduce the need to engage in the difficult behavior (Dunlap et al., 1998). Youth diagnosed with autism or Asperger Syndrome—a condition involving delays in social areas but not cognitive or language, may especially benefit from counseling in social skills programs, such as Circle of Friends (McTarnaghan, 1998) or Peer Mediated Intervention (Strain & Kohler, 1998).

Parents and families of students with physical and neurological disabilities may require direct services, too. These families may be dealing with restricted activities to accommodate the child's disability, stress and burnout from the demand of caregiving, or embarrassment in connection with their child's disabilities (Turnbull & Ruef, 1997). Counselors can offer parents individual, group, or family counseling to help them work on grief surrounding their child's disability, as well as their guilt, anger, and stress. They also may work on being overly protective and their feelings of hopelessness about their child's future (Taub, 2006).

When working with parents, counselors must be culturally sensitive because families from different cultural backgrounds hold culturally embedded beliefs about how to intervene with physical and neurological disabilities (Tarver-Behring & Tom-Galinas, 1998). For example, some families from Asian cultures may prefer indigenous healing practices, and African American or Latino families may want faith-based interventions in addition to, or instead of, traditional counseling interventions.

Counseling Students With Orthopedic Impairments

The counselor must be sure to recognize the student's strengths as well as disabilities. Frequently, adults who associate with these children and adolescents overlook their strengths by assuming deficits in all domains based upon the child's physical appearance. Often, the low self-esteem of these children and adolescents derives as much from having unrecognized strengths as from self-consciousness resulting from the physical disorder. In addition to supporting the child's strengths and helping the child to work with his or her disability, the counselor can assist parents in advocating for appropriate assessment and services at school and through community resources.

These children and adolescents should be included to the maximum extent possible to allow for optimal educational, self-care, vocational, and social opportunities (Downing, 1996). Counselors can coordinate services with other specialists to help parents and teachers reorganize physical environments, remove barriers, and obtain special equipment to facilitate inclusion in all areas of life. Counselors also can help parents and teachers avoid overprotectiveness and assist these children and adolescents in reaching their full potential (Taub, 2006).

Counseling Students With Multiple Disabilities

To coordinate services for children or adolescents with multiple disabilities, the counselor must understand disabilities in multiple areas and be able to work with all involved parties. Counselors can assist parents by advocating for school and community services and inclusive social and educational settings when appropriate, requesting appropriate modifications and communication or physical aids, and offering supportive counseling. They also can help the students directly in the areas of self-esteem, self-help, self-advocacy, and social skills if they have a high enough level of communication and cognitive functioning. Finally, counselors, in conjunction with the parents and the IEP team, should develop a plan to promote the long-term adjustment and post-high school transition plan with these children and adolescents (Taub, 2006).

Jen

Jen, a 3-year-old Chinese girl, was identified as having multiple disabilities during infancy. The family pediatrician confirmed, at her 6-month examination, that Jen had profound hearing and visual impairments. The mother reported that she had contracted rubella during the second trimester of her pregnancy and that her labor was long and difficult. The pediatrician recommended that the family contact a local counselor who might be able to suggest services for Jen.

That counselor first determined that the parents were comfortable speaking in English. After learning about the cultural value of privacy in this family, the counselor suggested that the parents, rather than joining a parent education group where discussing their child's difficulties in front of others could be shameful, instead suggested some parent education books for parents of young children with multiple disabilities to become better informed. The counselor would be available to discuss any questions they might have. The counselor also referred the family to a regional center, where the parents welcomed an intervention program designed specifically for them by experts specializing in vision and hearing impairments.

To address Jen's increasingly apparent language delay, the parents began to implement a variety of the recommended approaches. In addition, the counselor supported the parents in their seeking help from a healer from their culture who often assisted families from their community. At a 6-month follow-up visit at the regional center, the parents indicated that Jen's communication skills were developing slowly and that Jen acknowledged their presence and responded to specific structured stimuli.

The following year the counselor sought permission from both parents to refer the family to a public preschool program designed specifically to meet the needs of deaf–blind children. There, an individualized education program was developed for Jen, to be reviewed annually and to continue as Jen entered elementary school.

In the latest meeting the mother reported that the family was extremely happy with the intervention program at the preschool and noted dramatic improvements in Jen's interaction and communication skills. The family was invited to stay in contact with the counselor as needed in the future. The family honored the counselor for her assistance by giving her a gift from their country of origin, which she accepted.

Students With Attention-Deficit Hyperactivity Disorder

Attention-deficit/hyperactivity disorder (AD/HD) is a high-incidence disorder among children and adolescents in the United States and a common reason for referral for special services. Based on DSM-IV criteria, AD/HD is believed to occur in 7.4% of the population, and it appears three times more frequently in boys than girls (Barkley, 2006). The fourth edition of the *Diagnostic and Statistical Manual of Mental Disorders* (DSM-IV) defines the disorder as the presence of developmentally inappropriate hyperactivity, inattention, and impulsivity that is evident in the child by age 7 and leads to clinically significant impairment in social, academic, or occupational functioning across two or more settings, such as home and school (American Psychological Association, 2000).

Inattention includes difficulty in paying attention, sustaining task and play-related attention, listening, following instructions, organizing, and keeping track of things. In addition, the criteria include avoidance of tasks that require sustained mental effort, distractibility, and forgetfulness. Hyperactivity/impulsivity includes fidgeting, out-of-seat behavior, restlessness, overactivity, lack of quiet play, excessive talking, interrupting others, difficulty awaiting one's turn, and responding impulsively to questions.

As outlined in the DSM-IV, three subtypes of AD/HD are now recognized:

AD/HD, Predominately Inattentive Type: six or more inattentive symptoms, but fewer than six hyperactive-impulsive symptoms

AD/HD, Predominately Hyperactive-Impulsive Type: six or more hyperactive-impulsive symptoms but fewer than six inattentive symptoms; and

AD/HD, Combined Type: six or more inattentive symptoms and six or more hyperactive-impulsive symptoms.

In addition, the criteria for these subgroups must have been present for the last six months. The inattentive subtype has been described as exhibiting a sluggish cognitive tempo and social impassivity, in contrast to the distractible, impulsive, overactive, and emotionally volatile combined subtype (Barkley, 2006). The most recent theories on AD/HD have suggested that the social and behavioral challenges of children and adolescents with AD/HD are linked to difficulty with behavioral inhibition, and that inattentiveness also is related to deficits in executive functioning and self-regulation (Barkley, 2006). AD/HD symptoms often persist throughout adolescence and adulthood; with treatment, the symptoms often are lessened.

The cause of AD/HD has become clearer, with neurological variables and hereditary influences as contributors (Barkley, 2006). Diet and factors such as maternal behavior do not seem to contribute significantly to the presence of AD/HD, but the family characteristics and cultural contexts are being looked at as possible variables in predicting the outcome in hyperactive children.

Children and adolescents with AD/HD may or may not qualify for educational services. Although these children and adolescents frequently show some form of academic difficulty, such as attentional or organizational problems, their achievement deficits aren't always severe enough to fit a special education category. Children and adolescents with AD/HD qualify for special education services when the AD/HD occurs in combination with another disability, such as a specific learning disability, or when the AD/HD symptoms are so severe that achievement is delayed to the extent that the child or adolescent qualifies for the special education category of *other health impairment*.

Frequently, children and adolescents with AD/HD qualify for educational modifications under Section 504 guidelines; that is, they exhibit symptoms that affect learning to the extent that reasonable educational modifications are required, such as the implementation of a behavior management program, placement in a small, highly structured classroom, counseling, and the administration of medication (Zirkel & Gluckman, 1997). Classroom modifications and interventions for the child and adolescent with AD/HD usually are necessary regardless of whether the child qualifies for specific educational services.

Children who have AD/HD often are identified first at school, where their behavioral problems stand out in contrast to other children. To assess accurately for AD/HD, DuPaul and Stoner (2003) recommended that the initial screening be followed by multiple assessment techniques such as rating scales, behavioral observations, and evaluation of academic and organizational skills in both home and school settings.

Counseling Children and Adolescents With AD/HD

Children and adolescents with AD/HD face a variety of difficulties at school and at home that might require support from counselors. These students exhibit conduct problems, social skills deficits, academic difficulties, and poor educational outcomes in contrast to their non-AD/HD peers (DuPaul & Stoner, 2003). A comprehensive approach is recommended for effectively treating the child or adolescent with AD/HD, incorporating individualized, empirically supported interventions offered by a collaborative team of parents, teachers, and practitioners over the long term (DuPaul & Weyandt, 2006). Barkley (2006) has recommended that a combined treatment of psychosocial approaches, such as behavioral intervention, parent training, teacher consultation and academic strategies, and social skills training, in combination with stimulant medication offers the most effective approach at home and at school. Medication in combination with interventions such as behavior modification and parent training have been found to be especially beneficial with more severe cases of AD/HD and with co-morbidity of other disorders (Barkley, 2006).

Behavioral Modification

An effective treatment that counselors use to change behavior in children with AD/HD is behavior modification, especially with milder cases and when stimulant medication has not been effective (Barkley, 2006). Behavioral approaches should be modified to be age-appropriate for adolescents through the use of contracts, typical adolescent privileges, and negotiated rewards. Behavioral approaches can be organized into several categories (DuPaul & Weyandt, 2006). One behavioral approach involves modifying events that precede a behavior so as to decrease the behavior and increase alternative, more appropriate behaviors. An example is to give students choices of appropriate behaviors, such as a number of academic activities from which to choose. This strategy has received empirical support for increasing on-task behavior and reducing disruptive behavior (Dunlap et al., 1994). Other examples include modifying tasks, such as reducing the length of academic work and having classroom rules for behavior.

A second behavioral approach involves presenting an event after a behavior occurs to either increase or decrease its occurrence. With this approach, counselors can teach teachers and parents positive reinforcement strategies to increase the child's task-related attention and activity and decrease disruptive behavior at school and in the home. Ideally, preferred activities rather than concrete rewards should be used as reinforcement, frequent and specific behavioral feedback should be given, and redirection and/or mild consequences should be used following inappropriate behavior (DuPaul & Stoner, 2003). A successful application of this approach is to send a daily report card from school to home, in which the student is rewarded at home for good academic and behavioral performance at school (Pfiffner, Barkley, & DuPaul, 2006). For best results when using this strategy, goals should be worded positively and be few in number, feedback should be subject-specific, and parents should be involved in developing the behavior plan.

When developing behavior plans for children with AD/HD, reinforcement alone has been found to be less effective for increasing on-task behavior and positive social and academic performance than when this is combined with losing privileges for inappropriate behavior, called *response cost*, a term introduced by DuPaul, Guevremont, and Barkley (1992). In addition, a long-term plan must be in place to maintain appropriate behavior and generalize it to other settings or the results using behavioral interventions can be short-lived (Barkley, 2006).

Self-Management Strategies

In the self-management approach, self-control is taught through strategies such as self-monitoring, self-reinforcement, and self-evaluation. Children and adolescents with AD/HD use *self-reminder* statements to increase their awareness and control of their behavior when direct feedback is not available. *Self-reinforcement* operates on a principle similar to self-monitoring—teaching children ways to praise or reward themselves, such as a checkmark on a behavioral chart following positive behavior when external reinforcers are unavailable. Self-monitoring is most effective in combination with self-reinforcement for increasing on-task attention, peer interactions, and academic performance with children and adolescents who have AD/HD (Reid, Trout, & Schartz, 2005). With the *self-evaluation* strategy, children learn to follow a set of self-directed instructions for completing classwork, then evaluate their own performance.

Research indicates that self-management approaches, especially self-monitoring and self-reinforcement, are effective with milder AD/HD, and as an age-appropriate intervention with adolescents, especially to address organization issues (DuPaul & Stoner, 2003: Barkley, 2006). Self-management works best with specific situations that initially were managed successfully using an external reward system such as token reinforcement, and then faded to self-monitoring and self-reinforcement interventions (DuPaul & Weyandt, 2006). Self-management strategies require ongoing external monitoring and encouragement by the counselor, parent, and/or teacher; therefore, this approach should be used only in combination with other interventions (Barkley, 1995).

Social Skills Training

Programs that promote social adjustment are especially important because children and adolescents with AD/HD often have the most severe problems in social settings. Problems with attention and impulse control impact social situations in a number of ways, including disruptive entry behaviors; interruptions; inattentiveness or talking off topic during conversations; aggressive responses to interpersonal problems (DuPaul & Weyandt, 2006); and poor social problem solving, excessive talking, limited self-awareness, emotional overreactivity, and bossiness when initiating interactions (Guevremont, 1992). These social problems may lead to peer rejection and lower self-esteem, further complicating social adjustment. Inappropriate inattention, impulsivity, and hyperactivity exhibited by AD/HD children in social situations seem to be linked to a performance deficit in which the child has difficulty with delaying responses to the environment and with self-regulating behavior. Because these performance problems are found across a number of settings and social skills training does not automatically generalize to new social contexts (Gresham, 2002), ongoing interventions should be offered across situations by a team of parents, teachers, and counselors (DuPaul & Weyandt, 2006).

Several social skills programs are available for counselors to use with children or adolescents with AD/HD individually, in groups, or in classroom settings. One effective social skills program designed specifically for adolescents with AD/HD offers methods for joining social exchanges, conversational skills, conflict resolution, and anger control (Guevremont, 1990). This program also involves diversity in skill level of members, peer models, strategies for maintaining social success, and cognitive strategies.

In response to the need for empirically supported interventions that help to generalize behaviors, other programs offer a comprehensive approach, such as Sheridan's (1995) Tough Kids Social Skills program, in which small group, classwide, and schoolwide interventions are employed in the academic setting. Schoolwide programs using peers who have received training as social tutors or conflict mediators are effective in reducing playground violence and negative interactions with AD/HD students (Cunningham & Cunningham, 1998).

Stimulant Medication

Currently, stimulant medication has the most empirical support for managing AD/HD symptoms across a wide age range from preschool through adulthood (Barkley, 2006). Counselors might discuss with parents the option of obtaining a screening with a physician for medication for the child or adolescent with AD/HD, especially with more severe cases. Two newer medications that have been found to be effective over longer periods of time are Concerta and Adderall (Barkley, 2006). Approximately 75% of hyperkinetic children respond positively to initial doses of stimulant medication (Barkley et al., 1999). The most notable improvement has been seen in the areas of attention span, impulse control, reaction time, and fine-motor coordination, and is associated with increased academic accuracy and production in school-based settings. Medication also has been shown to improve the social interactions of children by increasing compliance, decreasing disruptiveness, and improving responsiveness to others. And stimulant medication has been found to improve the social judgment and interpersonal interactions in adolescents (Barkley, 2006).

Not all children and adolescents with AD/HD respond to stimulant medication, and some incur side effects. For these reasons, careful screening for the effectiveness of various medications must be conducted at home and at school. If medication is prescribed, it must be accompanied by ongoing drug monitoring by qualified physicians and child psychiatrists. Stimulant medication, in combination with other treatment modalities including behavioral strategies, can lead to the greatest improvement in social, family, and academic functioning (Conners et al., 2001). Other interventions for AD/HD, including self-management interventions (DuPaul & Stoner, 2003) and parent training (Barkley, 2006), seem to be more effective for improving behavior in children and adolescents with AD/HD when these interventions are used in combination with stimulant medication. The cultural values of the child and family always must be considered when discussing stimulant medication as an intervention.

Teacher Consultation

Because students with AD/HD often are included in the general education environment, teacher consultation is an effective intervention for counselors to support students with AD/HD, both with and without an individualized education program. Consultation can deter overreferral of students with AD/HD for special education assessment, as well as assist teachers in developing and implementing plans for students with an identified special education need. Counselors can collaborate with teachers in developing interventions, either student-specific or involving the whole class, such as a behavioral reward system.

When consulting with teachers, counselors should help teachers collect data about the effectiveness of interventions and remain involved until successful strategies have been identified. DuPaul and Weyandt (2006) recommend using data from a functional assessment when available, to identify problem behaviors and plan interventions in the classroom more efficiently and effectively. The role of the counselor–consultant in providing emotional support for teachers of AD/HD students is vital. Counselors also can inform teachers about federal laws pertaining to AD/HD, identify other school personnel with whom to create collaborative consultation teams, create teacher–parent connections, and identify classroom accommodations for the AD/HD students (Erk, 1999; Tarver-Behring & Spagna, 2000).

Classroom strategies include the use of behavioral techniques, such as modeling, token economies, and home–school reward systems. Other classroom strategies involve adapting instruction to highlight the main idea, giving the students prompts to respond, teaching the students to use organizers, working with them in small groups, using visual aids, using peer coaches, and teaching problem-solving strategies. Teachers also should offer structure, supervision, and support in classroom activities when working with AD/HD students, to offset disruption in executive functioning, self-regulation, and associated inattentiveness (Barkley, 2006).

Several other classroom interventions include altering the classroom layout, modifying tasks to work with the child's strengths and deficits, using computer-assisted instruction, improving self-monitoring, and adjusting interventions to be age-appropriate with teens (Barkley, 2006). Counselors can consult with teachers about cultural awareness, classroom strategies specific to the student's cultural background, and methods to collaborate with parents from diverse cultures (Tarver-Behring et al., 2000).

Family Counseling

A child or an adolescent with AD/HD can be disruptive to the entire family system because of the behavioral and developmental problems associated with this disorder. Marital discord, parental exhaustion, and sibling distress are among the problems in families with these children. (Hosie & Erk, 1993). For instance, the child's impulsivity and overactivity may keep the family in a constant state of arousal, and the child's inattention may require the parent to give repeated reminders (Bender, 1997).

In addition, the parents and AD/HD child may develop codependency as the parents try to establish normalcy through solving problems, organizing work, directing impulse control, completing tasks, and guiding social situations for the child who has difficulty in these areas. Adolescents with AD/HD may lie, steal, skip school, and exhibit similar antisocial behaviors (Barkley, 2006). The community may avoid these families because of the child's behavior, resulting in their social isolation (Erk, 1997).

A number of family interventions are available for helping a family with a child or adolescent with AD/HD. Through family counseling, the counselor can help all family members acquire knowledge, understanding, and strategies for coping with the child or adolescent with AD/HD without neglecting the needs of other family members. For example, parents can learn to channel their child's energies into productive activities that allow the child to attain success. Further, the counselor can help the family manage stress, establish balance for family members in relation to the high demands of the child with AD/HD, and envision a positive future for the child by informing the parents and child of college academic and vocational options and services available for adolescents with AD/HD.

A child or adolescent with AD/HD tends to disrupt the entire family system because of the many behavioral and developmental problems associated with this disorder. Further, the adolescent who is individuating moves away from the parents even though he or she still needs support, which causes additional friction. Adolescents can benefit from age-appropriate behavior management, problem solving, environmental adjustments, and self-monitoring to help with functioning at home and in other social settings (Barkley, 2006).

Support Groups

Parents of children and adolescents with AD/HD can be helped through support groups that target stress, guilt, and codependency issues. In addition, the group members can exchange information about causes, interventions, and community resources for AD/HD. Realizing that AD/HD is a neurochemically based disorder and not the result of poor parenting can be a relief to parents (Erk, 1999).

Parents working in groups are comforted when they realize that they are not alone in their feelings. Support group meetings can include lectures, demonstrations, question-and-answer sessions, or informal discussions. Counselors can help parents locate a recognized support group, such as CHADD (Children and Adolescents with Attention Deficit Disorder) or ADDA (Attention Deficit Disorder Association). Counselors also can facilitate their own local AD/HD parent-support groups. These groups often are organized around specific topics. A session on prescribed medications, for example, could feature a presentation by a qualified speaker or a group of experts having different points of view, followed by discussion.

Parenting Programs

Parent education programs are available for counselors to use with parents of children with AD/HD to reduce parent–child conflict, child defiance, and disruptive behavior. These include the Barkley Parent Training Program (Barkley, 1995), the Patterson Parent Training Program (Newby, Fischer, & Roman, 1991), and a parent training program by Lerner, Lowenthal, & Lerner (1995). All of these programs cover AD/HD behaviors and related parenting skills, methods for consistent, positive consequences for positive behaviors, and response-cost or time-out for negative behaviors. A session on anger control, for example, might involve teaching parents to role-model appropriate anger for their child, to encourage their child to self-monitor anger, and to administer rewards to the child for expressing anger appropriately. Other strategies taught to parents include altering environmental tasks and settings to increase success, and home–school monitoring systems (Barkley, 2006). Counselors can create their own parenting program, as well as provide local community resources for parents.

Parenting programs often are designed to target specific age groups with AD/HD. Parents can learn to use behavioral charts with younger children, listing three or four target behaviors in the home; the children can earn reinforcers each time they perform a positive behavior. Adolescents' behavior can be managed through behavioral contracts negotiated with the teenager, specifying ways to earn social activities and age-appropriate rewards (such as weekend activities). Parent training to collaborate with and access resources at school is essential for the successful education of students with AD/HD (Erk, 1999).

Direct Counseling with AD/HD Children and Adolescents

Children and adolescents with AD/HD often struggle with the effects of their disorder on their psychological well-being, stemming from social rejection. They tend to have a low sense of self-worth as a result of repeated negative feedback about their behavior. Among the therapeutic books available for use in individual counseling with children with AD/HD are *I Would If I Could* (Gordon, 1992) and *Putting on the Brakes* (Quinn, 1992). Games and other activities targeting AD/HD behaviors are available for the counseling setting (Taylor, 1994).

Group Counseling

Group counseling can help children and youth feel less different and more supported. Adolescent groups can promote the identification of positive role models and can help members set long-range goals as a tool for seeing themselves as having the potential for success. To help children and adolescents with AD/HD maintain attention and behavior during direct counseling, structured, time-limited sessions and more directive approaches are recommended.

▮▮Carlos

Carlos, age 6, recently entered kindergarten. His teacher, Mrs. Warner, contacted Carlos's parents soon after the school year began, because of his behavior. The teacher expressed concern that the boy needed to work on problems including remaining in his seat, paying attention to simple instructions, waiting to be called on, and completing his work. He tended to be distracted by classroom wall displays and interacted inappropriately with his peers. His mother concurred that she had observed many of these behaviors in Carlos at home, and his father said he had similar problems himself as a child.

The parents agreed to seek assistance from the school psychologist, who in turn referred the family to a counselor who worked with children with AD/HD and was trained in working with culturally diverse families in the community. This counselor discussed the issues with the parents in their primary language of Spanish. She then formed a collaborative team with Carlos, in which the boy would be rewarded in both settings for complying with specific rules in the classroom. The teacher would give him a star for each of four rules he complied with: complete work in class, keep his hands to himself, raise his hand and be recognized before talking, and stay in his seat. The teacher would send home a daily report. At home, Carlos would receive a sticker whenever he earned at least three stars at school.

Then the counselor consulted with the teacher about classroom modifications, such as minimizing distractions in the classroom, cuing on-task behavior, structuring class time to direct Carlos to specific activities, and modifying instruction to brief, specific tasks with frequent breaks, thereby reducing the need for long-term attention. The counselor advised the parents about their rights under federal legislation to request that these modifications be put into a written modification plan under the guidelines of Section 504, which would be reviewed annually at school.

The counselor also provided the teacher with a social skills program for the entire class, to assist other children having social problems, and to avoid singling out Carlos. In addition, the counselor provided the parents with parent training and short-term therapy to teach them specific parenting skills, such as the use of a home behavioral chart, to provide them with support and to help reduce their stress generated by Carlos's behavior. Finally, the counselor gave the parents information about the CHADD parent support group in their area.

After these interventions were tried, behavioral improvement was measured. Difficulties in paying attention and impulsive behavior, such as blurting out answers, still were evident. The counselor referred the parents to a child psychiatrist, and Carlos was placed on a low-dose trial of extended-release stimulant medication. The counselor worked with Carlos and his parents to help him understand the purpose of the medication.

The pediatrician conducted continual monitoring of the effects of the medication in collaboration with home and school. The counselor also taught Carlos some simple cognitive–behavior strategies for monitoring his own behavior at home and at school. These included a self-reward strategy in which Carlos would tell himself that he did a good job when he followed rules at home and school.

Following these interventions, Carlos's behaviors improved remarkably. The teacher and the counselor explained to the parents that Carlos did not require a referral for special education services at this time, but that they would monitor his behavior in the future.

Gifted Children and Adolescents

Gifted children and adolescents are one of the most misunderstood and politically controversial groups that counselors serve. Stereotypes abound about the gifted being socially isolated and emotionally unstable. In truth, many gifted children and adolescents are as well adjusted as their nongifted peers when functioning in educational, social, and familial environments that are supportive of their giftedness (Gottfried, Gottfried, Bathurst, & Guerin, 1994; LoCicero & Ashby, 2000). Gifted children who are most likely to face adjustment problems, including emotional sensitivity, isolation, and perfectionism, are those who are highly gifted (Peterson, 2006) children who are twice-exceptional, such as those who are gifted and have learning disabilities (Assouline et al., 2006) and gifted girls, who have difficulties in social status related to their high ability. (Ludwig & Cullinan, 1984). Therefore, although giftedness often does not lead to social isolation or emotional instability, it also does not necessarily guarantee mental health. Giftedness must be viewed as a complex set of characteristics for each individual.

Even more troubling, many people refuse to view giftedness as an exceptional educational category requiring appropriate educational programming (Colangelo, Assouline, & Gross, 2004), that other types of exceptionality are more in need of educational services than giftedness. The existing educational system does not accept the variation among individual learners and the need to provide academic and fiscal support equally to accommodate the educational process for individual learners.

Funding for gifted education has continued to decrease over the years in comparison to funding for other exceptional educational categories (Shaklee, 1997). And, although giftedness is recognized as an exceptional educational category by federal law (PL 103-382), no specific guidelines have been set forth for serving gifted students. As a result, educational services for the gifted may be inadequate or nonexistent. Most gifted children and adolescents do not receive differentiated instruction and often are in class settings in which they already have mastered much of the curriculum (Ross, 1993).

This generalized educational programming pattern is contrary to the finding that the most effective way to help highly capable students is through academic acceleration (Colangelo et al., 2004). Parents frequently must advocate for educational services for their gifted children, often in the face of considerable opposition from school personnel (Silverman, 1993). Alsop (1997) described how parents also experience negative and unsupportive reactions from friends, relatives, and community resources when seeking appropriate services for their gifted children. Similar to other exceptional children, the gifted student may hide his or her abilities to avoid the negative stereotyping associated with being different (Ross, 1993). The mismatch between ability and services increases the potential of adjustment problems—such as underachievement, behavioral problems, and frustration—for the gifted.

Another problem for this group is in the way in which giftedness is identified. The most frequently used indicator of giftedness is the intelligence quotient in combination with student achievement and teacher nominations. This approach has been found to be unreliable, with teachers often nominating compliant children and adolescents over outspoken, underachieving, or difficult ones who still may be deserving of gifted programs (Cioffi & Kysilka, 1997). In addition, European American students are overrepresented by 30-70% in gifted programs due to a biased assessment system that is based on the dominant culture (Peterson, 1999; Richert, 1997). And some types of giftedness, such as musical and artistic giftedness, often are overlooked in the identification process (Peterson, 2006).

For these reasons, the counselor must clearly understand the sociopolitical environment surrounding the gifted, as well as the individual issues that lead them to counseling. Counselors, too, must also be aware of methods for identifying a range of giftedness (Shaklee, 1997). These include methods that assess intrinsic motivation (Gottfried & Gottfried, 1997) that identify new types of giftedness, such as the gifted artist (Shaklee, 1997), that includes twice-exceptional students (Assouline et al., 2006) and recognizes cultural and contextual biases and more fairly includes students from culturally different backgrounds in the identification process (Peterson, 2006). Finally, counselors must be prepared to educate parents of the gifted, support parents in response to negative reactions to their gifted children, and advocate with parents and teachers for appropriate services for gifted children and adolescents.

Counseling Gifted Children

Much debate has been waged about the psychological well-being of gifted children and adolescents. A number of studies have described the social and emotional difficulties associated with giftedness, such as being overly sensitive, perfectionistic, anxious, socially isolated and depressed (Peterson, 2006), most acute in profoundly gifted youth. Other research has found gifted and nongifted youth to be similar in areas of maladjustment (LoCicero & Ashby, 2000), but gifted children and adolescents may be less likely to ask for help because they believe they can work out problems themselves (Peterson, 1998). Still other studies have identified psychological strengths associated with being gifted beyond intelligence and achievement, including the ability to cope with stress, excellent problem-solving abilities, a sense of humor, heightened moral regard, greater self-awareness, and higher self confidence (Peterson, 2006). In some cases, what originally were viewed as weaknesses, such as overexcitability, have been redefined as strengths that lead to positive adjustment, especially when supported by the children's environment (Tucker & Hafenstein, 1997).

Gifted students run the risk of being misunderstood or overlooked for services for a number of reasons. Teachers and parents may misunderstand areas of strength in a gifted child, thinking of them as problems, and do not realize that these patterns are normal and should be encouraged, especially when expressed appropriately. Still relevant are the subtypes of giftedness in adolescents identified by Orange (1997) that sometimes are perceived as dysfunctional, yet are more a reflection of the diversity within gifted groups. For example, the aggressive–independent subtype can be seen as confrontational and argumentative even though this behavior is more a reflection of self-sufficiency, inquisitiveness, and brightness than malicious intent.

In addition, gifted abilities may be misunderstood or overlooked in diverse children and adolescents. Therefore, counselors must promote services that are sensitive to the unique learning styles and contextual issues of culturally and linguistically diverse groups (de Barona & Barona, 2006). Finally, twice-exceptional students, who are both gifted and have special education needs, tend to be underidentified for gifted programs because educators may view these as mutually exclusive areas of need (Assoulinee et al., 2006). Clearly, counselors can promote positive adjustment for gifted children and adolescents in a number of ways.

Adjustment in the Academic Environment

Counselors can assist with the student's academic adjustment by consulting with teachers, assisting parents in advocating for services with school administrators and teachers, coordinating services and resources, and promoting systemic change toward new services that better serve this population. Counselors can assist teachers, as well as the parents and gifted children or adolescents themselves, to acquire accurate knowledge and understanding of characteristics associated with giftedness, thereby increasing understanding and dispelling negative attitudes. Counselors also can assist parents in seeking appropriate and fair educational assessment / identification, programs, and services for their child.

A frequent area of concern for gifted students is academic underachievement (Colangelo, 2003). Underachievement encompasses underperformance given intellectual potential, as well as failure to self-actualize in a broader psychological sense (Reis & McCoach, 2000). Frequently, students who underachieve are not educationally stimulated and can become unmotivated, passive, and even rejecting of unchallenging work (Reis, 1998). Another reason for underachievement may be the presence of strong verbal skills that the student has come to rely on, especially in middle school years, to the detriment of written work and organization (Baum, Owen, & Dixon, 1991).

Giftedness is multifaceted and complex, and students may be gifted in certain specific areas but not others. Some students have talents and interests outside of the academic environment, such as music or art, which take precedence over schoolwork (Ford, 1996). Elementary and secondary students who underachieve can have poor outcomes in postsecondary education and work, although sometimes the underachievement is reversed later in life. Developmental and contextual factors, as well as psychological stressors and resiliency, seem to influence the achievement pattern of gifted individuals over the lifespan (Peterson, 2006). By advocating for appropriate services, parents and counselors may prevent or eliminate behavior problems that result from boredom and frustration stemming from an unchallenging curriculum.

The counselor also can consult with general education teachers about classroom instructional methods that encourage gifted students' academic and unique strengths, and build upon areas that are less strong, such as written language or organization skills. Curricular consultation and gifted program development are especially needed, as many teachers lack training in gifted related education, and specific programs for the gifted often are minimal because of lack of support and funding (Shaklee, 1997).

Some methods that counselors can employ to support gifted students include:

- consulting with teachers about the unique strengths, weaknesses, and psychological characteristics of gifted students in their class;
- facilitating collaboration between school staff to make the educational curricula in the school appropriately challenging for gifted students, including advocating for an accelerated academic program (Colangelo et al., 2004);
- finding professional development opportunities and mentors in the gifted area for teachers;
- facilitating home–school communication to support student learning and for early detection of underachievement;
- providing proactive skills to gifted students through group guidance (ASCA, 2005) such as reflection, conflict resolution, and affective expression;
- creating noncompetitive and normalized opportunities for peer social interactions; and
- identifying career and vocational opportunities and linking them with academic activities as early as elementary age (Ross, 1993).

In addition, the counselor can facilitate college advisement and long-term career planning for gifted adolescents and can assist in identifying community resources that support talents and coordinating their services with the school. Finally, the counselor can offer counseling programs, such as the classic Developmental Model for Counseling the Gifted, which encourage self-awareness and acceptance of talents and career planning in relation to personal strengths, and conflict resolution to deal with negative reactions from others (Silverman, 1993).

Adjustment in the Home

Other counseling interventions can be directed to helping the child at home through family counseling, parent education, and parent consultation services. Parents can promote intellectual stimulation in the home, especially stimulation in response to the child's or adolescent's interests (Assouline et al., 2006). Gifted children and adolescents should be encouraged and supported when they express interest in activities such as a chess club, junior scientists, sports, educational books and television, and intellectually challenging projects in the home. Counselors can make referrals to other academic programs in the community applicable and relevant to children with high-level achievement and talents (Olzewski-Kubilius, 2004).

As another counseling intervention, counselors might work with parents who feel inadequate in comparison to their gifted child or adolescent, to help them manage these feelings. And some gifted children struggle with their identity as it differentiates from the family (Peterson, 2002). Counselors also can help parents manage their feelings about the additional demands, sibling jealousy, and tension associated with the gifted child in the home, while still facilitating the unique identity of the gifted child. Further, counselors can teach parents (as well as teachers) basic behavioral strategies designed to maintain control and fairness with gifted and nongifted children. Counselors can facilitate collaboration between home and school to promote student academic success and support. Finally, counselors can provide supportive counseling and teach coping skills to help parents deal with the negative and unsupportive reactions of school personnel, community resources, and friends toward their seeking educational placement in the best interest of their children.

Direct Counseling With the Gifted

Gifted children and youth require differentiated and specialized counseling services that address the specific concerns found in this population. For example, counselors may offer interventions for anxiety and depression in gifted young children who can perceive complex social situations and existential questions but lack the developmental and emotional resources to cope with these thoughts (Piechewski, 1997).

In individual counseling, the counselor can employ several strategies to assist the gifted child or adolescent with specific issues that may confront him or her. The counselor can teach cognitive strategies such as self-monitoring and self-discipline to help gifted children and adolescents make good choices, especially because they typically need to feel a sense of power and participation in decision-making. The counselor can help these students further by giving them an array of choices, as problem-solving has been found to be a strength in these children (Neihart, 2002).

The counselor can also assist in the child's or adolescent's appropriate expression of feelings, as well as self-advocacy, with gifted youth who are feeling misunderstood by teachers, parents, or peers.

Group Counseling

Group counseling can address positive social skills with peers who have similar abilities and interests (Peterson, 2003). Because friendships are based on cognitive similarities, age differences frequently are present in friendships among these children and adolescents. Group counseling also can promote identity development as this relates to their unique talents as well as relative weaknesses, offers outlets to normalize feelings in a safe, noncompetitive atmosphere, helps gifted youth to accept help for developmental and social emotional issues typical for their age group, and decreases the need to be self-sufficient and invulnerable. Finally, resources such as bibliotherapy and guided viewing of films can promote self-understanding for gifted students (Hébert & Neumeister, 2001).

The gifted have a tendency to be perfectionists. Although perfectionism can be a positive force toward high achievement, it can have negative aspects, such as compulsiveness, over concern for details, rigidity, and a tendency to set unrealistically high standards. Counselors can help their gifted clients set realistic short- and long-term goals, enjoy activities solely for pleasure, develop self-tolerance through the use of positive self-statements and exposure to less-than-perfect gifted role models, identify their strengths rather than limitations, and learn progressive relaxation or meditation techniques to counter the stressful aspects of perfectionism (Ford, 1996; Silverman, 1993).

Jasmine

Jasmine, an 11-year-old African American girl in the sixth grade, had achieved at uneven levels ever since entering school. She clearly seemed capable of exceptional work but sometimes rushed through assignments and made careless errors. In addition, her teachers perceived her as challenging authority because she shouted out answers in class, corrected teachers' mistakes, and questioned teachers' directives. Further, after finishing her classwork and before the rest of her classmates were done with theirs, Jasmine would wander around the classroom and talk to her peers.

Because Jasmine was seen as having behavioral problems, and perhaps because she was an African American, her teachers had not recommended her to be assessed for the gifted program. She was well liked by her peers, even seen as a leader. Her parents enjoyed her brightness but were frustrated by the demands and challenges she created in the home.

Jasmine and her parents met with a family counselor because of Jasmine's difficulties. The counselor recognized behavioral patterns often seen in gifted children and recommended that an assessment of Jasmine's cognitive and artistic abilities be requested of the school. Jasmine was found to be gifted in several areas, but she did not qualify for the school's criteria for giftedness because her grades were erratic and she lacked teacher nominations. The counselor advocated for Jasmine with the principal and Jasmine's sixth-grade teacher to allow Jasmine to be enrolled in the gifted program on a trial basis. The counselor also consulted with the teacher about how to find resources at school that were intellectually more appropriate for Jasmine.

An academically accelerated gifted curriculum for sixth graders was initiated with Jasmine. The parents and teacher worked with the counselor to place Jasmine on a positive reward system at home and school. The goals were for Jasmine to complete her schoolwork accurately, take turns talking with her classmates and siblings, and, to prevent boredom, finish her work before starting another project, which, when possible, would be identified for her as soon as she completed her current activity.

Jasmine was delighted to be in the gifted program and developed higher self-esteem as she began to see herself as a role model rather than as a child who was constantly in trouble. She completed her schoolwork and received excellent grades in both the general and gifted curricular activities. Because she had challenging material to engage her energies, her disruptiveness in class diminished greatly.

The counselor met with Jasmine's parents and teacher to provide more information on the behaviors of gifted children, which helped them to reframe Jasmine's actions in a more positive light. Jasmine enjoyed the reward system and chose to continue the program even after she had achieved all of the initial behavioral goals. Her parents met separately with the counselor to process their feelings about having a gifted child, to develop coping skills for negative reactions to Jasmine's giftedness, and to set realistic expectations for Jasmine, other children in the family, and themselves.

Summary

Exceptional children and adolescents comprise a diverse and complex group requiring a developmentally and culturally appropriate comprehensive approach to services dependent on their specific individual needs. Counselors must obtain information and training about educational laws, clinical and educational definitions, and appropriate interventions for children and adolescents with special educational needs, those who are gifted and twice-exceptional, and those who qualify as having a disability under Section 504 of the Rehabilitation Act.

The traditional counselor model is less effective with these populations than a broad-based service model in which the counselor creates a collaborative community with all individuals and resources necessary for the child or adolescent to experience success in every area of life to the greatest extent possible. Counseling with children and adolescents who have exceptional needs must be coordinated with educational services, medical and remedial specialists, family members, and the students themselves. Exceptional children and adolescents reap maximal benefits when comprehensive counseling services are offered in combination with a variety of other support services in the most normalized environment possible.

References

Abery, B., Schoeller, K., Simunds, E., Gaylord, V., & Fahnestock, M. (1997). *Yes I Can social inclusion program.* Minneapolis: University of Minnesota, Institute of Community Integration.

Albrecht, D. G. (1995). *Raising a child who has a physical disability.* New York: Wiley.

Alsop, G. (1997). Coping or counseling: Families of intellectually gifted students. *Roeper Review, 20,* 28–34.

American Association on Mental Retardation. (1992). *Mental retardation: Definition, classification, and systems of supports* (9th ed.). Washington, DC: Author.

American Psychological Association. (2000). *Diagnostic and statistic manual of mental disorders* (4th ed.). Washington, DC: Author.

American School Counselor Association. (2004). *The professional school counselor and students with special needs.* Retrieved July 24, 2007, from http://www.schoolcounselor.org/content.asp?contentid=218

American School Counselor Association. (2005). *The ASCA national model: A framework for school counseling programs* (2nd ed.). Alexandria, VA: Author.

American Youth Policy Forum and Center on Educational Policy. (2002). *Twenty-five years of educating children with disabilities: The good news and the work ahead.* Washington, DC: American Youth Policy Forum and Center on Educational Policy.

Amos, Patricia A. (2004). New Considerations in the Prevention of Aversives, Restraint, and Seclusion: Incorporating the Role of Relationships Into an Ecological Perspective. *Research and Practice for Persons with Severe Disabilities, 29,* 263–272.

Assouline, S, Nicpon, M., & Huber, D. (2006). The impact of vulnerabilities and strengths on the academic experiences of twice-exceptional students: A message to school counselors. *Professional School Counseling, 10*(1).

Banks, J. A. (2004). *Handbook of research on multicultural education.* San Francisco: Jossey-Bass.

Barkley, R. A. (1995). *Taking charge of AD/HD.* New York: Guilford.

Barkley, R. A. (2006). *Attention-deficit hyperactivity disorder: A handbook for diagnosis and treatment.* New York: Guilford.

Barkley, R. A., DuPaul, G. J., & Connor, D. F. (1999). Stimulants. In J. S. Werry & M. G. Aman (Eds.), *Practitioners guide to psychoactive drugs for children and adolescents.* (2nd ed., pp. 213–247.) New York: Plenum Medical Book.

Baum, S. M., Owen, S.V., & Dixon, J. (1991). *To be gifted and learning disabled: From identification to practical intervention strategies.* Mansfield, CT: Creative Learning Press.

Beail, N. (2003). What works for people with mental retardation? Critical commentary on cognitive-behavioral and psychodynamic psychotherapy research. *Mental Retardation, 41,* 468–472.

Beasley, J. B. (2004). Importance of training and expertise to assess "what works" for individuals with intellectual disabilities. *Mental Retardation, 42,* 405–406.

Bemak, R, & Chung, R. C. (2005). Advocacy as a critical role for urban school counselors: Working toward equity and social justice. *Professional School Counseling, 8,* 196–202.

Bender, W. N. (1997). *Understanding AD/HD: A practical guide for teachers and parents.* Englewood Cliffs, NJ: Prentice-Hall.

Bloomquist, M. L. (1996). *Skills training for children with behavioral disorders: A parent and therapist guidebook.* New York: Guilford.

Borland, J. H. (2004). *Issues and practices in the identification and education of gifted students from under-represented groups* (No. RM04186). Storrs: University of Connecticut, National Research Center on the Gifted and Talented.

Bullis, M., Tehan, C.J., & Clark, H.B. (2000). Teaching and developing improved community life competencies. In H.B. Clark and M. Davis, (Eds.), *Transition to adulthood: A resource for assisting young people with emotional or behavioral difficulties,* 107–131.

Carpenter, S. L., King-Sears, M. E., & Keys, S. G. (1998). Counselors + educators + families as a transdisciplinary team = more effective inclusion for students with disabilities. *Professional School Counseling, 2,* 1–9

Cioffi, D. H., & Kysilka, M. L. (1997). Reactive behavior patterns in gifted adolescents. *Educational Forum, 61,* 260-268.

Colangelo, N. (2003). Counseling gifted students. In N. Colangelo & G. A. Davis (Eds.), *Handbook of gifted education* (pp. 373–387). Boston: Allyn & Bacon.

Colangelo, N., Assouline, S. & Gross, M. (2004). *A nation deceived: How schools hold back America's brightest students.* Iowa City, IA: Templeton National Report on Acceleration.

Committee on Minority Representation in Special Education, Donovan, M. S., & Cross, C.T. (Eds.), (2002). *Minority students in special and gifted education.* Washington, DC: National Academies Press.

Conners, C. K., Epstein, J. N., March, J. S., Angold, A., Wells, K. C., Klaric, J., et al. (2001). Multimodal treatment of AD/HD in the MTA: An alternative outcome analysis. *Journal of the American Academy of Child and Adolescent Psychiatry, 40,* 159–167.

Cunningham, C. E., & Cunningham, L. J. (1998). Student-mediated conflict resolution programs. In R. A. Barkley (Ed.), *Attention-deficit hyperactivity disorder: A handbook for diagnosis and treatment* (2nd ed., pp. 491–509). New York: Guilford.

Davis, M., Geller, J., & Hunt, B. (2006). *State mental health authorities' capacities to help youth and young adults enter adulthood.* Manuscript submitted for publication.

de Barona, M. S., & Barona, A. (2006). School counselors and school psychologists: Collaborating to ensure minority students receive appropriate consideration for special educational programs. *Professional School Counseling, 10,* 3–13.

Downing, J. E. (1996). *Including students with severe and multiple disabilities in typical classrooms.* Baltimore, MD: Paul Brookes.

Downing, J. E., Eckinger, J., Williams, D., & Lilly, J. (1997). Inclusive education for students with severe disabilities: Comparative views of principals and educators at different levels of implementation. *Remedial and Special Education, 18*(3).

Dunlap, G., dePerczel, M., Clarke, S., Wilson, D., Wright, S., White, R., et al. (1994). Choice making to promote adaptive behavior for students with emotional and behavioral challenges. *Journal of Applied Behavior Analysis, 27,* 505–518.

Dunlap, G., Vaughn, B.J., & O'Neill, R. (1998). Comprehensive behavioral support: Application and intervention. In S. F. Warren & Reichle (Series Eds.) & A. M. Wetherby, S.F. Warren, & Reichle (Vol. Eds.), *Communication and language intervention series: Vol. 7. Transitions in prelinguistic communication* (pp. 343–374). Baltimore, MD: Paul H. Brookes Publishing.

DuPaul, G. J., Guevremont, D. C., & Barkley, R. A. (1992). Behavioral treatment of attention-deficit hyperactivity disorder in the classroom: The use of the attention training system. b*ehavior modification, 16,* 204–225.

DuPaul, G. J., & Stoner, G. (2003). *AD/HD in the schools: Assessment and intervention strategies* (2nd ed.). New York: Guilford.

DuPaul, G. J., & Weyandt, L. L. (2006). School-based intervention for children with attention deficit hyperactivity disorder: Effects on academic, social, and behavioral functioning. *International Journal of Disability, Development, and Education, 53,* 161–176.

Durodoye, B. A., Combes, B, H., & Bryant, R. M. (2004). Counselor intervention in the post-secondary planning of African American students with learning disabilities. *Professional School Counseling, 7,* 133–140.

Dwyer, K. P., Osher, D., & Hoffman, C.C. (2000). Creating responsive schools: Contextualizing early warning, timely response. *Exceptional Children, 66,* 347–365.

Echevarria, J. (2002). *The disproportionate representation of minority students in special education: Where do we go from here?* Paper presented at Oxford Round Table on Education and Human Rights, Oxford University, England, March 15, 2002.

Education for All Handicapped Children Act of 1975 (PL 94-142), 20 U.S.C. 1400 et seq. (1977).

Eichinger, J., & Woltman, S. (1993). Integration strategies for learners with severe multiple disorders. *Teaching Exceptional Children, 26,* 18.

Eisenman, L.T. (2003). Theories in practice: School-to-work transitions-for-youth with mild disabilities. *Exceptionality, 11*, 89–102.

Elksnin, L. K., & Elksnin, N. (2004). The social-emotional side of learning disabilities. *Learning Disability Quarterly, 27*, 3–8.

Erk, R. R. (1997). Multidimensional treatment of attention deficit disorder: A family oriented approach. *Journal of Mental Health Counseling, 19*, 3–22.

Erk, R. (1999). Attention deficit hyperactivity disorder: Counselors, laws, and implications for practice. *Professional School Counseling, 2,* 12–25.

Fertig, C. (Ed.) (2002, Winter). Twice exceptional (Special issue). *Understanding Our Gifted, 14,* 12–15.

Ford, D. Y. (1996). *Reversing underachievement among gifted black students.* New York: Teachers College Press.

Ford, D. Y., & Grantham, T. C. (2003). Providing access for culturally diverse gifted students: From deficit to dynamic thinking. *Theory into Practice, 42,* 217–225.

Frasier, M. M., Garcia, J. H., & Passow, A. H. (1995). *A review of assessment issues in gifted education and their implications for identifying gifted minority students* (No. RM95204). Storrs: University of Connecticut, National Research Center on the Gifted and Talented.

Frith, G. H., Clark, R. M., & Miller, S. H. (1983). Integrated counseling services for exceptional children: A functional, noncategorical model. *School Counselor, 30,* 387–391.

Gordon, M. (1992). *I would if I could.* DeWitt, NY: GCL.

Gottfried, A. E., & Gottfried, A. W. (1997). A longitudinal study of academic intrinsic motivation in intellectually gifted children: Childhood through early adolescence. *Gifted Child Quarterly, 40,* 179–183.

Gottfried, A. W, Gottfried, A. E., Bathurst, K., & Guerin, D. W. (1994). *Gifted IQ: Early developmental aspects.* New York: Plenum.

Gray, T., & Fleischman, S. (2005). Successful strategies for English language learners. *Educational Leadership, 62,* 84–85.

Gresham, F. M. (2002). Teaching social skills to high-risk children and youth: Preventive and remedial strategies. In M. R. Shinn, H. M. Walker, & G. Stoner (Eds.), *Interventions for academic and behavior problems II: Preventive and remedial approaches* (2nd ed., pp. 403– 432). Washington, DC: National Association of School Psychologists.

Guevremont, D. (1990). Social skills and peer relationship training. In R. A. Barkley (Ed.), *Attention deficit hyperactivity disorder: A handbook for diagnosis and treatment* (pp. 540–572). New York: Guilford.

Guevremont, D. (1992). The parent's role in helping the AD/HD child with peer relationships. *CHADDER, 6,* 17–18.

Heinrichs, R. R. (2003). A whole-school approach to bullying: Special considerations for children with exceptionalities. *Intervention in School and Clinic, 38,* 195–204.

Henley, M., Ramsey, R. S., & Algozzine, R. (1993). *Characteristics of and strategies for teaching students with mild disabilities.* Boston: Allyn & Bacon.

Hébert, T. P., & Neumeister, K. L. S. (2001). Guided viewing of film: A strategy for counseling gifted teenagers. *Journal of Secondary Gifted Education, 14,* 224–235.

Heward, W. L. (2003). *Exceptional children: An introduction to special education.* (7th ed.) Upper Saddle River, NJ: Merrill Prentice Hall.

Hosie, T. W., & Erk, R. R. (1993). ACA reading program: Attention deficit disorder. *American Counseling Association Guidepost, 35,* 15–18.

Hurley, A. D. (2005). Psychotherapy is an essential tool in the treatment of psychiatric disorders for people with mental retardation. *Mental Retardation, 43,* 448–450.

Individuals with Disabilities Education Act Amendments of 1997, PL 105-17, 105th Congress, 1st session.

Individuals with Disabilities Education Act of 2005 70 (118) U.S.C. 1221 e–3.

Isaacs, M. L., Greene, M., & Valesky, T. (1998). Elementary counselors and inclusion: A statewide attitudinal survey. *Professional School Counseling, 2*, 68–76.

Janiga, S. J., & Costenbader, V. (2002). The transition from high school to postsecondary education for students with learning disabilities: A survey of college service coordinators. *Journal of Learning Disabilities, 35*, 462–468.

Kauffman, J. M. (1997). *Characteristics of emotional and behavioral disorders in children and youth.* Columbus, OH: Merrill.

Kavale, K. A., & Forness, S. R. (1996). Social skills deficits and learning disabilities: A meta-analysis. *Journal of Learning Disabilities, 29*, 226–237.

Kay, P. J., & Fitzgerald, M. (1997). Parents + teachers + action research = real involvement. *Teaching Exceptional Children, 30*, 8–11.

Klein, S. D., & Kemp, J. D. (Eds.). (2004). *Reflections from a different journey: What adults with disabilities wish all parents knew.* New York: McGraw-Hill.

Klein, S. D., & Schive, K. (Eds.). (2001). *You will dream new dreams: Inspiring personal stories by parents of children with disabilities.* New York: Kensington.

Krebs, C. S. (2002*).* Self-advocacy skills: A portfolio approach. *RE: view, 33,* 160–163.

Lerner, J. W., Lowenthal, B., & Lerner, S. R. (1995). *Attention deficit disorders: Assessment and teaching.* Pacific Grove, CA: Brooks/Cole.

Lieberman, L. J., James, A. R., & Ludwa, N. (2004). Impact of inclusion in general physical education for all students. *Journal of Physical Education, Recreation & Dance, 75(5),* 37–42.

LoCicero, K. A., & Ashby, J. S. (2000). Multidimensional perfectionism in middle school age gifted students: A comparison to peers from the general cohort. *Roeper Review, 22,* 182–185.

Losen, D., & Orfield, G. (2002). *Racial inequity in special education.* Cambridge, MA: Harvard University, Civil Rights Project.

Ludwig, G., & Cullinan, D. (1984). Behavioral problems of gifted and non-gifted elementary school boys and girls. *Gifted Child Quarterly, 28*, 37–39.

Martella, R. C., Nelson, J. R., & Marchand-Martella, N. E. (2003). *Managing disruptive behaviors in the schools: A school wide, class-room, and individualized social learning approach.* Boston: Allyn & Bacon.

Masia-Warner, C., Nangle, D. W., & Hansen, D. J. (2006). Bringing evidence-based child mental health services to the schools: General issues and specific populations. *Education & Treatment of Children, 29,* 165–172.

McTarnaghan, J. (1998). *Circle of friends.* Unpublished training manuscript. Community Autism Resources, Fall River, MA.

Meyers, J., Parsons, R. D., & Martin, R. (1990). *Mental health consultation in the schools.* San Francisco: Jossey-Bass.

Milsom, A. (2002). Students with disabilities: School counselor involvement and preparation. *Professional School Counseling, 5,* 331–338.

Milsom, A. (2006). Creating positive school experiences for students with disabilities. *Professional School Counseling, 10,* 66–72.

Milsom, A., & Hartley, M., (2005). Assisting students with learning disabilities transitioning to college: What school counselors should know. *Professional School Counseling, 8,* 436–441.

Milsom, A., & Peterson, J. S. (2006). Introduction to special issue: Examining disability and giftedness in schools. *Professional School Counseling, 10,* 1–2.

Mishna, F. & Muskat, B. (2004). School based group treatment for students with disabilities: A group collaborative approach. *Children & Schools, 26,* 135–150.

National Center for Education Statistics. (2005). *Statistics of Public Elementary and Secondary School Systems.* Retrieved August 14, 2007, from http://www.ideadata.org/tables 26th/ar_aa7.htm

National Center for Learning Disabilities. (2007*). IDEA 2004 brief summary of changes and new provisions.* Retrieved July 24, 2007, from http://www.ncld.org/index.php?option= content&task=view&id=282

National Joint Committee on Learning Disabilities. (2005). *Responsiveness to intervention and learning disabilities.* Retrieved July 16, 2007, from http://www.ldanatl.org/pdf/rti 2005.pdf

Neihart, M. (2002). Risk and resilience in gifted children: A conceptual framework. In M. Neihart, S. M. Reis, N. M. Robinson, & S. M. Moon (Eds.), *The social and emotional development of gifted children: What do we know?* (pp. 113–122). Waco, TX: Prufrock Press.

Newby, R., Fischer, M., & Roman, M. (1991). Parent training for families of children with AD/HD. *School Psychology Review, 20,* 252–255.

Olenchak, F. R., & Reis, S. M. (2001). Gifted students with learning disabilities. In M. Neihart, S. M. Reis, N. M. Robinson, & S. M. Moon (Eds.), *The social and emotional development of gifted children: What do we know?* (pp. 177–191). Waco, TX: Prufrock Press.

Olszewski-Kubilius, P. (2004). Talent searches and accelerated programming for gifted students. In N. Colangelo, S. G. Assouline, & M. Gross (Eds.), *A nation deceived: How schools hold back America's brightest students* (pp. 69-86). Iowa City, IA: Connie Belin & Jacqueline N. Blank International Center for Gifted Education and Talent Development.

Orange, C. (1997). Gifted students and perfectionism. *Roeper Review, 20,* 39–41.

Orenstein, M. (2000). *Smart but stuck: What every therapist needs to know about learning disabilities and imprisoned intelligence.* New York: Haworth Press.

Oswald, D., Coutinho, M., & Best, A. (2000). *Community and school predictors of over representation of minority children in special education.* Paper presented at Minority Issues in Education Conference, sponsored by Civil Rights Project at Harvard University, November 17, 2000, Cambridge, MA.

Padilla, A. M. & Medina, A. (1996). Cross-cultural sensitivity in assessment: Using tests in culturally appropriate ways. In L. A. Suzuki, P. J. Meiler, & J. G. Ponteretto (Eds.), *Handbook of multicultural assessment: Reexamination, reconceptualization, and practical application* (pp. 3–18). San Francisco: Jossey-Bass.

Passaro, P. D., Moon, M., & Wiest, D. J., & Wong, E. H. (2004). A model for school psychology practice: Addressing the needs of students with emotional and behavioral challenges through the use of an in-school support room and reality therapy. *Adolescence, 39,* 503–517.

Peterson, J. S. (1998). The burdens of capability. *Reclaiming Children and Youth, 6,* 194–198.

Peterson, J. S. (1999). Gifted—through whose cultural lens? An application of the post positivistic mode of inquiry. *Journal for the Education of the Gifted, 22,* 354–383.

Peterson, J. S. (2002). A longitudinal study of post-high-school development in gifted individuals at risk for poor educational outcomes. *Journal of Secondary Gifted Education, 14,* 6–18.

Peterson, J. S. (2003). An argument for proactive attention to affective concerns of gifted adolescents. *Journal of Secondary Gifted Education, 14,* 62–71.

Peterson, J. S. (2006). Addressing counseling needs of gifted students. *Professional School Counseling, 10,* 43–51.

Pfiffner, L. J., Barkley, R. A., & DuPaul, G. J. (2006) Treatment of AD/HD in school settings. In Phelps, L. A. (2003). *High schools with authentic and inclusive learning practices: Selected features and findings (Research to Practice Brief 2).* Minneapolis: University of Minnesota, National Center for Secondary Education and Transition.

Phelps, L. A.(2003). *High schools with authentic and inclusive learning practices:Selected features and findings (Research to Practice Brief 2).* Minneapolis: University of Minnesota, National Center for Secondary Education and Transition.

Piechowski, M. M. (1997). Emotional intelligence: The measure of intrapersonal intelligence. In N. Colangelo & G. A. Davis (Eds.), *Handbook of gifted education* (2nd Ed., pp. 366-381). Boston: Allyn & Bacon.

Pierangelo, R., & Jacoby, R. (1996). *Parents complete special education guide.* West Nyack, NY: Center for Applied Research in Education.

Pollio, D., McClendon, C., North, D., Reid, D., & Jonson-Reid, M. (2005). *Children in schools, 27,* 111–115.

Polloway, E., Epstein, M., & Cullinan, D. (1985). Prevalence of behavior problems among educable mentally retarded students. *Education and Training of the Mentally Retarded, 20,* 3-13.

Public Law 93-380 (1974). *Federal Register, 41,* 24662-24675.

Public Law 94-142 (1975). *Federal Register, 42,* 42474-42518.

Public Law 101-476 (1990). *Federal Register, 54,* 35210-35271.

Public Law 105-17 (1997). *Federal Register, 62,* 55076-55126.

Public Law 108-446 (2004). *Federal Register, 71,* 46589-46638.

Quinn, P. (1992). *Putting on the brakes.* New York: Magination.

Razza, N. J., & Tomasulo, D. J. (2005). *Healing trauma: The power of group treatment for people with intellectual disabilities.* Washington, DC: American Psychological Association.

Reddy, L. A., & Richardson, L. (2006). School-based prevention and intervention programs for children with emotional disturbance. *Education and Treatment of Children, 29,* 379–404.

Reid, R., Trout, A. L., & Schartz, M. (2005). Self-regulation interventions for children with attention-deficit/hyperactivity disorder. *Exceptional Children, 71,* 361–377.

Reis, S. M., & McCoach, D. B. (2000). The underachievement of gifted students: What do we know and where do we go? *Gifted Child Quarterly, 44,* 152–170.

Renzulli, J. S., & Park, S. (2002). *Giftedness and high school dropouts: Personal, family, and school-related factors* (No. RM02168). Storrs: University of Connecticut, National Research Center on the Gifted and Talented.

Richert, S. (1997). Excellence with equality in identification and programming. In N. Colangelo & G. A. Davis (Eds.), *Handbook of gifted education* (2nd ed., pp. 75–88). Boston: Allyn & Bacon.

Roberts, M. C, Jacobs, A. K., Puddy, R. W., Nyre, J. E., & Vernberg, E. M. (2003). Treating children with serious emotional disturbances in schools and community: The intensive mental health program, *Professional Psychology: Research and Practice, 34,* 519–526.

Rosenberg, M. S., & Edmond-Rosenberg, I. (1994). *The special education sourcebook: A teacher guide to programs, materials, and information sources.* Bethesda, MD: Woodbine House.

Ross, R. O. (1993). *National excellence: A case for developing American talent.* Washington, DC: U.S. Department of Education.

Salend, S. (1983). Using hypothetical examples to sensitize nonhandicapped students to their handicapped peers. *School Counselor, 33,* 306–310.

Scarborough, J. & Gilbride, D. (2006). Developing relationships with rehabilitation counselors to meet the transition needs of students with disabilities. *Professional School Counseling, 10*, pp. 25–33.

Sciarra, D.T. (2004). *School counseling: Foundations and professional issues.* Belmont, CA: Thompson-Cole.

Shaklee, B. D. (1997). Gifted child education in the new millennium. *Educational Forum, 61,* 212–219.

Shechtman, Z. & Gilat, I. (2005). The effectiveness of counseling groups in reducing stress of parents of children with learning disabilities. *Group dynamics: Theory, research, and practice, 9,* 275–286.

Sheridan, S. M. (1995). *The tough kid social skills book.* Longmont, CO: Sopris-West.

Sheridan, S. M., Eagle, J. W., & Doll, B. (2006). An examination of the efficacy of conjoint behavioral consultation with diverse clients. *School Psychology Quarterly, 21,* 396–417.

Short, D., & Echevarria, J. (2005). Teacher skills to support English language learners. *Educational Leadership, 62,* 8–13.

Silverman, L. K. (1993). *Counseling the gifted and talented.* Denver, CO: Love.

Sinason, V (1997). *Your handicapped child.* Los Angeles, CA: Warwick.

Sitlington, P. L., Clark, G. M., & Kolstoe, O. P. (2000). *Transition education and services for adolescents with disabilities.* Needham Heights, MA: Allyn & Bacon.

Skiba, R.J., Poloni-Staudinger, L., Simmons, A. B., Feggins-Azziz, L. R., & Chung, C. (2005). Unproven links: Can poverty explain ethnic disproportionality in special education*? Journal of Special Education, 39,* 130–144.

Smith, D. (2001). *Introduction to special education: Teaching in an age of opportunity* (4th ed.) Boston: Allyn & Bacon.

Smith, S. L. (1991). *Succeeding against the odds: How the learning disabled can realize their promise.* New York: Penguin Putnam.

Stone, C. B., & Clark, M. A. (2001). School counselors and principals: Partners in support of academic achievement. *NASSP Bulletin, 85,* 46–67.

Strain, P. & Kohler, F. (1998). Peer mediated social intervention for children with autism. *Seminars in Speech and Language, 19,* 391–405.

Sturmey, P. (2005). Against therapy with people who have mental retardation. *Mental Retardation, 43,* 55–57.

Sue, D. W., & Sue, D. (2003). *Counseling the culturally diverse: Theory and practice* (4th ed.). New York: John Wiley.

Szymanski, E., & King, J. (1989). Rehabilitation counseling in transition planning and preparation. *Career Development for Exceptional Individuals, 12,* 3–10.

Tarver-Behring, S., Cabello, B., Kushida, D., & Murguia, A. (2000). Cultural modifications to current school-based consultation approaches reported by culturally diverse beginning consultants. *School Psychology Review, 29,* 354-367.

Tarver-Behring, S. & Ingraham, C. L. (1998). Culture as a central component to consultation: A call to the field. *Journal of Educational and Psychological Consultation, 9,* 57–72.

Tarver-Behring, S., & Spagna, M. E. (1997). School counselors as chance agents toward full inclusion. *Arizona Counseling Journal, 21,* 50–57.

Tarver-Behring, S., Spagna, M. E., & Sullivan, J. (1998). School counselors and full inclusion for children with special needs. *Professional School Counselor, 1,* 51–56.

Tarver-Behring, S. & Tom-Gelinas, Rosemary. (1996). School consultation with Asian American children and families. *California School Psychologist, 1,* 13–20.

Taub, J. (2006). Understanding the concerns of parents with disabilities: Challenges and roles for School Counselors. *Professional School Counseling, 10,* 52–57.

Taylor, J. F. (1994). *Helping your hyperactive/attention deficit child.* New York: Prima.

Taylor, J. L. (2005). In support of psychotherapy for people who have mental retardation. *Mental Retardation, 6,* 450–453.

Thurneck, D., Warner, P., & Cobb, H. (2007). Children and adolescents with disabilities and health care needs: Implications for intervention. In Thompson Prout, H. & Brown, D. (Eds.), *Counseling and Psychotherapy with children and adolescents: theory and practice for school and clinical settings* (pp. 419-453). Hoboken, NJ: Wiley.

Tucker, B., & Hafenstein, N. L. (1997). Psychological intensities in young children. *Gifted Child Quarterly, 41,* 66–75.

Turnbull, A. (2004). President's address 2004: "Wearing two hats": Morphed Perspectives on Family Quality of Life. *Mental Retardation, 42,* 383–399.

Turnbull, A. P., & Ruef, M. (1997). Family perspectives on inclusive lifestyle issues for people with problem behavior. *Exceptional Children, 63,* 211–227.

U.S. Department of Health and Human Services. (2000). *Report of the surgeon general's conference on children's mental health: A national action agenda.* Washington, DC: Author.

U.S. Department of Education. (2002). *A new era: Revitalizing special education for children and their families.* Washington, DC: Author.

Vander Stoep, A., Beresford, S. A., Weiss, N. S., McKnight,B., Cauce, A., & Cohen, P. (2000). Community-based study of the transition to adulthood for adolescents with psychiatric disorder. *American Journal of Epidemiology, 152,* 352–362.

Vaughan, M. (2002). An index for inclusion. *European Journal of Special Needs Education, 17,* 197-201.

Vogt, M. E., & Shearer, B. A. (2003). *Reading specialists in the real world: A sociocultural view.* Boston: Pearson Education.

Wagner, M. & Davis, M. (2006). How are we preparing students with emotional disturbances for the transition to young adulthood? *Journal of Emotional and Behavioral Disorders, 14,* 86–98.

Walker, H. M., Kavanagh, K., Stiller, B., Golly, A., Severson, H., & Feil, E. G. (1998). First step to success: An early intervention approach for preventing school antisocial behavior. *Journal of Emotional and Behavioral Disorders, 6,* 66–80.

Weinstein, C. S., Tomlinson-Clarke, S., & Curran, M. (2004). Toward a conception of culturally responsive classroom management. *Journal of Teacher Education, 55,* 25–38.

Westman, J. C. (1994). *Handbook of learning disabilities: A multisystem approach.* Boston: Allyn & Bacon.

Wetherby, A. & Prizant, B. (1999). Enhancing language and communication development in autism: Assessment and intervention guidelines. In D. Zager (Ed.), *Autism: Identification, education, & treatment* (pp. 141–174). Mahwah, NJ: Lawrence Erlbaum Associates.

Willner, P. (2005). The effectiveness of psycho-therapeutic interventions for people with learning disabilities: A critical overview. *Journal of Intellectual Disability Research, 49,* 77–85.

Winebrenner, S. (2003). Teaching strategies for twice-exceptional students. *Interventions in School and Clinic, 38*(3), 131–137.

Witt, N. (2004). Groups offer valuable life lessons. In S. D. Klein & J. D. Kemp (Eds.), *Reflections from a different journey: What adults with disabilities wish all parents* knew (pp. 184–188). New York: McGraw-Hill.

Wren, C., & Einhorn, J. (2000). *Hanging by a twig: Understanding and counseling adults with learning disabilities and ADD.* New York: W.W. Norton & Co.

Yell, M. L., & Shriner, J. G. (1997). The IDEA Amendments of 1997: Implications for special and general education teachers, administrators, and teacher trainers. *Focus on Exceptional Children, 30,* 1–20.

Ysseldyke, J. E., Algozzine, B., & Thurlow, M. L. (2000). *Critical issues in special education* (3rd. ed.). Boston: Houghton-Mifflin.

Zirkel, P. A., & Gluckman, B. (1997, May). ADD/AD/HD students and Section 504. *Principal,* pp. 47–48.

Counseling Children From Diverse Backgrounds

Darcie Davis-Gage

The U.S. population continues to become more diverse. The U.S. Bureau of the Census (2005) estimated that by the year 2050 the percentage of individuals identified as Hispanic, Asian, and Multiracial will double and individuals identified as Black will increase substantially. Religious and spiritual practices of children also have been changing as a consequence of education, the media, world-consciousness, and immigration Although the gender demographics stay fairly consistent, the gender expectations and socialization of young girls and boys continue to change and evolve (Brammer, 2004). Counselors working with youth will find these changes reflected in their caseloads and, therefore, must be aware of how to acknowledge these differences and incorporate appropriate interventions into their counseling practice.

As professional counselors work within educational and clinical settings, they inevitably will work with young people from diverse backgrounds. Therefore, the preamble to the Code of Ethics of the American Counseling Association (2005) states:

> Association members recognize diversity and embrace a cross-cultural approach in support of the worth, dignity, potential, and uniqueness of people within the social and cultural contexts. (p. 3).

The Association for Multicultural Counseling and Development identified 31 multicultural competencies, divided into three domains:

1. Awareness of personal bias and values
2. Awareness of the client's worldview
3. Knowledge about culturally appropriate interventions and strategies

The American School Counseling Association adopted a position statement regarding multiculturally competent counseling that was operationalized into the following checklist by Holcomb-McCoy (2004):

1. Multicultural counseling, consultation, and family counseling
2. Understanding racism, racial/ethnic development, and cross-cultural interpersonal interactions
3. Multicultural assessment
4. Social advocacy
5. Developing school-family-community partnerships

The checklist contains 51 statements of specific abilities related to providing multicultural competent counseling. For example, under the category of multicultural consultation, counselors would identify whether they met the following (Holcomb-McCoy, 2004):

1. I am aware of how culture affects traditional models of consultation.
2. I can discuss at least one model of multicultural consultation.
3. I recognize when racial and cultural issues are impacting the consultation process.
4. I can identify when the race and/or culture of the client is a problem for the consultee.
5. I discuss issues related to race/ethnicity/culture during the consultation process, when applicable. (p. 184)

The reality that the United States is becoming increasingly diverse is a compelling reason for counselors to become more culturally competent. Gaining knowledge about diversity is one means of doing so. This chapter provides information about ethnicity, gender, and spiritual considerations in working with children and adolescents. (Sexual orientation and socioeconomic status are covered elsewhere in this book.)

In addition to a strong knowledge base that includes awareness of various ethnic groups as well as the acculturation process and identity development models, counseling professionals have to be aware of their own cultural backgrounds and biases and understand how diversity influences the counseling process.

Improving Multicultural Competency

Examining one's own biases, assumptions, and belief system is a crucial first step in becoming a multiculturally competent counselor. Counselors can explore their bias and assumptions in a variety of ways, such as completing formal assessments and critically examining their own life. One formal assessment tool is the Counselors Self-Assessment of Cultural Awareness Scale (Vernon & Clemente, 2005). Completing this assessment tool provides counselors with a measure of their cultural awareness and informs them about the areas in which they may need to work. Counselors should recognize that increasing multicultural competency is a developmental process and has to involve interactions with others who are different.

Once counselors are able to identify areas in which they may need work, they can develop a plan of action. They should set goals for themselves by identifying readings, activities, and events to increase their multicultural competence. Counselors also could keep a journal about their thoughts, feelings, and reactions related to completing their goals. These journal entries can serve as a form of measurement and will illustrate growth and change over time.

Counselors who work with children and adolescents may consider the following ways to improve their multicultural competency in school and community mental health settings.

- Build knowledge by attending and becoming involved in cultural events in the community.
- Read autobiographies of diverse individuals.
- Develop cross-cultural relationships in personal and professional settings.
- Arrange the counseling office to include a variety of artifacts and artwork representing various cultures.
- Learn a language other than English.
- Be open to new learning experiences.
- Attend professional development workshops with various multicultural themes.

Acculturation and Identity Formation

When working with children and adolescents, counselors must consider acculturation issues as well as identity development, as these concepts often are interlinked.

Acculturation

Acculturation refers to how individuals blend their cultural beliefs and practices with the dominant beliefs and practices of a society (Robinson, 2005). Typically, individuals portray one of four patterns of acculturation, first identified by Berry (1998):

1. *Integration* (blending of culture of origin and dominant cultural practices)
2. *Assimilation* (replacing culture of origin practices with the dominant cultural practices)
3. *Separation* (rejecting of dominant culture and retaining culture-of-origin practices exclusively)
4. *Marginalization* (rejecting and separation from both culture of origin and dominant culture)

Children's and adolescents' patterns of acculturation may be different from those of their parents, and this may contribute to family conflicts. For example, children often are placed in situations where they must interpret for their parents, which impacts the hierarchy in the family and can contribute to these family conflicts (Sue & Sue, 2007).

Counselors should avoid placing children in those situations by using interpreters or learning other languages whenever possible. In addition, adolescents who have difficulty with acculturation are at risk for developing problems such as alcohol and nicotine use, (Unger et al., 2000) violence, (Samaniego & Gonzales, 1999) disordered eating, (Gowen, Hayward, Killen, Robinson, & Taylor, 1999) and high-risk sexual behavior. (Fraser, Piacentini, Van Rossem, Hein, & Rotheian-Borus, 1998).

Various assessment tools measure acculturation level for a variety of groups of individuals. Among these are

A Scale to Access African American Association (Snowden & Hines, 1999)
Male Arab Acculturation Scale (MAAS) (Barry, 2005)
The Asian Values Scale (Kim, Atkinson, & Yang, 1999)
Short Acculturation Scale for Hispanic Youth (SASH-Y) (Barona & Miller, 1994)
Rosebud Personal Opinion Survey (Hoffman, Dana, & Bolton, 1985).

The Acculturation, Habits, and Interests Multicultural Scale for Adolescents (AHIMSA) (Unger, Gallagher, et al., 2002) was created specifically for adolescents. This scale may be particularly useful to counselors because it can be used with adolescents coming from a variety of cultural backgrounds. The AHIMSA is ideal for adolescents because it is relatively short, is age-appropriate, and assesses multiple elements of acculturation.

Identity Formation

Many identity models have been developed to illustrate how healthy racial and cultural identify develops (Atkinson, Morton, & Sue, 1998; Cross, 1995; Helms, 1995; Garrett & Pichette, 2000). Two models most applicable to children and adolescents were developed by Bernal and colleagues (1993) and Marcia (1980). The model developed by Bernal and colleagues was designed to explain the ethnic identity development of Hispanic children but may be applicable to the identity development of other minority children as well (Thompson, Rudolph, & Henderson, 2004). In this step-by-step model,

1. children first develop *ethnic self-identity*, in which they are able to classify themselves within an ethnic group;
2. e*thnic constancy* occurs as children recognize that their ethnicity remains consistent over time and place;
3. children engage in cultural practices, customs and languages referred to as *ethnic role behavior*;
4. children exhibit *ethnic knowledge*, characterized by the recognition that many of their behaviors are important components of their ethnic heritages and practices; and

5. children develop *ethnic feelings and preferences* by expressing emotions and feelings related to their ethnic group.

A grasp of these concepts can assist counselors in helping children understand their cultural uniqueness and explore their feelings related to their culture.

As children grow and develop, their understanding of their ethnicity becomes more meaningful and complex. Marcia (1980) identified statuses of ethnic identity development of adolescents from various ethnic groups. In the first status, *identity diffusion* or *foreclosure*, adolescents have yet to explore their ethnic identity. During the exploration or *moratorium* status, adolescents spend time exploring their ethnic heritage, practices, and customs, which eventually leads them to commit to an ethnic identity. This status is referred to as *ethical identity achievement*.

Phinney (1989) conducted interviews with adolescents from a variety of ethnic backgrounds and found that about one-half of them were in the diffused/foreclosed status, one-quarter were in the moratorium status and about one-quarter had reached ethical identity achievement. Adolescents who were in the ethnic identity achievement status reported higher levels of self-mastery, social interaction, self-esteem, and psychosocial adjustment than individuals in the diffused/foreclosed status. In a later study achieved identity status was correlated positively with psychological well-being (Roberts, et al., 1999).

Knowledge of identity development is crucial when working with youth from diverse backgrounds. Based on the results of the above study, counselors may want to encourage children and adolescents to explore their cultural background, as this may contribute positively to their psychosocial development. If counselors are able to identify the stage of development, they might better tailor their techniques and interventions to meet the needs of the young people. This knowledge will be helpful in promoting ethnic identity.

Pope (2000) examined the relationship between psychosocial development and the culture identity of older adolescents. The conclusion was that counselors have to understand the connections between these concepts and to consider both when designing effective programs for adolescents because it will enhance healthy development.

Understanding identity development in youth may help them advocate for themselves. Astramovich and Harris (2007) outlined self-advocacy competences to encourage minority students to succeed in academic, career, and personal pursuits. When students are able to advocate for themselves, they become empowered and are better able to promote their ideas, needs, and rights. School counselors are in an ideal position to teach and encourage self-advocacy skills (Field & Baker, 2004).

Ethnically Diverse Children and Adolescents

Factors related to working with ethnically diverse groups are described next for African Americans, Arab Americans, Asian Americans, Latinos/as, and Native

Americans. Each section addresses strengths of the culture, values, typical present-ing problems, and counseling considerations and interventions.

African Americans

African Americans comprise 13% of the general populations, and that percentage continues to rise (U.S. Bureau of the Census, 2005). Although African Americans have been living in the United States for years, they continue to face considerable racism, oppression, and discrimination.

Williams, Yu, Jackson, and Anderson (1997) found that African Americans cope with stress better than European Americans, have more emotional flexibility, and have better support networks and community connections. Other strengths, includ-ing persistence, forgiveness, resistance, and resilience were identified by Exum, Moore, & Watt (1999) as characteristic of the African American community.

Values

When working with clients from diverse backgrounds, the Multicultural Counseling Competencies encourage counselors to understand their clients' worldview and out-line the awareness, knowledge, and skills needed to practice culturally competent counseling (Sue, Arrendando, & McDavis, 1992). Traditional African values center on seven principles of the Nguzo Saba and provide purpose and guidance in life:

1. Unity (umoja)
2. Self-determination (kujichagalia)
3. Purpose (nia)
4. Faith (imani)
5. Creativity (kuumba)
6. Cooperative economics (ujaama)
7. Collective work and responsibility (ujima)

Robinson (2005) outlined how these values can be used to develop healthy resistance and can be useful in counseling people with an African background. For example, counselors could support these values by encouraging youth to express their emo-tions through art projects or to engage in community service projects with other chil-dren and adolescents.

Woodard (1995) integrated music and African proverbs into the counseling process with young African American boys who have behavior problems such as physical fighting with other youth and being verbally disrespectful toward adults. As a result of the culturally sensitive counseling, the youth reported less aggression toward others and fewer school suspensions.

Family

African Americans tend to place a high value on family (Brammer, 2004). Many African American families have multiple generations living within the same household. And the family may extend beyond the nuclear family to people who are close to the family even though they may not be blood relatives. Care and discipline of the children often is shared by adults in the home.

Because of the strong family ties, counselors should consider how to involve the family in the counseling when feasible. The arrangement of African American families allows family members to adopt different roles in the family (e.g., provider, disciplinarian) (Sue & Sue, 2007). Counselors should help the family organize and use this arrangement and various roles as a strength and asset instead of viewing it as a deficit to be changed. Using a genogram is also useful in understanding family roles and relationships. Genograms allow counselors to develop a visual representation for clients that illustrates family dynamics and relationship patterns.

Presenting Problems of African American Youth

African American youth may seek or be referred for counseling for a variety of reasons, such as dealing with the adverse effects of stereotypes, racism, and oppression; poor academic achievement; physical developmental differences; and difficulty developing high self-esteem and a strong African American identity (Baruth & Manning, 2007).

Counselors must also keep in mind that these prejudices often contribute to African American youth being "sent" to counseling to be "fixed." To provide culturally competent counseling, counselors have to recognize the effects of prejudice and how they may contribute to the presenting problem.

Counseling Considerations and Interventions

The following suggestions will help counselors be more culturally sensitive in their work with African American youth.

1. Keep in mind that mental health professionals have tended in the past to pathologize and overdiagnose African Americans with schizophrenia and antisocial personality disorder (Strakowski, McElroy, Keck, & West, 1996). Early in the counseling process, cultural differences must be acknowledged and appreciated to enable the development of a trusting counselor–client relationship.
2. Integrating the seven principles of Nguzo Saba into the counseling process may make counseling more relevant and effective for African American youth and probably will match their worldview (Robinson, 2005).
3. Because African American youth tend to be tied to their community, counseling services might be utilized more often if they are offered in familiar settings. African American youth may receive more mental health services through the school than community-based mental health centers (Weist, Myers, Hastings, Ghuman, & Han, 1999).
4. African Americans tend to place less emphasis on being on time for an activity and more emphasis on the involvement in an activity. Counselors may consider

their concept of time, for example, if clients are late for appointments (Evans & George, 2008).

5. Counselors should consider the stage of identity development and incorporate ways to increase youths' knowledge about their cultural background and encourage them to share their cultural beliefs and practices. A well-developed ethnic identity has been correlated with higher self-esteem and positive psychosocial adjustment. (Roberts et al., 1999).

6. Family involvement may increase the effectiveness of counseling because, as we stated earlier, many African American families have multiple generations living in one household. In counseling, time can be spent helping define the roles of various members and identifying how caregivers can be supportive of youth with difficulties (Hines et al., 2005).

7. Psychoeducational and counseling groups tend to be particularly helpful when working with African American youth because these groups mirror the collective nature of their community (Bemak, Chi-Ying, Siroskey-Sabdo, 2005; Scott, 2001).

8. Counselors must become knowledgeable about typical spirituality practices of African American youth. Many traditional healing processes of African Americans involve music, chanting, and dancing. Incorporating these into counseling sessions can help youth connect the past, present, and future.

9. Integrating discussion and reflection on the effects of racism is crucial in providing competent counseling for African American youth (Sue & Sue, 2007).

Jackson

Jackson, a 7-year-old African American boy, was referred to his school counselor because he had become noticeably withdrawn in the classroom. His teacher described him as usually outgoing and having many friends but recently observed that he had stopped playing with other children at recess and had trouble paying attention in class. The counselor had started to see a change in Jackson about 3 weeks ago, and his normal interventions (talking with Jackson, giving him special jobs, partnering, and group work) did not seem to have any positive effects. In discussions with Jackson's family, the counselor learned that Jackson's aunt had recently died from cancer.

1. What other information would the counselor need to know to help Jackson?
2. What are some hypotheses about his behavior changes?
3. What cultural considerations are relevant to this case?
4. As the school counselor, what interventions would you choose? Why?

To best serve Jackson, the counselor should complete a contextual assessment of the situation to gather as much information as possible before arriving at any conclusions. The school counselor might start by visiting with the teacher to assess her expectations and cultural competency. Next, he should speak with the family about Jackson's issues, keeping in mind that the main caregiver might not be the mother or father.

Before meeting with Jackson, the counselor might consider what other cultural factors may be important in this case. If Jackson's aunt was his primary caregiver, her death may result in significant feelings of loss. Jackson's aunt may have provided for the family financially, and Jackson might be concerned about what will happen now. The counselor also might have to become more knowledgeable about the grieving process of African American families and the spiritual practices of Jackson's family. This would aid him in providing culturally appropriate counseling interventions.

Once the counselor has sufficient information about the problem and the context of the problem, he would set up a time to meet with Jackson individually to help him deal with his loss. Individual counseling with Jackson may include a discussion about what is causing his difficulties, what factors have contributed to these difficulties, and who he identifies as supportive people in his life. The counselor may use creative interventions such as art techniques or bibliotherapy. Group counseling with others who have lost a significant person also may be beneficial.

Arab Americans

Arab Americans, individuals of Middle Eastern descent, have been virtually invisible in the counseling literature until recently (Nassar-McMillian & Hakim-Larson, 2003). The American-Arab Anti-Discrimination Committee (ADC defines Arab Americans by their language, cultural practices, or countries of origin). Among them are people from Algeria, Egypt, Iraq, Kuwait, Lebanon, Libya, Morocco, Oman, Palestine, Qatar, Saudi Arabia, Somalia, Sudan, Syria, the United Arab Emirates, and Yemen. Because approximately 3 million Arab Americans reside in the United States, counselors will likely come into contact with Arab American youth in the schools and community mental health settings (Jackson & Nassar-McMillan, 2006).

As a result of the September 11, 2001, attacks on the United States, new government policies were put into place, affecting the lives of many Arab American youth. Arab American youth have experienced more discrimination and hostility in their schools and communities following this tragic event (Smith, 2004).

Values

Although many values that have been associated with Arab American families are rooted in Muslim traditions, not all Arab Americans identify as Muslim; a considerable number practice Christianity and other religions (Nassar-McMillian & Hakim-Larsen, 2003). Arab Americans as a whole value generosity, hospitality, prosperity, family honor, hard work, thrift, educational attainment, and economic advancement (Smith, 2004). Even though some of these values originated from Muslim practices, many values have been integrated into the cultural practices of Arab American families regardless of their religious practices (Nassar-McMillian & Hakim-Larson, 2003).

Family

Loyalty and commitment to family members are high priorities in Arab American families. These families tend to be structured in a hierarchical fashion with the father typically as the head of the household. The father's role usually includes providing economically for the family, acting as disciplinarian, and helping the family maintain honor, order, cohesiveness, and social standing. The mother's role tends to include education of the children and running of the household.

In Arab American families, children are allowed and encouraged to express their emotions, and childrearing practices in traditional Arab American families instill behaviors oriented toward interdependence versus autonomy and independence. These roles and communication patterns within families are essential to understand when working with Arab American youth.

Presenting Problems of Arab American Youth

Children in Arab American families are often allowed to express their emotions openly by crying, screaming, or shouting. Traditionally, this is believed to prevent future mental health issues such as anxiety or social withdrawal. These behaviors, however, may result in more referrals for counseling, so counselors should be aware of this cultural component and not assume that youngsters have a problem just because they are crying or screaming. Further, many Arab children and adolescents immigrating from war-torn countries have post-traumatic stress disorder, which may look like attention deficit/hyperactivity disorder or other behavioral disorders (Nassar-McMillian & Hakim-Larson, 2003). Counselors must consider experiences of trauma in completing a careful, contextual assessment.

Arab Americans tend to present with more somatic complaints and have high tolerance for emotional suffering and pain. Some Arab Americans believe that emotional problems have a spiritual or evil basis, so counselors should consider this in treatment and not pathologize the behavior. For example, Nassar-McMillian and Hakim-Larsen (2003) described working with an Arab client who was having trouble sleeping. After the counselor inquired about cultural traditions or rituals that might help her sleep, the client responded that she sprinkled salt outside of her door to ward off evil spirits. The culturally competent counselor supported this practice and encouraged the client to use this technique, which continued to be beneficial.

Counseling Considerations and Interventions

The following suggestions will facilitate counseling with Arab American children and adolescents.

1. Arab Americans tend to be highly sociable and have extensive social circles of same-sex friends. These friendships may provide beneficial support to children

and adolescents, especially when they are having difficulties (Timimi, 1995).

2. Counselors must consider the youth's level of acculturation and reasons for immigration because these factors can impact children and adolescents significantly and be significant in framing the presenting problems.

3. Goal-directed and concrete interventions may be used during the initial sessions, as many Arab American clients expect to leave the first session with some specific suggestions. This practice may help in retaining these clients in counseling (Smith, 2004).

4. Because the family is highly valued in Arab families, the family must be involved when counseling children and adolescents. In the schools the counselor might ask family members to volunteer or assist in a guidance lesson on diversity.

5. Counselors must be knowledgeable and respectful of the cultural and religious practices of children and adolescents.

6. Counselors should pay attention to physical complaints as many emotional issues are expressed as somatic problems (Timimi, 1995).

7. When working with adolescents, counselors should not expect a high level of individuation and autonomy (Smith, 2004).

8. Counselors should engage in outreach and advocacy activities that will provide opportunities to learn about the culture and build relationships with leaders in the Arab communities.

Farha

Farha is a 14-year-old eighth-grader in a prominently White, Christian, middle-class public school. Her parents, who were referred by their family doctor who attends their mosque, contacted the counselor to discuss a problem they were having with their daughter. Although they were reluctant to go outside of the family to discuss Farha's problem, they were encouraged by the family doctor to do so.

Farha, who had always been well behaved and had not questioned the family's traditional Muslim beliefs, had started to refuse to wear her headdress. Her usually high grades had begun to decline and her self-confidence had slipped. When the family discussed these concerns with leaders at the mosque, they learned that other families were dealing with the same issues with their teenagers.

Although Farha's parents did not necessarily desire individual counseling for Farha, they were interested in the counselor's recommendations because they did not want the problems to intensify.

1. As the counselor, what suggestions would you make?
2. How might you ensure that you are operating within Farha's worldview?
3. What interventions might you use?

In this case the counselor first familiarized herself with some Arab and Muslim practices by reading literature, consulting with a colleague who often worked with Arab Americans, and conversing with a local Muslim leader. The counselor invited Farha and her parents to attend an initial session, during which she explained to the parents that this session would help her get a complete picture of the situation so she could recommend how to proceed. During the session they discussed the problems the parents had noticed. Farha was open and honest about her feelings and said that she felt alienated at school and was most comfortable around her peers at the mosque.

After consulting with Farha's parents, the counselor volunteered to facilitate a psychoeducational group for young women from Farha's mosque. With her parents' cooperation, they facilitated a meeting between the counselor and some leaders in the Muslim community. As a result, a group was formed, co-facilitated by the counselor and a leader from the mosque.

The counselor prepared for this group by learning about Muslim and Arab traditions and worldview. In the group, members discussed healthy identity development, ways to balance traditional beliefs while living within Western culture, and effective ways to communicate with parents. As a follow-up, the counselors decided to offer an inservice for local school counselors, teachers, and administrators on how to foster inclusive learning environments.

Asian American and Pacific Island Youth

Asian American youth have a variety of backgrounds including Chinese, Japanese, Korean, Filipino, Vietnamese, Cambodian, Thai, Hmong, Laotian, and Samoan, among others (Maki & Kitano, 2002). Asian Americans and Pacific Islanders comprise 5% of the general population (U.S. Bureau of the Census, 2005). Asian Americans are characterized by a strong sense of humanity, interpersonal harmony in relationships, and benevolence.

Values

Asian American families are generally described as reserved, constrained, and emotionally self-controlled. As a group they tend to be a collective society and value group interests over individual interests. Children are taught obedience to authority and are highly conscious of saving face for the family as well as for themselves (Sue & Sue, 2007). Two values of which counselors should be aware of when working with Asian American youth are *Yuan* (influence of past relationships on present social relationships) and *Ren Qing* (social favors exchanged in the form of money, goods, and information) (Robinson, 2005).

Family

Asian families are arranged in a paternal hierarchy in which men and the elderly hold the highest status. Parents typically use a relaxed style with children younger than 7 years and a more authoritarian style as children get older (Jose et al., 2000). There are some within-group differences regarding parental approach. For example, Blair and Qian (1998) found that Japanese and Filipino families approach parenting from a more egalitarian perspective, and parents from Korea, China, and Southeast Asia tend to be more authoritarian. When assessing Asian American children and their families, counselors must do so carefully within a family and community context.

Presenting Problems of Asian American Youth

Typically, Asian American youth have problems similar to those of other minority youth, such as struggling with the differences in values between what is reinforced in schools versus what is reinforced at home, as well as difficulties with language differences (especially when families have recently immigrated). Because most Asian American families highly value academic achievement, youth who are struggling may present to counselors more often for academic and career issues than for emotional concerns (Brammer, 2004).

Tatman (2004) related some interventions to use with Hmong children in counseling. When many Hmong immigrated to the United States, they were relocated using a "scattering" (p. 224) process that spread them throughout the United States. This affected families because this is a close, collective society. Children from this culture may present with symptoms related to post-traumatic stress disorder and acculturation-related issues. When working with children and adolescents from the Hmong culture, Tatman (2004) suggested a problem-solving approach, acknowledging small successes, and using genograms. Developing genograms helps clients to visualize the patterns of their problems in a less threatening manner and may allow extra time to process the information.

Sandtray therapy—or Hakoniwa, as it is referred to in the Japanese culture—may be useful in working with Asian children, especially youth from Japan. Hakoniwa involves placing various figurines and miniatures in a shallow tray of sand, illustrating their inner world. For example, a child might be asked to construct a sandtray signifying a recent family interaction.

This technique is ideal for use with children and adolescents because it allows them to communicate nonverbally, encourages therapeutic work in the here-and-now, and can be a relaxing intervention for youth. Enns and Kasai (2003) said of this technique:

> Hakoniwa has been an important foundation for psychotherapy with adults and children in Japan, perhaps because of its connections to the arts and spiritual expression and the greater valuing of nonverbal and symbolic communication across life stages in Japan. (p. 95)

Counseling Considerations and Interventions

The following suggestions can be beneficial to counselors who are working with Asian American youth.

1. Asian youth may present with problems related to career and education concerns more often than social or emotional concerns (Schoen, 2005).

2. Because Asian Americans' concept of time tends to be more future-oriented, these clients may find treatment planning and goal-setting particularly helpful (Clemente, 2004).
3. Counselors may consider using a more task-orientated approach with Asian youth, asking about activities they enjoy rather than focusing on more personal topics related to relationships and feelings (Kim, Atkinson, & Umemoto, 2001).
4. Asian adolescents often present with acculturation difficulties such as conflicts with parents and struggling between autonomy and interdependence. Counselors may want to ask how their family views these conflicts and help the youth balance their needs with their family's needs (Sue & Sue, 2007).
5. Many Asian families emphasize academic achievement and success of their children. This can serve as a helpful support for children. Counselors may also want to help parents identify other positive behaviors and contributions of their children, especially when they are struggling academically (Sue & Sue, 2007).
6. Because Asian youth tend to focus more on thoughts than feelings, they may benefit from psychoeducational groups, which are more structured and place more emphasis on learning information (Cheng, 1996).
7. Counselors must understand the common spiritual practices of the Asian youth they are working with in counseling. This knowledge can assist in building a stronger therapeutic relationship with the child as well as the family (Hanna & Green, 2004).
8. Because Asian Americans are often referred to as the "model minority," some youth are at risk academically, socially, or emotionally, particularly children and adolescents who have immigrated recently (Smith, 2004).

Loon

Loon is a Hmong high school junior who is working with the school counselor to help her select a university to attend next year. She has been extensively involved with the school newspaper and yearbook. She tells the school counselor that she really likes writing but at the same time wants to find a university with a strong nursing program. She wavers back and forth between career paths. The counselor views Loon as indecisive and confused by her lack of commitment.

1. According to the Multicultural Competencies (Sue, Arredando, McDavis, 1992), what might Loon's school counselor work on?
2. What course of action might the counselor take to address Loon's decision making?

Loon's counselor has to develop his understanding of this problem from the client's worldview. He may accomplish this by reading counseling literature related to career counseling with Asian clients, examining his own feelings and frustrations within personal counseling sessions, seek consultation on the case from another counselor who works with Asian clients, and may decide to take professional development courses on becoming more culturally competent.

The counselor might start by discussing with Loon the concerns she and her family have about her higher education plans. Often in Asian families the parents have expectations about their children's career pursuits and might see nursing as a more appropriate career choice for Loon than a career in writing or journalism. Thus, the counselor may want to explore Loon's feelings about pursing a nursing program. Although she has a strong academic record, she may fear failure in the nursing program. The counselor may help Loon come to a decision that she and her parents will agree on. The counselor should consider inviting her parents to discuss these issues.

Latinos/Latinas

Latino/a youth comprise 15% of the general population in the United States and may identify as Puerto Rican, Cuban, Mexican, or other Latin heritage. High fertility rates make this one of the fastest growing minority populations (U.S. Bureau of the Census, 2005). Although Latinos have some within-group differences, the common use of the Spanish language is a unifying factor. Latino/a children and adolescents have many positive qualities. They engage in more active coping (i.e. information-seeking) skills, rely more on family members for support, and are more self reliant than non-Latino/a White youth.

Values

Robinson (2005) identified some values that have been associated with Latinos/Latinas as

- faith in family and friends (*familism*),
- respect (*respecto*),
- trust in others (*confianza*), and
- being a nice and gentle person (*simpatia*).

The counselor should keep these factors in mind when working with children and families, as they are essential in building strong trusting, therapeutic relationships.

Family

Latinos place a high value on family. Familism encourages a combination of collectivism and interdependence. Multiple generations often live within one household, especially families that have immigrated to the United States recently. In addition, families often share and pool resources and possessions that they own collectively. Children may refer to the weekly family meal or *la comida seminal* as a time when families join together and bond (Brammer, 2004). This may provide a good source of support to Latino/a youth. Children and adolescents who attend predominately non-Latino schools may especially value *la comida seminal* because it provides an important connection to family members and gives them an opportunity to speak Spanish and share concerns with people who can relate to their struggles.

Presenting Problems of Latino/a Youth

Villalba, Brunelli, Lewis and Orfanedes (2007) interviewed Latino parents, who indicated that their children had stress and transition problems in the public school system. In addition, these parents had difficulty dealing with inappropriate expectations of their children's behaviors and academic performance. Also, the parents expressed that some schools were "cold," in contrast to their cultural value of being warm and caring *(personlismo)*.

Latino children and adolescents may develop psychosocial difficulties resulting from poverty, language barriers, and discrimination (Clemente & Collsion, 2000). Too, language barriers may contribute to a misunderstanding of counseling services provided by schools and mental health agencies, as well as cause difficulties navigating through these systems. The need for Spanish-speaking counselors is great and could increase the use of counseling services by non-English speaking clients. Speaking someone's native language can foster strong therapeutic relationships and assist in assessing the presenting problems more accurately (Smith-Adcock et al., 2006).

Many Latino/a children and adolescents learn English as their second language. This sometimes is associated with problems in school adjustment, self-esteem, and expression of feelings (Crawford, 1999). Group work can be particularly helpful, as it offers children and adolescents an opportunity to practice their language skills, become more self-aware, and become comfortable with their peers. Villalba (2003) instituted a 6-week psychoeducational group devoted to processing feelings related to being identified as speaking English as a second language.

Cuento therapy uses culturally relevant folktales to convey messages about values, beliefs, and healthy behavior. Using stories and characters from a child's culture makes counseling more relevant to them and more aligned with their worldview. Costantino, Malgady, and Rogler (1986) found this therapy to be effective with Puerto Rican youth, Constantino and Malgady (1996) commented on its positive impact on the self-concept and ethnic identity of children with behavioral problems at school and home.

Counseling Considerations and Interventions

The following suggestions may facilitate counseling with Latino/Latina youth.

1. Parents indicate that their children are academically and emotionally more successful in environments where counselors serve as a resource and provide culturally relevant counseling (Villalba, Brunelli, & Lewis, 2007).
2. Counselors should consider providing services in Spanish when needed, and school and mental health administrators should consider hiring Spanish-speaking counselors.

3. Latinos/Latinas tend to take a less structured approach regarding time and give more emphasis to the present than the past and the future. Counseling may be more effective if counselors consider using a less structured, less formal approach in the sessions (Clemente, 2004).

4. When working with Latino/a clients, counselors should consider *personalismo* (intimacy). This can be accomplished by extending a warm greeting and spending time engaging in small talk about family and daily events, which will contribute to building rapport and trust (Robinson, 2005).

5. Counselors must be aware of the tendency of Latinos/as to express psychological problems in physical terms, such as stomach aches instead of depressed mood.

6. Latino/a youth are often concerned with the stigma attached to seeking counseling, so counselors must explain the counseling process and allow them to ask questions and express concerns. This will contribute greatly to a trusting therapeutic relationship (Smith, 2004).

7. Counselors have to remember that sense of time for Latino/a youths is different from the norm in schools. If they are late for counseling sessions, this may be the reason (Brammar, 2004).

Benita

Benita, a 4-year-old Mexican American, was referred to the local community mental health center by her preschool teacher. Benita was having a hard time separating from her mother when she was dropped off at preschool in the morning and would cry and be difficult to console. Recently, she became physically ill when her mother left the preschool. The intake counselor at the mental health center diagnosed Benita with separation anxiety disorder, and she was assigned for counseling.

1. How should the counselor proceed with Benita's treatment?
2. What cultural and developmental issues must be considered when counseling Benita?
3. How might Benita's family be involved in the counseling process?

After reviewing the intake, the counselor visited more extensively with the mother about Benita's issues. The counselor found that Benita does not have difficulty separating from her mother in other settings, such as when she stays with her grandparents. Her mother reported that Benita had met physical, social, and emotional developmental milestones appropriate for her age. The mother verified that Spanish was primarily spoken in the home and that Benita has had little exposure to the English language. At the preschool no one speaks Spanish, and the counselor believes this may be contributing to Benita's adjustment difficulties. Based on this additional information, the counselor decided that Benita does not meet the criteria for separation anxiety disorder. Her issues are much better explained by acculturation difficulties than a mental disorder.

While meeting with Benita's mother, the counselor wondered if she would be willing to teach the preschool teachers some commonly used phrases in Spanish. With the mother's permission, the counselor also called the preschool and advocated on behalf of the many Latino families served by the preschool and encouraged them to hire bilingual instructors or to engage in professional developmental courses to enhance their Spanish language communication. Once the staff started to use the Spanish phrases regularly with Benita, her difficulties dissipated.

Even though Benita's behavior improved, her mother continued to see the counselor to address her own stress level and to gain more parenting skills. Benita's mother admitted to the counselor that she had been reluctant to seek counseling because she thought counseling was for "crazy people," but as she witnessed the counselor advocate on her daughter's behalf in a culturally sensitive manner, she realized that she could trust the counselor and believed the counseling would be helpful for her.

Native Americans

Native American youth comprise 1% of public school enrollment. Almost 80% of Native American children and adolescents are educated in the public schools (Robbins, Tonemah, & Robbins, 2002). Although statistics often group all Native Americans into one category, counselors have to be aware that Native Americans belong to a variety of tribes, bands, and clans. Counselors should inquire about specific group affiliation because of the many within-group differences.

Too, Native American youth have been acculturated to different degrees (Brammer, 2004). And when working with Native American children and adolescents, counselors should inquire about their specific cultural practices to gain insight into the child's cultural environment and acculturation level.

Values

Among the values associated with Native American groups are sharing, noninterference, present time orientation (Smith, 2004), harmony with others, and valuing others beyond their possessions. The Circle of Life, a central component in the Native American culture and cultural practices, illustrates that all things are connected, have a purpose, and are worthy of respect. These concepts are threaded throughout most Native American communities and cultural practices (Hunter & Sawyer, 2006).

Family

Respect for elders is instilled in Native American youth. Elders convey oral histories and traditions to the younger members of their families and tribe. Childrearing practices encourage children to be self-sufficient and also to work in harmony with others, nature, and the spirits.

Presenting Problems of Native American Youth

Native American youth present with a variety of problems related to forced assimilation of their parents and grandparents and lack of recognition as a minority by many people (Smith, 2004). Native American youth sometimes present with concerns about career development because many career exploration programs do not take into consideration the cultural identity of Native American youth (Peavy, 1995).

Native American children may have difficulties developing a strong cultural identity and positive self-concept, have poor English proficiency, be misunderstood because of the nonverbal communication patterns in Native American culture, and have lower academic achievement than their non-Native American counterparts (Baruth & Manning, 2007). Adolescent problems tend to revolve around acculturation issues and being misunderstood by non-Native American school personnel. Hunter and Sawyer (2006) outlined numerous interventions that reinforce values associated with the Native American community. One intervention described is the "earth's gift" (p. 245), in which the child is asked to find a special object from nature and bring it to a session. The child then tells why he or she chose the object and what makes it special. This activity reinforces the connection between Native American youth and Mother Earth and reminds them to be thankful for the other gifts they receive from nature.

Another helpful intervention with Native American youth is pet therapy (Hunter & Sawyer, 2006). The counselor may have a pet in the office for the child to play with, or may ask the child to talk about a relationship with his or her own pet. Pet therapy can create a sense of connection.

Garrett and Crutchfield (1997) described a group intervention to promote harmony. In this activity youth are asked to choose a musical instrument from the leader's collection. The leader starts by establishing a rhythm, then, one by one, each member joins in playing the instrument and creating a song. The group leader then initiates a discussion of the Native American concepts of harmony and cooperation.

Counseling Considerations and Interventions

The following information may be useful in counseling Native American youth.

1. Descriptive statements or summaries may be more effective than questions, as directedness may be viewed as rude or make young children uncomfortable (Smith, 2004).
2. Native Americans tend to be more in tune with the earth's natural rhythms and take their cues from nature (e.g., sunrise) regarding time. They tend to see the beginning and end of an activity as depending on the activity and not according to the time on a clock (Garrett, 2008).
3. Underlying grief issues may have to be considered when working with Native American youth because of the high rates of suicide, alcohol use, and other health related problems within Native American communities (Indian Health Services, 2001).

4. The counselor should consider consulting with shamen, traditional healers, or spiritual leaders to increase their knowledge of the Native American worldview. They may be able to provide valuable education about spiritual practices, which in turn can demonstrate to youth and their families support and sensitivity toward these practices (Smith, 2004).

5. As a result of historical events, some Native Americans distrust European American professionals, so counselors will have to spend time building rapport with Native American youth (Baruth & Manning, 2007). Counselors must become knowledgeable about cultural practices and value systems such as limiting eye contact, slowing the pace of the conversation, and not interrupting the client (Brammer, 2004).

6. Adolescents may have difficulty planning for future academic or career work because of their "present time" orientation. Career interventions, therefore, should follow a structured, step-by-step approach. Incorporating Native American role models or elders from the community is a good idea, too. The narrative approach advanced by Peavy (1995) may help Native American youth find or rewrite their career aspiration stories.

7. Pet and nature therapy may be particularly useful with Native American youth because of their strong cultural ties to nature. These therapies help them form strong emotional bonds and develop empathy (Hunter & Sawyer, 2006).

Yuma

Yuma, a Native American fourth grader, was referred to the school counselor because of his recent behavior in the classroom. His teacher reported that he had withdrawn socially and had become aggressive at recess. The counselor knows that Yuma's family is active in Cherokee cultural practices and activities and that the parents encourage and support a strong bicultural identity. When the counselor invited Yuma to his office, he responded positively. As the counselor explored his feelings related to school and fourth grade, he learned that Yuma was troubled by how other children talked about Native Americans, that these comments made him sad and angry. Yuma was particularly concerned about an upcoming play the class was producing about a history lesson, saying that he did not like the play or how the children were told to portray Native Americans (as violent and angry).

1. How should the counselor proceed with Yuma?
2. How might the counselor address some of these issues using classroom guidance lessons?
3. What might be included in consultation with faculty and staff?

The counselor met with Yuma for several individual sessions and brought up healthy ways by which he could deal with his anger, employing various forms of nature therapy. For example, the counselor asked Yuma to find an object from nature that makes him feel calm. He found a smooth rock, which he carried in his pocket and stroked whenever he started to feel angry.

After working with Yuma, the counselor realized that this issue also had to be addressed with the teachers and then with the students in the classroom. First, he conveyed his concerns about the play to the fourth-grade teachers and invited them to meet with him. The teachers were open to modifying the play, and the counselor provided them with resources to help make some of their lessons more culturally appropriate. The counselor also arranged for diversity training at the next inservice for the teachers and staff. The teachers also agreed that a classroom guidance session about understanding and accepting differences would be helpful. The counselor asked for Yuma's help in preparing and developing a guidance lesson to present to all fourth-grade sections. Yuma seemed to enjoy this activity and became more empowered.

Gender

Gender is a significant variable that counselors must consider when working with children and adolescents. Gender roles and expectations are influenced by society, and also by culture, family, and spiritual practices. Although children's and adolescents' gender expectations may be influenced by their cultural and spiritual practices, some general gender issues warrant mentioning when working with youth, including gender awareness, gender socialization, and counseling considerations. Failure to recognize important gender differences has resulted in substantial harm over the past 30 years (Sax, 2005).

Gender Awareness

Most children become aware of gender differences at approximately 2 years of age and are able to consistently label their own gender correctly (Bigler & Liben, 1993). Although the youth that most counselors work with identify as male or female, some children do not fit into either category. Fausto-Sterling (2000) estimated that approximately 1% to 4% percent of children are born intersexed—having various combinations of male and female organs and genitalia. Black, Crether, Dermer, and Luke (2007) suggested defining gender on a continuum rather than two distinct categories, to provide a more accurate reflection of all youth and to be more inclusive in terms of diversity. When counselors acknowledge this factor, it may allow children who struggle with gender identity to share their thoughts and feelings.

Gender Socialization

Children are socialized in their gender roles early in life. Their socialization is influenced in many ways by parents, teachers, family members, and the media, including television, books, and the Internet.

Girls are often socialized to be passive, helpful to others, the object of men's sexual desires, and dependent on others. Girls are found to have higher self-esteem, have more confidence in their abilities, and are more optimistic about the future at age 9, but these positive beliefs and traits decline as they reach their adolescent years (AAUW, 2008). Gilligan's (1990) earlier interviewing of many adolescent girls yielded similar results and findings that relationships are crucial in young girls' development. Sax (2005) suggested that girls' strong bonds with one another help them to feel more comfortable in school, which impacts their performance positively. When young females come to counseling, they often reveal problems related to body image, sexuality, relationships, and victimization (Baruth & Manning, 2007). Girls are found to be at higher risk than boys for alcohol abuse (Sax, 2005).

Boys are socialized into roles that at times are more harmful than helpful. Boys are encouraged to be assertive, to feel superior to women, and to be self-reliant, and they are also taught to restrict their emotions, act tough, and avoid all things feminine (Gilbert & Scher, 1999). As a result, boys tend to have difficulty expressing emotions other than anger. Boys and young men often present to counselors with more externalizing problems, such as aggression, attention-seeking behavior, and substance-abuse issues (Baruth & Manning, 2007). Boys also are at-risk for not doing well in school (Sax, 2005).

Counseling Considerations and Interventions

Among the many effective things that counselors can do when working with gender issues are the following:

1. Counselors must avoid gender stereotypes when working with youth because these can contribute to misdiagnosis and treatment of young boys and girls (Baruth & Manning, 2007).
2. Counselors may consider using girls-only or boys-only group work, as research has shown that children excel when information and approaches are tailored toward their gender preferences and differences (Sax, 2005).
3. Girls often spend time in face-to-face conversations and interactions and tend to spend their time sharing secrets, personal doubts, and difficulties with friends. Boys, by contrast, spend time in shoulder-to-shoulder activities such as playing video games together and engaging in physical activities. When counselors choose interventions and activities, they may want to consider these factors and incorporate appropriate interventions. Counselors also may suggest that teachers work with young girls face-to-face and with boys side-by-side (Sax, 2005).
4. When working with adolescents, keep in mind how girls and boys satisfy their needs. Girls tend to meet their needs through relationships, whereas boys tend to meet their needs though mastery and competition (Feldman, 2004).
5. Bem (1987) suggested that parents encourage gender schemas that encompass both female and male characteristics. For example: Encourage young girls to be sensitive and caring but also assertive and independent.

6. Counselors should recognize that some fluidity in gender identity is normal in prepubescent children and does not always lead to gender identity disorder (Zucker, 2005).
7. Nondirective play therapy may be used with gender-variant children, as it fosters acceptance, which may encourage young children to explore their gender identity (Landreth, 2002).
8. When working with gender-variant children, family therapy may assist the family in coping with ambiguity and learn open communication and how to combat feelings of isolation (Black et al., 2007).

Spirituality and Religion

Spirituality and religion can play an important role when working with children. The Competencies for Integrating Spirituality into Counseling, created by the Association for Spiritual, Ethical, and Religious Values in Counseling (ASERVIC), may be considered when incorporating aspects of a client's faith practices.

An Introduction to Less Dominant Faiths

The most common faiths may be better understood, so here we will briefly introduce some of the less dominant faiths—Judaism, Buddhism, Islam, and Hinduism.

Judaism

Judaism goes beyond religion and has also been referred to as culture, ethnicity, and a set of traditions (Langman, 2000). Approximately 14 million people practice the Jewish faith worldwide, and they usually belong to one of three groups: Orthodox, Reformed, or Conservative. Group affiliations affect how individuals practice their faith. For example, the children and adolescents in schools may have dietary restrictions, celebrate holidays that many school districts do not recognize, and may encounter anti-Semitism. For example, some young Jewish children wear small head coverings called yamakas, and classmates may ridicule them (Smith, 2004).

Islam

Approximately 1.1 billion individuals worldwide practice Islam (Kosmin, Mayer, & Keysar, 2001), whose practices are based on the following Five Pillars of Faith:

1. There is only one God, and Muhammad is his messenger.
2. Those who practice Islam pray five times daily at predetermined times.
3. Practitioners are encouraged to give to the poor.
4. Practitioners should fast during Ramadan.
5. If possible, individuals should make a pilgrimage to the Mecca.

Youth who practice the Islamic religion may follow dietary restrictions and fast during certain times of the year, wear traditional dress, and pray throughout the day (Smith, 2004; Nassar-McMillian & Hakim-Larson, 2003).

Hinduism

Approximately 775,000 people in the United States practice Hinduism (Kosmin, Mayer, & Keysar, 2001). People of the Hindu faith believe in multiple deities, and the concept of Karma is a central component of Hinduism. Hindis often practice yoga and meditation to transcend into the spiritual realm. Most families that practice Hinduism have a spiritual teacher or guru, who works like a counselor. When working with Hindi youth, counselors may want to incorporate spiritual practices such as meditation into counseling sessions (Hanna & Green, 2004).

Buddhism

Buddhism is practiced by 1 million individuals in the United states and focuses on the end of suffering and producing a sense of liberation (Kosmin, Mayer, & Keysar, 2001). This faith is based on the four noble truths, which explore suffering (Smith, 2004):

1. Human suffering exists (Dukkha).
2. There is a cause for the suffering (Samudaya).
3. The suffering will end (Nirodha).
4. One must follow specific practices to end the suffering (Magga).

Counselors already may be using some practices connected to Buddhism, such as meditation and mindfulness, and, if not, may want to consider them.

Counseling Considerations and Interventions

The faith practices of children and adolescents confer many benefits on them, such as an extended social network of friends. Difficulties that children and adolescents face regarding their faith and faith practices may have more to do with practicing their religion in a society dominated by Christian beliefs and practices. For example, they may be required to attend school on their religious holidays or make crafts and projects in schools that don't incorporate their religious beliefs (Schlosser, 2003). Counselors also may consider the following when working with youth.

1. Counselors should educate themselves about various religious and spiritual practices and belief systems and may consider attending religious or spiritual events that differ from their own practices.
2. School counselors may develop a calendar acknowledging the religious holidays of various faiths. This demonstrates sensitivity to these faiths and also could be consulted by faculty and staff when planning school events.
3. Knowledge and utilization of the ASERVIC competencies are crucial for counselors when integrating religion and spiritual practices into their work with youth.

4. School counselors should learn what accommodations can be made for students who engage in their religious practices at school (e.g., dietary restrictions) and the steps involved in making these accommodations.

5. Counselors have to be flexible in setting appointments and schedules so as not to conflict with weekly religious services and holiday celebrations.

6. Counselors must remember that all family members may not practice the same religion or have the same spiritual belief system.

7. Counselors may want to build relationships with local religious and spiritual leaders and consult them when working with clients who have spiritual or religious backgrounds that are different from their own.

Counseling Interventions With Diverse Youth

Many culturally appropriate interventions are appropriate when working with children and adolescents from a variety of backgrounds. Because youth are influenced by their numerous identities (e.g., ethnicity, gender), some general interventions merit review.

Creative Arts

Counseling interventions incorporating the creative arts may be particularly helpful in connecting with young clients from diverse backgrounds. The arts are present in one form or another in all cultures and can be used to help clients and counselors transcend their differences. Henderson and Gladding (1998), pioneers in utilizing the creative arts, suggested their use with diverse youth because the arts (a) draw individuals out of self-consciousness and into self-awareness, (b) have universal appeal, and (c) provide clients with a concrete representation of their therapeutic work, which clients can take with them.

Counselors could also incorporate the arts by having a young client draw a *Cultural Coat of Arms* (Bowman, 1998). In this activity the child is provided with art materials and a blank shield. The child is asked to write words or draw symbols representing key aspects of their culture, gender, and spiritual practices. In processing the activity, the child is asked to explain the various elements on the shield. In this way, the counselor learns what the child finds important about his or her culture, and it may also help the counselor assess the level of identity development.

Music

Music is another form of art that can be incorporated readily into counseling sessions. Counselors may encourage adolescents to bring in a song that represents their values and belief systems. The counselor asks them how they made their selection or what parts of the song are most significant to them. The counselor may also want to collect compact discs representing various cultures, from which clients could select. The collection would demonstrate cultural sensitivity and interest to anyone who visits the counselor's office. The use of music with children and adolescents gives them a medium to express their emotions, is a creative way for a counselor to introduce a topic, or can be used to suggest a new manner of coping with a problem (Gladding, 2005).

Genogram

Similar to selecting a song, children could be asked to bring an item representing their culture or spiritual practices. This provides a way for children to share information about their culture and spiritual practices. This activity has the capacity to help build cultural pride and allows the counselor to understand important aspects of their culture and spirituality.

McGoldrick, Gerson, and Shellenberger (1998) described the *cultural genogram,* which can be a useful intervention when working with diverse youth. In the genogram, counselors help clients construct a visual representation of their family tree by identifying family members from each generation and how they are related. Counselors should be flexible in constructing the genogram, as youth from some cultural groups may consider non-blood relatives as "family." Completing a cultural genogram provides a visual representation of how the child's ideas about ethnicity, gender, and spirituality are passed down through the generations. This intervention may also help older children and adolescents explore their identity. Counselors may have the youngster interview family members to help the youth attain information and involve the family in the process as well.

Bibliotherapy

When working with diverse children, bibliotherapy is another useful tool. Incorporating books into counseling can be a creative way to teach coping skills and healthy development (Cole & Valentine, 2000). The appendix to this chapter lists selections that counselors could use with young children, including representations of children from various ethnic backgrounds.

First Language

When working with children whose first language is different from their counselor's language, the counselor may want to learn a few key phrases in the child's native language. This will demonstrate an interest in and sensitivity toward the child's culture. Counselors who often work with non-English speaking clients may consider learning a second language as part of their professional development.

Office Arrangement

Arrangement of the counselor's office is an important aspect in working with diverse children. Clemente (2004) suggested that counselors consider the furnishings, aroma, space, and sound in making their office a welcoming place for all children. Furnishings should reflect a balance of professional articles and personal artifacts, and counselors may consider how well their pictures, books, and artwork represent diverse groups and what messages they send about who the children are as individuals. In addition, different cultures interpret the concept of personal space differently depending on one's background. Counselors, therefore, should arrange their office in a manner that allows for flexibility.

Summary

Counseling children and adolescents from diverse backgrounds can be complex, as counselors have to assess acculturation level and ethnic identity development of the children and adults to ensure culturally appropriate interventions. Counselors must continue to educate themselves about multicultural issues and continue to examine themselves as cultural beings. Ongoing personal reflections will enhance a counselor's ability to provide effective counseling to all youth. Counselors also should engage in activities outside the counseling office, such as advocating on behalf of diverse youth when they witness discrimination, providing inservicing for school and agency personnel, or volunteering at cultural events in the community to build relationships with leaders of various groups.

References

American Counseling Association (2005). *ACA Code of Ethics*. Richmond, VA: Author.

Astramovich, R. L., & Harris, K. L. (2007). Promoting self-advocacy among minority students in school counseling. *Journal of Counseling and Development, 85,* 269–276.

Atkinson, D. R., Morten, G., & Sue, D. W. (1998). *Counseling American minorities.* Boston: McGraw-Hill.

Barona, A., & Miller, J. A. (1994). Short acculturation scale for Hispanic youth (SASH-Y): A preliminary report. *Hispanic Journal of Behavioral Sciences, 16,* 155–162.

Barry, D. T. (2005). Measuring acculturation among male Arab immigrants in the United States: An exploratory study. *Journal of Immigrant Health, 7,* 179–184.

Baruth, L. G., & Manning, M. L. (2007). *Multicultural counseling and psychotherapy: A life-span perspective (3rd ed.).* Upper Saddle River, NJ: Merrill Prentice Hall.

Bem, S. (1987). Gender schema theory and its implications for child development: Raising gender schematic children in a gender schematic society. In M. R. Walsh (Ed.), *The psychology of women: Ongoing debates.* New Haven, CT: Yale University Press.

Bemak, F., Chi-Ying, R., & Siroskey-Sabdo, L. A. (2005). Empowerment groups for academic success: An innovative approach to prevent high school failure for at-risk, urban African American youth. *Professional School Counseling, 8,* 377–389.

Bernal, M. E., Knight, B., Garza, C., C. Ocampo, K., & Cota, M. K. (1993). *Ethnic identity: Formation and transmission among Hispanics and other minorities.* Albany: State University of New York Press.

Berry, J. W. (1998). Acculturative stress. In P. B. Organista, K. M. Chun, & B. Marin (Eds.), *Readings in ethnic psychology* (pp. 113–117). New York: Routledge.

Bigler, R. S., & Liben, L. S. (1993). A cognitive-development approach to racial stereotyping and reconstructive memory in Euro-American children. *Child Development, 64,* 1507–1518.

Black, L. L., Crethar, H. C., Dermer, S. B., & Luke, M. (2007). My name is Samantha, not Sammy: Gender Identity. In S. M. Dugger and L. A. Carlson (Eds.), *Critical incidents in counseling children.* Alexandria, VA: American Counseling Association.

Blair, S. L., & Qian, Z. (1998). Family and Asian students' educational performance. *Journal of Family Issues, 19*, 355–374.

Bowman (1998). *Individual Counseling Activities for Children.* Chapin, SC: Youthlight, Inc.

Brammer, R. (2004). *Diversity in counseling.* Belmont, CA: Brooks/Cole-Thomson Learning.

Cheng, W. D. (1996). Pacific perspective. *Together, 24*(2), 10.

Clemente, R. (2004). Counseling culturally and ethnically diverse youth. In A. Vernon (Ed.), *Counseling children and adolescents* (pp. 227–256). Denver, CO: Love.

Clemente, R., & Collison, B. (2000). Interdependent perspective of functions and relations perceived by school counselors, ESL teachers, European American, and Latino students. *Professional School Counselor, 3*, 339–348.

Cole, E. M., & Valentine, D. P. (2000). Multiethnic children portrayed in children's picture books. *Child and Adolescent Social Work Journal, 17*, 305–317.

Constantino, G., & Malgady, R. G. (1996). Culturally sensitive treatment: Cuento and hero/heroine modeling therapies for Hispanic children and adolescents. In P. S. Jensen & E. D. Hibbs (Eds), *Psychosocial treatments for child and adolescent disorders: Empirically based strategies for clinical practice.* (pp. 639–669). Washington, DC: American Psychological Association.

Crawford, J. (1999). Bilingual education: History, politics, theory, and practice (4th ed.). Los Angeles: Bilingual Educational Services.

Cross, W. E. (1995). The psychology of Nigrescence: Revisiting and Cross Model. In J. G. Ponterotto, J. M. Casas, L. A. Suzuki, & C. M. Alexander (Eds.), *Handbook of multicultural counseling* (pp. 93–122). Thousand Oaks, CA: Sage.

Enns, C. Z., & Kasai, M. (2003). Hakoniwa: Japanese sandplay therapy. *Counseling Psychologist, 31*, 93–112.

Evans, K. M., & George, R. (2008). African Americans. In G. McAuliffe (Ed.), *Culturally alert counseling: A comprehensive introduction* (pp. 146–187). Los Angeles: Sage Publications.

Exum, H. L., Moore, Q. M., & Watt, S. K. (1999). Transcultural counseling for African Americans revisited. In McFadden, John (Ed), *Transcultural counseling* (2nd ed., pp. 171–219). Alexandria, VA: American Counseling Association.

Fausto-Sterling, A. (2000). *Sexing the body: Gender politics and the construction of sexuality.* New York: Basic Books.

Feldman, R. S. (2004). *Child development* (3rd ed.). Upper Saddle River, NJ: Pearson-Prentice Hall.

Field, J. E., & Baker, S. (2004). Defining and examining school counseling advocacy. *Professional School Counseling, 8*, 56–63.

Fraser, D., Piacentini, J., Van Rossem, R., Hien, D., & Rotheram-Borus, M. J. (1998). Effects of acculturation and Psychopathology on sexual behavior and substance use of suicidal Hispanic adolescents. *Hispanic Journal of Behavioral Sciences, 20*, 83–101.

Garrett, M. T. (2008). Native Americans. In G. McAuliffe (Ed.), *Culturally alert counseling: A comprehensive introduction* (pp. 220–254). Los Angeles: Sage Publications.

Garrett, M. T., & Crutchfield, L. B. (1997). Moving full circle: A unity model of group work with children. *Journal for Specialists in Group Work, 22*, 175–188.

Garrett, M. T., & Pichette, E. F. (2000). Red as an apple: Native American acculturation and counseling with or without reservation. *Journal of Counseling and Development, 78*, 3–13.

Gilbert, L. A., & Scher, M. (1999). *Gender and sex in counseling and psychotherapy.* Boston: Allyn & Bacon.

Gilligan, C. (1990). Teaching Shakespeare's sister. In C. Gilligan, N. Lyons, & T. Hamner (Eds.), *Making connections: The relational worlds of adolescent girls at Emma Willard School.* Cambridge, MA: Harvard University Press.

Gladding, S. T. (2005). *Counseling as an art: The creative art in counseling* (3rd ed.). Alexandria, VA: American Counseling Association.

Gowen, L.K., Hayward, C., Killen, J.D., Robinson, T.N., & Taylor, C. B. (1999). Acculturation and eating disorders symptoms in adolescent girls. *Journal of Research on Adolescence, 9,* 67–83.

Hanna, F. J., & Green, A. (2004). Asian shades of spirituality: Implications for multicultural school counseling. *Professional School Counseling, 7,* 326–333.

Helms, J. (1995). An update of Helm's white and people of color racial identity models. In J. G. Ponterotto, J. M. Casas, L. A. Suzuki, & C. M. Alexander (Eds.), *Handbook of multicultural counseling* (pp. 181–198). Thousand Oaks, CA: Sage.

Henderson, D. A., & Gladding, S. T. (1998). The creative arts in counseling: A multicultural perspective. *The Arts in Psychotherapy, 25,* 183–187.

Hines, P. M., Almeida, R., Preto, N. G., Weltman, S., & McGoldrick, M. (2005). Culture and the family life cycle. In B. Carter & M. McGoldrick, *The Expanded Family Life Cycle.* New York: Allyn & Bacon.

Hoffman, T., Dana, R., & Bolton, B. (1985). Measured acculturation and MMPI-168 performance of Native American adults. *Journal of Cross-Cultural Psychology, 16,* 243–256.

Holcomb-McCoy, C. (2004). Assessing the multicultural competence of school counselors: A checklist. *Professional School Counselor, 7,* 178–186.

Hunter, D., & Sawyer, C. (2006). Blending Native American spirituality with individual psychology in work with children. *Journal of Individual Psychology, 62,* 234–250.

Indian Health Service (2001). Trends in Indian Health. Retrieved August 2, 2007 from http://www.ihs.gov/NonMedicalPrograms/IHS_Stats/Trends00.asp 007

Jackson, M. J., & Nassar-McMillan, S. C. (2006). Counseling Arab Americans. In C. C. Lee (Ed.), *Multicultural issues in counseling: New approaches to diversity* (3rd ed.). Alexandria, VA: American Counseling Association.

Jose, P.E., Huntsinger, C. S., Huntsinger, P. R., & Liaw, L. (2000). Parent values and practices relevant to young children's social development in Taiwan and the United States. *Journal of Cross-Cultural Psychology, 431,* 677–701.

Kim, B., Atkinson, D., & Umemoto, D. (2001). Asian cultural values and the counseling process: Current knowledge and directions for future research. *Counseling Psychologist, 29,* 570–603.

Kim, B. S. K., Atkinson, D. R., & Yang, P. H. (1999). The Asian values scale: Development, factor analysis, validation, and reliability. *Journal of Counseling Psychology, 46,* 342–352.

Kosmin, B. A., Mayer, E., & Keysar, A. (2001). *American Religious Identification Survey, 2001.* New York: The Graduate Center of the City University of New York.

Landreth, G. L. (2002). *Play therapy: The art of the relationship.* New York: Brunner-Routledge.

Langman, P. F. (2000). Including Jews in multiculturalism. In M. Adams, W. J. Blumfield, R. Castaneda, H. W. Hackman, M. L. Peters, & X. Zuniga (Eds.), *Readings for diversity and social justice* (pp. 169–177). New York: Routledge.

Maki, M., & Kitaono, H. (2002). Counseling Asian Americans. In P. Pedersen, J. Draguns, W. Lonner, & J. Trimble (Eds.), *Counseling across cultures* (pp. 109–131). Thousand Oaks, CA: Sage Publications.

Marcia, J. (1980). Identity in adolescence. In J. Adelson (Ed.), *Handbook of adolescent psychology* (pp. 159–187). New York: Wiley.

McGoldrick, M., Gerson, R., and Shellenberger, S. (1998). *Genograms in family assessment* (2nd ed.), New York: Norton.

Nassar-McMillan, S. C., & Hakim-Larson, J. (2003). Counseling considerations among Arab Americans. *Journal of Counseling and Development, 81,* 150–159.

Peavy, R. V. (1995). *Career counseling with Native clients; Understanding the context.* ERIC Clearinghouse Doc. ED 399485.

Phinney, J. S. (1989). Stages of ethnic identity development in minority group adolescents. *Journal of Early Adolescence, 9,* 34–49.

Pope, R. L. (2000). The relationship between psychosocial development and racial identity of college students of color. *Journal of College Student Development, 41,* 302–311.

Robbins, R., Tonemah, S., & Robbins, S. (2002). Project eagle: Techniques for multi-family psycho-educational group therapy with gifted American Indian adolescents and their parents. *Journal of the National of American Indian and Alaska Native Programs, 10,* 56–74.

Roberts, R. E., Phinney, J. S., Masse, L. C., Chen, Y. R., Roberts, C. R., & Romero, A. (1999). The structure of ethnic identity of young adolescents from diverse ethnocultural groups. *Journal of Early Adolescence, 19,* 310–322.

Robinson, T. L. (2005). *The convergence of race, ethnicity, and gender: Multiple identities in counseling.* Upper Saddle River, NJ: Merrill Prentice Hall.

Samaniego, R. Y., & Gonzales, N. A. (1999). Multiple mediators of the effects of acculturation status on delinquency for Mexican American adolescents. *American Journal of Community Psychology, 27,* 189–210.

Sax, L. (2005). *Why gender matters: What parents and teachers need to know about the emerging science of sex differences.* New York: Doubleday.

Schlosser, L. Z. (2006). Affirmative psychotherapy for American Jews. *Psychotherapy: Theory, Research, Practice, and Training, 43,* 424–435.

Schoen, A. A. (2005). Culturally sensitive counseling for Asian American/Pacific Islander. *Journal of Instructional Psychology, 32,* 248-252

Scott, C. C. (2001). The sisterhood group: A culturally focused empowerment group model for inner city African American youth. *Journal of Child and Adolescent Group Therapy, 11,* 77–85.

Smith, T. B. (2004). *Practicing multiculturalism: Affirming diversity in counseling and psychology.* Boston: Allyn & Bacon.

Smith-Adcock, S., Daniels, M. H., Lee, S. M., Villalba, J. A., & Indelicato, N. A. (2006). Culturally responsive school counseling for Hispanic/Latino students and families: The need for bilingual school counselors. *Professional School Counseling, 10,* 92–101.

Snowden, L. R., & Hines, A. M. (1999). A scale to assess African American acculturation. *Journal of Black Psychology, 25,* 36–47.

Strakowski, S. M., McElroy, S. L., Keck, P. E., & West, S. A. (1996). Racial influence on diagnosis in psychotic mania. *Journal of Affective Disorders, 39,* 157–162.

Sue, D. W., Arredondo, P., & McDavis, R. J. (1992). Multicultural counseling competencies and standards: A call to the profession. *Journal of Counseling and Development, 70,* 477–486.

Sue, D. W., & Sue, D. (2007). *Counseling the culturally diverse: Theory and practice* (5th ed.). New York: John Wiley & Sons.

Tatman, A. W. (2004). Hmong history, culture, and acculturation: Implications for counseling the Hmong. *Journal of Multicultural Counseling, 32,* 222–233.

Thompson, C. L., Rudolph, L. B., & Henderson, D. (2004). *Counseling children* (6th ed). Belmont, CA: Thomson Brooks/Cole.

Timimi, S. B. (1995). Adolescence in immigrant Arab families. *Psychotherapy, 32*, 141–149.

Unger, J. B., Cruz, T. B., Rohrbach, L. A., Ribisl, K. M., Baezconde-Garbanti, L., & Chen, X. (2000). English language use as a risk factor for smoking initiation among Latino and Asian American adolescents: Evidence for medication by tobacco-related beliefs and social norms. *Health Psychology, 19*, 403–410.

Unger, J. B., Gallaher, P., Shakib, S., Ritt-Olson, A., Palmer, P.H., & , C. A. (2002). The AHIMSA acculturation scale: A new measure of acculturation for adolescents in a multicultural society. *Journal of Early Adolescence, 22*, 225–250.

U.S. Bureau of the Census (2005). Selected characteristics of the population of citizenship: 2004. Retrieved from http://sss.census.gov/population/socdemo/race/api

Vernon, A., & Clemente, R. (2005). *Assessment and interventions with children and adolescents: Developmental and multicultural approaches* (2nd ed.). Alexandria, VA: American Counseling Association.

Villalba, J. A. (2003). A psychoeducational group for limited-English proficient Latino/Latina children. *Journal for Specialists in Group Work, 28*, 261–276.

Villalba, J. A., Brunelli, M., Orfanedes, D., & Lewis (2007). Experience of Latino children attending rural elementary schools in the southeastern US: perspectives from Latino parents in burgeoning Latino communities. *Professional School Counseling, 10*, 506–509.

Weist, M. D., Myers, C. P., Hastings, E., Ghuman, H., Han, Y. L. (1999). Psychosocial functioning of youth receiving mental health services in the schools versus community mental health centers. *Community Mental Health Journal, 35*, 69–81.

Williams, D. R., Yu, Y., Jackson, J. S., & Anderson, N. B. (1997). Racial differences in physical and mental health: Socio-economic status, stress and discrimination. *Journal of Health Psychology, 3*, 335–351.

Woodard, S. L. (1995). Counseling disruptive black elementary school boys. *Journal of Multicultural Counseling and Development, 23*, 21–28.

Zucker, K. J. (2005). Gender identity disorder in children and adolescents. *Review of Clinical Psychology, 1*, 467–492.

Appendix to Chapter 8
Multicultural Resources

African American

Adoff, A. (1973). *Black is Brown is Tan*. New York: HarperCollins Publishing.*
Bradman, T. (1986). *Through My Window*. New Jersey: Silver Burdett Co.*
Heath, A (1992). *Sofie's Role*. New York: Four Winds Press.*
Hooks, B., & Raschka, C. (1999). *Happy to be Nappy*. New York: Hyperion Books for Children.**
Hooks, B., & Raschka, C. (1999). *Be Boy Buzz*. New York: Hyperion Books for Children.**

Arab American

Gilliland, J. H. (1995). *A Day of Ahmed's Secret*. New York: Mulberry Books.**
Hickox, R. (1999). *The Golden Sandal: A Middle Eastern Cinderella Story*. New York. Holiday House.**
Mobin-Uddin, A. (2005). *My Name is Bilal*. Honesdale, PA: Boyds Mills Press.**
Nagada, A. W. (2000). *Dear Whiskers*. New York: Scholastic.**

Asian American

Friedman, I (1984). *How My Parents Learned to Eat*. Boston: Houghton Mifflin.*
Igus, T. (1996). *Two Mrs. Gibsons*. Los Angeles: Children's Book Press.*
Mills, C. (1992). *A Visit to Amy-Claire*. New York: Macmillan.*
Rattigan, J. K. (1993). *Dumpling Soup*. Boston: Little Brown.*
Welber, R. (1972). *The Train*. New York: Pantheon Books.*

Latinos/Latinas

Cisneros, S. (1994). *Hairs/Pelitos*. New York: Knopf.*
Machado, A. M. (1996). *Nina Bonita*. New York: Kane/Miller Books.*
Bunting, E. (1994). *A Day's Work*. New York: Clarion Books.**

Native American

Bruchac, M. M. (1993). *A Picture Book of Sitting Bull*. New York: Holiday House.**
Hamm, D. J. (1997). *Daughter of Suqua*. Morton Grove, IL: Albert Whitman and Co.**
Lacapa, M. (1992). *Antelope Woman: An Apache Folktale*. Flagstaff, AZ: Northland Publishing.**
McCain, B. R. (2001). *Grandmother's Dream Catcher*. Morton Grove, IL: Albert Whitman and Co.**
Taylor, J. C. (1993). *How Two-Feather Was Saved From Loneliness*. Plattsburgh, NY: Tundra Books.**

---

* Cole and Valentine (2000) reviewed numerous children's picture books depicting children from a variety of ethnic backgrounds and identified these to be non-biased and affirming.

** The World of Difference Institute has identified these resources as anti-biased. (http://www.adl.org/bibliography/default.asp)

Counseling Children and Adolescents With Special Needs

William McFarland and Toni Tollerud

While growing up, children and adolescents find themselves in many circumstances over which they have little control. All young people have the potential to become at risk and are influenced by pressures from family, school, peers, and society (Capuzzi & Gross, 2006). As they attempt to deal with these pressures, children and adolescents often make choices that result in new problems such as substance abuse, gang involvement, sexually transmitted diseases, and pregnancy. Understanding how young people respond to situations that are out of their control—such as a parent who drinks too much or divorcing parents—is essential for counselors who want to help children and adolescents respond to these life events using healthy coping strategies.

Problems over which children and adolescents have little choice can bring difficulties, pain, and sorrow that prevent them from functioning effectively in their world. In this chapter we explore the family circumstances of divorce, blended families, adoption, and what counselors need to know to work effectively with children and adolescents to create resilient behaviors. In addition, we explore grief and loss; living with alcoholic parents; growing up gay, lesbian, bisexual, or transgender; having eating disorders; and coping with the psychological effects of terror attacks. The empowerment model suggested here is intended to develop and enhance resilient behaviors in the children and adolescents that counselors serve.

Resilience

Resilience is the ability to adjust to special problems and achieve positive outcomes. It is

> [a] trait that has a major influence on successful adaptive and coping behaviors and forms the foundation for many other positive character skills including patience, tolerance, responsibility, compassion, determination, commitment, self-reliance, and hope. The essence of resiliency is the ability to bounce back from adversity, frustration, and misfortune. (Janas, 2002, p. 117)

Werner and Smith (2001) explained the results of a longitudinal study of more than 200 children who experienced poverty, perinatal stress, family discord, divorce, parental alcoholism, and parental mental illness. By 18 years of age, one-third of these children were described as competent young adults, and by age 32, most of those who had problems coping as adolescents had become more effective and competent in adult roles.

Resilient children have positive outcomes. Kwok, Hughes, and Luo (2007), who investigated a measurement model of personality resilience with a sample of ethnically diverse children, reported that a resilient personality in first grade was linked to subsequent school achievement. Bogar and Hulse-Killacky (2006) investigated the resiliency determinants and process among female adult survivors of childhood sexual abuse and reported that

> participants in this study strongly suggested that the ability to refocus on more productive or rewarding aspects of their lives, thereby minimizing thoughts of their abuse experiences, was essential to their recovery process and their ability to become resilient adults (p. 324).

Characteristics of Resiliency

Children and adolescents from adverse backgrounds develop the ability to cope effectively with challenges that might lead to difficulties. Harvey (2007) listed the following characteristics of these resilient students:

- Having positive social relationships with friends, relatives, and neighbors
- Having positive peer relationships
- Having positive feelings toward school and academics
- Encouraging oneself to try
- Being determined to persevere until success is attained
- Applying a problem-solving approach to difficult situations
- Demonstrating feelings of hardiness

Hollister–Wagner, Foshee, and Jackson (2001) detailed protective factors that foster the development of resiliency as having

- a close relationship with an adult,
- a high value of religion,
- self-esteem,
- relationship competence,
- good communication skills, and
- an ability to deal with anger constructively

The salient point for counselors is that protective factors—including the child's temperament, alternative sources of support in the family, and mentoring by role models in the community—can help children overcome adversity and mature into successful adults.

Interventions

As children cope with difficult situations, they develop the following resiliencies (Desetta, Wolin, & Wolin, 2000):

- *Insight*: the ability to figure things out
- *Independence*: being able to do for oneself
- *Relationships*: finding support and mentoring outside the family
- *Initiative*: figuring out strategies to stay safe
- *Humor*: laughing at adverse circumstances
- *Creativity*: expressing feelings through artistic expression
- *Morality*: a promise not to do what has been done to them

As the counselor listens to young clients relate their stories of stress and pain, he or she can reframe these experiences as resiliencies or strengths. For example, adolescents who don't want to go home immediately after school because it might not be safe may spend time in the school library or with friends. This strategy clearly demonstrates insight and initiative because the teenager knows that going home might pose danger and takes actions to stay safe. The counselor can encourage the continued development of these strategies and reframe the situation as one of building resilience.

Counselors working in the schools can teach resiliency skills through classroom guidance lessons or in small-group counseling sessions (Wolin, Desetta, & Hefner, 2000). Examples include training in conflict resolution, interpersonal skills, assertion training, problem solving, and rational-emotive education. Elementary and middle school counselors could use the game "Bounce Back: A Game That Teaches Resiliency Skills" (Shapiro, 2002) to build resiliency skills in children and teens. Arman (2002) described a six-session brief group counseling model to increase the resiliency of students with mild disabilities. The topics for the group sessions were: setting group norms, educating students about resiliency, identifying dependable and trustworthy people in the lives of the students, appreciating the need for high expectations, involvement in meaningful community or school-related activities, and wrapping up unfinished business.

Racial socialization and racial identity are protective factors that can promote resiliency in African American adolescents as well as other minority groups (Miller, 1999). Parents socialize their children regarding racial issues such as prejudice, thereby creating a buffer against a hostile environment. A well-developed racial identity can help minority adolescents overcome the stigma of negative social stereotypes.

Perkins and Jones (2004) identified several protective factors that increase the likelihood that physically abused adolescents will not engage in at-risk behaviors but will increase the likelihood of abused adolescents for engaging in thriving behaviors. These protective factors offer a framework for interventions to develop or enhance protective factors.

1. Peer group characteristics (the more positive behaviors the peer group exhibited, the more thriving behaviors the at-risk youth displayed)
2. Positive school climate
3. Religiosity
4. Adult support
5. Family support
6. View of the future
7. Involvement with extracurricular activities

Wong and colleagues (2006) investigated the impact of behavioral control and resiliency in the onset of alcohol and illicit drug use in children of alcoholics. They concluded that children with greater initial resiliency were less likely to begin using alcohol.

By reframing difficult, stressful situations in terms of the development of resiliencies and by working to enhance protective factors within children, within their families, and within the school and community, counselors can tilt the balance for these young clients from vulnerability to resiliency. Counselors can play a critical role in facilitating the development of competent, successful, resilient children.

Nontraditional Families

A major contributor to the development of children is the family. Problems that may be present in the internal functioning of the family include the way family members communicate within the family or the rules it follows. Externally, problems may be based on the family structure. Certainly, children growing up in the traditional two-parent family are subject to difficulties, but children and adolescents in families with nontraditional structures are much more prone to self-defeating behaviors (Capuzzi & Gross, 2006; Goldenberg & Goldenberg, 2007).

The traditional definition of "family" is no longer applicable. We now readily acknowledge and accept diversity in how families are constituted and what special needs they have. Gladding (2007) has defined four distinct single-parent family lifestyles in which the family make-up is changed—based on divorce, choice, death, and when one parent is absent from the home. Children and adolescents who lack resilience may become casualties in these families. As their family structure goes through new phases, they are susceptible to a variety of self-defeating behaviors and special problems.

Counseling Children and Adolescents of Divorce

Ever since World War II, the divorce rate in the United States has been increasing dramatically. In the 40 years between 1960 and 2000, the divorce rate in the United States tripled. In the United States the divorce rate for first marriages is approximately 50%: for second marriages, 67%; and for third marriages, 74% (www.divorcerate.org). Even though most children live with both biological parents, estimates suggest that more than half of them will spend some time in an alternative family structure by their 18th birthday (Cavanagh & Huston, 2006). And children of divorce are much more likely to have relationship problems and school problems (DeLucia–Waack & Gerrity, 2001).

Characteristics

Most children and adolescents from divorced families face the following issues to varying degrees (Wallerstein & Kelly, 1996):

- Fear
- Sadness or feelings of loss
- Loneliness
- Rejection
- Conflicting loyalties
- Anger

Within 2 to 3 years after the divorce, most parents and children adjust to their new life (Dacey, Kenny, & Margolis, 2000). How well children adjust depends on the following factors:

1. The *cumulative stress* of children following a divorce (Hetherington, as cited in Dacey, Kenny, & Margolis, 2000). The stress is greater if the household has a significant loss of income, significant change in methods of discipline, or a move to a new location and school.
2. *Temperament and personality*. If children have been able to adapt readily to change prior to the divorce, adjustment to the divorce may not be as difficult and children can call upon their personal assets to deal with subsequent stressful life events (Dacey, Kenny, & Shapiro, 2000).

3. The *child's age*. Adolescents are more able than younger children to understand the causes and consequences of the divorce because of their ability to think more abstractly. With peer contacts outside the family, adolescents also may have developed a better support system than younger children.

4. *Gender*. The father most often is the one who leaves the home, and the effects are more negative for male than female children, according to Dacey, Kenny, and Margolis (2000). Many girls from divorced families, however, develop adjustment problems similar to boys (Hetherington, 1991). In a study examining the effect of parental divorce on attitude transmission, Kapinus (2004) concluded that "…young adults whose parents divorce are more likely to espouse pro-divorce attitudes, although this is more true of daughters than sons" (p. 132). This is significant because individuals who have pro-divorce views have lower levels of marital satisfaction and are more likely to divorce (Amato & Rogers, 1999).

Rather than viewing the impact of divorce as an isolated single event, researchers increasingly are viewing parents' marital disruption as a continuous process in which children are affected prior to and after a parental divorce or separation (Sun & Li, 2002). Marital disruption may begin years before the divorce itself, and children living in such a stressful environment will have to cope with those stressors. The results of a pooled time-series analysis with a sample of 9,524 students showed that the detrimental effects of parents' marital disruption occurred from about 3 years before to 3 years after the divorce (Sun & Li, 2002). Further highlighting the impact of family dysfunction and divorce on children, Strohschein (2005) found that even before the marital breakup, children whose parents later divorce exhibit higher levels of anxiety/depression and antisocial behavior than children whose parents remain married.

Interventions

Resiliency is an important factor in a child's ability to adapt to divorce (Chen & George, 2005). Wallerstein and Blakeslee (1996) described the following six psychological tasks that children of divorce must resolve. As they work through these tasks, they can become more resilient. These tasks provide a framework for counselor interventions.

1. *Acknowledging the reality of the marital rupture*. Younger children often fantasize about and deny the reality of the family breakup. Counselors can consult with the parents and encourage them to discuss the divorce with their children. Counselors can listen to children's concerns, validate their feelings, and develop lists of topics the children may want to explore with their parents. Pardeck (1998) suggested having older children compose a "Dear Abby" letter describing their family situation. They also suggested that younger children might use pictures and words cut from magazines to create a collage describing their family situations.

2. *Disengaging from the parental conflict and distress and resuming customary pursuits*. Counselors can recommend to parents that they maintain familiar routines and continue to encourage involvement of the parents in school and extracurricular activities. Counselors may suggest the use of structured procedures to ensure that homework is completed and study time is scheduled.

3. *Resolving the loss*. Resolving the many losses of children of divorce may be the most difficult task for them (Wallerstein, 1987). The counselor can encourage the absent parent to maintain contact with the children and also help the children develop connections with other adults outside the family who can offer support.

4. *Resolving anger and self-blame*. Counselors may have to address the cognitive distortions that children often have about the divorce. Using puppets is a good way for young children to project and express their feelings. Another excellent technique is bibliotherapy, in which young people read about peers who have gone through what they are going through. This helps them understand the divorce and identify with issues and feelings of the characters in the story (Pardeck, 1998).

   Useful books include, among others, *Don't Fall Apart on Saturdays* (Moser & Melton, 2000), *What in the World Do You Do When Your Parents Divorce?* (Winchester & Beyer, 2001), *Two Homes* (Masurel, 2001), *It's Not Your Fault, Koko Bear* (Lansky, 1998), *Mom's House, Dad's House for Kids* (Ricci, 2006), and *My Two Homes* (Magsamen, 2007).

5. *Accepting the permanence of the divorce*. Counselors may have to work with children who relentlessly hold firm to the idea that their parents will reconcile. The counselor can ask children to draw their families before the divorce and after the divorce. Or the counselor can place "feeling words" on 3 × 5 cards and ask the children to place the card on the picture of the family member that best describes their feelings toward that person.

6. *Achieving realistic hope regarding relationships*. Adolescents who have experienced parental divorce may struggle with creating satisfying intimate relationships. Counselors can use cognitive–behavioral techniques to help these teens realize the irrationality of their fears, asking questions such as: Where is the proof that…? Is it true that…? Does it make sense that because you experienced…, this means….?

For children in elementary school, DeLucia-Waack and Gerrity (2001) suggest a group-counseling intervention that

1. brings the divorce situation into the real world of the child so he or she can cope with the reality of the situation;
2. normalizes the child's common experiences and feelings;
3. creates a safe and supportive environment so each child can talk about the divorce;
4. helps each child label, understand, and express his or her feelings;

5. fosters new coping strategies and skills; and

6. emphasizes that the divorce is not the child's fault.

Some positive factors enhance children's resiliency and assist with a positive adjustment and decrease maladaptive conduct in response to parental divorce (Chen & George, 2005). The more resilient they are, the more likely they will be able to function successfully and not resort to unhealthy ways of coping with the potentially devastating effects of parental divorce. Resiliency is especially important with this issue because, as Goldenberg and Goldenberg (2007) noted, within 3 years of the divorce, three-fourths of the women and five-sixths of the men remarry, creating a blended family.

Counseling Children and Adolescents in Stepfamilies and Blended Families

The stepfamily represents a substantial portion of families in the United States. Gladding (2007) states that, "By the beginning of the 21st century, 1 million of the 2 million marriages in the United States each year involved at least one formerly married person." (p. 288). Visher and Visher (1996) defined a stepfamily, as "a household in which there is an adult couple, at least one of whom has a child by a previous relationship" (p. 3). Gladding (2007) used the term "remarried" families. Other authors referred to this family structure as the blended family (Becvar & Becvar, 2005; Fenell & Weinhold, 2003; Lambie & Daniels-Mohring, 2000). Blending is a more positive concept that seems to fit the resiliency model in a proactive perspective in that it implies an active approach toward addressing difficulties and using problem-solving techniques toward healthy adjustment for all participants.

Blending can cause difficulties within the family on a variety of levels. A major issue is the desire for the new members of the family to reconstitute a traditional family structure. This wish for "instant readjustment," in which members believe that once the remarriage takes place, everyone will live "happily ever after," is a myth for the blended—and, for that matter, any—family (Becvar & Becvar, 2005).

Characteristics

In a pioneering effort, Walsh (1992) suggested 20 major issues that blended families encounter as they blend. He organized these issues into four topical categories, noting that these issues impact children and adolescents because what happens in the family affects all members.

Initial Family Issues

The first category, *initial family issues*, occurs early in the development of the blended family unit. Issues may revolve around loyalty, in which a child believes that loving anyone other than the biological parent is disloyal. Children also may worry that the new stepparent is trying to take away the love from the biological parent. This fear may cause parents to be competitive or to undermine the other family members' relationships.

Children and adolescents also may need time to deal with the loss and grief still present from the divorce. Attachment issues and the loss of significant others can further disrupt children's development, or they may hold on to a fantasy that their biological parents will reconcile and the original family will be a unit again.

For adolescents who are coping with these initial family issues, the remarriage may challenge their own development around identity, sexuality, and the need for individuation from the family. Issues of attachment can become complicated as the adolescents seek to become more independent at a time when the new family is working to bond and attach. Watching their new parents act out the rituals of love may be embarrassing and conflictual and may influence the development of their own dating and peer relationships.

Some children and adolescents who have been living in single-parent households have served in parental roles, shouldering responsibility and playing prominent roles in their families. Although the remarriage may be a source of relief, it also may demote youngsters from positions of power they held in their families previously. Finally, the remarriage may cause problems around parenting time with the noncustodial parent, feelings of rejection, and the potential of moving the family to a new location.

Developing Family Issues

The second category, *developing family issues*, surfaces after initial formation of the blended family. As they cope with these developing family issues, children and adolescents deal with potentially difficult family dynamics such as discipline, role assignments within the family, sibling conflict, competition for time with the noncustodial parent, and going between families for visits. In addition, the reconstituted family members bring into the new family most of the personal issues from the former marriage and divorce, such as grief and loss issues, insecurity, low self-esteem, and anger.

Feelings About Self and Others

In the third category, *feelings about self and others*, children and adolescents are influenced by society's concept of remarriage. For example, the school system often reinforces the conflict and hurt feelings by its insensitivity to issues such as parent/teacher conferences, graduations, and other events. Classroom assignments that deal with drawing or talking about parents or family can become stressful for these children and adolescents. Being called or labeled as a member of a "stepfamily" still represents a negative image in U. S. society. Children who feel stress in the new family may act out in school or have difficulty concentrating. If the new parents conceive children of their own, this introduces another factor: Often, this new child, living with both biological parents, receives most of the attention and affection in the family, leaving stepchildren to feel less valued.

Adult Issues Related to the New Family

The fourth category involves *adult issues related to the new family* including financial concerns such as child support and alimony, competition with the noncustodial parent, blended remarried family that can put young people in the middle. For example, who will pay for college may become the topic of a bitter fight, creating stress for adolescents. Also, as adolescents begin to mature and become young adults, their personal values and beliefs about love, marriage, and their future families may be influenced strongly by living in a blended family situation. These young adults may be much more sensitive and critical about how they build their future and how they intend to rear their own children.

Interventions

Counselors who work with children and adolescents in families of divorce and blended families can help them with their concerns about loss, loyalty, and lack of control. Cobia and Brazelton (1994) described procedures using kinetic family drawings with children in remarriage families, in which the counselor asks the children to draw a picture of everyone in their family, including themselves, doing something. Counselors should ask their clients to include family members from both households. After the children have completed the drawings, the counselor asks clarifying questions to explore the issues the drawings suggest.

Also, counselors can ask older children and adolescents to keep journals and record their thoughts and feelings about the transition to a blended family. Within the counseling sessions they can develop insights about their issues, work on troublesome relationships, and gain some control over their lives by identifying and employing effective coping strategies.

Counselors should help children and adolescents in blended families overcome their feelings of helplessness by exploring developmentally appropriate behaviors such as visiting friends where they formerly lived, getting involved in extracurricular activities at school or in the community, finding private space in the home, or asking for one-on-one time with the birth parent without the presence of the stepparent or stepsiblings. Allowing children and adolescents to make choices can lead to a sense of independence, freedom, and control in one's life. Good books about blended families include *Louie's Search* (Keats, 2001), *My Family's Changing* (Thomas, 1999), *When a Parent Marries Again* (Heegaard, 1993), and *All Families Are Different* (Gordon & Cohen, 2000).

Further, counselors also must be willing to get involved and join the family members in understanding the frustrations of each person's role within the blended family unit (Fenell & Weinhold, 2003). Gladding (2007) encourages counselors to help family members realize that they do not have to give up old loyalties. Children can be encouraged to talk about their "past lives." Many times, the adults in the family put unrealistic expectations on the children or are so consumed with their own issues of adjustment that they do not support the children through this transitional time.

Advocating for children helps adults recognize children's unique needs and assists them in developing appropriate solutions and options that empower the family. School counselors have an important role in establishing communication between all those involved in the child's life, including stepparents, social workers, and school personnel. In addition, counselors can suggest parenting strategies or introduce family meetings to open up communications among all members of the blended family.

Being in a blended family may complicate adolescents' normal developmental changes. Those who seemed to be adjusting well to the blended family at first may later exhibit anger, acting-out behavior, or withdrawal. Knowing what behaviors are typical for adolescents can be helpful to stepparents. Counselors should encourage adolescents to talk about their feelings and concerns and suggest books to help them gain insights. Good resources include: *Step Kids: A Survival Guide for Teenagers in Stepfamilies* (Getzoff & McClenahan, 1984); *Stepliving for Teens: Getting Along with Stepparents and Siblings* (Block & Bartell, 2001); *Finding Your Place: A Teen Guide to Life in Blended Family* (Leibowitz, 2000); and *Step Trouble: A Survival Guide for Teenagers with Step Parents* (Coleman, 1993).

Finally, adolescents may develop problems involving sexuality. They may withdraw from stepsiblings or stepparents in reaction to their emerging sexual feelings. At the same time, discussing sexuality may be taboo in the family. Counselors should bring up the subject in counseling and help adolescents explore their feelings about their sexuality. Counselors may work with adolescents and their significant adults to discuss the importance of peer relationships, dating, and trust.

Knowing that certain students are living in blended families can be helpful in addressing classroom problems, academic failures, and personal or social problems. School counselors must work toward normalizing the blended family, along with all types of families, in the school. Teachers should be informed about children and adolescents from blended families so they can be sensitive to issues such as parent conferences, sending notes home, stepsiblings, and academic or behavioral problems (Lambie & Daniels-Mohring, 2000). Programs and developmental guidance lessons for all students should address diverse families and assist children and adolescents in understanding and developing tolerance of peers from various family constellations.

Counseling Children and Adolescents Who Are Adopted

Children who are aware that they have been adopted might have issues related to abandonment, family attachment, and loyalty (Jarratt, 1997). In addition, children who are adopted may feel insecure, angry, guilty, and blame themselves or their biological parents (Lambie & Daniels-Mohring, 2000). The circumstances surrounding the adoption have a strong impact on children and adolescents. In many cases, children are adopted because of unwanted pregnancies, abuse or neglect, or circumstances that have depleted all the family's emotional and economic resources.

An important component in adjustment is the adoptee's feelings of belonging in the adopting family. Early studies by Benson, Sharma, and Roehikepartain (1994) of children who had been adopted indicated that they developed good coping strategies and grew into happy, successful adolescents. Van IJzendoorn and Juffer (2005) looked at the cognitive development of adopted children to see how they differed from children who remained in institutional care or in their birth families. They found that adopted children scored higher on IQ tests and performed better in school than unadopted peers who stayed in care. Compared to children who remained in their birth families, however, school performance and language lagged. IJendoorn and Juffer (2005) also found that adopted children were twice as likely to be referred to special education.

Tan's (2006) research revealed that children with a history of neglect in infancy were less likely to participate in extracurricular activities and were less successful in academic achievement and overall competence. And adopted children are disproportionately more likely to experience psychological distress.

Characteristics

Children who are adopted before they are old enough to be in school go through little adjustment because they do not understand exactly how they differ from other children. Counseling may be beneficial with the adoptive parents, however, to help them deal with their possible infertility issues and bonding with the adopted child. Parents also may need to consider how they want to address the adoption issue as their adopted children get older and enter school.

At the point when they enter school, children become more capable of understanding the meaning of adoption. Brodzinsky and Schechter (1993) suggested that during this phase parents tell children about the adoption and create a safe environment where they can feel free to ask questions. Helping them feel that they belong in this family and that they are "chosen" assists with their adjustment.

As later childhood approaches and children move from concrete thinking to more abstract reasoning, they are better able to understand that being chosen into a family also means that another family rejected them. At this point, children become aware of the loss they sustained. They may react with feelings of uncertainty and insecurity, as well as anger at the parents who "gave me up." They may want to know more about their birth family and the circumstances surrounding the adoption.

When children approach adolescence, their adoption may add to the normal problems of development and growth. Adolescents typically are struggling with issues of identity formation (Erikson, 1968), and these issues are confounded for adopted adolescents who are searching for answers to "Who am I?" Because they do not live with their birth parents, they may look different from their adoptive parents and siblings, be unaware of their medical histories, and have questions about their biological parents. In addition, the normal fears and confusion of adolescence may be exacerbated and adolescents may worry about their adoptive family rejecting them.

Sexuality may become another issue for adopted adolescents. Benson and colleagues (1994) compared sexual behaviors of adopted and unadopted adolescents and found no differences. Sorosky, Baran, and Pannor (1989), however, found that adopted female adolescents acted out sexually. Those authors concluded that some adopted female adolescents desired to become pregnant to identify with their birth mothers and to connect with a blood relative, their own child.

Interventions

Dealing with children and adolescents who have been adopted means being aware that at critical periods in their growth and development, new issues and concerns may surface around the adoption. Adopted children who have been adjusting well may find that at the onset of adolescence, they suddenly face major problems relating to the adoption. Janus (1997) suggested that "normal" problems might be intensified for children and adolescents who have been adopted.

The older the child at the time of placement, the greater is the probability that the child will have behavioral and emotional difficulties (Zirkle, Peterson, & Collins-Marotte, 2001).

If adopted children are referred for counseling as preschoolers, working with the parents may be more helpful. Typical issues with the parents may center on infertility, parenting skills, and setting realistic expectations. Adopted children often are only children in the family, and parents may have unrealistic expectations for them (Lambie & Daniels-Mohring, 2000).

A form of adoption that can be complicating during this time is the *open adoption*. In an open adoption the birth parent or parents are involved with the adoption family before, during, and after the adoption. Although this can have advantages, it may create controversy in childrearing practices and confusion as children try to understand why they have two sets of parents.

As adopted children begin to understand what makes them different, they realize that they have had a loss in their life. When working with these children, counselors should help them deal with the issue of being different and the feelings related to loss. Adopted children may have problems with trust, self-esteem, and a fear of being rejected (Lambie & Daniels-Mohring, 2000). They need to know that they belong, have support, and feel a sense of stability. Counselors can engage adopted children in the therapeutic process using a variety of developmentally appropriate techniques including drawing, journaling, storytelling, incomplete sentences, role-play, puppets, and play therapy. Listening to their stories, affirming their feelings, and offering support can facilitate adopted children's adjustment.

At this point, counselors should involve the family, encouraging the parents to discuss aspects of the adoption openly with the children. There is potential damage to children who are not involved in learning about their past and the circumstances around the adoption. And children may have difficulty drawing a family tree or talking about their parents, for instance.

Sometimes counselors encounter school personnel who have mistaken assumptions about adopted children. School counselors can offer assistance and lead inservice workshops to increase educators' awareness and understanding.

Over time, group counseling has been helpful in working with adopted children (Kizner & Kizner, 1999; Morganett, 1990, 1994, 2000). Kizner and Kizner proposed a 12-session group counseling unit for children, supporting the belief that children need help in understanding their thoughts and feelings about adoption. Group counseling allows children who have common experiences to feel normal, to share their stories with others who can understand them, and to gain support in knowing they are not the only one who has been adopted.

In counseling adolescents the picture becomes more complicated because of the physical, social, and emotional changes characteristic of adolescence, which can trigger new feelings about being adopted. As adolescents struggle with their self-identity, they question their heritage, are concerned with how they look, worry about their intelligence, and wonder about health problems they might have inherited from their birth parents.

Specific interventions can allow adolescents to tell their stories and develop new insights and understandings about their lives. Encouraging them to keep a journal about their questions, concerns, and feelings is helpful, as is bibliotherapy. Assisting teens to recognize where they can take control of their lives and relate effectively to their adoptive family, friends, and, in some cases, their birth parents, promotes healthy adjustment. Older adolescents may raise issues about sexuality and family planning for the future.

The book *Maybe Days* (Wilgocki & Wright, 2002) is written specifically for children in foster care. In the children's book *Bringing Aska Home* (Krishnaswami, 2006), children read about how a family changes when a new person is adopted into it. Adopted adolescents may want to search for or meet their birth parents (Krueger & Hanna, 1997), and this can be traumatic, especially if the adolescent is immature or harbors anger and resentment. Adopted teens may exhibit external behaviors such as signs of stress, inability to sleep, trouble concentrating, inability to eat, irritability, or acting out in school. Counselors can help them sort through their feelings, provide support, and help them identify issues involved in possibly meeting their birth parent(s), as well as processing the effects of the meeting after it has taken place.

Counseling Children and Adolescents of Alcoholic Parents

In the United States, 7.6% (18.2 million individuals) aged 12 and older meet the criteria for alcohol dependence or abuse (SAMHSA, 2002). An estimated 9.6 million children under age 17 are living with an adult who is abusing alcohol, and one in every four children is exposed to alcohol abuse or dependence in the family some time before the age of 18 (Grant, 2000). Lambie (2005) estimated that an average school counselor caseload would include approximately 120 students who have been or will be exposed to alcohol abuse or dependence in their family. Gagliardi and colleagues (2006) suggest that the stress involved in alcoholic families results in increased physical, mental, social, and emotional difficulties for children.

Characteristics

Children who grow up in an alcoholic system are severely affected developmentally and are asked to cope with a unique set of difficulties (Lewis, Dana, & Blevins, 2002). When counselors work with children of alcoholic parents, several themes may be evident, including role reversal, low self-esteem, and role confusion (Black, 2002; Lewis, Dana & Blevins, 2002). These children have learned to curb many childhood behaviors as they try to anticipate their parents' reactions, which may be unpredictable and inconsistent. They sometimes appear extremely responsible, competent, and high-achieving and display no outward signs of distress. Having lived their early years behaving like adults, they later describe their experience as "growing up without a childhood."

Alcohol abuse can extend across generations in a family. Children of alcoholics (COAs) are four times more likely than non-COAs to develop alcohol abuse or dependence themselves (Brook et al., 2003). Similarly, children of alcoholics are at increased risk for abusing alcohol and other substances as they get older (Rice et al., 2006). This risk may be influenced by a variety of factors including poor parenting, family conflict and fighting, cognitive dysfunction, and the development of a difficult temperament in the child.

Children who live with alcoholic parents have role confusion because they are expected to be mature like adults when they are at home but are treated as typical children or adolescents by their teachers and peers in school. Determining when to act like a grown-up and when to allow themselves to be a child can be difficult because of the inconsistency of parents who show extreme variations in interactions with their children, ranging from warm to cold, affectionate to distanced, engaged to ignored (Lewis, Dana & Blevins, 2002).

The Research

Some children of alcoholic parents have an elevated risk for psychological, behavioral, and substance abuse problems, but the majority do not (Ohannessian et al., 2006). In this research adolescents were more likely to be influenced by their mother's use of substances than their father's use. Also, adolescents who worry a great deal about their mothers were more likely to have psychological adjustment issues.

In her research, Skibbee (2001) noted that adolescent boys have more stress than girls when they are growing up with an alcoholic parent, either mother or father. The boys in her study had lower self-esteem scores and higher depression scores, and they reported more family disruption and fewer family rituals than the girls did. Christensen and Bilenberg (2000) reported that daughters of alcoholics were more impaired than sons of alcoholics, as measured by the *Child Behavior Check List* (CBCL). They concluded that children of alcoholics should be regarded as a risk group but with heterogeneous consequences in response to parental alcoholism.

In their research with adult children of alcoholics (ACOAs), Anda and colleagues (2002) examined how growing up with alcoholic parents and having adverse childhood experiences are related to the risk of alcoholism and depression in adulthood. In this cohort study, 9,346 adults completed a survey about nine adverse childhood experiences: experiencing childhood emotional, physical, and sexual abuse; witnessing domestic violence; parental separation or divorce; and growing up with drug-abusing, mentally ill, suicidal, or criminal household members. The results showed that the risk of having had all nine of the adverse childhood experiences was significantly greater among the 20% of participants who reported parental alcohol abuse. The researchers concluded that

> children in alcoholic households are more likely to have adverse experiences …. Depression among adult children of alcoholics appears to be largely, if not solely, due to the greater likelihood of having had adverse childhood experiences in a home with alcohol-abusing parents. (p. 1001)

Roles

Historically, children in alcoholic families are said to adopt one of the following roles to maintain the balance of the family system (Alford, 1998; Wegscheider-Cruse, 1989):

1. Family hero
2. Scapegoat
3. Lost child
4. Mascot

Van Wormer and Davis (2003) point out that these roles have not been validated by empirical research and caution against using them to label or stereotype individuals. The counselor should also be mindful that families not having alcohol abuse-related issues may also fit this model and individual children may have qualities from more than one role.

Family Hero

The family hero is usually the oldest child in the family. "Heroes" believe they can push the family toward "normalcy" by being overly responsible (Alford, 1998). Parents may reinforce these behaviors in their children, living their lives vicariously through the hero's achievements. Nonalcoholic parents may turn to the oldest child for emotional support, relying on him or her to meet their need for intimacy.

Heroes feel burdened because of the overwhelming pressure to perform and appear flawless. These children may be lonely and isolated, fearful of allowing anyone to get close to them and discover the great "cover-up." The hero's world is one of perfectionism, isolation, emotional numbness, constantly being on the alert, and feeling hopeless.

Scapegoat

Scapegoats are targets in the family. They are blamed for the family's stress and dysfunction. The scapegoat draws the attention of the parents away from each other. Rather than the adults directing their attention to their abuse of alcohol, they direct their time and effort toward managing the misbehavior of children in the scapegoat role (Wegscheider-Cruse 1989). Parents do not define their alcohol abuse as the source of the family's dysfunction. Instead, they target the scapegoat as the cause of the stress in the family.

These children and adolescents may live out this self-fulfilling prophecy by engaging in troublesome behaviors such as acting-out in school, running away, or engaging in drug use or promiscuous sexual behavior. They typically feel angry, rejected, and hurt.

Lost Child

The "lost child" is commonly the middle child. Lost children feel confused because no one is explaining the reasons for the turmoil, violence, and stress in the family (Wegscheider-Cruse, 1989). They feel lost as to how they fit in the family or what is expected of them as they try to cope. These children and adolescents may be shy, withdrawn, and reluctant to reach out to others for support.

Mascot

The youngest child often assumes the "mascot" role, in which the children are shielded from the effects of the parent's alcoholism (Fields, 2004; Wegscheider-Cruse, 1989). These children may not have the opportunity to become aware of the issues the family is struggling to manage. Because mascots tend to be overindulged by their caregivers, they take on the behaviors of the family jokester or clown. Children in the mascot role may attempt to capture and hold the attention of adults and peers. Acting silly to control situations is common in children and adolescents in the mascot role.

Interventions

Children from alcoholic homes feel powerless to influence the fundamental cause of the family's dysfunction—the parents' drinking. Children in dysfunctional families must try to function in school despite the lack of support from their family (Baker &

Gerler, 2004). Counselors can help their clients understand that, even though they cannot control their parent's drinking, they can manage their own behaviors, feelings, and attitudes in healthy ways and strive for success in school.

Emshoff and Valentine (2006) offer a strength-based program composed of six factors:

1. *Goals.* In supporting children of alcoholics, goals should be to provide information about alcohol, how it affects them and their family, and assure them that they are not alone in this lifestyle.

2. *Participants.* Including others from the family in an intervention increases the likelihood of success, especially if there is a nonalcoholic parent. Grandparents, siblings, faith-based communities, and others should be considered.

3. *Group work.* The children or adolescents should be given opportunities to improve their social skills and social support by networking. This often increases their self-esteem and strengthens relationships.

4. *Teaching coping skills and ways to reduce stress.* Many children of alcoholics attempt to deal with their situation by expecting perfection from themselves. Counselors can help by teaching healthy emotions and problem-solving skills that are developmentally appropriate for the child, with time built-in for practicing these skills.

5. *Fun.* Children and adolescents involved in this family situation are often uptight and hypervigilant, so they should be encouraged to have fun, to relax and play.

Another approach for the counselor is to determine which role children may be filling in the family and then to identify the resiliencies that role may enhance (Wolin & Wolin, 1993). For example:

- Children in the hero role may develop the resiliency of initiative, in which they gain a sense of competence by concentrating on achievement at school or other interests. To strengthen resiliency, counselors can encourage them to become successful and competent and also help them manage their unhealthy drive for perfection.

- Children in the role of scapegoat may have developed the resiliency of insight concerning the families' troubles. Counselors can encourage these children to see things for what they are and help them develop strategies to manage their behavior and emotions that are not self-defeating.

- In the role of lost child, children often develop the resiliency of morality—quietly deciding not to act in hurtful ways toward others. Counselors can encourage their sense of not wanting to harm others and help them build bridges to people outside the family who can offer support and guidance.

- Mascots develop a sense of humor to cope with threatening emotions and use humor to diffuse unpleasant and dangerous situations in the home. Counselors can encourage their humor and at the same time help these children to identify and appropriately express other feelings.

Children from alcoholic families are likely to see the professional school counselor as a safe adult who they may feel comfortable approaching (Lambie, 2005). Because COAs often require mental health services that school counselors are not trained to deliver, school counselors can initiate referrals to agencies such as community mental health and substance abuse treatment centers when indicated.

Counseling Grieving Children and Adolescents

Children and adolescents do not always have the opportunity to grieve because many adults do not understand how they react to loss and, therefore, deny them the opportunity to discuss their grief. Children in the United States are growing up in a society that tends to avoid grief and deny the inevitability of death (Willis, 2002). Many of the social rituals for grieving, such as funerals, were developed to meet adults' needs, and children and adolescents often are not permitted to participate in those activities despite the evidence that participating in these activities helps children and adolescents cope with loss (Andrews & Marotta, 2005).

An estimated 2% of children are bereaved before the age of 18 (Kmietowicz, 2000). The leading cause of deaths of children is accidents, and as they move into the teen years, homicides and suicides are additional leading causes of death, suggesting that a peer's death is often unexpected and the circumstances of the death are often violent (Anderson, 2002). Manifestations in adolescents who have suffered a loss in this way include depression, anxiety, and behavioral disturbances (Kaufman & Kaufman, 2005). Other losses common in the lives of children and adolescents include the death of grandparents, parents, siblings, and teachers. And children and adolescents also grieve the death of pets.

Characteristics

Childhood grief and adult grief differ (Willis, 2002). Children's ages and levels of cognitive development influence their understanding of death. During the preoperational stage of development (ages 2–7) children exhibit magical thinking and egocentricity, are unable to distinguish between thoughts and deeds, and cannot comprehend the irreversibility of death. Therefore, children at this developmental level may believe they caused the death of a loved one because they had a fight with that person. Children may believe that if they wish the person back to life, it will happen, or they may wonder how the deceased can breathe or eat while they are confined inside a coffin (Cohen, et al., 2002; Webb, 2002).

During the concrete operational stage of development (ages 7–11), children demonstrate reduced egocentricity and greater ability for reasoning. These children understand that death is irreversible but may not believe it could happen to them. Their understanding of time permits them to place the inevitability of their own death in the distant future. These children believe that death happens mainly to people who are elderly and sick. The children might personify death as skeletons and ghosts who can chase down potential victims and therefore can be escaped or run away from if one is quick and strong (Webb, 2002).

By the age of 9 or 10, or shortly before they reach formal operational thinking, which begins around age 11 or 12, children perceive death as irreversible, inevitable, and universal (Webb, 2002). These children begin to understand concepts of spirituality and life after death (Cohen et al., 2002). Although age references cannot be taken too literally because they describe only general patterns, the critical point is that children's conception of death progresses over the years from an immature to a mature understanding and will have an impact on the way they grieve the loss.

Webb (2002) suggested that, when children have had a loss, counselors do an assessment to help these children understand how they are experiencing their grief. The assessment involves three groups of factors:

1. Individual factors
2. Factors related to the death
3. Family, social, and religious/cultural factors

Individual Factors

When assessing individual factors, counselors should consider the child's age, developmental level, and temperament. In assessing temperament the counselor is concerned with how children approach routine and stressful life events. For example, children who have approached new situations with difficulty probably will experience more stress in response to a loss than those who approach new situations more comfortably. Though past coping and adjustment may not predict precisely how children will cope with current stress, well adjusted children are likely to have less trouble adjusting to the loss than those who don't deal well with routine daily stresses.

Other individual factors that the counselor can assess are the overall psychological, social, and school functioning by ratings on the global assessment of functioning of the *Diagnostic and Statistical Manual—IV-TR*, Axis V, medical history, because children who are ill have diminished resources for grieving; and past experience with death or loss, as cumulative losses impact the grief response.

Factors Related to the Death

The first factor related to the death is the type of death—anticipated or sudden; preventable; if pain, violence, or trauma accompanied the death; and any stigma surrounding the death. For example, if a child was playing with a friend yesterday and the friend was killed today in an automobile accident, the child likely will feel more anxiety than if a friend who had a terminal illness died and death had been anticipated.

Another factor associated with the death that should be assessed is contact with the deceased—whether the child was given the opportunity to participate in rituals surrounding the death, including being present at the death, viewing the body, attending ceremonies, or visiting the grave. Webb (2002) recommended that children be given the choice of attending these rituals after having been told what these entail. A related factor is the expression of good-bye. Children may benefit from doing something concrete such as writing a poem or placing flowers at the grave.

In addition, the relationship to the deceased is an important factor. The closer the relationship to the person who died, the more of an impact the death is likely to have. Finally, one must consider grief reactions—the feelings the child described or what the family observed about the child, including signs of sadness, anger, confusion, guilt, or relief.

Family, Social, Religious, and Cultural Factors

Family factors include how the family perceives the death and to what extent children are involved in the family's mourning rituals. Some families believe in shielding children from pain, and adults in some families do not express their feelings about the death. In other families adults and children mourn together. In the social area, the counselor can assess the reaction of bereaved children's friends and peers. When children are going through a loss, their friends may treat them differently, resulting in stress because of their desire to fit in.

In the religious and cultural area, the counselor may benefit from knowing what the children have been taught either formally or informally. The counselor should attempt to obtain a sense of their religious beliefs about death, life after death, and their thoughts and feelings about those ideas. Learning as much as possible will aid the counselor in understanding the ways in which specific children process grief.

Mourning may become more complicated if children have more than one stressor, such as the divorce of the parents along with the death of a family member. In mourning the loss of an intact family, such as in the case of a divorce, children get confused because they are mourning the loss of a parent who is not dead.

Sometimes the counselor has difficulty distinguishing between normal grief and symptoms of post-traumatic stress disorder (PTSD) (Cohen et al., 2002; Webb, 2002). The criteria for a PTSD diagnosis include a distressing experience (such as a death or divorce), reexperiencing the traumatic event (commonly upon the anniversary of the loss), avoiding trauma-related stimuli/numbing (forgetting circumstances that surround the loss), increased arousal (becoming irritable), and symptoms that have persisted at least 1 month. Counselors will better understand the grief responses of children and adolescents if they can describe the child's grieving process as normal grief, complicated grief, or post-traumatic stress disorder.

Andrews and Marotta (2005) used a phenomenological approach to study how a sample of children aged 4 to 9 coped with the death of a family member. Five themes emerged from the analysis of the research findings. The two themes of *relationship* and *containment* appeared frequently in the qualitative data. The researchers noted that "primary attachment figures such as parents and friends, even same-age peers, and secondary attachments to pets served as comfort to grieving children and as containment of the intensity of emotions associated with grieving" (p. 43). These researchers also noted that family routines served a containment role because children felt less anxious when the usual routines of household, school, and play were maintained.

The third theme to emerge in the way children coped with loss was the use of *linking objects* as a way of maintaining and developing their relationship with the deceased family member. The children would carry around objects or display objects in their homes, such as photographs, toys, items of clothing belonging to the deceased, or jewelry. These linking objects often were included in the children's drawings about their loss.

The fourth theme, labeled *connections*, describes the spiritual connections that evolve for the children. The authors noted that "the children who had been told that God was also sad about the death were free to be sad themselves" (p. 44).

In the fifth theme, *meaning making*, the authors noted that participants in the study had not made meaning of the deaths. The children could talk about the finality of death but could not link the death to any larger purpose or to how they were deeply impacted by the loss.

Interventions

Worden (2007) offered the following guidelines for counselors to help young clients work through a grief situation and come to resolution:

1. Help survivors actualize the loss. Encouraging them to talk about the facts surrounding the loss can facilitate this.
2. Help them to identify and express feelings such as anger, guilt, anxiety, and helplessness.
3. Assist survivors to live without the deceased, by fostering decision-making and problem-solving.
4. Facilitate emotional withdrawal from the deceased by encouraging the survivors to form new relationships.
5. Allow them time to grieve by explaining that grief takes time and anniversaries of the loss may be particularly painful.
6. Interpret normal behavior by reassuring survivors that these new experiences are common for people in similar situations.
7. Allow for individual differences by reassuring them that not everyone grieves in the same way and that there may be dramatic differences within the same family.
8. Provide continuing support by being available at least for the first year following the loss.
9. Examine the child's defenses and coping styles. After trust has developed, help the survivors examine their coping style and evaluate its effectiveness.
10. Identify any pathology and make an appropriate referral, as some survivors need special interventions to cope with the loss.

Baker, Sedney, and Gross (1992) described the grief process in bereaved children as a series of psychological tasks extending over early, middle, and late phases.

Counselors can use these tasks to structure interventions. For example, the tasks for the early phase of grief for children are to gain an understanding of what has happened. Many children use self-protective mechanisms to protect against being overwhelmed by emotions relating to the loss. Therefore, psychoeducational guidance for the entire family in this phase is appropriate. Counselors can encourage significant adults to explain the circumstances of the loss to answer children's questions. When talking to a child about death, adults should be specific, honest, and concrete, and answer the child's questions as clearly as possible (Willis, 2002).

Cooper (1999) reported that grieving children tend to recall dreams more frequently than non-grieving children do. Therefore, she encourages counselors to introduce the topic of dreams in individual and group counseling sessions with grieving children. She points out that counselors frequently discuss nightmares that children have but overlook asking them about dreams that lack elements of fear. She suggests that these dreams may be a safe starting point for a child to begin examining his or her feelings.

To help families cope during this initial phase of grief, counselors might give parents resources that explain how to talk about death with children. Good sources include *Talking About Death: A Dialogue Between Parent and Child* (Grollman, 1991), *Life & Loss: A Guide to Help Grieving Children* (Goldman, 1999), *Helping Children Cope with Death* (Schuurman, Hoff, Spencer, & White, 1997), and *Thirty-Five Ways to Help a Grieving Child* (Barrett et al., 1999). Web resources are also prevalent, such as *All Kids Grieve* (allkidsgrieve.org) and *Kidsaid* at kidsaid.com. Parents should be cautioned about how children might react to this information. For example, to avoid pain, children may not want to talk about the loss, or after hearing about the loss, they may continue with normal activities such as play while showing no apparent impact. Parents need to know that this is normal.

By providing information and answering questions, including an explanation of their own feelings surrounding the loss, parents can encourage development of the resiliency of insight in their children. Children also may better understand death by reading, so counselors can use bibliotherapy with bereaved children. Good sources include *I Remember Miss Perry* (Brisson, 2006), *Michael Rosen's Sad Book* (Rosen, 2005), *When a Friend Dies: A Book for Teens About Grieving and Healing* (Gootman, 2005), *The Fall of Freddie the Leaf* (Buscaglia, 2002), *Nana Upstairs and Nana Downstairs* (Depaola, 1998), *When I Feel Sad* (Spelman, 2002), *Tear Soup, A Recipe for Healing After Loss* (Schweibert & DeKlyen, 1999), *Where Do People Go When They Die?* (Portnay, 2004), and *After a Suicide: A Workbook for Grieving Kids* (Lindholm, Schuurman, & Hoff, 2001).

Play is an avenue of healing for grieving children (Andrews & Marotta, 2005). The importance of play throughout the grieving process is significant for children who have experienced a loss because through play, they can exercise some control over their grieving. Counselors can use drawings, sand, or puppets to assist children in processing their grief.

In the middle phase of grief, tasks include accepting and reworking the loss and tolerating the psychological pain associated with the loss. During this second phase counselors can use a variety of individual counseling techniques in which the children

- are asked to answer incomplete sentence stems such as, "The memory that I like best of my loved one is when we…," "I'm glad my loved one and I got to….";
- write a story about grief, draw a memory of the deceased person, or draw a picture of what they remember about the funeral;
- write about happy and sad memories of the deceased and keep these stories and drawings in a book;
- write a letter to the deceased person expressing their feelings; and
- keep a journal in which they record thoughts and feelings about the loss.

Bereavement groups are suited to the tasks of the middle phase of grief (Haasl & Marnocha, 2000a, 2000b). Children who have had a loss may feel different from their peers, so being a member of a bereavement group allows them to be with others in a similar situation, which reduces their sense of being different. Groups composed of children in different stages of the grieving process are especially beneficial because middle-phase children tend to be more likely to rework their own loss when they hear how children in the later stage have coped.

Morganett (1994) outlined an eight-session group-counseling intervention for bereaved children. It is designed to help children realize that others have experienced loss, to label and express feelings about the loss, to say good-bye to a deceased person, to understand that funerals are not to be feared, to understand the stages of grief, to understand the causes of death, and to express sympathy to a grieving person. Murphy and colleagues (1997) developed a 10- to 12-week trauma/grief-focused group psychotherapy model for elementary school children.

At the late phase of grief for children, tasks include consolidating the child's identity and resuming normal developmental tasks. These children also can be resources for children who are in the early phases of grieving. Offering support to children in the earlier phases of grief can help children in the later phase to integrate the loss they suffered and begin getting on with their lives (Yalom & Leszcz, 2005).

Children and adolescents cannot be protected from loss. To try to shelter or protect them is futile. Instead, an approach that involves calmly presenting the reality of the situation, answering questions honestly, helping them find support so they don't feel different, and acknowledging that their grief will be different from adults' grief will assist them in dealing with loss in ways that build resiliency.

Counseling Gay and Lesbian Youth

According to Gutierrez (2006), "queer adolescents are the least visible of the adolescent minority groups" (p. 331). Since the 1990s, lesbian, gay, and bisexual youth have moved from invisibility to an awareness of the development of sexual identity in childhood and adolescence. Even so, dealing with the realization of adolescent homosexuality is still both challenging and complicated (Huegel, 2003).

Gay and lesbian youth experience harassment and abuse as they try to discover who they are in a predominantly heterosexual society (Varjas et al., 2006). They struggle to cope with a variety of issues including isolation, as most adolescents try to keep their orientation hidden; family issues such as parental rejection; health risks including AIDS, drug and alcohol abuse, and suicide; and educational issues, because many schools do not promote tolerance and acceptance of homosexuality (Cooley, 1998). Gay and lesbian youth also struggle in school and sometimes show poor academic performance, have relationship problems, and become the targets of school violence (Varjas et al., 2006). Gutierrez (2006) refers to these youth as the "invisible" group because they generally hide their true feelings from others. Gay and lesbian youth most likely will need assistance in coping with these difficult situations.

Characteristics

Gay and lesbian youth are four times more likely than other teens to attempt suicide. Suicide attempts by lesbian and gay youth range from 20% to 42% of this population, in comparison to a rate for heterosexual high school students of 8% to 13% (Ryan & Futterman, 2001a). The increased suicide rates for gay and lesbian teens are affected by factors that inhibit the development of a positive gay identity, such as emotional deprivation, physical or sexual abuse, stress, and prejudices. Lesbian and gay youth, for example, often report chronic stress as a result of verbal or physical abuse, or harassment from family members or peers.

Homosexual identity itself does not cause suicide. A study conducted by Rutter (2006) indicates that gay, lesbian, and bisexual (GLB) youth score higher on suicidal ideation scales, and they express hopelessness to a significantly higher degree than their heterosexual counterparts. Rutter further reported that these GLB youth lacked social support from friends, family, and school staff, as well as a sense of belonging. This led to feelings of disconnectedness.

This is exacerbated by marginalization of gay, lesbian, bisexual, and transgender (GLBT) youth that is fed by hatred and prejudice in the community (Gutierrez, 2006). Granello and Granello (2007) described this as a "widespread stigmatization and institutionalized discrimination against the GLBT population (that) leads both to externally derived hostility and internalized homophobia" (p. 136). Because most gay and lesbian youth lack positive adult models and support systems, they can easily conclude that they have little hope of becoming happy or productive adults (Owens, 2001).

Previously, gays and lesbians were less vocal because their survival depended on separating their social, professional, and emotional lives. Today's generation of gay and lesbian youth have an opportunity to live fully integrated lives. The average age of self-identification has been decreasing. Gay and lesbian adults indicated that their self-identification occurred between the ages of 19 and 23, and lesbian and gay adolescents reported self-identification at age 16 (Ryan & Futterman, 2001b). For some youth, the recognition that they may be attracted to a person of the same sex may occur as early as age 10 (McClintock & Herdt, 1996). Self-identification at a younger age means more stress, more negative social pressure, and more need for support. Because the students are struggling with these critical issues, the school counselor must be prepared to assist them appropriately.

Approximately 15% of acquired immunodeficiency syndrome (AIDS) cases in the United States through 2005 are young men and women in their 20s (Centers for Disease Control, 2007). Because people with HIV are typically asymptomatic for 7 to 10 years prior to the AIDS diagnosis, they most likely were infected during their teens. Young men who have sex with men (MSM), especially those of minority races or ethnicities, are at high risk for HIV infection (Centers for Disease Control, 2005).

Gay and lesbian youth encounter academic and social problems in school. After interviewing 119 GLB adults, Rivers (2004) reported that 26% of the subjects in his study indicated they had been or continued to be distressed regularly by recollections of bullying in school. They have increased social risk factors including high school dropout, and a sense of social isolation and loneliness contributes to their difficulty at school (Remafedi & Shelby, 1998). They often lack peer-group identification because they withdraw from typical adolescent peer-group experiences. Socializing with either gender is difficult because if they date the opposite sex, they could be discovered, and acting toward same-sex friends in any way that demonstrates intimacy might lead to discovery. The result is isolation and feeling like "I'm the only one" and "I don't fit in anywhere."

Homophobia and unsupportive social institutions affect their emotional and social development. Most gay and lesbian adults have been targets of anti-gay verbal abuse or threats. The average high school student hears anti-gay remarks 25 times a day, and teachers who hear these remarks fail to respond most of the time (Callahan, 2001). Nearly 17% of reported hate crimes were motivated by a bias toward the victim's sexual orientation (U.S. Department of Justice, 2001). Ryan and Futterman (2001a) reported, "Surveys of bias-related experiences among adult lesbian and gay men show that during their lifetimes, more than half had experienced some kind of violence because of their sexual orientation" (p. 6). A survey of more than 4,000 students in the landmark Youth Risk Behavior Study (Massachusetts Department of Education, 1999) found that gay males and lesbians were twice as likely to report being in a physical fight in school, three times as likely to be threatened with a weapon, and almost four times more likely to miss school than their non-gay peers.

Gay adolescents quickly learn that knowledge of their sexual orientation may have a negative effect on their treatment by family, friends, and social institutions such as schools, churches, and employers. But several recent court cases, as well as changes in the federal Title IX guidelines prohibiting sex discrimination, have created a clear duty for school districts to protect gay and lesbian students from sexual harassment (McFarland & Dupuis, 2001). School administrators now must ensure that gay and lesbian students are provided a safe educational environment, and ignoring this type of sexual harassment could be costly.

To remain hidden, these students engage in various coping behaviors. They sometimes date the opposite sex even though they are not erotically or emotionally attracted to their dates. They may avoid gym class. Some vocally denounce homosexuality as a way to prove to others that they are not gay. Young lesbians have even become pregnant in some cases to show that they are heterosexual. Still other gays and lesbians turn to casual sex with strangers so they can separate or keep their sexuality hidden from other facets of themselves. For gays and lesbians, the result of all these coping behaviors can be a sense of inferiority and worthlessness and a tearing apart of the person rather than integrating their sexual orientation into their identity.

Interventions

School counselors can serve as a first resource for sexual-minority youth (Stone, 2003). Educational information about gay and lesbian topics that has been developed for English, history, and social studies classes can be shared with all students. Curriculum materials such as Project 10 (Urbide, 1991) address issues such as challenging the myths and stereotypes surrounding homosexuality, exploring issues related to families of gay and lesbian youth, and correcting misinformation about homosexuality.

All students can be given the opportunity to learn about homosexuality through contact with positive gay and lesbian adult role models. Reading lists of positive books regarding gay and lesbian lives can be made available. Good resources for individuals who want to learn more include:

Is it a Choice? (Marcus, 2005)
Challenging Lesbian and Gay Inequalities in Education (Epstein, 1994)
Children of Horizons: How Gay and Lesbian Teens are Leading a New Way Out of the Closet (Herdt & Boxer, 1996)
Dangerous Liaisons: Blacks, Gays, and the Struggle for Equality (Brandt, 1999)
Gay Parents, Straight Schools: Building Communication and Trust (Casper & Schultz, 1999)
GLBTQ: The Survival Guide for Queer and Questioning Teens (Huegel, 2003)
One Teacher in Ten: Gay and Lesbian Educators Tell Their Stories (Jennings, 2005)
Transliberation: Beyond Pink and Blue (Feinberg, 1998)
School's Out: The Impact of Gay and Lesbian Issues on America's Schools (Woog, 1995)
Straight Parents, Gay Children: Inspiring Families to Live Honestly and with Greater Understanding (Bernstein, 1999)
Strong Women, Deep Closets: Lesbians and Homophobia in Sport (Griffin, 1998)
Free Your Mind: The Book for Gay, Lesbian, and Bisexual Youth and Their Allies (Bass & Kaufman, 1996)
The Shared Heart: Portraits and Stories Celebrating Lesbian, Gay, and Bisexual Young People (Mastoon, 2001).

Effective support groups for gay and lesbian youth or for their parents need not explore in-depth the psychological issues but, rather, attend to developmental issues such as decision-making and elevating the self-esteem (Gutierrez, 2006). Muller and Hartman (1998) outlined a 15-session group counseling intervention for sexual-minority youth. Topics of the group sessions include relationships with parents, stages in the coming-out process, coping with homophobia, clarifying values, adult male and female homosexual speakers, and field trips to gay and lesbian community centers.

School counselors can play a significant role in assisting student in their coming-out process. Some counselors do this well, but others do not seem to be prepared to handle this concern. In a seminal study called *Hatred in the Hallways* (Human Rights Watch, 2006) the researchers report that there are "attacks on the human rights of lesbian, gay, bisexual, and transgender youth who are subjected to abuse on a daily basis by their peers and in some cases by teachers and school administrators" (p. 3). This study reported some negative feedback regarding counselors who were misinformed or who held strong negative attitudes. Of significance was the importance of maintaining confidentiality when students confide in their counselor. Students reported that their counselors did not discuss confidentiality concerns with them and, even more unethical, some counselors "outed" students to parents or to administrators (Human Rights Watch, 2006).

In research conducted by Varjas and colleagues (2006), the students reported a lack of willingness to utilize school counselors because of confidentiality concerns. Davis, Williamson, and Lambie (2005) strongly suggest that school counselors raise awareness regarding their own biases, values, and prejudices and confront these if they are to work in a school setting. If counselors want to be trusted by gay, lesbian, or questioning youth, they will have to prove themselves to be ethical and trustworthy.

Teachers and parents may need information and support as they try to understand the issues of gay and lesbian youth. Parents of gay and lesbian youth may be served through support groups such as Parents and Friends of Lesbians and Gays (PFLAG), to discuss their concerns with other parents in similar situations. The National Education Association encourages schools to establish policies and programs that recognize and support GLBT youth (National Education Association (2007). Inservice programs can be developed to educate the school and agency staff about gay and lesbian youth. Counselors should be aware of appropriate referral sources within their communities for serving gay and lesbian youth and their families.

Although models of homosexual identity development vary, the general pattern seems to be one of moving from early awareness, through confusion, to an initial embracing of the gay identity, and finally to an affirmation of the gay identity. In his review of identity development models, Savin-Williams (2005) cautions against the use of a comprehensive theory of sexual identity development. Instead, he proposes that the sexual identity development of adolescents unfolds within a framework based on the following four tenets:

1. Same-sex-attracted teenagers are similar to all other adolescents in their developmental trajectories.

2. Same-sex-attracted teenagers are dissimilar from heterosexual adolescents in their developmental trajectories.

3. Same-sex-attracted teenagers vary among themselves in their developmental trajectories, and this can be similar to the ways in which heterosexual teens vary among themselves.

4. The developmental trajectory of a given person is similar to that of no other person who has ever lived. (p. 84)

Gay and lesbian youth may have fewer traumas as they construct their identities if they view their development and its challenges as opportunities for enhancing resiliencies (Savin-Williams, 2005).

> Given the documented levels of intimidation and harassment young gay people receive, the fact that the vast majority of them do not attempt suicide is noteworthy; it suggests that these teenagers have exceptional, but unacknowledged, coping skills and resiliency (p. 184).

When parents are informed about their child's homosexuality, they commonly react with shock, disappointment, grief, or denial. Because parents may be preoccupied with their own adjustment, gay or lesbian youth might have to develop supportive relationships outside the family.

Contact with other gay and lesbian youths and adults can be critical in establishing a positive identity. And gay and lesbian youth need access to accurate information about homosexuality so they can acquire insight into their thoughts, feelings, and behaviors and work through their confusion resulting from the presumption of heterosexuality. Counselors can acknowledge and facilitate the development of resiliencies such as insight and relationships in gay and lesbian youth so they may develop into successful adults who are secure in their sexual orientation and excited by the limitless possibilities for their future.

Counseling Children and Adolescents With Eating Difficulties

Children and adolescents get caught in and succumb to destructive cultural messages about body weight. These messages can become an obsession that fills young people with shame, depletes their energy, and inhibits them from normal development and feelings of success. The problems that children and adolescents face regarding eating are staggering (Berg, 2001). Neumark-Sztainer (2007) defined these problems as "significant public health problems in adolescents because of their high prevalence and their harmful physical, behavioral, and psychosocial consequences" (p. 11).

According to Wright (2006), "The standard for body size and weight is socially determined. It is a cultural phenomenon that demands that the current ideal physique is slim" (p. 167). When children become indoctrinated by messages such as this, they begin to fear food and, in essence, quit eating for fear of becoming fat.

Eating disorders have increased rapidly over the last three decades (Wright, 2006). Scott and Sobczak (2002) differentiated disordered eating problems that are problematic, such as fear of being fat, bingeing, restrictive dieting, and compulsive exercise from eating disorders that are clinical—more serious issues including anorexia, bulimia, and binge eating.

More than half of adults are dieting at any given time. An estimated one in 10 teens is struggling with a potentially fatal eating disorder (Berg, 2001). Results of the National Eating Disorders Screening Project, as reported by Austin and colleagues (2001), found that 30% of high school girls and 16% of high school boys participated in disordered eating behaviors including bingeing, vomiting, fasting, compulsive exercise, and consuming laxatives and diet pills. Children as young as third grade speak of "watching my weight." Berg (2001) claims that "weight issues have become an obsessive concern for American girls and boys of all ages, of every racial and ethnic heritage" (p. 18).

Characteristics

Poor eating habits in children and adolescents set the stage for more severe eating disorders such as anorexia nervosa (self-imposed starvation) and bulimia (cyclic bingeing and purging of food). Adolescents are at high-risk for developing eating disorders that seem to interact with the stress, anxiety, and vulnerability that coincide with puberty and maturation. In addition to age, Wright (2006) identified some risk factors associated with eating disorders, as follows:

1. *Gender.* More females than males report anorexia and bulimia, although males also are susceptible, especially to bulimia. Girls who previously were open to many options for careers and futures suddenly are placing an inordinate amount of energy on how they look rather than developing their identity, as well as developing peer attachments. There is a growing incidence of adolescent males with eating disorders, especially boys involved in athletics, boys struggling with their sexual identity, and those with family problems (Ray, 2004).

2. *Socioeconomic level.* The popular view permeating U.S. society has suggested that anorexia and bulimia tend to affect people from the middle to upper-middle socioeconomic class and obesity is associated with lower status. This is more of a myth that is perpetuated because families with resources tend to get help and treatment more often. "Eating disturbances are equally common among all socioeconomic and ethnic groups" (Scott & Sobczak, 2002, p. 13).

3. *Family characteristics.* Families with eating disorders tend to have other dysfunctional patterns such as alcoholism, emotional disorders, and dysfunctional conflict (Vandereychen, 2002).

4. *Social norms.* Certain social norms are also associated with eating disorders. Adolescent girls are taught early that, to be acceptable, they must sacrifice parts of themselves. The message sent to them is that they will be judged by their

appearance and thinness, not their talent, creativity, or ability. Girls use these unrealistic standards to judge their suitability for belonging and being accepted by their peers, including boys. This causes girls to develop a false self, one that is culturally based and the one they present in public (Pipher, 2005). The media saturate girls in how to do this, with emphasis on make-up, clothing, and weight. At the same time, the real issues that girls struggle with, such as careers, sports, hobbies, and maturity, are played down (Pipher, 2005). Boys, too, are caught in this un-nurturing web. They are taught to be "macho," take control, and exploit femaleness.

Eating Patterns

Children and adolescents who have eating difficulties present several different eating patterns to counselors. Berg (2001) organized eating patterns, as well as the effects of negative eating on normal development and relationships, into three categories: normal eating, dysfunctional eating, and eating disorders. Counselors can assess their clients' eating patterns according to these three categories.

Normal Eating

Children with normal eating patterns tend to eat regularly throughout the day, eat for nourishment as well as social reasons, and report feeling good about eating. Their weight is acceptable within a wide range of normal weight.

Disordered Eating

Disordered eaters are involved in a more chaotic, irregular eating pattern, skipping meals and overeating at others. They eat for reasons other than nourishment, such as shaping the body, reducing stress or anxiety, boredom, or loneliness. Children and adolescents who show disordered eating behaviors may develop physical symptoms such as feeling tired, lacking energy, or appearing apathetic. Their growth may be retarded or the onset of puberty delayed.

Often, disordered eating is linked to other serious at-risk behaviors such as use of drugs, alcohol, and tobacco, unprotected sex, dating violence, and even suicide (Scott & Sobczak, 2002). Mentally, these students tend to be less alert and unable to concentrate, which can influence their school performance negatively. They may lose interest in their friends and school and isolate themselves. They may have mood swings and become easily upset or irritable. Dieting impairs a person's ability to think and to learn effectively (U.S. Department of Health and Human Services, Office on Women's Health, 2000). As their dysfunctional eating habits escalate, they may develop an eating disorder (Berg, 2001).

Eating Disorders

Nearly 10% of high school students have some kind of eating disorder. Adolescents with eating disorders report eating for purposes other than nourishment or enjoyment. They are motivated by external or internal controls such as stress, anger, or pain.

Early on, Omizo and Omizo (1992) summarized the physical symptoms of anorexia and bulimia as including extreme weight loss, hair loss, edema (swelling), skin abnormalities, lethargy, and discoloration of teeth. They reported behavioral signs as frequent trips to the bathroom, avoiding snack foods, abnormal eating habits, frequent weighing, substance abuse, and social avoidance. These researchers reported common psychological signs including low self-esteem, external locus of control, feelings of helplessness, depression, anxiety, anger, perfectionism, and over-concern with body size. Victims may spend more than 90% of their waking time focusing on food, hunger, and weight issues (Berg, 2001).

In a study conducted by the National Center for Health Statistics (Centers for Disease Control, 2003), the prevalence of overweight children increased more than 100% between 1980 and 2000, with more than 15% of children 6–11 years of age considered overweight. For adolescents, the percentage of overweight children has increased 150%, from 5% in 1980 to more than 15% in 2000. Although some children and adolescents become overweight for genetic reasons, the most frequent reason cited is that children are less active. Based on the cultural pressure to be thin, overweight youngsters often develop shame and hatred for their bodies. Dieting should be discouraged as a meaningful intervention because most of the time it is unsuccessful and actually does more harm than good to students.

Interventions

Scott and Sobczak (2002) offered a new approach to working with children and adolescents, stating, "To resist dieting and eating disorders, people must embrace their bodies as they are, and pursue lifestyle changes that include healthy eating and exercise" (p. 15). In this "Body Positive's Body Aloud" approach, Scott and Sobczak suggested five principles to prevent eating disorders:

1. Help the young person find his or her own solutions to problems with eating and body image. Listen actively, ask appropriate questions, and honor the student's experiences and perceptions.
2. Help young people say no to dieting. Instead, encourage students to eat healthy. Allow them to reclaim their own natural physiological cues that tell them when to eat and when to stop.
3. Help children and adolescents to feel shame-free about their bodies and to care for their bodies by promoting health no matter what their size.
4. Help students to decode their "I feel fat" messages. Every time children say this about themselves, they pay an awful price that leads to discouragement and despair. Create a supportive and safe environment.
5. Support multidimensional change in the lives of students. This includes the need to talk with teachers, students, parents, and health providers to improve the environment in which young people live.

To assess an eating problem, especially an eating disorder, the services of a physician are needed. Collaborating with the medical expert can assist the counselor in understanding medications and proper diets and watching for side-effects. If the medical condition of the person is severe, close monitoring or even hospitalization may be necessary.

Counselors must develop a strong therapeutic relationship with the student and work to establish trust and support. Eclectic approaches (Wright, 2006), behavioral approaches (Thompson, Rudolph, & Henderson, 2004), and family approaches (Vandereychen, 2002) are helpful in treating eating disorders. To be effective, treatment must be directed to the behavioral, cognitive, emotional, and interpersonal difficulties of children and adolescents. The counselor may have to challenge the irrational beliefs inherent in their thinking about body image and self-esteem. Determining how they handle stress and emotions also provides insight into possible dysfunctional behaviors. The counselor's goal is to increase students' awareness so they can express their feelings and develop resiliency, as well as positive coping strategies.

The counselor might start a disordered-eating support group to complement individual counseling with these young people (Omizo & Omizo, 1992). In a group, members often feel less alone with their symptoms, and they receive feedback from peers. Group members can challenge each other's beliefs and values while offering support for each other during their recovery. Group sessions should challenge stereotypical thinking about traditional female and male role behaviors, encourage sharing their fears about sexuality and adulthood, and teach social competency skills to deal with peer, parent, and societal pressures.

Parenting skills may have to be addressed so parents can help to set realistic expectations for their children and adolescents. Parents can help to debunk pressures from media, peers, and the culture regarding gender role differences for their sons and daughters so their children do not have to compromise their development of a true self (Pipher, 2005). School counselors and teachers should be trained in how to detect early signs of potential eating problems (Bardick et al., 2004; Wright, 2006). Students who are having eating difficulties should be referred to the school counselor and specialists early, when interventions can be most effective.

Bardick and colleagues (2004) suggested that cognitive behavior therapeutic approaches are the most successful for youth who have eating disorders. They suggested that school counselors consider three phases in working with students who have an eating disorder: "(a) restoration of a healthy weight and/or normalization of eating, (b) significant changes in thought and behavior, and (c) relapse prevention" (p. 171).

Interventions directed at improving body image are critical to helping youth who struggle with disordered eating. Choate (2007) proposed a model that school counselors can use with girls that identifies five protective factors to build resilience and helps girls resist sociocultural pressures to be thin. Strategies for working with boys to address their body image suggested by Stout and Wiggins-Frame (2004) include both individual and group counseling, as well as consulting efforts with parents and school staff. Ray (2004) also addressed the need to focus on boys because factors associated with athletics, sexual identity, mental disorders, and family issues are risk factors for eating disorders.

School personnel must be cognizant of the particular risk factors for students who are cheerleaders, drill team members, wrestlers, track team members, and gymnasts. These students already live in a society that encourages perfectionism and competitiveness, in which weight and appearance are critical to survival, success, and worth. Educational and prevention programs should include these groups of students and others in building awareness and providing early intervention for those who are struggling with early symptoms (Wright, 2006). The National Association for Anorexia Nervosa and Associated Disorders (ANAD) is a good resource.

Counseling School-Age Children and Adolescents Affected by Terrorist Acts

Students of all ages who witness, experience, or hear about acts of terrorism are likely to incur severe psychological effects. Children in the United States who never witnessed an attack on their country before September 11, 2001, had no frame of reference for that event or how to respond. Early television coverage of the attacks on the World Trade Centers included images of airplanes crashing into skyscrapers and people jumping to their deaths from the burning buildings. Young children saw these horrific pictures, and Chibbaro and Jackson (2006) suggested that "school-aged students in the United States are one of the most vulnerable populations in the event of a terrorist act" (p. 314).

Characteristics

"Studies of the effects of disasters and tragedies that have occurred during the past 20 years have taught that youth are influenced by the salient events surrounding them" (Burnham, 2007, p. 465). In her research, Burnham found that television exposure had a strong and negative effect on children, with a greater effect on younger children. She also observed that the fears of younger children who were cognitively less developed were more vivid and intense. Her study indicated that the availability of counseling services after a disaster are beneficial for children, especially when the interventions are developmentally relevant.

Although a precise reaction to a devastating event such as a terror attack is difficult to predict, children and adolescents will have some probable responses. First, a traumatic event can impact children's assumptions about how safe and secure their world is. Secure children turn into frightened children. Denial is another typical initial reaction. While in denial, they may appear to be unaffected by what is going on around them. Other common reactions include nightmares, sleep disturbances, and changes in eating patterns. Some children regress emotionally or act younger than their chronological age. Parents may notice that their children are more clingy and unhappy or more demanding of parental time and attention. Some families see increased levels of aggression and violence in their children. Children also may complain of headaches, stomachaches, or sweating (National Association of School Psychologists, 2002).

Fear may be the major reaction—fear about the safety of themselves and their families or the threat of further terrorism. Media coverage may magnify their sense of danger. Another emotional response in children is loss of control as they realize that neither they nor adults can control the attackers. Many children and adolescents have reacted with anger, possibly blaming people in other countries for the attacks. Another emotional response is the loss of trust and sense of security as a result of the unsettling effect of the attack on the child's sense of stability. Children who have relatives or friends where the attack occurs may worry about the safety of their friends (American School Counselor Association, 2001).

Some children and adolescents act out traumas through repeated dreams or in the way they play. Other children react by withdrawing from people or refusing to talk about their irritability, anger, sadness, fear, or guilt. Many children are reluctant to initiate a conversation about the event, and others talk sporadically about it, concentrating on certain aspects of the tragedy. They avoid any activities that remind them of the event.

Children and adolescents may react to acts of terrorism by losing interest in school and showing poor concentration in activities that normally interest them. Because children react to how their caregivers respond to the events, students will be disturbed to the extent that they see disturbance in adults. Symptoms vary, and the more severe symptoms could indicate that a student is experiencing post-traumatic stress disorder or depression (National Association of School Psychologists, 2002).

In a study by Auger, Seymour, and Roberts (2004), the 89 school counselors surveyed were asked about their perceptions of the impact of 9/11 on their students. They reported high levels of student distress immediately following the attack, but this distress dissipated over the next 6 weeks. School counselors reported using a variety of activities to meet students' mental health needs, including providing more access to counselors, giving information to parents and teachers, and offering support groups for students.

Interventions

To help students cope with reactions to a terrorist act, the counselor's main goal is to help them describe the impact the event has had on them. Asking questions is more important than giving advice. Counselors can reassure students about how safe they really are and point out that people are available to assist them and be near them as they work through the impact of this event. Counselors should give clear messages about not showing disrespect to any people involved or shifting the focus to the negative effects of hatred and intolerance.

Other recommendations for counselors who work with children and adolescents include the following (American School Counselor Association, 2001):

- Provide support, rest, comfort, food, and an opportunity to play or draw.
- Clarify issues about which students are confused.
- Provide emotional labels for the children's reactions.
- Tolerate regressive symptoms in a time-limited fashion.

- Permit the students to talk and act it out; address distortions; acknowledge the normalcy of their feelings and reactions.
- Encourage students to express fear, anger, sadness, and other emotions in your supportive presence.
- Offer to help the children tell their parents how they are feeling.
- Allow time for the students to work through their responses to the event and to grieve.

Counselors might suggest to parents how they can be helpful to their children as they cope with this event (American School Counselor Association, 2001):
- Tolerate regression.
- Give special indulgences and extra nurturing.
- Help children put their words to what this means to them.
- Don't feed their fears—don't give them additional things to worry about.
- Limit their exposure to television coverage.
- Keep them from becoming engulfed in seriousness all the time. Encourage normal routine activities including play.

Juhnke (2002) described the Adapted Family Debriefing Model for school students, developed as an assessment and intervention method specifically for school-age children and adolescents exposed to violence. This first requires a debriefing with a group of the students' parents (usually fewer than 12), then a joint student–parent debriefing. The primary goals of the parent session are to inform the parents of possible symptoms their children may exhibit, to offer referral sources, and to explain the parental role as validating their children and normalizing the children's concerns.

During the joint student–parent debriefing, two circles are formed. Five or six students sit in the inner circle, and the parents sit behind their children. The model prescribes three roles for team members.

1. The leader explains the debriefing process, creates a supportive atmosphere, identifies those with excessive levels of emotional discomfort, and directs the other team members via hand signals to intervene with distraught students or parents. The leader discusses normal reactions, as well as more severe symptoms, with the students and parents
2. Co-leaders add comments to support the leader. The primary role of the co-leaders is to offer immediate support to students and parents who become emotionally distraught.
3. The doorkeeper prevents non-participants from entering the session and distraught students or parents from bolting from the session.

The debriefing process is composed of seven steps:

1. *Introduction.* The team leader identifies members of the team and establishes rules for the debriefing, explains confidentiality and the purposes of the

debriefing as: to help student survivors of terrorism to better understand their feelings, increase their coping skills, and gain solace.

2. *Fact-gathering*. The leader may begin by asking what the students saw on television. The emphasis is on the students telling the facts of what each saw or encountered. At this stage, participants are not asked to describe their feelings.

3. *Thought*. This is a transitional step from cognitive to affective responses. The leader asks questions to elicit students' thoughts at the time of the terrorist act.

4. *Reaction*. Participants discuss the most difficult or surprising part of seeing or hearing about the incident. This is the step at which strong emotions are expressed.

5. *Symptom*. The leader facilitates the group's movement from the affective step back to the cognitive domain. The leader may ask about any physical, cognitive, or affective symptoms that anyone in the group has experienced since the violent episode. Symptoms might include nausea, trembling hands, inability to concentrate, or feelings of anxiety. The leader might ask for a show of hands of those who had any of these symptoms.

6. *Teaching*. The leader normalizes the symptoms described by the participants. Possible future symptoms, such as recurring dreams of being attacked, are described briefly. The leader inquires about what the participants have done to help them handle the situation. Young children might report active fantasy such as a cartoon hero protecting them. Older students might report turning to peers for support.

7. *Re-entry*. The leader asks group members to mention any other concerns or thoughts they have. Then the debriefing team makes a few comments about the group's progress or visible group support. The team might distribute a handout for students and one for adults discussing common reactions or symptoms.

Juhnke (2002) recommended that after the session, team members should mingle with parents and children, serve refreshments, and pay particular attention to those who appear shaken. Those in severe distress should be encouraged to meet individually with a counselor. Counselors can offer critically important services to children and their families as they attempt to cope with effects of overwhelming violent acts.

A preventive, strategic model (Chibbaro & Jackson, 2006, p. 317) has been suggested for school counselors, which can be used to prepare students to cope with terrorism by alleviating their fear and strengthening resilience, as follows.

1. Stay reality-based.
2. Express emotions.
3. Develop concepts of life and death.
4. Develop self-efficacy and a sense of control.
5. Develop coping skills.
6. Encourage action by engagement in humanitarian efforts.

This model offers a way to educate students about living in a world where terrorism exists and shows how school counselors can provide a means to minimize students' fears and develop necessary coping skills for the 21st century.

▮▮Jessie

Jessie's father, who had divorced his wife a year ago, brought 15-year-old Jessie to the counselor. Less than a month previously, his former wife had been killed in an auto accident.

Jessie and her father agreed to six sessions with the counselor. When the counselor asked about her mother's death, Jessie was unresponsive. The counselor empathized how difficult that must be and then asked Jessie about her parents' divorce, if she had questions about the divorce that she still wanted to ask her dad. Jessie responded that she understood that her parents just couldn't get along and realized that the divorce might have been best for everyone. She said she was able to talk with a favorite grandparent about her parents and all their problems.

In subsequent sessions the counselor asked Jessie to describe her feelings about the divorce, how she dealt with those feelings, and what she said to herself that helped her deal with these feelings. The counselor validated Jessie's emotions and explained that adolescents typically feel this way prior to, during, and after a divorce. The counselor complimented Jessie on her insight about her parents' divorce, her initiative in developing self-statements to cope with this difficult situation, and the supportive relationship with her grandparent. The counselor pointed out that not all teenagers could do these things.

During the sixth session the counselor asked Jessie if she wanted to contract for another six sessions. Jessie and her father agreed to additional counseling sessions. During their next meeting the counselor asked Jessie about her goals for counseling. Jessie responded that she wanted to talk about her mom's death. Since then, she had been having trouble sleeping, couldn't concentrate on her schoolwork, and was feeling sad. Jessie had been with her mother only two days before the accident, and she felt shocked when she was told her mother had died. The counselor asked Jessie if she had attended her mother's funeral, and Jessie replied that she had. The counselor asked about her thoughts and feelings at the funeral. Jessie said she felt sad, cried, hurt inside, and wished she had said some important things to her mother while she was alive. The counselor assessed Jessie's mourning as complicated rather than normal because of her parents' recent divorce and the unexpectedness of her mother's death.

The counselor suggested that Jessie write a letter to her mother telling her the things she wished she had said. She brought the completed letter to their next meeting and read it to the counselor, who reflected the themes and feelings. Jessie cried as she read the letter. The counselor gave her a book, *How It Feels When a Parent Dies* (Krementz, 1988), and asked her to read several of the interviews with children and adolescents who had lost a parent.

During their next session the counselor asked Jessie to complete another homework assignment—writing a final letter to her mother to say good-bye and listing ways she would remember her mom. When Jessie returned for the sixth session, she read the good-bye letter to the counselor, who reflected its themes and feelings. Jessie said she would remember her mom by carrying her picture with her always.

The counselor complimented Jessie on her creativity and her ability to express honest feelings. Then she asked Jessie if she would like more counseling sessions to talk about her mom. Jessie responded "no" but indicated that her dad was going to remarry and she was worried. The counselor asked Jessie if she wanted to contract for six more sessions, and she and her father agreed.

Jessie explained that since her mom's death, her dad expected her to be the "woman of the house." She felt angry about all the responsibility but she also liked "having more say around the house." She could decide when to go to bed, how much television to watch, and no one except her dad could tell her what to do. She was worried that when he would remarry, her stepmother would try to "run my life." The woman her father planned to marry had a son, older than Jessie, and Jessie was concerned that he would "take over the house." The counselor empathized with her story, validated her feelings, and encouraged Jessie to keep a personal journal to record her thoughts, feelings, and questions about the remarriage. The counselor asked Jessie if she would agree to the counselor's informing Jessie's father about her concerns. Jessie agreed to the counselor's speaking with her dad.

The counselor told the father that Jessie had concerns about her impending role in the blended family and suggested that he explain to Jessie what the roles of everyone in the new family would be—especially who would be responsible for discipline. The counselor explained to him that, as a typical adolescent, Jessie may be confused and angry as she tries to figure out how "close" or how much "space" she needs from people in the stepfamily. The counselor pointed out that it is normal for adolescents in newly blended families to struggle with strong emotions such as anger, helplessness, jealousy, guilt, and fear as they give up the special role they had prior to the remarriage.

Later in counseling with Jessie, the counselor gave her the book *Stepliving for Teens: Getting Along with Stepparents and Siblings* (Block & Bartell, 2001). The counselor discussed the book with her, encouraged her to investigate additional activities at school to develop new interests, helped her develop a list of topics to discuss with her father, and discussed the results of those dialogues between Jessie and her dad. Although still feeling she might be "betraying my real mom," Jessie was becoming less anxious and fearful about the new stepfamily.

During their final session the counselor asked Jessie to summarize what she considered to be the most important aspects of their work. Jessie indicated that she was glad she had an opportunity to say good-bye to her mother, and to blend into the new stepfamily without "too much trouble."

The counselor shook Jessie's hand one last time, wished her well, and invited her to return if she felt the need. The counselor was inspired by this young person's incredible life, as she had encountered major issues beyond her control, faced them, and moved toward becoming a resilient, integrated, competent, and successful adult.

Summary

Many children and adolescents encounter traumatic situations as they grow up. They are challenged to adjust to issues over which they can exercise little control. Counselors may not be able to understand all the issues young clients face: what they face going home to an impulsive, violent, alcoholic parent; what it is like to have the family split apart by divorce; adjusting to a new stepfamily; how to deal with loss and grief; what underlies an eating disorder; the challenge of answering the question, "Who am I" while confused and scared about sexual orientation; and how best to minimize student fears related to violence and terrorism.

By applying appropriate developmental assessment and interventions (Vernon & Clemente, 2005; Vernon, 2002), counselors can help these young clients cope with difficult life events in self-enhancing rather than self-defeating ways. The initial challenge for counselors is to empower them to survive stressful and often traumatic events and conditions. The greater challenge—and the one that ultimately will prove more beneficial—is for the counselor to identify resilient traits in these youths and use interventions that will enhance their strengths. Students may not be aware, and may not initially accept the notion, that they have developed remarkable assets in response to overwhelmingly stressful situations. Therefore, counselors have to be patient and persistent in assuring these young clients that, in addition to their pain, they are acquiring and enhancing aspects of themselves that can assist them to become successful adults.

Counselors may develop a refreshing new attitude toward their work with these children and adolescents as they shift their emphasis from centering strictly on the problem and what is wrong to identifying resiliencies and the positive aspects these clients are gaining from these experiences. Counselors will be empowering their young clients, and counselors themselves may feel empowered as they observe with wonder the strengthening of these young people that results from their personal trials and challenges.

References

Alford, K. M. (1998). Family roles, alcoholism, and family dysfunction. *Journal of Mental Health Counseling, 20*(3), 250–261.

Amato, P. R., & Rogers, S. J. (1999). Do attitudes toward divorce affect marital quality? *Journal of Family Issues, 20* (1), 69–86.

American School Counselor Association (2001). Crisis management: Supporting students, staff, and parents. Retrieved June 10, 2002, from http://www.schoolcounselor.org/cont net.cfm? L1=1000L2=50

American School Counselor Association (2002). Response to terrorism. Retrieved June 10, 2002, from http://www.school counselor.org/content.cfm?L1=1000L2=48

Anda, R. F., Whitfield, C. L., Felitti, V. J., Chapman, D., Edwards, V. J., Dube, S. R., & Williamson, D. F. (2002). Adverse childhood experiences, alcoholic parents, and later risk of alcoholism and depression. *Psychiatric Services, 53*, 1001–1009.

Anderson, R. N. (2002). *Deaths: Leading causes for 2000. National vital statistics reports* 50(16). Hyattsville, MD: National Center for Health Statistics.

Andrews, C. R. & Marotta, S. A. (2005). Spirituality and coping among grieving children: A preliminary study. *Counseling and Values, 50*, 38–50.

Arman, J. F. (2002). A brief group counseling model to increase resiliency of students with mild disabilities. *Journal of Humanistic Counseling, Education, and Development, 41*, 120–128.

Auger, R. W., Seymour, J. W., & Roberts, W. B. (2004). Responding to terror: The impact of September 11 on K-12 schools and schools' responses. *Professional School Counseling, 7*(4), 222–230.

Austin, B., Ziyadeh, N., Keliher, A., Zachary, A. & Forman, S. (2001). Screening high school students for eating disorders: Results of a national initiative. *Journal of Adolescent Health, 28*(2), 96.

Baker, J. E., Sedney, M. A., & Gross, E. (1992). Psychological tasks for bereaved children. *American Journal of Orthopsychiatry, 62*(1), 105–116.

Baker, S. B., & Gerler, E. R. (2004). *School counseling for the twenty-first century*. Upper Saddle River, NJ: Pearson Education.

Bardick, A. D., Bernes, K. B., McCulloch, A. R. M., Witko, K. D., Spriddle, J. W., & Roest, A. R. (2004). Eating disorder intervention, prevention, and treatment: Recommendations for school counselors. *Professional School Counseling, 8*(2), 168–174.

Barrett, M. R., Spencer, D. W., Schuurman, D. L., & Hoff, J. S. (1999). *Thirty-five ways to help a grieving child*. Portland, OR: Dougy Center for Grieving Children.

Bass, E., & Kaufman, K. (1996). *Free your mind: The book for gay, lesbian, and bisexual youth and their allies*. New York: HarperCollins.

Becvar, D. S., & Becvar, R. J. (2005). *Family therapy: A systemic integration* (6th ed.). Boston: Allyn & Bacon.

Benson, P. L., Sharma, A. R., & Roehikepartain, E. C. (1994). *Growing up adopted: A portrait of adolescents and their families*. Minneapolis: Search Institute.

Berg, E. M., (2001). *Children and teens afraid to eat: Helping youth in today's weight obsessed world*. Hettinger, ND: Healthy Weight Publishing Network.

Bernstein, R. (1999). *Straight parents, gay children: Inspiring families to live honestly and with greater understanding*. New York: Thunder Mouth Press.

Black, C. (2002). *It will never happen to me: Growing up with addiction as youngsters, adolescents, adults*. Center City, MN: Hazelden Foundation.

Block, J. D., & Bartell, S. S. (2001). *Stepliving for teens: Getting along with stepparents and siblings*. East Rutherford, NJ: Penguin Putnam Books.

Bogar, C. B., Hulse-Killacky, D. (2006). Resiliency determinants and resiliency processes among female adult survivors of childhood sexual abuse. *Journal of Counseling and Development, 84*(3), 318–327.

Brandt, E. (Ed.) (1999). *Dangerous liaisons: Blacks, gays, and the struggle for equality*. New York: New Press.

Brisson, P. (2006). *I remember Miss Perry*. New York: Dial Books.

Brodzinsky, D. M., & Schechter, M. D. (1993). *Being adopted: The lifelong search for self*. New York: Doubleday.

Brook, D. W., Brook, J. S., Rubenstone, F., Zhang, C., Singer, M., & Duke, M. R. (2003). Alcohol use in adolescents whose fathers abuse drugs. *Journal of Addictive Disease, 2*(1), 11–43.

Burnham, J. (2007). Children's fears: A pre-9/11 and post: 9/11 comparison using the American fear survey schedule for children. *Journal of Counseling and Development, 85*, 461–466.

Buscaglia, L. (2002). *The fall of Freddie the leaf* (anniversary ed.). New York: Henry Holt & Co.

Callahan, C. (2001). Protecting and counseling gay and lesbian students. *Journal of Humanistic Counseling, Education and Development, 40*(1), 5–10.

Capuzzi, D., & Gross, D. R. (2006). *Youth at risk: A prevention resource for counselors, teachers, and parents* (4th ed.). Upper Saddle River, NJ: Pearson Education.

Casper V., & Schultz, S. (1999). *Gay parents, straight schools: Building communication and trust*. New York: Teachers College Press.

Cavanagh, S. E., & Huston, A. C. (2006). Family instability and children's early problem behavior. *Social Forces, 85*(1), 551–581.

Centers for Disease Control and Prevention. (2003). Overweight children and adolescents 6-10 years of age, according to sex, age, and race. Retrieved December 3, 2007, at http://www.cdc.gov/nchs/ data/hus/tables/2002/02hus071.pdf

Centers for Disease Control and Prevention (2005). *HIV/AIDS among youth*. Retrieved January 8, 2008, from http://www.ced.gov/hiv/resources/factsheets/youth

Centers for Disease Control and Prevention (2007). *HIV/AIDS: Basic Statistics*. Retrieved January 8, 2008, from http://www.cdc.gov/hiv/topics/survaillance/basic

Chen, J., & George, R. A. (2005). Cultivating resilience in children from divorced families. *Family Journal: Counseling and Therapy for Couples and Families, 13*(4), 452–455.

Chibbaro, J. S., & Jackson, C. M. (2006). Helping students cope in an age of terrorism: Strategies for school counselors. *Professional School Counseling, 9*(4), 314–321.

Christensen, H. B., & Bilenberg, N. (2000). Behavioral and emotional problems in children of alcoholic mothers and fathers. *European Child & Adolescent Psychiatry, 9*(3), 219–226.

Choate, L. H. (2007). Counseling adolescent girls for body image resilience: Strategies for school counselors. *Professional School Counseling, 10*(3), 317–326.

Cobia, D. C., & Brazelton, E. W (1994). The applications of family drawing tests with children in remarriage families: Understanding familial roles. *Elementary School Guidance and Counseling, 29*, 129–136.

Cohen, J. A., Mannarino, A. P., Greenberg, T., Padlo, S., & Shipley, C. (2002). Childhood traumatic grief: Concepts and controversies. *Trauma, Violence, & Abuse, 3*(4), 307–327.

Coleman, W. L. (1993). *Step trouble: A survival guide for teenagers with stepparents*. Center City, MD: Hazelden Information & Educational Services.

Cooley, J. J. (1998). Gay and lesbian adolescents: Presenting problems and the counselor's role. *Professional School Counseling, 1*, 30–34.

Cooper, C. A. (1999). Children's dreams during the grief process. *Professional School Counseling, 3*(2), 137–140.

Dacey, J., Kenny, M., & Margolis, D. (2000). *Adolescent development* (3rd ed.). London: Thomas Learning Publication.

Davis, K. M., Williamson, L. L., Lambie, G. W. (2005). Sexual minority adolescents: Professional school counselors' ethical responsibilities. *Journal of LGBT Issues in Counseling, 1*(1), 127–140.

DeLucia-Waack, J. L., & Gerrity, D. (2001). Effective group work for elementary school-age children whose parents are divorcing. *Family Journal: Counseling and Therapy for Couples and Families, 9*(3), 273–284.

Depaola, T. (1998). *Nana upstairs and Nana downstairs* (reissue ed.). New York: G.P. Putnam's Sons.

Desetta, A., Wolin, S. & Wolin, S. (2000). *Struggle to be strong: True stories by teens overcoming tough times*. Minneapolis: Free Spirit Publishing.

Emshoff, J. & Valentine, L. (2006). Supporting adolescent children of alcoholics. *Prevention Researcher, 13*(4), 18-20.

Epstein, D. (Ed.) (1994). Challenging lesbian and gay inequalities in education. New York: Taylor & Francis.

Erikson, E. (1968). *Identity: Youth and crisis*. New York: Norton.

Feinberg, L. (1998). *Transliberation: Beyond pink or blue*. Boston: Beacon Press.

Fenell, D. L., & Weinhold, B. K. (2003). *Counseling families* (3rd ed.). Denver, CO: Love.

Fields, R. (2004). *Drugs in perspective: A personalized look at substance use and abuse* (5th ed.). New York: McGraw-Hill.

Gagliardi, C. J., Gloria, A. M., Kurpius, S. E. R., & Lambert, C. (2006). "I can't live without it": Adolescent substance abuse. In D. Capuzzi and D. Gross (Ed.), *Youth at risk* (pp. 373-400). Upper Saddle River, NJ: Pearson Education.

Getzoff, A., & McClenahan, C. (1984). *Step kids: A survival guide for teenagers in stepfamilies*. New York: Walker and Co.

Gladding, S. (2007). *Family therapy: History, theory, and practice* (4th ed). Upper Saddle River, NJ: Pearson Education.

Goldenberg, L., & Goldenberg, H. (2007). *Family therapy: An overview* (7th ed.). Pacific Grove, CA: Brooks/Cole.

Goldman, L. (1999). *Life & loss: A guide to help grieving children* (2nd ed). Muncie, IN: Accelerated Development.

Gootman, M. (2005). *When a friend dies: A book for teens about grieving and healing*. Minneapolis: Free Spirit Publishing.

Gordon, S., & Cohen, V. (2000). *All families are different*. Amherst, NY: Prometheus Books.

Granello, D. H., & Granello, P. F. (2007). *Suicide: An essential guide for helping professionals and educators*. Boston: Pearson Education.

Grant, D. F. (2000). Estimates of U. S. children exposed to alcohol abuse and dependence in the family. *American Journal of Public Health, 90*(1), 112–115.

Griffin, P. (1998). *Strong women, deep closets: Lesbians and homophobia in sport*. Champaign, IL: Human Kinetics Publishers.

Grollman, E. A. (1991). *Talking about death: A dialogue between parent and child* (3rd ed). Boston: Beacon Press.

Gutierrez, F. J. (2006). Counseling queer youth: Preventing another Matthew Shepard. In D. Capuzzi & D. R. Gross (Eds.), *Youth at risk: A prevention resource for counselors, parents, and teachers* (pp. 331–352). Upper Saddle River, NJ: Pearson Education.

Haasl, B., & Marnocha, J. (2000a). *Bereavement support group program for children: Leader manual* (2nd ed.). Muncie, IN: Accelerated Development.

Haasl, B., & Marnocha, J. (2000b). *Bereavement support group program for children: Participant workbook* (2nd ed). Muncie, IN: Accelerated Development.

Harvey, V. S. (2007). Raising resiliency school wide. *Education Digest. 72*(7), 33–39.

Heegaard, M. (1993). *When a parent marries again: Children can learn to cope with family change*. Chapmanville, WV: Woodland Press.

Herdt, G., & Boxer, A. (1996). *Children of Horizons: How gay and lesbian teens are leading a new way out of the closet* (2nd ed). Boston: Beacon Press.

Hetherington, E. M. (1991). Families, lies, and videotapes. *Journal of Research on Adolescence, 1*, 323–348.

Hollister-Wagner, G. H., Foshee, V. A., & Jackson, C. (2001). Adolescent aggression: Models of resiliency. *Journal of Applied Social Psychology, 31*(3), 445–466.

Huegel, K. (2003). *GLBTQ: The survival guide for queer and questioning teens*. Minneapolis: Free Spirit Publishing.

Human Rights Watch (2006). Hatred in the hallways: Violence and discrimination against lesbian, gay, bisexual, and transgender students in the U.S. schools. Retrieved May 31, 2006, from http://www.hrw.org/reports/2001/uslgbt/toc.htm

Janas, M. (2002). Build resiliency. *Intervention in School and Clinic, 38*(2), 117–121.

Janus, N. G. (1997). Adoption counseling as a professional specialty area for counselors. *Journal of Counseling and Development, 75*, 266–274.

Jarratt, C. J. (1997). *Helping children cope with separation and loss* (2nd rev.). Boston: Harvard Common Press.

Jennings, K. (2005). *One teacher in ten: Gay and lesbian educators tell their stories* (2nd ed.). Boston: Alyson Publications.

Juhnke, G. (2002). *Intervening with school students after terrorist acts*. ERIC/CASS Resources for Helping Youth and Adults with Traumatic Events. Retrieved June 10, 2002, from http://ericcass.uncg.edu/juhnke

Kapinus, C. A. (2004). The effect of parents' attitudes toward divorce on offspring's attitudes: Gender and parental divorce as mediating factors. *Journal of Family Issues, 25*(1), 112–135.

Kaufman, K., & Kaufman, N. (2005). Childhood mourning: Prospective case analysis of multiple losses. *Death Studies, 29*, 237–249.

Keats, E. (2001). *Louie's search*. New York: Scholastic.

Kizner, L. R., & Kizner, S. R. (1999). Small-group counseling with adopted children. *Professional School Counseling, 2*(3), 226–229.

Kmietowicz, S. (2000). More services needed for bereaved children. *British Medical Journal*, 7239, 893.

Krementz, J. (1988). How it feels when a parent dies. New York: Knopf.

Krishnaswami, U. (2006). *Bringing Aska home*. New York: Lee & Low Books.

Krueger, M. J., & Hanna, E. J. (1997). Why adoptees search: An existential treatment perspective. *Journal of Counseling and Development, 75*, 195–202.

Kwok, O., Hughes, J. N., & Luo, W. (2007). Role of resilient personality on lower achieving first grade students' current and future achievement. *Journal of School Psychology, 45*(1), 61–82.

Lambie, G. W. (2005). Children of alcoholics: Implications for professional school counseling. *Professional School Counseling, 8,* 266–273.

Lambie, R., & Daniels-Mohring, D. (2000). *Family systems within educational contexts* (2nd ed). Denver, CO: Love.

Lansky, V. (1998). *It's not your fault, Koko bear.* (For parents and young children during divorce.) Minnetonka, MN: Publisher Group Web.

Leibowitz, J. (2000). *Finding your place: A teen guide to life in a blended family.* New York: Rosen Publishing Group.

Lewis, J. A., Dana, R. Q., & Blevins, G. A. (2002). *Substance abuse counseling.* Pacific Grove, CA: Brooks/Cole.

Lindholm, A. B., Schuurman, D. L., & Hoff, J. S. (2001). *After a suicide: A workbook for grieving kids.* Portland, OR: Dougy Center for Grieving Children.

Magsamen, S. (2007). *My two homes: Practical and hopeful wisdom for families, from families, when parents separate or divorce.* New York: Sterling Pub.

Marcus, E. (2005). *Is it a choice?* San Francisco: Harper/Collins Publishers.

Massachusetts Department of Education. (1999). Youth risk behavior study. Retrieved on line at http://www.doe.mass.edu/hssss/

Mastoon, A. (2001). *The shared heart: Portraits and stories celebrating lesbian, gay, and bisexual young people.* New York: HarperCollins Children's Books.

Masurel, C. (2001). *Two homes.* Cambridge, MA: Candlewick Press.

McClintock, M., & Herdt, G. (1996). Rethinking puberty: The development of sexual attraction. *Current Directions in Psychological Science, 5,* 178–183.

McFarland, W. P. & Dupuis, M. (2001). The legal duty to protect gay and lesbian students from violence in school. *Professional School Counseling, 4*(3), 171–179.

Miller, D. B. (1999). Racial socialization and racial identity: Can they promote resiliency for African–American adolescents? *Adolescence, 34*(135), 493–502.

Morganett, R. S. (1990). *Skills for living: Group counseling activities for young adolescents.* Champaign, IL: Research Press.

Morganett, R. S. (1994). *Skills for living: Group counseling activities for elementary students.* Champaign, IL: Research Press.

Morganett, R. S. (2000). *Skills for living: Group counseling activities for young adolescents* (Vol. 2). Champaign, IL: Research Press.

Moser, A. & Melton, D. (2000). *Don't fall apart on Saturdays!: The children's divorce–survival book.* Kansas City, MO: Landmark Editions.

Muller, L. E., & Hartman, J. (1998). Group counseling for sexual minority youth. *Professional School Counseling, 1,* 38–41.

Murphy, L., Pynoos, R. S., & James, C. R. (1997). The trauma/grief focused group psychotherapy module of an elementary school based prevention/intervention program. In J. Osofsky (Ed.), *Children in a violent society* (pp. 223–255). New York: Guilford.

National Association of School Psychologists. (2002). Children's reaction to trauma: Suggestions for parents. Retrieved June 10, 2002, from http://www.naspcenter.org/safe_ schools/trauma

National Education Association. (2007). The National Education Association encourages school policies and programs. Retrieved December, 26, 2007, at http://pflag.community-point.org/nea_encourages.pdf.

Neumark-Sztainer, D. (2007). Addressing the spectrum of adolescent weight-rated problems: Engaging parents and communities. *Prevention Researcher, 14*(3), 11–14.

Ohannessian, C. M., Hesselbrock, V. M., Ruddy, K., & Kramer, J. (2006). Parental substance use and adolescent adjustment: A micro-level approach. *Prevention Researcher, 13*(4), 7–9.

Omizo, S. A., & Omizo, M. M. (1992). Eating disorders: The school counselor's role. *School Counselor, 39*, 217–224.

Owens, R. E. (2001). Counseling with lesbian, gay, and bisexual youth. *Prevention Researcher, 8*(1), 9–13.

Pardeck, J. T. (1998). *Using books in clinical social work practice: A guide to bibliotherapy.* Binghamton, NY: Haworth Press.

Perkins, D. F., & Jones, K. R. (2004). Risk behaviors and resiliency within physically abused adolescents. *Child Abuse & Neglect, 28*, 547–563.

Pipher, M. (2005). *Reviving Ophelia.* New York: Ballantine Books, Random House.

Portnay, M. A. (2004). *Where do people go when they die?* Minneapolis: Kar-Ben Publishing.

Ray, S. L. (2004). Eating disorders in adolescent males. *Professional School Counseling, 8*(1), 98–101.

Remafedi, G. C. & Shelby, P. (1998). *Isolated and invisible: Gay, lesbian, bisexual and transgendered youth. Report for South Fraser Regional Health Board, March 1998.* (Report No. 6028728) Canada: British Columbia 1998-03-00.

Ricci, I. (2006). *Mom's house, dad's house for kids.* New York: Fireside.

Rice, C. E., Dandreaux, D., Handley, E. D., & Chassin, L. (2006). Children of alcoholics: Risk and resilience. *Prevention Researcher, 13*(4), 3–6.

Rivers, I. (2004). Recollections of bullying at school and their long-term implications for lesbians, gay men, and bisexuals. *Crisis, 25*(4), 169–175.

Rosen, M. (2005). *Michael Rosen's sad book.* Cambridge, MA: Candlewick Press.

Rutter, P. A. (2006). Young adult suicide and sexual orientation: What should counselors know? *Journal of LGBT Issues in Counseling, 1*(3), 33-48.

Ryan, C., & Futterman, D. (2001a). Experiences, vulnerabilities, and risks of lesbian and gay students. *Preventative Researcher, 8*(1), 6–8.

Ryan, C., & Futterman, D. (2001b). Lesbian and gay adolescents: Identity development. *Preventative Researcher, 8*(1), 1–5.

Savin-Williams, R. (2005). *The new gay teen.* Cambridge, MA: Harvard University Press.

Schuurman, D. L., Hoff, J. S., Spencer, D. W., & White, C. (1997). *Helping children cope with death.* Portland, OR: Dougy Center for Grieving Children.

Schwiebert, P., & DeKlyen, C. (1999). *Tear soup: A recipe for healing after loss.* Portland, OR: Grief Watch.

Scott, E. & Sobczak, C. (2002). *Body aloud! Helping children and teens find their own solutions to eating and body image problems.* Berkeley, CA: Body Positive.

Shapiro, L. (2002). *Bounce back: A game that teaches resiliency skills.* The Farm, MD: Childswork/Childsplay.

Skibbee, D. B. (2001). The relationship between parental mental health, family rituals, family environment, and the resiliency of adolescents of alcoholic parents. *Dissertation Abstracts International, 62*(1–B), 565. (University Microfilms No. 0419–4217)

Sorosky, A. D., Baran, A., & Pannor, R. (1989). *The adoption triangle.* San Antonio, TX: Corona.

Spelman, C. M. (2002). *When I feel sad.* Morton Grove, IL: Albert Whitman & Co.

Strohschein, L. (2005). Parental divorce and child mental health trajectories. *Journal of Marriage and Family, 67*(5), 1286–1300.

Stone, C. B. (2003). Counselors as advocates for gay, lesbian, and bisexual youth: A call for equity and action. *Multicultural Counseling and Development, 31*, 143–155.

Stout, E. J. & Wiggins-Frame, M. (2004). Body image disorder in adolescent males: Strategies for school counselors. Professional School Counselor, 8(2), 176-182.

Substance Abuse and Mental Health Services Administration (SAMHSA), (2002). Substance abuse and mental health statistics. Retrieved December 31, 2007, from http://www.samhsa.gov

Sun, Y. & Li, Y. (2002). Children's well-being during parents' marital disruption process: A pooled time-series analysis. *Journal of Marriage and Family, 64*(2), 472–488.

Tan, T. X., (2006). History of early neglect and middle childhood social competence: An adoption study. *Adoption Quarterly, 9*(4), 59–72.

Thomas, P. (1999). *My family's changing.* Hauppauge, NY: Barrons Ed. Series.

Thompson, C. L., Rudolph, L. B. & Henderson, D. (2004). *Counseling children* (6th ed). Pacific Grove, CA: Brooks/Cole.

Urbide, V. (1991). *Project 10 handbook: Addressing lesbian and gay issues in our schools.* Los Angeles: Friends of Project 10.

U.S. Department of Health and Human Services, Office of Women's Health. (2000). *Body-Wise Handbook.* Washington, DC.

U.S. Department of Justice, Federal Bureau of Investigation. (2001). *Hate crime statistics: 1999.* (FBI Uniform Crime Reports), Washington, DC: Government Printing Office.

Vandereychen, W. (2002). Families of patients with eating disorders. In C. G. Fairburn & K. D. Brownell (Eds.), *Eating disorders and obesity* (pp. 215–220). New York: Guilford Press.

van IJzendoorn, M. H., & Juffer, F. (2005). Adoption is a successful natural intervention enhancing adopted children's IQ and school performance. *Current Directions in Psychological Science, 14*(6), 326–330.

Van Wormer, K., & Davis, D. R. (2003). *Addiction treatment: A strengths perspective.* Pacific Grove, CA: Brooks/Cole Thomson Learning.

Varjas, K., Mahan, W., Meyers, J., Birckbichler, L., Lopp, G., & Dew, B. J. (2006). Assessing school climate among sexual minority high school students. *Journal of LGBT Issues in Counseling, 1*(3), 49–76.

Vernon, A. (2002). *What works when with children and adolescents: A handbook of individual counseling techniques.* Champaign, IL: Research Press.

Vernon, A., & Clemente, R. (2005). *Developmental assessment & intervention with children & adolescents: Developmental and cultural approaches.* Alexandria, VA: American Counseling Association.

Visher, E. B., & Visher, J. S. (1996). *Therapies with stepfamilies.* New York: Brunner/Mazel.

Wallerstein, J. S. (1987). Children of divorce: Report of a ten-year follow-up of early latency-age children. *American Journal of Orthopsychiatry, 57*(2), 199–211.

Wallerstein, J. S., & Blakeslee, S. (1996). *Second chances.* New York: Ticknor & Fields.

Wallerstein, J. S., & Kelly, J. (1996). *Surviving the breakup: How children and parents cope with divorce.* New York: Basic Books.

Walsh, W. M. (1992). Twenty major issues in remarriage families. *Journal of Counseling and Development, 70*(6), 709–715.

Webb, N. B. (2002). *Helping bereaved children: A handbook for practitioners.* New York: Guilford.

Wegscheider-Cruise, S. (1989). *Another chance: Hope and health for the alcoholic family* (2d ed.). Palo Alto, CA: Science and Behavior Books.

Werner, E. E., & Smith, R. S. (2001). *Journeys from childhood to midlife: Risk, resilience, and recovery.* Ithaca, NY: Cornell University Press.

Wilgocki, J., & Wright, M. K. (2002) *Maybe days: A book for children in foster care.* Washington, DC: Magination Press.

Willis, C. A. (2002). The grieving process in children: Strategies for understanding, educating, and reconciling children's perceptions of death. *Early Childhood Education Journal, 29*(4), 221–226.

Winchester, K., & Beyer, R. (2001). *What in the world do you do when your parents divorce?* Minneapolis: Free Spirit Press.

Wolin, S., Desetta, A. & Hefner, K. (2000). *A leader's guide to the struggle to be strong.* Minneapolis: Free Spirit Press.

Wolin, S., & Wolin, S. (1993). *The resilient self: How survivors of troubled families rise above adversity.* New York: Villard.

Wong, M. M., Nigg, J. T., Zucker, R. A., Puttler, L. L., Fitzgerald, H. E., Jester, J. M., Glass, J. M., & Adams, K. (2006). Behavioral control and resiliency in the onset of alcohol and illicit drug use: A prospective study from preschool to adolescence. *Child Development, 77*(4), 1016–1033.

Woog, D. (1995). *School's out: The impact of gay and lesbian issues on America's schools.* Boston: Alyson.

Worden, J. W. (2007). *Grief counseling and grief therapy: A handbook for the mental health practitioner* (3rd ed.). New York: Springer.

Wright, K. S. (2006). The secret and all-consuming obsessions: Eating disorders. In D. Capuzzi & D. Gross (Eds.), *Youth at risk* (pp. 167–209). Upper Saddle River, NJ: Pearson Education.

Yalom, I., & Leszcz, M. (2005). *The theory and practice of group psychotherapy* (5th ed.). New York: Basic Books.

Zirkle, D. S., Peterson, T. L., & Collins-Marotte, J. (2001). The school counselor's role in academic and social adjustment of late-adopted children. *Professional School Counseling, 4*(5), 366–369.

10

Counseling At-Risk Children and Adolescents

Ellen Hawley McWhirter and Jason J. Burrow-Sanchez

In our complex and ever-changing society numerous social, demographic, and economic factors have weakened the ability of families to provide healthy and developmentally appropriate environments for their children. For example, poverty and economic instability have led to some families living in substandard housing with inadequate nutrition, in neighborhoods plagued with crime and violence. Social changes and new technologies have affected the marketplace dramatically, altered family circumstances, and created new sets of influences and experiences for children and adolescents. Marital transitions and changes in family composition (such as increases in the numbers of single-parent, blended, and foster families), increasing hours of the day that are unsupervised by adults, the rising number of media figures who model sexual permissiveness, irrational risk-taking, and the use of violence to cope with frustration and anger, have contributed to a societal context that provides fewer supports and greater risks than in the past (McWhirter, McWhirter, McWhirter, & McWhirter, 2007).

Children today have fewer adults helping them develop skills such as responsibility and self-discipline, and much of the adult contact for adolescents is via television and the Internet, in which adults routinely display aggression, self-centeredness, superficiality, and poor communication skills. Counselors face the challenge of finding ways to assist their young clients to negotiate their environments and thrive in spite of the many risk factors. In this chapter we first detail some of the risk factors for children and adolescents in three primary socializing systems—families, peers, and schools. Then we present a framework for prevention and intervention. Finally, we review three specific problems that place children and adults at particular risk—depression, suicide, and substance abuse.

Socializing Systems

Of the three primarily socializing systems, we begin with the earliest context, the family.

The Family Context

The theory that guides our understanding of family systems and functioning reflects in large part the perspectives of the dominant European American culture. Bearing that in mind, counselors must explore a family's norms, values, and practices within the family's cultural context, tailoring their application of family systems theories to the individual family. Because of the large within-group differences of any racial or ethnic minority group and the variation within European American subgroups as well, counselors have to avoid making assumptions about the cultural appropriateness of specific interventions.

To understand the nature of the stresses on families and the dysfunction within families that place children at risk, counselors must understand the characteristics of healthy families. From a family-systems perspective, a healthy family is an open system that interacts with the environment and is capable of adaptation and flexibility. Within this open system the family is able to maintain the stability necessary to allow the development of its members, and family members must make accommodations to environmental changes as necessary. In contrast, a closed system is isolated from and does not adapt to the environment, and does not accommodate the changing developmental needs of its members.

Parenting behavior can be described in terms of three continua or dimensions that emerge across numerous studies, though the labels vary across studies (McWhirter et al., 2007):

1. The *permissiveness–restrictiveness dimension*: reflects control and power in the parents' behaviors
2. The *hostility–warmth dimension*: reflects levels of support and affection that parents give to children
3. The *anxious/emotional involvement–calm detachment dimension*: reflects the parents' emotional engagement or connectedness

In healthy families, parents' practices fall near the middle with respect to the permissive/restrictive continuum, and on the warmth and calm detachment ends of the other continua.

As discussed in chapter 9, parental divorce and the blending of families place significant stress on children and adolescents in these families. Compounding the stress of changes in the nuclear family, extended family support from grandparents, aunts, uncles, and cousins is no longer as available to the vast majority of young people as it was in the past.

An additional stressor in some instances is domestic violence, which leads to loss of self-esteem and confidence in children, increases in stress disorders and other psychological problems, with an increased probability that children will engage in violent behavior in their adult relationships (Ehrensaft et al., 2003). Child abuse, including physical and emotional abuse, neglect, and sexual abuse, also places children at high risk for future problems. Physical violence against children ranges from hair-pulling and slapping to severe beatings. Emotional abuse includes harsh criticism and ridicule, withholding of affection, irrational punishment, and inconsistent expectations (Gershoff, 2002). Gay and lesbian youth are at particular risk for verbal and physical abuse by family members (McWhirter et al., 2007).

Child sexual abuse is a predictor of many physical and psychological problems (Bauman, 2008), including severe depression, lower impulse control, eating disorders, anxiety disorders, substance abuse, somatization, post-traumatic stress disorder, dissociative identity disorder, high-risk sexual behaviors, adolescent pregnancy, a number of medical conditions, and difficulties with interpersonal relationships (Brown, Lourie, Zlotnick, & Cohn, 2000; Neumark-Sztainer et al., 2000; Wonderlich et al., 2000). Girls with a history of being sexually abused are three times more likely to develop psychiatric and substance abuse disorders than girls with no such history (Kendler et al., 2000).

Children who have been victimized by sexual abuse may feel stigmatized as "different," and may feel isolated from their peers. Children often are not believed when they disclose sexual abuse and may be blamed for the abuse, threatened by their perpetrators, and come to believe that they are to blame for the abuse, which can lead to intense feelings of guilt and shame (Finkelhor, 1995; Wolf, 1993).

The Peer Context

The influence of the peer group is another major socializing agent for children and adolescents. The peer group typically becomes more influential with the onset of adolescence. Young people influence and are influenced by their peer groups or "peer clusters" in a dynamic process (Beauvais, Chavez, Oetting, Deffenbacher, & Cornell, 1996; Oetting & Beauvais, 1987). For example, a well-known risk factor for adolescent drug use is the use of drugs by the adolescent's peer group (Hawkins, Catalano, & Miller, 1992). Peer groups provide adolescents with a micro-environment that supports their engagement in the behaviors the group deems appropriate. The dynamics of peer clusters explain the failure of many prevention and intervention programs targeted at changing the behavior of at-risk adolescents. When adolescents return to their original peer cluster after receiving an intervention, they are again reinforced for engaging in the risk behaviors that are normative for that group.

Peer-group interventions are designed to influence youth behavior positively by simultaneously influencing peer groups. McWhirter et al. (2007) provide a review of the major peer support interventions used in school settings, including cooperative learning, peer support networks, and peer tutoring. Heterogeneous groups of students expose them to differing skill sets and levels. Cooperative learning groups are frequently used in school settings for students with differing academic performance. When lower academically performing students are grouped with higher-performing students to complete a group task, the performance of the lower-performing students typically improves. Cooperative learning groups are linked to positive outcomes such as improved academic performance and intergroup relationships among students from different backgrounds (e.g., disability/ability, cultural), as well as increases in self-esteem and internal locus of control (Kutnick, 2005). Peer mediation programs have resulted in reduced school violence and shown significant benefits for at-risk students who were trained as mediators (Blake, Wang, Cartledge, & Gardner, 2000). These positive outcomes provide support for utilizing well-structured interventions that promote youth learning from their peers.

A possible drawback of peer interventions is that young people may teach and reinforce deviant behavior in each other. In an early study, Dishion and his colleagues (1999) found that middle school students at risk for antisocial behavior who participated in a peer group preventive intervention had worse outcomes on some measures than students who did not receive the intervention. Based on findings such as this, some researchers have warned of the potential for "deviancy training" when at-risk students are grouped together for intervention (Dishion & Dodge, 2005). These negative peer effects have been associated mostly with secondary preventive interventions rather than treatment interventions. Secondary preventive interventions are targeted toward youth who are exhibiting negative behaviors (e.g., delinquency, substance use) but have not yet fully developed a clinical disorder, whereas treatment interventions target youth who have developed a clinical disorder such as conduct disorder or a substance-abuse disorder.

Kaminer (2005) concluded that empirical evidence supports the effectiveness of group interventions for adolescents, and to minimize the risk for deviancy training, recommends utilizing group leaders who are well trained, providing effective supervision, using well structured intervention protocols (i.e., manualized) and including some adolescents with good social skills to provide group heterogeneity.

The School Context

The school is a third major socializing agent. Healthy school environments are characterized by strong instructional leadership, a curriculum that emphasizes academics, a collaborative atmosphere among teachers and staff members, a sense of commitment and a feeling of belonging among students, and student discipline that is fair, clear, and consistent (McWhirter et al., 2007; Taylor, Pressley, & Pearson, 2000). If a school is to be truly effective, community support is important. The level of community support depends, in large part, on the community's "social capital"—the network of nuclear and extended families, the neighborhood and church community, and social services and other community agencies—uniting in beliefs and values regarding, among other things, the nature and role of education (McWhirter et al., 2007).

Deficient social capital in present-day society constrains school systems, as does the lack of financial support for educational systems. Indicators of a healthy student climate include positive self-concept and self-esteem among students, support for the development of student decision-making and problem-solving skills, structures that facilitate and encourage self-monitoring of behavior and school progress, and promoting an attitude of shared responsibility for learning.

School structure, size, and philosophy influence the learning environment. Smaller schools can increase the sense of community and personal identity for students. Classroom structures can help students feel a sense of empowerment, safety, and influence over their environment, enhancing their acceptance and appreciation of differences, creativity, and personal autonomy. This, in turn, may lead to improvements in mental health and overall quality of learning. Curricula that include social-skills training, problem-solving, and critical thinking can be highly beneficial to at-risk students (McWhirter et al., 2007).

School Dropout

When school environments are unhealthy, when social and economic resources are strained, and when students do not experience success or belonging, they are at greater risk for dropping out. A dropout is defined as a student who leaves school before his or her program of study is complete—that is, before graduation and without transferring to another school. The dropout rate in many states is as high as one in four students, and the problem likely is even more pronounced in large cities (McWhirter et al., 2007). Hispanic students are much more likely to drop out of school than their White and African American counterparts (Laird, DeBell, Kienzl, & Chapman, 2007).

Risk factors for dropping out of school include low academic motivation, a history of problems with school authorities or police, frequent absences, pregnancy or marriage, working outside of school because of financial need, family conflict, substance-abuse problems, membership in a minority group, or having fallen 2 or more years behind grade level. Thus, the young people who are most likely to drop out of school are those already at risk, and dropping out of school compounds their difficulties. School dropout is associated with future economic and social consequences such as lower earning potential, unemployment, dissatisfaction with self and the surrounding environment, and lack of opportunities (McWhirter et al., 2007).

School Violence

Violence within schools and the surrounding communities is a growing concern that can create a climate of fear for young people. During the 2004–05 academic year there were 21 homicides and 7 suicides in schools across the nation. Projections for 2004 were that 1.4 million students would be victims of nonfatal crimes, including 863,000 thefts and 583,000 violent crimes (Dinkes et al., 2006). One study of students in grades 9–12 found that fighting and intimidation were problems in schools; 14% of students reported they had been involved in a fight at school, and 6% reported they had carried a weapon on campus in the past 30 days (Dinkes et al., 2006).

Funding shortages, teacher quality concerns, and efforts to comply with legislation such as No Child Left Behind, in conjunction with problems such as school violence, all create stress in the school microsystem in ways that affect students directly and indirectly. Next we propose a larger framework that integrates the contexts of family, peers, and school for at-risk children and adolescents. This conceptual framework sets the stage for providing effective prevention and intervention programs.

A Framework for Prevention and Intervention

Because families, schools, communities, and society clearly play a role in developing and maintaining the above risk factors, models of prevention and intervention must be comprehensive to produce lasting effects. Counselors working with children and adolescents will be most effective if their prevention and intervention strategies account for the family, peer, and school contexts of children's lives. Here we describe a framework for conceptualizing the prevention and intervention efforts of counselors (McWhirter et al. 2007). This framework involves three distinct continuua: the at-risk continuum, the approach continuum, and the context continuum.

At-Risk Continuum

The at-risk continuum reflects the degree to which children and adolescents are at-risk for serious behaviors such as substance abuse, risky sexual activity, depression, violence, gang involvement, and conduct disorders. The continuum ranges from minimal risk to imminent risk.

1. Young people characterized by *minimal risk* are those who enjoy favorable demographics; that is, they have higher socioeconomic status, have positive family, school, and social interactions, and are exposed to only limited psychosocial and environmental stressors. These young people certainly are not invulnerable to problems. The key is that they have many buffers and supports for coping with adverse experiences and for responding to pressures and challenges.

2. Young people at *remote risk* have less favorable demographic characteristics, such as lower socioeconomic status or a less cohesive community life; and they may be members of a family that is under stress, perhaps because of poverty, divorce, remarriage, or job loss. Family functioning may be affected by these demographic variables, and school and social interactions are less positive. The effects of these risky demographic characteristics are additive; the more of these demographic characteristics are present, the greater is the risk of developing problems.

3. *High risk* is characterized by negative family, school, and social interactions (such as domestic violence and school performance problems), numerous stressors, and individual characteristics such as negative attitudes, poor self-regulation, and academic and social skill deficiencies.

4. Young people at *imminent risk* are those who, in addition to having several or many of the preceding characteristics, have developed gateway behaviors. Gateway behaviors typically (though not inevitably) lead to more negative behavior. For example, smoking may occur with or precede alcohol use, which may be a gateway to the use of illegal substances such as marijuana, cocaine, and other illicit drugs. Involvement in negative peer networks may lead to juvenile offenses, aggression, rejection by other peers, family distancing, and later to gang involvement and more serious offenses.

5. At *highest risk* are youth engaged in serious problem behaviors such as violence, risky sexual behavior, and drug use, as well as those who are depressed or suicidal.

Approach Continuum

The approach continuum reflects the types of prevention and intervention approaches that are most appropriate for different levels of risk.

1. Paralleling the at-risk continuum, the approach continuum begins with *universal approaches* that correspond to minimal risk. Universal approaches are considered to be appropriate for all children, not just those who are presumed to be at risk, and they target all children in a given catchment area. An example is a life-skills curriculum that is implemented across all grades in a given school. In such a curriculum, developmentally appropriate personal, social, and cognitive skills in areas such as communication, conflict resolution, and problem solving are most effective when these are taught early and supported throughout elementary, middle, and secondary school.

2. *Selected approaches* are aimed at groups of young people who share some circumstance or experience that increases their likelihood for developing problems in the future. Examples of selected programs are Head Start, which is directed toward low-income children, and school-based, small-group interventions for children whose parents are divorcing or divorced. Universal and selected programs are not mutually exclusive and overlap actually is often preferable. That is, children whose parents are divorcing would benefit from a school curriculum that promotes life skills such as communication plus participation in a small group specific to their current experience.

3. Next on the continuum are *booster sessions*, which review and reinforce components of universal and selected approaches.

4. These are followed on the continuum by *indicated treatment approaches*, which are used with children and adolescents who are at imminent risk for serious problems or who have just begun to engage in serious problem behaviors. An adolescent who is considering suicide, has begun to skip classes, and is brought to counseling because she came home intoxicated, for example, would require an indicated treatment approach. The goals of treatment would include helping him to develop coping skills that could prevent him from committing suicide, from dropping out of school, and from developing a substance-abuse problem.

5. At the end of the approach continuum are *second-chance programs*, designed for young people who have engaged in severe problem behavior already. They may, for example, regularly use alcohol or drugs, be pregnant, or be clinically depressed. Second-chance programs provide an opportunity for them to develop the skills and the network of support they need to engage in and sustain different and healthier behaviors.

Context Continuum

Finally, the prevention and intervention framework incorporates a context continuum, which reflects the manner in which three important contexts—family, school, and society/community—are involved in early, broad-based prevention efforts, early intervention efforts that coordinate support and training activities, and treatment approaches that incorporate a variety of education, training, and counseling efforts.

1. With respect to the *family context*, prevention may involve providing culturally appropriate family-strengthening opportunities that increase interaction and communication between family members and increase support for families. Providing family access to prenatal and health-care programs is another important prevention strategy. Parent training and other kinds of family support programs constitute early intervention. At the treatment end of the continuum are family counseling and programs designed to address child abuse, neglect, and domestic violence.

2. *School-based prevention* includes early compensatory programs such as Head Start and before- and after-school programs that provide safe, nurturing environments for children whose parents are not available at those times. Participating in quality after-school programs can have significant learning, career, social, and health benefits (Durlak & Weissberg, 2007). Prevention also includes generic programs infused in the curriculum to provide life skills including decision making and social skills. At the treatment end of the continuum are second-chance, school-based programs, such as alternative high schools and school-based health clinics that provide a variety of treatment services.

3. Finally, with respect to the *society/community context*, prevention involves improving economic conditions, increasing the availability of low-cost housing and affordable, quality child care, increasing job opportunities, providing an umbrella of community-based support services, and promoting prosocial norms and values.

We recommend that counselors working with children and adolescents utilize this framework to conceptualize their work. Is the target all children, at-risk children, groups engaged in problem behaviors, or individuals? How are family, peer, and school contexts addressed in the prevention or intervention strategy? Evaluation of outcomes should include attention to multiple contexts in recognition of their dynamic influences. For example, evaluation of the effects of a school-based group intervention for adolescents with high anxiety should not simply be directed to post-treatment anxiety levels but also to factors such as stress in the home environment, school attendance, and satisfaction with peer support. Such an approach will help the counselor identify a wider range of potential benefits.

Specific Problem Areas

We will review three specific problems that affect children and adolescents: depression, suicide, and substance abuse. Each is examined in the context of the conceptual framework for prevention and intervention, providing a brief problem description as well as suggestions for counselors.

Depression

Depression is a serious condition that can affect children and adolescents. Symptoms include depressed mood, markedly diminished interest or pleasure in most activities, significant weight loss or gain, insomnia or hypersomnia, psychomotor agitation or retardation, fatigue, feelings of worthlessness or inappropriate guilt, diminished ability to concentrate, and recurring thoughts of death or suicidal ideation (APA, 2000). Children and adolescents also may say they are "bored," "down," "sad," or "blue." Symptoms of *dysthymia*—a chronic sense of dysphoria that is less intense than depression—include either poor appetite or overeating, low energy or fatigue, low self-esteem, poor concentration or indecision, and feelings of hopelessness (APA, 2000).

Although efforts have been made to differentiate adolescent and adult depression, counselors often apply to children the criteria that have been developed to define adult depression, without taking into account developmental considerations that may affect the cause, course, and outcome of depression in children and adolescents (Cicchetti & Toth, 1998). Signs that may be associated with depression in children and adolescents include frequent physical complaints such as headaches, stomachaches, muscle aches or fatigue, school absence or poor performance in school, talking about running away or efforts to run away from home, outbursts of anger, irritability or crying, boredom and lack of interest in previous activities, alcohol or substance abuse, heightened social sensitivity and difficulty in relationships, and fear of death (National Institute of Mental Health [NIMH], 2000). Depression in children and adolescents is also associated with anxiety disorders, disruptive behaviors, substance-abuse disorders, physical illnesses such as diabetes, and increased risk of suicidal behaviors (NIMH, 2000).

At any given time, depression affects approximately 30% of the adolescent population (Lewinsohn et al., 1993) and 2–5% of younger children (Milling & Martin, 1992). Risk factors for the onset of depression include having a parent or other close relative with a mood disorder, severe stressors such as divorce in the family, traumatic experiences or a learning disorder, low self-esteem, low self-efficacy, a sense of helplessness and hopelessness, living in poverty, and being female (Beardslee & Gladstone, 2001). Thus, risk factors include individual, family, and environmental characteristics. In general, females are twice as likely as males to experience depression. Gender role socialization pressures that result in excessive caregiving and difficulties in being assertive may be linked to the gender differences in depression that emerge in adolescence (Aube et al., 2000).

The results of a longitudinal study of low-SES families showed that adverse early family environments, including maternal depression, abuse, deficits in supportive early care, and overall maternal stress are particularly associated with prepubertal-onset depression (Duggal et al., 2001). In the same study, maternal depression was associated with the development of depression in adolescent females, and lack of supportive early care was associated with adolescent depression in males. This finding is consistent with another study showing that mothers' history of depression was significantly associated with higher levels of depressive symptoms in their adolescent children (Garber, Keiley, & Martin, 2002).

Counselors, therefore, should not minimize depression during childhood and adolescence as being a part of a "phase." Depressive disorders are not normal developmental events, nor are they short-lived problems that will pass with time (Kovacs, 1989). Depressive episodes predict the development of recurring depressive disorder, as well as co-occurring diagnoses of anxiety disorders, alcohol or substance abuse, and suicide attempts (Cicchetti & Toth, 1998). Counselors must understand that depression in youth involves the interplay of biological, psychological, and social processes.

Theories of and interventions with depression in adults may not always be appropriate when working with depressed youth (McWhirter & Burrow-Sanchez, 2004). Intervention approaches always should consider a client's environment, attitude toward therapy, cognitive development, and maturity, and adolescents are likely to differ from adults in each of these areas. Issues such as degree of separation from family, cultural norms, adolescent identity development, interpersonal challenges (e.g., peer groups), and physical and cognitive milestones also should be considered within the context of treatment (Mueller & Orvaschel, 1997; Williams, 2003). School and peer contexts influence adolescent psychological and academic adjustment, and depressive symptoms have been shown to increase during the middle school years (Cicchetti & Toth, 1998; Goldman, 2001).

Hector

West High is located in a major metropolitan area and serves a diverse student body. Mr. Warner has been a counselor at West High School for 3 years. One day he met with Hector, a 16-year-old, 10th-grade Mexican American student. Hector was referred by one of his teachers because she noticed recent behavior changes, such as isolating himself from peers and reduced participation in class. The counselor noticed that Hector seemed down or depressed, although Hector described this as being "bored."

When Mr. Warner inquired about other symptoms of depression, Hector reported that he had lost his appetite and was sleeping less during the night. He also said that he stopped hanging out with his friends on the weekends—something he previously enjoyed. Mr. Warner asked about any recent stressful events, and Hector said that his parents had been arguing a lot and were considering divorce. Hector was worried about the possibility of his parents divorcing and how it could affect his family.

In talking with Hector, Mr. Warner began to understand how much responsibility Hector shouldered for the well-being of his family. The counselor also realized that Hector partially blamed himself for the parents' difficulties.

Mr. Warner talked with Hector's mother and explained the situation. She admitted that things had been more difficult at home lately. The counselor provided Hector's mother with some referrals for family counseling in the community that serve Latino families. Hector's mother was concerned about her son and gave Mr. Warner permission to work with him.

As an intervention, Mr. Warner asked Hector to keep a "thought log" of what he was thinking about during times when he was feeling bored, sad, or down. Hector wrote, "It's my fault my parents may get divorced" and "I'm bad" when he was feeling down.

The counselor taught Hector how to challenge these negative thoughts by looking for evidence that the thoughts were not true. Then he taught Hector how to replace these negative thoughts with more positive statements such as, "It's not my fault that my parents are having trouble" and, "I'm a good son, and I'm trying to do what I can to help my family."

Because Mr. Warner knew that pleasurable activities tend to alleviate symptoms of depression, he encouraged Hector to return to activities such as hanging out with friends on the weekends, using statements such as, "It's okay to have fun with my friends even if things are tense at home" and, "Staying home all the time won't fix the problem."

The counselor scheduled weekly meetings with Hector to check-in on his progress. Within a few weeks Hector stated that he was beginning to feel like his old self again. He said that his parents had gone to see one of the family therapists that Mr. Warner had recommended. Hector also said that things were still difficult at home between his parents but that he was working on not blaming himself. Mr. Warner reviewed Hector's thought log with him, and they discussed how to make adjustments as needed. Hector's teacher reported that he had begun participating in class again.

The intervention acknowledged the family context that influenced Hector's depression. His encouraging the parents to get counseling met with success, which may have helped Hector to feel less responsible for "fixing" his parents and helped the parents recognize how their struggles were affecting Hector's well-being. Mr. Warner's response to Hector's depression resulted in internal changes that also affected Hector's behavior in school in a positive way. Finally, the intervention included reengaging Hector in his peer group, which provided an additional source of support.

Prevention and Treatment of Depression

From the perspective of the prevention/intervention framework described by McWhirter and colleagues (2007), counselors working with depressed youth should implement prevention, early intervention, or treatment strategies that involve the family, the school, and the community. A family approach to prevention and treatment might include both family therapy and parent training that promote open and healthy communication, training in problem solving and conflict resolution, and training in active listening skills.

When working with minority and majority culture families alike, family approaches must take cultural variables into account. Prevention and intervention in the school setting can include programs with specific topics (e.g., "When a friend is depressed") or a more general focus on life-skills training (e.g., "5 steps to solving problems"). Prevention at the community level might be directed to reducing the social stigma associated with seeking treatment for a mental disorder, promoting increased awareness of the availability and effectiveness of treatments for depression (e.g., free depression screenings), and educating the public about the consequences of depressive disorders and the importance of intervention (Cicchetti & Toth, 1998).

Treatment of adolescent depression requires developmentally appropriate interventions that are consistent with the ways in which adolescents express depression (Mueller & Orvaschel, 1997). This may require that counselors modify existing programs that are adult-focused, although depression interventions designed for the adolescent age group are increasing. Cognitive behavior therapy, the most frequently researched psychosocial intervention for adolescent depression, has demonstrated success (Evans et al., 2005). Other promising psychosocial interventions such as interpersonal therapy and family therapy for adolescent depression have been studied, but their outcomes are not as well understood because of the relative lack of studies (Evans et al., 2005).

In addition, antidepressant medications such as selective serotonin reuptake inhibitors (SSRIs) have shown positive outcomes in studies of adolescent depression; however, most researchers argue that more studies are needed to understand more clearly the potential short-term and long-term effects of prescribing antidepressant medication to children and adolescents (Evans et al., 2005). Finally, emerging data from studies using a combination of cognitive behavior therapy and medication for treating adolescent depression indicate that this approach shows promise (March et al., 2004).

One of the most serious symptoms of depression is suicidal thoughts and behaviors. This is where we turn next.

Suicide

Suicide is the third leading cause of death in the United States for ages 10–24, and annually about 142,000 youth are treated medically for self-inflicted injuries in the nation's emergency rooms (CDC, 2007). Suicide is the leading cause of death of gay and lesbian youth (see chapter 9). American Indian adolescents have the highest rate of suicide compared to youth from other racial/ethnic groups (see Gould & Kramer, 2001), and these rates have been attributed to substance-abuse, child abuse/neglect, and high rates of unemployment and lack of economic prosperity (Middlebrook et al., 2001). Some research has indicated higher rates of suicide for Hispanic adolescents than for European American and African American adolescents. For example, a study of risky youth behaviors (Kann et al., 1998) reported that 13% of Hispanic adolescents had attempted suicide compared to 7% for European American and African American youth.

Gender differences have been found in regard to suicide attempts and completions. Females are three times more likely than males to attempt suicide; however, males are five times more likely that females to complete a suicide (Hoyert et al., 2001). Females tend to use more passive, low-lethality suicide methods such as pills, whereas males are more apt to use violent and highly lethal methods such as guns (McWhirter et al., 2007).

Risk factors for adolescent suicide include family interactions characterized by anger, emotional ambivalence, and ineffective communication (McWhirter et al., 2007). These types of interactions deprive young people of opportunities to develop skills for coping effectively within their families and with their own negative affect. They may engage in aggression or withdrawal, reducing the likelihood that they will receive nurturing and support from others in their environment. Intrapersonal and psychological risk factors for youth suicide include loneliness (e.g., peer rejection, isolation), impulsivity (e.g., low tolerance for frustration), risk-taking (e.g., daredevil reactions to stressors), low self-esteem (e.g., poor self-concept, a sense of worthlessness), faulty thinking patterns (e.g., negative beliefs about oneself, strictly dichotomous thinking patterns, decreased ability to solve problems), and alcohol or drug use (McWhirter et al., 2007). To screen suicidal youth effectively, counselors should be familiar with these risk factors.

Assessment of Suicidality

A multifaceted approach is necessary to assess an adolescent's suicidality. The clinical interview is an effective method of assessing the risk and lethality of the adolescent's ideation. Risk factors include a family history of suicide, any previous suicide attempts, substance abuse, anxiety, hopelessness and depression, current family problems, and other current stressors. Suicide ideation may be communicated in poems, journals, diaries, or artwork. Any signs of poor impulse control, acting out, or rage should be explored further, as should mood swings, changes in sleeping or eating patterns, evidence of cognitive constriction, acting-out behaviors in school, and statements such as, "I wish I were dead" or, "I won't be around much longer."

Self-report measures such as the *Suicide Risk Screen* (Thompson & Eggert, 1999), the *Beck Hopelessness Scale* (Beck, Weissman, Lester & Trexler, 1974) and the *Beck Scale of Suicidal Ideation* (Beck, Kovacs, & Weissman, 1979) may be helpful for assessing adolescent suicidality.

Prevention of and Intervention for Suicide

Suicide prevention efforts should be directed to the underlying environmental and interpersonal characteristics linked to suicide, such as depression, lack of social support, poor problem-solving skills, and hopelessness. Schools are an excellent setting for primary prevention efforts (King et al., 2000; McWhirter et al. 2007). A number of model programs are available to teach young people how to build their self-esteem, learn to problem-solve, develop a repertoire of social skills, manage their anger and anxiety, and learn ways to assert themselves positively (for reviews, see Bauman, 2008; Hendin et al., 2005; McWhirter et al., 2007).

Follow-up or booster sessions that foster additional adaptive skills and competencies are essential to a program's long-term effectiveness. Garland and Zigler (1993) argue that the inclusion of family support programs are an important and effective adjunct to suicide-prevention efforts. These programs are designed to empower whole families by teaching them new ways to cope with life's stressors, such as poverty, single parenthood, substance abuse, and teen pregnancy.

Early intervention efforts are aimed at minimizing the frequency and severity of the suicide ideation of adolescents who exhibit some or all of the characteristics described earlier. Garland and Zigler (1993) suggest that group screening processes are the easiest and least expensive method to identify those who may be at high risk for suicide, but these types of screenings are likely to produce a number of false positives, which can be upsetting to the misclassified youth. To reduce the number who are misclassified, suicide-screening methods can be nested within the context of other health-related screening programs.

Schools, however, may be reluctant to allow suicide screenings. The first author (E. H. McWhirter) was involved in an attempt to conduct a suicide-ideation screening in a middle school as part of a research project. It took approximately a year to secure permission to enter one school district. When a suicide occurred just prior to the scheduled screening, permission for the screening was withdrawn because the school administrators feared that attention to the topic would result in copycat behavior.

In addition to screening, many researchers have emphasized the need for schools to develop interdisciplinary crisis teams to include teachers, school counselors, school nurses, parents, and others in the community (Allen et al., 2002; King, et al., 2000). Such teams are responsible for a number of activities including (a) developing prevention and early intervention programs, (b) establishing networks with other mental health agencies in the community, (c) making educational presentations in the schools and community, and (d) keeping the programs up-to-date and running smoothly. Many schools have districtwide crisis-response teams that are prepared to respond to a variety of school-related tragedies, including suicide.

McWhirter and colleagues (2007) delineated four steps to be followed in managing a suicide crisis.

1. The school counselor should assess the lethality of the threat (e.g., existence of a plan, lethality of the plan, and feasibility of carrying out the plan).
2. The counselor and the adolescent should develop a written agreement establishing that the client will contact the counselor before attempting suicide. The counselor also should provide the client with 24-hour emergency crisis line numbers as another source of support and safety.
3. The counselor should develop a plan for carefully monitoring the client and closely tracking his or her behavior for 1 to 3 days, depending on the severity of the risk. In cases in which the client will not agree to a contract or in which the counselor assesses the likelihood of an attempt to be high, the counselor may have to arrange for hospitalization or otherwise secure the client's safety.
4. When the client is a child or an adolescent, the counselor has a legal and ethical responsibility to inform the client's parents when the counselor is aware of their child's threat of suicide. Thus, the counselor must explain to the child or adolescent the limits of confidentiality so he or she will not feel betrayed if the counselor makes a disclosure to parents.

In addition to these four steps, counselors should consult with other professionals.

Substance Abuse

Substance abuse is a concern that often emerges in conjunction with depression and suicidal behavior. Experimentation with substances is typical for many youth. Unfortunately, some go on to develop significant substance-abuse problems. Almost 20% of youth in the eighth grade reported using alcohol in the past 30 days, and for drugs such as marijuana and inhalants, more than 10% of 8th-graders reported using one of these illicit substances in the past 30 days (Johnston, O'Malley, Bachman, & Schulenberg, 2006).

In general, high school students report higher substance-use levels than their middle school counterparts. In U.S. high schools approximately 34% of 10th-grade students and 45% of 12th-grade students reported using alcohol in the past 30 days, and almost 18% of 10th-grade students and 22% of 12-grade students reported using an illicit substance in the past 30 days (Johnston et al., 2006).

There are differences when drug use is compared across racial and ethnic groups. In the 8th grade, Hispanic students reported the highest levels of alcohol use (25.3%) compared to their White (20.1%) and African American (15.5%) counterparts in the past 30 days (Johnston et al., 2004). White students reported the highest alcohol use levels in the 10th (38.7%) and 12th grades (52.3%), followed by Hispanic students (10th = 37.1%, 12th = 46.4%) and African American students (10th = 23.7%; 12th = 29.9%).

Contrary to many harmful stereotypes, African American students reported the lowest level of alcohol use in the past 30 days among all three groups. American Indian students have disproportionately high use rates for drugs such as alcohol, tobacco, marijuana, and stimulants when compared to other racial/ethnic groups (Wallace et al., 2003). Hispanic students report higher levels of crack and heroin use than Whites and African Americans (Johnston et al., 2004).

The drugs used most frequently by adolescents in the United States are alcohol, tobacco, and marijuana, respectively. About 10% of youth between ages 12 and 17 are considered to be current illicit drug users, and 8% of them could be diagnosed with a substance-abuse or dependence disorder (SAMHSA, 2006). Research suggests that a substantial number of youth with a substance-use disorder simultaneously experience another disorder such as conduct disorder (60%–80%), attention deficit/hyperactivity disorder (30%–50%), depression (15%–25%), anxiety disorders (15%–25%), and bipolar disorder (10%–15%) (Riggs, 2003).

Risk factors for adolescent substance abuse are generally categorized into the five major areas of individual, peer, family, school, and community factors (Burrow-Sanchez & Hawken, 2007).

1. *Individual factors.* Adolescents' characteristics and behaviors include aggressiveness toward others, negative moods, withdrawal, and impulsivity, as well as mental health problems such as conduct disorder, attention-deficit hyperactivity disorder (ADHD), depression, or a learning disorder. In general, the earlier these behaviors appear in adolescent development, the more strongly they predict a later substance abuse problem.

2. *Peer factors.* Adolescents who associate with drug using peers are more likely to use drugs themselves.

3. *Family factors.* The likelihood of drug use increases when an adolescent comes from a family in which a parent or older sibling uses drugs (Brook, Whiteman, Gordon, & Brook, 1990; Johnson, Schoutz, & Locke, 1984). Other family-related risk factors for adolescent substance abuse include high levels of family conflict or stress, as well as poor parenting practices such as low levels of parental supervision for children, parents' use of inconsistent and harsh discipline, poor display of problem-solving skills by parents, and low levels of emotional support.

4. *School factors.* Risk factors for adolescent substance abuse in the school context include things such as academic failure and subsequent dropout. Students who drop out of school are more likely to use substances than their in-school counterparts (Freudenberg & Ruglis, 2007; Mensch & Kandel, 1988). Other risk factors include displaying inappropriate classroom behavior such as overt aggression toward others or excessive withdrawal. Certain school characteristics that can serve as risk factors include schools in which personnel have low expectations for students, settings that are disorganized and unsafe, and schools that do not have clear expectations regarding appropriate student behavior (Mayer, 1995; Skiba & Peterson, 1999; Sugai, Horner, & Gresham, 2002).

5. *Community factors.* Risk factors in the community and neighborhood include poverty, adult and community norms that favor drug use, lax drug laws, and high availability of drugs (NIDA, 2003). The more available drugs are in a given community, the more likely adolescents will report using them. (Maddahian, Newcomb, & Bentler, 1988). Data from the National Survey on Drug Use and Health provided estimates that more than 50% of adolescents ages 12–17 consider marijuana "fairly easy" or "very easy" to acquire in their communities (SAMHSA, 2003). Another community-based factor that creates risk for adolescent substance abuse is a disorganized and unsafe neighborhood (Hawkins et al., 1992; Newcomb, 1995). Disorganized and unsafe neighborhoods are typically a function of poverty and its sequelae, including high crime and a general lack of physically maintaining buildings and homes.

Prevention and Treatment of Substance Abuse

Preventive interventions for adolescent substance abuse typically occur in school settings and may be universal, selected, or indicated interventions. Fortunately, evidence-based substance-abuse prevention programs can be implemented in schools at all levels of prevention (see Burrow-Sanchez & Hawken, 2007 for a review of prevention programs). In contrast, substance-abuse treatment generally occurs outside of the school setting in community mental health clinics, residential settings, or medical centers.

The most common treatment approaches for adolescent substance abuse identified by Muck and colleagues (2001) include 12-step (e.g., AA), cognitive-behavioral, family-based, and therapeutic communities. Further, these approaches are most likely found in the following treatment formats: outpatient, day-treatment, inpatient and residential (see Burrow-Sanchez & Hawken, 2007, for a review of treatment programs). Students who participate in community treatment will likely need support from school counselors to reintegrate successfully into the school setting and resist negative peer influences upon completion of treatment.

School Intervention

Some schools have a Student Assistance Program (SAP) to which counselors can refer students who have drug use problems. SAPs generally include a drug-abuse counselor and other school professionals (Moore & Forster, 1993). Counselors in many schools, however, do not have this option and thus will have to establish a positive working relationship with the adolescent to better understand his or her problem and subsequently make an appropriate referral to a school or community-based intervention program (Burrow-Sanchez & Hawken, 2007).

A potential difficulty that counselors may find in working with students who have substance-abuse problems is their reluctance to talk about the issue openly and a tendency to underreport drug use (Winters, Stinchfield, Henly, & Schartz, 1992). In many school settings, student substance problems fall under zero-tolerance polices and students are generally punished (e.g., suspension, expulsion) for drug-related behavior. Thus, in general, students are keenly aware that disclosing their substance use may lead to negative consequences rather than support. Students also may anticipate that adults in positions of authority, such as counselors, will tell them things such as, "You must stop using immediately" and, "This is a bad thing you are doing." Therefore, students with substance-abuse problems frequently resist adults in school settings (Burrow-Sanchez & Hawken, 2007).

Using strategies from Motivational Interviewing (MI), counselors can work with a student's resistance, rather than against it, as an initial step in developing a positive working relationship (Miller & Rollnick, 2002). Building a sense of trust and understanding early in the working relationship will help to reduce the student's resistance to talking about a potential substance-abuse problem. One strategy is to initiate a discussion with the student about what will be done with the information discussed (Burrow-Sanchez & Hawken, 2007). For example, most students are apprehensive to discuss their drug-use history because they fear that they will be punished or that the information will be divulged to others such as parents or school administrators (e.g., principal). Thus, counselors are encouraged to initiate a discussion with the student about issues such as confidentiality and substance-abuse-related policies for their specific school setting.

A second MI strategy for lowering resistance is to listen for challenges the student is currently facing, such as disciplinary consequences at school or problems at home, and use the skills of reflection to echo his or her statements in a way that communicates understanding of the situation (Miller & Rollnick, 2002). Generally, adolescents respond better when discussing a sensitive topic such as substance use when they perceive the environment to be supportive, nonthreatening, and with an emphasis on understanding the problem instead of placing blame on the student (Baer & Peterson, 2002). Therefore, lowering a student's resistance, as described above, will allow him or her to communicate more openly about the substance-abuse problem and will lead to more accurate information-gathering by the counselor (Burrow-Sanchez & Hawken, 2007).

Sara

A European American 11th-grade senior, Sara, was referred to the school counselor by her teacher, Mr. Martinez, who said he smelled alcohol on Sara's breath. The school counselor, Mrs. Carn, asked Sara if she knew why she had been referred to her. Sara said that Mr. Martinez was out to get her and that he "made up a story" about smelling alcohol on her breath. Sara also stated that she did not have a problem with alcohol and wasn't sure why everybody was so worried about it.

Mrs. Carn immediately noticed Sara's hesitancy in talking about the issue, so she employed motivational interviewing strategies to help lower the resistance in the interaction. She did this initially by responding to Sara with reflective statements such as, "Sounds like Mr. Martinez and others are out to get you and that you don't have a problem with alcohol."

Sara generally agreed with Mrs. Carn's reflective statements and related more about her situation as a result. Mrs. Carn successfully used this strategy to lower Sara's resistance, as well as to learn how she perceived the problem.

When Mrs. Carn asked Sara who else seemed to be worried about her drinking, she responded, "My mom has been on my case for the past few weeks because she thinks I party too much on the weekends."

The counselor reflected, "Sounds like your Mom is also concerned about your drinking." She then asked Sara if *she* had any concerns about her drinking.

Sara admitted that a couple of times she had "blacked out" after drinking too much, and this did concern her. She also disclosed that her dad drank a lot and that she sometimes wondered if she would turn out like her dad.

Mrs. Carn responded, "So, it sounds like you're concerned that you may drink too much at times and that you may drink as much as your father in the future." She sensed that Sara would likely benefit from talking with someone in more detail about her drinking. She asked Sara if she would be open to talking with a counselor who had more training in this area about the concerns she had expressed.

Sara said she was open to talking to someone but stated, "I can't promise anything."

Mrs. Carn said she understood her position and offered her a referral to the Student Assistance Program (SAP) at the high school. She provided her with information on how SAPs work, to further her understanding and lower her resistance regarding this program. She also offered Sara the opportunity to meet with her again, if needed. The interested reader can find additional information on specific techniques and strategies for working with students on substance abuse issues in Burrow-Sanchez and Hawken (2007).

Summary

The primary socializing systems that contribute to young people's well being and level of risk are the family, peer group and school. We have emphasized the complex influences of these contexts and noted the importance of conceptualizing all young clients within these contexts. The framework for prevention and intervention provides counselors with a means of conceptualizing the range of risk, contexts, and approaches to consider in designing programs and implementing strategies. We reviewed three specific problems faced by many youth, depression, suicide and substance abuse, providing descriptive information as well as suggestions for intervention. Two case studies illustrate intervention approaches.

Awareness of the complexity of the problems faced by today's youth, together with knowledge of the range of community and school programs and resources that are locally available, can help counselors deliver more comprehensive and effective interventions. Advocacy for broader social and policy change is a necessary adjunct to the direct work that counselors do with young people and will help lay the foundation for a better future.

References

Allen, M., Burt, K., Bryan, E., Carter, D., Orsi, R., & Durkan, L. (2002). School counselors' preparation for and participation in crisis intervention. *Professional School Counseling*; 6(2), 96–102.

American Psychiatric Association. (2000). *Diagnostic and statistical manual of mental disorders* (4th ed., text rev.). Washington, DC: Author.

Aube, J., Fichman, L., Saltaris, C., & Koestner, R. (2000). Gender differences in adolescent depressive symptomatology: Towards an integrated social–developmental model. *Journal of Social and Clinical Psychology, 19*(3), 297–313.

Baer, J. S., & Peterson, P. L. (2002). Motivational interviewing with adolescents and young adults. In W. R. Miller & S. Rollnick, *Motivational interviewing: Preparing people for change* (2nd ed., pp. 320–332). New York: Guilford Press.

Bauman, S. (2008). *Essential topics for the helping professional*. Boston: Allyn & Bacon.

Beardslee, W. R., & Gladstone, T. R. G. (2001). Prevention of childhood depression: Recent findings and future prospects. *Biological Psychiatry, 49*, 1101–1110.

Beauvais, F., Chavez, E. L., Oetting, E. R., Deffenbacher, J. L., & Cornell, G. R. (1996). Drug use, violence, and victimization among White American, Mexican American, and American Indian dropouts, students with academic problems, and students in good academic standing. *Journal of Counseling Psychology, 43*, 292–299.

Beck, A. T., Kovacs, M., & Weissman, A. (1979). Assessment of suicidal intention: The scale for suicidal ideation. *Journal of Clinical and Consulting Psychology, 47*(2), 343–352.

Beck, A. T., Weissman, A., Lester, D., & Trexler, L. (1974). The measurement of pessimism: The hopelessness scale. *Journal of Consulting and Clinical Psychology, 42*(6), 861–865.

Blake, C., Wang, W. Cartledge, G., & Gardner, R. (2000). Middle school students with serious emotional disturbances serve as social skills trainers and reinforcers for peers with SED. *Behavioral Disorders, 25*, 280–298.

Brook, J. S., Whiteman, M., Gordon, A. S., & Brook, D. W. (1990). The role of older brothers in younger brothers' drug use viewed in the context of parent and peer influences. *Journal of Genetic Psychology, 151*, 59–75.

Brown, L. K., Lourie, K. J., Zlotnick, C., & Cohn J. (2000). Impact of sexual abuse on the HIV-risk-related behavior of adolescents in intensive psychiatric treatment. American Journal of Psychiatry, *157*(9), 1413–1415.

Burrow-Sanchez, J. J., & Hawken, L. S. (2007). *Helping students overcome substance abuse: Effective practices for prevention and intervention*. New York: Guilford Press.

Centers for Disease Control (2007). *Youth suicide*. Retrieved August 28, 2007, from http://www.cdc.gov/ncipc/dvp/Suicide/youthsuicide.htm

Cicchetti, D., & Toth, S. L. (1998). The development of depression in children and adolescents. American Psychologist, 53(2), 221–241.

Dinkes, R. Cataldi. E. F., Kena, G., & Baum, K. (2006). *Indicators of school crime and safety: 2006* (NCES 2007-03/NCJ 214262). Washington, DC: U.S. Departments of Education and Justice.

Dishion, T. J. & Dodge, K. A. (2005). Peer contagion in interventions for children and adolescents: Moving towards an understanding of the ecology and dynamics of change. *Journal of Abnormal Child Psychology, 33*(3), 395–400.

Dishion, T. J., McCord, J., & Poulin, F. (1999). When interventions harm: Peer groups and problem behavior. *American Psychologist, 54*(9), 755–764.

Duggal, S., Carlson, E. A., Sroufe, L. A., & Egeland, B. (2001). Depressive symptomatology in childhood and adolescence. *Development and Psychopathology, 13*, 143–164.

Durlak, J. A., & Weissberg, R. P. (2007). *The impact of after-school programs that promote personal and social skills.* Chicago: Collaborative for Academic, Social, and Emotional Learning.

Ehrensaft, M. K., Cohen, P., Brown, J., Smailes, E., Chen, H., & Johnson, J. G. (2003). Intergenerational transmission of partner violence: A 20-year prospective study. *Journal of Consulting and Clinical Psychology, 71*(4), 741–753.

Evans, D. L., Beardslee, W., Biederman, J., Brent, D., Charney, D., Coyle, J. et al. (2005). Treatment of depression and bipolar disorder. In D. L. Evans, E. B. Foa, R. E. Gur, H. Hendin, C. P. O'Brien, M. E. P. Seligman, & B. T. Walsh (Eds.), *Treating and preventing adolescent mental health disorders: What we know and what we don't know* (pp. 30–54). New York: Oxford.

Finkelhor, D. (1995). The victimization of children: A developmental perspective. *American Journal of Orthopsychiatry, 65*(2), 177–193.

Freudenberg, N., & Ruglis, J. (2007). Reframing school dropout as a public health issue. *Prevention of Chronic Disease*, 4(4*)*. Accessed October 31, 2007, from http://www.cdc.gov/pcd/issues/2007/oct/07_0063.htm

Garber, J., Keiley, M. K., & Martin, N. C. (2002). Developmental trajectories of adolescents' depressive symptoms: Predictors of change. *Journal of Consulting and Clinical Psychology, 70*(1), 79–95.

Garland, A. E., & Zigler, E. (1993). Adolescent suicide prevention: Current research and social policy implications. *American Psychologist, 48*(2), 169–182.

Gershoff, E. (2002). Corporal punishment by parents and associated child behaviors and experiences: A meta-analytic and theoretical review. *Psychological Bulletin, 128*, 539–579.

Goldman, W. T. (2001). Depression in children. Retrieved July 28, 2002, from http://www.keepkidshealthy.com/cgi-bin/MasterPFP.cgi

Gould, M. S., & Kramer, R. A. (2001). Youth suicide prevention. *Suicide and Life Threatening Behavior, 31*(Suppl.), 6–31.

Hawkins, J. D., Catalano, R. F., & Miller, J. Y. (1992). Risk and protective factors for alcohol and other drug problems in adolescence and early adulthood: Implications for substance abuse prevention. *Psychological Bulletin, 112*(1), 64–105.

Hendin, H., Brent, D. A., Cornelius, J. R., Coyne-Beasley, T., Greenberg, T., Gould, Madelyn et al. (2005). Youth suicide. In D. L. Evans, E. B. Foa, R. E. Gur, H. Hendin, C. P. O'Brien, M. E. P. Seligman, & B. T. Walsh (Eds.), *Treating and preventing adolescent mental health disorders: What we know and what we don't know* (pp. 434–493). New York: Oxford.

Hoyert, D. L., Anas, E., Smith, B. L., Murphy, S. L., & Kochanek, K. D. (2001). *Deaths: Final data for 1999. National Vital Statistics Reports, 49*(8). Hyattsville, MD: National Center for Health Statistics. (DHHS Publication Number (PHS) 2001–1120).

Johnson, G. M., Schoutz, F. C., & Locke, T. P. (1984). Relationships between adolescent drug use and parental drug behaviors. *Adolescence, 19*, 295–299.

Johnston, L. D., O'Malley, P. M., Bachman, J. G., & Schulenberg, J. E. (2004). *Demographic subgroup trends for various licit and illicit drugs, 1975–2003* (Monitoring the Future Occasional Paper No. 60). Ann Arbor, MI: Institute for Social Research.

Johnston, L. D., O'Malley, P. M., Bachman, J. G., & Schulenberg, J. E. (2006). *Monitoring the Future national results on adolescent drug use: Overview of key findings 2005* (No. NIH Publication No. 06-5882). Bethesda, MD: National Institute on Drug Abuse.

Kaminer, Y. (2005). Challenges and opportunities of group therapy for adolescent substance abuse: A critical review. *Addictive Behaviors, 30*(9), 1765–1774.

Kann, L., et al. (1998). Youth risk behavior surveillance–United States 1997. *Journal of School Health 68*(9), 355–369.

Kendler, K. S., Bulik, C. M., Silberg, J., Hettema J. M., Myers, J., Prescott, C. A. (2000). Childhood sexual abuse and adult psychiatric and substance use disorders in women. *Archives of General Psychiatry, 57*, 953–959.

King, K. A., Price, J. H., Telljohann, S. K., & Wahl, J. (2000). Preventing adolescent suicide: Do high school counselors know the risk factors? *Professional School Counseling, 3*(4), 255–263.

Kovacs, M. (1989). Affective disorders in children and adolescents. *American Psychologist, 44*, 209–215.

Kutnick, P. (2005). Co-operative learning: The social and intellectual outcomes of learning in groups. *European Journal of Special Needs Education, 20*(1), 117–121.

Laird, J., DeBell, M., Kienzl, G. & Chapman, C. (2007). *Dropout rates in the United States: 2005* (NCES 2007-059). U.S. Department of Education. Washington, DC: National Center for Education Statistics. Retrieved September 6, 2007, from http://nces.ed.gov/pubsearch

Lewinsohn, P. M., Hops, H., Roberts, R., Seeley, J. R., & Andrew, J. (1993). Adolescent psychopathology: I. Prevalence and incidence of depression and other DSM-III-R disorders in high school students. *Journal of Abnormal Psychology, 102*(1), 133–144.

Maddahian, E., Newcomb, M. D., & Bentler, P. M. (1988). Adolescent drug use and intention to use drugs: Concurrent and longitudinal analyses of four ethnic groups. *Addictive Behaviors, 13*, 191–195.

March, J., Silva, S., Petrycki, S., Curry, J., Wells, K., Fairbank, J., et al. (2004). Fluoxetine, cognitive behavioral therapy, and their combination for adolescents with depression: Treatment for Adolescents with Depression Study (TADS) randomized controlled trial. *Journal of the American Medical Association*, *292*(7), 807–820.

Mayer, G. R. (1995). Preventing antisocial behavior in the schools. *Journal of Applied Behavior Analysis, 28*, 467-478.

McWhirter, B. T., & Burrow-Sanchez, J. J. (2004). Preventing and treating depression and bipolar disorders in children and adolescents. In D. Capuzzi & D. R. Gross (Eds.) *Youth at risk: A prevention resource for counselors, teachers, and parents* (4th ed., pp. 117–141). Alexandria, VA: American Counseling Association.

McWhirter, E. H. (1994). *Counseling for empowerment*. Alexandria, VA: American Counseling Association.

McWhirter, E. H. (1997). Empowerment, social activism, and counseling. *Counseling & Human Development, 29*(8), 1–11.

McWhirter, E. H. (1998). An empowerment model of counselor training. *Canadian Journal of Counselling, 32*(1), 12–26.

McWhirter, E. H. (2001, March). Social action at the individual level: In pursuit of critical consciousness. In P. Gore & J. Swanson (chairs), *Counseling psychologists as agents of social change*. Paper presented at Fourth National Conference on Counseling Psychology, Houston, TX.

McWhirter, J. J., McWhirter, B. T., McWhirter, A. M., & McWhirter, E. H. (2007). *At-risk youth: A comprehensive response* (3d ed.). Pacific Grove, CA: Brooks/Cole.

Mensch, B. S., & Kandel, D. B. (1988). Dropping out of high school and drug involvement. *Sociology of Education, 61*(2), 95–113.

Middlebrook, D. L., LeMaster, P. L., Beals, J., Novins, D. K., & Manson, S. M. (2001). Suicide prevention in American Indian and Alaska Native communities: A critical review of programs. *Suicide and Life Threatening Behavior, 31*(Suppl.), 132–149.

Miller, W. R., & Rollnick, S. (2002). *Motivational interviewing: Preparing people for change* (2nd ed.). New York: Guilford Press.

Milling, L. & Martin, B. (1992). Depression and suicidal behavior in preadolescent children. In C. E. Walker & M. C. Roberts (Eds.), *Handbook of clinical child psychology* (2nd ed., pp. 319–339). New York: Wiley.

Moore, D. D., & Forster, J. R. (1993). Student assistance programs: New approaches for reducing adolescent substance abuse. *Journal of Counseling and Development, 71*, 326–329.

Muck, R., Zempolich, K. A., Titus, J. C., Fishman, M., Godley, M. D., & Schwebel, R. (2001). An overview of the effectiveness of adolescent substance abuse treatment models. *Youth and Society, 33*(2), 143–168.

Mueller, C. & Orvaschel, H. (1997). The failure of "adult" interventions with adolescent depression: What does it mean for theory, research, and practice? *Journal of Affective Disorders, 44*, 203–215.

National Institute of Drug Abuse (NIDA). (2003). Preventing drug use among children and adolescents: A research-based guide for parents, educators, and community leaders (2nd ed.). Washington DC: Author. Retrieved August 11, 2007, from http://www.drugabuse.gov/pdf/prevention/RedBook.pdf

National Institute of Mental Health (2000). Depression. Retrieved August 28, 2007, from http://www.nimh.nih.gov/publicat/depression.cfm

Neumark-Sztainer, D., Story, M., Hannan, P., Beuhring, T., & Resnick, M. (2000). Disordered eating among adolescents: Associations with sexual/physical abuse and other familial/psychosocial factors. *International Journal of Eating Disorders, 28*(3), 249–258.

Newcomb, M. D. (1995). Identifying high-risk youth: Prevalence and patterns of adolescent drug abuse. In E. Rahdert & D. Czechowicz (Eds.), *Adolescent drug abuse: Clinical assessment and therapeutic interventions* (DHHS Publication No. 95-3908, NIDA Research Monograph No. 156, pp. 7-38). Rockville, MD: U.S. Department of Health and Human Services.

Oetting, E. R., & Beauvais, E. (1987). Peer cluster theory, socialization characteristics, and adolescent drug use: A path analysis. *Journal of Counseling Psychology*, 34(2), 205–213.

Riggs, P. D. (2003). Treating adolescents for substance abuse and comorbid psychiatric disorders. *NIDA Science and Practice Perspectives, 2*(1), 18–28.

Skiba, R. J., & Peterson, R. L. (1999). The dark side of zero tolerance: Can punishment lead to safe schools? *Phi Delta Kappan, 80*, 372–376.

Substance Abuse and Mental Health Services Administration, Office of Applied Studies. (2003). *Results from the 2002 National Survey on Drug Use and Health: National Findings* (NSDUH Series H-22. DHHS Publication No. SMA 03-3836). Rockville, MD: Author.

Substance Abuse and Mental Health Services Administration (SAMHSA), Office of Applied Studies. (2006). *Results from the 2005 National Survey on Drug Use and*

Health: National Findings (NSDUH Series H-30. DHHS Publication No. SMA 06-4194). Rockville, MD: Author.

Sugai, G., Horner, R. H., & Greshman, F. M. (2002). Behaviorally effective school environments. In M. R. Shin, H. M. Walker, & G. Stoner (Eds.), *Interventions for academic and behavior problems II: Preventive and remedial approaches.* Bethesda, MD: National Association of School Psychologists.

Taylor, B., Pressley, M., & Pearson, D. (2000). *Research-supported characteristics of teachers and schools that promote reading achievement.* Ann Arbor, MI: Center for the Improvement of Early Reading Achievement.

Thompson, E. A., & Eggert, L. L. (1999). Using the suicide risk screen to identify suicidal adolescents among potential high school dropouts. *Journal of the American Academy of Child and Adolescent Psychiatry, 38*(12), 1506–1514.

Wallace, J. M., Jr., Bachman, J. G., O'Malley, P. M., Schulenberg, J. E., Cooper, S. M., & Johnston, L. D. (2003). Gender and ethnic differences in smoking, drinking and illicit drug use among American 8th, 10th, and 12th grade students, 1976–2000. *Addiction, 98,* 225–234.

Williams, J. S. (2003). Multiculturalism at Least as Effective as Cultural Specificity in Test of Prevention Program. *NIDA Notes Research Findings*, 18(3). Retrieved August 11, 2007 from http://www.nida.nih.gov/NIDA_Notes/NNVol18N3/Multiculturalism.html

Winters, K. C., Stinchfield, R. D., Henly, G. A., & Schwartz, R. H. (1992). Validity of adolescent self-report of alcohol and other drug involvement. *International Journal of the Addictions, 25,* 1379–1395.

Wolf, V. B. (1993). Group therapy of young latency age sexually abused girls, *Journal of Child and Adolescent Group Therapy, 3*(1), 25–39.

Wonderlich, S. A., Crosby, R. D., Mitchell, J. E., Roberts, J., Haseltine, B., Demuth, G. & Thompson, K. (2000). Relationship of childhood sexual abuse and eating disturbance in children. *Journal of the American Academy of Child and Adolescent Psychiatry, 39*(10), 1277–1283.

11

Small-Group Counseling

James J. Bergin and James F. Klein

According to Yalom (2005),

> human beings have always lived in groups that have been characterized
> by intense and persistent relationships among members and that the
> need to belong is a powerful, fundamental, and pervasive motivation.
> (p. 19)

This sense of belonging is paramount in the lives of children and adolescents. Group counseling provides a microcosm of life as well as the opportunity to safely explore how members relate to the world around them. Small-group counseling with children and adolescents is becoming more popular in school and community settings (Myrick, 2002). The American School Counselor Association (2003) considers group counseling to be an ideal treatment modality for delivering direct services as part of a comprehensive developmental school counseling program.

This chapter explores the benefits of group counseling with children and adolescents, the stages of group, the counselor's role, ethical considerations in group work with minors, and logistics of group formation. The chapter concludes with a description of three types of counseling groups, with references for designing group activities.

Benefits of Group Counseling With Children and Adolescents

A major benefit of group counseling is that it creates the opportunity for individuals to gain knowledge and skills that will assist them in making and carrying out their own choices. The intent is to promote personal growth and resolve problems and conflicts. To this end, the group process engages individuals in activities that explore personal thoughts, feelings, attitudes, values, and interests and the way these factors influence personal choices. It also examines the individual's skills in communication, cooperation, and decision-making, particularly as these skills pertain to interpersonal interaction and problem-solving (Baker, 2000).

Group counseling is well suited to the needs of elementary, middle, and secondary school students. Developmentally, most children and adolescents lack the knowledge and skills needed to deal with all of the challenges of growing up. Much of the curriculum that covers these areas is addressed appropriately through large-group guidance activities. If students require additional assistance, more personalized information, or emotional support, group counseling provides an atmosphere that is conducive to remedial training, self-exploration, and peer support (Sandhu, 2001).

Further, group counseling is a valuable supplement to individual counseling. Students who are being counseled individually may present problems and concerns that can be addressed best in a group context. For example, a student who has difficulty making decisions and committing to a course of action may benefit a great deal from a group that addresses the tasks of communication and cooperative decision-making. Similarly, young children who have trouble articulating their thoughts and feelings, perhaps because of delayed language development, can enhance their vocabulary and expressive skills by participating in a "feelings" group.

Group counseling with children differs from group work with older students in some respects. Although the basic principles of group counseling apply to all ages, groups for young children must use language that is developmentally tailored to them (Corey & Corey, 2006). Young children tend to feel most natural in play and activity groups because they are accustomed to acting out their needs as a way of expressing themselves (Gladding, 1998). Small groups (two to four members) that use play media as the main vehicle for communication are often recommended for preschoolers and primary-grade youngsters (Kaduson & Schaefer, 2000).

During the elementary and middle school years, children rapidly gain verbal ability, which enables them to participate readily in the verbal exchange that typifies most counseling groups. Hence, most groups in this age range use activities similar to those used with adolescents. Even though these students may be articulate and expressive, many require some training in social interaction, especially in functioning as a member of a group. Therefore, counselors in elementary and middle schools incorporate into group procedures the opportunity for participants to learn group roles and to practice active listening skills that will facilitate the group process. Some practitioners have developed specialized group activities targeting the acquisition of these skills for group participants (Bergin, 1991; Myrick, 2002).

Group counseling may be the preferred intervention for adolescents. Adolescents strongly desire peer acceptance and affiliation, and the group context affords them easy access to peer feedback and support. Moreover, the struggle for independence from authority and the preoccupation with self that characterize this developmental stage can make adolescents reluctant to seek individual counseling with an adult. Unlike younger children, who trust counselors more readily, adolescents tend to feel threatened by any suggestion that they seek counseling. The invitation to join a group and to work with peers is more appealing, as it reduces the chances of being put on the "hot seat." At the same time, it increases the opportunity to relate with peers and gain their approval. Other than the additional emphasis on trust and peer acceptance, group counseling procedures with adolescents are generally the same as those used with adult groups.

Group Stages

Groups typically proceed through four stages: initial, transition, working, and termination. Movement from stage to stage is seldom smooth and uniform.

Initial Stage

In the initial stage, activities are geared to bring about cohesion among group members. Icebreaker activities frequently are employed to introduce members and help them feel comfortable interacting with other participants. In this stage the group's purpose and objectives are explained and members discuss their commitment to work with and help one another (Capuzzi & Gross, 2001). The group agrees on and establishes the rules, and each rule is clarified for the group to ensure understanding, especially concerning confidentiality. Once these issues have been clarified, the group sets about building rapport by demonstrating caring, attention, and a desire to know and understand one another.

An excellent example of an effective and creative icebreaker is Bergin's (1989) "Group Logo" activity. This icebreaker strives to build group identity and promotes cohesion. In this activity the members cooperate in drawing overlapping shapes on a large piece of posterboard. Together they agree upon a picture they see emerging from the lines they have drawn, and then outline, color, and title the picture. The title and picture become the group's logo, which can be displayed throughout subsequent group sessions.

Following this group-building activity, the counselor invites the students to identify personal concerns they want to bring up in subsequent sessions. The counselor can facilitate the group's discussion by asking questions such as:

Why do you think joining this group can be helpful to you?
What do you think about the group logo?
How can you feel more comfortable in the group?
What are you looking forward to?

Transition Stage

The transition stage is characterized by resistance. This may be in the form of avoidance behaviors such as coming late to sessions, failing to listen attentively to others, engaging in chitchat, or withholding ideas and opinions from the group. Or it may take the form of challenges to the counselor. Participants might question the "real" purposes of the group, why the members were chosen for the group, and how confidentiality can be guaranteed.

The key ingredient in group success is trust—trusting oneself, other members, and the process. The group facilitator can provide the impetus for individual members to confront the others' concerns in a caring and accepting manner, thereby reinforcing others' trust and commitment to the group's progress.

Another way in which the group facilitator can address resistance is by illuminating and/or activating the "here-and-now" (Yalom, 2005). According to Yalom, each sentiment, or behavior for that matter, is composed of invisible and unvoiced layers. For example, illuminating and activitating the here-and-now could be as simple and meaningful as deliberately addressing a member's "lateness" to the group and processing how this has affected the group. In essence, they bring into the group what is happening in real time and acknowledge its contribution (i.e., positively or negatively) to the group process and other members.

Working Stage

The group reaches the working stage when it addresses its primary purpose of helping individual members deal with their present concerns. These concerns may revolve around a developmental need, a situation, or an experience common to many or all group members, or it may be an issue of immediate concern to an individual member. The group assists individual members in clarifying their concerns and exploring alternative ways of achieving their personal goals. Activities such as role-playing and modeling afford group members the opportunity to express themselves, receive feedback from others, and observe, practice, and learn new ways of behaving, which they can transfer to their environments outside the counseling group.

Termination

The major function of the termination stage is to help members evaluate their progress toward personal goals during their involvement in the group process. Members engage in self-evaluation, provide feedback to one another, and are reinforced for their participation in the group. They formulate and discuss plans for implementing what each member has learned. To facilitate the discussion, the counselor might ask questions such as the following:

- How do you feel about your concerns right now?
- How would you describe the growth you've made as a result of this group experience?

- What must you continue to do to maintain your positive growth?
- What is the next step you should take?
- What things have you learned in this group that will help you reach your goals?

The counselor should encourage members to make positive statements, reinforcing one another for their communication and cooperation while they are in the group. The counselor and members then plan a follow-up session. Follow-up and evaluation arrangements also are made during the termination stage.

The Counselor's Role

In groups for children and adolescents, the counselor is the primary facilitator of the group process. The counselor's role as facilitator involves numerous components during the following three phases: (a) before, (b) during, and (c) after.

Before: Logistics and Collaboration

These groups often take place in the school setting, with the group counselor as facilitator. Initially he or she assesses the students' needs, defines the group's purposes and objectives, identifies and selects prospective group members, arranges permission for members to join, organizes the schedule of sessions, plans the group activities, and arranges space for the group to meet. While carrying out these responsibilities, the counselor enlists the support of parents, school administrators, teachers, and other faculty members.

During: Facilitating Group Processes

During the group process the counselor concentrates on promoting the development of group interaction, establishing rapport among group members, leading the group progressively through all four stages, and encouraging individual members' self-exploration and personal decision making. The counselor guides the group as it discusses individual and joint concerns, models appropriate attending and responding behaviors, and reinforces members for supporting one another during their individual self-exploration. In addition, the counselor confronts resistance sensitively, redirects negative behavior, and encourages the group's efforts to become self-regulatory. The counselor safeguards the group's integrity by reminding members of the collaboratively agreed-upon rules.

After: Evaluation and Accountability

After completion of the group process, the counselor evaluates the group as a whole and helps the group conduct an evaluation of the group process. After the final session, in which members assess their personal progress and contributions to the group, the counselor conducts a follow-up evaluation with the members to gain their opinions of the group's effectiveness. The counselor may ask the group members to fill out a brief questionnaire or rating sheet. Thompson and Rudolph (2000) recommend using the following evaluation instrument (developed by Bruckner and Thompson, 1987, p. 398), which contains six incomplete statements and two forced-choice items:

1. I think coming to the group room is (response).
2. Some things I have enjoyed talking about in the group room are (response).
3. Some things I would like to talk about that we have not talked about are (response).
4. I think the counselor is (response).
5. The counselor could be better if (response).
6. Some things I have learned from coming to the group room are (response).
7. If I had a choice, I (would)/(would not) come to the group room with my class.
8. Have you ever talked with your parents about things that were discussed in the group? (yes)/(no).

In addition to evaluating the group as a whole, school counselors facilitating groups with children and adolescents are facing increasing pressure to empirically demonstrate how their specific intervention contributes positively to school outcomes and supports the overall school mission. School counselors in the 21st century work in a culture of assessment and accountability. A considerable percentage of the push for accountability emanates from the No Child Left Behind Act of 2001.

The American School Counselor Association (ASCA) (2005) asserts that accountability and evaluation of school counseling programs and services are an absolute necessity. As a result, school counselors must consider collecting available descriptive data (attendance rates, grade-point averages, behavioral referrals, etc.) for pre- and post-test analyses. The ability to aggregate and disaggregate data to demonstrate positive growth as well as academic achievement are critical skills for the contemporary school counselor.

Ethical Considerations in Group Work With Minors

When engaging children and adolescents in group counseling, one of the counselor's primary responsibilities is to protect the welfare of each member. Adult clients presumably have the ability to care for themselves and make wise choices regarding their present and future behavior. Minors, however, are dependent upon their parents or guardians to assist them. Therefore, the counselor has to accept ethical responsibility for advising children and adolescents of their rights to choose how they participate in the group process and deal with their personal feelings, beliefs, values, and behaviors.

Likewise, because parents and guardians normally have a deep interest in their children's welfare, as well as being legally responsible for them, the counselor should collaborate with parents and keep them apprised of the children's progress and needs as revealed through the counseling group process (Schmidt, 2002). And other adults who actively participate in the child's growth and development, such as teachers and school administrators, too, have ethical and legal rights to be informed of the counselor's work with group members, especially if the parents grant these other adults these privileges.

The counselor should prepare an information sheet describing the group process, purpose, activities, rules, and number of sessions to present to parents. Some counselors also request that parents give written consent allowing the child to participate in the counseling group. The counselor must clarify and emphasize the group rule regarding confidentiality. The group counseling context offers less assurance than individual counseling for maintaining confidentiality, and the counselor cannot guarantee to the group anyone's confidentiality other than his or her own.

Some group members may question whether the counselor is adhering to the rules of confidentiality when they know that he or she is consulting with their parents, teachers, and other adults. Therefore, during pre-group interviews and again in the first session, the counselor must explain the importance of maintaining confidentiality, inform members of the potential consequences of intentionally breaching confidentiality, and clarify the specific conditions under which he or she will reveal information about a member to parents, guardians, teachers, or others.

Corey and Corey (2001) presented a number of guidelines concerning the issue of confidentiality when working with minors. They recommended that the counselor ask participants to sign a contract agreeing not to discuss outside of the group what happens in the group, obtain written parental consent even when state law does not required it, and scrupulously abide by school policies regarding confidentiality. Counselors must practice within the boundaries of local and state laws, especially laws regarding child neglect and abuse, molestation, and incest. Group leaders who videotape or audio-record sessions should inform members of the ways the recordings will be used and the manner in which their security will be maintained.

Logistics of Group Formation

In forming a group, logistical considerations include the selection of participants, a determination of how many to include, and the duration and number of group sessions. Also, the rules must be clearly defined.

Selecting Group Participants

When considering children and adolescents, the selection of group participants is critical and also highly interactive. Multi-level interactions happen in many ways and include, but are not limited to identifying and/or securing potential members, as well as pre-screening interview processes. Embedded in these processes should be sensitivity to thorough informed consent procedures, as well as applicable ethical and state standards/laws. Selection of participants should be as transparent as possible without sacrificing confidentiality and should be responsive to the multiple stakeholders involved (school counselors, clients/students, parents/guardians, etc.).

With respect to identifying or securing potential group members, Hines and Fields (2002) suggested that members emanate from the school counselor's connections with key stakeholders (i.e., students, teachers, families, community leaders, etc.). These connections can potentially produce rich and detailed thematic information that can be utilized for group topics.

Once potential members have been identified, Corey, Corey, Callanan, and Russell (2004) suggested securing written permission from parents or legal guardians prior to enrolling the members. In addition to written permission, Corey et al. recommend inviting parents and students to a meeting in which the group process is discussed, along with an opportunity for questions and answers. Being proactive is a key dimension of selecting participants, as not all students are ready and/or suited for group counseling. Determination of suitability is often apparent during pre-screening interviews.

The American Counseling Association (2005) and the Association for Specialists in Group Work (2000) both support the value and use of screening potential group members. According to Newsome and Gladding (2007) the pre-screening interview is a time to discuss the group process, its purpose, and expectations, as well as assess for readiness and willingness to engage in the group experience. Readiness and willingness includes emotional readiness and/or willingness to participate, interact, and give and receive feedback (Greenberg, 2003). If the student is deemed to be a good fit for the proposed group, a letter should be sent home, followed by contact with parents or guardians that is consistent with school board policies and procedures. Finally, counselors should recognize that not all students are ready or willing to take part in the group process but have significant enough concerns to suggest individual counseling.

Determining Size of the Group

In determining the number of members to include in the group, the leader's primary consideration is his or her ability to manage the group's interactions. With primary-grade youngsters engaged in play therapy, group size should be limited to 3 or 4 members. Groups for older children and adolescents usually have 6 to 8 members but can range from 5 to 10 members depending on the group's focus and the skills of the members and their counselor. A group of older children or adolescents with fewer than five members runs the risk of limiting the opportunities for members to interact with a variety of peers and benefit from a broader range of suggestions and support.

The counselor also must take into account student absenteeism. Young students are prone to childhood diseases, and absentee rates of at-risk students tend to be higher than those of their peers. Transience in the student population also portends dropouts. Expanding the group membership beyond 10, however, strains the counselor's ability to attend and respond to all the interactions in the group. Larger groups can be managed by the counselor working with a co-leader, and some experts highly recommend co-leaders for smaller groups as well. By collaborating in planning and managing the group process, a co-leader helps the counselor broaden his or her skills as a leader.

Determining Length and Number of Group Meetings

Groups need time to warm up, to build cohesion, to address their problems, and to come to closure. To maintain continuity and momentum, groups ideally should meet weekly for 90 to 120 minutes per session. Counselors in public schools, however, often are restricted in the amount of time they can arrange for group counseling. Convincing teachers and parents to release students from class for an extended time each week is difficult, especially when state officials and the public pressure the schools to assume more accountability for student achievement. Further, once-a-week sessions often are disrupted by school special events and holidays.

Therefore, many school counselors arrange for their groups to meet for a normal class hour once or twice a week over 8 to 12 weeks. Groups for younger students usually meet for one or two 30-minute sessions each week, as this timeframe more closely fits their regular instructional class periods and their average attention spans.

Counselors have different preferences in scheduling. Some find that group continuity and momentum are enhanced by meeting more frequently over a shorter timeframe. This schedule might be especially advantageous for topic-specific groups directed at crises such as coping with suicide or dealing with a death or natural disaster. Developmental groups for elementary school students often are scheduled to meet daily for 2 weeks. Holding the sessions during a different class session each day minimizes the amount of time students miss a given instructional period (Myrick, 2002).

Setting Group Rules

One of the first tasks in which a group engages is to establish group rules. This activity is most effective when it is done collaboratively because it promotes a sense of ownership in the group process. Group members typically commit to voluntary membership, attendance, willingness to participate in group activities, work on their issues, provide helpful feedback to others, maintain confidentiality, and adhere to co-constructed rules. The counselor and the members are bound by the rules they establish, and they share responsibility for maintaining the rules.

According to Heckenlaible-Gotto and Roggow (2007), as the group matures, members assume more responsibility for holding each other accountable to the rules. More specifically, this natural maturation allows for children and adolescents to "practice positive skills, such as how to be assertive and stand up for themselves, express their thoughts and emotions, and find alternative ways to deal with unhealthy choices" (p. 223), which can lead to an improved sense of self.

Types of Counseling Groups

Counseling groups for children and adolescents can be divided into three types: (a) problem-centered, (b) developmental, and (c) topic-specific. An overview of the common elements associated with each group is followed by detailed descriptions for each type, along with associated examples.

Common Elements

First, all groups must have a definite purpose, which the counselor clearly defines and states. Group purposes are defined and delineated in the goals and objectives the counselor prepares for the group process prior to selecting members. The goals may target the needs of an identified group of students who, for example, are deficient in certain academic, vocational, or interpersonal skills, or the goals may be based on the expressed needs and interests of individual students, such as dealing with bullying or living in a stepfamily. In addition, groups may be targeted to developmental tasks that students need to master at various developmental stages, such as learning to deal with peer pressure or exploring careers. Regardless, the goals direct the group process from its inception through post-group evaluation.

The objectives clarify the goals by stating expected outcomes for members to derive from the group experience. The objectives, too, guide the counselor in selecting activities and discussion procedures to use during the group sessions and form the basis for evaluating how well the group attains its purposes (Furr, 2000).

Second, all three types of groups must have requirements for members' participation and enforce rules for membership. Group members are expected to commit to the rules and be accountable to the group itself. If the group convenes within an educational institution and the group members are minors, the group must operate within certain legal restrictions, organizational policies, and the expectations of parents, teachers, and school administrators.

Third, all three types of groups must include structured procedures. Each type of group proceeds through the same four stages of group development. For each type of group, the length of sessions and duration of the meetings are predetermined. Although the roles of the counselor and the members vary depending on the purpose of the group, the age and characteristics of the students, and the counselor's theoretical orientation, the counselor and the group collaborate through the structural procedures to bring about cohesion among the members and sustain an atmosphere of mutual trust, caring, understanding, acceptance, and support. This dynamic interaction is what provides the core structure for all of the group's activities.

Incorporating structured activities into the group process is intended to be a stimulus for group interaction and self-reflection. The activities should not be used to limit the thoughts and expressions of group members or to substitute for lack of communication among group members. The leader is responsible for helping members identify their unique personal reactions (thoughts, feelings, opinions, and values) as they emerge in the context of the group process, what Yalom (2005) identified as the "activation" and "illumination" of the here-and-now.

Problem-Centered Groups

The problem-centered group is open-ended, and topics are determined by whatever is of concern to individual participants at the time of the meeting. The group members each may be working on different problems, and each member has the opportunity to receive the group's full attention to his or her individual concerns. Members' commitment to the group consists of agreeing to help the others with their concerns and to foster problem-solving processes.

The emphasis is on here-and-now experiences of individual group members. They are encouraged to explore their problems, examine the alternatives open to them, consider the probable consequences of each alternative, and decide upon a course of personal action. The counselor and other group members attempt to empower the individuals to take action on their decisions by providing support, feedback, and the opportunity to practice new behaviors within the group. In addition, the counselor encourages members to try out new behaviors as homework between scheduled group meetings.

In schools, membership in problem-centered groups is open to all students, but members preferably have skills in articulating personal concerns, skills in attending and responding to others, and some knowledge of their personal needs and aspirations. Intermediate, junior-high, and senior-high students, because of their level of maturation and social experience, are more likely to have these skills than are primary-grade students. For younger students, play therapy techniques can be effective in promoting problem-solving skills. To facilitate communication in problem-centered groups, counselors first might involve students in developmental groups designed specifically to teach listening skills and cooperative behaviors that will enhance appropriate interaction in group-counseling activities.

Because the group members usually are close in age and share the same school environment, their concerns tend to be similar and common topics often emerge in the group sessions. For instance, an increasing number of children and adolescents experience "stressful life events that have a detrimental impact on their emotional well-being, social life, and school performance" (Shechtman, 2002, p. 293). More specifically, according to the American Psychiatric Association (2000) a number of stressful situations (e.g., family breakups, parental neglect, parental abuse, death, war, and disasters) affect the functioning of children and adolescents. The following example offers a highly adaptable template for a "generic" problem-centered group.

A Problem-Centered Group

Target population: Children or adolescents

Group goals:

- To build group cohesion, communication, and cooperation
- To define and analyze personal concerns
- To generate solutions to personal concerns through problem-solving
- To establish personal plans of action to resolve problems
- To accept responsibility for transferring what is learned in the group process to solving problems in one's personal life

Session 1

Objectives:

- To demonstrate cooperative behaviors
- To establish group rules and develop group cohesion
- To self-disclose concerns the individual wishes to address in the group

Procedure:

The counselor leads the group in discussing the group's purpose and goals and in establishing rules for the group. (Rules should be written on posterboard and displayed during each session.) Members sign the contracts they negotiated in the individual counselor/member interviews, which represent commitment to the group process. Individuals introduce themselves by sharing one thing that others can't tell by looking at them.

The counselor then employs an inclusion activity, "Group Logo" (Bergin, 1989), to begin to build group identity and promote cohesion. In this activity the members cooperate in drawing overlapping shapes on a large piece of posterboard. Together they agree upon a picture they see emerging from the lines they have drawn and then outline, color, and title the picture. The title and picture become the group's logo, which can be displayed throughout subsequent group sessions. Following this group-building activity, the counselor invites the students to identify personal concerns they want to bring up in subsequent sessions. The counselor can facilitate the group's discussion by asking questions such as:

- Why do you think joining this group can be helpful to you?
- What is your reaction to Group Logo?
- How can you feel more comfortable in the group?
- What are you looking forward to?

Sessions 2–8:

Objectives:

- To identify individual problems
- To brainstorm ways to solve these problems

- To encourage self-disclosure of feelings, concerns, and opinions
- To try out new behaviors and responses to problem situations through role-playing
- To establish plans for resolving personal problems

Procedure:

Individual members identify their personal concerns and describe their thoughts, behaviors, and feelings about those problems in the here-and-now. Members respond to one another to clarify their feelings, perceptions, and concerns, and the counselor leads the group in brainstorming problem-solving behaviors. The members suggest alternative courses of action and identify and evaluate probable consequences of these proposed solutions. Role-playing may be used to try out alternative behaviors. The counselor also suggests homework assignments to help members try out new behaviors and encourages members to report the results during subsequent sessions. For closure, the counselor can initiate a round-robin sharing of an "I learned," "I feel," or "I will" statement relative to the issues discussed.

To stimulate dialogue, the counselor might briefly review and summarize what happened in the previous session and then ask group members to tell how their problem-solving "plans" worked or how the problem has evolved since the last session. During the sessions the counselor prompts members to speak directly to one another and links members by pointing out similarities in the problems, feelings, or experiences they describe.

The group must adhere to the rules it has established. The counselor must insist that members wait their turn and allow everyone to have the opportunity to speak. The counselor must allow reticent members to proceed slowly until they are comfortable with self-disclosure. The counselor can encourage the group by making statements such as:

I'd like to hear each of you give your opinion about what Jill has told us.
When Trent is ready, he will tell us more about his feelings.
Kara, you seem to understand how Andy and Chago are feeling. Can you tell us how your feelings are similar?

Session 9:

Objectives:

- To share what was learned during group sessions
- To share with the group personal goals and strategies for resolving the problems shared

Procedure:

The counselor initiates a discussion in which group members exchange what they have learned during the group process in regard to themselves and their personal problems. Each member defines a plan for applying these problem-solving skills in his or her environment. To facilitate the discussion, the counselor might ask questions such as:

- How do you feel about your problems right now?
- What progress do you think you've made toward resolving the problems?
- What must you continue to do to resolve the problems?
- What is the next step you need to take?
- What things have you learned in this group that will help you reach your goals?

Members make positive statements, reinforcing one another for their communication and cooperation while they are in the group. The counselor and members then plan a follow-up session.

Developmental Groups

Developmental groups help children and adolescents meet the challenges of everyday, normal activity in the process of growing up. Like large-group guidance activities, they address the individual's need to gain knowledge and acquire skills in the areas of personal identity, interpersonal interaction, emotional and behavioral development, academic achievement, and career planning. These groups are oriented toward growth and prevention rather than remediation and are directed toward developing specific behaviors and skills that will enhance the individual's ability to function independently and responsibly.

Although group membership is open to all students, it usually is targeted to children and adolescents who are developmentally delayed in comparison to their peers of the same ability levels and social and academic backgrounds. Prospective group members often are identified by parents or teachers, in consultation with the counselor, as students who are experiencing underachievement, absenteeism, tardiness, low self-esteem, or lack of social involvement with peers. In addition, individuals volunteer for developmental groups to enhance their skills or learn how to cope with what they currently are experiencing in the process of growing up.

The groups usually have a central theme related to the students' level of understanding, perceived needs, and developmental stage. Based upon the developmental milestones described by Vernon and Clemente (2005), Vernon (2004), and other specialists in human growth and development, the counselor selects an issue for the group theme that is appropriate to the members' ages, abilities, and social/emotional maturity and is relevant to the developmental tasks at their stage of development. The group is designed to address the developmental needs of all individuals at this age level, to promote their personal growth regarding the issue, and to prevent problems with their dealing with the issue in the future.

Specific group themes vary according to age level, although the general issues may be continuous throughout childhood and adolescence. For example, a group dealing with interpersonal communication skills might be called "The Friendship Group" for younger students and deal primarily with identifying friendship behaviors and how to maintain them. For adolescents, the theme still may be interpersonal relationships but within the context of dating, so the group might be called "Dating Conversation Made Easy."

When establishing developmental groups for children and adolescents, the counselor must draw on his or her knowledge of, and sensitivity to, specific developmental issues. The counselor has to address the general issues related to a specific theme during the group and also must identify for inclusion in the group those students for whom these issues are a serious concern.

In analyzing student behavior, the counselor must use his or her skills in assessment and intervention techniques to distinguish between behavior caused by situational stressors and those resulting from developmental issues. For example, an adolescent whose academic performance is slipping and who appears uncharacteristically withdrawn in his or her social interactions may actually be caught up in personal identity issues rather than academic or social skills concerns. Appropriate for this student would be a developmental counseling group addressing these specific identity issues. Developmental groups frequently incorporate media such as videos, films, and books. Games, worksheets, simulations, and role-plays also can encourage discussion.

Issues covered in developmental groups for children and adolescents include:

- interpersonal communication and assertiveness (Morganett, 2002a; Myrick, 2002; Pearson & Nicholson, 2000),
- dealing with feelings and managing stress (Akos, 2000; Morganett, 2002a, b; Vernon, 1998a, b, c),
- social skills and friendship (LeCroy, 2005; Morganett, 2002b; Thompson, 1998; Vernon, 1998a, b, c),
- academic achievement, motivation, and school success (Erford & Mazzuca, 2004; Hines & Fields, 2004; Morganett, 2002a),
- self-concept, self-esteem, and identity (Morganett, 2002a, b; Vernon, 1998b, c; Vernon, 2006a, b),
- career awareness, exploration, and planning (Pope & Minor, 2000; Sears, 2004; Niles, Trusty, & Mitchell, 2004; Jackson & Grant, 2004), and
- problem solving and decision making (Bergin, 1991; Vernon, 1998a, b, c).

The following is a developmental group example from which to work, adapt, or replicate:

A Developmental Group: Relationship Development 101

Target population: Adolescent females

Group goals:

- To build group cohesion, communication, and cooperation
- To use popular culture (e.g., film) to generate discussion of various significant relationships in adolescent female lives (e.g., parents or guardians, siblings, friends, significant others, and society at-large)

- To use film as a metaphor for discussing how people relate to the world around them
- To encourage self-disclosure of feelings, concerns, and opinions
- To establish goals for growth and development relative to relationships and begin discussions of "how-to" generalize what was learned in the group to the "real" world

Session 1:

Objectives:

- To demonstrate cooperative behaviors
- To establish group rules and group identity

Procedure:

The central theme of the first session is to develop an overall group identity. Identity is one of the most important developmental aspects of adolescence and thus is critical to the initial group process. In addition to developing and discussing the group's purpose, goals and rules, members introduce themselves by relating one thing they would like to get from the group. In addition, the counselor employs Bergin's (1989) "Group Logo" activity to build group identity and promote cohesion (see Session 1 of the problem-centered group example for a more detailed description of the "Group Logo" delivery). Finally, the counselor can facilitate group processing by asking questions such as:

- Why do you think joining this group can be helpful to you?
- How do you feel about the group's chosen identity?
- What are you looking forward to?

Sessions 2–6:

Objectives:

- To generate in-depth discussion of various significant relationships
- To explore the role of media and pop culture
- To explore decision-making processes
- To discuss differences in positive and challenging boundaries

Procedure:

Interpersonal learning is both an explicit and an implicit goal of group counseling. This group targets female adolescents and seeks to explore all meaningful relationships in their lives (parents or guardians, siblings, friends, significant others, and society at-large). Because media and technology are prominent features of their day-to-day lives, a contemporary film chronicling the ups and downs of being an adolescent female will be used to structure and facilitate this group.

The movie "Mean Girls" (Waters et al., 2004) has been chosen because of its content and critical acclaim. Twenty-minute segments of the movie will be shown over five sessions (i.e., Sessions 2–6). Following each 20-minute segment, the group facilitator will process the films content by broaching the following questions. These questions are only suggestions and can be modified or not used depending on the culture and maturity of the respective groups:

- What thoughts and/or feelings have this 20-minute clip generated?
- How would you describe the nature of the relationship between the main character and her _____ (parent or guardian, sibling, friends, significant others, or society at large)?
- What elements of this interaction or others from previous clips fit your story?
- How is, or is not, this film a metaphor for how relationships look in your life?
- What is one thing you can do to promote positive growth in terms of relationship development between now and the next group meeting and how can we hold you accountable?

Session 7:

Objectives:

- To explore relationships through an interactive and generalizable closing activity
- To share what was learned during the group experience
- To share strategies for continued growth

Procedure:

To close the group experience, the counselor initiates the following activity, entitled "Making and Keeping Friends" (LeCroy and Daley, 2005).

> This session is designed to teach friendship skills and provide group members with an arena in which they can practice these skills. Group leaders help girls to identify and practice using tools to start conversations (for example, making eye contact, asking someone a question, and saying something positive about the other person). We also discuss and practice how to communicate positive feelings and how to deal with friction when it arises in a friendship. In addition to role-plays, the girls brainstorm different ways to build, maintain, and mend friendships. They write these ideas down on strips of paper and then place them in a "friendship tool box," which they decorate and keep. (p. 132)

To facilitate discussion, the counselor might ask questions such as:

- How might this experience and/or knowledge be generalized to other relationships?
- What sort of movement have you made during this group experience?
- What must you continue to do to grow in all of your relationships?

LeCroy and Daley (2005) have developed a complete 13-session group experience for adolescent girls, entitled, "Empowering Adolescent Girls: The Go Grrrls Social Skills Training Program."

Topic-Specific Groups

Topic-specific groups are designed to meet the needs of individuals who are having difficulty with situational circumstances that create negative feelings and stress, which interfere with normal functioning. These groups are similar to developmental groups in that new knowledge and skills are taught to the members, but topic-specific groups are intended to help members handle more serious, immediate, or situational concerns rather than to help them address or resolve typical developmental problems.

In topic-specific groups members all share similar concerns about a given situation or condition such as learning how to cope with parental alcoholism, moving, or death of a friend. Because of the commonality of problems, topic-specific groups also have similarities to problem-centered groups, which center on open discussion about current issues that all group members do not necessarily share.

Group membership usually is targeted to individuals who are having difficulty with a specific issue or are considered to be at-risk. Some members, however, may be chosen because of their past experience with the issue and their success in coping with it. These individuals can help stabilize the group atmosphere and build a sense of hope and confidence that the group process will lead to similar successes for all group members. They also serve as role models who exemplify the coping skills that group members desire.

Topic-specific groups give members the opportunity to understand the issue in more depth, to explore and express feelings, and to identify coping strategies. Group members learn that their feelings are normal, that their peers often feel the same way, and that they have options to help them deal more effectively with the problems and thereby reestablish personal autonomy and happiness. They also receive feedback and support from members who understand what they are experiencing because they have similar problems.

As in developmental groups, counselors facilitating topic-specific groups frequently use media and structured activities to stimulate discussion of the topic and present relevant information to the members. They may make extensive use of role-play and homework exercises to promote specific coping skills. Topic-specific groups often arise out of crisis events such as a classmate's accidental death or suicide. In such instances, the immediate purpose of the group is to provide support to group members who are dealing with the crisis situation. Later, a follow-up group can be organized to help the members explore the incident more fully, as well as to explore any other concerns related to the larger issue, such as coping with death (Myrick, 2002).

Issues covered in topic-specific groups for children and adolescents include:

■ physical and sexual abuse and violence (Lee, 2004),
■ grief and loss (Huss, 2004; Lehmann, Jimerson, & Gaasch, 2001; Morganett, 2002b),
■ aggressive behavior (Nelson, Dykeman, Powell, & Petty, 1996; Rainey, Hensley, & Crutchfield, 1997),

- divorce and separation (DeLucia-Waack, 2001; Hage & Nosanow, 2000; Morganett, 2002a),
- suicide, fear, and stress (Brooks, 2004; Morganett, 2002a),
- substance abuse and alcohol (Coker, 2004; McNair & Arman, 2000)
- Adoption (Kizner & Kizner, 1999), and
- lesbian, bisexual, gay, transgendered, and questioning (Gustavsson & MacEachron, 2005; Smith & Chen-Hayes, 2004).

The following is a topic-specific group example from which to work, adapt, and/or replicate.

A Topic-Specific Group: Support Group for Divorce

Target population: Children

Group Goals:

- To build group cohesion, cooperation, and communication
- To develop mutual support
- To correct misinformation about the causes of divorce
- To identify and express feelings about divorce
- To plan strategies for coping with divorce

Session 1:

Objectives:

- To establish rules for the group
- To demonstrate cooperative behaviors
- To develop group cohesion and commitment
- To state what members hope to achieve while in the group

Procedure:

The counselor leads the group members in a discussion of the group's purpose and goals. The members then are asked to establish group rules and sign individual contracts, negotiated during counselor–client interviews, symbolizing the individual's commitment to the group. The counselor or a volunteer from the group writes the group rules on a large piece of posterboard for display throughout each session. The counselor then asks each member to introduce himself or herself to the group and initiates an icebreaker activity as follows:

The counselor distributes a magazine and a 9-inch square of tagboard to each student. Each student cuts out a picture describing himself or herself and pastes it on the tagboard. Then the students cut their tagboard into four to six pieces and put the pieces in an envelope. The students exchange envelopes, put the puzzles together, and tell what they have learned about each other from the "people puzzle" (Vernon, 1980).

Following this activity the counselor describes the group goals and invites the members to say what they would like to learn. Questions such as the following may stimulate this:

- What do you want to learn while you are in this group?
- Now that you have heard everyone tell what they want to learn, what do you have in common?
- How did you feel about describing your goals to the group?

Session 2:

Objectives:

- To describe the changes the divorce has made on the family
- To identify similarities and differences in experiences with divorce

Procedure:

The counselor distributes paper and colored markers to group members and tells them that they will use this material in drawing pictures of their families and their homes. The counselor instructs the members to divide their paper into six spaces and draw pictures, one per space, to represent the following:

- Their family
- A good time they've had with their family
- How their family has changed recently
- What they miss about the way their family used to be
- A good thing about the way their family is now
- How they feel about the way things are now

The counselor then asks each member to display his or her "family picture" and tell the group about it. Other members listen and then relate their own experiences, which may be similar or dissimilar. The following questions can stimulate discussion:

- How did it feel to describe your family picture?
- What changes has divorce made in your family life?
- After hearing others in the group describe the changes in their lives, what changes do you think are similar for everyone?

Session 3:

Objectives:

- To encourage expression of feelings
- To learn to express feelings through pantomime
- To identify feelings common to all group members
- To identify ways to cope with negative feelings

Procedure:

The counselor leads the group members in an activity in which they express their feelings through pantomime. The counselor has the participants take out of a sack a piece of paper labeled with a feeling word (such as "bored," "angry," "happy," "sad," "confused," "worried" or "frustrated") and asks them to show how they look or act when they are feeling that way. Each group member is able to see the expressions on the other faces and identify with those feelings.

Following the pantomime, the participants are invited to draw out of the bag a piece of paper labeled with a situation, such as the following, and identify how they feel:

- Mom is angry with Dad (or Dad is angry with Mom).
- You are home alone.
- You don't get to see Mom or Dad very often.
- You think you're the cause of your parents' divorce.
- Your parents don't have as much time to spend with you.
- Your friend makes fun of your family.

The counselor encourages the group member drawing a card to verbalize his or her feelings and helps the group think of ways to cope with the feelings. The members describe what they do to relieve sad, angry, or lonely feelings. They are encouraged to brainstorm ways of coping by doing positive things. The counselor records on a large piece of posterboard all of the positive suggestions to use in later sessions. He or she then debriefs the activity by asking students:

- Was it hard to identify your feelings?
- Did others share similar feelings?
- What did you learn about ways to deal with negative feelings?

Session 4:

Objectives:

- To observe other children struggling through divorce
- To generate a sense of hope that things can improve

Procedure:

Members view the video "Dealing with Divorce" found on the PBSkids (2005) website entitled "It's My Life." The video documents how children have been adjusting to life post-divorce. The counselor can utilize the PBSkids (2005) discussion guide that asks the following "It's My Life" video-related questions on divorce:

- What types of problems did the kids face before their parents separated or divorced?

- How did the kids' living situations change after the divorce?
- How did having parents that lived in separate homes make things difficult for the kids?
- In what ways did life improve after divorce?

Session 5:

Objectives:

- To describe the negative situations that divorce causes
- To listen to and reflect others' feelings

Procedure:

The counselor asks each group member to describe the divorce-related events that bother him or her most. The counselor then helps the group set up a role-playing activity in which members can act out some of these events. Volunteers take turns acting out problem events for the other group members, who then attempt to help the individual clarify the reasons the events bother him or her the most. The counselor and the other group members express their appreciation for the individual's willingness to share his or her experiences and feelings with the group. The counselor then asks questions such as the following:

- Are your situations similar or dissimilar to the others' situations?
- How do you feel about discussing things that bother you?
- Is it helpful to have others listen and understand?

Session 6:

Objectives:

- To express concerns about divorce to a divorced adult
- To simulate parent–child discussions about divorce
- To identify strategies to cope with the changes precipitated by divorce

Procedure:

The counselor invites a divorced parent to attend the group session and respond to members' questions about divorce. The counselor emphasizes the importance of parent/child dialogue to help children and parents adjust to the changes in their lives resulting from the divorce.

Following the question-and-answer session, the counselor asks volunteers to use adult and child puppets to demonstrate situations precipitated by divorce that can be stressful for children. These situations could include:

- talking with the custodial parent and the noncustodial parent about the divorce,
- meeting new adults in their parents' lives,
- adjusting to changes in the home environment, and
- taking on new responsibilities that parents may place on the child.

After each simulation, the counselor leads the group and guest in a discussion of the simulation. To facilitate the discussion, the counselor may ask questions such as the following:

- What is the child feeling in this situation?
- How does the parent feel?
- How does the other adult feel?
- What are the puppets saying and doing that make the parent and/or child feel bad?
- How can they make each other feel better?
- How can they make themselves feel better?

Session 7:

Objectives:

- To state personal goals for coping with divorce
- To identify strategies to help reach the goals
- To identify people who can offer support after the group ends

Procedure:

Based on work done in previous sessions, the counselor encourages and helps each member make a plan for coping with his or her own problems relating to the divorce. The counselor leads the group in brainstorming a list of people such as peers, family members, clergy, and significant others who can provide support to group members. The counselor can facilitate these activities by asking the following kinds of questions:

- What things continue to upset you the most about divorce?
- When do you feel most upset?
- What can you do to feel better?
- What can other people do to help you?

Session 8:

Objectives:

- To express current feelings about the divorce
- To state what members have learned during the group sessions
- To offer support and encouragement to one another

Procedure:

The counselor distributes index cards to the participants and invites them to write the following on the cards:

- One thing you have learned from being in the group
- Something you can do about your negative feelings

- Someone who can help you if you need help
- One way you've changed because of the group

The counselor encourages members to exchange the statements they wrote on their cards and offer one another feedback and positive suggestions for coping. The group and the counselor plan a follow-up session. Then the counselor brings closure to the group by asking questions such as these:

- How do you feel now compared to how you felt when you first became a member of the group?
- How have the other group members been helpful to you?
- What do you plan to do to help yourself between now and the group follow-up session?

Summary

Group counseling can be a valuable intervention in schools as well as agency settings. Given the developmental concerns of children and adolescents, counselors see group counseling as an efficient, effective, and viable approach for helping more children and adolescents both remedially and preventively. Further, group counseling provides for immediate feedback and support from peers and the opportunity to gain knowledge and skills they can use in decision-making and problem-solving.

The primary differences between group counseling with children and group counseling with adolescents involve the group members' verbal capacities and their ability to conceptualize problems based on their developmental level. For this reason, group activities, topics, and methods have to be tailored to the targeted age level.

Although group counseling has many advantages, it is not intended to replace individual counseling or classroom guidance. In many cases, group counseling may be suggested to complement individual counseling. Group counseling is a powerful, strategic intervention for addressing problems and enhancing human development in both the agency and the school setting. The concepts and examples in this chapter will aid counselors to effectively incorporate group work into their practices.

References

Akos, P. (2000). Building empathic skills in elementary school children through group work. *Journal for Specialists in Group Work, 25*(2), 214–223.

American Counseling Association. (2005). *Code of ethics.* Alexandra, VA: Author.

American Psychiatric Association. (2000). *Diagnostic and statistical manual of mental disorders* (4th ed., text rev.). Washington, DC: Author.

American School Counselor Association. (2003). *The ASCA national model: A framework for school counseling programs.* Alexandria, VA: Author.

American School Counselor Association. (2005). *The ASCA national model: A framework for school counseling programs* (2nd ed.). Alexandria, VA: Author.

Association for Specialists in Group Work. (2000). Association for specialists in group work: Professional standards for the training of group workers. *Journal for Specialists in Group Work, 25*, 327-342.

Baker, S. B. (2000). School counseling for the twenty-first century (3rd ed.). Upper Saddle River, NJ: Prentice-Hall.

Bergin, J. (1989). Building group cohesiveness through cooperation activities. *Elementary School Guidance and Counseling, 24*, 90–95.

Bergin, J. (1991). *Escape from pirate island* [Game]. Doyleston, PA: Mar*Co Products.

Berk, L. (1998). *Development through the life span.* Boston: Allyn & Bacon.

Brooks, V. (2004). Stress management: The school counselor's role. In R. Perusse & G. E. Goodnough (Eds.), *Leadership, advocacy, and direct service strategies for professional school counselors* (pp. 328–352). Belmont, CA: Brooks/Cole.

Bruckner, S., & Thompson, C. (1987). Guidance program evaluation: An example. *Elementary School Guidance and Counseling, 21*, 193–196.

Canfield, J. (1976). *100 ways to enhance self-concept in the classroom.* Englewood Cliffs, NJ: Prentice–Hall.

Capuzzi, D., & Gross, D, (2001). *Introduction to group counseling* (3rd ed.). Denver: Love Publishing.

Coker, J. K. (2004). Alcohol and other substance abuse: A comprehensive approach. In R. Perusse & G. E. Goodnough (Eds.), *Leadership, advocacy, and direct service strategies for professional school counselors* (pp. 284–327). Belmont, CA: Brooks/Cole.

Corey, G. (1999). *Theory and practice of group counseling* (5th ed.). Pacific Grove, CA: Wadsworth.

Corey, G., Corey, M., Callanan, R., & Russell, J. (1992). *Group counseling techniques* (2nd ed.). Pacific Grove, CA: Brooks/Cole.

Corey, G., Corey, M., Callanan, R., & Russell, J. (2004). *Group techniques* (3rd ed.). Pacific Grove, CA: Brooks/Cole.

Corey, M., & Corey, G. (2001). Groups: Process and practice (6th ed.). Pacific Grove, CA: Brooks/Cole.

Corey, M.., & Corey, G. (2006). *Groups: Process and practice* (7th ed.). Belmont, CA: Thomson.

DeLucia–Waack, J. L. (2001). *Using music in children of divorce groups: A session-by-session manual for counselors.* Alexandria, NC: American Counseling Association.

Erford, B. T., & Mazzuca, S. A. (2004). Improving academic achievement through an understanding of learning styles. In R. Perusse & G. E. Goodnough (Eds.), *Leadership, advocacy, and direct service strategies for professional school counselors* (pp. 34–70). Belmont, CA: Brooks/Cole.

Furr, S. R. (2000). Structuring the group experience: A format for designing psychoeducational groups. *Journal for Specialists in Group Work, 25*(10), 29–49.

Gladding, S. (1998). *Counseling as an art: The creative arts in counseling* (2nd ed.). Alexandria, VA: American Counseling Association.

Greenberg, K. R. (2003). *Group counseling in K-12 schools: A handbook for school counselors.* Boston: Allyn & Bacon.

Gustavsson, N., & MacEachron, A. (2005). Case studies in group treatment: Gay youth and safe spaces. In C. W. LeCroy & J. M. Daley (Eds.), *Case studies in child, adolescent, and family treatment* (pp. 151–156). Belmont, CA: Brooks/Cole.

Hage, S. M., & Nosanow, M. (2000). Becoming stronger at broken places: A model for group work with young adults from divorced families. *Journal for Specialists in Group Work, 25*(1), 50–66.

Heckenlaible-Gotto, M. J., & Roggow, L. (2007). Supporting peers lives and solving hassles: The SPLASH program. *Reclaiming Children and Youth, 15*(4), 220–226.

Hines, P. L., & Fields, T. H. (2002). Pregroup screening issues for school counselors. *Journal for Specialists in Group Work, 27*, 358–376.

Hines, P. L., & Fields, T. H. (2004). School counseling and academic achievement. In R. Perusse & G. E. Goodnough (Eds.), *Leadership, advocacy, and direct service strategies for professional school counselors* (pp. 3-33). Belmont, CA: Brooks/Cole.

Huss, S. N. (2004). Loss and grief in the school setting. In R. Perusse & G. E. Goodnough (Eds.), *Leadership, advocacy, and direct service strategies for professional school counselors* (pp. 262–283). Belmont, CA: Brooks/Cole.

Jackson, M., & Grant, D. (2004). Equity, access, and career development: Contextual conflicts. In R. Perusse & G. E. Goodnough (Eds.), *Leadership, advocacy, and direct service strategies for professional school counselors* (pp. 125–153). Belmont, CA: Brooks/Cole.

Kaduson, H., & Schaefer, C. (Eds). (2000). *Short-term play therapy for children.* New York: Guilford Press.

Kizner, L., & Kizner, S. (1999). Small group counseling with adopted children. *Professional School Counseling, 2*(3), 226–229.

LaFountain, R., & Garner, N. (1996). Solution-focused counseling groups: The results are in. *Journal for Specialists in Group Work, 21*, 128–143.

LeCroy, C. (2005). Social skills group for children. In C. W. LeCroy & J. M. Daley (Eds.), *Case studies in child, adolescent, and family treatment* (pp. 107–115). Belmont, CA: Brooks/Cole.

LeCroy, C., & Daley, J. (2005). Empowering adolescent girls: The go grrrls social skills training program. In C. W. LeCroy & J. M. Daley (Eds.), *Case studies in child, adolescent, and family treatment* (pp. 127–141). Belmont, CA: Brooks/Cole.

Lee, V. (2004). Violence prevention and conflict resolution education in the schools. In R. Perusse & G. E. Goodnough (Eds.), *Leadership, advocacy, and direct service strategies for professional school counselors* (pp. 222–261). Belmont, CA: Brooks/Cole.

McNair, R., & Arman, J. (2000). A small group model for working with elementary school children of alcoholics. *Professional School Counseling, 3*(4), 290–293.

Morganett, R. (2002a). *Skills for living: Group counseling activities for elementary students* (2nd ed.). Champaign, IL: Research Press.

Morganett, R. (2002b). *Skills for living: Group counseling activities for young adolescents* (2nd ed.). Champaign, IL: Research Press.

Myrick, R. (2002). Developmental guidance and counseling: A practical approach (4th ed.). Minneapolis: Educational Media.

Nelson, J., Dykeman, C., Powell, S., & Petty, D. (1996). The effects of a group counseling intervention on students with behavioral adjustment problems. *Elementary School Guidance and Counseling, 31*, 21–33.

Newsome, D. W., & Gladding, S. T. (2007). Counseling individuals and groups in school. In B. T. Erford (Ed.), *Transforming the school counseling profession* (2nd ed., pp. 168–194). Columbus, OH: Pearson.

Niles, S. G., Trusty, J., & Mitchell, N. (2004). Fostering positive career development in children and adolescents. In R. Perusse & G. E. Goodnough (Eds.), *Leadership, advocacy, and direct service strategies for professional school counselors* (pp. 102–124). Belmont, CA: Brooks/Cole.

PBSkids. (2005). *It's my life*, CastleWorks, Inc. Retrieved September 20, 2007, from http://pbskids.org/itsmylife

Pearson, Z., & Nicholson, J. (2000). Comprehensive character education in the elementary school: Strategies for administrators, teachers, and counselors. *Journal of Humanistic Counseling, Education, and Development, 38*(4), 243–251.

Pope, M., & Minor, C. (Eds.). (2000). *Experiential activities for teaching career counseling classes and for facilitating career groups.* Columbus, OH: National Career Development Association.

Rainey, L., Hensley, E., & Crutchfield, L. (1997). Implementation of support groups in elementary and middle school student assistance programs. *Professional School Counseling, 1*(2), 36–40.

Sandhu, D., (Ed.). (2001). *Elementary school counseling in the new millennium.* Alexandria, VA: American Counseling Association.

Sears, S. (2004). Investigating the world of work. In R. Perusse & G. E. Goodnough (Eds.), *Leadership, advocacy, and direct service strategies for professional school counselors* (pp. 71–101). Belmont, CA: Brooks/Cole.

Schmidt, J. (2002). *Counseling in schools: Essential services and comprehensive programs* (4th ed.). Boston: Allyn & Bacon.

Shechtman, Z. (2002). Child group psychotherapy in the school at the threshold of a new millennium. *Journal of Counseling & Development, 80*, 293–299.

Smith, S. D., & Chen-Hayes, S. F. (2004). Leadership and advocacy for lesbian, bisexual, gay, transgendered, and questioning (LBGTQ) students: Academic, career, and interpersonal success strategies. In R. Perusse & G. E. Goodnough (Eds.), *Leadership, advocacy, and direct service strategies for professional school counselors* (pp. 187–221). Belmont, CA: Brooks/Cole.

Sunburst Communications. (1990). *I like being me: Self-esteem.* [Video]. Pleasantville, NY: Author.

Thompson, C., & Rudolph, L. (2000). *Counseling children* (5th ed.). Pacific Grove, CA: Brooks/Cole.

Vernon, A. (1980). *Help yourself to a healthier you: A handbook of emotional education exercises for children.* Washington, DC: University Press of America.

Vernon, A. (1989). *Thinking, feeling, behaving: An emotional educational curriculum for adolescents.* Champaign, IL: Research Press.

Vernon, A. (1993). *Developmental assessment and intervention with children and adolescents.* Alexandria, VA: American Counseling Association.

Vernon A. (1998a). *The Passport Program: A journey through emotional, social, cognitive, and self-development/grades 1–5.* Champaign, IL: Research Press.

Vernon, A. (1998b). *The Passport Program: A journey through emotional, social, cognitive, and self-development/grades 6–8.* Champaign, IL: Research Press.

Vernon, A. (1998c). *The Passport Program: A journey through emotional, social, cognitive, and self-development/grades 9–12.* Champaign, IL: Research Press.

Vernon, A. (2002). *What works when with children and adolescents: A handbook of individual counseling techniques.* Champaign, IL: Research Press.

Vernon, A. (2004). Working with children, adolescents, and parents: Practical application of developmental theory. In A. Vernon (Ed.), *Counseling children and adolescents* (3rd ed;, pp. 1–34). Denver: Love Publishing.

Vernon, A. (2006a). *Thinking, feeling, behaving: An emotional education curriculum for adolescents.* Champaign, IL: Research Press.

Vernon, A. (2006b). *Thinking, feeling, behaving: An emotional education curriculum for children.* Champaign, IL: Research Press.

Vernon, A., & Clemente, R. (2005). *Assessment and intervention with children and adolescents: Developmental and multicultural considerations.* Alexandria, VA: American Counseling Association.

Waters, M. (Director), Wiseman, R. (Writer), & Fey, T. (Writer). (2004). *Mean girls* [Motion picture]. Los Angeles: Paramount Pictures.

Yalom, I. D. (2005). *The theory and practice of group psychotherapy* (5th ed.). New York: Basic Books.

12

Designing a Developmental Counseling Curriculum

Toni R. Tollerud and Robert J. Nejedlo

For most adults, remembrances about a school counselor are vague, minimal, or negative. Often they visited the high school counselor for assistance in setting up their schedule or to explore future career options. Some may have had to see the counselor if they were in trouble. Certainly they would have few, if any, recollections of the counselor being in the classroom or conducting small-group counseling activities—although this might have been the case if they had an elementary counselor in their school.

Over the past decades, school reform has been a consistent theme at the national level. Notwithstanding the wave of educational reform and changes to schools, however, school counseling programs and school counselors were not part of the picture. As Stone and Dahir (2006) noted:

> School counseling programs and school counselors were absent from many of the early conversations that spoke to changes in curriculum, instruction, and pedagogy. Thankfully this is no longer the situation. (p. 6)

A transformation began to impact school counseling in the 1990s as the profession looked ahead to the 21st century to identify how counseling could best meet the needs of students. Today the concept of transformation is a hot topic in the field as authors work to define it and address its ramifications for the profession.

> Transforming school counseling involves changing its substance and appearance…(and) encourages professional school counselors to become agents of educational reform and change. (Erford, House & Martin, 2007, p. 1)

387

Stone and Dahir (2006) suggested that "the transformed school counselor acts, influences, and impacts" (p. xi). This proactive approach is in sharp contrast to the traditional counselor role, which, according to Sink (2005), was reactive, remedial, and crisis-oriented and served only a small percentage of students (Stone & Dahir, 2006). Sink challenged contemporary school counselors to "move beyond their conventions and fully implement a systemic-programmatic approach—one that is proactive, prevention-oriented, and developmental in focus" (p. xx).

As early as 1991, Ellis described new changes in the field that give more credence to the role of school counselors as integral to a student's academic development and personal growth within the educational process. Over the 17 years since Ellis, much has transpired to professionalize and integrate the field of school counseling into the school climate. School counselors no longer have been left out of the school reform agenda. In 1996 a grant was awarded that resulted in the Transforming School Counseling Initiative, with the explicit goal to help school counselors become more responsive to student needs (Education Trust, 1997).

According to House and Hayes (2002), school counselors have to become more involved as key players in educational reform and strive to close the achievement disparity between students of color and low-income students compared to those with more economic advantages. This aligns the role of the school counselor with national concerns over student success and achievement.

Additional contributions to school reform were generated by the American School Counseling Association, which developed national standards for school counseling programs in 1997 (Campbell & Dahir, 1997) and the ASCA National Model in 2003 (ASCA, 2005). These models addressed important elements of school reform by providing proactive responses for school improvement, program development that is comprehensive, developmental, and outcome-based, and directed to students' career, academic, and personal–social developmental needs.

In a historical account of the evolution of the profession, Gysbers (2004) emphasized what school counselors have begun to do to hold themselves accountable for how their work contributes to student success and academic achievement. He advised that just talking about this is not enough. Rather, accountability is an ongoing responsibility, and school counselors must assume a leadership role in addressing this challenge. Brott (2006) recommended identifying specific teaching and learning strategies, as well as an active-oriented research project as methods for training school counselors in the practice of accountability. Included is a classroom guidance project that usually is undertaken during the internship experience.

At the core of school counseling reform is the development of comprehensive guidance programs. Gysbers and Henderson (2006), Myrick (1997), and Paisley and McMahon (2001) emphasized the need for comprehensive guidance programs fostering the academic, career, and personal/social development of students that contributes to their success. Gysbers (2001) further supported the integration of these school counseling programs into the educational framework in ways that promote students' academic success and assist them in reaching their personal and career goals. He stated, "Our mission, then, is to use the wisdom of the past to further strengthen the work of school counselors within a comprehensive guidance and counseling program framework for today and tomorrow" (p. 104).

To meet these challenges, contemporary counselors have to broaden their roles. Dealing with crises and doing remedial work will continue to be important, but school counselors must move into an arena that includes the developmental/preventive component—which means that they also will be taking on a teaching role. To accomplish this, the ideal school counselor has to be culturally and technologically competent and responsive. Paisley and McMahon suggested that counselors should

> intentionally and collaboratively design responsive school counseling programs. They would hold themselves accountable rather than wait for someone else to. They would evaluate their programs and share the results with the school community, and use the results to enhance the programs to more effectively meet student needs and support student learning. (p. 114)

Baker and Gerler, Jr. (2008) extended these roles even further by suggesting that school counselors must know what they need to do and work to develop the skills to be proficient in this work. This is critical because it garners support from significant stakeholders to whom school counselors must be accountable—parents, students, teachers, and administrators. Erford and colleagues (2007) identified the role of a development classroom guidance specialist as essential. School counselors must be proficient at designing and implementing or teaching a developmental counseling curriculum within the classroom to increase students' academic performance, as well as to build skills and awareness for well-being and future planning. By addressing these challenges and opportunities, school counselors will be contributing positively to the climate of school reform and will assist the profession in moving away from the traditional service provider role to a role that promotes optimal success for all students.

Developmental/Preventive School Counseling Programs

In 1979 the American School Counselor Association adopted the following definition of developmental guidance:

> Developmental guidance is that component of all guidance efforts which fosters planned interventions within educational and other human services programs at all points in the human life cycle to vigorously stimulate and actively facilitate the total development of individuals in all areas: i.e., personal, social, career, emotional, moral–ethical, cognitive, and aesthetic; and to promote the integration of the several components into an individual's life style. (American School Counselor Association [ASCA], 1979)

Several models of school counseling advocate a strong developmental/preventive emphasis. Developmental guidance and counseling models (Gysbers & Henderson, 2006; Myrick, 1997; VanZandt & Hayslip, 1994, 2001; Vernon & Strub, 1990–1991) came on the scene in the early 1990s. Gysbers and Henderson (2006) suggested an organizational structure consisting of four elements and four components. The four elements are

1. *content*—student competencies achieved in the activity that is grade-level-appropriate and grouped around the career, academic, or personal/social domain;
2. the *organization framework*, consisting of the structural and program components;
3. *resources*, including human, financial, and political support to deliver the guidance program; and
4. *development, management, and accountability*. Gysbers and Henderson added this fourth element in 2006. It includes an emphasis on the planning, design, implementation, evaluation, and enhancement of the comprehensive guidance and counseling program.

The four program components are presented under the second element. They clarify the organizational structure and describe how the program will be delivered to students. These components are

1. the counseling curriculum,
2. responsive services (student initiated activities),
3. individual planning (counselor initiated activities), and
4. system support (activities and services that establish, maintain, and enhance the counselor's work).

The guidance curriculum component is composed of activities and learning opportunities taught in the classroom that help students to gain information, learn techniques, and master important skills. In the classroom these components become part of an organized and intentional curriculum, similar to other school disciplines.

The early work of Gysbers and Henderson in constructing their developmental model was influential in the development of the ASCA standards in 1997, which used the original three domains as standards around which to organize student competencies. These three domains are essential to the model and indicate the focus for working with students in the areas of career/vocational development, academic/learning development, and personal/social development. These domains, along with the four program components, were included in the ASCA model published in 2003 and provide a common language for school counselors. As Stone and Dahir (2006) stated:

> Comprehensive, developmental, results-based, national standards-based school counseling programs have established our presence and will define our future. (p. 228)

The developmental guidance and counseling approach integrates a counseling curriculum into the total educational process for all students in the school, rather than seeing it as peripheral or tangential. Myrick (1997) was one of the leaders in defining and implementing key principles of a developmental approach:

1. Developmental guidance is for all students.
2. Developmental guidance has an organized and planned curriculum.
3. Developmental guidance is sequential and flexible.
4. Developmental guidance is an integrated part of the total educational process.
5. Developmental guidance involves all school personnel.
6. Developmental guidance helps students learn more effectively and efficiently.
7. Developmental guidance includes counselors who provide specialized counseling services and interventions. (p.35)

Today, a new vision of developmental school counseling has been proposed by Lee and Goodnough (2007). This model builds upon the essential parts of previous models but adds critical components grounded in systems theory to become more inclusive of all student populations within a school system. The authors stated that their approach embraces "a truly systemic data-driven school counseling program rooted in educational equity for all students, especially students from traditionally underserved populations" (p. 122). The vision is unique for each school and contains a commitment to social justice, striving for equitable access to the school counseling program for *all* children in the school.

Built into the new vision is a data-driven program that is integrated with other educational programs in the school and is evaluated on its effectiveness to close the achievement and access gap between groups in the school. This model has a strong connection to some of the outcomes sought through No Child Left Behind and other reform efforts. Effective classroom activities and programs intentionally developed for students will require design and implementation skills by the professional school counselor to meet these standards.

Counseling All Students in the Classroom

The core component of a developmental guidance and counseling program is its preventive aspect. Certainly, prevention can be integrated into individual and small-group counseling, but its primary infusion for children and adolescents comes through the counseling and guidance curriculum offered in the classroom. This type of counseling program is available to all students in the school. Through the classroom curriculum, students at every grade level, throughout the entire academic year, are offered programming that attends to their developmental level and personal needs.

Developmental guidance and counseling models span the K–12 grades. They are based on the concept that children pass through various developmental stages as they grow and mature. For children to develop in a healthy manner, they must progress successfully through certain kinds of learning and development. Therefore, within the models, student competencies, based on developmental learning theory and national standards, are identified (Campbell & Dahir, 1997). Using these standards as guides, professional school counselors can develop specific competencies for each grade level, reflecting the developmental characteristics and needs of students for that grade.

For example, a first-grade competency might be to learn how to set a goal for getting work done in class during the day. In middle school the student may take a situation and set a short-term, intermediate, and long-term goal for a class project. High-school students may address the competency by establishing goals for postsecondary education or employment. These student competencies become the objectives from which the school counselor begins to develop a counseling curriculum.

Student competencies differ among school districts and states. Some state have developed their own student competencies by grade level that can assist school districts and teachers in determining what to emphasize and what skills to introduce at an appropriate level. The American School Counselor Association is planning to develop a national list of standards by grade level, which should be helpful (Jill Cook, Assistant Director of ASCA, personal communication, January 28, 2008). States and school districts will be able to use these guidelines to write their own list of competencies applicable to their situations and settings. In developing counseling programs, student competencies typically are organized around the three domains of development—personal/social, career/vocational, and academic/learning—as discussed in detail later in this chapter. Comprehensive developmental guidance programs can be taught to all students by the school counselor or by classroom teachers. In some schools, teachers and counselors collaborate to present the material. The key is to include all students in the activities and lessons conducted in the developmental counseling program. This ensures that all students are learning the skills and competencies identified in the curriculum.

As Lee and Goodnough (2007) stressed, there is an ethical responsibility to include all children, those with special needs and those from diverse groups, in the program and to tailor the material so all have equitable access to the school counseling program. In most schools where the counselor-to-student ratio exceeds 1:350, developmental classroom guidance is the primary way to engage all students. This trend is growing in schools that are utilizing a comprehensive, developmental approach. Some reasons for this national trend are the following.

1. Today's children are trying to grow up in a complicated and fast-changing society. Their complex needs for personal and social adjustment, academic proficiency, and career and vocational awareness can be met best through a comprehensive integrative program.
2. Counselors in the schools cannot effectively use a one-to-one counseling approach alone, as it provides services to only a few students. Developmental programming

in the classroom enables counselors, teachers, and people in the community to impact all students in their personal, academic, and career development.

3. As the developmental approach is implemented, it becomes cost-effective by providing services to all students in an accountable manner.

Subsequent to Gysber's seminal work on developmental guidance and counseling, developmental models have been adopted in most states throughout the country by state departments of education (e.g., Wisconsin, Oklahoma, Louisiana, Alaska, Indiana) and by school districts (e.g., San Antonio, Texas, and Lincoln, Nebraska). Miller (2006) reported on a successful collaboration between state officials in Minnesota where school counselors positively influenced student counseling practices. As a result of the state initiated study, school counselor certification standards were updated, counselor functions were clarified and strengthened, counselor education training programs were improved, and school counseling development and preventive guidance programs were initiated and supported in both elementary and high schools. This outcome contributed to the support of the National Standards for School Counseling Programs (ASCA, 1997). As Gysbers (2006) reiterated, the importance of involving state supervisors of guidance and counseling in collaborative efforts is paramount to promoting effective and accountable comprehensive guidance and counseling programs.

Presentations and workshops are offered on how to design and implement developmental and prevention based school counseling programs nationally. For example, the National School Counselor Training Initiative funds workshops to train school counselors and administrators on the transforming role of school counselors (Stone & House, 2002).

The Counselor's New Role as Educator

In the past some counselors entered the field of counseling to escape the classroom. Today's school counselors see the classroom as the "front line" of their work. In returning to the mainstream of education, counselors must have the professional skills to fulfill all the roles they will be called upon to perform— teacher, therapist, group facilitator, career specialist, crisis manager, mediation trainer, consultant, administrator, researcher, college specialist, test interpreter, and so forth. When administrators hear an explanation of the integrated counseling curriculum, they usually are highly supportive and willing to help make it possible.

In support, Chata and Loesch (2007) surveyed future school principals—with positive results. Principals were able to identify the roles that ASCA recommended for school counselors. This should be helpful in supporting transformational counseling in schools to meet student needs, including having school counselors in the classroom.

Many counselors wonder how they will have the time to implement a counseling curriculum. With good administrative support and program management skills, implementing a fully developed counseling curriculum typically requires only 20%–25% of the counselor's time. It is a matter of administrative support and program management. The following time utilization plan has been shown to be workable at the high school level:

individual and group counseling	25–30%
developmental programming	20–25%
placement (internal and external)	18%
administrative coordination	15%
information-giving	10%
testing	5%
evaluation/follow-up	2%

Even though large-group counseling is vital to the developmental/preventive focus, counselor time must be allocated to small-group counseling and individual counseling, as well as other aspects of the counselor's role.

In their model for a developmental school program, Gysbers and Henderson (2006) suggested the percentages in Table 12.1 for distributing time across the four program components.

The recommended percentages do differ based upon the setting, but it should be noted that curriculum implementation still should occur at the high school level. Careful planning is required to integrate the counseling curriculum at this level when classroom teachers may not see the value of the developmental counseling program or are unwilling to take minutes away from teaching their curriculum. School counselors may have to advocate for the developmental curriculum at the upper grade levels.

Field and Baker (2004) argued that advocacy is a central theme in school counseling and that school counselors must invest energy into identifying and clarifying their unique position in the school. They stated: "The professional school counselor is the ideal agent for organizing and leading advocacy efforts on behalf of students" (p. 63).

As with any comprehensive program, developmental programming must incorporate a team approach if it is to meet the needs of all students effectively. Thus, teachers must be active participants. Counselors who are trained and prepared in the

TABLE 12.1   Distribution of Counselor Time

	Elementary School	Middle School	High School
Guidance Curriculum	35–45%	25–35%	15–25%
Individual Planning	5–10%	15–25%	25–35%
Responsive Services	30–40%	30–40%	25–35%
System Support	10–15%	10–15%	15–20%

developmental model take the lead in establishing the curriculum, but they do so by strongly collaborating with teachers, drawing upon their expertise.

Further, team teaching is encouraged. School counselors can train teachers in the types of lessons and the process desired for a counseling curriculum. As counselors meet with the large groups, they can model the teaching of personal/social, academic, and career lessons that enhance and promote academic growth.

Ideally, classroom teachers will assume some of the responsibility for teaching the lessons and meeting the objectives identified in the counseling curriculum because counselors cannot do all of the classroom guidance and still have time to do the individual and small-group counseling for which they are uniquely trained. For example, the counselor and teacher would collaborate on an assignment that involves writing an essay on a career option for an English class.

Because time during the school day is at a premium, creative planning is necessary to implement developmental programming. This may be simpler at the grade-school level because the suggested 30 minutes a week for counselors to come into the classroom is easier to fit into the teacher's schedule. In the upper grades, when students are attending classes in periods, the school counselor may have to negotiate alternatives for leading classroom programs. In some schools, teachers in English, science, social studies, physical education, or other classes allow the counselor to deliver the curriculum in the classroom within agreed-upon timeframes. In other schools, a guidance and counseling period has been established around homerooms or split lunch periods. Myrick (1997) suggested implementing a program in which teachers, serving as student advisors, become involved in developmental guidance and counseling during homeroom or other designated periods.

The use of student advisory periods has become a popular way to implement a developmental program, especially at the middle school and high school levels. An advisory period is an identified period in the school day lasting from 15–30 minutes that can be used for delivering a curriculum that addresses student needs. In identifying the teacher as student advisor, Myrick (1997) emphasized the work that teachers must do to build a personal relationship with students.

In a survey conducted by the Consortium for School Improvement at the University of Chicago (Sebring et al., 1996), students overwhelmingly indicated that they did not have a personal relationship with their teachers and believed that no one really cared about their development in high school. The Chicago Public Schools (1997–98) addressed this need by establishing student advisories for freshmen in many high schools, with two primary purposes:

1. to establish a personal relationship between students and at least one adult in the school, and
2. to help students develop life skills that will enable them to achieve in school and experience success.

In the many schools that have student advisory periods, teachers, administrators, and school counselors use this time collaboratively to address students' competencies and needs. In other schools, the developmental curriculum is presented predominantly by the counselor, who develops units and goes into general classes to deliver the material. In these cases cooperation is vital to planning and delivering an effective program. The counselor is under heavy scrutiny to use classroom time effectively and efficiently, because students, faculty, and administrators are critics of how the program is evolving.

To establish accountability, the counselor must put in place an evaluation procedure that measures outcomes of the student competencies and objectives of the established curriculum. Reporting outcomes to the faculty and administration is a positive step in gaining support. In addition, the evaluation procedure can help counselors improve the effectiveness in future student programming.

Reforming school counseling—changing it from an ancillary role to an integral role in the total educational process—is no easy task. What seems to be the emphasis for the school counselor of the 21st century is a fusion between counseling and guidance and education. This can be accomplished by encouraging school counselors to attend to the following (Sink, 2002):

> Developing and updating the skills needed to serve all students; exploring innovations in educational and counseling theory and practice; advocating for themselves and their programs; implementing well-designed comprehensive programs; collaborating with one another, other school personnel, and with community agencies and programs; measuring student and program accomplishments and needs; creating a sense of community in their schools; and demonstrating a high degree of professionalism. (p. 161)

Working as an educator in the classroom may require major shifts in the counselor's role and behaviors. Infusing objectives from a counseling curriculum into other areas of teaching requires creativity by classroom teachers. With careful planning, however, this change can be highly productive and is well worth the effort. Students will benefit from a counseling curriculum that assists in their positive development throughout their school years and helps them to refine their skills for living by increasing their decision-making, self-awareness, and coping abilities. Schools will benefit from a curriculum that addresses the complex personal developmental needs of its students in addition to their academic subject-matter needs. The curriculum will give students the tools to approach life's challenges and therefore will help to minimize the number and severity of student difficulties.

Goodnough, Perusse, and Erford (2007) addressed the importance of developmental classroom curriculum, and the need for the school counselor to take this role seriously and intentionally. They wrote:

> Professional school counselors have not consistently focused on designing academically rigorous lesson plans, activities sensitive to diverse-learner needs, and assessment and follow-up procedures to determine the effectiveness and continuity of classroom guidance activities. The

school reform movement, with its emphasis on academic performance, requires this of classroom teachers. The same is expected of the transformed professional school counselor. (p. 142)

For school counselors the new role of educator means becoming more active and taking an integral role in the total school curriculum. It means moving into the classroom, becoming curriculum specialists, and holding themselves and their programs accountable. The profession no longer can hide behind closed doors or have unclear goals. To move into the developmental program is to put one's expertise on display and to be accountable for one's work. It is a worthy challenge.

Major Principles in a Counseling Curriculum

A counseling curriculum is based on the premise that all students need assistance throughout their school years to accomplish developmental tasks. Acquiring the necessary skills can lead each student to a sense of personal fulfillment and enhance the student's quality of life as a productive person in society.

The counseling curriculum provides a systematic approach for exposing students to age-appropriate lessons that will help them learn, understand, and eventually master aspects of personal/social development, vocational/career development, and academic/educational development. The primary goal is to help students develop healthy ways to cope and deal with situations that arise during their life journeys. Students can work through developmental and situational crises if they are able to call upon the skills they learned to confront difficulties when they arise.

As an example, students might role-play appropriate ways of handling their feelings when they are angry at school. Having the students explore alternative ways of reacting and consider the consequences of their behaviors in situations that are not emotionally charged will help them gain a better understanding without the emotional component. When the students are faced with a real situation in their personal lives, they will be able to make more appropriate, positive decisions.

Like any other curriculum in the educational schema, a counseling curriculum must be comprehensive, ongoing, and sensitive to the students' readiness to learn. Lessons emphasizing prevention should begin at the elementary level and progress to more difficult or abstract levels as the students develop cognitive and emotional capabilities. All students can benefit from lessons that promote positive self-esteem, for example, but the way the counselor approaches this topic will be quite different depending on the grade level. For example, first graders may learn to identify their physical characteristics, middle school students may learn to deal with self-consciousness, and high-school students may learn how to identify individual strengths that relate to career interests. The main ideas and themes (self-esteem, for example) must be repeated at each grade level through different activities that reflect developmental tasks and challenges and enhance students' learning.

Some counselors establish monthly themes for the entire student body as a part of their developmental curriculum. The units taught during a given month reflect that month's theme in developmentally appropriate lessons. The example below, for elementary level, utilizes themes that relate to the time of the school season or to holidays.

August:	Getting Acquainted/Orientation/Transition
September:	Academic Fitness/Self-Evaluation/Goal Setting
October:	Choices and Consequences/Decision Making
November:	Liking Me/Self-Esteem
December:	Family
January:	Wellness/Lifestyles/Stress Management
February:	Friendship/Interpersonal Relationship Skills
March:	Citizenship/Civic and Social Responsibility
April:	Feelings/Communication/Coping
May:	Careers/Exploration/Planning

Monthly themes also may be developed around topics based on age-appropriate developmental issues. For example, elementary-school students may benefit from themes of sibling rivalry, tattling, and good touch/bad touch. Middle school students may be good candidates for units on cliques, peer relationships, study skills, or managing emotional ups and downs. High-school students might benefit from units on college planning, applying for jobs, dating, and developing a sexual identity.

Counselors also may identify situational topics, which usually are presented to students following a specific event or catastrophe. After the September 11th attacks on the Trade Centers, for example, counselors presented units addressing students' fear, terrorism, death, and safety. As another example, a unit on loss and grief may be appropriate following the death of a student or staff member.

Regardless of the topic, the counseling curriculum must be well organized and planned intentionally. Goals and competencies for each grade level must be identified, followed by units and lesson plans containing sequential, developmentally appropriate activities that follow a lesson plan format. Students, faculty, staff, and parents all must see the counseling curriculum as an integral component within the total instructional program, and this can be accomplished only if the curriculum is organized, evaluated, and accountable.

Developing the curriculum to fit the needs of a school system is a major task. Counselors must be willing to scrutinize the plethora of materials available from publishers and glean from them the activities or ideas they believe will be the most appropriate. Curriculum resources can be organized into three-ring binders so they can be shared readily with other counselors in the school district or neighboring districts. The materials that can be used in classroom guidance and counseling programming should be reviewed and customized according to the unique characteristics of the setting. (Designing a lesson plan for a developmental program and suggestions for teaching the lesson in the classroom are discussed in detail later in this chapter.)

A counseling curriculum also must be flexible. As new areas of need arise, the curriculum should be revised and embellished. The toughest time will be at the start, when guidance and counseling units have to be created. After a unit has been taught, additional lessons can be added and changes made. When appropriate, outside experts can serve as resources. For example, local police officers might come into the classroom to teach a unit on drug awareness or personal safety. Some school districts hire a representative from a local substance-abuse center to teach a prevention program to students. Flexibility enables the counseling curriculum to fit the ever-changing needs and circumstances of the setting and the students.

Finally, a counseling curriculum must be accountable, and this requires good planning from the beginning. Goals and objectives for the curriculum should be written in behavioral and measurable terms. An evaluation should be done at the end of each unit to determine whether the students understood and grasped the topic or issue presented. The evaluation activity might be a game or an informal test that would not be graded. Accountability should be built into the program when it is data-driven (Cobia & Henderson, 2007). In this process, school counseling programs are systematically planned based on identified student needs or age-appropriate competencies, and goals are set and evaluated on the extent to which the desired outcomes were achieved.

Students' progress can be monitored through results on standardized tests, grades, or retention rates, but school counselors have not done a good job of providing evidence to show if their counseling program is effective (Studer, Oberman & Womack, 2006). As a result, in some cases school counseling programs have been eliminated and school counselors have been reassigned to non-counseling tasks that do not meet student needs.

An example of a program with built-in skills for school success with the goal of improving academic and social competence was implemented for students in grades 5, 6, 8, and 9 (Brigman, Webb, & Campbell, 2007). Accountability was measured by looking at the achievement outcomes on math and reading tests, as well as teacher-rated student behavior surveys. Students who were part of the program showed significantly higher scores in math and substantially better classroom behavior compared to a similar group of students who were not in the program. The results give credence to this classroom developmental counseling intervention as beneficial for students. Once stakeholders see the value to children and how it meets students' development, support is strengthened for the program and for the counselor's role.

A Student Development Program Model

Recall that a thorough counseling curriculum carefully considers three components within each of the general domains: personal/social, career/vocational, and academic/learning. These components originated from work by Drum and Knott (1977) and refer to the identification of life themes, life transitions, and life skills that affect growth and development The student development program model illustrates step-by-step how these components that give focus to live themes, life transitions, and life skills can be incorporated effectively into a counseling curriculum.

The student development program is a structured, sequenced, large-group activity directed to the needs and interests of all students in a school, while being sensitive to the developmental competencies and interests of students at different grade levels. It is a helping process in which the counselor or teacher presents a series of lessons representing a curriculum of counseling. Figure 12.1 depicts the student development program model and the interrelatedness of each aspect with the developmental domains described next. The developmental approach targets the accomplishment of student competencies in three domains of living:

1. *Personal/social*: The curriculum identifies competencies that will assist students in understanding and expressing self and in looking at how they relate to others as individuals and in groups. It helps students see how their thoughts, feelings, and behaviors shape their personality, their being, and their interpersonal relationships.
2. *Career/vocational*: The curriculum targets competencies that will assist students in exploring career possibilities and opportunities, helps students with career decision making, and enables them to make a successful transition from school to work.
3. *Academic/learning*: The curriculum provides activities and experiences that develop competencies leading to a student's educational success and promotes optimum development of each student's learning potential.

When students are taught a curriculum emphasizing these three domains at every grade level, the preventive aspect is clear. The goal is to teach the students how to deal with normal developmental issues in a way that will increase their self-awareness, self-esteem, and positive relationships with others and will improve their goal-setting, decision-making, career exploration, and study skills. These competencies then can be translated into skills or tools that will lead to healthy choices and responses when students face difficulties or decisions.

Student development program planners also identify specific goals, issues, and situations to be addressed in the classroom in the following areas.

1. *Life themes*: major recurring situations and issues throughout the lifespan that can be addressed developmentally so people can respond adequately to and deal with them. Certain situations occur again and again throughout life. Each time they appear, they may have to be addressed differently, perhaps at a more intensive level, requiring modifications or different skills. Life themes are best approached by teaching life skills that relate to specific recurring situations. As people grow and mature, the best method to handle or cope with these situations may change. Examples of life themes are friendship and love, stress, personal safety, and responsibility.
2. *Life transitions*: major changes and passages throughout the lifespan that influence a person and necessitate adapting and restructuring current behaviors and realities. Life transitions are specific points in a person's life at which significant

changes transpire. Some of these transitions occur at times common to most individuals, such as starting school and obtaining a driver's license. Other transitions come at varying times, such as first job, first love, moving, and the death of a significant grandparent or parent. Some students go through painful life transitions before most people do, such as a serious illness or injury that alters their life, or parents divorcing, for example. Including life transitions in the curriculum is vital so students can begin to prepare for anxious times and crises by identifying life skills that may help them cope effectively when such situations do present themselves.

3. *Life skills*: learned behaviors that enable a person to perform the essential tasks of normal developmental growth throughout the lifespan. These are taught continually in the counseling curriculum. Most relate heavily to the personal/social area and include self-acceptance, listening, communication, problem solving, values clarification, identifying and expressing feelings, and so forth.

Life themes and life transitions necessitate that individuals learn life skills that can help them handle recurring situations, issues, changes, and life passages. As counselors identify the themes and transitions in the lives of preschool–grade 12 students, they should design and implement programs that will

1. create awareness of the dynamics involved in each life theme and transition,
2. help individuals understand how the themes and transitions affect them, and
3. teach students how to change or modify their behaviors to adjust to or resolve specific life themes or transitions.

For example, lessons on stress management will help students realize that sometimes unpleasant circumstances result in an upset stomach or other physical manifestation. These lessons should allow for students' discussing how they feel about unpleasant situations and the effects of these situations, and they should teach students how to develop coping skills to deal with unpleasant situations.

Working Within the Structural Framework

As a counseling curriculum is developed, the school counselor has to plan to include certain essential topics. Counselors are encouraged to prioritize the essential topics and develop units and lessons one topic at a time across the K–12 curriculum. For example, a planner may set up their curriculum emphasizing decision making in fifth grade and friendships in sixth grade. Counselors should avoid this type of haphazard or inconsequential planning, as students at all grade levels need to learn developmentally appropriate information about each topic at each grade level to assure more comprehensive learning. Suggested topics are listed in Table 12.2.

A school or community may institute another set of topics, termed "special needs," depending on the unique needs or characteristics of the local community. For example, a unit on death or loss may be needed if a district or school has had a series

TABLE 12.2	Essential Topics to be Covered in a Counseling Curriculum	
Life Themes	**Life Transitions**	**Life Skills**
	Personal/Social Domain	
Self-Concept Development	Family Changes (new	Self-Awareness
Friendship and Love	siblings, death, divorce)	Self-Acceptance
Change	New School Orientation	Listening Skills
Conflicts	Significant Life Events	Communications Skills
Stress	(puberty, driver's	Values Clarification
Values	license, first job)	Problem Solving
Personal Safety	Loss of Friends and	Relationship Skills
Responsibility	Loved Ones	Coping Skills
Grief and Loss		Behavior Management
Death		
	Career/Vocational Domain	
Career Exploration	Career Fantasy to	Planning
Use of Leisure Time	Career Exploration	Goal Setting
Attitude Toward Work	Exploration to Tentative	Career Decision Making
Dual-Career Couples	Career Choice	Employment-Seeking
Career Decisions		Skills
	Academic/Learning Area	
Motivations	Preschool to Elementary	Study Skills
Learning Styles	Elementary to Middle	Time Management
Learning Deficiencies	School	Speech and Test Anxiety
Discipline vs. Procrastination	Middle School to High	Reduction
Lifelong Learning	School	Critical Thinking
	High School to College	Analysis and Synthesis
	High School to Work	

of suicides or catastrophic deaths, or a unit on eating disorders or self-mutilation if the district or school has a high prevalence of these behaviors.

Figure 12.1 contains a structural framework form to assist counselors in designing classroom guidance and counseling programs. Often the hardest step in a developmental guidance and counseling program is getting started. This format can be used to begin a new program or to reassess an ongoing program. Prior to using the form, the counselor should do the following.

1. Identify students' needs based on developmental level (a review of ASCA student competencies, national standards, or another source addressing student needs will be helpful).

Steps:	**Definitions:**
1. Identify school level (i.e., elementary, middle, or high school). 2. Identify developmental tasks and needed competencies. 3. Utilize professional assessment and/or needs assessment. 4. Identify developmental program based on the model.	**Life Themes:** Major recurring situations and issues throughout the lifespan that need to be addressed developmentally so that people can adequately respond to these situations and cope with these issues. **Life Transitions:** Major changes and/or passages throughout the lifespan that impact on a person in such a way as to necessitate adaption and restructuring of current behaviors and realities. **Life Skills:** Learned behaviors that enable a person to perform the essential tasks of normal developmental growth throughout the lifespan (e.g., problem solving).

	Life-Themes	**Life Transitions**	**Life Skills**
Academic			
Personal/ Social			
Career			

FIGURE 12.1 **Structural Framework Form for a Developmental Counseling Program**

2. Consider the ASCA model as an aid to foster a strong theoretical foundation for the curriculum. This can help the school counselor in setting priorities.
3. Conduct a formal needs assessment of students, teachers, parents, and administrators when initiating a comprehensive program. This allows the school counselor to gain insights into their perceptions, needs, and issues (Gysbers & Henderson, 2006).
4. Regularly use informal assessment on a regular basis that allows for students' changing needs.

5. Consider state policies and requirements that have to be addressed in the school. For example, many states require classroom programming on bullying, sexual harassment, social–emotional development, or character education.
6. Select a grade level and the specific domain desired.
7. In the appropriate column on the form in Figure 12.1, list important life themes, life transitions, and life skills to be addressed at that grade level.

The suggested essential K–12 topics for a student development counseling curriculum, as listed in Table 12.1, cover the personal/social, career/vocational, and academic/learning domains. Within each domain the three components—life skills, life themes, and life transitions—add meaningful organization to the specific units. This structural framework enables counselors to identify the core areas of the counseling curriculum, topics essential for all programs, and topics unique to the individual school setting.

Identifying topics is only the first step, though. Objectives or competencies should be developed for each topic from kindergarten through the senior year in high school. These objectives will serve as the basis for creating lessons and units on each of these topics and for developing a sequential, grade-level curriculum. To illustrate, we present the objectives that Vernon (1998a, b, c) identified for the topic of Self-Acceptance.

Self–Acceptance (Grades 1–12)

Grade 1

- To learn that everyone has strengths as well as weaknesses
- To learn that everyone is worthwhile regardless of weaknesses
- To identify what children like about being who they are
- To develop an attitude of self-acceptance
- To identify ways in which children are physically growing and changing
- To identify competencies associated with physical changes

Grade 2

- To develop awareness of abilities and attributes
- To learn to accept oneself with these abilities and attributes
- To recognize that strengths and limitations are part of one's self-definition
- To learn not to put oneself down because of limitations
- To identify individual strengths
- To learn a strategy to help remember good things about oneself

Grade 3

- To learn that how one acts determines self-worth
- To learn that nobody is perfect

- To learn to accept oneself as less than perfect
- To identify characteristics of self, including strengths and weaknesses
- To learn to accept compliments
- To identify personal strengths

Grade 4

- To learn that mistakes are natural
- To learn that making mistakes does not make one a bad person
- To identify strengths and weaknesses in the areas of physical, social, and intellectual development
- To recognize ways to get approval from others and ways to approve of oneself
- To learn that others' approval is not required to be worthwhile
- To learn more about individual preferences, characteristics, and abilities

Grade 5

- To identify one's positive attributes
- To differentiate between making mistakes and being a total failure
- To identify specific characteristics that are like or unlike oneself
- To identify feelings associated with varying rates of development

Grade 6

- To identify self-characteristics
- To learn that self-characteristics may change over time
- To normalize the self-conscious feelings that begin to occur during this period of development and to learn more about the physical changes occurring during this period of rapid growth
- To learn that all individuals have strengths and weaknesses and not to rate oneself globally as good or bad
- To learn to take multiple perspectives into account when forming opinions about oneself
- To learn to separate others' negative perceptions from one's sense of self-worth

Grade 7

- To learn not to equate self-worth with performance
- To normalize feelings of self-consciousness during early adolescence
- To explore ways to deal with self-conscious feelings
- To develop a better understanding of the self-definition process and how this applies to oneself
- To identify ways one is like and unlike one's peers

- To develop awareness of social, emotional, and physical problems associated with eating disorders

Grade 8

- To develop an understanding of the frequent changes in the way one thinks, feels, and behaves
- To identify feelings associated with changes during early adolescence
- To develop an understanding of adolescent egocentricity
- To learn how adolescent egocentricity affects oneself as well as others
- To normalize feelings of self-consciousness and develop effective strategies for dealing with those feelings
- To develop a clearer picture of whom one is

Grade 9

- To learn more about personal values
- To learn more about one's identity
- To clarify values and beliefs
- To learn that one is not invincible
- To identify consequences of believing that one is invincible
- To learn that performance in one area is not a reflection of one's total worth as a person

Grade 10

- To distinguish between all-or-nothing self-rating and rating one's individual traits
- To clarify aspects of self-identity
- To learn facts about anorexia and bulimia
- To identify the social, emotional, cognitive, and physical problems associated with eating disorders
- To compare self-image with one's perceptions of how others see one
- To learn not to equate self-worth with others' perceptions of one

Grade 11

- To learn more about whom one is becoming in one's identity quest
- To learn how to accept oneself and to identify one's positive qualities
- To identify ways one puts oneself down
- To differentiate between self-respect and disrespect
- To identify ways to change things one doesn't respect in oneself but to accept oneself as worthwhile regardless of these things
- To identify what it means to be independent, ways one is independent, and feelings associated with independence

Grade 12

- To assess personal strengths
- To identify present and future roles
- To distinguish between abuse and self-abuse
- To identify strategies to deal with self-abusive behaviors or abusive behaviors inflicted by others
- To clarify how one sees oneself in the future
- To identify what it means to be dependent, ways one is dependent, and feelings associated with dependence

How to Design a Lesson

Once grade-level objectives have been established, the counselor is ready to design the lessons and units to address the objectives or competencies.

Format for Developing Counseling Lessons and Units

The most common approach for developing a counseling curriculum is to organize units around a theme, central idea, or developmentally age-appropriate topic that may arise out of the life-themes, life-transitions, or life-skills components discussed earlier. The unit may evolve as the result of a needs assessment or an outcome desired by the students, or it may reflect grade-level developmental competencies based on developmental needs and tasks.

Gysbers and Henderson (2006) compared the development of a classroom curriculum to the development of curricula in other subject areas such as social studies, math, and science. Of significance is the involvement of school counselors in design of the curriculum as the experts in their field. Goodnough, Perusse, and Erford (2007) strongly advise a data-driven, outcome-based curriculum.

Myrick's (1997) suggested that many units be presented yearly, adjusted to target the appropriate readiness skills for each grade level, and that other units be created in response to specific needs or events. For example, if the school is beginning to see gang activity, the counselor might elect to introduce a unit on gang awareness, taking care to provide lessons that match the students' developmental level.

Units usually have an overall theme and are composed of several lessons or sessions. Although the number of sessions varies with the topic, time allocation, and age level, anywhere from four to 10 sessions is appropriate. When designing a unit or series of lessons, the counselor should specify the general objectives and goals that he or she intends to meet throughout the sessions. The unit format should include

grade level,
unit name or topic,
appropriate grade-level competencies,
national or state competencies,

rationale for the unit,
unit purpose,
unit objectives,
number of sessions,
detailed procedures of all activities, and
evaluation criteria and method.

In addition to being included in the unit format, a brief rationale for the unit, explaining why it is important, should be included in the curriculum at times. This rationale can be presented to the administration, staff, and faculty to summarize the "what and why" of the curriculum. This is especially needed if the counselor develops units on sensitive issues such as AIDS or death and loss.

The classroom lesson is the heart of the developmental counseling program. Building upon a model developed by Vernon (1998a,b,c; 2006a,b), each lesson should contain the following components:

1. *Purpose and objectives*

When developing a lesson, the counselor should begin by writing down the purpose and objective that he or she intends to accomplish in that lesson. The objective should be written in the specific terms of a performance/measurable outcome. For example: "The student will respond to another by using an 'I message' appropriately." To be avoided are broad objectives such as, "The student will develop an understanding of better communication skills."

2. *Stimulus activity/procedure*

Then the counselor should design a well-planned activity to assist in fulfilling that objective. This stimulus activity may be a story, a film, role-play, a speaker, simulation, a reading assignment, or other activity. The counselor should make sure that the activity will not take up all of the time allotted for the session. The activity is not the most important part of the lesson. It should only "set the stage" for what the counselor wants to accomplish with the students. A list of the materials and/or supplies needed for the activity should be included here.

3. *Content-level discussion*

The next part of the lesson should consist of a discussion of the stimulus activity at a content level. For example, the counselor might ask the students to tell a partner what was going on in the story or might have the students discuss in small groups the main problem in the video. This section of the lesson should be relatively short and simple with a focus on what the students did in the activity or what they learned about the content of the activity.

4. *Personal-level discussion*

The stimulus activity then should be discussed at a personal level. For example, the counselor may ask the students to think of a time when they might have had a similar experience and, if so, how they felt. The counselor could have the students brainstorm ideas about what they think should be done, or what they would do, to handle the situation. In this component the students apply the main concepts of the lesson to their personal situations. The counselor should allow ample time for this component, as it is the key to the lesson. Counselors will find that most of the published materials applicable to counseling units do not contain questions directed to the personal level. Thus, counselors have to pay special attention to personal-level discussion and spend time developing appropriate questions.

5. *Closure*

At this stage the counselor processes the session and brings closure to the group. The counselor can utilize group-process skills in asking the students what they learned in the session. The discussion may reveal students' insights about themselves or about others.

6. *Evaluation*

The final step in developing a counseling unit is to plan the evaluation. Evaluation is essential for reporting the value and benefit outcomes to administrative and school board personnel. It also benefits the classroom teacher and the students by calling attention to the work the students are doing and the impact that work is having on the students' thinking, feelings, behaviors, and achievement.

Curriculum evaluation can be done at the end of each session or at the end of a unit. The evaluations should be simple and appropriate to the grade level, and they can be creative, using art or creative writing projects. The students might form small groups and role-play what they have learned for the rest of the class. They might be asked to complete checklists or surveys that pinpoint the objectives identified at the start of the unit. Most important, the counselor should gain insight into the effectiveness of the unit so he or she can decide if or how the unit should be changed when it is taught again.

Curriculum evaluations can have a major influence on the effectiveness of the overall developmental counseling program. These results contribute to the overall data on which the accountability of the school counseling program is based. The results also contribute to the data-driven and outcome-based results that are critical components in the program's accountability (Cobia & Henderson, 2007; Lapan, 2001). These results are planned systematically and are driven by pre-identified objectives and competencies that should benefit all students in the school.

Examples include monitoring student progress on standardized testing or with grades, closing the achievement gap by increasing competence, enhanced feelings of belonging, higher levels of motivation for at-risk groups in the school, higher graduation rates, improved retention of students, better attendance records, and improved school climate (Cobia & Henderson, 2007). School counselors must make it their priority to gather these data and report their results to stakeholders including administrators, parents, and teachers. This emphasis provides accountability for the school counseling program—an outcome that can no longer be avoided or overlooked.

Unit development and lesson design are challenging tasks that require creativity. Ideas can be created, found in affective education materials, or borrowed from other counseling programs. When using ready-made materials, the counselor should adapt them, as necessary, to the unique needs and objectives of his or her situation. A resource list of suggested affective education resources is provided at the end of this chapter.

The lesson plan format discussed here and outlined in Figure 12.2, was used to develop the following sample lessons, one for elementary students and one for middle school. Both lessons are related to emotional development and illustrate how to design lessons around the same theme but relate the concepts to developmental tasks at each level: Elementary students are just developing feeling vocabularies and becoming aware of their emotions; young adolescents need to learn how to deal effectively with painful emotions.

Lesson # _____ Topic _____

(1) Lesson Objectives _____

_____

Materials _____

(2) Stimulus Activity _____

(procedure) _____

_____

(3) Content-Level Discussion Questions

    a) _____

    b) _____

    c) _____

(4) Personal-Level Discussion Questions

    a) _____

    b) _____

    c) _____

(5) Closure _____

Evaluation (may be optional) _____

Notes:

FIGURE 12.2   **Lesson Plan Format**

Sample Lesson: Emotions

Grade 2

This lesson is taken from *The Passport Program: A Journey through Emotional, Social, Cognitive, and Self-Development*, by Ann Vernon (Champaign, IL: Research Press, 1998a, pp. 91–92).

Title: *A Lot or a Little?*
Lesson Objective: To learn to differentiate the intensity of emotions and to learn that everyone doesn't feel the same way about the same situation
Materials: Chalkboard, a ruler, sheet of paper, and pencil for each student
Stimulus Activity/Procedure:

1. Introduce the activity by having the students use their rulers to draw a line across their papers (in a horizontal position).
2. On the model line, write the words "very happy" at one end and the words "very unhappy" on the other end. Write the other words (on) the line as illustrated:

very happy   pretty happy   pretty unhappy   very unhappy

3. Ask the children to listen carefully as you read the following situations, one at a time. After each, ask them to put an X on the line to illustrate how they might feel if they were in this situation: very happy, pretty happy, pretty unhappy, very unhappy.

    Your teacher tells you that you did very well on your spelling test.
    Your sister gets to stay up later than you do.
    Your best friend didn't walk to school with you today.
    Your dad yelled at you because you hadn't picked up your room.
    Your neighbor's dog chewed your new tennis shoes.
    Your big brother took you for a ride on his bike.
    Your cousin let you use her new rollerblades.
    You can't go out for recess because it is raining.
    Your class is going on a field trip to the zoo.
    You missed two problems on your math paper.

    When you have finished reading the first situation, ask the children to raise a hand if they marked this situation "very happy," "pretty happy," and so on. Count each response and put the total on the chalkboard beside each feeling on the continuum. Then proceed to the next situation and follow the same procedure of identifying and tallying the responses.

4. After all the situations have been read and recorded, process the activity by asking the Content and Personalization Questions.

Content Questions:

1. Looking back at the responses, did this group have all of the marks on the "very happy" end of the line? Did this group have all of the marks on the "very unhappy" end of the line? Why do you think this group had marks at several different places on the line?
2. Did you have difficulty deciding how you felt about some of these situations? If so, why do you think it was hard?
3. Do you think everyone always feels the same way about the same things? Why or why not?

Personalization Questions

1. Think about your day today. Have you felt only "very happy" or "very unhappy," or have you also felt "pretty happy" or "pretty unhappy?"
2. Have you ever had a disagreement with someone because that person felt differently than you about something? Invite sharing of examples.
3. Based on this lesson, what should you remember about feelings?

Closure (to the leader)

At this age children are concrete thinkers. Consequently, they have difficulty understanding the concept of a continuum of feelings. As a result, they frequently assume that someone is either very angry or very unhappy about something without recognizing the range of intensity of emotions. Without this understanding, misinterpretation is common. It is possible to teach children how to develop a broader perspective as part of their emotional development.

Grade 8

This lesson is reprinted from *The Passport Program: A Journey through Emotional, Social, Cognitive, and Self-Development,* by Ann Vernon (Champaign, IL: Research Press, 1998b, pp. 203–204).

Title:	*Pain Relievers*
Lesson Objective:	To distinguish healthy and unhealthy ways to relieve emotional pain
Materials:	A chalkboard, magazines, scissors, glue, large sheet of tagboard, and markers for every group of four students

Stimulus Activity/Procedure:

1. Introduce the activity by having students quickly brainstorm examples of painful emotions. As they identify examples, write them on the board. Next discuss the difference between healthy and unhealthy ways of dealing with painful emotions. For example, anger can be a painful emotion. An unhealthy way to deal with anger would be to get drunk. A healthy way to deal with it would be to talk it out.

2. Divide students into groups of four and distribute the materials. Instruct them to make two columns on the bottom half of the tag board poster and to label one side "Healthy ways to deal with painful emotions" and the other side "Unhealthy ways to deal with painful emotions." Ask each group to list several painful emotions at the top of the poster. Then have them look through the magazines for pictures representing healthy or unhealthy ways to deal with these emotions. If they can't find appropriate pictures, have them draw symbols or use words to represent their suggestions.

3. After the posters have been completed, have the small groups share them with the total group.

4. Discuss the Content and Personalization questions.

Content-Level Discussion Questions:

1. Which was harder to identify—healthy or unhealthy ways to deal with painful emotions?

2. In general, were the small groups in agreement with each other? Did one group label as unhealthy any ideas that you might have considered healthy, and vice versa? Share examples.

3. What makes the unhealthy methods unhealthy? Do you think they help relieve pain in the long-term? Why or why not?

Personal-Level Discussion Questions:

1. Are your "pain relievers" generally healthy or unhealthy? Why?

2. If you have tried unhealthy methods in the past, how has this affected your life? If you had it to do over, what might you do differently, if anything?

3. Did you learn anything from this lesson that will be helpful to you in dealing with painful emotions? Invite sharing.

Closure (to the Leader):

To young adolescents, feelings such as discouragement, ambivalence, depression, shame, and confusion often seem unbearable. Too often they numb their feelings in unhealthy ways. This activity can help them learn more effective means of dealing with painful emotions. As a follow-up you could make available novels that portray healthy ways of dealing with painful emotions.

How To Conduct Classroom Guidance and Counseling Lessons

School counselors who have been trained in a teacher-preparation program have a distinct advantage in developing classroom developmental counseling lessons because they know how to write lesson plans. They also have had training in motivation and classroom management. Counselors who have not had formal training should at least familiarize themselves with the following.

A Knowledge Base of Teaching Skills

Good (1979), and Hunter (1976), developed early instructional programs that provided classroom teachers with a format and process for teaching that has been shown to be effective. These programs and others that offer innovative techniques for use in the classroom can increase the knowledge and confidence of school counselors who work in the large-group setting. One of these approaches is *cooperative learning* (Johnson & Johnson, 1994). According to Jones and Jones (2006), a cooperative learning approach has a positive impact on students' self-esteem and relationship building by enhancing learning and building positive attitudes. Because self-esteem is always a by-product, and sometimes even the prime objective in a classroom guidance unit, methods that enhance its potential are imperative.

Another method with a strong impact was introduced by Purkey and Schmidt (1996) and Purkey and Novak (1996). Called *invitational learning*, this approach attempts to elevate the importance of school and learning in an environment that heavily emphasizes the unique worth, respect, and dignity of each student. It moves beyond the premise that self-esteem is something that should be the theme of an occasional classroom activity and, instead, holds that the entire educational experience should validate individual worth.

Marzano (2007) offers a current model for classroom instruction and management designed as a comprehensive framework. This framework serves as a starting point that allows each school or school district to develop its own model. Marzano proposed three components of effective classroom pedagogy:

1. Effective instructional strategies
2. Classroom management strategies
3. Classroom curriculum design strategies

He stated that "the most basic issues a teacher can consider is what he or she will do to establish and communicate learning goals, track student progress, and celebrate success" (p. 9). His model organizes strategies for effective instruction around key elements including helping students to interact, deepen and understand new knowledge, engage students in learning, maintain rules and procedures in the classroom, build effective relationships, communicate high expectations for all students, and develop effective lessons (Marzano, 2007).

Jones (2007) taught a series of tools that help teachers to manage successful classrooms. His classroom instruction program proposed four key elements in effective teaching:

1. Fundamental classroom strategies that include "working smart" in the classroom
2. Instructional practices that make learning interactive and independent, and discourage the helpless hand-raiser
3. Strategies that motivate students through internalized values of hard work and conscientiousness

4. Strategic management of discipline in the classroom to provide a structure that makes cooperation and responsible behavior a matter of routine in the classroom (Jones, 2007)

Goodnough, Perusse, and Erford (2007) emphasized the importance of maintaining discipline in the classroom and that it is influenced strongly by having a well-designed and smooth-flowing lesson. At the same time, the school must have a plan for how to deal with problematic behavior in the classroom when students are disruptive. The general impression by guests in the classroom is that the school counselor would follow the rules that the classroom teacher already has in place. At times this can create a difficult, even ethical dilemma for the school counselor who does not want to act with too much authority and jeopardize individual counseling relationships that may take place at other times.

School counselors and teachers must act in a way that makes school inviting to children (Purkey & Schmidt, 1996). By modeling and demonstrating concrete behavior, the counselor and teacher can help the student relate to the environment, become assertive by developing a sense of control within the classroom, be willing to try new things and make mistakes, and be able to cope with the world. Becoming knowledgeable about models such as those described above provides a base of knowledge for the counselor who will be active in the school setting as the large-group teacher. Using these models, the counselor will be able to create a learning environment that encourages the transfer of knowledge and experiences from the classroom to the entire school, the family, and the community.

Some skills important to teaching a counseling curriculum successfully include the following:

Classroom management
Operation of technological equipment
Time management
Delivery of a presenting stimulus or lecturette
Directing small group to whole-class structured activities
Active listening
Open-ended questioning
Facilitating the group process
Nonjudgmental responses
Pacing
Balancing flexibility and staying on task
Involving all students
Noting cues for follow-up work with individual students

Developing a Counseling Curriculum

For counselors, conducting guidance and counseling lessons in a classroom is much different from counseling in an office. Counselors with prior teaching experience may find the rewards of classroom teaching to be an enjoyable part of their total counseling work. In conducting classroom guidance units, several options have been highlighted in the examples in this chapter. For example, the counselor could be totally responsible for the design and implementation of the entire classroom unit, or the counselor could be responsible for design and the teacher for implementation.

Another option involves a collaborative effort in which the counselor and the teacher work together to deliver the unit. The counselor would teach some of the lessons, and other lessons would be led by the classroom teacher or qualified community people. For example, the counselor might teach the first three sessions and the teacher the last three sessions. Ultimately, the school counselor is the one who is responsible for implementing the counseling curriculum and for assisting and coordinating the teachers who are also involved. This assistance may include inservice training, team teaching, or modeling by the counselor.

In contrast to typical classroom teaching, which centers on subject matter, teaching a counseling curriculum, or developmental programming, centers on content that is much more personalized. The content of the counseling curriculum (life themes, life transitions, and life skills) necessarily means that the counselor or teacher has to personalize the content to each student. Teachers have to differentiate teaching academic content from teaching a curriculum that is more process-focused and phenomenological. The goal is for students to integrate what they learn in the counseling curriculum into their own individual, family, and social environments. Thus, the counselor and the teacher alike strive to have the students internalize the content as it relates to their academic, vocational, and personal/social life and then make behavioral changes.

A counseling curriculum also involves teaching elements that are more factual and objective. A unit on self-awareness, for example, may include information on nutrition, stress reduction, or using positive self-statements. Those objectives can be infused intentionally into the total school curriculum and become part of a health, English, or reading lesson. As another example, career exploration may be incorporated into a social studies class. In these ways the counseling curriculum can be integrated within the total curriculum and help to meet the needs of the whole student. The key to this approach is for classroom teachers to be consistent in how they address the objectives within the counseling curriculum so students are exposed to developmental, sequential programming. The counselor should administer this curriculum and be responsible for seeing that age-level competencies and objectives are met clearly and appropriately.

Teaching a counseling curriculum is one of the most effective and efficient ways of developing students' potential, as the content is developmental and preventive and the counselor or teacher is working with 15 to 30 or more students at the same time. Teaching a developmental counseling curriculum can further the potential of many individuals.

Steps in Classroom Lessons

Counselors and teachers may find the following suggestions useful in conducting classroom lessons:

1. Prepare materials and handouts in advance.
2. Place all materials for a given lesson in a file folder that can be pulled later to update and reuse. (Portfolios work well here.)
3. Arrange ahead of time for any audiovisual equipment, know how to operate it, or arrange for someone else to do it.
4. Be generally knowledgeable and familiar with the entire unit and totally familiar with the lesson that is to be taught that day.
5. Arrive early, and start on time.
6. Keep the classroom atmosphere relaxed, but maintain proper decorum using appropriate classroom-management skills.
7. Follow the structure of the lesson plan, and teach the lesson using group-process skills.
8. Strive to personalize the content with a balance of task orientation and flexibility while keeping an eye on the time.
9. Utilize various-sized groups (dyads, triads, groups of six, or total group) for maximum effectiveness in given activities.
10. Vary the traditional classroom style by having students sit in a circle or on the floor.
11. Make use of student demonstrations, role-plays, or homework with nonthreatening assignments.
12. Conclude by generalizing the content to applicable situations in the students' world.

Leading classroom lessons has some pitfalls that can be avoided just by being aware of what could happen. For one, detailed storytelling by the facilitator and students could bore students or get the lesson off track and should be avoided. Or if the counselor is overly flexible, students could ramble in their discussions. If the content contains sensitive material for students and their families (e.g., sexual responsibility), the counselor can avoid resistance by letting the parents know about the material in advance. Tactfully presenting the issue to parents might defuse any negative reactions.

School counselors who are not familiar with teaching in the classroom must also be cautious in identifying and teaching learning goals within their lessons. Sometimes the temptation as a counselor in the classroom is to lead it more like a small-group experience and not as a classroom, learning-based activity. School counselors can use student-centered and student-friendly approaches, but they still must be identified as the expert in addressing learning outcomes.

For example, in a lesson on stress and anxiety, beginning the class by having students articulate examples of stress in their lives, would build interest. These examples could be listed on the board. Eventually, though, the lesson has to provide examples of common stressors not covered in the student discussion, as well as information that addresses the learning objectives of the lesson. This might include a list of strategies for reducing stress and anxiety at school for students with these feelings. The school counselor might utilize a PowerPoint presentation, clever over-heads, role-plays, or videos to convey this information within the lesson. Students need to take away new information, new skills, or increased understanding as a result of the lesson. Differentiating the school counselor's roles when teaching a large classroom lesson and small groups is necessary.

Finally, school counselors who are teaching a lesson in the classroom must be cautious about raising the issue of confidentiality in the classroom. In most cases, students who participate in a comprehensive developmental guidance and counsel-ing classroom do not bring in signed parental slips for participation. The classroom experience should be geared to all students and must be broad enough to meet the diverse needs and abilities of students who make up the class. Without parental per-mission, it is paramount to not raise confidentiality as a requirement for participa-tion in the classroom. The school counselor who is teaching this lesson must be ready to intervene if a student begins to reveal information that is too personal or that may place the student in a vulnerable position.

The Future of Developmental Programming and Classroom Guidance and Counseling

The benefits to be gained by developmental programming far outweigh the pitfalls. Developmental programming through classroom lessons averts students' problems, or "nips them in the bud." This programming intentionally addresses students' needs regarding their career, academic, and personal/social development and how these contribute to academic success and personal well-being. Because the content of developmental programming is preventive in nature, students should be enabled to reach their potential sooner than they would without this intervention.

Sink (2005, p. 190) proposed five benefits that students can achieve through par-ticipation in classroom guidance lessons. He stated that children and youth

1. hear or are exposed to others' comments or feelings about issues with which they may be grappling,
2. can participate in the group even though they may not choose to speak in the group,
3. have opportunities to try out their ideas and receive feedback from their peers,
4. acquire important information or knowledge that they can use to make effective decisions, and
5. gain skills needed to deal with problems at school or in their daily lives.

At a time when students' personal and developmental needs are increasing and schools are focused overwhelmingly on testing and test scores, the role of the school counselor as an integral component in meeting student needs has never been more urgent. The benefits that Sink identified help students at all grade levels to become successful, knowledgeable, skilled individuals. As this chapter has addressed, though, school counselors must be intentional in working to these ends. School counselors must design and deliver a comprehensive developmental guidance and counseling curriculum as a part of their work in schools. They must understand and utilize exceptional classroom instructional strategies and classroom management skills, and strive to maintain the high standards of the teaching profession. And they must plan and follow-through with evaluative techniques that confer the highest accountability on their programs.

The school counselor of the 21st century must practice a transformational counseling model that embraces a new vision. Professional counselors exhibit strong leadership, advocate for themselves, their students, and the profession, utilize a team and collaborative approach, are masterful in counseling and consultation, and constantly use assessment and data to hold themselves and their programs accountable (Erford, House, & Martin, 2007). This focus is mandated if school counselors are to participate in the educational reform movement currently under way.

Outcome-based research must continue in school counseling to delineate programs that are effective when delivered through a developmental guidance and counseling curriculum. Curricular programs on social skills development, career awareness, academic skills, conflict resolution, violence prevention, and other issues that plague students must be researched and reported. Practical research is needed to determine the extent to which developmental programming is helpful in problem solving, fosters achievement, reduces dropout rates, alleviates social/emotional problems, promotes readiness for major transitions, and so on.

Research by Lapan, Gysbers, and Sun (1997) with high-school students indicated that when intentional developmental guidance programs were in place, the students rated the school climate as more positive, felt safer, and reported a greater sense of belonging, indicated less disruption and better behavior from peers, and believed more career and college information was presented. Similar results were reported by Lapan, Gysbers and Petroski (2001) with middle-school students.

The Social Decision Making-Social Problem Solving curriculum (Elias & Butler, 2005) has been shown to have a positive impact on the academic test scores of students in elementary school. Webb and Brigman (2006), who created the Student Success Skills program to develop academic skills and social competence, found that it significantly impacted math achievement scores and improved classroom behaviors in 5th, 6th, 8th, and 9th graders.

But more must be done to demonstrate effectiveness. Issues of accountability and program evaluation have to be intentionally addressed. These must include outcome data, as well as the impact of school counseling programs on students' achievement and positive behavior in schools (Paisley & McMahon, 2001). The counselor's role in creating and implementing a comprehensive school guidance and counseling curriculum holds much promise in developing students' potential and achievement in the learning/academic, career/vocational, and personal/social domains.

Summary

A developmental counseling curriculum reaches all students and is delivered by school counselors in collaboration with other student services staff, teachers, and community resource persons. Properly trained teachers have an integral role in the delivery of this curriculum when the content of their class activities relates directly to the topics in the counseling curriculum. The curriculum is based on identification of students' age-appropriate developmental needs.

The model curriculum has three domains: (a) learning/academic, (b) career/vocational, and (c) personal/social. In each of the domains, the curriculum addresses age-appropriate life themes, life transitions, and life skills. A developmental counseling curriculum is an effective and productive means for students to succeed academically, interpersonally, and vocationally. In this model, counselors are viewed as providing an essential part of the total school curriculum designed to facilitate learning and develop the potential of all students.

References

American School Counselor Association. (1979). *Standards for guidance and counseling programs*. Falls Church, VA: ASCA.

American School Counselor Association. (1990). *Counseling paints a bright future: Student competencies and guide for school counselors*. Alexandria, VA: ASCA.

American School Counselor Association. (1997). *Executive summary: The national standards for school counseling programs*. Alexandria, VA: ASCA.

American School Counselor Association. (2005). *The ASCA national model: A framework for school counseling programs* (2nd ed.).Alexandria, VA: ASCA.

Baker, S. B., & Gerler, Jr., E. R. (2008). *School counseling for the twenty-first century* (5th ed.). Englewood Cliffs, NJ: Merrill.

Brigman, G. A., Webb, L. D., & Campbell, C. (2007). Building skills for school success: Improving the academic and social competence of students. *Professional School Counseling, 10*(3), 279–288.

Brott, P. E. (2006). Counselor education accountability: Training the effective professional school counselor. *Professional School Counseling, 10*(2), 179–187.

Campbell, C. A., & Dahir, C. A. (1997). *The national standards for school counseling programs*. Alexandria, VA: American School Counselor Association.

Chata, C. C., & Loesch, L. C. (2007). Future school principals' view of the roles of professional school counselors. *Professional School Counseling, 11*, 35–41.

Chicago Public Schools. (1997–1998). *The student's advisory handbook* (working draft). Chicago: Author.

Cobia, D. C., & Henderson, D. A. (2007). *Developing an effective and accountable school counseling program* (2nd ed.). Upper Saddle River, NJ: Pearson Education Inc.

Drum, D. J., & Knott, J. E. (1977). *Structured groups for facilitating development: Acquiring life skills, resolving life themes, and making lift transitions*. New York: Human Sciences Press.

Education Trust. (1997). *Working definition of school counseling*. Washington, DC: Author.

Elias, M. J., & Butler, L. B. (2005). *Social decision making, social problem solving: Skills and activities for academic, social, and emotional success.* Champaign, IL: Research Press.

Ellis, T. (1991). Guidance—The heart of education: Three exemplary approaches. In G. R. Walz (compiler), *Counselor quest* (p. 70). Ann Arbor: University of Michigan. (ERIC Counseling and Personnel Services Clearinghouse)

Erford, B. T., House, R. M., & Martin, P. J. (2007). Transforming the school counseling profession. In B.T. Erford (Ed.), *Transforming the school counseling profession* (2nd ed., pp. 1–12). Upper Saddle River, NJ: Pearson Education.

Field, J. E., & Baker, S. (2004). Defining and examining school counselor advocacy. *Professional School Counseling, 8*(1), 56–63.

Good, T. (1979). Teacher effectiveness in the elementary school. *Journal of Teacher Education, 30*, 52–64.

Goodnough, G. E., Perusse, R., & Erford, B. T. (2007). Developmental classroom guidance. In B.T. Erford (Ed.), *Transforming the school counseling profession* (2nd ed., pp. 142–167). Upper Saddle River, NJ: Pearson Education.

Gysbers, N. C. (2001). School guidance and counseling in the 21st century: Remember the past into the future. *Professional School Counseling, 5*, 96–105.

Gysbers, N. C. (2004). Comprehensive guidance and counseling programs: The evolution of accountability. *Professional School Counseling, 8*(1), 1–14.

Gysbers, N. C. (2006). Improving school guidance and counseling practices through effective and sustained state leadership. *Professional School Counseling, 9*(3), 245–247.

Gysbers, N. C., & Henderson, P. (2006). *Developing and managing your school guidance program* (4th ed.). Alexandria, VA: American Counseling Association.

House, R. M., & Hayes, R. L. (2002). School counselors: Becoming key players in school reform. *Professional School Counseling, 5*, 249–256.

Hunter, M. (1976). *Improved instruction.* El Segundo, CA: TIP.

Johnson, D., & Johnson, R. (1994). *Learning together and alone: Cooperative, competitive, and individualistic learnings* (4th ed.). Englewood Cliffs, NJ: Prentice–Hall.

Jones, F. (2007). *Tools for teaching* (2nd ed.). Santa Cruz, CA: Fredric H. Jones & Associates.

Jones V. E., & Jones, L. S. (2006). *Comprehensive classroom management: Motivating and managing students* (8th ed.). Boston: Allyn & Bacon.

Lapan, R. T. (2001). Results-based comprehensive guidance and counseling program: A framework for planning and evaluation. *Professional School Counseling, 4*, 289–299.

Lapan, R. T., Gysbers, N. C., & Petroski, G. F. (2001). Helping seventh graders be safe and successful: A statewide study of the impact of comprehensive guidance and counseling programs. *Journal of Counseling & Development, 79*, 320–330.

Lapan, R. T., Gysbers, N. C, & Sun, Y. (1997). The impact of more fully implemented guidance programs on the school experiences of high school students: A statewide evaluation study. *Journal of Counseling & Development, 75*, 292–302.

Lee, V. V., & Goodnough, G. E. (2007). Creating a systemic, data-driven school counseling program. In B.T. Erford (Ed.), *Transforming the school counseling profession* (2nd ed., pp. 121–141). Upper Saddle River, NJ: Pearson Education.

Marzano, R. J. (2007). *The art and science of teaching: A comprehensive framework for effective instruction.* Alexandria, VA: Association for Supervision and Curriculum Development.

Miller, G. D. (2006). How collaboration and research can affect school counseling practices: The Minnesota story. *Professional School Counseling, 9*(3), 238–244.

Myrick, R. D. (1997). *Developmental guidance and counseling. A practical approach* (3d ed.). Minneapolis: Educational Media Corporation.

Paisley, P. O., & McMahon, G. (2001). School counseling for the 21st century: Challenges and opportunities. *Professional School Counseling, 5*, 106–115.

Purkey, W. W., & Novak, J. M. (1996). Inviting school success. A self-concept approach to teaching and learning (3d ed.). Belmont, CA: Wadsworth.

Purkey, W. W., & Schmidt, J. J. (1996). *Invitational counseling: A self-concept approach to professional practice*. Pacific Grove, CA: Brooks/Cole.

Sebring, P, Sebring, P., Bryk, A. S., Roderick, M., Camburn, E., Luppescu, S., Thum, Y. M., Smith, B., & Kahne, J. (1996). *Charting reform in Chicago: The students speak.* Chicago: Consortium on Chicago School Research.

Sink, C. A. (2002). In search of the profession's finest hour: A critique of four views of 21st century school counseling. *Professional School Counseling, 5*, 156–163.

Sink, C. A. (2005). *Contemporary school counseling: Theory, research, and practice.* Boston: Lahaska Press.

Stone, C. B., & Dahir, C. A. (2006). *The transformed school counselor.* Boston: Lahaska Press.

Stone, C. B., & House, R. (2002, May–June). Train the trainers program transform school counselors. *ASCA Counselor,* 20–21.

Studer, J. R., Oberman, A. H., & Womack, R. H. (2006). Producing evidence to show counseling effectiveness in the schools. *Professional School Counseling, 9*(5), 385–391.

VanZandt, C. E., & Hayslip, J. B. (1994). *Your comprehensive school guidance and counseling program.* New York: Longman.

VanZandt, Z., & Hayslip, J. (2001). *Developing your school counseling program: A handbook for systemic planning.* Pacific Grove, CA: Brooks/Cole.

Vernon, A. (1998a). *The Passport Program: A journey through emotional, social, cognitive, and self-development, grades 1–5.* Champaign, IL: Research Press.

Vernon, A. (1998b). *The Passport Program: A journey through emotional, social, cognitive, and self-development, grades 6–8.* Champaign, IL: Research Press.

Vernon, A. (1998c). *The Passport Program: A journey through emotional, social, cognitive, and self-development, grades 9–12.* Champaign, IL: Research Press.

Vernon, A. (2006a). *Thinking, feeling, behaving: An emotional education curriculum (Grades 1–6).* Champaign, IL: Research Press.

Vernon, A. (2006b). *Thinking, feeling, behaving: An emotional education curriculum (Grades 7–12).* Champaign, IL: Research Press.

Vernon, A., & Strub, R. (1990–1991). *Developmental guidance program implementation* (Counseling and Human Development Foundation Grant Project). Cedar Falls: University of Northern Iowa, Department of Educational Administration and Counseling, University of Northern Iowa, Cedar Falls.

Webb, L.D., & Brigman, G. A. (2006). Student success skills: Tools and strategies for improved academic and social outcomes. *Professional School Counseling, 10*(2), 112–120.

Selected Resources for Developing a Counseling Curriculum

Elementary Level

Begun, R. W. (2005). *Ready-to-Use Social Skills Lessons and Activities for Grades 1–3 and Grades 4–6*. Champaign, IL: Research Press.
> A program that teaches positive behavior skills to students through classroom activities addressing sharing, listening, anger management, and self-control.

Berne, P., & Savary, L. (1999). *Building Self-Esteem in Children* (new expanded ed.). New York: Crossroads/Herder & Herder.
> 68 effective, practical techniques to help parents, educators, and other concerned adults develop healthy relationships with children and foster attitudes and atmosphere in which self-esteem can flourish.

Canfield, J., & Wells, H. (1994). *100 Ways to Enhance Self-Concept in the Classroom* (2d ed.). Englewood Cliffs, NJ: Prentice–Hall.
> A good source for quotations, cartoons, and activities that can be used in developing self-awareness and enhancing positive self-concept. K–12.

Chapman, D. B. (1997). *My Body Is Where I Live*. Circle Pines, MN: American Guidance Service.
> Picture book and cassette tape to help children develop an appreciation of their bodies and an understanding of the dangers of drugs.

Coombs-Richardson, R. (1997). *Connecting with Others: Lessons for Teaching Social and Emotional Competence, Grades K–2 and Grades 3–5*. Champaign, IL: Research Press.
> A program that teaches social and emotional skills to promote competence through instructional strategies in the classroom; includes cultural and ethnic diversity issues.

Davis, S., & Davis, J. (2007). *Schools Where Everyone Belongs: Practical Strategies for Reducing Bullying* (2nd edition). Champaign, IL: Research Press.
> A curriculum covering all grade levels and containing practical ideas as well as proven ideas for addressing bullying utilizing a whole-school approach.

Devencenzi, J., & Pendergast, S. (1999). *Belonging: Self and Social Discovery for Children and Adolescents* (revised). San Luis Obispo, CA: Sovereignty Press.

Elias, M. J., & Butler, L. B. (2005). *Social Decision Making, Social Problem Solving (Grades 2–3 and Grades 4–5)*. Champaign, IL: Research Press.
> A research-based approach to reduce school violence, foster social and emotional learning, improve academics, develop multicultural sensitivity, and prevent at-risk youth from giving up on school.

Goldstein, A. P., & McGinnis, E. (1997). *Skillstreaming for the Elementary School Child*. Champaign, IL: Research Press.

Horne, A. M., Bartolomucci, C. L., & Newman-Carlson, D. (2000). *Bully Busters: A Teacher's Manual for K–5*. Champaign, IL: Research Press.
> Proven research strategies that address prevention and intervention activities around bullying.

Horne, A. M., Stoddard, J., & Bell, C. (2008). *Parent Guide to Understanding and Responding to Bullying*. Champaign, IL: Research Press.
> A recent publication that involves parents in the bullying program in a school setting.

Jolin, J., & Randolph, D. (1999). *How to . . . Career Activities for Every Classroom: Grades 4–6* (D. Caulum & R. Lambert, Project Directors). Madison: University of Wisconsin/ Wisconsin Alumni Research Foundation.

Jones, P. (2003). *104 Activities That Build: Self-esteem, Teamwork, Communication, Anger Management, Self-Discovery, Coping Skills*. Plainview, NY: Rec Room Publishing.

Kreidler, W J. (1997). *Conflict Resolution in the Middle School: A Curriculum and Teacher's Guide*. Cambridge, MA: Educators for Social Responsibility.
   Methods for improving pupils' communication skills, cooperation, tolerance, and positive emotional expression; helps students deal with anger, fear, prejudice, and aggression in the K–6 classroom.

Loomans, D. (1996). *Today I Am Lovable: 365 Positive Activities for Kids*. Tiburon, CA: Kramer.

Shure, M. (2001). *I Can Problem Solve: Kindergarten and Primary Grades*. Champaign, IL: Research Press.
   A program for primary and kindergarten that teaches children *how* to think rather than *what* to think; pre-problem-solving skills and problem-solving skills help children process information to solve problems including caring, sharing, cooperation, and working with others.

Smead, M. (1994). *Skills for Living: Group Counseling Activities for Elementary Students*. Champaign, IL: Research Press.
   Details the skills and steps needed to design, organize, conduct, and evaluate a multi-session group-counseling experience; includes eight developmentally appropriate topics for groups, including self-esteem, peacemaking, responsibility, and divorce.

Taylor, J. V., & Trice-Black, S. (2007). *G.I.R.L.S. Girls in Real Life Situations: Group Counseling Activities for Enhancing Social and Emotional Development, Grades K–5*. Champaign, IL: Research Press.
   More than 80 activities to encourage girls to share their feelings and struggles in a safe and supportive environment.

Teolis, B. (1996). *Self-Esteem and Conflict-Solving Activities for Grades 4–8*. West Nyack, NY: Center for Applied Research in Education.

VanZandt, Z., & Buchan, B. A. (1997). *Lessons for Life: Career Development Activities Library* (Vol. 1: Elementary Grades). West Nyack, NY: Center for Applied Research in Education.

Vernon, A. (1998). *The Passport Program: A Journey Through Emotional, Social, Cognitive, and Self-Development: Grades 1–5*. Champaign, IL: Research Press.
   A comprehensive developmental curriculum based on typical developmental issues that children need to master; interactive, creative lessons focus on self-acceptance, emotional development, decision making, and interpersonal relationships.

Vernon, A. (2006). *Thinking, Feeling, Behaving: An Emotional Education Curriculum for Children (Grades 1–6), Revised Edition*. Champaign, IL: Research Press.
   A comprehensive developmental curriculum including chapters on feelings, behavior management, self-acceptance, problem solving, and interpersonal relationships.

Secondary Level

Begun, R. W. (2005). *Ready to Use Social Skills Lessons and Activities.* Champaign, IL: Research Press.
> Classroom activities to teach students positive behavioral skills that promote sharing, listening, self-control, and anger management.

Bodine, J., & Crawford, D. K. (1998). *The Handbook of Conflict Resolution: A Guide to Building Quality Programs in the Schools.* San Francisco: Jossey-Bass.

Capacchione, L. (2001). *The Creative Journal for Teens.* North Hollywood, CA: New Castle Publishing.

Carlock, J. C. (Ed.). (1999). *Enhancing Self-Esteem* (3rd Edition). New York: Taylor & Francis.
> Techniques for enhancing self-esteem presented in a specific sequence and progression; for children, adolescents, and adults.

Cohen, L. M. (1996). *Coping for Capable Kids: Strategies for Parents, Teachers, and Students.* Waco, TX: Prufrock Press.

Coombs-Richardson, R. (2001). *Connecting with Others: Lessons for Teaching Social and Emotional Competence, Grades 9–12.* Champaign, IL: Research Press.

Elias, M. J., & Butler, L. B. (2005). *Social Decision Making, Social Problem Solving for Middle School Students.* Champaign, IL: Research Press.
> Research-based approach to reduce school violence, foster social and emotional learning, improve academics, develop multicultural sensitivity, and prevent at-risk youth from giving up on school.

Fitzell, S. G. (2006). *Transforming Anger to Personal Power: An Anger Management Curriculum for Grades 6–12.* Champaign, IL: Research Press.
> A program to help middle and high school students take control of their lives and their emotions and choose healthy responses to anger.

Goldstein, A. P., Glick, B., & Gibbs, J. (1998). *Aggression Replacement Training: A Comprehensive Intervention for Aggressive Youth.* Champaign, IL: Research Press.
> Developed for grades 6–12, teaches youth to understand and replace antisocial behaviors with positive alternatives.

Horne, A. M., Bartolomucci, C. L., & Newman-Carlson, D. (2000). *Bully Busters: A Teacher's Manual, Grades 6–8.* Champaign, IL: Research Press.
> Proven strategies for effective bullying prevention and intervention through classroom modules that address increasing awareness, recognizing the bully, the victim, and the bystander, and learning coping and relaxation strategies for personal growth.

Jackson, T. (1995). *More Activities That Teach.* Cedar City, UT: Red Rock Publishing.

JIST Works. (Eds.). (1998). *Creating Your High School Portfolio: An Interactive School, Career, and Life Planning Workbook.* Indianapolis: Author.

Johnson, D. W. (1997). *Reaching Out* (6th ed.). Boston: Allyn & Bacon.
> A comprehensive source for exercises in interpersonal relations, goal setting, self-awareness, and communication.

Jolin, J., & Randolph, D. (1997). *How to...Career Activities for Every Classroom: Grades 7–9* (Caulum, D. & Lambert, R. Project Directors). Madison: University of Wisconsin/ Wisconsin Alumni Research Foundation.

Schrumpf, F., Crawford, D. K., & Bodine, R.J. (1997). *Peer Mediation: Conflict Resolution in Schools*. Champaign, IL: Research Press.

> Classroom activities with an emphasis on social and cultural diversity, to teach students how to mediate difficult situations around name-calling, put-downs, rumors, prejudice and threats.

Shure, M. (2001). *I Can Problem Solve, Intermediate Grades*. Champaign, IL: Research Press.

> Program for intermediate grades that teaches children *how* to think rather than *what* to think; pre-problem-solving skills and problem-solving skills help children solve problems, including caring, sharing, cooperation, and working with others.

Smead, R. (1990). *Skills for Living: Group Counseling Activities for Young Adolescents*. Champaign, IL: Research Press.

> Details the skills and steps needed to design, organize, conduct, and evaluate a multi-session group counseling experience; includes eight developmentally appropriate topics for groups, including anger management, grief and loss, and divorce.

Taylor, J. V., & Trice-Black, S. (2007). *G.I.R.L.S. Girls in Real Life Situations: Group Counseling Activities for Enhancing Social and Emotional Development, Grades 6–12*. Champaign, IL: Research Press.

> More than 80 activities that encourage girls to share their feelings and struggles in a safe and supportive environment.

VanZandt, Z., & Buchan, B. A. (1997). *Lessons for Life: Career Development Activities Library* (Vol. 2: Secondary Grades). West Nyack, NY: Center for Applied Research in Education.

VanZandt, Z., & Hayslip, J. (2001). *Developing Your School Counseling Program: A Handbook for Systematic Planning*. Belmont, CA: Wadsworth/Thompson Learning.

Vernon, A. (1998). *The Passport Program: A Journey Through Emotional, Social, Cognitive, and Self-Development: Grades 6–8*. Champaign, IL: Research Press.

> A comprehensive curriculum that includes creative, interactive lessons on self-acceptance, emotions, problem solving/decision making, feelings, and interpersonal relationships; based on typical developmental issues that young adolescents face during this period of development.

Vernon, A. (1998). *A Journey Through Emotional, Social, Cognitive, and Self-Development: Grades 9–12*. Champaign, IL: Research Press.

> A comprehensive developmental curriculum that includes creative, interactive lessons on self-acceptance, feelings, behavior management, problem solving, and interpersonal relationships; based on typical developmental issues that adolescents face during this period of development.

Vernon, A. (2006). *Thinking, Feeling, Behaving: An Emotional Education Curriculum for Children (Grades 7–12): Revised Edition*. Champaign, IL: Research Press.

> A comprehensive curriculum that includes lessons on self-acceptance, feelings, rational thinking and problem solving, and interpersonal relationships.

Working With Parents

Ann Vernon

As I write this chapter, our first grandchild is 3 weeks old. When I held this beautiful little girl just minutes after she was born, I was flooded with memories of bringing her father into our family three decades ago. At that moment I was relieved that he was perfectly normal, overjoyed that he had finally graced us with his presence, and overcome with awe. Several days later, as we left the hospital to go home, I recall being overwhelmed and anxious because he didn't come with operating instructions! How would we know what to do or when to do it? What if we inadvertently did something wrong? With such a precious commodity, learning by trial and error just didn't seem right.

Not surprisingly, Elia's parents had similar emotions and questions. Even though they had received more education than we did "back then," the irony is that childrearing is the most important thing we will ever do as parents, yet the need for more parenting support continues, not just when a child is born but throughout their childhood and adolescence.

More and more, school and mental health professionals are interacting with parents in various ways about issues related to their children. Although parenting has never been easy, the stressors on families in today's society make parenting even more difficult, and this is complicated in that families now are more diverse in both membership and functioning. "In today's society, the home is not so simple" (Thompson, Rudolph, & Henderson, 2004, p. 7). Single-parent, teen-parent, blended, and never-married families are prevalent, as are dual-worker families struggling to juggle home and work responsibilities.

A negative and alarming trend is that many families are breaking down and are not coping with life effectively (Karpowitz, 2000). These families are characterized by more violence and tension, less parental supervision, and lack of emotional stability; children in these families manifest more psychopathology (Lindahl, 1998). Glenn and Nelson (2000) discussed how families have changed historically, expressing concern that increasing numbers of children have fewer opportunities to experience a meaningful role in family life and social institutions. The upshot is that these children will have difficulty developing a sense of meaning, purpose, and significance. Clearly, these trends have significant implications for school and mental health counselors.

The tendency has been to blame the increase of problems in childhood and adolescence on family dysfunction, poverty, alternative family structures, or a conflict-ridden society. Certainly these factors may contribute to the difficulties of children and adolescents that necessitate professional intervention. In recent years, however, research indicates that these children are not the only ones at risk. According to Levine (2006), there is a mental health epidemic among privileged youth who "defy the stereotypes commonly associated with the term 'at risk'" (p. 17). These teens and pre-teens are from affluent, well-educated families, and "in spite of their economic and social advantages, they experience among the highest rates of depression, substance abuse, anxiety disorders, somatic complaints, and unhappiness of any group of children in this country" (Levine, 2006, p. 17). Clearly, our definition of who is at risk has been too simplistic.

Kennedy (2001) alluded to the "good old days" (p. 3) when the traditional family was supposedly ideal and children were problem-free. He challenged this myth, concluding that many who grew up during that time can recall painful memories of abuse, neglect, or other bad experiences. The reality is that there never has been any such thing as a perfect family, and even those who look more "perfect" because they have money, education, power, and prestige are by no means immune to problems.

Gordon (2000) raised an important point: Mental health professionals, teachers, administrators, and law-enforcement officials, among others, blame parents for the troubles of youth and for the problems that young people cause. Yet, Gordon asks, who is helping parents?

> How much effort is being made to assist parents to become more effective in rearing children? Where can parents learn what they are doing wrong and what they might do differently?" (Gordon, 2000, p. 1)

Gordon's points are well taken. Certainly in the present day, parents need various forms of assistance, not blame, as the problems they face make parenting more stressful and challenging than ever (Kennedy, 2001; Vernon, 2002).

More and more parents are expressing feelings of inadequacy about family relationships, and some parents simply don't know what to do with their children (Levy & O'Hanlon, 2001). Traditional patterns of parental authority no longer are effective, but at the same time, parents often feel uncomfortable and uncertain about changing what has become familiar (Nelson & Lott, 2000; Shapiro, Friedberg, & Bardenstein, 2006). And, though good parenting always has been a full-time effort and continues to be one of the most challenging tasks a person will undertake, we receive more instruction about balancing a checkbook and changing a tire than we do about how to be parents.

Although the concept of parent education has been around since the 1920s (Fine, Voydanoff, & Donnelly, 1993), the development and marketing of parenting programs is only a few decades old (Ayers, 2000). Parents now seem to be more interested in education and training for their role. Without a doubt, parents need help in managing the contemporary challenges of parenting. They also need to develop skills to help themselves and their children deal successfully with developmental stressors and opportunities. In addition to practical skills, they have to understand how their irrational beliefs about themselves as parents or about their children contribute to negative emotional and behavioral reactions that can prevent them from implementing effective parenting skills (Vernon, 2002).

School and mental health counselors can assist parents through parent counseling, parent education, and consultation. In *parent counseling* the counselor works with the parent on personal issues related to the emotions about parenting (Shapiro et al., 2006). This is a role that a mental health professional, not a school counselor, would assume. *Parent education* that is preventive and psychoeducational in nature is valuable for all parents. *Parent consultation* is recommended for parents who have specific problems after receiving parent training or whose children are having difficulties for which more intensive help is indicated. In contrast to parent counseling, consultation is triadic—helping the parent develop more effective skills for dealing with the child rather than working on the parent's personal issues with the child.

This chapter addresses the importance of parent education and consultation and the counselors' role in providing these services to parents. The information includes effective parenting practices, how to develop and implement parent education groups, and how to employ a consultation model.

Definitions

Fine (1989), whose definition continues to be relevant and descriptive, stated that parent education is "concerned mainly with the imparting of information and skills which are supportive of good parenting" (p. 13). Parent education is based on the belief that the influential role of parents produces considerable responsibility for them to provide appropriate guidance for their children. Parent education increases parents' knowledge and helps them develop skills. The focus is preventive: As parents learn to parent more effectively, they will reduce the potential for problems arising from ineffective parenting practices.

Parent consultation is recommended for parents who have specific problems with their child. Consultation is a "one-to-one interaction between the counselor and a significant adult in the child's life…with the purpose of finding ways of assisting children to function more effectively" (Thompson, Rudolph, & Henderson, 2004, p. 480). Parents may contact a counselor to discuss their concerns about a variety of matters—for example, their child's behavior or growth and development (Thompson et al., 2004), school performance, or emotional and social adjustment; specific issues related to developmental or learning disabilities (Knowlton & Mulanax, 2000; Lancaster, 2000) and other special needs (Romano & Hermann, 2007; Taub, 2006); or severe problems such as depression (Abrams, Theberge, & Karan, 2005; Evans, VanVelsor, & Schumacher, 2002), self-injury (Kress, Drouhard, & Costin, 2006), or eating disorders (Vernon & Clemente, 2005).

Although education may be part of the consultation process, consultation deals more specifically with an existing problem. School counselors often use consultation techniques within the responsive services component of a developmental program (Clemens, 2007). As a result, consultees gain skills and knowledge about how to respond to a specific situation, and this also empowers them to respond to similar problems in the future more effectively. Thus, consultation has a preventive aspect as well.

Outcomes of Parent Education and Consultation

Parent education and consultation are essential components of the counselor's role. Many parents are anxious to learn new techniques or alleviate their anxiety about problems they are having with their children. Parent education and consultation can best be understood by considering some of the expected outcomes of these processes. Stone and Bradley (1994) identified a number of outcomes and benefits of parent education and consultation. This list underscores the value of working with parents.

1. *Improved parent–child relationships.* The primary goal of parent education is to improve relationships between parents and children. As parents become more understanding and accepting, children are less likely to misbehave, and the relationship between parents and children improves.
2. *Improved behavior at home and school.* Parental participation in education groups can result in positive changes in parents' attitude toward children, positive changes in children's behavior, and an improved family atmosphere. An early study conducted by Kottman and Wilborn (1992) discovered that parents who participated in study groups initiated by counselors had significantly more positive attitudes toward their children than parents who were not exposed to study groups.
3. *Improved acceptance of responsibility.* In their work with parents, both in parent study groups and when conducting consultations, Stone and Bradley (1994) found that as the relationship between children and their parents improved, children were willing to accept more responsibility.

4. *Parent involvement in the school.* Parents who have positive relationships with their children and whose children are more likely to accept responsibility are more likely to become involved with the school. Parents' involvement with the school often begins with parent education. As parents' attitudes toward their children and toward the school improves, parents likely will become more involved with the school.

5. *Improvement in school achievement.* Parent education and consultation seem to initiate a chain reaction. When the child's behavior starts to improve, he or she begins to accept more responsibility, the relationship with the parents improves, the parents are more inclined to become involved with the school, and the child's schoolwork improves correspondingly. Because this tends to be a linear process, children's feelings about the relationship with their parents are extremely important to their motivation and school achievement. Children's potential for success in school is enhanced when parents are actively involved in their children's education; and parent involvement in schools helps children cope with challenges so they have a clear path to reach their full potential (Harris & Coy, 2004).

For the counselor, the need for parent education and consultation becomes obvious. This is not a matter of whether to offer parent education and consultation but, rather, where, when, and in what format it should be provided. Edwards (2000) suggested that it should be offered to all who function in a parental role, including grandparents rearing grandchildren. Single and low-income parents, teenage parents, and never-married parents also should be targeted (Bogenschneider & Stone, 1997).

Generally speaking, research has shown that as a consequence of attending a parent program, parents became less angry and felt less guilty and simultaneously became more effective in helping their children solve problems. While the child may have a problem, the parents themselves have problems dealing with the child or with their own issues about the child' problem (Vernon, 2002). Therefore, if practitioners work only with the child, they are neglecting an important part of the problem.

Cultural Considerations

Our population increasingly is becoming more ethnically diverse (Rubel & Ratts, 2007), and if predictions are accurate, underrepresented ethnic groups will make up 50% of the population in the United States by the year 2050 (U.S. Bureau of Census, 2004). According to a more recent U.S. Bureau of Census (2005) report, Latinos are the largest ethnic group—14.1% of the total population in the United States. In the year 2000 Latinos comprised the largest minority group in U.S. public schools, accounting for 17% of the total enrollment (U.S. Bureau of Census, 2003). Needless to say, cultural and ethnic diversity have to be addressed if we intend to provide successful parenting services to a variety of populations (McDermott 2000; Vernon & Clemente, 2005). Thompson, Rudolph, and Henderson (2004) stressed how important it is for counselors to value multiple perspectives when working with parents, providing support and building self-efficacy.

Even if parent education and consultation are tailored to the values and cultures of specific groups, however, accessing the individuals and groups needing assistance is a challenge because many ethnic minorities fear or distrust the services or feel ashamed about admitting that they need help (Harris & Coy, 2004). Ethnic minorities may not understand how talking about problems could be helpful, or they may be embarrassed when strangers ask them personal questions (Shapiro et al., 2006).

Professionals working with parents should be aware that the European-American culture is more individualistic than some others, valuing independence and autonomy, directness and self-assertion, competition, and hard work (Shapiro et al., 2006). This prevailing culture places a premium on time and an action-orientation characterized by structure and problem resolution (McDermott, 2000). We cannot assume that all groups share these values, so we must become familiar with the characteristics of each group and how their values and characteristics affect their parenting practices. For example, Euro-Americans generally understand that children will express their opinions and that parents and children will have disagreements at times, which are often resolved by compromise. In contrast, many other cultures place a high priority on parental authority and would not allow children to disagree (Shapiro et al., 2006).

For African Americans, the extended family, as contrasted with the nuclear family, is extremely important. In the African American family, children belong to the entire group; friends, neighbors, and relatives help discipline and care for the children (Clemente, 2004; Shapiro et al., 2006). Asian American families also value the extended family, and they generally do not talk about personal problems outside this family circle (Clemente, 2004). This culture is group-oriented, placing priority on harmonious relationships and fulfilling others' needs rather than their own (Shapiro et al., 2006).

The extended family also is central to Latino Americans. Loyalty to the family and obedience to the father are expected. The parenting style typically is authoritarian, and children are expected to value family cohesion over individual preferences (Shapiro et al., 2006).

In the Native American culture, children may live in a nuclear family with many family members or even in different homes as part of the tribal system (Red Horse, 1982, as cited in McDermott, 2000). Interconnectedness and interdependence are emphasized, along with indirect communication, in contrast to open expression of emotions.

Understanding the cultural characteristics of various groups is necessary because counselors otherwise could easily label behavior as pathological, failing to take into account culturally normative behaviors. Also, counselors must not make generalizations about groups, as many factors determine the individual's actual lifestyle (Clemente, 2004). Gender must be taken into consideration because both sexes have commonalities within their own group that are irrespective of ethnicity (Hays, 1996). Age is another important variable; older members of the ethnic group may have very different values than younger members (Baruth & Manning, 1991).

Because different cultural and ethnic groups perceive and define parenting differently, knowledge about and sensitivity to these variables will promote the success of parent education and consultation. As professionals, we need to know our limitations and seek advice and consultation when in doubt.

Parent Education Programs

Parent education frequently is done through groups, as the group format provides an opportunity to reach many parents in a relatively short time. The group structure enables counselors to expand their contact with parents and at the same time make use of the group to provide direction and support for each parent. Parents who struggle with their parenting role typically feel alone in this situation ("Other parents don't have trouble with their kids"). By bringing parents together, they can quickly gain a sense of commonality in that they face concerns similar to those of other parents.

Identifying parents' needs and concerns is essential in developing good programs. In a parent education approach, Stone and Bradley (1994) suggested taking time to ensure that the approach will provide appropriate information to meet parents' needs, as well as to provide a philosophical foundation that addresses those needs. A program's flexibility in meeting the changing needs of the family as well as the cultural context is a prerequisite for effectiveness.

In selecting the appropriate approach, the parents' level of education and income should be considered. Other factors, such as cost, special training of the leaders, and availability and appropriateness of the materials, should be taken into account as well. In addition, the developmental needs of children must be considered in formulating any program, as research has indicated that parents have different concerns about their children at different stages (Levine, 2006; Nelson & Lott, 2000; Vernon & Al–Mabuk, 1995; Vernon & Clemente, 2005).

Hundreds of books about parenting are available, along with many parent education models (Gordon, 2000). If counselors are aware of historical and current trends in parent education, programs can be modified to better meet parents' specific needs. Because parent education has no magic approach, counselors often develop the most effective program by selecting materials from various sources and compiling a program that best addresses the needs of a given group of parents through materials and approaches that are relevant and culturally appropriate.

Stone and Bradley (1994) stressed that parents are not a homogeneous body; they have different needs at different times. These authors noted that parent groups do not have to be large, that timing is crucial, and lack of attendance does not necessarily reflect a lack of concern.

Format and Topics

Parent education can take several forms, including support groups, parent study groups, and parent education. Support groups typically are not as structured as education groups. The primary goal of these groups is to create an environment in which parents can come together to share concerns about their children and receive some assistance. Support groups may be organized around specific topics, such as a support group for parents of children who are hyperactive, have disabilities, or are gifted, or support groups for single parents, teenage parents, or parents in blended families.

Support groups also can be convened by a leader who facilitates interaction among parents about any parenting issue they want to discuss. This type of support group has no identified topic; members bring their current concerns, and other members respond with suggestions and encouragement. Although support groups may have some educational aspect, the basic purpose of these groups is to encourage discussion and interaction among parents relative to their specific concerns about their children. They gain knowledge primarily from other parents who share their ideas and experiences, although the leader may introduce content as appropriate.

In contrast, parent education and parent study groups are more highly structured. While discussion and interaction are encouraged, the primary goal is to develop parenting skills and impart information through a variety of methods such as small-group activities, videos, role-play, and specific skill-building activities. In these types of groups, the leader is more active and directive in presenting information, facilitating skill-development opportunities and discussion, and encouraging parents to apply the content to their own situations.

Topics for support, education, and study groups often are the same. The format and basic goals differ. Topics may address general parenting practices, selected topics, or topics applicable to children at specific developmental levels.

Topics for *general parenting practices* groups include:

- communication techniques ("I versus you" messages, assertive communication, active listening),
- understanding stages of child and adolescent development,
- methods of discipline (behavior modification, time-out, logical consequences),
- parenting styles (authoritarian, authoritative, ignoring, permissive), and
- parent involvement (over-involved, under-involved).

Topics for groups organized around *selected topics* may be:

- parenting gifted children,
- parenting children with learning disabilities, ADHD, or other disabilities,
- parenting children with eating disorders, anxiety, or depression,
- parenting oppositional children, and
- parenting children with chronic illnesses.

Examples of groups organized around issues pertinent to *specific developmental levels* are:

- dealing with preschoolers' separation anxiety,
- helping elementary-aged children develop positive peer relationships,

- understanding and dealing with issues related to puberty,
- helping teens deal with peer pressure, and
- dealing with the transition out of high school.

Many more topics could be included in each category. The distinction between general parenting practices, topics pertaining to specific development levels, and selected topics should offer counselors a variety of ways to approach parenting programs. The groups should be organized around developmental levels because even general parenting practices differ depending on developmental level. For example, discipline techniques that work well with younger children might not be applicable to adolescents.

In addition to topics, parenting programs can assume a variety of formats. For example, support groups may be *time-limited* (6 to 8 weeks or biweekly sessions lasting from 1 hour to 2 hours for each session), or they may meet monthly for 6 months, or they could be ongoing. Parent study groups and education groups may meet weekly or biweekly for 1 to 2 hours for 6 to 8 weeks, or they may be single-session meetings on selected topics. These single-session meetings may be offered sporadically throughout the year. For example, a counselor may offer four sessions on general parenting practices. Parents could choose to attend all sessions or select the ones they find most applicable to their needs.

Another format is the *mini-conference*, a brief, single-session held during the day or an evening. For example, the conference may last 3 hours, and during this time parents could opt to extend the meetings to three hour-long sessions on topics such as establishing family rules, conducting family meetings, or helping children develop responsible behaviors. The conference topics could target issues pertinent to specific developmental levels or address selected topics or general parenting matters.

An additional format especially applicable to a parent study group is to organize the group around books that all parents could read and discuss, such as: *SOS! Help for Parents* (Clark, 1996), *P.E.T.—Parent Effectiveness Training* (Gordon, 2000), *Try and Make Me!* (Levy & O'Hanlon, 2001), *Positive Discipline A-Z* (Nelson, Lott, & Glenn, 2007), *The Encouraging Parent* (Kennedy, 2001), *Positive Discipline for Teenagers* (Nelson & Lott, 2000), *Kids, Parents, and Power Struggles* (Kurcinka 2000), *Raising Self-Reliant Children in a Self-Indulgent World* (Glenn & Nelsen, 2000), or *The Price of Privilege: How Parental Pressure and Material Advantage are Creating a Generation of Disconnected and Unhappy Kids* (Levine, 2006).

Of the many good parenting resources available, the leader should select books that are relatively short and easy to read so they are appropriate for various reading levels. If participants have to purchase the book themselves, cost must be taken into account. And the books must be culturally appropriate for the population served.

Each type and format has advantages and disadvantages, and counselors are encouraged to do a brief needs assessment to see which format would be most relevant to their specific population. Although ongoing groups provide more opportunities to build support, gain knowledge, and develop skills, many parents cannot afford to hire sitters or give up valuable time with their children. Therefore, the mini-conference or the series of single-session programs is often more practical and reaches more parents. Edwards (2000) suggested offering child care, as well as door prizes and refreshments, to encourage attendance.

Skills for the Leader

Jacobs, Masson, and Harvill (1998, pp. 113–120) identified a number of leadership skills that counselors possess by virtue of their training. The following are applicable to parent education.

1. Communication skills, which usually include active listening, reflection, clarification, questioning, and summarizing.
2. Mini-lecturing and information-giving for the purpose of providing interesting, relevant, and stimulating material in a short time.
3. Setting a climate in the group that is encouraging and supportive of parents and also appropriate in tone to underscore the material being discussed.
4. Leader modeling and self-disclosure to provide parents with an example of effective behavior in interacting with others and a sense of comfort in being able to share their thoughts.
5. The leader's voice intonation and eye contact to stimulate the group and set the tone for each session by reinforcing members' participation and energizing the group to participate. The leader assumes an important role in creating an atmosphere of inclusion for all members.
6. The leader as a group manager who has to know how to direct the flow of conversation by bringing members into the conversation and tempering the participation of overly active members.

Group leaders have to be able to accept participants as individuals, recognizing that members will vary considerably in the extent to which the leader can expect participants to change their behaviors and integrate the information. Leaders also have to be able to alter the pacing in terms of content in an educational group, as well as demonstrate sensitivity to members' needs (Fine & Wardle, 2000). Finally, leaders must take cultural considerations into account.

Approaches to Parent Education

A number of approaches for parenting education have emerged. They share the same general objective: to help parents learn ways of relating to their children that will promote healthy development. These programs differ in content and also in the use of cognitive, behavioral, and affective modalities to achieve their goals. Each approach emphasizes reeducating parents. Examples of a number of commercially developed programs are:

Parenting without Hassles (Stone & Bradley, 1992)
Systematic Training for Training Parenting (STEP) (Dinkmeyer, McKay, & Dinkmeyer, 1997)

How To Talk So Kids Will Listen and Listen So Kids Will Talk (Faber & Mazlish, 1999)

P.E.T.: Parent Effectiveness Training (Gordon, 1970, 2000)

Active Parenting Today (Popkin, 1995)

In addition, literally hundreds of parenting programs and resources are available over the Internet. Among them is *1-2-3 Magic Parenting* (www.parentmagic.com/123Magic), a popular parenting program that teaches discipline techniques. A program that helps parents get their children to behave is www.addadhdadvances.com and parents can get answers to their questions and join a support network through www.ivillage.com. Parents even can take a quiz to find out what parenting style fits them, at www.AreYouASlackerMom.com. Counselors must take care to select materials that aren't stereotypical and should choose programs that best address the needs of the parent populations with whom they are working.

Organizing a Parent Education Program

Parent education programs can be organized in many different ways, and more and more materials are available to use in developing the program. Some counselors prefer commercially developed programs such as those suggested above. Other counselors believe that designing their own program is a more effective way to address the specific needs, cultural values, and interests of the target groups.

The first step in organizing a parent education program is to appoint a committee of professionals and parents (Stone & Bradley, 1994). The committee's primary goal is to decide which parent education approach best fits the parents' needs. After the committee has been established, its members can develop a brief needs assessment, which could take the form of a checklist of potential topics and formats for the program.

Based on the results of the needs assessment, the committee can determine the nature of the program—a support group, single or ongoing sessions, a mini-conference, or a multi-session topical education group. Topics also can be identified. Next, the time and place of the meetings can be decided, then implementation begins. The following steps are suggested for implementation:

1. Promote the program through flyers, newsletters, personal contact with parents, commercial media, and parent–teacher organizations through the school.
2. Prepare for the parenting sessions. This will include a thorough review of the materials and consideration of how to create a good learning environment, including building a "sense of community" by involving parents in some ice-breaker activities. The physical arrangement of the meeting place should enhance good communication through visual contact between all participants and the leader. Good preparation and planning will help to establish credibility as a leader and provide the parents with positive feelings about the program.
3. Establish a means for getting parents to participate through planned activities and assignments that will enable them to identify with the material presented.

4. Order materials that may be used as a supplement to the parenting sessions.

5. Establish an evaluation procedure, the primary purpose of which is to ensure that the parents' needs have been met, to solicit feedback on the quality of the program, and to provide the leader with input for self-improvement. Evaluations can be oral or written.

A Sample Parent Education Program

Counselors are in an ideal position to help parents and children interact well with one another. The parent–child relationship can be enhanced by helping parents communicate more effectively, employ positive behavior-management strategies, adopt more effective parenting styles, and tailor their parenting strategies to the developmental needs of their children. The intent is to bring together parents and children in a way that might stimulate ongoing interaction rather than distancing them from each other as the children grow older.

A six-session program on general parenting practices with an emphasis on communication is presented below. This model parent–child communication program identifies the content-and-program sequence. The program could be delivered either through a parent education group or modified for use in parent consultation. Careful selection of material and the use of examples will enable parents to identify with the concepts and incorporate the material more readily into their own parenting styles. The material here has been adapted from a variety of sources including *Parent Effectiveness Training* (Gordon, 2000) and *Positive Discipline for Teenagers* (Nelson & Lott, 2000).

Session 1: Parent Awareness Activity

Objectives:

- To build a sense of community in the group
- To sensitize parents to their interactions with their children
- To help parents differentiate effective and ineffective communication
- To help parents appreciate the value of effective communication

Procedure:

In the first session it is important to build a "sense of community" so the parents feel less self-conscious, which in turn facilitates sharing and participation. A simple nonthreatening technique is to engage participants in "Find Someone Who…." Participants move around the room and find other parents who can sign their initials behind a sentence starter that depicts their family, such as:

More than three children in the family _____
Twins in this family _____
Children are involved in sports_____

Child or children share household responsibilities_____
In this family, we use time-out when children misbehave_____

Depending on the topics, this activity introduces parents to a variety of issues and conveys to parents that they all have some things in common.

Another simple strategy is to have half of the participants place their chairs in an inner circle while the other half places theirs in an outer circle, sitting opposite someone in the inner circle. The leader states a topic, and the inner circle member has 1 minute to respond to his or her partner. When time is up, the procedure is repeated but with the outer-circle member sharing. After a minute the outer circle rotates so there are new partners, another new topic, and so forth. Sample topics include:

The best part about parenting is....
A worry I have as a parent is....
One of my favorite memories of my firstborn was....
Something that frustrates me as a parent is....
As a parent, I wish I were better at....

Once again, the topics are nonthreatening and normalize the joys and concerns of parenting. Depending on how open the group is, another get-acquainted activity may be introduced in the next session as well.

The opening session is intended to sensitize parents to the nature of their communication by first helping them to consider their typical interactions with their children. Although counselors can provide awareness through didactic presentations, experiential activities may be more effective in helping parents review their own behaviors. The latter can be addressed through the introspective consideration of parent and child interchanges.

Ask parents to divide a sheet of paper into four squares. Then invite them to think about the last positive interchange they had with one of their children, and to write in the first square a few words describing what they think made this exchange positive. Next, ask them how they felt about this interchange and write their feeling in the second square. Then ask them to think about the last time they had an unsatisfactory discussion or exchange with one of their children. Instruct them to think about what made that exchange so negative and write that in the third square. Finally, ask how they felt about the negative discussion and write that in the last square.

To facilitate sharing, play some music and invite the parents to circulate throughout the room, selecting a partner when the music stops. Invite them to share the information on their first two squares. After 10 minutes, start the music and instruct them to find another partner and share their last two squares when the music stops.

Ask the parents to tell what it was like to identify the positive and negative exchanges, and the characteristics that described these interchanges. Write this information on newsprint, along with a list of the feelings they had about each of the types of interactions. This information will set the stage for a discussion with parents in which they identify for themselves how their communication is effective and what should be improved.

Next ask for a volunteer to play the role of a child, and you as leader will assume the role of a parent. Use a typical example such as checking to see if the child has done his or her homework. In the role play, use as many of the following communication roadblocks as possible (Gordon, 2000): ordering, commanding, and directing; warning and threatening; moralizing and preaching; advising, offering solutions or suggestions; teaching, lecturing, or giving logical arguments; judging, criticizing, disagreeing, or blaming; praising, agreeing; name-calling, ridiculing, or shaming; interpreting, analyzing, and diagnosing; reassuring, sympathizing, consoling, and supporting; questioning, probing, interrogating; and withdrawing, distracting, humoring, or diverting (pp. 49–52).

After presenting the role-play, ask the parents to say what they thought was effective or ineffective about the exchange. Provide more explanation of the road-blocks (Gordon, 2000), and then divide the parents into small groups and have them discuss roadblocks they may use. Emphasize that all parents use these roadblocks from time to time and that the purpose of this session is to help them realize that communication with children isn't easy but that in this group they will have an opportunity to learn new skills and unlearn ineffective behaviors.

As a homework assignment, ask the parents to pay attention to their communication and eliminate as many roadblocks as possible.

Session 2: Undoing the Roadblocks: Effective Listening Skills

Objective:

- To help parents learn and practice effective listening skills

Procedure:

Begin this session by reviewing the information from the last session and checking on the homework assignment. Then discuss how listening is the primary skill necessary for good communication. Being a good listener requires verbal and nonverbal skills, eye contact, and a posture that indicates "I'm listening." Listening requires paying close attention to what the child is saying, and concentrating on the meaning. By paying close attention to the child, parents can communicate understanding and acceptance (Gordon, 2000).

Introduce the concept of *active listening* (Gordon, 2000). Active listening is just that: It means that the receiver of a message listens empathically to what the sender is saying and refrains from using the communication roadblocks. Active listening promotes a relationship of warmth between parent and child and requires close attention, sensitivity to feeling, and the ability to express what the child is feeling. Kennedy (2001) stressed the importance of nonverbal communication, noting that body language and tone of voice are powerful cues because emotions are more accurately communicated nonverbally. He also indicated that nonverbal communication is more honest.

At this point the leader should ask for a volunteer to role-play a teenager who is upset about receiving a bad grade on a test. Invite the other group members to be observers. As the leader, you play the role of the parent and demonstrate active listening. For example, the teenager says, "I'm no good at math. I got a terrible grade on the test." The parent might reflect, "You're discouraged about your ability to perform well in math." In this example the parent attempts to understand what the child feels and means and then states this meaning to the child so he or she feels understood and accepted. The parent is nonjudgmental and encourages the child to feel heard and to continue talking.

After discussing the role-play, invite the parents to work in triads as parent, child, and observer, to practice active listening. After they each have had a turn to play the role of the active listener, discuss their reactions and encourage them to practice this skill throughout the week.

Session 3: The Language of Acceptance

Objectives:

- To help parents develop techniques for communicating acceptance of their children
- To sensitize parents to their own thoughts and actions regarding their children

Procedure:

Communicating acceptance extends beyond understanding what the child is saying; it conveys acceptance of the child. Through the language of acceptance, children can believe they are part of the environment and the world of their important adults (Dinkmeyer, McKay, & Dinkmeyer, 1997). The language of acceptance frees children to talk about their feelings and problems and lets them know that they are accepted for who they are, not as they should or could be (Gordon, 2000).

Inform parents that they can show acceptance by listening passively—doing nothing but offering encouragers such as "Oh?" "I see," "Mm–hmm" (Gordon, 2000, pp. 44–45). Verbal acceptance can be offered in the form of "door openers" (p. 57), which convey acceptance of the child and respect for him or her as a person. Examples of door openers are: "Your thoughts and feelings are important," "I'm interested in hearing about your experiences," and "I really want to hear your ideas."

As an activity to demonstrate the language of acceptance, lead a discussion with the parents regarding each of the following concepts: acceptance, confidence, appreciation, and recognition of effort. Using newsprint to record their responses, ask parents to provide examples of each form of acceptance. Post the examples on the wall, and divide parents into triads. Instruct them to take turns role-playing parent–child interactions that would give them opportunities to practice the language of acceptance. Invite them to "contract" with members of their triad to practice a certain number of acceptance statements during the following week.

Session 4: "I" Messages

Objective:

- To help parents use "I" messages instead of "you" messages

Procedure:

Open this session with a general discussion about "I messages" and "you messages"—a concept fundamentally attributed to Gordon (1970). "I messages" are nonjudgmental responses about how we feel. Vernon and Al–Mabuk (1995) referred to "I messages" as a clear way of communicating to the child how you as a parent are feeling without the child becoming defensive. These authors noted that "I messages" are more effective than shaming and blaming. "I messages" give children an opportunity to change their behavior without losing face and help them learn to be more responsible.

To deliver a good "I message," parents must state clearly how they are feeling and why, and then give the message using the following formula: "When you … (describe the unacceptable behavior in a nonjudgmental way), I feel … (describe your feelings), because … (share what effect the behavior has on you)" (Gordon, 2000, p. 130).

By contrast, "you messages" tend to put children on the defensive and accuse them of inappropriate behavior, attitude, or motive. When children feel they are being accused of something, they resist. "You messages" are more likely to evoke argumentative behaviors. An example of a "you message" is: "You never pick up your clothes. Why can't you ever do anything right?" Overgeneralizations like the last sentence often accompany "you messages."

To further differentiate "I messages" and "you messages," use a typical example of a child not coming home on time. "You message": "You never obey the rules. You were supposed to be home an hour ago. Why can't you follow the rules?" Note that this message is often a put-down and contains many of the communication roadblocks described in a previous session. In contrast, an "I message" is: "When you don't come home on time, I feel worried and angry because I don't know where you are, and you're not obeying the rule."

Following this demonstration, group the parents in triads and have them practice "I messages," taking turns playing the role of the parent, the child, and an observer. After each triad has worked-through all three roles, lead a discussion about their reactions to the use of "I messages."

Session 5: Encouragement

Objectives:

- To help parents better understand the concept of encouragement
- To help parents demonstrate competence in using encouragement

Procedure:

As with the previous session, begin with a presentation of the following information about encouragement: The process of encouragement is based on communication skills and is designed to improve a child's sense of self. All people want to succeed at the activities they undertake. This is a natural human desire. Unfortunately, many people are discouraged, and our society is good at pointing out mistakes. The slogan has been, "We learn from our mistakes," but what is often overlooked with this strategy is that only the strongest can withstand constant bombardment of their errors and persevere.

Inform parents that a more useful strategy is to accentuate the positive and eliminate the negative. If parents want to help children develop a positive self-concept, the key lies in emphasizing what young people can do rather than what they can't do. Parents need to learn how to encourage because it helps children feel good about themselves and enhances their sense of self-control (Vernon & Al–Mabuk, 1995). Encouragement is not a single act on a single occasion. It is ongoing as children attempt to succeed and gain mastery in their world. By expressing faith in children as they are, and not as they could or should be, children feel more self-confident.

Encouragement—the language of acceptance—is based on respect for the child as a human being. It differs from reinforcement in that reinforcement is a reward given after the child has successfully completed a task, whereas encouragement is given before a task has begun or after the child has failed. In these instances, when children may feel insecure, discouraged, or self-doubting, support and positive words help. Dinkmeyer and Losoncy (1980) described an encourager as someone who listens effectively, focuses on the positive, is accepting, inspires hope, and recognizes effort and improvement.

Parents can show acceptance by saying things such as, "I like the way you picked up your room," with the emphasis on the task rather than an evaluation of the child. In accordance with the philosophy, you would not say, "You're a good kid because you picked up your room," as that would equate self-worth with performance.

Various authors (e.g., Kennedy, 2001; Vernon & Al–Mabuk, 1995) identified the following ways to encourage children:

1. Emphasize strengths; encourage children to be good people.
2. Minimize weaknesses and failure.
3. Show you care; be your child's number-one cheerleader.
4. Spend time together.

5. Develop patterns of learning, to build success.
6. Value silence as a means to reduce discouragement.
7. Support effort, not just success.
8. Try to understand the child's point of view.
9. Be positive for both of you.
10. Remember that both adults and children have the right to a bad day.

After the input on encouragement, ask parents to take each of these 10 methods of encouraging and individually develop a list of examples of when they have used or could use each one. Then have them share their examples with others in a small group. Suggest that they make a plan to incorporate at least three methods at home during the following week.

Session 6: Family Meetings

Objective:

■ To teach parents how to conduct family meetings to foster open communication

Procedure:

Family meetings provide an opportunity for family members to feel a sense of belonging and work together to improve communication and problem-solving skills (Glenn & Nelson, 2000; Nelson & Lott, 2000). During family meetings, issues such as family rules, routines, decisions, chores, and family outings can be discussed. Reminding family members that all of their thoughts and feelings are considered important conveys acceptance and reinforces the notion that everyone in the family unit is valued, which in turn enhances communication because individuals feel safe to express their point of view.

After this explanation of the purpose of the family meeting, distribute the following guidelines for effective family meetings and invite discussion about them (Nelson & Lott, 2000, p. 173).

1. Start with compliments and appreciations.
2. Prioritize items on the agenda. Ask if any items can be eliminated because they have been handled already. Ask if any should be top priority.
3. Set a timeline for the meeting. Use a timer and a designated timekeeper.
4. Discuss each item and let everyone voice his or her opinion without comments or criticism from others.
5. If the problem calls for more than a discussion—which is more often than not—brainstorm for solutions.
6. Choose one solution that everyone can live with (consensus), and try it for a week.
7. Table difficult issues to discuss at the next regularly scheduled family meeting.

To further clarify the process, ask for four volunteers to assume roles as family members (with at least one as the parent), and conduct a short family meeting according to the guidelines. They are to assume that this is a first meeting with no prior agenda; everything brought up will be a new agenda item. Give them 15 minutes to conduct this mock meeting and indicate that you will serve as a coach to facilitate the process as needed. During the demonstration other participants should keep notes on questions they have so these can be addressed at the end of the role-play.

Following the demonstration, ask family members to tell how they felt about the process, and encourage discussion from other participants, including any personal experiences with family meetings within their own family units.

This is the last session, so the following activity could be used for closure: Ask parents to reflect on three things and write them on an index card: (1) what they learned by participating in the group, (2) something they have done differently as a result of what they learned, and (3) what they would like to continue to work on in their parenting role. To encourage sharing, give one of the participants a ball of yarn and ask him or her to share one of his or her responses. Then, while holding the end of the yarn, he or she is to toss the ball of yarn to another parent, who shares, and so forth. Continue in this manner until everyone has had an opportunity to share at least once. When everyone has been "connected" through this activity, invite discussion and closing comments.

Consultation

One of the best ways to foster child/adolescent development is through the counselor's consultation with parents. Even though consultation is one of the counselor's roles, many counselors hesitate to consult with parents, in part because counselors are uncertain about the exact nature of consulting and because they believe parents will not be receptive to consultation. Contrary to this belief, most parents who are aware of the availability of consultation will request or accept assistance when needed.

Consulting is distinguished from counseling by the nature of the relationship between the consultant and the consultee (parent). Unlike counseling, in which the counselor works directly with the client, consultation is an indirect process, in which the counselor (consultant) works with the consultee (parent) to bring about change in the client (child) (Gibson, 2004). Dougherty (2000) defined consultation as

> a process in which a human service professional assists a consultee with a work-related (or caregiving-related) problem with a client system, with the goal of helping both the consultee and the client system in some specified way. (pp. 10–11)

Kampwirth (2003) described consultation as a process in which

> one person, the consultatnt, develops interventions for referral problems with a consultee who is primarily, if not solely, responsible for carrying out the recommended interventions. (p. 3)

A goal of consultation is to create positive change. It is collaborative in that the consultant and consultee work together to solve the problem (Gibson, 2004; Kampwirth, 2003). Consultation is intended to improve consultees' functioning with their child and also to develop consultees' skills so they can handle similar problems independently in the future. Consultees are perceived as parents or anyone else who works with young people and can benefit from consultation. The consultee is a partner with the consultant in a shared problem-solving process in which the concern is to improve parents' functioning with their children.

Various consultation models have been developed, with specific counseling techniques for each. Brown, Pryzwansky, and Schulte (2001) presented a representative model consisting of the stages with reference to the Case Study of Sonja.

Sonja

Sonja, a 14-year-old eighth-grader, has been in a continual battle with her single-parent mother over family rules. In particular, Sonja leaves home for extended periods without letting her mother know where she is going and when she will return, often coming home well after midnight. Her mother is concerned that Sonja may be involved with a 21-year-old man. The mother wonders if Sonja is sexually active and experimenting with alcohol or drugs. The mother has contacted you for assistance with Sonja.

Stage One: Phasing-In

The first stage primarily involves relationship-building. The counselor as consultant has to develop and be able to exhibit specific relationship skills including listening, understanding, empathy, and, if appropriate, self-disclosure. In the case of Sonja, the consultant would spend the first meeting gathering information regarding the mother's (consultee's) concerns about Sonja, the frequency and intensity of the problem, some background information about the family, and the nature of the relationship between mother and daughter. The counselor should work to gain the mother's trust and be supportive.

Stage Two: Problem Identification

The consultant's priority is to clarify the main problem. The appropriate skill during this stage is to provide focus. Additional skills include paraphrasing, restating, goal-setting (establishing priorities), and obtaining commitment. In this stage the consultant and the consultee attend to the various concerns that the consultee has expressed, and to prioritize these concerns. In the scenario here, time is spent on actions the mother has taken regarding her concerns with Sonja. Possibly, the consultant will want to determine how the mother reacts when Sonja comes home late and what discussions or arguments have arisen about the family rules and the mother's expectations.

Stage Three: Implementation

The counselor/consultant helps the consultee explore strategies to solve the identified problem. A major skill is the ability to give feedback, and additional skills include dealing with resistance and demonstrating patience and flexibility. The consultant also can provide recommendations for action. In this stage the consultant helps the consultee examine the actions the latter has taken in terms of the success or the extent to which they have worsened the situation. Also, the consultee—the mother in this case—possibly has tried to remedy the situation by imposing stricter rules, which have been to no avail.

The goals at this stage in the above case are to establish something the mother can do differently or to reinforce strategies that have been successful in the past. The consultant might look at ways for the consultee to spend more time with Sonja doing things they mutually enjoy and helping the mother develop reasonable rules and establish consequences. They should identify specific strategies the mother can accept and implement. Often, when the problem is complex and involves several concerns, a sequence for addressing the various issues should be established. The consultant should provide support and encouragement in helping the consultee implement the plan of action.

Stage Four: Evaluation

In this stage the counselor/consultant and consultee evaluate progress. The evaluation stage ends when the consultee is satisfied with the outcome. This stage involves monitoring the implementation and evaluation strategies. Within a reasonable timeframe to allow the consultee to implement the strategies discussed, the counselor and the consultee identify and review what has transpired. Often this session includes a detailed review of how things have been going between the mother and Sonja. The intent is to reinforce the things that are working and to consider precisely what has happened with the things that have not worked. Usually, adjustments are made in the plan of action, and the consultee's commitment to trying different strategies is reaffirmed.

This session may be repeated several times over the next few weeks to months until the consultee believes the relationship has improved. Another possible outcome is that the consultant may refer the consultee—in this case, Sonja's mother—for counseling for her own issues.

Stage Five: Termination

The consultant signifies an ending to the consultation by bringing closure to a consultation agreement. Together the consultant and the consultee review both the positive and the negative outcomes derived from the change in strategy. Although similar to the preceding stage, the purpose at this stage is to provide closure by emphasizing the progress the mother has made and reinforcing her for the behaviors she has adopted in her relationship with Sonja. Although some provision can be made to allow the mother to reinitiate the consultation at later date, the purpose of this last stage is to terminate the relationship.

As the case of Sonja illustrates, the consultation process can be an effective way to empower parents and resolve parent-child issues. In this role consultants must have good communication and interpersonal skills (Kampwirth, 2003).

General Parenting Information

Counselors who work with parents recognize the value of having a knowledge base to draw on when working in various capacities. The following information summarizes several useful topics.

Myths About Parenting

When consulting with parents or delivering some form of parent education, counselors should keep in mind that some parents think parenting is instinctive and, therefore, should be easy. This is an unrealistic view that is hard to let go of because most parents wish it were this way (Vernon & Al–Mabuk, 1995). Other myths about parenting that Vernon and Al–Mabuk identified are that children should be perfect, that what works with one child will work with another, and that whatever parenting methods their parents used with them will automatically be best for their own children. When parents cling to these myths, they often feel guilty, anxious, frustrated, angry, or uncomfortable.

Irrational Beliefs About Parenting

Along with the myths about parenting, irrational beliefs contribute to negative feelings and inappropriate parenting behaviors. Vernon and Al–Mabuk (1995) and Vernon (2002) and Wenning (1996) identified the following irrational beliefs that have a significantly negative impact on parents' behavior and emotions:

1. *Demands*: requiring children to behave perfectly. Demands result in anger, which in turn can result in aggressive punishment instead of effective discipline. Demanding that children behave is useless, as all children will misbehave to some extent some of the time. Rather than making rigid demands, parents should establish developmentally appropriate behavioral standards but not upset themselves by demanding perfect behavior.
2. *Self-downing*: equating self-worth as parents with their child's performance. Parents who engage in self-downing think they are a failure if their children misbehave or don't live up to parental expectations. Parents need to remember that they do the best they can but they can't control every aspect of their children's lives. If their children mess up, the parents aren't worthless.

3. *Awfulizing* or *catastrophizing*: blowing things out of proportion and overgeneralizing about the effects of a specific action. For example, many parents think it
   is the end of the world if their children don't always keep their rooms clean or
   if their teenager has blue hair and wears baggy clothes. Although parents might
   not prefer this, they should look at situations realistically and put them in perspective: Things could be worse.

4. *Low tolerance for frustration or discomfort anxiety*: demanding that parenting
   should be easy; that parents shouldn't have to go through inconvenience or discomfort. Parents have to expect that parenting will be a challenge with hassles
   and hurdles, although that certainly will vary from child to child. Parents who
   have discomfort anxiety are afraid to enforce rules, for example, because they are
   afraid they can't stand their child's being upset if he or she doesn't like the rules.

When parents hold one or more of these irrational beliefs, it interferes with their
ability to be effective. Helping them understand that they are not to blame if something goes wrong with their child, that it is better to prefer than demand, and that
they can tolerate the discomfort that is naturally associated with parenting will
increase their competence.

Parenting Style

For some time, coercive parenting styles, inconsistency, and lack of parental involvement clearly have been associated with more pathology in children (Lindahl, 1998).
Vernon (2002) and Vernon and Al–Mabuk (1995) delineated the parenting styles of
authoritarian, authoritative, permissive, and ignoring. They distinguished between
authoritarian and authoritative by suggesting that *authoritarian* parents are demanding and rigid, using harsh punishment to try to change behavior. In contrast, *authoritative* parents maintain a reasonable amount of control but do it in a collaborative
way based on mutual respect. Authoritative parents have reasonable rules and consequences, and they are supportive of their children.

Permissive parents think they can't stand conflict, so they give in because it is
easier. These parents generally have few rules, and they are underinvolved in their
children's lives. *Ignoring* parents put their own needs first and provide children with
little parental guidance. A parenting style that includes clear explanations, moderate
and realistic limit-setting, consequences instead of physical punishment, reasonable
consistency and involvement, and communication of warmth results in children who
have higher self-esteem, better school achievement, more positive social skills, and
more personal happiness (Karpowitz, 2000).

Nelson and Lott (2000) identified three discouraging (short-term) parenting
styles and one encouraging (long-term) parenting style. Short-term styles are

1. controlling/punitive/rewarding,
2. permissive/overprotective/rescuing, and
3. neglectful/giving up on being a parent.

These styles take away power from children and do not help them learn to be responsible or to become self-reliant. By contrast, kind and firm parenting, which is similar to the authoritative parenting style, provides opportunities for children to learn and grow.

Glenn and Nelson (2000) described other parenting styles including

- hostile autonomy (the parent shows lack of interest, is uninvolved, and lets the child have free rein),
- loving autonomy (the child decides what he or she wants to do but lacks guidelines and is not required to be responsible),
- hostile control (parental control is characterized by lack of love and respect), and
- loving control (limits are set, but in a loving, collaborative manner).

Counselors also may want to share with parents information about myths, irrational beliefs, and parenting styles, as well as the following information on discipline—another topic with which parents generally need help.

Discipline

Levine (2006) made an excellent point:

> We can learn all kinds of "techniques" for disciplining, but they are bound to fail unless, at heart, we have a loving relationship with our child. (p. 154)

Certainly that is an important message to convey to parents. It is also imperative that we help them understand that discipline and punishment are not synonymous. Discipline, on the one hand, is about caring. It is a balance of firmness and kindness (Nelson, Lott, & Glenn, 2007). On the one hand, discipline is not intended to belittle but, rather, to help children learn appropriate behavior and to teach self-discipline, responsibility, and cooperation (Vernon & Al–Mabuk, 1995). Punishment, on the other hand, is delivered in anger (Levy & O'Hanlon, 2001) and is characterized by endless scolding, blaming, shaming, ridicule, and harsh physical measures to thwart unwelcome behavior.

When parents try to teach children responsibility by demanding, they often punish harshly when children don't comply. The problem with this approach is that, when children are punished, they punish the parent in return. Needless to say, how parents discipline their child affects the quality of the parent–child relationship.

Although children need limits and controls, these must be reasonable to enable children to become more self-reliant and responsible. Rudolph Dreikurs, a prominent psychiatrist, suggested that parents become knowledgeable leaders of their children instead of authority figures (Dreikurs & Soltz, 1964), that parents should influence their children rather than overpowering them.

An effective discipline strategy that helps children develop responsibility and puts parents in the role of leaders rather than authoritarians is to use consequences. Consequences are of two types: natural and logical (Levy & O'Hanlon, 2001).

1. *Natural consequences* follow the natural order of the universe. For example, if you go outside in below-zero temperatures with no coat, you'll probably catch cold.
2. *Logical consequence* are arranged by parents. For example, a logical consequence of coming home an hour late is that the child will have to come home an hour earlier the next day, or if he or she breaks another child's toy, he or she should have to figure out how to replace it.

Logical consequences should relate directly to the specific problem, be respectful to the child and adult, and be reasonable to both parties (Glenn & Nelson, 2000).

In applying consequences, parents should be both kind and firm. Giving children a choice is a good idea: "You can either eat your dinner without playing with your food, or you have to leave the table now and not plan on a snack later. Which do you choose?" Tone of voice can indicate a desire to be kind, and the follow-through can demonstrate firmness. There can be a thin line between punishment and consequences. In applying consequences, your tone of voice, attitude, and willingness to accept the child's choice are important. If your voice is harsh and your tone is angry, the child might view the consequence as punishment. Parents must delay the consequence long enough so they can deliver it effectively and calmly (Levy & O'Hanlon, 2001).

In the following situations the use of consequences is not helpful.

1. Don't use consequences when they can't be carried out—such as when the consequence would result in breaking the law or violating rules or regulations.
2. Don't use consequences that are detrimental. For example, making a child go without lunch if the child doesn't use good manners or interact appropriately at the table is not a good idea.
3. Don't use consequences when the child may be placed in a dangerous situation, such as if the child is playing with matches. In this situation, simply remove the matches; don't give the child a choice. If a logical consequence is not appropriate, take action and try to use as few words as possible.
4. Don't use consequences if anger gets in the way. This is when a consequence turns into punishment through tone of voice and actions.

Consequences can be effective in managing children's behavior because the consequence links them with the reality of their behavior. Through the use of consequences, parents are able to form a relationship with their children based on mutual rights and mutual respect.

Another discipline strategy that can be effective, especially with younger children, is the *time-out*. Although time-out does not teach children how you want them to behave, they do learn what the results will be when they continue to misbehave

(Levy & O'Hanlon, 2001). Time-out allows children to cool down and regroup. The area designated for time-out should be a boring place, and the adult in charge will determine the length of the time-out. The goal of time-out is to help children think about what put them there and how they have to act differently. It can be an effective way to modify behavior.

Problem-Solving

It is natural for parents and children to have differences of opinion and, therefore, to have conflicts. To resolve the conflict satisfactorily, parents must move beyond listening to working-through the issue at hand. The following problem-solving steps are useful for parents (Friend & Cook, 1992), particularly with older children and adolescents.

1. *Understand the problem*. Parents and children should arrive at a common understanding of the problem and the responsibility each person might have in this situation. All too often parents assume that they know the basis of the problem, and they act from that perception. This step is designed to arrive at a common understanding.

2. *Consider the alternatives*. This step is extremely important when the problem affects both parent and child, because each will bring his or her own expectations to the situation. For this step to work, each must actively participate in generating possible alternatives. Although this is hard for most adults, it works best when both parties suggest possible solutions without being judgmental. What is important is to create a number of ideas. If the parent and the child can cooperate in this way, each will feel free to bring forward thoughts and expectations.

3. *Select the best mutual alternative*. Critically consider each suggestion. This is when the hard work and effective communication come into play. Both parent and child must be willing to listen to the other, and each must be willing to express his or her ideas and evaluate the pros and cons of each alternative. This is a most important step, and quite possibly the most time-consuming, because it involves negotiation and compromise. Here, the parent and the child will work out a mutually satisfactory solution. If the decision is not satisfying to both, the solution probably will not work. Therefore, both must be willing to compromise to reach a satisfactory solution.

4. *Discuss the probable results of the chosen solution*. This is an opportunity to examine how to implement the alternatives selected. Two questions must be addressed: What will make the solution work? What will make it fail? By considering the answers to each of these questions, both parties begin to gain a perspective on their investment to ensure success.

5. *Establish a commitment*. Once the probable results have been examined, each party knows what he or she must do to be successful. In this step both parent and child are asked to make a commitment to carry out the solution.

6. *Plan an evaluation*. This last step is a safety net for the whole process. Before embarking on new actions, the parent and child should set a specific time to

review their solution to the problem. By setting a specific timeframe for review, they have provided a means for checking out their solution and making the necessary adjustments. Possibly they will have to return to the second step—reexamine the alternatives, and consider another choice.

Problem-solving is a rather simple model, which parents too often "short-circuit" by not following the entire process. If done well, it is a highly useful technique for working-through conflicts especially with older children and adolescents.

Summary

Counselors engage in parent education and consultation on behalf of children at all school levels, as well as in mental health settings. Given the struggles that parents face today, coupled with the difficulties that young people face as they grow up, both parent education and consultation are vital services.

Parent education imparts information and skills that support good parenting. Three approaches are (a) parent study groups, (b) support groups, and (c) parent education. In support groups, which generally are not as structured as education groups, the primary goal is to create an environment in which parents can come together to share common concerns about their children. Parent education and parent study groups are more structured and have the primary objective of developing parenting skills and disseminating information. Leaders of such groups need good communication skills, including active listening, reflection, clarification, questioning, and summarizing. They also set an encouraging and supportive group climate and modeled effective behavior.

Parent consultation is suited for parents who have specific problems with a child. It is different from parent education in that it is indirect; the consultant works with the consultee, the parent, to bring about change in the child. A typical model has five stages: phasing-in, problem identification, implementation, evaluation, and termination.

Counselors who work with parents are advised to educate them about irrational beliefs that have a negative impact on parenting. Rational parents are better equipped to parent with an authoritative style that results in collaboration, problem solving, mutual respect, and reasonable rules and consequences. In accordance with authoritative parenting, discipline is designed to help children learn responsibility and cooperation as well as self-discipline. It is done in a caring manner, as opposed to a punitive, harsh approach.

References

Abrams, K., Theberge, S. K., & Karan, O.C. (2005). Children and adolescents who are depressed: An ecological approach. *Professional School Counseling, 8*, 284–292.

Ayers, L. (2000). Gender issues in parenting: parenting teenage girls. In M. J. Fine & S. W. Lee (Eds.), *Handbook of diversity in parent education: The changing faces of parenting and parent education* (pp. 15–35). San Diego: Academic Press.

Baruth, L. G., & Manning, M. L. (1991). *Multicultural counseling: A lifespan perspective* (2d ed). Upper Saddle River, NJ: Macmillan.

Bogenschneider, K., & Stone, M. (1997). Delivering parent education to low and high risk parents of adolescents via age-paced newsletters. *Family Relations, 46*(2), 123–134.

Brown, D., Pryzwansky, W. B., & Schulte, A. C. (2001). *Psychological consultation: Introduction to theory and practice* (5th ed.). Boston: Allyn & Bacon.

Clark, L. (1996). *SOS! Help for parents: A practical guide for handling common everyday behavior problems.* Bowling Green, KY: Parents Press.

Clemens, E. (2007). Developmental counseling and therapy as a model for school counselor consultation with teachers. *Professional School Counseling, 10*, 352–359.

Clemente, R. (2004). Counseling culturally and ethnically diverse youth. In A. Vernon (Ed.), *Counseling children and adolescents* (3rd ed., pp. 227–256). Denver: Love.

Dinkmeyer, D., & Losoncy, L. E. (1980). *The encouragement book.* Englewood Cliffs, NJ: Prentice–Hall.

Dinkmeyer, D., McKay, G., & Dinkmeyer, D. (1997). *Systematic training for effective parenting.* Circle Pines, MN: American Guidance Service.

Dougherty, A. M. (2000). *Psychological consultation and collaboration in school and community settings.* Belmont, CA: Brooks/Cole.

Dreikurs, R., & Soltz, V. (1964). *Children the challenge.* New York: Hawthorn.

Edwards, O. W. (2000). Grandparents raising grandchildren. In M. J. Fine & S. W. Lee (Eds.), *Handbook of diversity in parent education: The changing faces of parenting and parent education* (pp. 199–210). San Diego: Academic Press.

Evans, J. R., VanVelsor, P., & Schumacher, J. E. (2002). Addressing adolescent depression: A role for school counselors. *Professional School Counseling, 5,* 211–219.

Faber, A., & Mazlish, E. (1999). *How to talk so kids will listen and listen so kids will talk* (3rd ed.). New York: Avon.

Fine, M. (Ed.). (1989). *The second handbook on parent education.* New York: Academic Press.

Fine, M. A., Voydanoff, P., & Donnelly, B. W. (1993). Relation between parental control and warmth in child well-being in stepfamilies. *Journal of Family Psychology, 7,* 222–232.

Fine, M. J. & Wardle, K. F. (2000). A psychoeducational program for parents of dysfunctional backgrounds. In M. J. Fine & S. W. Lee (Eds.), *Handbook of diversity in parent education: The changing faces of parenting and parent education* (pp. 134–152). San Diego: Academic Press.

Friend, M., & Cook, L. (1992). *Interactions: Collaboration skills for school professionals.* White Plains, NY: Longman.

Glenn, H. S. & Nelsen, J. (2000). *Raising self-reliant children in a self-indulgent world.* New York: Three Rivers Press.

Gibson, D. M. (2004). Consulting with parents and teachers: The role of the professional school counselor. In B. Erford (Ed.), *Professional school counseling: A handbook of theories, programs, & practices* (pp. 349–335). Austin, TX: Pro-Ed.

Gordon, T. (1970). *Parent effectiveness training: The proven program for raising responsible children.* New York: Wyden.

Gordon, T. (2000). *Parent effectiveness training: The proven program for raising responsible children.* New York: Three Rivers Press.

Harris, H. L., & Coy, D. R. (2004). Parent involvement in schools. In B. Erford (Ed.), *Professional school counseling: A handbook of theories, programs, & practices* (pp. 851–858). Austin, TX: Pro-Ed.

Hays, P. A. (1996). Addressing the complexities of culture and gender in counseling. *Journal of Counseling and Development, 74,* 332–338.

Jacobs, E., Masson, R., & Harvill, R. (1998). *Group counseling: Strategies and skills* (3d ed.). Pacific Grove, CA: Brooks/Cole.

Kampwirth, T. J. (2003). Collaborative consultation in the schools: *Effective practices for students with learning and behavior problems* (2nd ed.). Upper Saddle River, NJ: Merrill Prentice Hall.

Karpowitz, D. H. (2000). American families in the 1990's and beyond. In M. J. Fine & S. W. Lee (Eds.), *Handbook of diversity in parent education: The changing faces of parenting and parent education* (pp. 3–12). San Diego: Academic Press.

Kennedy, R. W. (2001). The *encouraging parent: How to stop yelling at your kids and start teaching them confidence, self-discipline, and joy.* New York: Three Rivers Press.

Knowlton, E., & Mulanax, D. (2000). Education programs for parents and families of children and youth with developmental disabilities. *Handbook of diversity in parent education: The changing faces of parenting and parent education* (pp. 299–312). San Diego: Academic Press.

Kottman, T., & Wilborn, B. L. (1992). *Parents helping parents: Multiplying the counselor's effectiveness. School Counselor, 40,* 10–14.

Kress, V. E., Drouhard, N., & Costin, A. (2006). Students who self-injure: School counselor ethical and legal considerations. *Professional School Counseling, 10,* 203–209.

Kurcinka, M. S. (2000). *Kids, parents, and power struggles.* New York: Harper.

Lancaster, P. E. (2000). Parenting children with learning disabilities. In M. J. Fine & S. W. Lee (Eds.), *Handbook of diversity in parent education: The changing faces of parenting and parent education* (pp. 233–250). San Diego: Academic Press.

Levine, M. (2006). *The price of privilege: How parental pressure and material advantage are creating a generation of disconnected and unhappy kids.* New York: Harper Collins.

Levy, R., & O'Hanlon, B. (2001). *Try and make me! Simple strategies that turn off the tantrums and create cooperation.* New York: St. Martin's Press.

Lindahl, K. M. (1998). Family process variables and children's disruptive behavior problems. *Journal of Family Psychology, 12*(3), 420–436.

McDermott, D. (2000). Parenting and ethnicity. In M. J. Fine & S. W. Lee, (Eds.), *Handbook of diversity in parent education: The changing faces of parenting and parent education* (pp. 73–94). San Diego: Academic Press.

Nelson, J., & Lott, L. (2000). Positive *discipline for teenagers: Empowering your teen and yourself through kind and firm parenting* (2d ed.). Roseville, CA: Prima Publishing.

Nelson, J., Lott, L, & H. S. Glenn (2007). *Positive discipline A-Z* (2d ed.). Rocklin, CA: Prima.

Popkin, M. H. (1995). *Active parenting today.* Atlanta: Active Parenting.

Romano, D. M., & Hermann, M. A. (2007). Advocates for all. *ASCA School Counselor, 44,* 86–89.

Rubel, D,J., & Ratts, M. (2007). Diversity and social justice issues in counseling and psychotherapy. In D. Capuzzi & D. Gross (Eds.), *Counseling and psychotherapy: Theories and interventions (4th ed)* (pp. 47-67). Upper Saddle River, NJ: Pearson Prentice Hall.

Shapiro, J. P., Friedberg, R. D., & Bardenstein, K. K. (2006). *Child and adolescent therapy: Science and art.* Hoboken, NJ: John Wiley & Sons.

Stone, L. A. & Bradley, F. O. (1992). *Parenting without hassles: Parents and children as partners*. Salem, WI: Sheffield.

Stone, L. A., & Bradley, F. O. (1994). *Foundations of elementary and middle school counseling*. White Plains, NY: Longman.

Taub, D. J. (2006). Understanding the concerns of parents of students with disabilities: Challenges and roles for school counselors. *Professional School Counseling, 10*, 80–89.

Thompson, C. L., Rudolph, L. B., & Henderson, D. (2004). *Counseling children* (6th ed.). Belmont, CA: Brooks/Cole.

U.S. Bureau of Census (2003, August). School enrollment: 2000 (U.S. Census Bureau No. C2KBR-26). Washington, DC: U.S. Government Printing Office,.

U.S. Census Bureau (2004). *U.S. interim projections by age, sex, race, and Hispanic origin*. Retrieved August 20, 2004, from http://www.census.gov/ipc/www/usinterimproj/natpro jtab01a.xls.

U.S. Bureau of Census (2005, June 9). *Census Bureau reports: Hispanic population passes 40 million*. Retrieved June 13, 2005 from http://www.census.gov/Press-release/www. releases/archives/population/005164.html

Vernon, A. (2002). *What works when with children and adolescents: A handbook of individual counseling techniques*. Champaign, IL: Research Press.

Vernon, A., & Al–Mabuk, R. H. (1995). *What growing up is all about: A parent's guide to child and adolescent development*. Champaign, IL: Research Press.

Vernon, A., & Clemente, R. (2005). *Assessment and intervention with children and adolescents: Developmental and multicultural considerations*. Alexandria, VA: American Counseling Association.

Wenning, K. (1996). *Winning cooperaton from your child! A comprehensive method to stop defiant and aggressive behavior in children*. Northvale, NJ: Jason Aronson.

Family Counseling in the Schools

Carol Klose Smith

The message that Lynn's stepfather left on my answering machine was brief. He simply requested that I set up a meeting with Lynn, himself, and his wife to discuss their 15-year-old daughter's problems. I returned the call, leaving a message that I would be available after school if that would be convenient for them. I was somewhat apprehensive because this would be my first family session as a school counselor, but I recognized that it might be helpful to meet and, if necessary, refer them for family counseling.

As the family entered my office for the meeting, it was readily apparent that Lynn was not happy to be here. Her nonverbals said it all. My contact with Lynn had been minimal before now, as it was relatively early in the school year and I only recently had begun a series of career guidance lessons in her classroom.

I began by asking for a bit of background information about the family. Lynn's parents were divorced 7 years ago, Lynn and her mother had lived alone for 3 years after Mrs. Brown's first divorce, and Mrs. Brown remarried 4 years ago when Lynn started middle school. This was Mr. Brown's first marriage, so the family configuration did not include other children.

Then I asked what I could do to help them, and Mr. Brown began discussing the recent changes he had witnessed in Lynn, including changes in her friends, her belligerent attitude, and a decline in grades in most subjects. He also indicated that she had begun lying and had recently sneaked out of her room and walked to a friend's house several blocks away to stay for the night. Mr. Brown said they couldn't trust her and didn't know what to do. He had taken away her phone and Internet privileges and had grounded her for 2 months. The day after he had announced this punishment, Lynn didn't come home from school, and after hours of calling around and looking for her, they finally found her late that night with a girl they had never met before. Lynn's step-father explained that he wanted to guide Lynn in making "better choices" and in "minding her parents."

Throughout the step-father's frustrated and emotionally charged account of her behavior, Lynn remained silent, staring at the floor. Mrs. Brown occasionally nodded her head in agreement with her husband, and when pressed, reported that the arguments between Lynn and her step-father had intensified, making things difficult at home.

This family clearly was at a standstill because the parents wanted Lynn to change and saw her as "the problem." Mr. Brown said they had tried everything to get Lynn to "clean up her act" but nothing seemed to be working. After listening to the parents, I expected Lynn to be sullen and argumentative when I asked for her perspective, but to my surprise, she teared up and said she didn't like to hear her parents arguing about how to handle her. With some prompting, she said that her step-dad refused to listen to her side of the story and didn't understand teenagers; he just wanted to be the boss, and her mom let him take that role, which Lynn resented.

After talking with Lynn, a clear pattern was emerging. A high-school sophomore, she wanted more autonomy, her step-father wanted his authority to be respected, and Lynn's nonassertive mother was caught in the middle, alternating between defending her daughter to her husband and defending her husband's actions to her daughter. When Lynn broke the rules, the step-father reacted by restricting her choices, which Lynn resisted even more, perpetuating the pattern.

It was interesting to note that each family member had labeled the same situation in very different ways. They each had their own "truth." For example, when Lynn sneaked out of the house and stayed overnight at a friend's place, Lynn's step-father called her "a runaway," his wife called it "rebellion," and Lynn called it "an escape." Also clear was the notion of "fixing the problem" and identifying one family member as "the problem" instead of the problem being the family system. The parents were worried about Lynn and were not sure what to do. The normal pattern of responding had failed to work. Even as inexperienced as I was, it seemed obvious that all these family members would have to make some changes to reach their goals.

As the vignette illustrates, working with families can be challenging. It would have been far easier to label Lynn as the problem and work with her in individual counseling sessions. Certainly, I would have been far more comfortable engaging in individual counseling. Unfortunately, taking such an approach would have reinforced the notion with the parents that Lynn was the problem. Instead, I reframed the problem by encouraging the family to look at the circular process that had been shaping their communication and behavior. This approach had a three-pronged goal:

1. to encourage each family member to examine how his or her own communication and behavior contributed to a negative loop;
2. to gain a perspective that each member was also responsible for the solution; and
3. to begin to construct small steps that could be accomplished each week.

Family Stressors

Today's families face many difficulties and challenges, including poverty, lack of access to health care, drug and alcohol addiction, and exposure to violent crime, to name just a few. These external stressors may affect families' ability to provide opportunities for their children to learn and to engage in the education of their children (Honig, Kahne, & McLaughlin, 2001). For example, maternal stress related to living in poverty has been connected to both internalizing (withdrawn and depressed) and externalizing (aggressive and impulsive) behaviors at school (Conger et al., 2002). Children in families dealing with substance-use issues have an increased risk for disruptive behavior in the school setting (Loukas et al., 2003). Clearly, family stressors can impact the academic, social, and behavioral functioning of children in school.

Families can also have internal stressors. Even healthy families are challenged by the normal ongoing developmental changes in a family as it matures and grows. Often, the transition into a new developmental stage is characterized by stress, chaos, and conflict. For example, families with young children will be challenged by (Carter, 2005)

- adjusting the marital/partner subsystem to make space for a child or children,
- assuming parenting roles,
- handling the roles of work and child care,
- learning parenting, and
- realigning the extended family relationships to include grandparents and others.

Too, families have to deal with normative stressors, such as when a child begins school. Families need to find ways to adapt to the new demands of the educational system—establishing new routines, completing homework, and managing their child's developing social lives and activities—all of which become more complicated for families with nonstandard work schedules or variable work shifts (Hsueh & Yoshikawa, 2007).

As families mature and children reach adolescence, other tasks have to be mastered, including (Preto, 2005)

- negotiating the adolescent's physical and the emotional changes,
- giving greater autonomy to the child and renegotiating family relationships,

- focusing on mid-life marital/partner and career concerns, and
- planning care for the older generation.

Families adapt in different ways to these normative changes. Some families do so with little effort, while other families have more difficulty achieving the transition and demonstrate more stress, which may impact a child's ability to learn.

In addition, more children are growing up in a variety of family configurations, including single-parent, biracial, blended, same-gender, and grandparent-headed households—all influenced by culture, ethnicity, and socioeconomic status (Worden, 2003). Although school buildings and classrooms may look the same as they did two decades ago, the issues that families are dealing with have changed. With the ever-increasing diversity and social challenges facing today's families, school counselors have to be prepared to assist children in the traditional approaches of classroom guidance and small-group or individual counseling and use strategies that have proven to be effective through interventions aimed at the family level within the schools (Caffery, Erdman & Cook, 2000; Nelson, 2006). Family counseling strategies in conjunction with more traditional approaches can support the significant role of school counselors in promoting students' success and helping them achieve at a higher level.

Rationale for Family Counseling in the Schools

Why is family counseling appropriate in schools? Why intervene at the school level? Does family counseling work in the schools? We will address these questions next.

Why Is Family Counseling Appropriate in Schools?

Children from the ages of 5 to 18 spend approximately half of their waking hours from September through May in a school setting. The school environment and the family environment become focal points for children and their families at these ages, as these two environments are inextricably linked (Nelson, 2006). The family environment provides the social, cultural, and emotional support that children need so they can function well in school. In turn, the school environment offers children opportunities for academic growth, as well as positive peer and adult interactions in a manner that supports their continued development and learning. Consequently, the family and the counselor should work toward common goals that facilitate optimum growth in children. Children benefit most when families and schools work together (Cox, 2005).

When children exhibit problems at school, these may be connected to the family. Some children become symptomatic at school when a crisis occurs at home, and the symptoms can alert educational professionals that these children need help, because many of them cannot articulate their needs adequately. In these situations, interventions that involve only the child are less effective in terms of improving their academic success, because treating only the symptoms will not address the concerns where the problem originated—in the family.

Children who have stressors at home often display a variety of reactions that can cause behavioral or academic difficulties at school. Recurrent acting out in class, repeated verbal and physical aggression, truancy, or excessive daydreaming can all be signs that a child needs attention. Other behavior and psychological indicators of family difficulties at home may be more subtle—such as fatigue, tardiness, difficulties concentrating, or changes in academic performance. In addition, the stressors associated with families living in poverty correlate with poor social outcomes in schools, aggressive or impulsive behavior, and higher stress levels (Evans & English, 2002). These stressors are varied and can influence a child's behavior, social interactions, and academic performance.

Why Intervene at the School Level?

Parents' involvement in their children's education is widely accepted as desirable and even essential to effective education (Fan & Chen, 2001). The school may favor involved parents (Miller, (2002b). These parents feel more comfortable in the school setting and model a more positive commitment to education to their children, which in turn helps children reap the full benefits of the school environment.

Researchers have studied the impact of families on the educational outcomes of preschool through school-aged children (Bates, 2005; Cox, 2005; Fan & Chen, 2001; Valdez, Carlson, & Zanger, 2005). This research has demonstrated that families seem to be a critical component in determining academic success. In a meta-analytic study on student achievement, Fan and Bates (2005) concluded that family variables contributed in a meaningful way to students' academic achievement. In another review of the literature, Henderson and Berla (1995) found that when schools provided support to families, children had higher test scores and grades, better attendance, fewer referrals for special education services, improved graduation rates, and increased enrollment in post-secondary education.

Many families, however, may not understand the importance of their involvement in their child's education. Issues such as inconveniently scheduled times for meetings, child care for other children, perceived lack of relevancy and power, prior negative experiences, and the cultural assumption that education should be held in high regard may inhibit families from participating fully in their child's educational experience (Miller, 2002a).

Despite the mounting evidence that parental involvement in the schools is important in the child's education, not until the late 1980s and 1990s was significant attention directed to how educators and school counselors might work with families to enhance students' learning and achievement (Fan & Chen, 2001). Facilitating this type of involvement requires specific skills to confront the complex dynamics in today's families, schools, and community systems. This person must be able to confront and resolve highly emotional and conflictual situations that are common in today's schools, as well as the evolving complexity within families. Because of their training, counselors are in the unique position to navigate the complex systems of family, school, and community to provide the best possible outcomes for today's youth (Nelson, 2006; Stone & Dahir, 2006).

Does Family Counseling Work in Schools?

Counselors are often more comfortable providing individual, small-group, and classroom interventions than family counseling. Yet, research indicates that family systems counseling is not only important, but efficacious as well. It is important to begin work with children and families when the difficulties begin to become apparent, before patterns of responding become entrenched and more difficult to change. Qualitative reviews (Alexander & Barton, 1996) and meta-analytic studies (Shadish et al., 1993) concluded that family counseling is an effective method for working with a wide range of behavioral and emotional difficulties.

Research has demonstrated that involving families in treatment, no matter which approach is used, has been effective in improving the academic performance of students who have problems with violence (Stein et al., 2002), attention-deficit/hyperactivity disorder (Edwards, 2002), antisocial behavior (Connell et al., 2007), school refusal (Heyne et al., 2001), behavioral difficulties (Valdez, Carlson, & Zanger, 2005), early childhood problems, conduct disorder, and substance abuse (Connell et al., 2007; Rones & Hoagwood, 2000), and difficulties encountered in adolescence (Rones & Hoagwood, 2000).

The family systems approach has proven to be at least as effective, if not more so, than other therapies, and it produces positive change quickly (Carter & McGoldrick, 2005; Mullis & Edwards, 2001). Family systems theory is a viable approach for conceptualizing the behavior of the student, understanding the context of family, and providing services to the family. An example would be a child who demonstrates withdrawal from school by not completing assignments, not playing during recess, and not interacting as much with the teacher.

One may ask, "What's going on? Has something changed for this child, or has something changed in the child's environment?" The child's problem may be a response to the parents' recent separation. To fully understand the child's problems, communication with the family is important in formulating a solution (Birdsall, 2002). Clearly, counselors will want to include the family in gathering information and, if appropriate, provide family counseling. In some situations family counseling may be the most efficacious treatment available to promote the child's academic success and adjustment, as well as create parent–school collaboration.

Compelling arguments have been raised for using systems-based family counseling in the schools (Nelson, 2006). Often, families with young children do not have the financial means to seek out private counselors. Some families think they have exhausted all resources available in the community and are frustrated because their children continue to have difficulties. Also, school personnel may be the first to recognize the emotional and behavioral problems that are impacting a child negatively.

A counselor's desire to assist a child through the use of family counseling has to be balanced against the constraints within today's schools. Many school counselors have large caseloads and other non-counseling duties that may make it difficult to add more responsibilities (Stone & Dahir, 2006). Some school counselors have difficulty asking parents to be involved (Vanderbleek, 2004). School administrators may not be comfortable with offering family counseling within the purview of the duties of the counselor (Vanderbleek, 2004). Last, some school counselors lack the necessary education and supervision to work with families (Terry, 2002). The question is not whether school counselors are asked to work with the many problems a child may have but, rather, the most efficacious ways of doing so.

Multicultural Considerations

One of the most difficult aspects of working with culturally diverse families is in assessing the acculturation levels of each family member. Counselors must balance the needs of parents who may be more embedded and committed to their culture of origin, and the needs of the children who often spend more of their time in the dominant culture (O'Connor, 2005). Therefore, counselors should recognize that ethnicity may impact the child and parents differently, especially when examining how parents and children choose to negotiate between the dominant culture, the family's culture of origin, and their rapidly acculturating child. For example, a local school district had a recent influx of new immigrant families. As a group, the children are having difficulty adjusting within the school. How can a school counselor assist with these types of concerns? What are some problems in providing counseling services to various cultural groups?

A key challenge for counselors when engaging in culturally sensitive work is in some of the expectations that counselors have for their clients. One assumption is that counselors encourage children and families to express their feelings as a step in effective problem solving and conflict resolution (O'Connor, 2005). Yet, many cultures place restrictions on expressing emotions directly. Instead, these families may rely on more indirect and subtle forms of communication. For example, Korean families tend to avoid expressing intense emotions, especially negative affect. Thus, encouraging their direct expression of feelings may be interpreted as disrespectful and confrontational in a family system that values a hierarchical structure (Kim & Ryu, 2005). Problem-solving and psychoeducational approaches that respect the family's hierarchical structure can be effective in working with Korean families.

Another issue in emotional expressiveness is that of nonverbal communication. When the family has learned English as a second language or when a different language is spoken at home, the family may rely heavily on the counselor's tone of voice, expressions, and body movements to understand what he or she is saying (O'Connor, 2005). Even some indigenous U.S. cultures focus more strongly on nonverbal communication. Kanuha (2005) noted that native Hawaiian children are often more attuned to indirect communication, gestures, and body language.

Another consideration when working with families from diverse cultural backgrounds is the expectation that families and children will communicate voluntarily and spontaneously to the counselor (O'Connor, 2005). Parents are expected to tell the counselor about both the difficulties and the successes of the previous week so counseling can respond to the new developments. Similarly, the child is expected to communicate about his or her experiences so these may be addressed in the course of counseling. But voluntary disclosure of personal information to someone outside of the family—someone who is considered a virtual stranger—is not consistent with the social values of many cultural groups, including African Americans, Hispanic Americans, Asian Americans, and Southeast Asian Americans, who may tend to believe that problems should be handled within the family (O'Conner, 2005).

Families of Southeast Asian descent may be reluctant to disclose personal information and are unlikely to do so unless they are questioned directly, because the counselor is viewed as an authority figure to whom they should not speak unless spoken to (Leung & Boehnlein, 2005). Similarly, when Japanese families enter family counseling, they do not necessarily believe that problems can be resolved by talking about them, and they prefer to avoid conflict (Shibusawa, 2005). Clarifying the counseling process and specific communication about confidentiality can help parents understand the process and show respect to the families (Leung & Boehnlein, 2005).

Finally, traditional Western thinking emphasizes linear and logical problem-solving strategies (O'Connor, 2005), whereas many non-Western groups feel more comfortable with holistic and intuitive approaches. For example, family counselors working with Native American families should be alert to any contact their clients may have with a medicine person and should consider such contact as potentially beneficial (Sutton & Broken Nose, 2005).

O'Connor (2005) identified several errors by counselors working with families from a culture with which they are not familiar.

1. Counselors may either overestimate or underestimate the importance of one or more cultural values in their clients' lives. When counselors underestimate the impact of cultural factors on their clients' lives, they may concentrate on the shared experience of being a family. This trivializes and denies the realities of cultural identification.
2. Family counselors may fail to adequately differentiate the various subcultural groups. For example, American Indian tribes differ greatly in their values, organizational structures, beliefs, and cultural practices.
3. Many novice family counselors make the mistake of recognizing the culture of their specific clients but not understanding how that cultural group behaves in other environments. Thus, the counselor may have trouble recognizing the difference between cultural issues and more idiosyncratic issues of a child or family.

Systemic Approaches

A systems perspective is the cornerstone of many family therapy theories. Systems theory differs from individual counseling theories in a few key ways, such as the system theory emphasis on interpersonal relationships, homeostasis, and circular causality. In describing the differences between individual interpersonal theories and the systems perspective, the metaphor of a camera has been used. The interpersonal perspective is a zoom lens directed at the person standing in isolation. One gets a good perspective on the client's thoughts, feelings, and experience, which results in a phenomenological perspective of the person. This perspective is the cornerstone of individual counseling.

Systems theory, in contrast, widens the focus of the camera lens. With this wide-angle lens, one is able to view individuals within the context of their relationships to others. Specifically, it allows counselors to gain perspectives on the patterns of interaction among family members, the family's structure/organization, and the family's belief structure, which includes the family's cultural and ethnic background.

The systems perspective, then, allows the family to be viewed as a whole unit. This process of expanding the focus can be easily seen in the initial stages of working with parents and children. Suppose, for example, that parents are concerned about their child's lack of academic progress. One parent explains, in detail, all of the attempts to help the child attain higher grades. Because the parent believed that the child was deliberately not trying, the failure of all of these attempts to motivate the child was laid on the child. Often, individuals examine the world from an inside-out perspective because it is easier to see others as contributing to the problem, which reflects a more unilateral influence (Gladding, 2007). From the systems perspective, the child's behavior is not about self-motivation that leads to poor performance but, instead, the perception and role that this behavior plays within the family.

Upon examining the problem of poor academic performance, it becomes clear that the parent–child interaction is focused solely on the child's poor academic performance. The parent does not spend much time interacting with the child in a positive manner or in other activities. The child and parent are both caught in a no-win situation. The child seeks out the only predictable interaction from the parent—battling over homework. The counselor in this situation can provide information about the circular nature of their interactions and seek ways, in conjunction with the family, to negotiate more time for fun activities with the parent and reward the child's small, incremental steps toward meeting the academic goals that are determined by both the parent and the child.

Another difference between the individual counseling and the family systems perspectives is the concept of linearity versus circular causality. *Linearity* examines immediate events and possible consequences (i.e., A leads to B), whereas *circular causality* helps one examine all of the possible related events through multiple interrelationships and dynamics (Gladding, 2007). Like the ripples on a pond, an event can impact many family members in multiple ways. From a family counseling perspective, family problems are seen as the result of mistaken interactional patterns that develop between people. These patterns are mutually reinforcing and serve to maintain the problem. For example, one of the most basic beliefs in family counseling is not to assign blame but, instead, to examine more effective ways of interacting with one another. The counselor reframes the problem as a difficulty that everyone in the family shares, explaining that everyone can contribute to the solution. This step is essential in family counseling and requires skill in working with people because the counselor is asking families to adjust the way they think about the problem.

Almost any human difficulty can be treated through either individual or family counseling, but certain problems are more suited to a family approach, and chief among these are problems related to children (Nichols & Schwartz, 2006). Regardless of how effective individual counseling or educational intervention can be, at the end of the day, children return home to their families. If the difficulties at school are symptoms of family difficulties, when a child returns home, he or she will encounter the same stresses and concerns that created the problem in the first place. Family interventions, coupled with the traditional approaches used in the schools, may induce change for the child and the rest of the family.

Overview of Theories

Family counseling can take many forms and may reflect the counselor's perspective and training (interpersonal or systems) or the composition of the people in counseling. Family counseling can involve an individual, a couple, a parent, a child or children, members of an extended family, and unrelated people living in the same home, in nuclear or intergenerational situations. All of the family theories have one trait in common: Family counseling is about changing the entire family. When one individual in a family changes, all other members of the system are impacted. In this chapter we briefly review a few of the classic family theory approaches: humanistic, structural, solution-focused, strategic, and social constructionism.

Humanistic Approaches (Existential and Human Validation)

Virginia Satir has been credited with founding the humanistic approach to family therapy, which purports that the root cause of problems in the family is emotional suppression (Gladding, 2007). Although children must learn that they cannot always do whatever they feel like doing, many parents try to influence their children's actions by controlling their feelings. As a result, children in these families learn to suppress their feelings. Thus, existential family counseling works from the inside out by helping individuals express their honest feelings and then assists them in developing more genuine family interactions from the enhanced authenticity. This approach emphasizes teaching open communication among family members.

Satir used techniques from a wide variety of approaches to help families express empathy and self-disclose. Family members are active participants in the counseling process and engage in active and spontaneous interventions. In this approach, family therapy is seen as an emotional encounter, but simply getting in touch with one's feelings through catharsis is not, in itself, a sufficient model of psychotherapy. Still, ignoring or rationalizing unhappy emotions may result in cheating clients out of the opportunity to get to the center of their difficulties. Thus, the emphasis of the experiential approach on emotional expression continues to offer a valuable alternative to the reductionism emphasis on behavior and cognition common in many of the popular problem-solving approaches (Miller, 2002a).

Structural Approach

The structural approach to family therapy, developed by Salvador Minuchin, is concerned with the boundaries and the hierarchy among family members. Family boundaries are the acknowledged or unacknowledged rules that guide behavior and communication among family members. In part, *boundaries* help to provide a balance between privacy and openness within a family; they are physical and emotional barriers that enhance the integrity of the individuals, subsystems, and families (Nichols & Schwartz, 2006). Family hierarchy relates to the various subsystems in the family: parental, sibling and spousal.

The *parental subsystem* is the relationship between the parents and the children. Sometimes referred to as the executive subsystem, the parental subsystem has the responsibility of setting and establishing the rules for the children, as well as providing for the basic needs of the family. In the structural approach a healthy system requires a parental subsystem (parents, couples, or an adult) that accommodates each individual family member's uniqueness (Miller, 2002b). Security, rules, consequences, and support are developed for the sibling subsystem by the parental subsystem. The *sibling subsystem* includes the children and/or step-children in the family and deals with the relationship among the children. The *spousal subsystem* involves the relationship between the parents within the family.

Clear and consistent boundaries are essential to healthy families. Having clear boundaries between parents and children allows children to interact with their parents but excludes them from the spousal subsystem. A common problem among parents of young children is parents' repeatedly relinquishing time together because of the demands of the children, which may place stress on the spousal subsystem (Carter, 2005). In addition to maintaining privacy for the couple, a clear boundary is essential to establish a hierarchical structure. This structure allows parents to occupy a position of leadership to maintain the executive subsystem. According to this theory, as children get older, they should be included in the decision-making process, but the final decisions rest with the parents. Providing for autonomy and still maintaining leadership with the family is a delicate balance, especially as a child approaches and reaches adolescence.

From a structural perspective, according to Nichols and Schwartz (2006), three solutions may have predominately maintained a family's problems:

1. The solution the family has chosen is to deny that a problem exists; action is necessary but not taken. For example, parents continue to maintain the status quo despite growing evidence that their teenage child is heavily involved with drugs.
2. The solution is an effort to solve a problem that isn't really a problem; action is taken when it shouldn't have been taken. For example, parents punish a child for not completing homework fast enough.
3. The solution is an ineffective effort to solve a problem; there is too much effort, or way too little effort. For example, a divorced father brings expensive gifts to cajole his unhappy children into being cheerful, when spending more time doing activities with the children would have been more effective.

Solution-Focused Approach

Solution-focused therapy follows the work of the constructivists such as Steve de Shazer and Bill O'Hanlon. It holds that reality is co-created by the counselor and the family, and the reality of the contentious situation is redefined with the help of the family counselor (Walsh, 1996). The solution-focused counselor acknowledges that how the parties attempt to solve the problem is more important than the problem itself. This approach emphasizes the processes of decision making. The model emphasizes an orientation to the future and to change with quick, concrete, working solutions. The presenting problem is viewed behaviorally, with no inclination toward pathology. This model is empowering because of its emphasis on solutions and strengths rather than on the problem (Gunn, Haley, & Lyness, 2007).

The counselor's role is to validate the family's experience, to guide family members as they shift their behavior (what they do) and/or their perceptions of (how they view) the problem, and to build on the family's existing strengths, resources, and success (Gunn, Haley, & Lyness, 2007). As a facilitator of change, the counselor works to find a proper fit between the family's strengths and the therapeutic interventions (Gladding, 2007). The counselor helps the family identify when the problem behavior does not occur: "When doesn't it happen? When don't you feel this way?" The aim is to encourage the family to make small, rapid changes to impact the behavior and the family's perception of the behavior.

Strategic Approach

The strategic approach is time-sensitive and oriented to the present (Nelson, 2006). Developed by Jay Haley and Milton Erickson this perspective views the family system as needing to maintain *homeostasis*—the mechanism by which families go back to equilibrium in the face of a disruption (Nichols & Schwartz, 2007). Maintaining homeostasis may be seen in a family that becomes stuck coping with problems in the same manner even when confronted with the reality that those solutions are not working. The family may continue to act in ways that are familiar instead of adapting to new ways of thinking or changing behaviors toward the problem. Thus, this process serves as a resistance to change.

For example, parents of a child who is not completing his or her homework on time may nag, cajole, nudge, or yell to motivate the child to do homework. They follow this pattern regardless of the success of the strategy, because they find some comfort in the certainty of the pattern when they do not know what else to do. Homeostasis may also relate to the emotions inherent in the situation, with the attention being on the child who has the problem completing homework.

According to the strategic approach, families are goal-directed and rule-governed systems. Strategic counselors are problem-focused and prescriptive in their approach to helping families. They view problems as families being stuck rather than sick, and the counselor's job is to get families moving again. This approach emphasizes the problem and how it relates to the family's interactional sequence (Nelson, 2006). In addition, most strategic counselors assign homework to be completed between sessions. These directives do not include lengthy discussions or rationale; rather, they are an attempt to disrupt the interactional patterns that have been maintaining the presenting concern (Nelson, 2006).

Social Constructionism and the Narrative Approach

Social constructionism is based upon the belief that knowledge or meaning is constructed through social interaction (Worden, 2003). This approach is concerned with how clients understand the world around them, what meanings they create to explain the world, and how these meanings are constructed. In this approach, individuals are not just passive recipients of their world but, instead, are active in shaping their perceptions when constructing their view of the world. When a counselor views reality as socially constructed, family therapy shifts from the problem-centered approach that considers counseling as a meaning- and language-generating process. The social construction process involves the counselor creating meaning with the client.

Currently, the influence of social constructionism can be seen in the narrative approaches to therapy. As a family enters into counseling, each individual story is heard and accepted as reality for the respective family members. These initial narratives often are problem-saturated and can lead to singling out members of the family as the cause of the difficulties the family is encountering (Gladding, 2007).

The counselor engages the family members in conversation in which they are encouraged to retell their stories to include hope and previously unacknowledged alternatives. As the stories are retold, strengths are uncovered and hidden interpretations emerge. The narrative approach allows the counselor to be a collaborator with the family. Together they co-construct healthy narratives to replace the problem-saturated ones.

Brief Family Counseling Model

Demands on school counselors' time include individual counseling, small-group counseling, classroom intervention, and consultation with parents, teachers, and administrators, plus other tasks. To assume that a school counselor has the time to engage in long-term family counseling is unrealistic, but even if family counseling is not fully embraced, gaining understanding of systems theory will help the counselor to conceptualize students' problems. Further, the brief family counseling model is realistic for school counselors to use.

The family counseling process is similar to the individual counseling process in that both include the steps of building rapport, an initial assessment, the working phase, and termination. For the process to be effective, the school counselor must promote and develop rapport with each family member. Building rapport should begin at the initial contact by having all family members introduce themselves and asking family members to each provide their individual perspective on the presenting concerns (Worden, 2003).

Rapport developed during the initial stages of counseling assists the counselor during the working stage and facilitates engagement in termination and follow-up. The family counselor must make sure that everyone is heading in the same direction, as well as attending to the goals established to assist in the students' progress and goals. If family counseling is successful, the child will attain his or her educational and personal goals and the family unit will function more effectively in the present as well as the future.

In the following brief family counseling (BFC) model for conducting family counseling in the schools, step 1 represents some considerations for the counselor when considering brief family intervention; and steps 2 through 4 outline the process of building rapport with a family. If these steps are completed, step 5 (or the working phase) will begin, eventually leading to termination, step 6. Figure 14.1 diagrams the steps in brief family counseling. Table 14.1 provides sample assessment questions.

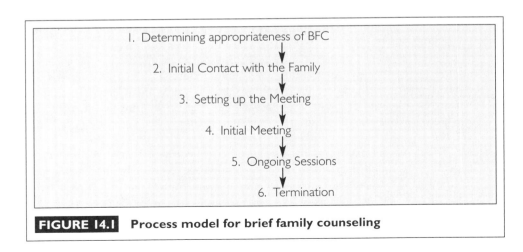

1. Determining appropriateness of BFC

2. Initial Contact with the Family

3. Setting up the Meeting

4. Initial Meeting

5. Ongoing Sessions

6. Termination

FIGURE 14.1   **Process model for brief family counseling**

TABLE 14.1	Assessment Questions for Families
Type of Question	**Sample Questions**
Investigating the problem	What behavior has the teacher noticed in the classroom? What behavior has the parents/siblings noticed at home? What did the child do? How did the teacher/parents/siblings respond to the behavior? What did the teacher/parents/siblings feel during this incident?
Coping questions	How have you managed so far? What has prevented the problem from getting worse?
Family history	Has your family has experienced or is experiencing a life transition such as death, divorce, separation, job change, relocation, children leaving home, new family member, illness or retirement? Is there or has there been a major or minor family conflict? Do you as parents agree on rules and discipline for your child or children? Are any members of the family currently having difficulty in life?
Exception-finding questions	Describe to me when the problem does not happen? Is there any part of the day when the problem is better? Is there a certain place where the problem does not occur? Are there people who never see this problem?
Miracle question	If a miracle happened and the problem no longer existed, what would you be doing differently? Or what would be family be doing differently?
Scaling question	On a scale from 1 to 10, 1 being the problem is totally in control and 10 being the family is in control of the problem, where is each family member today? Where would the family like to be next week, next month?
Goal-development questions	What is one thing that each family member can do to help in just a small amount? What is one small goal the family can set to encourage a new behavior?

Step 1: Determining the Appropriateness of Brief Family Counseling

Even though many children and their families can benefit from family counseling, brief family intervention is not appropriate for all families. Some families need more assistance than the brief model proposed here can provide. One of the pitfalls is that many counselors concentrate on the evolution of the problem. Although that is important, one of the underlying premises of brief counseling is that small changes lead to big change. So the question becomes: Which families are candidates for a BFC intervention, and which families will require more intensive family counseling?

Within any brief model intervention, the first aspect to consider is the willingness of the family to accept help. Families who approach the school counselor for assistance are already a few steps ahead of families who have to be approached and asked to participate in family counseling. Those who have requested counseling have already acknowledged a difficulty and are seeking solutions to help their child.

Counselors also have to be aware of their own comfort level. They ask themselves: "Is this family concern within my professional expertise? Should I request supervision or make a referral in this instance?" The counselor must determine whether this family's problems seem to be of long duration and may require more time than BFC would allow. Not every family's difficulties will fit neatly into a BFC model. Some families may be better served in a community mental-health setting. If the BFC is determined not to be appropriate, the school counselor should refer the family for counseling within the community and consider maintaining contact with the family, acting as the liaison between the school and the mental health center.

Step 2: Initial Contact with the Family

Before making initial contact with the family, the counselor should keep several considerations in mind. First, talking with the child's teachers and other school personnel can yield important information about the perceived impact of the family's concerns on the child's education outcome.

Second, BFC can involve any combination of children, parents, step-parents, and caregivers. Therefore, counselors must not presume that children come from a traditional nuclear family. Family roles differ in different cultures and may include individuals who may or may not be related by blood (Miller, 2002a). The family itself determines who will attend family counseling, and the school counselor should be sensitive to the concerns of family members who are seeking help.

Third, parents and other family members may be reluctant or even hostile to the idea that the family is need of assistance because they think they are being singled out as a "problem family." One challenge at this stage is to convince reluctant siblings and other family members to attend family counseling sessions. Family counseling benefits more than just the child with the problem behavior and the parents. Research has shown that the older siblings of preschoolers referred for family counseling have benefited from counseling as well (Brotman et al., 2005).

Fourth, cultural considerations are especially important at this juncture. Some cultures, such as Irish-Americans, hesitate to accept help because they may feel embarrassed about sharing their feelings with anyone, especially other family members. Generally, they believe that family concerns should be handled privately (McGoldrick, Giordano, & Garcia-Preto, 2005.) Other families may be entirely comfortable in talking about personal experiences. For example, in the Jewish culture, analyzing and discussing their experiences are important to finding meaning in life. And in families of Italian descent, the interaction and the emotional relationship—not the words—have the deepest meaning (McGoldrick et al., 2005).

Last, in many of the families that are good candidates for BFC, the parents may have talked with teachers about their child already but classroom interventions have not been successful. Parents sometimes say that they think the teacher is blaming them for their child's difficult behavior in the classroom. The parents or caregivers may be frustrated and blame the teacher for the child's difficulty at school, citing problems such as the child's not liking the teacher or the teacher's having inappropriate expectations. The counselor can help establish and restore important relationships with school personnel that allow everyone to work toward a common goal. The school counselor must join with the family without taking sides and without passing judgment.

With all of these factors in mind, the tone of the initial contact is crucial. The parents and/or caregivers should be approached as equals (Miller, 2002a). The communication should be clear, honest, directed at the presenting problem, and conveyed with the authentic desire to help the student with the problem. The school counselor should provide clear examples to illustrate why the meeting should take place. Additional information about the process and purpose of the meeting can be included to help the family become more receptive to counseling. In short, the counselor must stress that the goal of the meeting is to assist the family in helping the child.

Step 3: Setting up the Meeting

Establishing a meeting time to accommodate various individuals can be difficult. A vast majority of parents work outside of the home or have other children involved in a variety of activities, so conflicts are to be expected. If families cannot take time off during the day, alternative meeting times, such as evening hours or the hour before school or work, should be considered (Pena, 2000).

An essential consideration for counselors at this stage is getting to know the family members and how they perceive their values and world view. Expectations regarding appropriate child behavior, independence of the child from the family, and how children are disciplined are examples of how families may vary from culture to culture. For example, families may react differently to a child diagnosed with a specific disability based on their family's cultural or ethnic heritage. In some instances a family's cultural values make it more difficult or easier to accept and cope with the child's problem.

According to Winton (1988), "The values of some cultures encourage passivity and ascribe events to fate or outside uncontrollable sources. For these families, a simple acceptance of the handicapped child may be their natural response; reliance on outside help may be minimal" (pp. 213). In other cases such news is broadcast throughout wide kinship ties, and numerous calls and inquiries will begin. In still other cases families are suspicious toward outsiders. The counselor will have to exhibit patience and skill in building a trusting relationship and working with families from their unique perspectives.

Step 4: Initial Meeting

After greeting each member of the family who is present, the school counselor can begin establishing rapport by defining the problem and clarifying expectations (Miller, 2002). Each family member must have a voice in this process. Gathering information from a variety of viewpoints allows the counselor to assess the problem for both content and process (Worden, 2003). The subsequent steps are to:

1. *Discuss meeting format.* The counselor begins by explaining the counseling process: discussing the role of each person within counseling, including the school counselor; the time parameters involved; confidentiality and its limits; and scheduling follow-up sessions. Families may not know what to expect, so the counselor should encourage questions and take the time to answer them to the satisfaction of the family members.

2. *Establish rules.* The family should be encouraged to discuss what rules will be necessary to be able to work together on the concern. A family in a highly emotionally charged situation can quickly escalate to shouting and interrupting. Therefore, explicit rules are established at the onset and quickly reinforced when the session begins to tip toward unproductive verbal communication—rules such as, "No name calling," "no put-downs," "no interruptions," and "everyone gets a chance to talk." Establishing rules for the family counseling session also can serve as valuable role modeling for parents who are having trouble establishing and maintaining household rules.

3. *Identify the problem.* The session now begins to get to the heart of the matter. All family members are asked to express their impression of the difficulty. The school counselor should ask family members to give their thoughts through behavioral descriptions (Worden, 2003). Family members may generalize by using words such as "lazy," "slow," "obstinate," "impulsive," and even misuse labels such as "attention deficit disorder," "oppositional defiant," or "learning disabilities" without the benefit of a diagnosis. Such labeling may lead to an inadequate understanding of the problem (Miller, 2002a). Asking for specific descriptions of the behavior, and the various family members' reactions toward the behavior, will help to clarify it.

For example, a third-grade child who recently moved into a new school has been having difficulty making friends. The teacher noted that he often sits alone at lunch and on the playground. When asked by the counselor about the child's behavior, the parents responded, "He *always* holds himself apart. He's *always* shy and withdrawn around people he doesn't know." With some clarification, however, it was learned that the child did have some neighborhood friends that he had played with regularly since he was a young child. He had transferred from a small, private grade school, where the class size was small, to a larger school.

In addressing the problem initially, the parents and teacher had tried gentle encouragement. In this case, though, encouraging a child to "go make friends" wasn't enough, and classroom interventions of intentional small-group activities did not have the desired result. At this point the school counselor was consulted to assist the child in establishing relationships. The counselor helped the child express his feelings about meeting new children and joining others at lunch and on the playground. The young boy replied that "…sometimes I really want to be alone" and found encounters with others to be overwhelming. After observing the child at lunch and on the playground, the counselor surmised that the child lacked a skill set that his parents and teacher had assumed he had learned already. Providing support, listening to the child, and clarifying the problem as a skill-learning process helped everyone turn in a productive direction, defining goals and interventions for home and school.

Important to the school counselor is to gain a history of the problem, as well as to find out when the problem does *not* occur. If the problem is always present, a skill might be learned to solve it. If the behavior is intermittent, the behavior might be a response to interactions or some other factor within the environment. Examining when the behavior does not occur helps the family recognize that the child also does many good things.

When gathering history about the problem, some families launch into a detailed account of the child's misdeeds. This should be discouraged. Rather, the counselor should elicit information about any recent changes within the family, such as the death of a family member or pet, birth of a sibling, separation, divorce, or relocation. The behavior should be then reframed. *Reframing* is when the counselor explains the child's behavior to the parents in such a way that it allows for equal ownership of the problem. Reframing structures the problem from a linear way of thinking to a circular family systems perspective and removes any blaming that may be occurring. In the above example, if a counselor reframed by pointing out a lack of knowledge about establishing friendships, providing an intervention of learning how to make and maintain friends to allow the parents a clear forward direction. Second, and concurrently, the reframe could explain that his new environment had changed from a small, intimate classroom to a larger classroom in a much bigger school and encourage all stakeholders to add some extra support. Therefore, the teacher could help by creating small learning environments within the classroom to assist with the transition and the parents could help by providing play dates with another classmate in the child's home.

4. *Ask about a typical day.* This can help the counselor understand the family's tempo and temperament, as well as reveal information about the amount of time spent with non-family individuals, activities the family may engage in, typical sibling interactions, and how responsibilities are divided among the family members. This is also an effective means of determining the family's strengths. Acknowledging strengths can assist the counselor in establishing rapport, developing goals, and planning interventions.

5. *Ascertain prior solutions.* The counselor should attempt to find out if the family has made prior attempts to solve the problem. Families who have been struggling with their difficulty for some time understandably become frustrated. The counselor should be sensitive to their feelings and respect their past attempts to resolve the problems. The counselor should let the family members know that they are not alone in trying to find a solution.

Family patterns sometimes are maintained by using the same flawed solution (Nichols & Schwartz, 2006). As an analogy, if the only thing a person has in his or her toolbox is a hammer, all problems begin to look like a nail. Perhaps the hammer no longer works, just as parenting strategies that might be effective with a 7-year old may no longer work with a 12-year-old. At times it is difficult to change to a new tool when the old hammer is so comfortable, but school counselors should encourage parents to try a variety of solutions. If one solution does not work, they should not continue to repeat the same solution with the hope that the next time will be different.

School counselors should also assess whether the family can use basic information to assist them with the difficulty. Some parents are so overwhelmed by their child's behavior that they have given up trying to change the behavior or have no idea where to start. Parents in this situation may benefit from support and information on setting and establishing routines involving homework or bedtimes, establishing clear and consistent expectations appropriate to the child's developmental child's developmental level, and connecting to important community resources.

Reframing the Problem

During this portion of the first session, discovering the function that the behavior has within the family can provide important clues that allow reframing the problem as a shared responsibility of all family members. Often families blame one member for the problem. This is a simplistic notion of problems within families and reflects linear thinking. To encourage all members of the family to share in the solution to the problem, counselors can help families recognize the circular nature of communication and behavior within the family (Worden, 2003). This process, called reframing, can be initiated by the counselor's sharing his or her thoughts and feelings about the problem, empathizing how the problem is causing difficulty for each family member. Shared responsibility for the problem and the solution should be emphasized.

Goal Setting

Goals should be thought of in terms of small steps toward longer-term goals. Goals ideally are developed by the counselor and the family together. Initially, the family and the counselor can choose one step toward the goal, with each member agreeing to it. Every member should have a role within the plan, and every attempt to make the initial goal achievable, which will foster the family's confidence in the plan. The counselor encourages adherence to the plan, even if not implemented perfectly, or even if it appears to be unsuccessful initially. Behaviors sometimes worsen initially as a child tests the new solution, so preparing parents for this possibility is critical.

Before the end of the session, the counselor brings up the need for further meetings and elicits the family's thoughts about this. If necessary, the counselor can coordinate the efforts with the child's educators. Consistency between the school and family environments is important. Getting a release of information to assist with the collaboration between the family and the school is important and will establish a precedent for future contact with the family. In addition, this step ensures that parents and educators are not working at cross-purposes.

Step 5: Ongoing Sessions

Depending on the severity and the nature of the concern, several sessions may be beneficial. Ongoing sessions may take different paths—sessions with the student in individual counseling to develop a new skill or practice a new way of interaction; phone conversations with the parents to fine-tune an intervention and to provide further suggestions; or one or more family sessions.

Step 6: Termination

Once the family seems to be functioning well, the counselor should reduce the frequency of contacts but is advised to check in with the family a few weeks later to determine if the family needs additional support. If the family continues to have difficulties and BFC has been unsuccessful, the counselor should consult with another professional or provide a referral for more intensive family counseling.

Techniques

Because children may be somewhat intimidated by family counseling, the counselor should try to make the context of the session as family-friendly as possible. Depending on the family's developmental level, the counselor can offer refreshments such as juice and cookies and a child-friendly waiting room with toys. The following techniques can be implemented during family counseling sessions. Ages of the children, cultural background, and the family's developmental stage must be taken into account in selecting or adapting techniques for use with families.

Genogram and Family Lifeline

The genogram and the family lifeline are two techniques that are particularly useful early in the counseling process. They can help with assessment of the family and clarify complicated family relationships, especially for homes with parents who have had multiple divorces and/or children from different partners (McGoldrick, Gerson, & Shellenberger, 2008). These tools can be more effective with children if they are presented as a game.

In the modified genogram, the counselor draws a family map with circles representing girls and squares as boys. Every family member must have a name and an age. Parents and partners are usually placed at the top of the genogram. Marriages are denoted with a solid line and divorce by two short diagonal lines bisecting the solid line (See Figure 14.2). All related and unrelated family members should be included. This is an excellent way to allow participants to indicate who they consider part of the family.

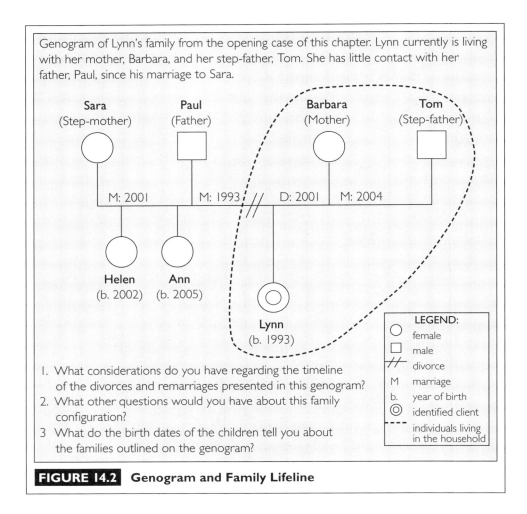

Genogram of Lynn's family from the opening case of this chapter. Lynn currently is living with her mother, Barbara, and her step-father, Tom. She has little contact with her father, Paul, since his marriage to Sara.

Sara
(Step-mother)

Paul
(Father)

Barbara
(Mother)

Tom
(Step-father)

M: 2001   M: 1993   D: 2001   M: 2004

Helen
(b. 2002)

Ann
(b. 2005)

Lynn
(b. 1993)

1. What considerations do you have regarding the timeline of the divorces and remarriages presented in this genogram?
2. What other questions would you have about this family configuration?
3. What do the birth dates of the children tell you about the families outlined on the genogram?

LEGEND:
○ female
□ male
// divorce
M marriage
b. year of birth
◎ identified client
- - - individuals living in the household

FIGURE 14.2   **Genogram and Family Lifeline**

When the genogram is completed, family members can use stickers or draw different faces to indicate their relationship to each member of the family (Carr, 2002). These faces can be kept simple for younger children—happy, mad, sad, and glad. The counselor then can engage in conversation with family members in how they view their relationships with each other, examining how they are alike and how they are different. Most families readily identify individuals who are close to one another and individuals who are more distant. This technique also serves as a gauge of the family's emotional atmosphere.

A developmental family history can be constructed with a family timeline. Children supply their birthdays and other significant information about the family. Timelines can include information such as marriage dates, dates of each child's birth, family moves or relocations, deaths, divorces, and other major life events. Placing the timeline on newspaper print and using stickers or small drawings for major life events allows the family to self-define major life events, assists in giving the family a more personalized story, and provides a greater voice for individuals with a different cultural background.

Play Therapy Techniques

Play therapy techniques can be incorporated into family counseling. One meta-analytic review of the literature of 93 play therapy outcome studies demonstrated the efficacy of this intervention among children who had been treated for a variety of emotional and behavioral concerns (Bratton, Ray, Rhine, & Jones, 2005). Further analyses from the Bratton and colleagues study revealed that including parents in play therapy produced the largest gains.

Play is an essential part of children's lives and provides an outlet for feelings and thoughts, and it helps children identify their likes and dislikes in their own language (Miller, 2002b). In family counseling sessions, play therapy creates a climate that can ease fears about family counseling for the whole family. Play therapy should be client-driven and provide an encouraging and nurturing environment that facilitates the exploration of feelings, personal growth, and identification of potential solutions to problems (Cheung, 2006). Through play, children become more aware of what they feel, what they need, who they are, and choices about their behaviors and attitudes. The counselor can view recurrent themes such as loss, abandonment, inconsistent rules, and the like, and offer suggestions for coping at home and school (Miller, 2002b; Norton & Norton, 2006).

Many play therapy techniques can be adapted for use with the family. The Kenetic family drawing technique can be used with families whose members are at a variety of developmental stages. It involves each family member drawing a picture of the family doing something. Every family member must be included and must be drawn engaging in some activity. This is a projective technique, which is interpreted as to how each person thinks and feels about the family. It reveals which family members are interacting and which family members are on the periphery, which family members are getting along and which family members are not. As a caution: Sometimes a child does not draw a realistic depiction of the family and instead draws how he or she hopes the family would get along.

Cindy

Cindy, a 12-year-old African-American female, was enrolled in special education. She and her family were recommended for counseling because Cindy had begun to have angry outbursts at school. After the initial session the family was given the Kenetic family drawing project to complete individually for the next session. The parents were asked to provide a time to limit the project but to allow Cindy the opportunity to draw whatever she wanted.

During the next session both parents revealed their drawings, which reflected tensions in the family as family members were engaged in activities separately. Cindy had drawn the family from a "happier time": The family was at a picnic at a park, and everyone was together, with smiling faces.

From this drawing it was increasingly clear that Cindy was missing the closeness that the family had once shared. The parents said that Cindy was their youngest, and the two older children were increasingly independent and not doing as many things with the family as they had previously. As the older siblings began driving and asserting more independence, they argued with the parents more often. Cindy seemed to be having difficulty navigating these normative family changes.

Role-Playing

Tracking sequences of interactions can be helpful in understanding problem solving in a family. Often, children notice things in a behavioral sequence that adults do not notice or will not admit, so discovering how others in the family view the interactions in the family can be valuable (Carr, 2002). Role-playing is effective in this regard. Two role-plays can be done—one that sheds light on the sequence of behavior around the difficulty and another in which the patterns of interaction are slightly different, or a similar situation when the behavior is not occurring. Comparing these two sequences can shed light on the interactions and possibly point to improved ways of interaction. At the very least, these role-plays will increase awareness about the behavioral sequences in the home.

If it is difficult to find a secondary role play for comparison. role modeling a positive sequence during the session can be useful. With young children, these sequences may be dramatized using stuffed animals, action figures, or dolls, and/or the sequence may be drawn on a large posterboard or whiteboard. Using a board helps the family visualize the behavioral sequence and allows for comparison between the two role-plays without trying to remember all of the details.

The Dollhouse

Similar to other interventions, the dollhouse enactment allows the child and family members to express their feelings about their home life, thereby giving the counselor insight into the child's life at home. Using small figures can encourage the child and other family members to enact scenes. "Toys become representative to the child's identity and provide an avenue toward security to express him- or herself safely. Simply put, toys become extensions of a child's being, projections of the child's thoughts and feelings" (Norton & Norton, 2006, pp. 32). Through play, a child can change his or her perceptions and feelings about an event and provide a new perspective to other family members. In addition, miniature toys can assist in the child's practicing new skills and in encouraging little-used skills.

Bibliotherapy

Bibliotherapy can be a powerful tool as an adjunct to traditional counseling. In practice, bibliotherapy incorporates many different media (e.g., print, video) and creative processes (e.g., writing, painting, sculpting, movement) through which people can communicate their stories. In bibliotherapy, family members read stories and can empathize with others, feel less isolated, and gain hope for their future. Many media are useful in working with the family, so the counselor has to discover the medium that works for each family member. Books and movies that have multiple levels of meaning are most effective with a variety of age ranges and wide variety of clients. In addition, cultural considerations and metaphors in the assignment should be addressed.

Children's books have often have themes that are relevant for families (Ivey, Ivey, Myers, & Sweeney, 2005), but some adults may perceive children's books as too simplistic and may think the counselor considers them unintelligent. As with any technique, accurate assessment of clients' needs is essential.

As follow-up to the homework assignment in which the family has been asked to read a book or view a movie, two guidelines are helpful (Ivey, Ivey, Myers, & Sweeney, 2005).

1. Ask if the family has followed through with the assignment and, if so, ask for reflections on the book.
2. Allow the each family member to express his/her emotions and impressions of the assignment.

In this assignment family members are encouraged to explore important themes, characters, and reactions to the assignment. For example, if a family is asked to watch a movie together, each member should be given the time to process the movie with consideration to their developmental and cognitive level. This is a good activity to help; families learn to accept differences of opinion in a nonthreatening way.

The Mobile

When the entire family has been asked to attend counseling, the child or children not having identified problems will complain that they do not need to be involved. One technique to explain the interdependence of family members is to demonstrate with a mobile or a wind chime. The counselor asks a family member to move one piece of the mobile or the wind chime so he or she can see that when one piece is moved, the entire mobile moves, or when one part of the wind chime moves, the whole wind chime begins to make music. The counselor can point out that when one person has a problem, the entire family is affected and all can help with a solution.

The Rope/Pass the Animal

At times in family sessions, family members may interrupt each other or speak for one another. Here, the rope technique can be useful. The person speaking holds one end of the rope, and the one who interrupts or speaks for another members holds the other end of the rope (Carr, 2002). When someone is interrupted, he or she pulls the rope as a gentle reminder to allow the other individual to speak.

In a similar technique, a stuffed animal or a Nerf ball is used to designate who is speaking. Each family member who wishes to speak can indicate nonverbally to "pass the animal." After speaking, he or she passes the animal to the next person. Only those who are holding the animal are allowed to speak. This technique can help regulate families who speak over one another. Providing clear rules for taking turns is essential in this technique (Carr, 2002).

A variation requires the individual who receives the animal to paraphrase what was stated by the person who just spoke, before making his or her own point. Counselors can pay attention to those who are speaking by examining their nonverbal behavior. What do they do with their hands and to the animal while they are speaking?

Humor

The viability of humor within family counseling cannot be underestimated. Taking a humorous approach can reduce barriers and move people from resistance to greater openness. Puns, non sequiturs, and jokes can change families from a negative orientation to a positive perspective. Asking family members to bring jokes or cartoons to counseling sessions can be a fun way to initiate or lighten up a session.

Summary

Providing family counseling in the schools can be an efficacious intervention with children, adolescents and their families. Research supports that working with the families of school-aged children and adolescents assists with their academic and personal growth. Brief family counseling (BFC) approaches offer strategies for increasing the visibility and the effectiveness of counseling in the school environment while simultaneously providing optimal services to the school, the student, and their families.

References

Alexander, J. F., & Barton, C. (1996). Family therapy research. In R. H. Mikesell, D. Lusterman, & S. H. McDaniel (Eds.), *Integrating family therapy: Handbook of family psychology* (pp. 199–216). Washington, DC: American Psychological Association.

Bates, S. L. (2005). Evidence-based family-school interventions with preschool children. *School Psychology Quarterly, 20*(4), 352–370.

Birdsall, B. (2002). Creating solution-focused families: Tools for the school counselors. In L. D. Miller & J Carlson (Eds.), *Integrating school and family counseling: Practical solutions* (pp. 53–71). Alexandria, VA: American Counseling Association.

Bratton, S. C., Ray, D., Rhine, T., & Jones, L. (2005). The efficacy of play therapy with children: A meta-analytic review of treatment outcomes. *Professional Psychology: Research and Practice, 36*(4), 376–390.

Brotman, L. M., Dawson-McClure, S., Gouley, K. K., McGire, K., Burraston, B., &

Caffery, T., Erdman, P., & Cook, D. (2000). Two systems/one client: Bringing families and school together. *Family Journal: Counseling and Therapy for Couples and Families, 8*(2), 154–160.

Carr, A. (2002). Compendium of practices for including children in family session. In L. D. Miller & J Carlson (Eds.). *Integrating school and family counseling: Practical solutions.* Alexandria, VA: American Counseling Association.

Carter, B. (2005). Becoming parents: The family with young children. In B. Carter & M. McGoldrick (Eds.), *The expanded family life cycle: Individual, family, and social perspective* (3rd ed., pp. 249–273). Boston: Allyn & Bacon.

Carter, B., & McGoldrick, M. (Eds.). (2005). *The expanded family life cycle: Individual, family, and social perspective* (3rd ed.). Boston: Allyn & Bacon.

Cheung, M. (2006). *Therapeutic games and guided imagery: Tools for mental health and school professionals working with children, adolescents, and their families.* Chicago: Lyceum.

Conger, R. D., Wallace, L., Sun, Y., Simons, R. L., McLoyd, V., & Brody, G. H. (2002). Economic pressure in African American families: A replication and extension of the family stress model. *Developmental Psychology, 38,* 179–193.

Connell, A. M., Dishion, T. J., Yasui, M., & Kavanagh, K. (2007). An adaptive approach to family intervention: Linking engagement in family-centered intervention to reductions in adolescent problem behavior. *Journal of Consulting and Clinical Psychology, 75*(4), 568-579.

Cox, D. D. (2005). Evidence-based interventions using home-school collaboration. *School Psychology Quarterly, 20*(4), 473–497.

Edwards, J. H. (2002). Evidence-based treatment for child ADHD: "Real world" practice implications. *Journal of Mental Health Counseling, 24,* 126–139.

Evans, G. W., & English, K. (2002). The environment of poverty: Multiple stressor exposure, psychophysiological stress, and socioemotional adjustment. *Child Development, 73,* 1238–1248.

Fan, X., & Chen, M. (2001). Parental involvement and student's academic achievement: A meta-analysis. *Educational Psychology* Review, *13*(1), 1–22.

Gladding, S. T. (2007). *Family therapy: History, theory, and practice* (4th ed.). Upper Saddle River, NJ: Pearson Education.

Gunn, W. B., Haley, J., & Lyness, A. M. P. (2007). Systemic approaches: Family therapy. In H. T. Prout & D. T. Brown (Eds.), *Counseling and psychotherapy with children and adolescents: Theory and practice for school and clinical set*tings (4th ed., pp. 388–418). Hoboken, NJ: John Wiley & Sons.

Henderson, A. T., & Berla, N. (1995). *A new generation of evidence: The family is critical to student achievement.* Washington, DC: Center for Law and Education.

Heyne, D., King, N. J., Tonge, B. J., & Cooper, H. (2001). School refusal: Epidemiology and management. *Paediatr Drugs, 3,* 719–732.

Honig, M. I., Kahne, J., & McLaughlin, M. W. (2001). School-community connections: Strengthening opportunity to learn and opportunity to teach. In V. Richardson (Ed.), *Handbook of research on teaching* (4th ed., pp. 998–1028). Washington, DC: American Education Research Association.

Hsueh, J., & Yoshikawa. H. (2007). Working nonstandard schedules and variable shifts in low-income families: Associations with parental psychological well-being, family functioning, and child well-being. *Developmental Psychology, 43*(3), 620–632.

Ivey, A., Ivey, M., Myers, J., & Sweeney, T. (2005). *Developmental counseling and therapy: Promoting wellness over the lifespan.* Boston: Lahaska Press.

Kanuha, V. K. (2005). Na 'Ohana: Native Hawaiian families. In M. McGoldrick, J. Giordano, & N. Garcia-Preto (Eds.), *Ethnicity and family therapy* (3rd ed., pp. 64-76). New York: Guilford.

Kim, B., & Ryu, E. (2005). Korean families. In M. McGoldrick, J. Giordano, & N. Garcia-Preto (Eds.), *Ethnicity and family therapy* (3rd ed., pp. 349–362). New York: Guilford.

Leung, P. K., & Boehnlein, J. K. (2005). Vietnamese Families. In M. McGoldrick, J. Giordano, & N. Garcia-Preto (Eds.), *Ethnicity and family therapy* (3rd ed., pp. 363–373). New York: Guilford.

Loukas, A., Zucker, R. A., Fitzgerald, H. E., & Krull, J. L. (2003). Developmental trajectories of disruptive behavior problems among sons of alcoholics: Effects of parent psychopathology, family conflict and child under control. *Journal of Abnormal Psychology, 112*(1), 119–131.

McGoldrick, M., Gerson, R., & Shellenberger, S. (2008). *Genograms: Assessment and interventions* (3rd ed.). New York: W. W. Norton.

McGoldrick, M., Giordano, J., & Garcia-Preto, N. (2005). Overview: Ethnicity and family therapy. In M. McGoldrick, J. Giordano, & N. Garcia-Preto (Eds.). *Ethnicity and family therapy* (3rd ed., pp. 1–42). New York: Guilford.

Miller, L. D. (2002a). Overview of family systems counseling in a school setting. In L. D. Miller & J Carlson (Eds.), *Integrating school and family counseling: Practical solutions* (pp. 3–30). Alexandria, VA: American Counseling Association.

Miller, L. D. (2002b). Working with individual children from a family system perspective. In L. D. Miller & J Carlson (Eds.), *Integrating school and family counseling: Practical solutions* (pp. 109–128). Alexandria, VA: American Counseling Association.

Mullis, F., & Edwards, D. (2001). Consulting with parents: Applying family systems concepts and techniques. *Professional School Counseling, 5,* 116–127.

Nelson, J. A. (2006). For parents only; A strategic family therapy approach in school counseling. *Family Journal: Counseling and Therapy for Couples and Families, 14*(2), 180–183.

Nichols, M. P., & Schwartz, W. C. (2007). *Family therapy: Concepts and methods* (8th ed.). Boston: Pearson.

Norton, C. C., & Norton, B. E. (2006). Experiential play therapy. In C. E. Schaefer & H. G. Kaduson (Eds.), *Contemporary play therapy: Theory, research and practice* (pp. 28–54). New York: Guilford.

O'Connor, K. (2005). Addressing diversity issues in play therapy. *Professional psychology: Research and Practice, 36*(5), 566–573.

Pena, D. C. (2000). Parent involvement: Influencing factors and implications. *Journal of Educational Research, 94*(1), 42–54.

Preto, N. G. (2005). Transformation of the family system during adolescence. In B. Carter & M. McGoldrick (Eds.), *The expanded family life cycle: Individual, family, and social perspective* (3rd ed., pp. 274–286). Boston: Allyn & Bacon.

Rones, M., & Hoagwood, K. (2000).School-based mental health services: A research review. *Clinical Child and Family Psychology Review, 3,* 223–241.

Shadish, W. R., Montgomery, L., Wilson, P., Wilson, M., Bright, I., & Okwumabua, T. (1993). Effects of family and marital psychotherapies: A meta-analysis. *Journal of Consulting and Clinical Psychology, 61,* 992–1002.

Shibusawa, T. (2005). Japanese families. In M. McGoldrick, J. Giordano, & N. Garcia-Preto (Eds.), *Ethnicity and family therapy* (3rd ed., pp. 339–348). New York: Guilford.

Stein, B. D., Kataoka, S., Jaycox, L. H., Wong, M., Fink, A., Escudero, P., & Zaragoza, C. (2002). Theoretical basis and program design of a school-based mental health intervention for traumatized immigrant children: A collaborative research partnership. *Journal of Behavioral Health Services Research, 29*, 318–326.

Stone, C. B., & Dahir, C. A. (2006). *The transformed school counselor.* Boston: Houghton Mifflin.

Sutton, C., & Broken Nose, M. A. (2005). In M. McGoldrick, J. Giordano, & N. Garcia-Preto (Eds.), *Ethnicity and family therapy* (3rd ed., pp. 43–54). New York: Guilford.

Terry, L. L. (2002). Family counseling in the schools: A graduate course. *Family Journal: Counseling and Therapy for Couples and Families, 10*(4), 419–428.

Valdez, C. R., & Carlson, C., & Zanger, D. (2005). Evidence-based parent training and family interventions for school behavior change. *School Psychology Quarterly, 20*(4), 403–433.

Vanderbleek, L. M. (2004). Engaging families in school-based mental health treatment. *Journal of Mental Health Counseling, 26*(3), 211–224.

Walsh, W. M. (1996). *Essentials of family therapy.* Denver: Love.

Winton, P. J. (1988). Effective communication between parents and professionals. In D. B. Bailey, Jr., & R. J. Simmeonsson (Eds.), *Family assessment in early intervention* (pp. 207–228). Columbus, OH: Merrill.

Worden, M. (2003). *Family therapy basics* (3rd ed.). Pacific Grove, CA: Brooks/Cole.

Name Index

Subject Index